AHA Hospital Statistics™

W9-BPM-948

2013 Edition

4/13
MATT.
@ 250.00

FSC
www.fsc.org
MIX
From responsible
sources
FSC® C099992

AHA Institutional Members $190
Nonmembers $250
AHA Catalog NUMBER 082013
Telephone ORDERS 1-800-AHA-2626

ISSN 0090-6662
ISBN-13: 978-0-87258-909-4

Copyright © 1999 by Health Forum an American Hospital Association company
Copyright © 2000-2012 by Health Forum LLC, an affiliate of the American Hospital Association

All rights reserved. No portion of Hospital Statistics may be duplicated or reproduced
without prior written consent of Health Forum, LLC.
Printed in the U.S.A.

Contents

Acknowledgements & Advisements

Acknowledgments

The 2013 edition of AHA Hospital Statistics is published by Health Forum, an affiliate of the American Hospital Association, Richard J. Umbdenstock, President and CEO.

Advisements

The data published here should be used with the following advisements: The data are based on replies to an annual survey that seeks a variety of information, not all of which is published in this book. The information gathered by the survey includes specific services, but not all of each hospital's services. Therefore, the data do not reflect an exhaustive list of all services offered by all hospitals. For information on the availability of additional data, please contact Health Forum, (800) 821-2039.

Health Forum does not assume responsibility for the accuracy of information voluntarily reported by the individual institutions surveyed. The purpose of this publication is to provide basic data reflecting the delivery of health care in the United States and associated areas, and is not to serve an official and all-inclusive list of services offered by individual hospitals.

Emerging Health Care Delivery, Payment Models and Care Coordination Practices

By Kevin Kenward and Nathan Bostick

  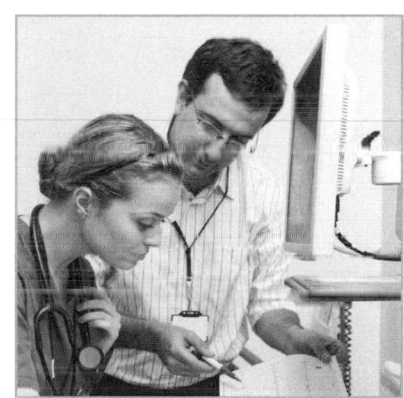

Hospital Statistics is a comprehensive compilation of data on trends in the hospital field through 2011 based on the results of the American Hospital Association's (AHA) Annual Survey of Hospitals. Overall, Hospital Statistics identifies both long-standing and emerging trends, in addition to offering insights into what the future may hold for hospitals.

Background

The Patient Protection and Affordable Care Act (PPACA) of 2010 includes a number of policies to help physicians, hospitals, and other caregivers to improve the safety and quality of patient care, while also serving to make health care more affordable. By focusing on the needs of patients and linking payments to outcomes, these delivery systems are expected to help improve the health of individuals and communities, while additionally slowing the increase in overall health care costs. As the Affordable Care Act is implemented, there is an increased likelihood there will be changes in payment models that reward provider performance and enhance coordination of care.

Delivery Models

Medical Homes

The Affordable Care Act officially codified the medical home as formal public policy. The patient-centered medical home is a model of care in which "patients have a direct relationship with a provider who coordinates a cooperative team of healthcare professionals, takes collective responsibility for the care provided to the patient, and arranges for appropriate care with other qualified providers as needed."[1] Approximately 15 percent of hospitals responding to the AHA Annual Survey indicated they have an established medical home program.

Accountable Care Organizations

While the patient-centered medical home model is designed to improve the coordination of care among physicians, ACOs have the broader goal of coordinating care across the entire continuum of health care, from physicians to hospitals to other clinicians. The idea is that,

by improving care coordination within an ACO and reducing fragmented care, costs can be controlled and outcomes improved.

Just six percent of hospitals reported participating in an ACO in 2011. Hospitals participating in an ACO were generally larger than non-ACO hospitals (249 vs. 160 beds). They were also more likely to be not-for-profit institutions, as compared to investor-owned, for-profit organizations. ACO participants also tended to be teaching hospitals and to be Joint

Table 1: ACO Demographics

Characteristic	Non-ACO	ACO
Bed Size	160	249
Government-Non-Federal	21%	2%
Not-for-Profit	62%	87%
Investor Owned For-Profit	17%	10%
Government-Federal	1%	1%
Teaching Hospital	8%	19%
Joint Commission Accredited	69%	85%
New England	4%	7%
Mid Atlantic	10%	7%
South Atlantic	14%	5%
East North Central	17%	40%
East South Central	6%	4%
West North Central	12%	11%
West South Central	23%	9%
Mountain	7%	6%
Pacific	7%	11%
Associated Areas	0%	0%
Mean Net Revenue	$10,247,967	$22,393,284

---

[1] National Committee for Quality Assurance (NCQA). Leveraging health IT to achieve ambulatory quality: the patient-centered medical home (PCMH).www.ncqa.org/Portals/0/Public%20Policy/HIMSS_NCQA_PCMH_Factsheet.pdf. Accessed October 2, 2012.

Commission accredited. Geographic variations in ACO participation were also observed, with ACOs being more prevalent in the New England, East North Central and Pacific regions and less prevalent in the Mid Atlantic, South Atlantic, East South Central, and West South Central regions (Table 1). ACO participating hospitals also had twice the net revenue, on average, as non-ACO participating hospitals.

In order to be eligible to receive payments under the Affordable Care Act, all ACOs will be required to have at least 5,000 Medicare beneficiaries assigned to it, although some exceptions will be made for rural and other shortage areas, or areas with critical access hospitals. Of the hospitals or health systems that have established an accountable care organization, 58 percent indicated that Medicare patients participated in the ACO. Furthermore, half of the hospitals indicated privately insured patients participated in the ACO and 27 percent said the ACO served Medicaid patients (Figure 1).

Payment Models

Interest in the Accountable Care concept lies in the concept of shared savings along with defined shared responsibility. Many feel that the achievement of cost controls that effectively maintain quality and access to care will require physicians, hospitals, and other providers that ultimately impact those costs to share in the overall savings. That is where the "shared savings" concept of Accountable Care is derived.

An option is for ACOs to participate in a "one-sided risk" model—which means that they would share in any savings they achieve without being at financial risk if their costs exceed their spending target—for the duration of the three-year performance period. Providers could choose to share a larger proportion of savings under a "two-sided risk" model, but they also would be liable for a share of any excess costs. Providers just starting to form ACOs, or with limited experience taking financial risk, may find it more appealing to

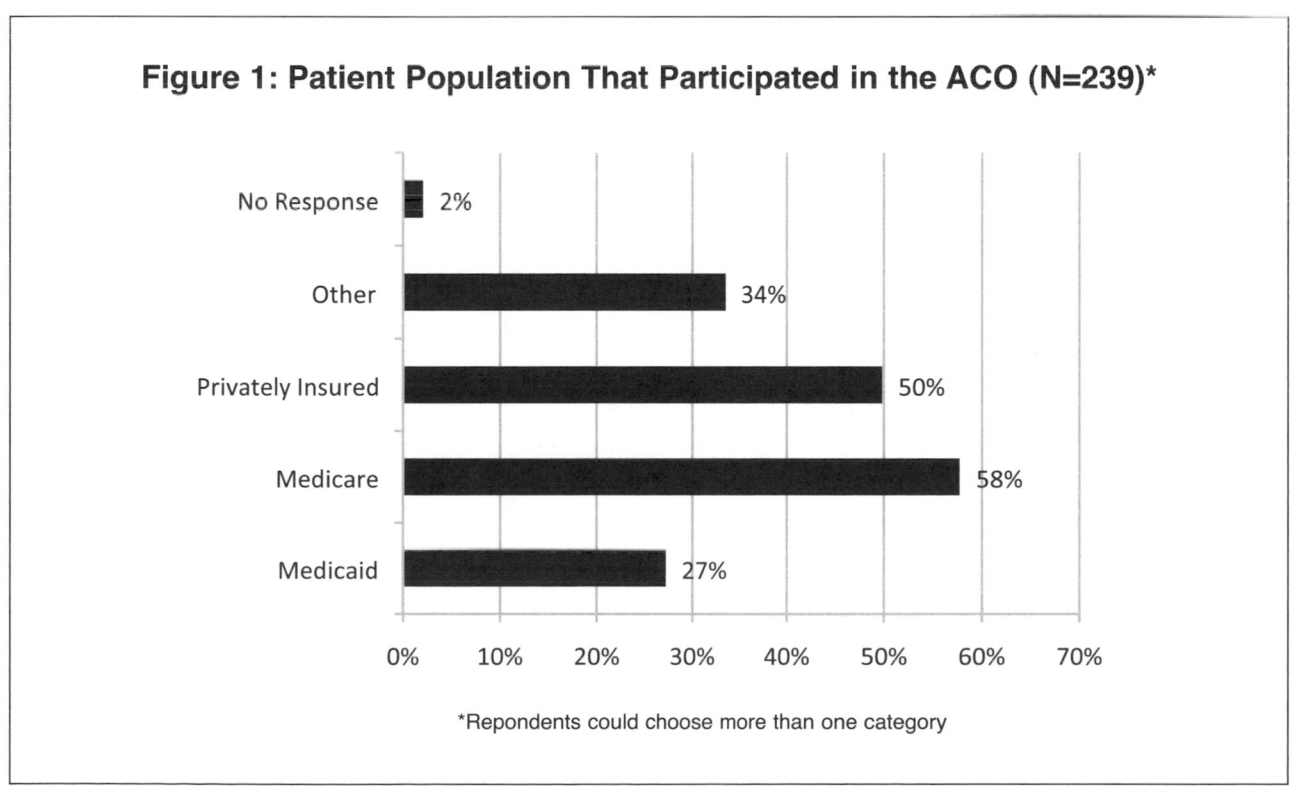

Figure 1: Patient Population That Participated in the ACO (N=239)*

- No Response: 2%
- Other: 34%
- Privately Insured: 50%
- Medicare: 58%
- Medicaid: 27%

*Repondents could choose more than one category

stay in a one-sided model for a longer period of time. This currently appears to be the case as, on average, less than 1 percent of hospitals' net patient revenue is paid on a shared risk basis.

Bundled Payments

There are three basic payment models. Fee-for-service, or volume-based reimbursement, encourages the provision of more care. Capitation, or prepayment, is a fixed monthly payment for a defined set of services for each patient assigned to the practice. Prepayment forces providers to switch their emphasis from merely treating sickness to also maintaining or improving health to prevent costly avoidable illness and unnecessary care. Because providers would not receive additional payment for extra treatment resulting from an unintended consequence of care, such as a hospital-acquired infection and readmission, providers are faced with an incentive to improve the quality of care as a means of preventing costly complications.

In between fee-for-service and capitation is a model known as "bundled payment." "Bundled payment" refers to a single payment for all care related to a treatment or condition—a payment that is then divided up among multiple providers across many settings. In a bundled payment system, providers take on more financial responsibility for outcomes than in a fee-for-service model. This mechanism is designed to address overutilization by discouraging the duplication of services that provide little or no benefit. When multiple providers in various settings are held accountable for the total cost of care through shared payment, they have a financial incentive to coordinate care and use resources wisely.

Six and a half percent of responding hospitals participated in a bundled payment program involving inpatient, physician, and/or post-acute care services where the hospital receives a single payment from a payer for a package of services and then distributes payments to participating providers of care (such as a single

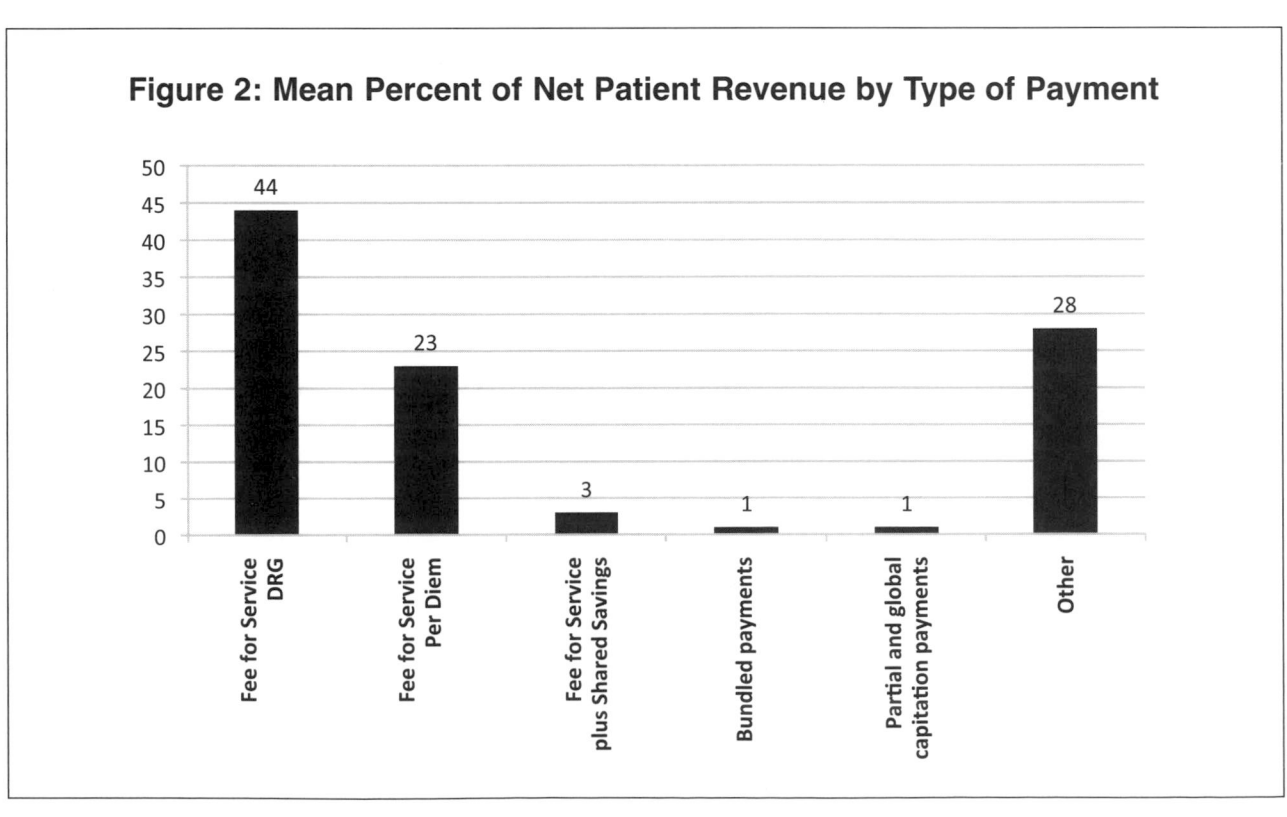

Figure 2: Mean Percent of Net Patient Revenue by Type of Payment

fee for hospital and physician services for a specific procedure, e.g. hip replacement, CABG). On average, these bundled payments represent slightly less than one percent of net patient revenue among hospitals whose responses across the payment categories added up to 100 percent. Fee-for-service remains the predominant form of payment revenue, representing 67 percent of net patient revenue (Figure 2). And less than 1 percent of net patient revenues are in risk sharing arrangements.

Care Coordination

The fee-for-service model, in which the payer has the full insurance risk, has resulted in poor coordination of care and overutilization largely due to the fact that coordination is generally not reimbursed. A failure to coordinate care can often lead to patients not getting the care they need, receiving duplicative care, and being at an increased risk of suffering medical errors. Each year, on average, one in seven Medicare patients admitted to a hospital has been subject to a harmful medical mistake in the course of their care. Furthermore, nearly one in five Medicare patients discharged from the hospital is readmitted within 30 days[1]— a readmission many patients could have avoided if the care that they received outside of the hospital had been more aggressive and better coordinated. Improving coordination and communication among physicians, other providers and suppliers will help improve the care patients receive, while also helping to lower aggregate costs.

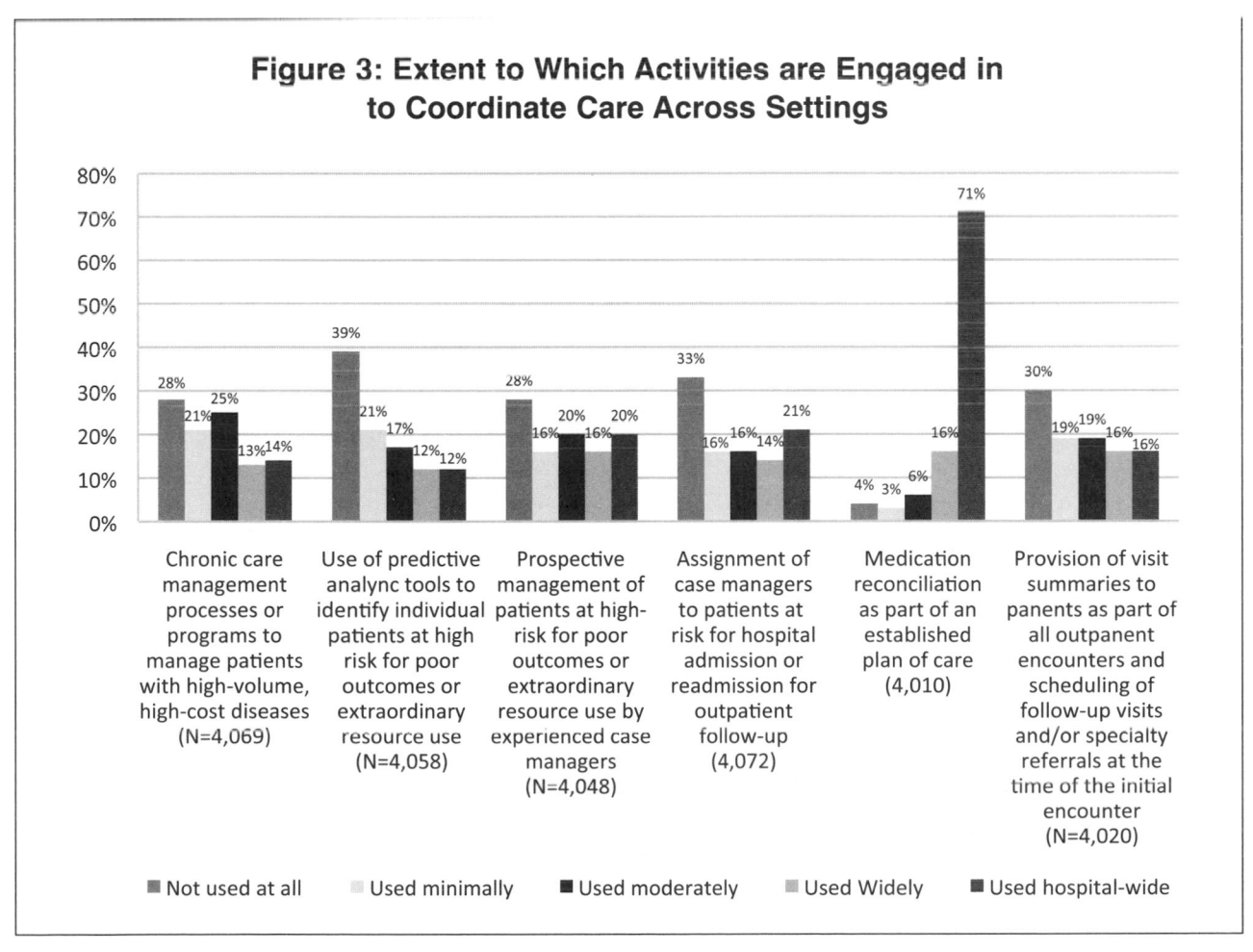

Figure 3: Extent to Which Activities are Engaged in to Coordinate Care Across Settings

[1] Jencks, Stephen F. , Williams, Mark V. , and. Coleman, Eric A . Rehospitalizations among Patients in the Medicare Fee-for-Service Program. *N Engl J Med* 2009; 360:1418-1428

At this time hospitals are engaged in a variety of coordination of care activities. The activity most engaged in is the reconciliation of medication, which 71 percent of hospitals use hospital-wide. Between one-quarter and one-third of hospitals either widely use or use hospital-wide chronic care management processes, analytic tools to identify high-risk patients, prospective management of high-risk patients, case managers for patients at risk for hospital admission or readmission, or visit summaries. However, between one-quarter and one-third of hospitals are not engaged in these same coordination of care activities at all.

ACO hospitals were significantly more likely to widely-use or use hospital-wide all forms of care coordination relative to non-ACO institutions. This suggests that the accountable care model may indeed be a successful means of better coordinating patient care, and may therefore also bear the potential to reduce overall health care costs (Table 2).

Ensuring Safe Transitions

Overall, ACO hospitals were appear to be actively working to ensure patients' safe transitions between care settings. ACO hospitals were significantly more likely to identify patients' transitions between settings of care, to share clinical information between settings, and to provide discharge summaries to primary care and other providers. ACO hospitals were less likely, however, to report tracking the status of patients' transitions (Table 3).

Table 2: Widely or Hospital-wide Used or Care Coordination Among ACO and Non-ACO Hospitals

Care Coordination Component	Non-ACO	ACO
Chronic care management processes or programs to manage patients with high-volume, high-cost diseases	26%	45%
Use of predictive analytic tools to identify individual patients at high risk for poor outcomes or extraordinary resource use	23%	34%
Prospective management of patients at high-risk for poor outcomes or extraordinary resource use by experienced case managers	36%	49%
Assignment of case managers to patients at risk for hospital admission or readmission for outpatient follow-up	34%	38%
Medication reconciliation as part of an established plan of care	87%	93%
Provision of visit summaries to patients as part of all outpatient encounters and scheduling of follow-up visits and/or specialty referrals at the time of the initial encounter	31%	51%
Post-hospital discharge continuity of care program with scaled intensiveness based upon a severity or risk profile for adult medical-surgical patients in defined diagnostic categories or severity profiles	20%	27%
Arrangement of home visits by physicians, advanced practice nurses or other professionals for homebound and complex patients for whom office visits constitute a physical hardship	27%	37%

Meaningful User of Electronic Health Records

Electronic health records play a critical role in obtaining a higher quality, safer, and more effective health care system. Through the Medicare and Medicaid EHR Incentive Programs, the Centers for Medicare & Medicaid Services (CMS) provide incentive payments to hospitals that adopt, implement, upgrade, or demonstrate meaningful use of certified electronic health record (EHR) technology. Health care providers now have additional funding to support the meaningful use of electronic health records, as well as guidelines that can help them implement them in a way that improves care for their patients.

To be eligible for the payments, physicians must use the technology in a meaningful manner, which includes utilizing e-prescribing; exchanging electronic health information to improve the quality of care; having the capacity to provide clinical decision support (CDS) to support practitioner order entry; and submitting clinical quality measures—and other measures—as selected by the Secretary of Health & Human Services (HHS).

Approximately 27 percent of hospitals have some kind of electronic health record system.[2] Almost one-fifth (18%) of responding hospitals had already attested as a meaningful user of certified EHR technology by September 2011. Another 24 percent either had or were planning on having attested by September 2012. Twenty-three percent expect to become meaningful users by 2013. An additional five percent expect to become meaningful users by 2015. Three percent say they are not planning on becoming a meaningful user and another three percent indicated they are not eligible for CMS incentive payments to become a meaningful user. An additional thirteen percent of hospitals said they did not know when they might become a meaningful user of certified EHR technology (Figure 4).

Table 3: Safe Transition Practices Among ACO and Non-ACO Hospitals

Standard Safe Transition Practices	Non-ACO	ACO
Identifying patients who transition between settings of care	75%	79%
Sharing clinical information between settings of care	78%	85%
Providing patient discharge summaries to primary care providers	71%	78%
Providing patient discharge summaries to other providers	70%	77%
Tracking the status of transitions including the timing of information exchange	47%	39%

---

[2] DesRoches, CM, Worzala, C, Joshi, MS, Kralovec, PD, and Jha, AK. (2012). Small, Nonteaching, and Rural Hospitals Continue to be Slow in Adopting Electronic Health Record Systems. *Health Affairs,* vol. 31, no. 5.

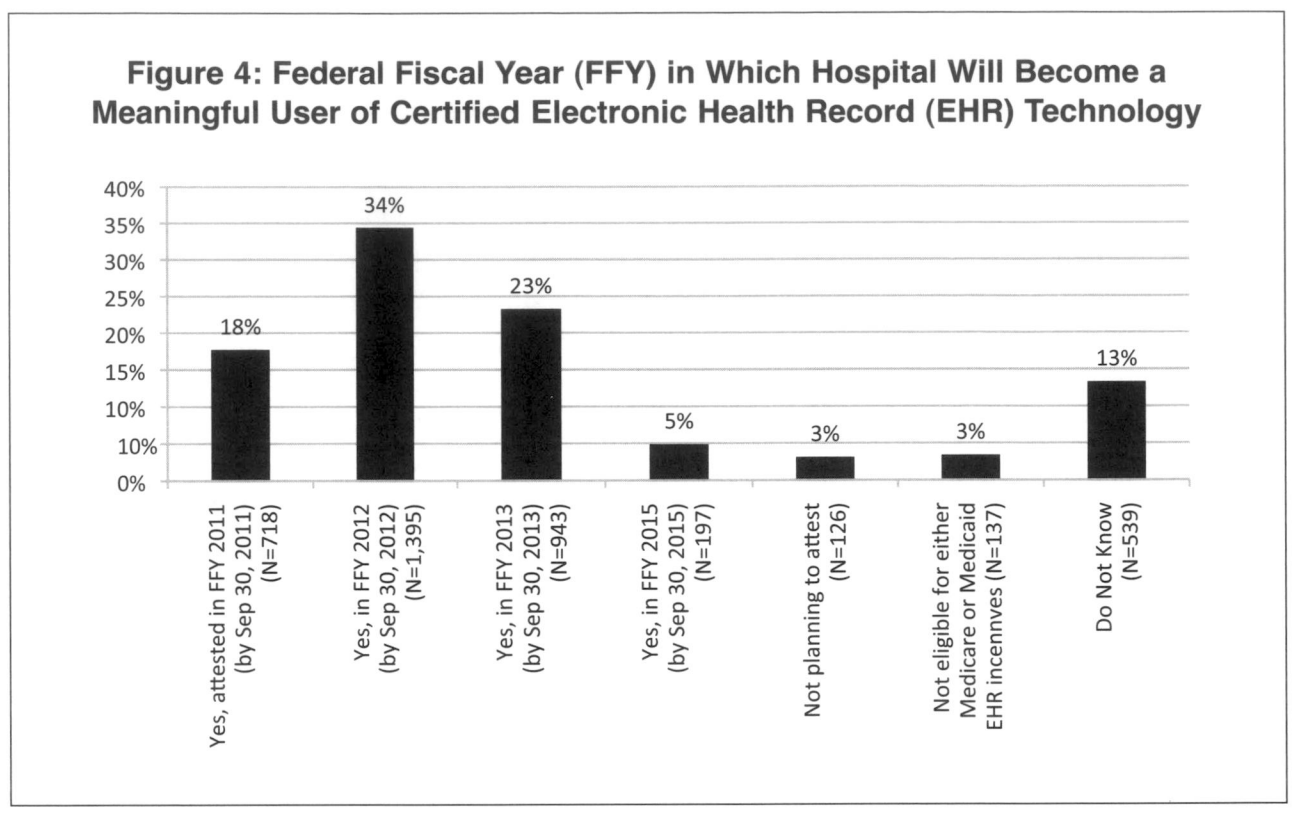

Figure 4: Federal Fiscal Year (FFY) in Which Hospital Will Become a Meaningful User of Certified Electronic Health Record (EHR) Technology

- Yes, attested in FFY 2011 (by Sep 30, 2011) (N=718): 18%
- Yes, in FFY 2012 (by Sep 30, 2012) (N=1,395): 34%
- Yes, in FFY 2013 (by Sep 30, 2013) (N=943): 23%
- Yes, in FFY 2015 (by Sep 30, 2015) (N=197): 5%
- Not planning to attest (N=126): 3%
- Not eligible for either Medicare or Medicaid EHR incennves (N=137): 3%
- Do Not Know (N=539): 13%

Conclusion

Only a small proportion of surveyed hospitals reported participating in an ACO arrangement. Why this is so is unclear. It may be that hospitals were waiting for the final ACO rules to be released (which they were in October 2011) before committing to participate in an ACO. Alternatively, it could be they did not have the capital for start-up costs, which are estimated by the American Hospital Association (AHA) to be between $5.3 and $12 million, dependent upon a hospital's size.[3] If CMS estimates are correct, however, the level of shared savings payments made to providers should be worth roughly three times the amount of money they will need for start-up investment and annual costs.[4]

Overall, hospitals embracing the ACO model appeared to be more progressive in terms of care coordination and transition activities, as well as the achievement of meaningful use criteria, relative to non-ACO institutions. This suggests that the accountable care model may well improve upon the traditional fee-for-service model by better incentivizing the enhanced care of patients. These findings may warrant further studies to determine if such improved care methods serve to functionally reduce the overall cost of medical care provision.

---

[3] What are ACO start-up costs? – FierceHealthcare http://www.fiercehealthcare.com/story/what-are-acos-start-costs/2011-10-26#ixzz27mGesir9. Accessed October 2, 2012.

[4] Remington Report. ACO Final Regulations Give Providers More Flexibility. http://remingtonreport.com/news-across-the-healthcare-delivery/1247-aco-final-regulations-give-providers-more-flexibility. Accessed October 2, 2012.

How to Use this Book

For more than seven decades, *AHA Hospital Statistics*™ has reported aggregate hospital data derived from the AHA Annual Survey and is the definitive source when doing trend analysis with data by bed size category, U.S. Census Divisions, States, and Metropolitan Statistical Areas (MSAs). As the health care delivery system changes, so have the data tracked by the survey and presented in this report. Recent additions include:

- **Community health indicators** that offer readers a connection to the community for their analysis and planning: the data are broken down into beds, admissions, inpatient days, ER outpatient visits, and other indicators per 1000 population, as well as expense per capita.

- **Utilization, personnel and finance** by all MSAs in the United States.

- **Five-year trend data** on physician models, insurance products, and managed care contracts enable you to identify changes in relationships between hospitals and other health care systems and providers.

- **Tables 3 through 6 have been organized** to show breakdowns between inpatient and outpatient care to better reflect market shifts toward outpatient-centered care. Additional clarity is gained by the breakdown between total facility data (which includes nursing home type units under the control of the hospital) and hospital units (which exclude the nursing home data).

TABLE 6	**Sample State**				
	U.S. Registered Community Hospitals				
	(Nonfederal, short-term general and other special hospitals)				
	Overview 2007–2011				
	2011	**2010**	**2009**	**2008**	**2007**
Physician Models					
Independent Practice Association........	14	17	17	17	14
Group Practice without Walls...........	4	5	5	8	4
Open Physician-Hospital Organization....	20	21	24	23	18
Closed Physician-Hospital Organization...	21	17	18	17	11
Management Service Organization.......	14	18	20	14	9
Integrated Salary Model...............	35	29	30	26	24
Equity Model.......................	4	3	4	6	3
Foundation........................	9	8	23	21	19
Insurance Products					
Health Maintenance Organization.......	20	22	23	24	19
Preferred Provider Organization.........	39	47	52	53	37
Indemnity Fee for Service.............	7	12	14	12	6
Managed Care Contracts					
Health Maintenance Organization.......	64	67	62	49	42
Preferred Provider Organization........	97	93	92	87	72

Example of five-year trend data

- **Facilities and Services information** on more than 100 categories of hospital facilities and services in Table 7. At a glance, you can determine the number and percentage of hospitals offering a specific service such as Oncology, Angioplasty, Palliative Care Program, Complementary Medicine, Women's Health Services and Tobacco Cessation.

- **Plus, System and Network involvement along with Group Purchasing Organizations** that demonstrate ways in which organizations are linked.

The survey instrument and the glossary

A good place to begin your analysis is the AHA Annual Survey instrument. Found on page 215, it includes the instructions, questions, and terms that were used to gather the data for fiscal year 2011. This can be extremely valuable for a clearer understanding of the data we collect and the tables presented in *AHA Hospital Statistics*.

Please also review the glossary in the back of the book. The glossary contains complete definitions for specific terms used in the tables and text of *AHA Hospital Statistics*. These definitions will clarify how terminology is being used.

As mentioned above, it is important to note that the primary focus of the most detailed data contained in *AHA Hospital Statistics* is community hospitals. As defined, community hospitals are all non-federal, short-term general and special hospitals whose facilities and services are available to the public. If the majority of a hospital's patients are admitted to units where the average length of stay is 30 days or less, a hospital may still be classified as short-term even if it includes a nursing- home-type unit. (For a more complete definition of community hospitals, please see the glossary definition, located on page 201.)

Getting the most out of
AHA Hospital Statistics
This section of the book provides an introduction for getting the most out of your *AHA Hospital Statistics* 2013 edition. Here, you'll find a guide to the book, with insights into each table.

Equity model: An arrangement that allows established practitioners to become shareholders in a professional corporation in exchange for tangible and intangible assets of their existing practices.

Expenses: Includes all expenses for the reporting period including payroll, non-payroll, and all nonoperating expenses. *Payroll expenses* include all salaries and wages. *Non-payroll expenses* are all professional fees and those salary expenditures excluded from payroll. *Labor related expenses* are defined as payroll expenses plus employee benefits. *Non-labor related expenses* are all other non-payroll expenses. *Bad debt* has been reclassified from a "reduction in revenue" to an expense in accordance with the revised AICPA Audit Guide. However, for purposes of historical consistency, the expense total that appears throughout *AHA Hospital Statistics does not include "bad debt" as an expense item*. Note: Financial data may not add due to rounding.

Extracorporeal shock wave lithotripter (ESWL): A medical device used for treating stones in the kidney or urethra. The device disintegrates kidney stones noninvasively through the transmission of acoustic shock waves directed at the stones.

Fitness center: Provides exercise, testing, or evaluation programs and fitness activities to the community and hospital employees.

Example of Glossary definitions.

Table 1	Historical Trends in Utilization, Personnel, and Finances for Selected Years from 1946 through 2011

CLASSIFICATION	YEAR	HOSPITALS	BEDS (in thousands)	ADMISSIONS (in thousands)	AVERAGE DAILY CENSUS (in thousands)	ADJUSTED AVERAGE DAILY CENSUS (in thousands)
Total United States	1946	6,125	1,436	15,675	1,142	—
	1950	6,788	1,456	18,483	1,253	—
	1955	6,956	1,604	21,073	1,363	—
	1960	6,876	1,658	25,027	1,402	—
	1965	7,123	1,704	28,812	1,403	—
	1970	7,123	1,616	31,759	1,298	—
	1971	7,097	1,556	32,664	1,237	—
	1972	7,061	1,550	33,265	1,209	—
	1973	7,123	1,535	34,352	1,189	—
	1974	7,174	1,513	35,506	1,167	—
	1975	7,156	1,466	36,157	1,125	—
	1976	7,082	1,434	36,776	1,090	—
	1977	7,099	1,407	37,060	1,066	—
	1978	7,015	1,381	37,243	1,042	—
	1979	6,988	1,372	37,802	1,043	—
	1980	6,965	1,365	38,892	1,060	—
	1981	6,933	1,362	39,169	1,061	—
	1982	6,915	1,360	39,095	1,053	—
	1983	6,888	1,350	38,887	1,028	—
	1984	6,872	1,339	37,938	970	—
	1985	6,872	1,318	36,304	910	—
	1986	6,841	1,290	35,219	883	—
	1987	6,821	1,267	34,439	873	—
	1988	6,780	1,248	34,107	863	—
	1989	6,720	1,226	33,742	853	—
	1990	6,649	1,213	33,774	844	—
	1991	6,634	1,202	33,567	827	—
	1992	6,539	1,178	33,536	807	—
	1993	6,467	1,163	33,201	783	—
	1994	6,374	1,128	33,125	745	—
	1995	6,291	1,081	33,282	710	—
	1996	6,201	1,062	33,307	685	—
	1997	6,097	1,035	33,624	673	—
	1998	6,021	1,013	33,766	662	—
	1999	5,890	994	34,181	657	—
	2000	5,810	984	34,891	650	—
	2001	5,801	987	35,644	658	—
	2002	5,794	976	36,326	662	—
	2003	5,764	965	36,611	657	—
	2004	5,759	956	36,942	658	—
	2005	5,756	947	37,006	656	—

Example of Table 1

Table 1 — Historical Trends in Utilization, Personnel and Finances for Selected Years from 1946 through 2011

Table 1 at a Glance

This table is used to evaluate historical data and allows you to examine long-term trends in health care with data dating back more than sixty years. Table 1 reports on all AHA registered hospitals in the United States. One important note: To be considered an AHA-registered hospital, a hospital does not need to be an AHA member. Rather, the hospital must meet particular certification or satisfy a number of requirements. These Registration Requirements immediately follow this section and begin on page (xxiv.)

This table segments the data into various organizational structure categories. Here's a brief look at these different classifications:

- Total United States Hospitals
- Total Non-Federal Short-term and other special hospitals
- Community hospitals
- Non-government not-for-profit community hospitals
- Investor-owned (for-profit) community hospitals
- State and local government community hospitals

Table 1 also provides input on nationwide utilization, personnel and finance trends. You'll find answers to questions such as: *Over the past 25 years, what trends do I see comparing the average length of stay at government and non-government not-for-profit community hospitals and investor-owned for-profit community hospitals?* or *What has been the trend in outpatient visits?*

Table 2 — 2010 U.S. Registered Hospitals: Utilization, Personnel and Finances

Table 2 at a Glance

This table takes a closer look at U.S. Registered Hospitals for 2011. It offers a snapshot of utilization, personnel and finance statistics, and breaks down this information for specialty hospitals. In addition, this is the only table that outlines data on federal hospitals. You'll be able to use this table to better understand the number of beds set-up and staffed, how many personnel and trainees are on the payroll, and what the financial implications of these may be.

TABLE 3

TOTAL UNITED STATES

U.S. Registered Community Hospitals
(Nonfederal, short-term general and other special hospitals)

**Utilization, Personnel, Revenue and Expenses,
Community Health Indicators 2007-2011**

	2011	2010	2009	2008	2007
TOTAL FACILITY (Includes Hospital and Nursing Home Units)					
Utilization - Inpatient					
Beds	839,988	853,287	862,352	872,736	902,061
Admissions	31,811,673	31,576,960	31,098,959	30,945,357	30,718,136
Inpatient Days	191,430,450	192,504,015	193,747,004	199,876,367	207,180,278
Average Length of Stay	6.0	6.1	6.2	6.5	6.7
Inpatient Surgeries	9,735,705	9,509,081	9,545,612	9,700,613	9,833,938
Births	3,726,233	3,742,191	3,723,871	3,764,698	3,809,367
HOSPITAL UNIT (Excludes Separate Nursing Home Units)					
Utilization - Inpatient					
Beds	758,186	769,505	782,504	794,502	824,969
Admissions	31,265,867	31,047,930	30,652,820	30,577,564	30,403,766
Inpatient Days	165,644,176	165,605,620	168,189,130	174,898,504	182,702,882
Average Length of Stay	5.3	5.3	5.5	5.7	6.0
Personnel					
Total Full Time	3,235,153	3,183,730	3,154,603	3,166,729	3,147,922
Total Part Time	1,213,426	1,214,232	1,153,790	1,146,082	1,122,957
Revenue and Expenses - Totals					
(Includes Inpatient and Outpatient)					
Total Net Revenue	$333,054,828,642	$322,459,942,930	$310,513,291,998	$298,519,717,355	$285,858,018,951
Total Expenses	314,709,758,455	301,905,101,393	290,128,641,153	282,372,557,487	272,840,121,437

Example of Table 3. Helps contrast acute and long-term care

Table 3 — Total United States

Table 3 at a Glance

This table provides a look at all U .S. Registered Community Hospitals, in terms of general overview with utilization by inpatient and outpatient, personnel, revenue, expenses and community health indicators. It provides a snapshot of the past five years, allowing you to track emerging trends.

This national information can be compared to local or regional trends, for benchmarking:

- Both inpatient and outpatient information is included, for better evaluation of data.

- Reporting by total facility *Includes hospital and Nursing Home Units* and hospital unit only *Excludes Separate Nursing Home Units* helps contrast acute and long-term care.

- Community health indicators can help uncover trends and help determine future facility needs.

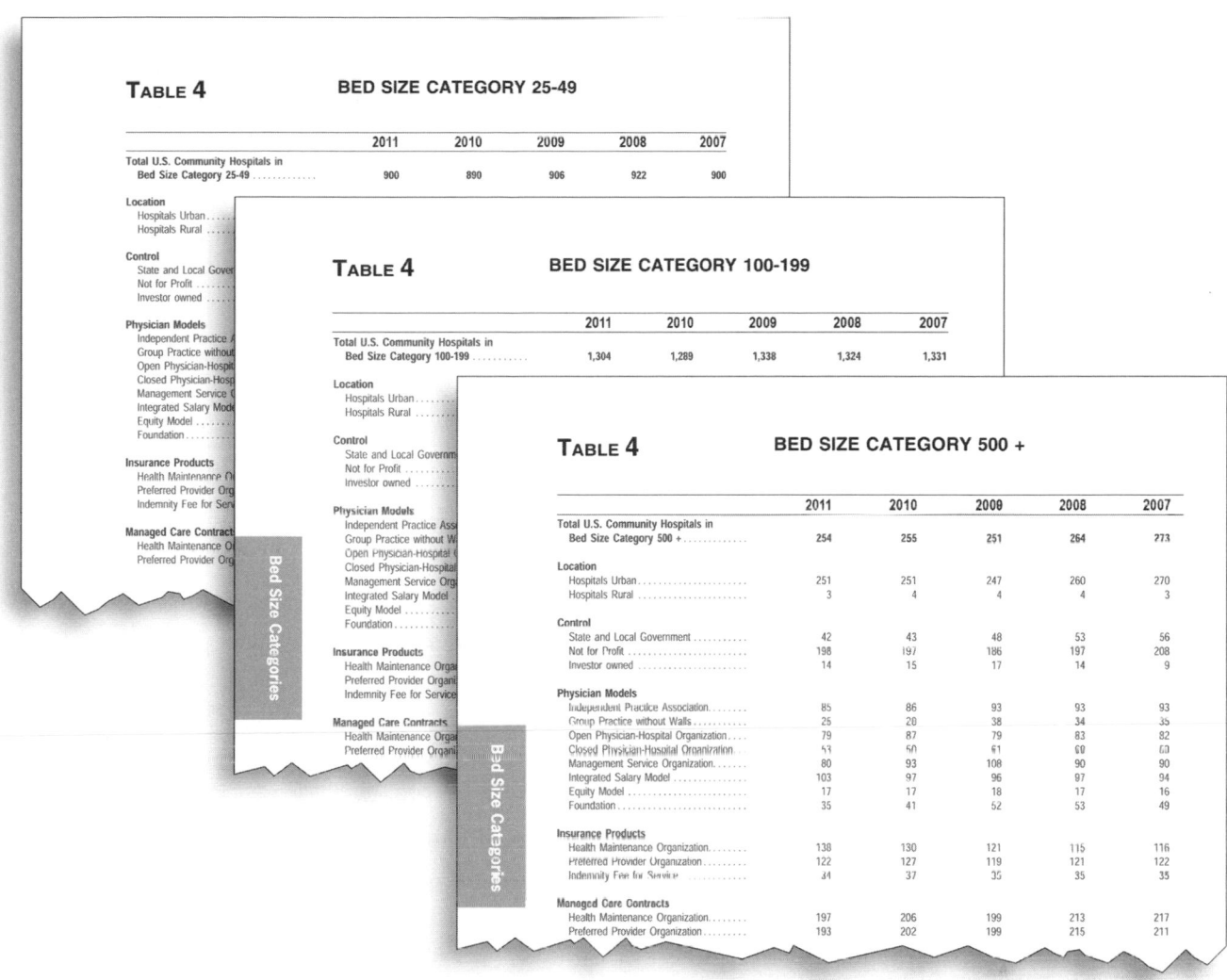

Example of Table 4. Compares facilities with peers.

Table 4 — Bed Size Categories

Table 4 at a Glance

This table provides a look at all U.S. Registered Community Hospitals, broken down by bed size. The table includes general overview, utilization, personnel, and revenue and expense information. These categories of bed sizes were developed by the AHA, and have become an industry standard. By categorizing each facility into a peer group, this table provides a snapshot of the past five years allowing you to compare facilities with their peers.

TABLE 5

U.S. CENSUS DIVISION 2: MIDDLE ATLANTIC

U.S. Registered Community Hospitals
(Nonfederal, short-term general and other special hospitals)

Utilization, Personnel, Revenue and Expenses, Community Health Indicators 2007-2011

	2011	2010	2009	2008	2007
COMMUNITY HEALTH INDICATORS PER 1000 POPULATION					
Total Population (in thousands) . . .	38,292	38,216	38,184	38,147	38,108
Inpatient					
Beds	3.6	3.8	3.9	4.0	4.1
Admissions	135.8	136.7	136.2	138.3	137.4
Inpatient Days	963.5	988.8	1,019.0	1,093.8	1,145.0
Inpatient Surgeries	42.2	41.4	41.2	42.7	43.6
Births	13.0	13.2	13.6	13.7	14.3
Outpatient					
Emergency Outpatient Visits	367.7	362.0	363.4	379.5	360.1
Other Outpatient Visits	1,970.9	1,802.3	1,767.7	1,680.3	1,573.9
Total Outpatient Visits	2,338.6	2,164.3	2,131.1	2,059.8	1,934.0
Outpatient Surgeries	67.8	62.4	59.9	55.4	53.5
Expense per Capita (per person) . . .	$1,494.9	$1,462.7	$1,428.6	$1,429.8	$1,369.2

Example of Table 5. Uncovers trends to determine future facility needs.

Table 5 — U.S. Census Divisions

Table 5 at a Glance
This table provides a look at all U.S. Registered Community Hospitals, broken down by Census Division. The table includes general overview, utilization, personnel, and expenses, and community health indicator information. It provides a snapshot of the past five years, allowing you to track trends on a regional level. In addition, this allows you to compare this data to other population based health indicators, offering a more comprehensive look than the survey data alone. Community health indicators can help uncover trends and help determine future facility needs.

Table 6 — States

Table 6 at a Glance
This table provides a look at all U.S. Registered Community Hospitals, broken down by State. The table includes general overview, utilization, personnel, revenue and expenses, and community health indicator information. It provides a snapshot of the past five years, allowing you to track trends on a state level.

Note:
You can use the information in tables 3, 4, 5 and 6 to make accurate comparisons across Total U.S., Bed Size Category, Census Division and State.

Table 7 — 2011 Facilities and Services in the U.S. Census Divisions and States

Table 7 at a Glance

This table examines facilities and services by both Census Division and State. A comprehensive alphabetical guide helps make each facility or service easy to find. This table will allow you to better understand what service lines are emerging and how many facilities offer a particular service in a discrete state or region.

This collection of facilities and services information data is unique to *AHA Hospital Statistics* and the list is continually growing. Recent additions include:

- Rural health clinic
- Adult cardiology services
- Pediatric cardiology services
- Assistive technology center
- Electrodiagnostic services
- Prosthetic and orthotic services
- Adult cardiac electrophysiology
- Pediatric cardiac electrophysiology
- Optical colonoscopy
- Robot-assisted walking therapy
- Simulated rehabilitation environment

Table7 (Continued)

CLASSIFICATION	HOSPITALS REPORTING	CASE MANAGEMENT Number	Percent	CHILDREN WELLNESS PROGRAM Number	Percent	CHIROPRACTIC SERVICES Number	Percent	COMMUNITY OUTREACH Number	Percent
UNITED STATES	4,797	2,980	62.1	783	16.3	61	1.3	2,725	56.8
COMMUNITY HOSPITALS	4,113	2,620	63.7	742	18.0	53	1.3	2,491	60.6
CENSUS DIVISION 1, NEW ENGLAND	230	157	68.3	63	27.4	6	2.6	169	73.5
Connecticut	42	32	76.2	15	35.7	3	7.1	32	76.2
Maine	39	20	51.3	9	23.1	0	0.0	30	76.9
Massachusetts	85	64	75.3	21	24.7	2	2.4	62	72.9
New Hampshire	31	20	64.5	10	32.3	0	0.0	23	74.2
Rhode Island	16	12	75.0	4	25.0	1	6.3	11	68.8
Vermont	17	9	52.9	4	23.5	0	0.0	11	64.7
CENSUS DIVISION 2, MIDDLE ATLANTIC	461	344	74.6	143	31.0	7	1.5	345	74.8
New Jersey	71	66	93.0	29	40.8	2	2.8	60	84.5
New York	194	146	75.3	61	31.4	2	1.0	140	72.2
Pennsylvania	196	132	67.3	53	27.0	3	1.5	145	74.0
CENSUS DIVISION 3, SOUTH ATLANTIC	734	484	66.9	123	17.0	8	1.1	460	62.2
Delaware	9	5	55.5	4	44.4	0	0.0	5	55.6
District of Columbia	17	13	76.5	3	17.6	2	11.8	10	58.8
Florida	138	117	84.8	23	16.7	3	2.2	89	64.5
Georgia	144	87	60.4	19	13.2	0	0.0	75	52.1
Maryland	64	47	73.4	10	15.6	1	1.6	46	71.9
North Carolina	119	84	70.6	20	16.8	1	0.8	71	59.7
South Carolina	71	25	35.2	25	35.2	0	0.0	64	90.1
Virginia	98	72	73.5	9	9.2	0	0.0	55	56.1
West Virginia	64	34	53.1	10	15.6	1	1.6	35	54.7
CENSUS DIVISION 4, EAST NORTH CENTRAL	741	478	64.5	140	18.9	15	2.0	494	66.6
Illinois	193	128	66.3	45	23.3	5	2.6	132	68.4
Indiana	110	68	61.8	20	18.2	1	0.9	76	69.1
Michigan	148	92	62.2	32	21.6	0	0.0	101	66.2
Ohio	156	108	69.2	34	21.8	9	5.8	109	69.9
Wisconsin	134	82	61.2	9	6.7	0	0.0	46	34.3
CENSUS DIVISION 5, EAST SOUTH CENTRAL	403	239	59.8	26	6.5	3	0.7	198	49.1
Alabama	94	80	63.8	5	5.3	1	1.1	52	55.3
Kentucky	104	64	61.5	12	11.5	0	0.0	49	47.1
Mississippi	106	45	42.5	0	0.0	0	0.0	56	52.8
Tennessee	99	60	60.6	9	9.1	2	2.0	41	41.4
CENSUS DIVISION 6, WEST NORTH CENTRAL	723	308	43.8	86	12.1	11	1.6	370	52.6
Iowa	120	65	54.0	13	10.8	2	1.6	98	54.0
Kansas	139	48	34.5	12	8.6	3	2.2	46	33.1
Minnesota	115	33	28.7	9	7.8	1	0.9	74	64.3
Missouri	151	106	70.2	23	15.2	4	2.6	97	64.2
Nebraska	81	28	34.6	5	6.2	0	0.0	45	55.6
North Dakota	35	7	20.0	5	14.3	1	2.9	16	45.7
South Dakota	56	18	32.1	6	10.7	0	0.0	24	42.9
CENSUS DIVISION 7, WEST SOUTH CENTRAL	777	492	63.3	76	9.8	4	0.5	316	40.7
Arkansas	65	44	67.7	5	7.7	0	0.0	27	41.5
Louisiana	111	70	63.1	18	16.2	1	0.9	44	39.6
Oklahoma	115	60	60.2	9	7.8	1	0.9	49	42.6
Texas	486	318	65.4	44	9.1	2	0.4	196	40.3
CENSUS DIVISION 8, MOUNTAIN	333	194	58.3	47	14.1	2	0.6	162	48.6
Arizona	54	44	81.5	8	14.8	0	0.0	25	46.3
Colorado	59	40	67.8	10	16.9	1	1.7	41	69.5
Idaho	39	17	43.6	5	14.3	0	0.0	19	54.?
Montana	54	12	22.2	7	13.0	0	0.0	14	25.?
Nevada	30	15	75.0	3	15.0	0	0.0	10	50.?
New Mexico	40	22	55.0	7	17.5	0	0.0	18	45.0
Utah	44	20	59.1	6	13.6	1	2.3	20	45.5
Wyoming	27	18	66.7	1	3.7	0	0.0	15	55.6
CENSUS DIVISION 9, PACIFIC	425	284	69.2	80	18.8	5	1.2	251	59.1
Alaska	15	9	60.0	1	6.7	0	0.0	6	40.?
California	280	209	74.6	55	19.6	3	1.1	173	61.8
Hawaii	16	10	62.5	3	18.8	0	0.0	8	50.0
Oregon	52	28	53.8	11	21.2	0	0.0	31	59.?
Washington	62	38	61.3	10	16.1	2	3.2	33	

Example of Table 7.

These new categories reflect the trends as hospitals expand their service lines to mirror the needs of their patients. For example, services such as acupuncture or massage therapy are now accounted for in the Complementary Medicine service item.

This table can answer questions such as: *What percentage of hospitals in the United States offer complementary medicine or wound management?* or *How are these new services distributed by state?*

Table 8 — Utilization, Personnel and Finances in Community Hospitals by MSAs for 2011

Table 8 at a Glance

This table provides a look at all U.S. Registered Community Hospitals, broken down by Metropolitan Statistical Area (MSA). The table includes general overview, utilization, personnel, and finance information. It provides a snapshot of the past year.

Additional Resources

Again, in the back of the book you will find the comprehensive glossary and the 2011 annual survey questionnaire. The survey itself can be a valuable resource to understanding what was asked in order to gather the data in the book. This survey is also used to produce the *AHA Guide*® and AHA Annual Survey Database™.

AHA-Registered Hospitals

Any institution that can be classified as a hospital according to the requirements may be registered if it so desires. Membership in the American Hospital Association is not a prerequisite.

The American Hospital Association may, at the sole discretion of the Executive Committee of the Board of Trustees, grant, deny, or withdraw the registration of an institution.

An institution may be registered by the American Hospital Association as a hospital if it is accredited as a hospital by The Joint Commission or is certified as a provider of acute services under Title 18 of the Social Security Act and has provided the Association with documents verifying the accreditation or certification.

In lieu of the preceding accreditation or certification, an institution licensed as a hospital by the appropriate state agency may be registered by AHA as a hospital by meeting the following alternative requirements:

Function: The primary function of the institution is to provide patient services, diagnostic and therapeutic, for particular or general medical conditions.

1. The institution shall maintain at least six inpatient beds, which shall be continuously available for the care of patients who are nonrelated and who stay on the average in excess of 24 hours per admission.

2. The institution shall be constructed, equipped, and maintained to ensure the health and safety of patients and to provide uncrowded, sanitary facilities for the treatment of patients.

3. There shall be an identifiable governing authority legally and morally responsible for the conduct of the hospital.

4. There shall be a chief executive to whom the governing authority delegates the continuous responsibility for the operation of the hospital in accordance with established policy.

5. There shall be an organized medical staff of fully licensed physicians* that may include other licensed individuals permitted by law and by the hospital to provide patient care services independently in the hospital. The medical staff shall be accountable to the governing authority for maintaining proper standards of medical care, and it shall be governed by bylaws adopted by said staff and approved by the governing authority.

6. Each patient shall be admitted on the authority of a member of the medical staff who has been granted the privilege to admit patients to inpatient services in accordance with state law and criteria for standards of medical care established by the individual medical staff. Each patient's general medical condition is the responsibility of a qualified physician member of the medical staff. When nonphysician members of the medical staff are granted privileges to admit patients, provision is made for prompt medical evaluation of these patients by a qualified physician. Any graduate of a foreign medical school who is permitted to assume responsibilities for patient care shall possess a valid license to practice medicine, or shall be certified by the Educational Commission for Foreign Medical Graduates, or shall have qualified for and have successfully completed an academic year of supervised clinical training under the direction of a medical school approved by the Liaison Committee on GAT Medical Education.

7. Registered nurse supervision and other nursing services are continuous.

8. A current and complete‡ medical record shall be maintained by the institution for each patient and shall be available for reference.

9. Pharmacy service shall be maintained in the institution and shall be supervised by a registered pharmacist.

10. The institution shall provide patients with food service that meets their nutritional and therapeutic requirements; special diets shall also be available.

Types of Hospitals

In addition to meeting these 10 general registration requirements, hospitals are registered as one of four types of hospitals: general, special, rehabilitation and chronic disease, or psychiatric. The following type of hospital and special requirements for registration are employed:

General

The primary function of the institution is to provide patient services, diagnostic and therapeutic, for a variety of medical conditions. A general hospital also shall provide:

- diagnostic x-ray services with facilities and staff for a variety of procedures
- clinical laboratory service with facilities and staff for a variety of procedures and with anatomical pathology services regularly and conveniently available
- operating room service with facilities and staff.

Special

The primary function of the institution is to provide diagnostic and treatment services for patients who have specified medical conditions, both surgical and nonsurgical. A special hospital also shall provide:

- such diagnostic and treatment services as may be determined by the Executive Committee of the Board of Trustees of the American Hospital Association to be appropriate for the specified medical conditions for which medical services are provided shall be maintained in the institution with suitable facilities and staff. If such conditions do not normally require diagnostic x-ray service, laboratory service, or operating room service, and if any such services are therefore not maintained in the institution, there shall be written arrangements to make them available to patients requiring them.
- clinical laboratory services capable of providing tissue diagnosis when offering pregnancy termination services.

Rehabilitation and Chronic Disease

The primary function of the institution is to provide diagnostic and treatment services to handicapped or disabled individuals requiring restorative and adjustive services. A rehabilitation and chronic disease hospital also shall provide:

- arrangements for diagnostic x-ray services, as required, on a regular and conveniently available basis
- arrangements for clinical laboratory service, as required on a regular and conveniently available basis
- arrangements for operating room service, as required, on a regular and conveniently available basis
- a physical therapy service with suitable facilities and staff in the institution
- an occupational therapy service with suitable facilities and staff in the institution
- arrangements for psychological and social work services on a regular and conveniently available basis

---

* Physician–Term used to describe an individual with an M.D. or D.O. degree who is fully licensed to practice medicine in all its phases.

‡ The completed records in general shall contain at least the following: the patient's identifying data and consent forms, medical history, record of physical examination, physicians' progress notes, operative notes, nurses' notes, routine x-ray and laboratory reports, doctors' orders, and final diagnosis.

- arrangements for educational and vocational services on a regular and conveniently available basis
- written arrangements with a general hospital for the transfer of patients who require medical, obstetrical, or surgical services not available in the institution.

Psychiatric

The primary function of the institution is to provide diagnostic and treatment services for patients who have psychiatric-related illnesses. A psychiatric hospital also shall provide:

- arrangements for clinical laboratory service, as required, on a regular and conveniently available basis
- arrangements for diagnostic x-ray services, as required on a regular and conveniently available basis
- psychiatric, psychological, and social work service with facilities and staff in the institution
- arrangements for electroencephalograph services, as required, on a regular and conveniently available basis.
- written arrangements with a general hospital for the transfer of patients who require medical, obstetrical, or surgical services not available in the institution.

The American Hospital Association may, at the sole discretion of the Executive Committee of the Board of Trustees, grant, deny, or withdraw the registration of an institution.

Data Comparability

The economic climate, demographic characteristics, personnel issues, and health care financing and payment policies differ by region, state, and city across the country. *Differences in these factors must be taken into account when using the data.* In addition, the profiles of hospitals across comparison groups vary. For example, states will differ in terms of the number and percentage of hospitals by size, ownership, services provided, types of patients treated, and so forth. *Differences in these variables also must be taken into consideration when doing a comparative analysis.*

Notes on the Survey

The 2013 edition of *AHA Hospital Statistics*™ draws its data from the 2011 AHA Annual Survey of Hospitals. It is the statistical complement to the 2013 edition of the *AHA Guide*®, which contains selected data about individual hospitals.

The AHA Survey was mailed to all hospitals, both AHA-registered and nonregistered, in the U.S. and its associated areas: American Samoa, Guam, the Marshall Islands, Puerto Rico, and the Virgin Islands. U.S. government hospitals located outside the U.S. were not included. Overall, the average response rate over the past five years has been approximately 83 percent.

Reporting Period

In completing the survey, hospitals were requested to report data for a full year, in accord with their fiscal year, ending in 2011. The statistical table present data reported or estimated for a 12-month period, except for data on personnel, which represent situations as they existed at the end of the reporting period.

Respondents

Data for Tables 1 and 2 include 5,724 AHA-registered hospitals in the U.S. Data on community hospitals (nonfederal, short-term general and other special hospitals) only are presented in Tables 3-6, and Table 8.

It is important to note that the AHA-registered hospitals included in *AHA Hospital Statistics* are not necessarily identical to those included in *AHA Guide*. The institutions listed in the 2013 edition of AHA Guide include all of those institutions CMS certified, Joint Commission accredited, or AHA registered as of September 2011. Tables 1-6 in *AHA Hospital Statistics* present data for AHA-registered hospitals that were in operation during the 12-month reporting period ending 2011.

Estimates

Estimates were made of data for nonreporting hospitals and for reporting hospitals that submitted incomplete AHA Annual Survey questionnaires. Estimates were not made for beds, bassinets and facilities and services. Data for beds and bassinets of nonreporting hospitals were based on the most recent information from those hospitals. (Note that in all statistical tables, whenever bed-size categories are listed, all eight categories appear, whether or not there are hospitals in every category.)

Missing revenue, expenses, admissions, births, inpatient days, surgical operations, outpatient visits, and full-time-equivalent personnel values are estimates from regression models. For all other variables the estimates were based on ratios such as per bed averages derived from data reported by hospitals similar in size, control, major service provided, length of stay, and geographical characteristics to the hospitals that did not report this information.

Tables 1–2

Table

1

Historical Trends in Utilization, Personnel, and Finances for Selected Years from 1946 through 2011

Data are for all AHA-registered hospitals in the United States. Data are estimated for nonreporting hospitals with the exception of newborn and outpatient data before 1972. Personnel data exclude residents, interns, and students from 1952 on; personnel data include full-time personnel and full-time equivalents for part-time personnel from 1954 on. As a result of the AHA Annual Survey validation process, the New York state expense data from 1976 were revised after the 1977 edition was published. The revised figures are included below. In order to provide trend data on a consistent basis, the 1970 and 1971 psychiatric and long-term data have been slightly modified. The 1982 FTE figures have updated to provide the most accurate data possible.

CLASSIFICATION / YEAR	HOSPITALS	BEDS (in thousands)	ADMISSIONS (in thousands)	AVERAGE DAILY CENSUS (in thousands)	ADJUSTED AVERAGE DAILY CENSUS (in thousands)	AVERAGE STAY (days)	OUTPATIENT VISITS (in thousands)	NEWBORNS Bassinets	NEWBORNS Births	FTE PERSONNEL Number (in thousands)	FTE PERSONNEL Per 100 Adjusted Census	TOTAL EXPENSES Amount (in Millions of dollars)	TOTAL EXPENSES Adjusted per Inpatient Stay (dollars)	TOTAL EXPENSES Adjusted per Inpatient Day (dollars)
Total United States														
1946	6,125	1,436	15,675	1,142	—	—	—	85,585	2,135,327	830	—	$1,963	—	—
1950	6,788	1,456	18,483	1,253	—	—	—	90,101	2,742,780	1,058	—	$3,651	—	—
1955	6,956	1,604	21,073	1,363	—	—	—	98,823	3,476,753	1,301	—	$5,594	—	—
1960	6,876	1,658	25,027	1,402	—	—	—	102,764	3,835,735	1,598	—	$8,421	—	—
1965	7,123	1,704	28,812	1,403	—	—	125,793	101,287	3,565,344	1,952	—	$12,948	—	—
1970	7,123	1,616	31,759	1,298	—	—	181,370	97,128	3,537,000	2,537	—	$25,556	—	—
1971	7,097	1,556	32,664	1,237	—	—	199,725	94,344	3,464,513	2,589	—	$28,812	—	—
1972	7,061	1,550	33,265	1,209	—	—	219,182	92,960	3,231,875	2,671	—	$32,667	—	—
1973	7,123	1,535	34,352	1,189	—	—	233,555	90,071	3,087,210	2,769	—	$36,290	—	—
1974	7,174	1,513	35,506	1,167	—	—	250,481	88,269	3,043,386	2,919	—	$41,406	—	—
1975	7,156	1,466	36,157	1,125	—	—	254,844	86,875	3,091,629	3,023	—	$48,706	—	—
1976	7,082	1,434	36,776	1,090	—	—	270,951	85,284	3,067,063	3,108	—	$56,005	—	—
1977	7,099	1,407	37,060	1,066	—	—	263,775	83,193	3,223,699	3,213	—	$63,630	—	—
1978	7,015	1,381	37,243	1,042	—	—	263,606	80,650	3,250,373	3,280	—	$70,927	—	—
1979	6,988	1,372	37,802	1,043	—	—	262,009	79,720	3,376,467	3,382	—	$79,796	—	—
1980	6,965	1,365	38,892	1,060	—	—	262,951	79,842	3,500,043	3,492	—	$91,886	—	—
1981	6,933	1,362	39,169	1,061	—	—	265,332	78,823	3,558,274	3,661	—	$107,146	—	—
1982	6,915	1,360	39,095	1,053	—	—	313,667	77,998	3,615,751	3,746	—	$123,219	—	—
1983	6,888	1,350	38,887	1,028	—	—	273,168	77,837	3,596,146	3,707	—	$136,315	—	—
1984	6,872	1,339	37,938	970	—	—	276,566	77,845	3,563,106	3,630	—	$144,114	—	—
1985	6,872	1,318	36,304	910	—	—	282,140	77,202	3,630,961	3,625	—	$153,327	—	—
1986	6,841	1,290	35,219	883	—	—	294,634	76,002	3,680,178	3,647	—	$165,194	—	—
1987	6,821	1,267	34,439	873	—	—	310,707	74,770	3,698,294	3,742	—	$178,662	—	—
1988	6,780	1,248	34,107	863	—	—	336,208	72,568	3,794,369	3,839	—	$196,704	—	—
1989	6,720	1,226	33,742	853	—	—	352,248	71,491	3,920,384	3,937	—	$214,886	—	—
1990	6,649	1,213	33,774	844	—	—	368,184	70,539	4,046,704	4,063	—	$234,870	—	—
1991	6,634	1,202	33,567	827	—	—	387,675	69,464	4,047,504	4,165	—	$258,508	—	—
1992	6,539	1,178	33,536	807	—	—	417,874	69,052	4,007,179	4,236	—	$282,531	—	—
1993	6,467	1,163	33,201	783	—	—	435,619	67,911	3,949,788	4,289	—	$301,538	—	—
1994	6,374	1,128	33,125	745	—	—	453,584	67,311	3,886,667	4,270	—	$310,834	—	—
1995	6,291	1,081	33,282	710	—	—	483,195	66,256	3,833,132	4,273	—	$320,252	—	—
1996	6,201	1,062	33,307	685	—	—	505,455	65,138	3,790,678	4,276	—	$330,531	—	—
1997	6,097	1,035	33,624	673	—	—	520,600	64,649	3,811,522	4,333	—	$342,334	—	—
1998	6,021	1,013	33,766	662	—	—	545,481	63,485	3,795,212	4,407	—	$355,450	—	—
1999	5,890	994	34,181	657	—	—	573,461	62,714	3,829,881	4,369	—	$372,933	—	—
2000	5,810	984	34,891	650	—	—	592,673	61,915	3,940,017	4,454	—	$395,391	—	—
2001	5,801	987	35,644	658	—	—	612,276	61,527	3,929,733	4,535	—	$426,849	—	—
2002	5,794	976	36,326	662	—	—	640,515	62,151	3,934,421	4,610	—	$462,222	—	—
2003	5,764	965	36,611	657	—	—	648,560	60,699	3,976,886	4,651	—	$498,104	—	—
2004	5,759	956	36,942	658	—	—	662,131	59,660	3,965,906	4,696	—	$533,853	—	—
2005	5,756	947	37,006	656	—	—	673,689	59,073	4,048,442	4,791	—	$570,534	—	—
2006	5,747	947	37,189	653	—	—	690,425	58,670	4,126,598	4,907	—	$607,355	—	—
2007	5,708	945	37,120	645	—	—	693,510	58,429	4,128,796	5,024	—	$641,124	—	—
2008	5,815	951	37,529	649	—	—	709,960	58,133	4,109,081	5,116	—	$690,074	—	—
2009	5,795	944	37,480	641	—	—	741,551	58,078	4,001,748	5,178	—	$726,671	—	—
2010	5,754	942	36,915	627	—	—	750,408	57,396	3,871,751	5,184	—	$750,602	—	—
2011	5,724	924	36,565	615	—	—	754,454	57,022	3,767,697	5,196	—	$773,547	—	—

Table 1 (Continued)

CLASSIFICATION: Total nonfederal short-term general and other special

YEAR	HOSPITALS	BEDS (in thousands)	ADMISSIONS (in thousands)	AVERAGE DAILY CENSUS (in thousands)	ADJUSTED AVERAGE DAILY CENSUS (in thousands)	AVERAGE STAY (days)	OUTPATIENT VISITS (in thousands)	NEWBORNS Bassinets	NEWBORNS Births	FTE PERSONNEL Number (in thousands)	FTE PERSONNEL Per 100 Adjusted Census	TOTAL EXPENSES Amount (In Millions of dollars)	TOTAL EXPENSES Adjusted per Inpatient Stay (dollars)	TOTAL EXPENSES Adjusted per Inpatient Day (dollars)
1946	4,444	473	13,655	341	—	9.1	—	80,987	2,087,503	505	—	$1,169	—	—
1950	5,031	505	16,663	372	—	8.1	—	86,019	2,660,982	562	—	$2,120	—	—
1955	5,237	568	19,100	407	—	7.8	—	93,868	3,304,451	826	—	$3,434	—	—
1960	5,407	639	22,970	477	—	7.6	—	98,127	3,678,051	1,080	224	$5,617	—	—
1965	5,736	741	26,463	563	620	7.8	92,631	96,782	3,413,370	1,386	224	$9,147	$316.37	$40.56
1970	5,859	848	29,252	662	727	8.2	133,545	93,079	3,403,064	1,929	265	$19,560	$604.59	$73.73
1971	5,865	867	30,142	665	736	8.0	148,423	90,444	3,337,605	1,999	272	$22,400	$667.44	$83.43
1972	5,843	884	30,777	664	739	7.9	166,983	89,315	3,119,446	2,056	278	$25,549	$747.42	$94.61
1973	5,891	903	31,761	681	768	7.8	178,939	86,851	2,987,089	2,149	280	$28,496	$793.88	$101.78
1974	5,977	931	32,943	701	793	7.8	194,838	85,208	2,947,342	2,289	289	$32,751	$883.04	$113.21
1975	5,979	947	33,519	708	806	7.7	196,311	83,834	2,998,590	2,399	298	$39,110	$1,024.72	$133.08
1976	5,956	961	34,068	715	816	7.7	207,725	82,307	2,962,305	2,483	304	$45,402	$1,172.25	$152.24
1977	5,973	974	34,353	717	820	7.6	204,238	80,228	3,117,756	2,581	315	$51,832	$1,316.70	$173.25
1978	5,935	980	34,575	720	841	7.6	204,461	78,090	3,156,570	2,662	323	$58,348	$1,470.13	$193.81
1979	5,923	988	35,160	729	841	7.6	203,873	77,277	3,287,157	2,762	328	$66,184	$1,631.16	$215.75
1980	5,904	992	36,198	748	861	7.6	206,752	77,539	3,408,699	2,879	334	$76,970	$1,844.19	$244.44
1981	5,879	1,007	36,494	754	876	7.6	206,729	76,567	3,465,683	3,039	347	$90,739	$2,167.70	$283.94
1982	5,863	1,015	36,429	753	882	7.6	250,888	75,739	3,514,761	3,102	353	$105,094	$2,493.09	$326.68
1983	5,843	1,021	36,201	750	869	7.6	213,995	75,471	3,450,629	3,102	357	$116,632	$2,775.55	$368.01
1984	5,814	1,020	35,202	703	824	7.3	216,474	75,587	3,456,467	3,023	367	$123,550	$2,984.00	$409.85
1985	5,784	1,003	33,501	660	780	7.1	222,773	74,899	3,521,296	3,003	385	$130,700	$3,238.94	$459.57
1986	5,728	982	32,410	631	774	7.1	234,270	73,688	3,564,530	3,032	392	$140,907	$3,529.60	$499.19
1987	5,659	961	31,633	624	780	7.2	247,704	72,516	3,602,416	3,120	400	$152,909	$3,848.79	$536.96
1988	5,579	949	31,460	622	795	7.2	271,436	70,361	3,706,748	3,209	404	$168,941	$4,194.39	$581.08
1989	5,497	936	31,141	619	805	7.3	287,909	69,436	3,831,051	3,307	411	$185,204	$4,572.23	$630.59
1990	5,420	929	31,203	620	820	7.3	302,691	68,443	3,958,646	3,423	417	$203,927	$4,929.93	$681.52
1991	5,370	926	31,084	612	828	7.2	323,202	67,440	3,965,489	3,539	427	$225,230	$5,345.63	$745.37
1992	5,321	923	31,053	606	832	7.1	349,397	67,095	3,925,024	3,624	436	$248,318	$5,788.52	$815.99
1993	5,289	921	30,770	593	834	7.0	368,358	66,060	3,870,392	3,681	441	$266,382	$6,120.94	$874.98
1994	5,256	904	30,739	569	814	6.8	384,880	65,728	3,809,367	3,697	454	$276,148	$6,230.33	$929.65
1995	5,220	874	30,966	549	811	6.5	415,710	64,742	3,764,756	3,718	458	$286,073	$6,220.54	$966.79
1996	5,160	864	31,116	531	800	6.2	440,845	63,646	3,723,907	3,728	466	$293,920	$6,225.95	$1,005.45
1997	5,082	855	31,595	529	813	6.1	450,907	63,247	3,742,240	3,794	467	$306,088	$6,266.24	$1,031.68
1998	5,039	842	31,830	527	821	6.0	474,366	62,162	3,726,234	3,835	467	$319,035	$6,387.53	$1,064.93
1999	4,977	831	32,377	527	835	5.9	495,850	61,534	3,760,295	3,840	460	$335,405	$6,512.44	$1,101.47
2000	4,934	825	33,102	527	850	5.8	522,970	60,845	3,880,166	3,916	461	$356,757	$6,650.68	$1,147.99
2001	4,927	828	33,834	534	866	5.8	539,316	60,454	3,873,395	3,990	461	$383,911	$6,979.29	$1,216.04
2002	4,949	823	34,501	541	887	5.7	557,336	59,974	3,870,191	4,072	459	$416,791	$7,353.17	$1,288.63
2003	4,918	815	34,800	540	895	5.7	563,864	59,662	3,915,842	4,112	459	$450,403	$7,798.19	$1,378.78
2004	4,942	810	35,098	542	910	5.6	573,125	58,710	3,931,508	4,151	456	$481,517	$8,168.06	$1,449.90
2005	4,956	804	35,265	542	930	5.6	587,295	58,195	3,937,766	4,260	458	$516,172	$8,538.30	$1,521.58
2006	4,947	805	35,403	540	940	5.6	599,597	57,832	4,075,193	4,347	462	$552,276	$8,972.85	$1,610.76
2007	4,915	803	35,370	535	944	5.5	603,411	57,546	4,077,962	4,468	473	$583,550	$9,377.82	$1,694.38
2008	5,026	810	35,776	538	963	5.5	624,185	57,301	4,073,724	4,552	473	$626,823	$9,789.69	$1,780.45
2009	5,023	807	35,603	529	973	5.4	643,420	57,302	3,950,432	4,594	472	$657,242	$10,042.56	$1,851.44
2010	4,995	806	35,160	520	974	5.4	651,617	56,610	3,818,399	4,603	473	$678,254	$10,316.07	$1,908.59
2011	4,983	799	34,852	514	983	5.4	657,071	56,290	3,730,342	4,654	473	$702,822	$10,542.09	$1,959.69

Table 1 (Continued)

CLASSIFICATION	YEAR	HOSPITALS	BEDS (in thousands)	ADMISSIONS (in thousands)	AVERAGE DAILY CENSUS (in thousands)	ADJUSTED AVERAGE DAILY CENSUS (in thousands)	AVERAGE LENGTH OF STAY (days)	OUTPATIENT VISITS (in thousands)	NEWBORNS Bassinets	NEWBORNS Births	FTE PERSONNEL Number (in thousands)	FTE PERSONNEL Per 100 Adjusted Census	EXPENSES Amount (in Millions of dollars)	EXPENSES Adjusted per Inpatient Stay (dollars)	EXPENSES Adjusted per Inpatient Day (dollars)
Total community hospitals	1975	5,875	942	33,435	706	798	7.7	190,672	83,829	2,998,552	2,392	300	$38,962	$1,030.34	$133.81
	1976	5,857	956	33,979	713	810	7.7	201,247	82,296	2,962,216	2,475	306	$45,240	$1,176.25	$152.76
	1979	5,842	984	35,099	727	833	7.6	198,778	77,266	3,287,012	2,756	331	$66,004	$1,641.67	$217.34
	1980	5,830	988	36,143	747	857	7.6	202,310	77,522	3,408,482	2,873	335	$76,851	$1,851.04	$245.12
	1981	5,813	1,003	36,438	763	873	7.6	202,768	76,561	3,465,401	3,033	347	$90,572	$2,171.20	$284.33
	1982	5,801	1,012	36,379	762	878	7.6	248,124	75,733	3,514,457	3,103	353	$104,876	$2,500.52	$327.37
	1983	5,783	1,018	36,152	749	864	7.6	210,044	75,465	3,490,254	3,096	358	$116,438	$2,789.18	$369.49
	1984	5,759	1,017	35,155	702	820	7.3	211,961	75,581	3,456,308	3,017	368	$123,336	$2,995.38	$411.10
	1985	5,732	1,001	33,449	649	777	7.1	218,716	74,893	3,521,135	2,997	386	$130,499	$3,244.74	$460.19
	1986	5,678	978	32,379	629	770	7.1	231,912	73,682	3,584,408	3,025	393	$140,654	$3,532.51	$500.81
	1987	5,611	958	31,601	622	776	7.2	245,524	72,510	3,602,296	3,114	401	$152,585	$3,850.16	$538.96
	1988	5,533	947	31,453	620	787	7.2	269,129	70,325	3,706,402	3,205	407	$168,722	$4,206.73	$586.33
	1989	5,455	933	31,116	618	796	7.2	285,712	69,405	3,830,615	3,303	415	$184,898	$4,587.87	$636.96
	1990	5,384	927	31,181	619	813	7.2	301,329	68,412	3,958,263	3,420	421	$203,693	$4,946.68	$686.83
	1991	5,342	924	31,064	611	820	7.2	322,048	67,434	3,965,396	3,535	431	$225,023	$5,359.56	$752.10
	1992	5,292	921	31,034	604	827	7.1	348,522	67,089	3,924,944	3,620	437	$248,095	$5,794.43	$819.83
	1993	5,261	919	30,748	592	828	7.0	366,885	66,054	3,870,376	3,677	444	$266,089	$6,132.06	$880.52
	1994	5,229	902	30,718	568	812	6.7	382,924	65,722	3,809,367	3,692	455	$275,779	$6,229.83	$930.71
	1995	5,194	873	30,945	548	809	6.5	414,345	64,736	3,764,698	3,714	459	$285,588	$6,215.51	$967.69
	1996	5,134	862	31,099	531	799	6.2	439,863	63,640	3,723,871	3,725	466	$293,755	$6,224.94	$1,006.14
	1997	5,057	853	31,577	528	811	6.1	450,140	63,241	3,742,191	3,790	467	$305,763	$6,261.93	$1,032.70
	1998	5,015	840	31,812	525	819	6.0	474,193	62,156	3,726,233	3,831	468	$318,834	$6,385.99	$1,066.96
	1999	4,956	830	32,359	526	833	5.9	495,346	61,528	3,760,295	3,838	461	$335,246	$6,511.72	$1,102.61
	2000	4,915	824	33,089	526	849	5.8	521,404	60,839	3,880,166	3,911	461	$356,564	$6,648.82	$1,149.40
	2001	4,908	826	33,814	533	865	5.7	538,480	60,448	3,873,395	3,987	461	$383,735	$6,979.53	$1,217.27
	2002	4,927	821	34,478	540	886	5.7	556,404	59,974	3,870,191	4,069	459	$416,591	$7,354.60	$1,289.87
	2003	4,895	813	34,783	539	894	5.7	563,186	59,662	3,915,842	4,109	460	$450,124	$7,796.41	$1,379.48
	2004	4,919	808	35,086	541	909	5.6	571,569	58,710	3,931,508	4,148	456	$481,247	$8,165.55	$1,450.35
	2005	4,936	802	35,239	540	929	5.6	584,429	58,195	3,987,766	4,257	458	$515,740	$8,534.90	$1,522.42
	2006	4,927	803	35,378	538	939	5.6	599,553	57,832	4,075,193	4,343	463	$551,835	$8,970.31	$1,612.23
	2007	4,897	801	35,346	533	943	5.5	603,300	57,546	4,077,962	4,465	474	$583,252	$9,377.17	$1,696.10
	2008	5,010	808	35,761	536	962	5.5	624,098	57,301	4,073,724	4,550	473	$626,577	$9,788.25	$1,782.28
	2009	5,008	806	35,527	528	970	5.4	641,953	57,282	3,959,605	4,585	472	$656,156	$10,045.15	$1,852.59
	2010	4,985	805	35,149	520	973	5.4	651,424	56,610	3,818,399	4,600	473	$677,968	$10,313.44	$1,909.64
	2011	4,973	797	34,843	513	982	5.4	656,079	56,290	3,730,342	4,650	473	$702,091	$10,532.52	$1,959.58

Table 1 (Continued)

CLASSIFICATION	YEAR	HOSPITALS	BEDS (in thousands)	ADMISSIONS (in thousands)	AVERAGE DAILY CENSUS (in thousands)	ADJUSTED AVERAGE DAILY CENSUS (in thousands)	AVERAGE LENGTH OF STAY (days)	OUTPATIENT VISITS (in thousands)	NEWBORNS Bassinets	NEWBORNS Births	FTE PERSONNEL Number (in thousands)	FTE PERSONNEL Per 100 Adjusted Census	EXPENSES Amount (In Millions of dollars)	EXPENSES Adjusted per Inpatient Stay (dollars)	EXPENSES Adjusted per Inpatient Day (dollars)
Nongovernment not-for-profit community hospitals	1975	3,339	658	23,722	510	574	7.8	131,435	57,496	2,131,057	1,712	298	$27,938	$1,040.21	$133.36
	1976	3,345	670	24,082	517	586	7.9	140,914	56,442	2,100,917	1,791	306	$32,764	$1,208.23	$152.94
	1979	3,330	690	24,874	528	603	7.7	139,565	52,859	2,308,548	1,999	332	$47,937	$1,684.40	$218.06
	1980	3,322	692	25,566	542	621	7.7	142,756	52,659	2,389,478	2,086	336	$55,780	$1,901.64	$245.74
	1981	3,340	706	25,945	555	636	7.8	143,380	52,302	2,455,033	2,213	399	$66,267	$2,225.17	$285.64
	1982	3,338	712	25,898	553	636	7.8	176,245	51,566	2,483,345	2,265	355	$76,806	$2,572.93	$330.41
	1983	3,347	718	25,827	544	629	7.7	150,839	51,649	2,465,604	2,270	362	$85,637	$2,868.80	$373.78
	1984	3,351	716	25,236	512	598	7.4	153,281	51,491	2,446,540	2,222	372	$90,814	$3,072.51	$415.04
	1985	3,349	707	24,179	476	569	7.2	158,953	51,424	2,507,288	2,216	389	$96,150	$3,307.41	$462.69
	1986	3,323	689	23,483	460	563	7.2	167,633	50,885	2,547,170	2,241	398	$103,524	$3,589.64	$503.64
	1987	3,274	673	22,937	455	566	7.2	177,413	50,133	2,557,294	2,298	406	$112,325	$3,914.23	$543.67
	1988	3,242	668	22,939	456	577	7.3	195,363	48,828	2,653,794	2,373	412	$124,703	$4,272.95	$591.13
	1989	3,220	661	22,792	455	584	7.3	209,091	48,305	2,751,426	2,454	420	$136,889	$4,649.22	$642.45
	1990	3,191	657	22,878	455	586	7.3	221,073	47,441	2,833,204	2,533	424	$150,673	$5,001.24	$692.36
	1991	3,175	656	22,964	451	603	7.2	238,204	47,229	2,845,995	2,624	435	$166,806	$5,393.30	$758.21
	1992	3,173	656	23,056	445	606	7.1	257,887	47,185	2,846,386	2,692	443	$183,793	$5,808.80	$828.44
	1993	3,154	651	22,749	432	602	6.9	270,738	46,214	2,802,164	2,711	451	$197,187	$6,177.69	$897.70
	1994	3,139	637	22,704	413	589	6.6	282,653	46,381	2,792,116	2,719	462	$204,219	$6,256.72	$950.31
	1995	3,092	610	22,557	393	578	6.4	303,851	45,198	2,725,641	2,702	468	$209,614	$6,279.17	$994.39
	1996	3,045	598	22,542	379	567	6.1	320,746	44,650	2,683,750	2,711	478	$215,950	$6,344.05	$1,042.04
	1997	3,000	591	22,905	376	575	6.0	330,215	44,484	2,698,086	2,765	481	$225,287	$6,392.74	$1,074.26
	1998	3,026	588	23,282	377	587	5.9	352,714	44,087	2,715,958	2,834	483	$237,978	$6,525.68	$1,110.50
	1999	3,012	587	23,871	381	605	5.8	370,784	44,172	2,746,453	2,862	473	$251,534	$6,607.51	$1,139.89
	2000	3,003	583	24,452	382	618	5.7	393,768	43,655	2,833,615	2,919	472	$267,051	$6,717.48	$1,182.32
	2001	2,998	585	24,983	385	628	5.6	404,901	43,640	2,829,691	2,971	473	$287,250	$7,051.76	$1,255.25
	2002	3,025	582	25,425	391	646	5.6	416,910	43,241	2,820,159	3,039	471	$312,726	$7,457.84	$1,328.81
	2003	2,984	575	25,668	389	647	5.5	424,215	42,965	2,854,764	3,059	473	$337,696	$7,904.93	$1,429.62
	2004	2,967	568	25,757	388	655	5.5	430,262	41,968	2,844,617	3,077	470	$359,414	$8,266.64	$1,501.09
	2005	2,958	561	25,881	388	667	5.5	441,653	41,585	2,876,677	3,155	473	$385,993	$8,670.83	$1,585.34
	2006	2,919	559	25,798	385	671	5.4	453,501	40,888	2,905,275	3,207	478	$412,868	$9,189.58	$1,685.62
	2007	2,913	554	25,752	380	673	5.4	455,825	40,681	2,907,002	3,286	488	$436,319	$9,592.93	$1,776.06
	2008	2,923	557	25,899	380	683	5.4	469,804	40,567	2,901,654	3,340	489	$468,080	$10,080.50	$1,875.78
	2009	2,918	556	25,783	375	690	5.3	485,935	40,467	2,822,527	3,369	488	$492,853	$10,379.09	$1,956.71
	2010	2,904	556	25,532	368	691	5.3	494,778	39,946	2,750,163	3,388	490	$510,744	$10,651.81	$2,025.05
	2011	2,903	548	25,185	362	694	5.2	496,643	39,651	2,692,577	3,427	494	$528,303	$10,932.55	$2,088.05

Table 1 (Continued)

CLASSIFICATION: Investor-owned (for-profit) community hospitals

YEAR	HOSPITALS	BEDS (in thousands)	ADMISSIONS (in thousands)	AVERAGE DAILY CENSUS (in thousands)	ADJUSTED AVERAGE DAILY CENSUS (in thousands)	AVERAGE LENGTH OF STAY (days)	OUTPATIENT VISITS (in thousands)	NEWBORNS Bassinets	NEWBORNS Births	FTE PERSONNEL Number (in thousands)	FTE PERSONNEL Per 100 Adjusted Census	EXPENSES Amount (in Millions of dollars)	EXPENSES Adjusted per Inpatient Stay (dollars)	EXPENSES Adjusted per Inpatient Day (dollars)
1975	775	73	2,646	48	53	6.6	7,713	4,062	141,392	139	263	$2,561	$876.48	$132.80
1976	752	76	2,734	50	54	6.6	8,048	4,044	144,751	147	272	$3,085	$1,031.91	$156.35
1979	727	83	2,963	53	59	6.6	9,289	4,110	174,843	174	300	$4,820	$1,476.42	$225.87
1980	730	87	3,165	57	62	6.5	9,696	4,439	199,722	189	304	$5,847	$1,675.85	$257.12
1981	729	88	3,239	58	63	6.5	9,961	4,523	207,405	203	322	$6,856	$1,952.56	$299.02
1982	748	91	3,316	60	63	6.6	13,193	4,736	219,675	212	320	$8,177	$2,224.75	$340.03
1983	757	94	3,299	59	66	6.5	10,389	5,039	228,883	213	323	$9,208	$2,517.53	$385.42
1984	786	100	3,314	57	64	6.3	11,090	5,807	242,088	214	335	$10,251	$2,748.51	$438.30
1985	805	104	3,242	54	63	6.1	12,378	6,117	266,839	221	350	$11,486	$3,033.06	$500.48
1986	834	107	3,231	54	65	6.1	14,896	6,305	291,112	229	354	$12,987	$3,341.79	$552.40
1987	828	106	3,157	54	66	6.2	16,566	6,391	306,492	242	367	$14,067	$3,617.19	$585.01
1988	790	104	3,090	53	66	6.2	17,926	6,254	308,828	249	379	$15,545	$4,022.77	$649.33
1989	769	102	3,071	53	67	6.3	19,341	6,354	325,711	261	390	$17,240	$4,406.20	$707.90
1990	749	101	3,066	54	69	6.4	20,110	6,261	340,555	273	396	$18,822	$4,727.27	$751.55
1991	738	100	3,016	52	69	6.3	21,174	6,358	359,115	281	409	$20,516	$5,133.53	$820.19
1992	723	99	2,969	51	69	6.3	22,900	6,519	357,776	285	412	$22,496	$5,548.24	$888.73
1993	717	99	2,946	51	69	6.2	24,936	6,395	363,358	289	417	$23,077	$5,643.21	$914.39
1994	719	101	3,035	50	70	6.1	26,443	6,329	354,477	302	434	$23,445	$5,528.91	$923.90
1995	752	106	3,428	55	77	5.8	31,940	7,164	408,339	343	443	$26,653	$5,425.20	$946.99
1996	759	109	3,684	56	82	5.6	37,347	7,441	444,697	359	437	$28,385	$5,207.44	$945.49
1997	797	115	3,953	60	89	5.5	40,919	8,026	465,919	385	433	$31,179	$5,218.69	$961.96
1998	771	113	3,971	60	90	5.5	42,072	7,895	466,025	383	425	$31,732	$5,262.44	$968.00
1999	747	107	3,905	58	86	5.5	39,896	7,486	467,585	362	422	$31,179	$5,350.07	$999.03
2000	749	110	4,141	61	90	5.4	43,378	7,792	503,497	378	418	$34,969	$5,642.18	$1,057.32
2001	754	109	4,197	63	92	5.4	44,706	7,413	494,669	379	413	$37,348	$5,971.81	$1,121.31
2002	766	108	4,365	64	93	5.3	45,215	7,467	496,988	380	407	$40,082	$6,161.44	$1,180.83
2003	790	110	4,481	65	95	5.3	44,246	7,491	515,693	391	411	$43,953	$6,589.91	$1,264.50
2004	835	113	4,599	68	100	5.4	44,962	7,763	534,503	406	406	$48,971	$7,139.13	$1,362.42
2005	868	114	4,618	68	101	5.3	46,016	7,714	546,307	421	418	$51,833	$7,351.96	$1,412.74
2006	890	115	4,735	68	103	5.2	44,237	8,012	574,113	423	413	$55,030	$7,422.08	$1,471.53
2007	873	116	4,626	66	101	5.2	43,943	7,760	555,670	432	429	$56,405	$7,823.44	$1,535.98
2008	982	121	4,839	70	109	5.3	44,897	7,791	562,711	450	414	$61,762	$7,984.62	$1,555.55
2009	998	122	4,887	70	112	5.3	47,281	7,965	553,233	464	414	$64,367	$8,037.18	$1,573.64
2010	1,013	125	4,925	71	113	5.3	48,201	7,965	525,427	474	420	$67,168	$8,336.16	$1,628.90
2011	1,025	128	5,060	73	119	5.3	50,013	8,137	508,330	485	409	$70,340	$8,262.74	$1,627.65

Table 1 (Continued)

Classification: State and local government community hospitals

YEAR	HOSPITALS	BEDS (in thousands)	ADMISSIONS (in thousands)	AVERAGE DAILY CENSUS (in thousands)	ADJUSTED AVERAGE DAILY CENSUS (in thousands)	AVERAGE LENGTH OF STAY (days)	OUTPATIENT VISITS (in thousands)	NEWBORNS Bassinets	NEWBORNS Births	FTE PERSONNEL Number (in thousands)	FTE PERSONNEL Per 100 Adjusted Census	EXPENSES Amount (in Millions of dollars)	EXPENSES Adjusted per Inpatient Stay (dollars)	EXPENSES Adjusted per Inpatient Day (dollars)
1975	1,761	210	7,067	148	171	7.6	51,525	22,271	726,103	540	316	$8,463	$1,030.86	$135.64
1976	1,760	210	7,163	146	170	7.5	52,286	21,810	716,548	537	315	$9,391	$1,132.50	$151.00
1979	1,785	211	7,262	146	171	7.4	49,924	20,297	803,621	583	341	$13,247	$1,561.04	$211.89
1980	1,778	209	7,413	149	174	7.3	50,459	20,424	819,282	598	343	$15,204	$1,750.13	$238.63
1981	1,744	210	7,255	150	174	7.6	49,427	19,736	802,963	618	354	$17,449	$2,071.57	$274.25
1982	1,715	210	7,165	149	175	7.6	58,685	19,431	811,437	627	320	$19,893	$2,364.09	$311.55
1983	1,679	207	7,025	145	170	7.6	48,816	18,777	795,767	613	360	$21,593	$2,621.28	$347.56
1984	1,622	201	6,606	133	158	7.3	47,590	18,283	767,680	581	368	$22,271	$2,823.13	$385.17
1985	1,578	189	6,028	119	145	7.2	47,386	17,352	747,008	561	387	$22,863	$3,106.14	$432.84
1986	1,521	182	5,665	114	142	7.4	49,383	16,492	746,126	555	391	$24,143	$3,404.69	$466.17
1987	1,509	180	5,507	113	144	7.5	51,544	15,986	738,510	573	399	$26,192	$3,717.77	$499.33
1988	1,501	175	5,424	112	145	7.6	55,840	15,243	743,780	583	403	$28,474	$4,033.67	$538.63
1989	1,466	170	5,253	110	145	7.7	57,179	14,746	753,478	589	406	$30,769	$4,430.12	$582.15
1990	1,444	169	5,236	111	148	7.7	60,146	14,710	784,504	614	415	$34,198	$4,837.76	$634.45
1991	1,429	168	5,084	108	148	7.8	62,670	13,847	760,286	630	424	$37,701	$5,339.75	$695.89
1992	1,396	166	5,008	108	152	7.9	67,734	13,385	720,782	643	424	$41,806	$5,870.76	$753.92
1993	1,390	169	5,054	109	157	7.8	71,311	13,445	704,854	676	430	$45,825	$6,205.52	$799.73
1994	1,371	164	4,979	104	154	7.6	73,328	13,012	662,774	672	438	$48,115	$6,513.39	$858.62
1995	1,350	157	4,961	100	154	7.4	78,354	12,374	630,718	670	435	$49,322	$6,445.18	$877.85
1996	1,330	155	4,873	96	150	7.2	81,770	11,549	595,424	654	437	$49,420	$6,418.65	$903.41
1997	1,260	148	4,720	92	148	7.1	79,007	10,731	578,186	640	433	$49,298	$6,475.07	$913.62
1998	1,218	139	4,559	87	142	7.0	80,008	10,174	544,250	614	433	$49,123	$6,612.23	$949.36
1999	1,197	136	4,583	86	143	6.9	84,667	9,870	546,257	614	430	$52,534	$6,923.35	$1,006.91
2000	1,163	131	4,496	83	140	6.7	84,858	9,392	543,654	614	438	$54,544	$7,106.05	$1,063.75
2001	1,156	132	4,634	85	145	6.7	88,873	9,395	549,035	637	442	$59,137	$7,400.01	$1,113.79
2002	1,136	130	4,688	84	147	6.6	94,280	9,266	553,044	651	434	$63,783	$7,772.93	$1,188.12
2003	1,121	129	4,634	84	152	6.6	94,725	9,206	545,385	658	434	$68,475	$8,205.10	$1,237.64
2004	1,117	128	4,730	85	154	6.5	96,545	8,979	552,388	666	431	$72,861	$8,473.18	$1,291.06
2005	1,110	128	4,740	85	161	6.5	96,760	8,896	564,782	681	424	$77,914	$8,793.26	$1,329.64
2006	1,119	128	4,848	86	166	6.5	101,645	8,932	595,835	713	433	$83,974	$9,147.40	$1,400.09
2007	1,111	131	4,967	87	168	6.4	103,532	9,105	615,290	747	443	$90,528	$9,523.22	$1,472.26
2008	1,105	131	5,023	86	171	6.3	109,398	8,943	609,139	760	446	$96,735	$9,826.94	$1,552.32
2009	1,092	127	4,857	83	163	6.2	108,738	8,850	583,845	751	447	$98,937	$10,067.96	$1,611.31
2010	1,068	125	4,693	80	163	6.2	109,045	8,699	542,809	738	437	$100,056	$10,283.35	$1,624.93
2011	1,045	121	4,598	78	170	6.2	109,423	8,502	529,435	738	434	$103,448	$10,531.65	$1,666.96

Table 2

2011 U.S. Registered Hospitals: Utilization, Personnel, and Finances

Excludes U.S.-Associated Areas, Puerto Rico, and nonregistered hospitals.

CLASSIFICATION	HOSPITALS	BEDS	ADMISSIONS	INPATIENT DAYS	ADJUSTED PATIENT DAYS	AVERAGE DAILY CENSUS	ADJUSTED AVERAGE DAILY CENSUS	AVERAGE STAY (days)	SURGICAL OPERATIONS	OUTPATIENT VISITS Emergency	OUTPATIENT VISITS Total	NEWBORNS Bassinets	NEWBORNS Births
UNITED STATES	5,724	924,333	36,564,886	224,158,421	—	614,543	—	—	27,599,912	133,440,767	754,454,093	57,022	3,767,697
6-24 Beds	489	8,348	218,636	1,039,794	—	2,850	—	—	316,133	1,909,661	13,424,487	468	15,715
25-49	1,272	41,092	1,246,660	6,913,097	—	18,943	—	—	1,376,984	8,771,649	52,360,244	3,075	121,256
50-99	1,173	83,863	2,482,122	17,960,904	—	49,301	—	—	2,165,122	12,214,311	72,979,584	5,342	234,570
100-199	1,200	170,800	6,502,921	38,950,799	—	106,755	—	—	5,180,716	27,245,284	140,958,945	11,708	677,951
200-299	675	164,255	6,848,156	39,361,987	—	107,997	—	—	4,902,642	25,558,704	134,987,800	10,554	676,516
300-399	402	139,345	6,019,606	34,840,197	—	95,439	—	—	4,136,672	19,906,133	105,798,940	9,145	661,840
400-499	199	88,586	3,914,492	22,490,960	—	61,748	—	—	2,780,352	11,971,405	68,627,396	5,398	410,117
500 or more	314	228,044	9,332,293	62,600,683	—	171,510	—	—	6,741,291	25,863,620	165,316,697	11,332	969,732
Psychiatric	431	75,896	789,421	23,620,900	—	64,711	—	—	17,455	153,728	11,058,620	0	0
Hospitals	424	72,462	789,162	22,325,920	—	61,164	—	—	17,455	153,728	11,058,620	0	0
Institutions for mentally retarded	7	3,434	259	1,294,980	—	3,547	—	—	0	0	0	0	0
General	4,734	803,972	34,991,410	189,703,815	—	520,092	—	—	27,194,710	132,868,745	727,740,528	56,278	3,717,146
Hospitals	4,721	802,280	34,981,251	189,166,086	—	518,621	—	—	27,192,901	132,814,692	726,483,743	56,278	3,717,146
Hospital units of institutions	13	1,692	10,159	537,729	—	1,471	—	—	1,809	54,053	1,256,785	0	0
TB and other respiratory diseases	2	125	148	26,785	—	73	—	—	0	0	874	0	0
Obstetrics and gynecology	8	1,460	73,815	319,147	—	875	—	—	55,609	51,641	760,161	577	45,881
Eye, ear, nose and throat	4	137	2,607	8,275	—	22	—	—	63,537	45,015	674,416	0	0
Rehabilitation	198	15,737	274,426	4,100,643	—	11,256	—	—	9,791	0	5,774,713	16	310
Orthopedic	24	1,147	49,793	176,240	—	483	—	—	104,786	13,074	851,879	0	0
Chronic Disease	5	290	1,564	65,561	—	180	—	—	313	9,021	91,614	0	0
Surgical	3	175	4,649	31,379	—	86	—	—	9,108	52,649	169,278	6	184
Cancer	8	1,759	79,765	518,118	—	1,418	—	—	66,893	21,137	3,544,258	0	0
Heart	5	416	21,755	81,274	—	222	—	—	9,954	9,600	93,323	0	0
Acute long-term care hospital	263	18,774	203,000	4,397,611	—	12,085	—	—	11,988	59,435	1,169,565	15	761
All other	39	4,445	72,533	1,108,673	—	3,040	—	—	55,768	156,722	2,524,864	130	3,415
Federal	208	38,065	892,189	9,604,475	—	26,309	—	—	668,234	3,755,457	87,974,613	726	37,355
Psychiatric	10	2,833	26,163	824,252	—	2,259	—	—	4,412	32,921	2,799,017	0	0
General and other special	198	35,232	866,026	8,780,223	—	24,050	—	—	663,822	3,722,536	85,175,596	726	37,355
Nonfederal	5,516	886,268	35,672,697	214,553,946	—	588,234	—	—	26,931,678	129,685,310	666,479,480	56,296	3,730,342
Psychiatric	421	73,063	763,258	22,796,648	—	62,452	—	—	13,043	120,807	8,259,603	0	0
Hospitals	414	69,629	762,999	21,501,668	—	58,905	—	—	13,043	120,807	8,259,603	0	0
Institutions for mentally retarded	7	3,434	259	1,294,980	—	3,547	—	—	0	0	0	0	0
TB and other respiratory diseases	2	125	148	26,785	26,785	73	73	181.0	0	0	874	6	0
Long-term general and other special	110	14,505	57,415	4,304,909	4,870,041	11,798	13,344	75.0	9,843	75,977	1,148,127	0	0
Short-term general and other special	4,983	798,575	34,851,876	187,425,604	358,639,611	513,911	983,344	5.4	26,908,792	129,488,526	657,070,876	56,290	3,730,342
Hospital units of institutions	10	1,172	8,791	353,591	353,591	967	967	40.0	1,080	26,868	991,934	0	0
Community Hospitals	4,973	797,403	34,843,085	187,072,013	358,286,020	512,944	982,377	5.4	26,907,712	129,461,658	656,078,942	56,290	3,730,342
6-24 Beds	445	7,616	197,272	888,064	3,835,087	2,433	10,504	4.5	307,124	1,702,152	10,530,884	410	14,880
25-49	1,177	37,680	1,173,246	6,091,172	19,075,220	16,690	52,301	5.2	1,326,319	8,170,484	45,097,853	2,918	112,584
50-99	955	67,844	2,104,041	13,720,587	33,771,850	37,690	92,660	6.5	2,041,740	11,503,565	56,126,118	5,094	223,326
100-199	1,005	143,843	6,022,274	31,348,118	66,959,629	85,926	183,557	5.2	4,987,411	26,551,709	120,555,140	11,604	677,253
200-299	582	141,308	6,463,753	32,799,097	61,401,874	90,021	168,481	5.1	4,766,460	24,513,239	109,900,663	10,389	660,610
300-399	353	122,269	5,850,631	29,754,662	52,416,123	81,506	143,610	5.1	4,027,857	19,606,197	95,282,246	9,145	661,840
400-499	184	81,699	3,862,877	20,364,896	35,046,853	55,922	96,254	5.3	2,774,131	11,929,789	66,428,305	5,398	410,117
500 or more	272	195,144	9,168,991	52,105,417	85,779,384	142,756	235,010	5.7	6,676,670	25,484,523	152,157,733	11,332	969,732
Nongovernment not-for-profit	2,903	547,804	25,185,197	131,862,854	253,012,597	361,508	693,662	5.2	19,671,846	91,534,375	496,643,082	39,651	2,692,577
Investor-owned (for profit)	1,025	128,371	5,059,930	26,657,368	43,215,607	73,221	118,699	5.3	3,712,576	18,104,420	50,012,883	8,137	508,330
State and Local Government	1,045	121,228	4,597,958	28,551,791	62,057,816	78,215	170,016	6.2	3,523,290	19,822,863	109,422,977	8,502	529,435

Table 2 (Continued)

U.S. Registered Hospitals

Column groups: **FULL-TIME EQUIVALENT PERSONNEL** (Physicians and Dentists, Registered Nurses, Licensed Practical Nurses, Other Salaried Personnel, Total Personnel); **FULL-TIME EQUIVALENT TRAINEES** (Medical and Dental Residents, Other Trainees, Total Trainees); **EXPENSES** — LABOR (Payroll, Employee Benefits), Total, Percent of Total, Amount; **TOTAL** (Adjusted per Admission, Adjusted per Inpatient Day).

CLASSIFICATION	Physicians and Dentists	Registered Nurses	Licensed Practical Nurses	Other Salaried Personnel	Total Personnel	Medical and Dental Residents	Other Trainees	Total Trainees	Payroll (in thousands)	Employee Benefits (in thousands)	Total (in thousands)	Percent of Total	Amount (in thousands)	Adjusted per Admission	Adjusted per Inpatient Day
UNITED STATES	135,150	1,409,995	110,020	3,540,379	5,195,544	105,571	16,928	122,499	$318,762,638	$87,095,658	$405,858,296	52.5	$773,546,800	—	—
6-24 Beds	1,484	12,185	3,304	45,214	62,187	32	29	61	$2,973,544	$756,779	$3,730,322	52.4	$7,123,594	—	—
25-49	8,180	55,649	10,782	195,200	269,811	439	686	1,125	$13,484,311	$3,565,776	$17,050,086	52.4	$32,509,193	—	—
50-99	9,532	96,110	14,286	285,386	405,314	1,321	576	1,897	$22,062,582	$5,947,363	$28,009,945	53.8	$52,050,817	—	—
100-199	18,505	226,875	22,558	591,195	859,133	5,475	1,563	7,038	$50,579,470	$13,507,451	$64,086,921	52.9	$121,108,650	—	—
200-299	19,843	244,047	18,956	599,724	882,570	11,552	6,464	18,036	$55,640,977	$15,236,740	$70,877,718	53.3	$133,050,503	—	—
300-399	16,989	215,863	13,596	508,414	754,862	10,357	1,161	11,498	$47,097,306	$13,144,627	$60,241,933	52.0	$115,757,088	—	—
400-499	11,259	152,414	7,443	343,371	514,487	16,233	1,003	17,236	$33,050,816	$8,930,994	$41,981,810	51.1	$82,157,939	—	—
500 or more	49,358	406,852	19,095	971,875	1,447,180	60,162	5,446	65,608	$93,873,633	$26,005,930	$119,879,563	52.2	$229,789,017	—	—
Psychiatric	3,886	26,689	7,194	148,318	186,087	409	676	1,085	$9,242,465	$3,034,645	$12,277,110	70.1	$17,514,814	—	—
Hospitals	3,850	26,399	6,623	139,497	176,369	409	497	906	$8,907,108	$2,929,444	$11,836,553	69.7	$16,992,147	—	—
Institutions for mentally retarded	36	290	571	8,821	9,718	0	179	179	$335,357	$105,230	$440,557	84.3	$522,667	—	—
General	125,819	1,338,839	96,480	3,253,728	4,814,866	103,925	15,096	119,022	$297,891,317	$81,026,069	$378,917,386	52.0	$728,636,768	—	—
Hospitals	125,641	1,337,888	96,124	3,248,175	4,307,838	103,920	15,057	118,977	$297,470,977	$80,901,197	$378,372,173	52.0	$727,739,025	—	—
Hospital units of institutions	178	941	355	5,553	7,028	6	39	45	$420,341	$124,872	$545,213	60.7	$897,744	—	—
TB and other respiratory diseases	0	37	32	205	274	0	0	0	$13,173	$4,826	$17,999	72.3	$24,902	—	—
Obstetrics and gynecology	162	3,098	58	4,558	7,876	56	8	64	$542,261	$147,767	$689,968	52.7	$1,310,298	—	—
Eye, ear, nose and throat	195	442	32	2,332	3,001	85	26	111	$151,680	$45,973	$197,653	45.6	$433,389	—	—
Rehabilitation	560	12,060	2,285	43,307	58,212	152	33	185	$2,871,019	$710,083	$3,581,102	59.0	$6,068,236	—	—
Orthopedic	466	2,074	113	6,900	9,453	62	13	75	$677,490	$198,913	$876,403	48.9	$1,793,370	—	—
Chronic Disease	26	241	40	1,196	1,503	0	13	13	$61,752	$20,794	$82,547	56.1	$147,070	—	—
Surgical	14	283	20	637	1,004	0	0	0	$60,343	$14,713	$75,055	45.9	$163,373	—	—
Cancer	2,660	7,456	130	28,320	38,556	683	622	1,305	$2,981,922	$858,138	$3,840,060	51.4	$7,472,379	—	—
Heart	5	638	18	974	1,635	3	0	3	$108,715	$26,291	$135,006	39.0	$346,473	—	—
Acute long-term care hospital	407	13,385	2,891	35,248	51,931	106	12	118	$2,675,032	$614,297	$3,289,329	51.6	$6,373,523	—	—
All other	950	4,753	727	14,706	21,136	89	129	218	$1,485,468	$393,210	$1,878,678	57.6	$3,262,204	—	—
Federal	19,432	64,740	15,046	232,273	331,491	5,719	8,039	13,758	$24,138,399	$6,953,693	$31,072,592	60.6	$51,237,830	—	—
Psychiatric	404	2,064	505	8,427	11,400	25	41	66	$864,140	$261,133	$1,125,278	57.9	$1,942,547	—	—
General and other special	19,028	62,676	14,541	223,846	320,051	5,694	7,998	13,692	$23,274,758	$6,672,556	$29,947,314	60.8	$49,295,284	—	—
Nonfederal	115,718	1,345,255	94,974	3,308,105	4,364,053	99,852	8,869	108,721	$294,623,740	$80,161,965	$374,785,705	51.9	$722,308,970	—	—
Psychiatric	3,482	24,625	6,689	139,891	174,687	384	655	1,039	$8,378,325	$2,773,507	$11,151,832	71.6	$15,572,268	—	—
Hospitals	3,446	24,335	6,113	131,070	164,969	384	456	840	$8,042,968	$2,668,307	$10,711,275	71.2	$15,049,600	—	—
Institutions for mentally retarded	36	290	571	8,821	9,718	0	179	179	$335,357	$105,200	$440,557	84.3	$522,667	—	—
TB and other respiratory diseases	0	37	32	205	274	0	0	0	$13,173	$4,826	$17,999	72.3	$24,902	$168,253.72	$929.68
Long-term general and other special	374	6,239	2,239	26,323	35,175	4	42	46	$1,946,098	$557,818	$2,503,917	64.4	$3,889,865	$57,043.67	$798.73
Short-term general and other special	111,862	1,314,354	86,014	3,141,687	4,653,917	99,464	8,212	107,676	$284,286,143	$76,825,814	$361,111,957	51.4	$702,821,936	$10,542.09	$1,959.69
Hospital units of institutions	121	728	194	3,259	4,302	6	14	20	$321,455	$98,573	$420,028	57.5	$730,902	$83,142.11	$2,067.08
Community Hospitals	111,741	1,313,626	85,820	3,138,428	4,645,615	99,458	8,198	107,656	$283,964,687	$76,727,241	$360,691,929	51.4	$702,091,034	$10,532.52	$1,959.58
6-24 Beds	1,015	10,433	2,612	35,864	49,924	11	16	27	$2,455,063	$628,533	$3,083,596	50.3	$6,128,100	$6,862.34	$1,597.90
25-49	5,468	51,740	10,136	163,423	236,767	216	663	879	$12,307,000	$3,198,206	$15,535,206	53.1	$29,219,812	$7,342.76	$1,531.82
50-99	5,330	78,770	10,555	225,735	320,390	513	222	735	$17,172,863	$4,506,886	$21,679,749	52.7	$41,141,854	$7,767.18	$1,218.23
100-199	13,750	204,262	17,335	504,177	739,524	4,657	729	5,386	$42,949,284	$11,379,431	$54,328,715	51.6	$105,195,692	$8,417.28	$1,571.03
200-299	16,675	222,988	13,738	521,195	774,596	8,250	717	8,967	$47,251,291	$12,575,288	$59,826,579	51.3	$116,575,733	$9,719.40	$1,998.57
300-399	13,816	204,534	10,261	456,264	684,375	10,072	748	10,820	$42,932,931	$11,898,525	$54,831,456	50.9	$107,750,738	$10,484.28	$2,055.68
400-499	10,676	149,888	6,511	330,004	497,079	16,201	916	17,117	$32,020,865	$8,657,677	$40,678,542	50.7	$80,196,968	$12,142.87	$2,288.28
500 or more	45,011	391,011	4,672	895,766	1,346,460	59,538	4,187	63,725	$86,875,390	$23,882,695	$110,758,085	51.3	$215,882,136	$14,281.18	$2,516.71
Nongovernment not-for-profit	90,349	959,230	52,138	2,324,851	3,426,568	68,937	6,319	75,256	$211,480,546	$57,223,240	$268,703,786	50.9	$528,303,066	$10,932.55	$2,088.05
Investor-owned (for profit)	3,167	160,546	14,351	307,214	485,278	3,723	200	3,923	$27,417,303	$6,102,534	$33,520,237	47.7	$70,340,004	$8,262.74	$1,627.65
State and Local Government	18,225	193,850	19,331	506,363	737,769	26,798	1,679	28,477	$45,066,838	$13,401,067	$53,467,905	56.5	$103,447,964	$10,531.65	$1,666.96

Tables 3–6

Total U.S.

TABLE 3

TOTAL UNITED STATES

U.S. Registered Community Hospitals
(Nonfederal, short-term general and other special hospitals)

Overview 2007–2011

	2011	2010	2009	2008	2007
TOTAL U.S. Community Hospitals............	**4,973**	**4,985**	**5,008**	**5,010**	**4,897**
Bed Size Category					
6-24	445	424	402	389	360
25-49	1,177	1,167	1,164	1,151	1,076
50-99	955	970	991	995	971
100-199	1,005	1,029	1,063	1,070	1,083
200-299	582	585	582	596	613
300-399	353	352	348	355	343
400-499	184	185	192	184	191
500 + ...	272	273	266	270	260
Location					
Hospitals Urban..........................	2,989	2,998	3,011	3,012	2,732
Hospitals Rural	1,984	1,987	1,997	1,998	2,165
Control					
State and Local Government................	1,045	1,068	1,092	1,105	1,111
Not for Profit............................	2,903	2,904	2,918	2,923	2,913
Investor owned	1,025	1,013	998	982	873
Physician Models					
Independent Practice Association	514	563	579	597	654
Group Practice without Walls................	161	159	175	160	166
Open Physician-Hospital Organization	622	630	649	672	691
Closed Physician-Hospital Organization	210	203	207	213	240
Management Service Organization	446	454	449	436	453
Integrated Salary Model....................	1,795	1,728	1,664	1,583	1,534
Equity Model.............................	76	80	92	97	75
Foundation..............................	263	261	237	248	236
Insurance Products					
Health Maintenance Organization	640	614	587	597	632
Preferred Provider Organization..............	744	740	693	685	842
Indemnity Fee for Service	253	260	235	250	292
Managed Care Contracts					
Health Maintenance Organization	2,665	2,677	2,702	2,670	2,655
Preferred Provider Organization..............	3,045	3,074	3,137	3,125	3,099
Affiliations					
Hospitals in a System.....................	3,007	2,941	2,921	2,868	2,730
Hospitals in a Network	1,535	1,508	1,485	1,490	1,472
Hospitals in a Group Purchasing Organization..	3,562	3,595	3,674	3,677	3,591

TABLE 3

TOTAL UNITED STATES

U.S. Registered Community Hospitals
(Nonfederal, short-term general and other special hospitals)

Utilization, Personnel, Revenue and Expenses, Community Health Indicators 2007–2011

	2011	2010	2009	2008	2007
TOTAL FACILITY (Includes Hospital and Nursing Home Units)					
Utilization - Inpatient					
Beds	797,403	804,943	805,593	808,069	800,892
Admissions	34,843,085	35,149,427	35,527,377	35,760,750	35,345,986
Inpatient Days	187,072,013	189,593,349	192,656,804	196,078,468	194,549,348
Average Length of Stay	5.4	5.4	5.4	5.5	5.5
Inpatient Surgeries	9,638,467	9,954,821	10,100,980	10,105,156	10,189,630
Births	3,730,342	3,818,399	3,959,605	4,073,724	4,077,962
Utilization - Outpatient					
Emergency Outpatient Visits	129,461,658	127,249,317	127,298,193	123,024,024	120,811,299
Other Outpatient Visits	526,617,284	524,174,400	514,655,249	501,074,272	482,489,075
Total Outpatient Visits	656,078,942	651,423,717	641,953,442	624,098,296	603,300,374
Outpatient Surgeries	17,269,245	17,357,177	17,357,534	17,354,282	17,146,334
Personnel					
Full Time RNs	1,071,952	1,055,118	1,029,828	984,649	950,064
Full Time LPNs	72,641	76,503	82,159	86,750	89,577
Part Time RNs	483,351	477,739	477,699	487,480	482,239
Part Time LPNs	26,448	29,164	31,647	35,602	38,213
Total Full Time	4,034,205	3,989,587	3,971,118	3,919,415	3,846,287
Total Part Time	1,446,076	1,427,136	1,434,492	1,460,487	1,441,216
Revenue - Inpatient					
Gross Inpatient Revenue	$1,275,806,742,970	$1,224,790,498,627	$1,154,085,466,645	$1,090,598,012,951	$1,013,168,556,764
Revenue - Outpatient					
Gross Outpatient Revenue	$968,928,635,990	$887,419,059,972	$802,893,402,009	$711,918,761,681	$632,728,034,044
Revenue and Expenses - Totals (Includes Inpatient and Outpatient)					
Total Gross Revenue	$2,244,735,378,960	$2,112,209,558,599	$1,956,978,868,654	$1,802,516,774,632	$1,645,896,591,708
Deductions from Revenue	1,545,016,281,249	1,435,826,277,742	1,309,916,141,834	1,191,615,889,365	1,072,315,472,850
Net Patient Revenue	699,719,097,711	676,383,280,857	647,062,726,820	610,900,885,267	573,581,118,858
Other Operating Revenue	43,297,884,991	41,269,017,419	38,997,453,520	37,136,577,114	35,765,948,073
Other Nonoperating Revenue	12,267,965,061	13,251,393,842	4,467,480,534	-4,453,107,631	17,000,138,209
Total Net Revenue	755,284,947,763	730,903,692,118	690,527,660,874	643,584,354,750	626,347,205,140
Total Expenses	702,091,033,815	677,968,038,012	656,156,258,314	626,576,957,912	583,252,287,933
HOSPITAL UNIT (Excludes Separate Nursing Home Units)					
Utilization - Inpatient					
Beds	749,181	755,091	755,286	753,905	743,401
Admissions	34,636,454	34,935,503	35,304,455	35,522,351	35,087,765
Inpatient Days	171,803,076	173,686,925	176,511,062	179,043,949	176,068,211
Average Length of Stay	5.0	5.0	5.0	5.0	5.0
Personnel					
Total Full Time	4,002,112	3,955,083	3,930,304	3,875,073	3,795,278
Total Part Time	1,428,754	1,407,838	1,413,237	1,436,850	1,416,918
Revenue and Expenses - Totals (Includes Inpatient and Outpatient)					
Total Net Revenue	$751,284,115,404	$726,685,542,179	$686,454,003,753	$639,389,781,304	$621,836,200,340
Total Expenses	698,572,269,130	674,188,184,839	652,470,080,058	622,828,801,705	579,272,589,469
COMMUNITY HEALTH INDICATORS PER 1000 POPULATION					
Total Population (in thousands)	311,592	309,051	307,007	304,375	301,580
Inpatient					
Beds	2.6	2.6	2.6	2.7	2.7
Admissions	111.8	113.7	115.7	117.5	117.2
Inpatient Days	600.4	613.5	627.5	644.2	645.1
Inpatient Surgeries	30.9	32.2	32.9	33.2	33.8
Births	12.0	12.4	12.9	13.4	13.5
Outpatient					
Emergency Outpatient Visits	415.5	411.7	414.6	404.2	400.6
Other Outpatient Visits	1,690.1	1,696.1	1,676.4	1,646.2	1,599.9
Total Outpatient Visits	2,105.6	2,107.8	2,091.0	2,050.4	2,000.5
Outpatient Surgeries	55.4	56.2	56.5	57.0	56.9
Expense per Capita (per person)	$2,253.2	$2,193.7	$2,137.3	$2,058.6	$1,934.0

Total U.S.

TABLE 4

BED SIZE CATEGORY 6-24

U.S. Registered Community Hospitals
(Nonfederal, short-term general and other special hospitals)

Overview 2007–2011

	2011	2010	2009	2008	2007
Total Community Hospitals in Bed Size Category 6-24	**445**	**424**	**402**	**389**	**360**
Location					
Hospitals Urban	114	113	111	103	81
Hospitals Rural	331	311	291	286	279
Control					
State and Local Government	178	165	154	148	138
Not for Profit	216	207	194	186	177
Investor owned	51	52	54	55	45
Physician Models					
Independent Practice Association	46	51	57	49	51
Group Practice without Walls	12	10	13	11	11
Open Physician-Hospital Organization	32	29	31	34	33
Closed Physician-Hospital Organization	8	5	6	9	6
Management Service Organization	16	17	20	18	15
Integrated Salary Model	149	120	116	110	99
Equity Model	5	3	2	6	5
Foundation	14	10	11	7	7
Insurance Products					
Health Maintenance Organization	37	40	36	34	35
Preferred Provider Organization	44	44	38	39	52
Indemnity Fee for Service	13	13	11	15	16
Managed Care Contracts					
Health Maintenance Organization	163	156	151	137	120
Preferred Provider Organization	231	218	210	203	190
Affiliations					
Hospitals in a System	185	172	166	158	141
Hospitals in a Network	138	129	122	116	103
Hospitals in a Group Purchasing Organization	306	291	286	263	242

TABLE 4

BED SIZE CATEGORY 6-24

U.S. Registered Community Hospitals
(Nonfederal, short-term general and other special hospitals)

Utilization, Personnel, Revenue and Expenses, Community Health Indicators 2007–2011

	2011	2010	2009	2008	2007
TOTAL FACILITY (Includes Hospital and Nursing Home Units)					
Utilization - Inpatient					
Beds	7,616	7,261	6,894	6,726	6,238
Admissions	197,272	198,692	196,599	204,522	199,900
Inpatient Days	888,064	854,226	846,228	835,702	792,847
Average Length of Stay	4.5	4.3	4.3	4.1	4.0
Inpatient Surgeries	35,479	36,003	33,615	36,519	39,047
Births	14,880	13,839	14,161	13,938	13,267
Utilization - Outpatient					
Emergency Outpatient Visits	1,702,152	1,658,487	1,558,802	1,505,235	1,399,997
Other Outpatient Visits	8,828,732	8,275,935	7,553,921	6,877,919	6,297,926
Total Outpatient Visits	10,530,884	9,934,422	9,112,723	8,383,154	7,697,923
Outpatient Surgeries	271,645	271,260	250,113	249,528	215,459
Personnel					
Full Time RNs	8,052	7,587	6,790	6,382	5,763
Full Time LPNs	2,104	2,113	1,992	1,996	1,633
Part Time RNs	4,752	4,701	4,212	3,931	3,232
Part Time LPNs	1,012	886	918	859	769
Total Full Time	40,408	38,328	34,290	32,101	29,210
Total Part Time	19,007	17,746	16,301	14,933	12,801
Revenue - Inpatient					
Gross Inpatient Revenue	$2,808,082,491	$2,786,370,995	$2,627,018,044	$2,459,057,974	$2,173,593,992
Revenue - Outpatient					
Gross Outpatient Revenue	$8,967,777,277	$8,039,286,106	$7,310,737,048	$6,343,851,906	$5,307,718,755
Revenue and Expenses - Totals					
(Includes Inpatient and Outpatient)					
Total Gross Revenue	$11,775,859,768	$10,825,657,101	$9,937,755,092	$8,802,909,880	$7,481,312,747
Deductions from Revenue	6,019,723,826	5,474,162,402	5,035,910,207	4,391,015,802	3,707,878,289
Net Patient Revenue	5,756,135,942	5,351,494,699	4,901,844,885	4,411,894,078	3,773,434,458
Other Operating Revenue	620,276,695	540,121,094	436,638,024	343,522,682	346,123,111
Other Nonoperating Revenue	107,732,522	103,852,868	70,082,709	69,707,381	85,878,584
Total Net Revenue	6,484,145,159	5,995,468,661	5,408,565,618	4,825,124,141	4,205,436,153
Total Expenses	6,128,099,984	5,644,509,939	5,099,918,468	4,510,451,244	3,898,795,232
HOSPITAL UNIT (Excludes Separate Nursing Home Units)					
Utilization - Inpatient					
Beds	7,610	7,225	6,852	6,693	6,214
Admissions	197,272	198,651	196,571	204,445	199,884
Inpatient Days	885,028	841,340	829,135	823,878	781,994
Average Length of Stay	4.5	4.2	4.2	4.0	3.9
Personnel					
Total Full Time	40,404	38,313	34,160	31,993	29,116
Total Part Time	19,087	17,743	16,225	14,902	12,723
Revenue and Expenses - Totals					
(Includes Inpatient and Outpatient)					
Total Net Revenue	$6,483,007,236	$5,990,190,925	$5,395,279,787	$4,821,483,710	$4,200,890,155
Total Expenses	6,127,873,361	5,642,553,901	5,092,088,584	4,508,680,031	3,896,171,176

Bed Size Categories

TABLE 4

BED SIZE CATEGORY 25-49

U.S. Registered Community Hospitals
(Nonfederal, short-term general and other special hospitals)

Overview 2007–2011

	2011	2010	2009	2008	2007
Total Community Hospitals in					
Bed Size Category 25-49..................	1,177	1,167	1,164	1,151	1,076
Location					
Hospitals Urban...........................	403	408	411	411	270
Hospitals Rural	774	759	753	740	806
Control					
State and Local Government................	366	381	391	397	399
Not for Profit............................	570	547	536	527	515
Investor owned	241	239	237	227	162
Physician Models					
Independent Practice Association	96	102	108	104	115
Group Practice without Walls...............	30	32	32	27	35
Open Physician-Hospital Organization	80	82	94	92	97
Closed Physician-Hospital Organization	25	23	23	24	28
Management Service Organization	56	54	56	54	54
Integrated Salary Model....................	353	344	350	309	298
Equity Model.............................	13	17	15	14	9
Foundation...............................	41	39	40	42	37
Insurance Products					
Health Maintenance Organization	93	86	90	83	81
Preferred Provider Organization..............	142	134	123	112	140
Indemnity Fee for Service	47	44	41	39	43
Managed Care Contracts					
Health Maintenance Organization	477	471	488	474	451
Preferred Provider Organization..............	631	636	658	649	622
Affiliations					
Hospitals in a System......................	620	598	593	580	499
Hospitals in a Network.....................	305	302	296	296	297
Hospitals in a Group Purchasing Organization..	781	791	805	795	775

Bed Size Categories

TABLE 4

BED SIZE CATEGORY 25-49

U.S. Registered Community Hospitals
(Nonfederal, short-term general and other special hospitals)

Utilization, Personnel, Revenue and Expenses, Community Health Indicators 2007–2011

	2011	2010	2009	2008	2007
TOTAL FACILITY (Includes Hospital and Nursing Home Units)					
Utilization - Inpatient					
Beds	37,680	37,446	37,338	37,142	34,350
Admissions	1,173,246	1,168,665	1,217,233	1,218,123	1,169,941
Inpatient Days	6,091,172	6,116,350	6,265,180	6,342,577	5,786,668
Average Length of Stay	5.2	5.2	5.1	5.2	4.9
Inpatient Surgeries	241,364	256,940	266,047	242,142	227,059
Births	112,584	107,380	113,460	106,334	109,618
Utilization - Outpatient					
Emergency Outpatient Visits	8,170,484	7,923,353	8,004,368	7,781,578	7,409,466
Other Outpatient Visits	36,927,369	35,175,869	34,456,501	32,947,438	31,766,431
Total Outpatient Visits	45,097,853	43,099,222	42,460,869	40,729,016	39,175,897
Outpatient Surgeries	1,084,955	1,092,740	1,067,767	1,022,034	927,021
Personnel					
Full Time RNs	39,915	37,943	37,289	34,935	32,045
Full Time LPNs	8,460	8,776	8,901	9,165	8,382
Part Time RNs	23,665	22,187	21,865	20,005	18,171
Part Time LPNs	3,365	3,605	3,815	3,809	3,590
Total Full Time	194,434	187,568	184,562	178,257	165,913
Total Part Time	86,421	81,895	80,350	76,222	69,915
Revenue - Inpatient					
Gross Inpatient Revenue	$23,060,034,924	$21,382,867,485	$20,489,409,044	$18,764,220,947	$15,192,815,130
Revenue - Outpatient					
Gross Outpatient Revenue	$43,836,287,394	$39,164,706,833	$36,064,974,499	$31,292,050,672	$26,532,671,728
Revenue and Expenses - Totals					
(Includes Inpatient and Outpatient)					
Total Gross Revenue	$66,896,322,318	$60,547,574,318	$56,554,383,543	$50,056,271,619	$41,725,486,858
Deductions from Revenue	38,545,311,880	34,313,307,874	31,432,916,209	26,923,199,398	21,510,609,136
Net Patient Revenue	28,351,010,438	26,234,266,444	25,121,467,334	23,133,072,221	20,214,877,722
Other Operating Revenue	2,558,100,321	2,209,537,503	2,229,830,552	1,982,012,610	1,814,575,058
Other Nonoperating Revenue	465,541,424	523,520,663	299,120,900	142,977,449	580,543,731
Total Net Revenue	31,374,652,183	28,967,324,610	27,650,418,786	25,258,062,280	22,609,996,511
Total Expenses	29,219,811,844	27,075,731,145	26,281,664,624	24,074,708,651	21,232,861,615
HOSPITAL UNIT (Excludes Separate Nursing Home Units)					
Utilization - Inpatient					
Beds	36,335	35,924	35,726	35,230	32,433
Admissions	1,171,231	1,166,430	1,213,515	1,215,522	1,166,976
Inpatient Days	5,661,438	5,638,505	5,745,424	5,747,460	5,198,062
Average Length of Stay	4.8	4.8	4.7	4.7	4.5
Personnel					
Total Full Time	193,678	186,670	182,894	176,408	164,033
Total Part Time	85,897	81,286	79,370	75,100	68,994
Revenue and Expenses - Totals					
(Includes Inpatient and Outpatient)					
Total Net Revenue	$31,292,864,199	$28,881,412,934	$27,550,727,504	$25,153,457,365	$22,466,173,311
Total Expenses	29,151,001,828	27,009,348,946	26,216,346,135	23,996,899,302	21,157,891,227

Bed Size Categories

TABLE 4

BED SIZE CATEGORY 50-99

U.S. Registered Community Hospitals
(Nonfederal, short-term general and other special hospitals)

Overview 2007–2011

	2011	2010	2009	2008	2007
Total Community Hospitals in					
Bed Size Category 50-99	955	970	991	995	971
Location					
Hospitals Urban...........................	484	483	483	480	415
Hospitals Rural	471	487	508	515	556
Control					
State and Local Government................	190	194	210	215	227
Not for Profit	478	485	501	508	506
Investor owned	287	291	280	272	238
Physician Models					
Independent Practice Association	66	84	86	97	112
Group Practice without Walls................	21	21	20	25	28
Open Physician-Hospital Organization	89	93	94	112	123
Closed Physician-Hospital Organization	32	33	29	34	36
Management Service Organization	48	54	54	61	68
Integrated Salary Model	292	288	280	277	268
Equity Model	10	12	13	14	8
Foundation...............................	35	40	35	45	41
Insurance Products					
Health Maintenance Organization	98	89	80	94	99
Preferred Provider Organization..............	129	128	124	135	171
Indemnity Fee for Service	40	49	44	56	56
Managed Care Contracts					
Health Maintenance Organization	426	444	435	456	447
Preferred Provider Organization..............	508	533	548	564	566
Affiliations					
Hospitals in a System......................	588	584	576	559	536
Hospitals in a Network.....................	256	260	257	271	278
Hospitals in a Group Purchasing Organization..	635	649	672	682	674

Bed Size Categories

TABLE **4**

BED SIZE CATEGORY 50-99

U.S. Registered Community Hospitals
(Nonfederal, short-term general and other special hospitals)

Utilization, Personnel, Revenue and Expenses, Community Health Indicators 2007–2011

	2011	2010	2009	2008	2007
TOTAL FACILITY (Includes Hospital and Nursing Home Units)					
Utilization - Inpatient					
Beds	67,844	69,470	71,012	71,477	69,974
Admissions	2,104,041	2,173,195	2,255,591	2,318,730	2,295,002
Inpatient Days	13,720,587	13,960,874	14,494,367	14,775,775	14,354,674
Average Length of Stay	6.5	6.4	6.4	6.4	6.3
Inpatient Surgeries	498,804	543,313	557,900	573,876	593,650
Births	223,326	228,035	245,282	252,752	257,346
Utilization - Outpatient					
Emergency Outpatient Visits	11,503,565	11,667,902	11,702,839	11,523,593	11,373,584
Other Outpatient Visits	44,622,553	46,033,464	45,633,323	45,219,692	42,938,775
Total Outpatient Visits	56,126,118	57,701,366	57,336,162	56,743,285	54,312,359
Outpatient Surgeries	1,542,936	1,592,532	1,625,749	1,608,622	1,564,443
Personnel					
Full Time RNs	61,781	60,774	59,702	58,276	56,028
Full Time LPNs	8,721	9,718	10,384	10,739	10,921
Part Time RNs	33,998	33,585	33,613	33,996	34,128
Part Time LPNs	3,685	4,125	4,537	4,911	5,415
Total Full Time	260,825	260,463	263,865	264,056	255,144
Total Part Time	120,605	118,372	119,501	121,026	120,860
Revenue - Inpatient					
Gross Inpatient Revenue	$53,109,381,343	$52,180,741,692	$48,434,688,539	$46,010,068,854	$42,120,063,662
Revenue - Outpatient					
Gross Outpatient Revenue	$66,009,645,599	$60,748,431,980	$57,539,780,471	$51,849,631,924	$45,947,957,640
Revenue and Expenses - Totals					
(Includes Inpatient and Outpatient)					
Total Gross Revenue	$119,119,026,942	$112,929,173,672	$105,974,469,010	$97,859,700,778	$88,068,021,302
Deductions from Revenue	76,709,358,028	71,250,437,701	65,093,252,794	59,144,961,432	52,387,575,211
Net Patient Revenue	42,409,668,914	41,678,735,971	40,881,216,216	38,714,739,346	35,680,446,091
Other Operating Revenue	1,689,476,095	1,566,850,196	1,628,159,436	1,598,169,545	1,434,537,429
Other Nonoperating Revenue	625,595,709	677,949,955	358,788,581	248,970,994	970,524,605
Total Net Revenue	44,724,740,718	43,923,536,122	42,868,164,233	40,561,879,885	38,085,508,125
Total Expenses	41,141,854,495	40,509,092,623	39,918,181,789	38,332,175,201	35,148,034,292
HOSPITAL UNIT (Excludes Separate Nursing Home Units)					
Utilization - Inpatient					
Beds	58,517	60,417	60,783	60,983	58,916
Admissions	2,086,226	2,152,715	2,200,384	2,293,835	2,271,564
Inpatient Days	10,790,706	11,108,738	11,303,044	11,528,634	10,951,518
Average Length of Stay	5.2	5.2	5.1	5.0	4.8
Personnel					
Total Full Time	255,669	255,262	257,466	257,784	248,223
Total Part Time	116,620	114,674	115,249	116,770	115,925
Revenue and Expenses - Totals					
(Includes Inpatient and Outpatient)					
Total Net Revenue	$44,157,904,896	$43,379,453,757	$42,231,656,619	$39,967,178,977	$37,463,316,808
Total Expenses	40,660,522,689	40,049,446,577	39,405,302,301	37,833,276,129	34,678,598,342

Bed Size Categories

TABLE **4**

BED SIZE CATEGORY 100-199

U.S. Registered Community Hospitals
(Nonfederal, short-term general and other special hospitals)

Overview 2007–2011

	2011	2010	2009	2008	2007
Total Community Hospitals in					
Bed Size Category 100-199	1,005	1,029	1,063	1,070	1,083
Location					
Hospitals Urban	707	707	726	726	704
Hospitals Rural	298	322	337	344	379
Control					
State and Local Government	135	149	159	162	166
Not for Profit	623	633	656	660	670
Investor owned	247	247	248	248	247
Physician Models					
Independent Practice Association	107	120	122	124	144
Group Practice without Walls	35	36	44	33	33
Open Physician-Hospital Organization	144	152	166	167	176
Closed Physician-Hospital Organization	51	47	53	53	63
Management Service Organization	102	103	102	91	97
Integrated Salary Model	343	332	317	308	302
Equity Model	20	17	25	26	20
Foundation	59	56	49	43	43
Insurance Products					
Health Maintenance Organization	132	124	116	108	126
Preferred Provider Organization	142	136	134	122	169
Indemnity Fee for Service	58	52	46	44	60
Managed Care Contracts					
Health Maintenance Organization	578	587	621	591	620
Preferred Provider Organization	624	641	675	668	677
Affiliations					
Hospitals in a System	667	655	665	661	652
Hospitals in a Network	280	278	298	296	302
Hospitals in a Group Purchasing Organization ..	705	724	779	792	800

Bed Size Categories

TABLE **4**

BED SIZE CATEGORY 100-199

U.S. Registered Community Hospitals
(Nonfederal, short-term general and other special hospitals)

Utilization, Personnel, Revenue and Expenses, Community Health Indicators 2007–2011

	2011	2010	2009	2008	2007
TOTAL FACILITY (Includes Hospital and Nursing Home Units)					
Utilization - Inpatient					
Beds...........................	143,843	148,090	152,655	153,488	155,291
Admissions.....................	6,022,274	6,124,987	6,337,184	6,304,036	6,341,170
Inpatient Days..................	31,348,118	32,616,034	34,162,392	34,742,992	35,016,507
Average Length of Stay...........	5.2	5.3	5.4	5.5	5.5
Inpatient Surgeries...............	1,520,872	1,602,340	1,687,965	1,670,856	1,728,464
Births...........................	677,253	706,284	747,784	765,495	777,562
Utilization - Outpatient					
Emergency Outpatient Visits.......	26,551,709	26,433,098	27,527,025	26,601,799	26,879,730
Other Outpatient Visits............	94,003,431	94,469,225	99,739,947	93,178,685	92,574,821
Total Outpatient Visits............	120,555,140	120,902,323	127,266,972	119,780,484	119,454,551
Outpatient Surgeries	3,466,539	3,551,479	3,694,985	3,653,497	3,645,361
Personnel					
Full Time RNs	162,016	163,437	161,715	154,376	150,102
Full Time LPNs	14,534	15,414	16,777	17,825	19,168
Part Time RNs...................	84,492	87,526	90,352	89,500	89,687
Part Time LPNs	5,653	6,135	6,982	7,788	0,022
Total Full Time.................	612,257	624,072	634,361	623,645	625,608
Total Part Time	265,264	270,145	275,686	274,371	277,630
Revenue - Inpatient					
Gross Inpatient Revenue...........	$181,129,764,497	$177,873,737,781	$172,022,467,282	$161,279,571,502	$149,688,308,624
Revenue - Outpatient					
Gross Outpatient Revenue	$172,260,570,520	$160,748,748,573	$148,908,204,845	$131,080,390,450	$119,230,252,656
Revenue and Expenses - Totals					
(Includes Inpatient and Outpatient)					
Total Gross Revenue..............	$353,398,335,017	$338,622,486,354	$320,930,672,127	$293,259,969,958	$268,918,561,280
Deductions from Revenue..........	245,217,347,870	231,276,346,434	216,014,370,801	195,921,601,786	175,628,976,504
Net Patient Revenue	108,180,987,147	107,346,139,920	104,916,301,326	97,338,368,172	93,289,584,776
Other Operating Revenue	4,265,506,812	4,194,548,704	3,845,471,488	3,635,678,864	3,559,652,278
Other Nonoperating Revenue	1,324,614,718	1,589,574,499	773,148,510	-86,795,995	2,031,003,137
Total Net Revenue...............	113,771,108,677	113,130,263,123	109,534,921,324	100,887,251,041	98,880,240,191
Total Expenses..................	105,195,692,008	104,618,604,747	103,165,948,166	96,955,948,353	92,365,463,660
HOSPITAL UNIT (Excludes Separate Nursing Home Units)					
Utilization - Inpatient					
Beds...........................	131,102	134,182	138,351	137,233	137,797
Admissions.....................	5,976,691	6,074,709	6,284,177	6,247,190	6,276,370
Inpatient Days..................	27,367,543	28,160,867	29,540,921	29,546,134	29,443,800
Average Length of Stay...........	4.6	4.6	4.7	4.7	4.7
Personnel					
Total Full Time..................	604,314	614,788	624,258	612,571	613,811
Total Part Time	260,194	264,091	269,719	267,530	270,208
Revenue and Expenses - Totals					
(Includes Inpatient and Outpatient)					
Total Net Revenue...............	$112,746,343,253	$112,109,514,588	$108,564,165,998	$99,832,442,896	$97,743,593,245
Total Expenses..................	104,375,763,548	103,732,105,185	102,320,666,510	95,982,012,829	91,367,396,890

Bed Size Categories

TABLE **4**

BED SIZE CATEGORY 200-299

U.S. Registered Community Hospitals
(Nonfederal, short-term general and other special hospitals)

Overview 2007–2011

	2011	2010	2009	2008	2007
Total Community Hospitals in					
Bed Size Category 200-299................	**582**	**585**	**582**	**596**	**613**
Location					
Hospitals Urban...........................	498	505	503	515	504
Hospitals Rural	84	80	79	81	109
Control					
State and Local Government................	58	63	58	62	61
Not for Profit	410	422	427	435	448
Investor owned	114	100	97	99	104
Physician Models					
Independent Practice Association	60	67	68	72	78
Group Practice without Walls................	23	18	23	26	21
Open Physician-Hospital Organization	108	111	104	110	102
Closed Physician-Hospital Organization	26	28	26	27	37
Management Service Organization	81	76	74	84	85
Integrated Salary Model...................	225	223	211	206	200
Equity Model	13	17	17	14	13
Foundation..............................	38	40	35	35	32
Insurance Products					
Health Maintenance Organization	95	93	89	93	96
Preferred Provider Organization..............	105	105	88	95	114
Indemnity Fee for Service	37	35	36	33	46
Managed Care Contracts					
Health Maintenance Organization	379	380	382	400	410
Preferred Provider Organization..............	399	402	406	421	425
Affiliations					
Hospitals in a System......................	392	386	381	377	378
Hospitals in a Network.....................	194	192	185	195	192
Hospitals in a Group Purchasing Organization..	443	448	452	475	460

Bed Size Categories

TABLE **4**

BED SIZE CATEGORY 200-299

U.S. Registered Community Hospitals
(Nonfederal, short-term general and other special hospitals)

Utilization, Personnel, Revenue and Expenses, Community Health Indicators 2007–2011

	2011	2010	2009	2008	2007
TOTAL FACILITY (Includes Hospital and Nursing Home Units)					
Utilization - Inpatient					
Beds	141,308	142,616	141,920	144,895	149,546
Admissions	6,463,753	6,569,492	6,684,169	6,866,533	7,009,011
Inpatient Days	32,799,097	33,301,779	33,902,236	35,165,769	36,324,208
Average Length of Stay	5.1	5.1	5.1	5.1	5.2
Inpatient Surgeries	1,749,337	1,896,663	1,871,675	1,945,775	2,006,491
Births	660,610	681,848	739,459	794,470	806,019
Utilization - Outpatient					
Emergency Outpatient Visits	24,513,239	24,171,792	24,181,322	24,185,692	23,913,978
Other Outpatient Visits	85,387,424	86,489,482	83,087,309	83,791,081	82,621,482
Total Outpatient Visits	109,900,663	110,661,274	107,268,631	107,976,773	106,535,460
Outpatient Surgeries	3,017,123	3,001,309	3,015,075	3,224,033	3,281,300
Personnel					
Full Time RNs	179,617	178,567	172,868	171,515	167,333
Full Time LPNs	11,593	12,698	13,435	14,215	15,105
Part Time RNs	86,739	84,923	85,762	88,610	92,245
Part Time LPNs	4,315	5,133	5,396	6,221	6,952
Total Full Time	655,559	657,452	650,138	651,645	656,376
Total Part Time	255,998	252,299	256,501	265,981	271,077
Revenue - Inpatient					
Gross Inpatient Revenue	$222,460,322,498	$216,302,711,528	$203,207,782,786	$197,533,594,288	$192,707,619,825
Revenue - Outpatient					
Gross Outpatient Revenue	$167,530,250,112	$152,845,016,955	$136,999,646,724	$124,669,613,502	$116,124,524,652
Revenue and Expenses - Totals					
(Includes Inpatient and Outpatient)					
Total Gross Revenue	$389,990,572,610	$369,147,728,483	$340,207,429,510	$322,203,207,790	$308,832,144,477
Deductions from Revenue	272,710,512,076	254,962,232,713	230,420,211,811	215,803,795,922	205,589,245,758
Net Patient Revenue	117,280,060,534	114,185,495,770	109,787,217,699	106,399,411,868	103,242,898,719
Other Operating Revenue	5,683,916,062	5,345,831,411	4,960,901,489	5,082,400,440	4,909,405,746
Other Nonoperating Revenue	2,100,529,841	2,413,672,808	869,665,589	-782,268,587	2,859,845,478
Total Net Revenue	125,132,506,437	121,944,999,989	115,617,784,777	110,699,543,721	111,012,149,943
Total Expenses	116,575,732,582	113,049,739,427	109,876,595,200	108,021,530,166	103,273,675,370
HOSPITAL UNIT (Excludes Separate Nursing Home Units)					
Utilization - Inpatient					
Beds	133,352	133,765	133,463	136,050	140,265
Admissions	6,414,383	6,516,545	6,624,904	6,806,537	6,944,618
Inpatient Days	30,290,801	30,497,421	31,155,392	32,384,629	33,356,376
Average Length of Stay	4.7	4.7	4.7	4.8	4.8
Personnel					
Total Full Time	649,600	650,650	642,802	642,916	649,221
Total Part Time	253,312	248,794	252,441	261,723	267,280
Revenue and Expenses - Totals					
(Includes Inpatient and Outpatient)					
Total Net Revenue	$124,426,000,759	$121,195,426,366	$114,847,552,059	$109,893,167,266	$110,282,485,903
Total Expenses	115,962,048,197	112,407,841,598	109,171,734,399	107,333,326,624	102,575,812,740

Bed Size Categories

TABLE 4

BED SIZE CATEGORY 300-399

U.S. Registered Community Hospitals
(Nonfederal, short-term general and other special hospitals)

Overview 2007–2011

	2011	2010	2009	2008	2007
Total Community Hospitals in					
Bed Size Category 300-399...............	353	352	348	355	343
Location					
Hospitals Urban..........................	332	329	327	331	317
Hospitals Rural	21	23	21	24	26
Control					
State and Local Government................	44	41	49	47	45
Not for Profit.............................	258	261	252	259	253
Investor owned	51	50	47	49	45
Physician Models					
Independent Practice Association	49	52	55	65	63
Group Practice without Walls...............	15	15	11	11	13
Open Physician-Hospital Organization	71	66	60	61	64
Closed Physician-Hospital Organization	28	28	29	29	23
Management Service Organization	49	57	54	50	52
Integrated Salary Model...................	165	161	143	140	133
Equity Model............................	4	5	5	8	6
Foundation..............................	27	27	20	25	24
Insurance Products					
Health Maintenance Organization	63	61	62	69	70
Preferred Provider Organization..............	65	66	65	67	65
Indemnity Fee for Service	19	18	19	22	27
Managed Care Contracts					
Health Maintenance Organization	264	263	251	250	242
Preferred Provider Organization..............	273	269	266	260	256
Affiliations					
Hospitals in a System.....................	237	234	228	227	217
Hospitals in a Network.....................	146	147	139	141	124
Hospitals in a Group Purchasing Organization..	291	296	287	287	272

Bed Size Categories

Table 4

BED SIZE CATEGORY 300-399

U.S. Registered Community Hospitals
(Nonfederal, short-term general and other special hospitals)

Utilization, Personnel, Revenue and Expenses, Community Health Indicators 2007–2011

	2011	2010	2009	2008	2007
TOTAL FACILITY (Includes Hospital and Nursing Home Units)					
Utilization - Inpatient					
Beds	122,269	121,749	120,201	122,363	118,160
Admissions	5,850,631	5,835,325	5,761,848	5,894,366	5,637,441
Inpatient Days	29,754,662	29,931,672	29,771,668	31,089,796	30,016,302
Average Length of Stay	5.1	5.1	5.2	5.3	5.3
Inpatient Surgeries	1,577,523	1,594,088	1,638,540	1,679,276	1,626,862
Births	661,840	669,356	669,093	678,865	676,761
Utilization - Outpatient					
Emergency Outpatient Visits	19,606,197	18,788,786	18,319,154	17,724,755	17,121,428
Other Outpatient Visits	75,676,049	71,726,267	68,364,695	72,894,987	64,549,780
Total Outpatient Visits	95,282,246	90,515,053	86,683,849	90,619,742	81,671,208
Outpatient Surgeries	2,450,334	2,401,308	2,371,683	2,340,405	2,279,223
Personnel					
Full Time RNs	166,975	159,878	157,652	151,208	143,484
Full Time LPNs	8,862	8,875	10,238	10,864	11,311
Part Time RNs	75,111	73,727	71,718	75,014	69,901
Part Time LPNs	2,778	3,090	3,461	4,125	4,365
Total Full Time	589,570	572,775	571,380	575,521	554,813
Total Part Time	212,248	211,094	206,711	215,729	204,796
Revenue - Inpatient					
Gross Inpatient Revenue	$216,619,573,502	$209,508,102,124	$192,767,208,267	$188,790,420,618	$169,713,323,276
Revenue - Outpatient					
Gross Outpatient Revenue	$149,199,860,634	$133,493,602,189	$118,085,940,332	$107,500,249,231	$91,813,591,084
Revenue and Expenses - Totals					
(Includes Inpatient and Outpatient)					
Total Gross Revenue	$365,819,434,136	$343,001,704,313	$310,853,148,599	$296,290,669,849	$261,526,914,360
Deductions from Revenue	256,798,261,828	239,740,752,936	213,449,294,445	201,399,629,121	176,791,285,927
Net Patient Revenue	109,021,172,308	103,260,951,377	97,403,854,154	94,891,040,728	84,735,628,433
Other Operating Revenue	6,181,177,363	5,624,897,632	5,833,232,696	5,496,095,330	4,775,900,317
Other Nonoperating Revenue	1,684,050,046	2,187,362,723	421,501,249	-735,779,905	2,352,647,862
Total Net Revenue	116,886,399,717	111,073,211,732	103,658,588,099	99,651,356,153	91,864,176,612
Total Expenses	107,750,738,297	102,319,306,727	97,985,067,095	96,680,861,169	85,991,812,527
HOSPITAL UNIT (Excludes Separate Nursing Home Units)					
Utilization - Inpatient					
Beds	116,402	115,138	114,177	115,956	111,008
Admissions	5,812,423	5,794,184	5,722,480	5,852,894	5,593,182
Inpatient Days	27,951,385	27,890,368	27,966,432	29,131,108	27,762,180
Average Length of Stay	4.8	4.8	4.9	5.0	5.0
Personnel					
Total Full Time	585,534	567,683	565,928	570,294	548,396
Total Part Time	210,406	208,623	204,570	212,975	201,430
Revenue and Expenses - Totals					
(Includes Inpatient and Outpatient)					
Total Net Revenue	$116,327,869,334	$110,402,770,436	$102,987,034,415	$98,992,882,329	$91,064,513,405
Total Expenses	107,307,019,085	101,715,147,145	97,429,327,288	96,149,983,308	85,383,983,393

Bed Size Categories

TABLE **4**

BED SIZE CATEGORY 400-499

U.S. Registered Community Hospitals
(Nonfederal, short-term general and other special hospitals)

Overview 2007–2011

	2011	2010	2009	2008	2007
Total Community Hospitals in					
Bed Size Category 400-499	184	185	192	184	191
Location					
Hospitals Urban	181	182	187	180	184
Hospitals Rural	3	3	5	4	7
Control					
State and Local Government	26	28	23	24	26
Not for Profit	141	139	148	142	149
Investor owned	17	18	21	18	16
Physician Models					
Independent Practice Association	31	27	28	34	35
Group Practice without Walls	14	13	16	15	11
Open Physician-Hospital Organization	40	35	41	39	45
Closed Physician-Hospital Organization	12	13	15	15	17
Management Service Organization	35	30	30	29	33
Integrated Salary Model	90	94	86	79	89
Equity Model	4	4	4	4	3
Foundation	24	24	22	23	25
Insurance Products					
Health Maintenance Organization	37	38	33	36	41
Preferred Provider Organization	40	41	37	40	54
Indemnity Fee for Service	13	15	9	12	17
Managed Care Contracts					
Health Maintenance Organization	148	149	147	134	148
Preferred Provider Organization	150	147	149	135	149
Affiliations					
Hospitals in a System	127	128	128	122	131
Hospitals in a Network	86	78	70	65	72
Hospitals in a Group Purchasing Organization . .	160	158	159	154	154

Bed Size Categories

TABLE 4

BED SIZE CATEGORY 400-499

U.S. Registered Community Hospitals
(Nonfederal, short-term general and other special hospitals)

Utilization, Personnel, Revenue and Expenses, Community Health Indicators 2007–2011

	2011	2010	2009	2008	2007
TOTAL FACILITY (Includes Hospital and Nursing Home Units)					
Utilization - Inpatient					
Beds	81,699	82,071	84,783	80,815	84,136
Admissions	3,862,877	3,869,124	4,049,002	3,895,152	4,043,595
Inpatient Days	20,364,896	20,521,474	21,675,972	20,830,426	21,561,191
Average Length of Stay	5.3	5.3	5.4	5.3	5.3
Inpatient Surgeries	1,150,202	1,178,350	1,220,457	1,133,598	1,241,437
Births	410,117	408,256	431,706	435,954	436,346
Utilization - Outpatient					
Emergency Outpatient Visits	11,929,789	11,546,221	12,078,252	10,828,538	11,467,478
Other Outpatient Visits	54,498,516	53,996,342	51,649,202	46,814,290	49,136,174
Total Outpatient Visits	66,428,305	65,542,563	63,727,454	57,642,828	60,603,652
Outpatient Surgeries	1,623,929	1,665,216	1,804,693	1,739,961	1,764,315
Personnel					
Full Time RNs	123,351	121,762	123,770	113,628	115,451
Full Time LPNs	5,525	6,176	6,578	7,035	7,749
Part Time RNs	53,067	53,293	55,922	52,946	57,353
Part Time LPNs	1,972	2,317	2,330	2,903	3,355
Total Full Time	439,370	441,431	458,527	435,911	450,198
Total Part Time	149,644	146,459	155,793	152,140	157,418
Revenue - Inpatient					
Gross Inpatient Revenue	$158,709,548,655	$150,837,747,313	$154,483,680,751	$134,562,622,630	$133,204,086,152
Revenue - Outpatient					
Gross Outpatient Revenue	$105,408,223,039	$98,160,076,960	$94,037,031,898	$77,496,854,013	$72,665,010,884
Revenue and Expenses - Totals (Includes Inpatient and Outpatient)					
Total Gross Revenue	$264,117,771,694	$248,997,824,273	$248,520,712,649	$212,059,476,643	$205,869,097,036
Deductions from Revenue	184,087,484,155	172,382,284,117	170,485,791,464	144,218,038,992	137,448,298,436
Net Patient Revenue	80,030,287,539	76,615,540,156	78,034,921,185	67,841,437,651	68,420,798,600
Other Operating Revenue	4,601,079,434	4,922,929,664	4,809,356,943	4,570,160,760	4,690,966,723
Other Nonoperating Revenue	1,374,562,424	1,471,629,299	576,751,753	-823,396,082	2,572,380,989
Total Net Revenue	86,005,929,397	83,010,099,119	83,421,029,881	71,588,202,329	75,684,146,312
Total Expenses	80,196,968,394	77,854,509,046	79,447,824,942	70,515,262,080	70,823,523,589
HOSPITAL UNIT (Excludes Separate Nursing Home Units)					
Utilization - Inpatient					
Beds	78,997	79,722	82,330	77,661	80,693
Admissions	3,848,071	3,854,485	4,034,937	3,878,278	4,023,773
Inpatient Days	19,494,041	19,770,661	20,873,864	19,817,710	20,501,012
Average Length of Stay	5.1	5.1	5.2	5.1	5.1
Personnel					
Total Full Time	437,087	439,282	455,941	431,434	446,149
Total Part Time	148,452	145,585	154,827	150,412	156,426
Revenue and Expenses - Totals (Includes Inpatient and Outpatient)					
Total Net Revenue	$85,724,707,161	$82,724,653,206	$83,143,956,566	$71,316,876,706	$75,352,413,590
Total Expenses	79,940,658,386	77,613,265,522	79,186,633,408	70,261,647,760	70,461,579,770

Bed Size Categories

TABLE 4

BED SIZE CATEGORY 500 +

U.S. Registered Community Hospitals
(Nonfederal, short-term general and other special hospitals)

Overview 2007–2011

	2011	2010	2009	2008	2007
Total Community Hospitals in Bed Size Category 500 +.................	**272**	**273**	**266**	**270**	**260**
Location					
Hospitals Urban...........................	270	271	263	266	257
Hospitals Rural	2	2	3	4	3
Control					
State and Local Government................	48	47	48	50	49
Not for Profit	207	210	204	206	195
Investor owned	17	16	14	14	16
Physician Models					
Independent Practice Association	59	60	55	52	56
Group Practice without Walls...............	11	14	16	12	14
Open Physician-Hospital Organization	58	62	59	57	51
Closed Physician-Hospital Organization	28	26	26	22	30
Management Service Organization	59	63	59	49	49
Integrated Salary Model...................	178	166	161	154	145
Equity Model............................	7	5	11	11	11
Foundation..............................	25	25	25	28	27
Insurance Products					
Health Maintenance Organization	85	83	81	80	84
Preferred Provider Organization..............	77	86	84	75	77
Indemnity Fee for Service	26	34	29	29	27
Managed Care Contracts					
Health Maintenance Organization	230	227	227	228	217
Preferred Provider Organization..............	229	228	225	225	214
Affiliations					
Hospitals in a System.....................	191	184	184	184	176
Hospitals in a Network....................	130	122	118	110	104
Hospitals in a Group Purchasing Organization..	241	238	234	229	214

Bed Size Categories

TABLE **4**

BED SIZE CATEGORY 500 +

U.S. Registered Community Hospitals
(Nonfederal, short-term general and other special hospitals)

Utilization, Personnel, Revenue and Expenses, Community Health Indicators 2007–2011

	2011	2010	2009	2008	2007
TOTAL FACILITY (Includes Hospital and Nursing Home Units)					
Utilization - Inpatient					
Beds	195,144	196,240	190,790	191,163	183,197
Admissions	9,168,991	9,209,947	9,025,751	9,059,288	8,649,926
Inpatient Days	52,105,417	52,290,940	51,538,761	52,295,431	50,696,951
Average Length of Stay	5.7	5.7	5.7	5.8	5.9
Inpatient Surgeries	2,864,886	2,847,124	2,824,781	2,823,114	2,726,620
Births	969,732	1,003,401	998,660	1,025,916	1,001,043
Utilization - Outpatient					
Emergency Outpatient Visits	25,484,523	25,059,678	23,926,431	22,872,834	21,245,638
Other Outpatient Visits	126,673,210	128,007,816	124,170,351	119,350,180	112,603,686
Total Outpatient Visits	152,157,733	153,067,494	148,096,782	142,223,014	133,849,324
Outpatient Surgeries	3,811,784	3,781,333	3,527,469	3,516,202	3,469,212
Personnel					
Full Time RNs	330,245	325,170	310,042	294,329	279,858
Full Time LPNs	12,842	12,733	13,854	14,911	15,308
Part Time RNs	121,527	117,797	114,255	123,478	117,522
Part Time LPNs	3,668	3,873	4,208	4,986	4,945
Total Full Time	1,241,782	1,207,498	1,173,995	1,158,279	1,108,995
Total Part Time	336,809	329,120	323,649	340,085	326,719
Revenue - Inpatient					
Gross Inpatient Revenue	$417,910,035,060	$393,918,219,709	$360,053,211,932	$341,198,456,138	$308,368,746,103
Revenue - Outpatient					
Gross Outpatient Revenue	$255,708,021,415	$234,219,190,376	$203,947,086,192	$180,786,111,977	$155,106,307,545
Revenue and Expenses - Totals					
(Includes Inpatient and Outpatient)					
Total Gross Revenue	$673,618,056,475	$628,137,410,085	$564,000,298,124	$521,984,568,115	$463,475,053,648
Deductions from Revenue	464,928,281,586	426,426,753,565	377,984,394,103	343,813,646,912	299,251,603,589
Net Patient Revenue	208,689,774,889	201,710,656,520	186,015,904,021	178,170,921,203	164,223,450,059
Other Operating Revenue	17,698,352,209	16,864,301,215	15,253,862,892	14,428,536,883	14,234,787,411
Other Nonoperating Revenue	4,517,338,377	4,283,831,027	1,098,421,243	-2,486,522,886	5,547,313,823
Total Net Revenue	230,905,465,475	222,858,788,762	202,368,188,156	190,112,935,200	184,005,551,293
Total Expenses	215,882,136,211	206,896,544,358	194,381,058,030	187,486,021,048	170,518,121,648
HOSPITAL UNIT (Excludes Separate Nursing Home Units)					
Utilization - Inpatient					
Beds	186,866	188,718	183,604	184,099	176,075
Admissions	9,130,157	9,177,784	8,994,487	9,023,650	8,611,398
Inpatient Days	49,362,134	49,779,016	49,096,850	50,064,396	48,073,269
Average Length of Stay	5.4	5.4	5.5	5.5	5.6
Personnel					
Total Full Time	1,235,826	1,202,435	1,166,855	1,151,673	1,096,329
Total Part Time	334,786	327,042	320,836	337,438	323,932
Revenue and Expenses - Totals					
(Includes Inpatient and Outpatient)					
Total Net Revenue	$230,125,418,566	$222,002,119,967	$201,733,630,805	$189,412,292,055	$183,262,813,923
Total Expenses	215,047,382,036	206,018,475,965	193,647,981,433	186,762,975,722	169,751,155,931

Bed Size Categories

Census Divisions

Census Division 1

New England
Connecticut, Maine, Massachusetts, New Hampshire, Rhode Island, Vermont

Census Division 2

Middle Atlantic
New Jersey, New York, Pennsylvania

Census Division 3

South Atlantic
Delaware, District of Columbia, Florida, Georgia, Maryland, North Carolina, South Carolina, Virginia, West Virginia

Census Division 4

East North Central
Illinois, Indiana, Michigan, Ohio, Wisconsin

Census Division 5

East South Central
Alabama, Kentucky, Mississippi, Tennessee

Census Division 6

West North Central
Iowa, Kansas, Minnesota, Missouri, Nebraska, North Dakota, South Dakota

Census Division 7

West South Central
Arkansas, Louisiana, Oklahoma, Texas

Census Division 8

Mountain
Arizona, Colorado, Idaho, Montana, Nevada, New Mexico, Utah, Wyoming

Census Division 9

Pacific
Alaska, California, Hawaii, Oregon, Washington

U.S. Census Divisions

TABLE 5

U.S. CENSUS DIVISION 1: NEW ENGLAND

U.S. Registered Community Hospitals
(Nonfederal, short-term general and other special hospitals)

Overview 2007–2011

	2011	2010	2009	2008	2007
Total Community Hospitals					
in Census Division 1, New England	204	203	203	200	202
Bed Size Category					
6-24	10	10	10	10	8
25-49	42	39	40	38	39
50-99	40	40	41	42	45
100-199	56	59	57	54	54
200-299	27	25	22	22	23
300-399	15	14	17	17	16
400-499	3	4	4	5	5
500 + ...	11	12	12	12	12
Location					
Hospitals Urban.	146	145	145	142	125
Hospitals Rural	58	58	58	58	77
Control					
State and Local Government.	4	4	5	5	6
Not for Profit	181	182	184	180	182
Investor owned	19	17	14	15	14
Physician Models					
Independent Practice Association	36	44	40	40	46
Group Practice without Walls.	9	11	8	7	7
Open Physician-Hospital Organization	47	52	51	50	51
Closed Physician-Hospital Organization	12	14	12	11	16
Management Service Organization	21	24	21	20	23
Integrated Salary Model.	105	107	98	98	92
Equity Model	4	4	6	6	5
Foundation.	16	13	10	8	12
Insurance Products					
Health Maintenance Organization	18	19	17	19	22
Preferred Provider Organization.	14	9	8	9	21
Indemnity Fee for Service	8	6	4	4	12
Managed Care Contracts					
Health Maintenance Organization	137	141	133	132	139
Preferred Provider Organization.	133	136	132	127	131
Affiliations					
Hospitals in a System.	93	89	77	74	75
Hospitals in a Network	80	75	69	69	74
Hospitals in a Group Purchasing Organization. .	157	166	159	164	171

U.S. Census Divisions

TABLE 5

U.S. CENSUS DIVISION 1: NEW ENGLAND

U.S. Registered Community Hospitals
(Nonfederal, short-term general and other special hospitals)

Utilization, Personnel, Revenue and Expenses, Community Health Indicators 2007–2011

	2011	2010	2009	2008	2007
TOTAL FACILITY (Includes Hospital and Nursing Home Units)					
Utilization - Inpatient					
Beds	33,693	33,974	33,672	33,743	34,140
Admissions	1,677,325	1,668,378	1,678,176	1,660,654	1,691,347
Inpatient Days	8,650,119	8,813,799	8,987,254	8,992,337	9,029,013
Average Length of Stay	5.2	5.3	5.4	5.4	5.3
Inpatient Surgeries	429,342	439,721	454,138	457,144	469,330
Births	159,359	152,389	156,346	163,857	165,858
Utilization - Outpatient					
Emergency Outpatient Visits	7,018,233	7,120,183	7,004,583	6,848,347	6,732,398
Other Outpatient Visits	40,285,469	39,615,363	38,999,668	37,188,267	34,540,452
Total Outpatient Visits	47,303,702	46,735,546	46,004,251	44,036,614	41,272,850
Outpatient Surgeries	954,123	1,018,591	980,423	996,495	1,010,447
Personnel					
Full Time RNs	46,138	44,258	44,777	43,571	42,761
Full Time LPNs	1,794	1,811	1,898	1,972	2,052
Part Time RNs	41,003	39,689	38,236	39,421	39,108
Part Time LPNs	1,361	1,359	1,508	1,768	1,863
Total Full Time	227,567	223,298	223,553	217,995	212,331
Total Part Time	128,182	123,799	118,235	121,345	120,603
Revenue - Inpatient					
Gross Inpatient Revenue	$49,993,866,945	$47,986,647,777	$46,367,979,779	$44,041,639,373	$41,786,910,589
Revenue - Outpatient					
Gross Outpatient Revenue	$55,511,810,142	$52,517,753,883	$49,137,348,602	$43,645,548,924	$38,945,410,783
Revenue and Expenses - Totals					
(Includes Inpatient and Outpatient)					
Total Gross Revenue	$105,505,677,087	$100,504,401,660	$95,505,328,381	$87,687,188,297	$80,732,321,372
Deductions from Revenue	62,731,335,770	59,098,902,583	55,719,745,134	50,488,459,964	45,898,543,565
Net Patient Revenue	42,774,341,317	41,405,499,077	39,785,583,247	37,198,728,333	34,833,777,807
Other Operating Revenue	4,641,150,617	4,151,761,895	3,962,230,864	3,637,620,235	3,373,305,081
Other Nonoperating Revenue	187,237,842	426,472,039	-167,328,782	-272,745,680	1,107,269,692
Total Net Revenue	47,602,729,776	45,983,733,011	43,580,485,329	40,563,602,888	39,314,352,580
Total Expenses	45,537,927,696	44,366,268,718	42,351,771,503	39,734,569,287	36,994,342,737
HOSPITAL UNIT (Excludes Separate Nursing Home Units)					
Utilization - Inpatient					
Beds	32,627	32,710	32,524	32,109	32,789
Admissions	1,674,145	1,662,431	1,673,090	1,654,586	1,682,524
Inpatient Days	8,384,172	8,377,660	8,601,239	8,442,410	8,577,083
Average Length of Stay	5.0	5.0	5.1	5.1	5.1
Personnel					
Total Full Time	226,972	222,354	222,494	215,906	210,754
Total Part Time	127,672	123,029	117,563	119,472	119,412
Revenue and Expenses - Totals					
(Includes Inpatient and Outpatient)					
Total Net Revenue	$47,525,027,006	$45,855,486,664	$43,455,515,086	$40,395,735,597	$39,176,727,876
Total Expenses	45,467,953,143	44,254,639,824	42,232,006,786	39,589,865,862	36,879,337,539
COMMUNITY HEALTH INDICATORS PER 1000 POPULATION					
Total Population (in thousands)	14,492	14,474	14,430	14,363	14,298
Inpatient					
Beds	2.3	2.3	2.3	2.3	2.4
Admissions	115.7	115.3	116.3	115.6	118.3
Inpatient Days	596.9	608.9	622.8	626.1	631.5
Inpatient Surgeries	29.6	30.4	31.5	31.8	32.8
Births	11.0	10.5	10.8	11.4	11.6
Outpatient					
Emergency Outpatient Visits	484.3	491.9	485.4	476.8	470.9
Other Outpatient Visits	2,779.8	2,737.0	2,702.7	2,589.2	2,415.7
Total Outpatient Visits	3,264.0	3,228.9	3,188.2	3,066.1	2,886.6
Outpatient Surgeries	65.8	70.4	67.9	69.4	70.7
Expense per Capita (per person)	$3,142.2	$3,065.2	$2,935.0	$2,766.5	$2,587.4

U.S. Census Divisions

TABLE 5

U.S. CENSUS DIVISION 2: MIDDLE ATLANTIC

U.S. Registered Community Hospitals
(Nonfederal, short-term general and other special hospitals)

Overview 2007–2011

	2011	2010	2009	2008	2007
Total Community Hospitals					
in Census Division 2, Middle Atlantic.......	**449**	**454**	**457**	**468**	**462**
Bed Size Category					
6-24	9	8	7	7	8
25-49	36	38	39	41	29
50-99	66	66	64	65	60
100-199	106	102	111	115	119
200-299	91	98	93	95	98
300-399	54	53	53	56	57
400-499	33	33	36	34	38
500 + ...	54	56	54	55	53
Location					
Hospitals Urban..........................	364	367	369	379	382
Hospitals Rural	85	87	88	89	80
Control					
State and Local Government...............	30	30	30	33	31
Not for Profit	362	373	381	388	397
Investor owned	57	51	46	47	34
Physician Models					
Independent Practice Association	53	54	54	63	69
Group Practice without Walls...............	12	17	20	20	19
Open Physician-Hospital Organization	39	40	41	55	55
Closed Physician-Hospital Organization	15	15	18	15	18
Management Service Organization	47	51	54	52	51
Integrated Salary Model...................	175	172	158	142	150
Equity Model	3	2	5	6	6
Foundation...............................	18	14	12	11	12
Insurance Products					
Health Maintenance Organization	90	80	66	83	78
Preferred Provider Organization.............	69	79	66	80	76
Indemnity Fee for Service	31	42	28	33	31
Managed Care Contracts					
Health Maintenance Organization	284	286	279	283	289
Preferred Provider Organization.............	274	277	264	270	271
Affiliations					
Hospitals in a System.....................	254	242	235	231	218
Hospitals in a Network....................	163	157	151	154	152
Hospitals in a Group Purchasing Organization..	321	321	305	308	315

U.S. Census Divisions

TABLE 5

U.S. CENSUS DIVISION 2: MIDDLE ATLANTIC

U.S. Registered Community Hospitals
(Nonfederal, short-term general and other special hospitals)

Utilization, Personnel, Revenue and Expenses, Community Health Indicators 2007–2011

	2011	2010	2009	2008	2007
TOTAL FACILITY (Includes Hospital and Nursing Home Units)					
Utilization - Inpatient					
Beds	118,152	120,495	120,666	122,511	123,639
Admissions	5,308,422	5,387,182	5,469,937	5,516,053	5,505,319
Inpatient Days	31,927,960	32,429,928	32,905,796	33,922,806	34,215,129
Average Length of Stay	6.0	6.0	6.0	6.1	6.2
Inpatient Surgeries	1,385,212	1,472,258	1,444,280	1,475,219	1,495,234
Births	473,951	473,143	481,966	493,580	498,628
Utilization - Outpatient					
Emergency Outpatient Visits	18,128,050	17,544,922	18,036,427	17,471,705	17,141,299
Other Outpatient Visits	89,610,828	90,638,433	92,532,690	91,694,245	89,970,276
Total Outpatient Visits	107,738,878	108,183,355	110,569,117	109,165,950	107,111,575
Outpatient Surgeries	2,612,230	2,662,613	2,672,246	2,667,312	2,673,530
Personnel					
Full Time RNs	163,685	159,336	157,599	154,609	153,296
Full Time LPNs	9,399	9,477	10,498	11,135	11,648
Part Time RNs	62,925	61,970	58,758	59,586	61,316
Part Time LPNs	3,059	3,392	3,492	3,915	4,192
Total Full Time	663,442	641,848	649,700	652,102	645,979
Total Part Time	201,876	193,048	188,250	187,630	190,730
Revenue - Inpatient					
Gross Inpatient Revenue	$224,663,669,372	$214,875,701,636	$207,428,274,807	$204,106,922,337	$191,802,352,802
Revenue - Outpatient					
Gross Outpatient Revenue	$142,077,957,104	$131,067,665,392	$119,608,818,446	$108,338,945,283	$97,230,945,480
Revenue and Expenses - Totals					
(Includes Inpatient and Outpatient)					
Total Gross Revenue	$366,741,626,476	$345,943,367,028	$327,037,093,253	$312,445,867,620	$289,033,298,282
Deductions from Revenue	258,245,571,725	241,791,805,319	226,954,454,439	217,335,551,911	198,289,740,098
Net Patient Revenue	108,496,054,751	104,151,561,709	100,082,638,814	95,110,315,709	90,743,558,184
Other Operating Revenue	7,014,856,042	6,773,917,247	6,240,458,318	5,905,669,784	6,338,357,464
Other Nonoperating Revenue	1,370,628,711	1,636,895,627	1,079,935,145	-522,530,088	2,136,486,090
Total Net Revenue	116,881,539,504	112,562,374,583	107,403,032,277	100,493,455,405	99,218,401,738
Total Expenses	112,027,433,487	107,964,477,816	104,601,314,499	101,341,325,573	94,889,661,651
HOSPITAL UNIT (Excludes Separate Nursing Home Units)					
Utilization - Inpatient					
Beds	108,920	112,240	112,737	114,721	115,326
Admissions	5,266,742	5,349,564	5,432,647	5,477,486	5,465,485
Inpatient Days	28,745,893	29,691,180	30,267,570	31,398,678	31,360,166
Average Length of Stay	5.5	5.6	5.6	5.7	5.7
Personnel					
Total Full Time	657,123	636,513	642,529	644,394	638,846
Total Part Time	198,919	189,998	184,726	184,048	187,399
Revenue and Expenses - Totals					
(Includes Inpatient and Outpatient)					
Total Net Revenue	$116,030,325,922	$111,642,685,649	$106,605,542,714	$99,744,284,282	$98,469,053,061
Total Expenses	111,216,627,510	107,117,179,018	103,815,232,446	100,633,830,609	94,212,728,480
COMMUNITY HEALTH INDICATORS PER 1000 POPULATION					
Total Population (in thousands)	41,029	40,943	40,854	40,698	40,581
Inpatient					
Beds	2.9	2.9	3.0	3.0	3.0
Admissions	129.4	131.6	133.9	135.5	135.7
Inpatient Days	778.2	792.1	805.4	833.5	843.1
Inpatient Surgeries	33.8	36.0	35.4	36.2	36.8
Births	11.6	11.6	11.8	12.1	12.3
Outpatient					
Emergency Outpatient Visits	441.8	428.5	441.5	429.3	422.4
Other Outpatient Visits	2,184.1	2,213.8	2,265.0	2,253.1	2,217.0
Total Outpatient Visits	2,625.9	2,642.3	2,706.4	2,682.4	2,639.4
Outpatient Surgeries	63.7	65.0	65.4	65.5	65.9
Expense per Capita (per person)	$2,730.4	$2,636.9	$2,560.4	$2,490.1	$2,338.3

U.S. Census Divisions

TABLE 5

U.S. CENSUS DIVISION 3: SOUTH ATLANTIC

U.S. Registered Community Hospitals
(Nonfederal, short-term general and other special hospitals)

Overview 2007–2011

	2011	2010	2009	2008	2007
Total Community Hospitals					
in Census Division 3, South Atlantic	759	758	759	762	735
Bed Size Category					
6-24	22	21	20	18	17
25-49	130	129	127	129	112
50-99	138	133	133	128	120
100-199	193	196	202	209	203
200-299	110	115	115	116	122
300-399	66	65	62	67	66
400-499	33	34	37	30	33
500 + ...	67	65	63	65	62
Location					
Hospitals Urban.........................	515	514	516	516	447
Hospitals Rural	244	244	243	246	288
Control					
State and Local Government...............	137	141	144	147	148
Not for Profit	404	398	402	406	394
Investor owned	218	219	213	209	193
Physician Models					
Independent Practice Association	49	52	51	52	51
Group Practice without Walls...............	23	23	26	24	24
Open Physician-Hospital Organization	78	79	77	80	81
Closed Physician-Hospital Organization	37	38	36	39	40
Management Service Organization	66	67	56	51	50
Integrated Salary Model....................	287	287	256	255	249
Equity Model............................	20	21	20	20	18
Foundation..............................	19	20	16	21	20
Insurance Products					
Health Maintenance Organization	78	74	72	62	64
Preferred Provider Organization..............	95	94	85	75	97
Indemnity Fee for Service	32	29	27	24	37
Managed Care Contracts					
Health Maintenance Organization	428	417	412	402	407
Preferred Provider Organization..............	455	448	452	435	446
Affiliations					
Hospitals in a System.....................	527	504	493	479	443
Hospitals in a Network....................	218	215	205	211	219
Hospitals in a Group Purchasing Organization..	522	538	535	542	490

U.S. Census Divisions

TABLE 5

U.S. CENSUS DIVISION 3: SOUTH ATLANTIC

U.S. Registered Community Hospitals
(Nonfederal, short-term general and other special hospitals)

Utilization, Personnel, Revenue and Expenses, Community Health Indicators 2007–2011

	2011	2010	2009	2008	2007
TOTAL FACILITY (Includes Hospital and Nursing Home Units)					
Utilization - Inpatient					
Beds	156,421	156,678	156,435	156,622	154,101
Admissions	6,995,044	6,970,769	7,001,234	6,958,360	6,913,804
Inpatient Days	37,874,666	37,775,346	37,871,460	38,331,279	38,540,724
Average Length of Stay	5.4	5.4	5.4	5.5	5.6
Inpatient Surgeries	1,922,638	1,978,051	2,014,276	2,003,768	1,998,114
Births	691,803	718,161	736,030	764,298	771,074
Utilization - Outpatient					
Emergency Outpatient Visits	25,719,396	25,132,194	25,680,948	24,482,937	24,095,446
Other Outpatient Visits	72,465,338	70,980,844	71,516,908	69,838,160	67,864,346
Total Outpatient Visits	98,184,734	96,113,038	97,197,856	94,321,097	91,959,792
Outpatient Surgeries	3,285,368	3,275,089	3,347,083	3,346,983	3,262,710
Personnel					
Full Time RNs	218,388	214,222	209,172	195,655	191,207
Full Time LPNs	13,119	14,299	15,153	16,133	17,055
Part Time RNs	71,740	73,321	75,692	79,445	77,184
Part Time LPNs	3,608	4,092	4,515	5,177	5,470
Total Full Time	764,221	753,621	746,110	731,035	718,204
Total Part Time	206,195	204,742	211,449	219,295	214,064
Revenue - Inpatient					
Gross Inpatient Revenue	$230,857,582,404	$221,881,724,341	$206,158,157,529	$190,255,383,250	$179,774,493,773
Revenue - Outpatient					
Gross Outpatient Revenue	$171,171,466,560	$156,997,699,889	$141,704,232,345	$123,592,865,886	$110,871,408,881
Revenue and Expenses - Totals					
(Includes Inpatient and Outpatient)					
Total Gross Revenue	$402,029,048,964	$378,879,424,230	$347,862,389,874	$313,848,249,136	$290,645,902,654
Deductions from Revenue	278,266,927,544	257,534,395,622	231,360,708,001	204,204,305,242	186,436,266,133
Net Patient Revenue	123,762,121,420	121,345,028,608	116,501,681,873	109,643,943,894	104,209,636,521
Other Operating Revenue	6,233,574,974	5,739,614,294	5,340,444,911	5,395,566,187	4,847,826,689
Other Nonoperating Revenue	1,983,730,368	2,153,138,363	702,305,382	-1,072,116,225	2,512,438,728
Total Net Revenue	131,979,426,762	129,237,781,265	122,544,432,166	113,967,393,856	111,569,901,938
Total Expenses	122,100,282,752	118,053,521,062	115,183,239,713	109,762,268,873	103,137,798,170
HOSPITAL UNIT (Excludes Separate Nursing Home Units)					
Utilization - Inpatient					
Beds	145,614	145,304	146,162	145,784	142,648
Admissions	6,952,755	6,925,183	6,957,697	6,913,674	6,864,373
Inpatient Days	34,472,561	34,041,050	34,447,166	34,834,753	34,608,173
Average Length of Stay	5.0	4.9	5.0	5.0	5.0
Personnel					
Total Full Time	756,853	745,348	737,233	723,355	706,613
Total Part Time	203,449	201,603	208,120	216,083	210,620
Revenue and Expenses - Totals					
(Includes Inpatient and Outpatient)					
Total Net Revenue	$131,160,884,248	$128,322,166,959	$121,761,391,092	$113,171,813,994	$110,708,005,981
Total Expenses	121,286,710,334	117,214,899,415	114,453,158,594	109,002,752,761	102,312,602,232
COMMUNITY HEALTH INDICATORS PER 1000 POPULATION					
Total Population (in thousands)	60,514	59,659	59,196	58,607	57,916
Inpatient					
Beds	2.6	2.6	2.6	2.7	2.7
Admissions	115.6	116.8	118.3	118.7	119.4
Inpatient Days	625.9	633.2	639.8	654.0	665.5
Inpatient Surgeries	31.8	33.2	34.0	34.2	34.5
Births	11.4	12.0	12.4	13.0	13.3
Outpatient					
Emergency Outpatient Visits	425.0	421.3	433.8	417.7	416.0
Other Outpatient Visits	1,197.5	1,189.8	1,208.1	1,191.6	1,171.8
Total Outpatient Visits	1,622.5	1,611.0	1,642.0	1,609.4	1,587.8
Outpatient Surgeries	54.3	54.9	56.5	57.1	56.3
Expense per Capita (per person)	$2,017.7	$1,978.8	$1,945.8	$1,872.8	$1,780.8

U.S. Census Divisions

TABLE 5

U.S. CENSUS DIVISION 4: EAST NORTH CENTRAL

U.S. Registered Community Hospitals
(Nonfederal, short-term general and other special hospitals)

Overview 2007–2011

	2011	2010	2009	2008	2007
Total Community Hospitals					
in Census Division 4, East North Central....	774	777	779	774	742
Bed Size Category					
6-24	45	43	40	37	31
25-49	204	198	196	193	171
50-99	155	163	166	162	150
100-199	155	151	161	159	169
200-299	93	100	96	99	101
300-399	56	56	52	56	50
400-499	27	26	29	29	33
500 + ...	39	40	39	39	37
Location					
Hospitals Urban..........................	501	503	504	499	456
Hospitals Rural	273	274	275	275	286
Control					
State and Local Government...............	89	96	99	103	107
Not for Profit	592	590	593	589	583
Investor owned	93	91	87	82	52
Physician Models					
Independent Practice Association	69	73	86	88	88
Group Practice without Walls...............	30	25	23	28	27
Open Physician-Hospital Organization	163	164	163	151	156
Closed Physician-Hospital Organization	52	51	45	47	67
Management Service Organization	82	87	93	96	94
Integrated Salary Model....................	321	312	303	295	281
Equity Model.............................	21	22	26	30	15
Foundation...............................	49	59	52	49	44
Insurance Products					
Health Maintenance Organization	151	145	143	140	154
Preferred Provider Organization..............	161	165	167	155	197
Indemnity Fee for Service	54	57	59	57	71
Managed Care Contracts					
Health Maintenance Organization	514	531	552	529	491
Preferred Provider Organization..............	547	568	597	576	535
Affiliations					
Hospitals in a System.....................	486	475	467	452	421
Hospitals in a Network....................	272	277	276	271	252
Hospitals in a Group Purchasing Organization..	608	632	645	643	598

U.S. Census Divisions

TABLE 5

U.S. CENSUS DIVISION 4: EAST NORTH CENTRAL

U.S. Registered Community Hospitals
(Nonfederal, short-term general and other special hospitals)

Utilization, Personnel, Revenue and Expenses, Community Health Indicators 2007–2011

	2011	2010	2009	2008	2007
TOTAL FACILITY (Includes Hospital and Nursing Home Units)					
Utilization - Inpatient					
Beds	122,555	124,528	124,648	124,957	123,858
Admissions	5,518,124	5,573,945	5,631,570	5,730,456	5,656,902
Inpatient Days	27,603,703	28,088,741	28,659,008	29,237,134	28,818,795
Average Length of Stay	5.0	5.0	5.1	5.1	5.1
Inpatient Surgeries	1,537,005	1,598,684	1,629,031	1,641,475	1,611,589
Births	531,487	549,668	569,683	590,869	595,181
Utilization - Outpatient					
Emergency Outpatient Visits	21,873,056	21,645,563	21,143,963	20,682,680	20,641,691
Other Outpatient Visits	110,723,087	110,255,848	106,866,440	102,419,976	100,771,454
Total Outpatient Visits	132,596,143	131,901,411	128,010,403	123,102,656	121,413,145
Outpatient Surgeries	3,152,571	3,207,896	3,184,812	3,147,665	3,131,378
Personnel					
Full Time RNs	171,026	166,190	159,198	154,002	148,084
Full Time LPNs	9,094	8,792	9,506	10,480	10,888
Part Time RNs	97,012	97,309	97,165	96,817	94,856
Part Time LPNs	4,841	5,200	5,538	6,489	6,726
Total Full Time	661,130	656,411	652,503	647,246	631,125
Total Part Time	301,819	305,777	309,198	306,273	296,396
Revenue - Inpatient					
Gross Inpatient Revenue	$176,586,489,578	$169,254,285,621	$159,626,875,101	$149,698,495,809	$138,385,536,623
Revenue - Outpatient					
Gross Outpatient Revenue	$167,198,588,978	$153,605,458,204	$139,937,321,698	$125,559,569,848	$112,453,910,765
Revenue and Expenses - Totals					
(Includes Inpatient and Outpatient)					
Total Gross Revenue	$343,785,078,556	$322,859,743,825	$299,564,196,799	$275,258,065,657	$250,839,447,388
Deductions from Revenue	224,785,581,163	206,741,773,300	188,295,725,972	169,876,753,425	151,738,136,454
Net Patient Revenue	118,999,497,393	116,117,970,525	111,268,470,827	105,381,312,232	99,101,310,934
Other Operating Revenue	7,235,875,567	6,838,675,527	6,706,843,261	6,300,528,903	5,973,060,158
Other Nonoperating Revenue	2,481,023,683	2,812,190,226	360,822,911	-2,457,450,887	3,688,479,320
Total Net Revenue	128,716,396,643	125,768,836,278	118,336,136,999	109,224,390,248	108,762,850,412
Total Expenses	118,844,737,908	116,021,099,796	112,388,231,445	108,029,056,637	100,228,770,592
HOSPITAL UNIT (Excludes Separate Nursing Home Units)					
Utilization - Inpatient					
Beds	117,051	118,315	118,136	118,085	116,254
Admissions	5,480,695	5,532,131	5,587,798	5,687,064	5,612,602
Inpatient Days	25,917,067	26,193,965	26,630,592	27,072,122	26,485,828
Average Length of Stay	4.7	4.7	4.8	4.8	4.7
Personnel					
Total Full Time	657,862	652,317	647,481	642,131	620,539
Total Part Time	298,789	302,371	305,428	302,441	292,478
Revenue and Expenses - Totals					
(Includes Inpatient and Outpatient)					
Total Net Revenue	$128,223,217,900	$125,272,982,180	$117,798,388,335	$108,726,765,462	$108,179,483,196
Total Expenses	118,428,199,417	115,557,672,594	111,947,643,021	107,600,938,852	99,700,838,980
COMMUNITY HEALTH INDICATORS PER 1000 POPULATION					
Total Population (in thousands)	46,519	46,522	46,501	46,389	46,299
Inpatient					
Beds	2.6	2.7	2.7	2.7	2.7
Admissions	118.6	119.8	121.1	123.5	122.2
Inpatient Days	593.4	603.8	616.3	630.3	622.5
Inpatient Surgeries	33.0	34.4	35.0	35.4	34.8
Births	11.4	11.8	12.3	12.7	12.9
Outpatient					
Emergency Outpatient Visits	470.2	465.3	454.7	445.8	445.8
Other Outpatient Visits	2,380.2	2,370.0	2,298.2	2,207.8	2,176.5
Total Outpatient Visits	2,850.4	2,835.3	2,752.9	2,653.7	2,622.4
Outpatient Surgeries	67.8	69.0	68.5	67.9	67.6
Expense per Capita (per person)	$2,554.8	$2,493.9	$2,416.9	$2,328.7	$2,164.8

U.S. Census Divisions

TABLE 5

U.S. CENSUS DIVISION 5: EAST SOUTH CENTRAL

U.S. Registered Community Hospitals
(Nonfederal, short-term general and other special hospitals)

Overview 2007–2011

	2011	2010	2009	2008	2007
Total Community Hospitals					
in Census Division 5, East South Central ...	440	441	446	449	441
Bed Size Category					
6-24	22	16	16	18	16
25-49	125	128	128	126	115
50-99	98	100	104	107	109
100-199	99	104	104	99	103
200-299	40	35	35	39	41
300-399	25	25	26	26	23
400-499	10	14	15	14	14
500 + ...	21	19	18	20	20
Location					
Hospitals Urban..........................	207	208	211	211	178
Hospitals Rural	233	233	235	238	263
Control					
State and Local Government................	112	112	115	119	118
Not for Profit	177	182	186	188	190
Investor owned	151	147	145	142	133
Physician Models					
Independent Practice Association	31	36	36	35	36
Group Practice without Walls...............	7	7	10	10	12
Open Physician-Hospital Organization	43	43	41	49	55
Closed Physician-Hospital Organization	10	8	11	17	14
Management Service Organization	46	39	34	34	39
Integrated Salary Model....................	111	114	102	94	84
Equity Model	1	1	3	2	1
Foundation...............................	21	22	23	22	21
Insurance Products					
Health Maintenance Organization	25	32	26	39	44
Preferred Provider Organization.............	80	75	70	83	90
Indemnity Fee for Service	18	21	15	28	27
Managed Care Contracts					
Health Maintenance Organization	165	165	164	176	160
Preferred Provider Organization.............	204	215	211	233	211
Affiliations					
Hospitals in a System.....................	294	289	289	286	275
Hospitals in a Network	91	101	105	111	108
Hospitals in a Group Purchasing Organization..	194	205	224	240	242

U.S. Census Divisions

TABLE 5

U.S. CENSUS DIVISION 5: EAST SOUTH CENTRAL

U.S. Registered Community Hospitals
(Nonfederal, short-term general and other special hospitals)

Utilization, Personnel, Revenue and Expenses, Community Health Indicators 2007–2011

	2011	2010	2009	2008	2007
TOTAL FACILITY (Includes Hospital and Nursing Home Units)					
Utilization - Inpatient					
Beds	62,478	63,079	63,252	63,626	64,505
Admissions	2,424,397	2,486,454	2,535,115	2,587,919	2,695,512
Inpatient Days	13,300,397	13,614,893	13,973,205	14,460,015	14,787,799
Average Length of Stay	5.5	5.5	5.5	5.6	5.5
Inpatient Surgeries	732,580	728,125	746,929	736,745	773,623
Births	207,943	221,646	233,974	245,061	253,405
Utilization - Outpatient					
Emergency Outpatient Visits	9,526,218	9,527,974	9,630,514	9,557,382	9,547,437
Other Outpatient Visits	25,425,473	25,726,751	25,948,613	25,382,539	24,408,334
Total Outpatient Visits	34,951,691	35,254,725	35,579,127	34,939,921	33,955,771
Outpatient Surgeries	1,386,491	1,344,976	1,337,590	1,309,219	1,361,522
Personnel					
Full Time RNs	75,308	73,350	73,191	70,022	71,100
Full Time LPNs	6,748	7,457	8,025	8,614	9,593
Part Time RNs	24,560	25,319	24,568	25,507	28,291
Part Time LPNs	1,692	2,052	2,168	2,568	2,954
Total Full Time	266,680	262,110	265,884	263,757	275,742
Total Part Time	68,968	72,591	71,457	74,148	81,297
Revenue - Inpatient					
Gross Inpatient Revenue	$75,686,751,272	$73,345,815,567	$70,177,022,070	$67,429,348,071	$64,100,535,279
Revenue - Outpatient					
Gross Outpatient Revenue	$61,846,614,466	$56,798,252,271	$52,231,598,393	$46,662,139,027	$43,516,710,261
Revenue and Expenses - Totals					
(Includes Inpatient and Outpatient)					
Total Gross Revenue	$137,533,365,738	$130,144,067,838	$122,408,620,463	$114,091,487,098	$107,617,245,540
Deductions from Revenue	99,633,059,934	92,627,817,898	85,830,854,030	79,115,671,773	72,599,542,258
Net Patient Revenue	37,900,305,804	37,516,249,940	36,577,766,433	34,975,815,325	35,017,703,282
Other Operating Revenue	1,532,546,010	1,479,335,426	1,540,908,813	1,625,010,586	1,664,289,342
Other Nonoperating Revenue	481,348,514	696,071,058	193,864,288	-19,706,728	964,949,462
Total Net Revenue	39,914,200,328	39,691,656,424	38,312,539,534	36,581,119,183	37,646,942,086
Total Expenses	36,909,370,915	36,471,494,399	36,466,730,541	34,933,934,594	35,466,530,096
HOSPITAL UNIT (Excludes Separate Nursing Home Units)					
Utilization - Inpatient					
Beds	58,770	58,946	58,982	59,075	59,580
Admissions	2,407,693	2,471,184	2,518,083	2,569,243	2,673,641
Inpatient Days	12,159,845	12,327,182	12,606,657	12,982,972	13,211,639
Average Length of Stay	5.1	5.0	5.0	5.1	4.9
Personnel					
Total Full Time	262,518	258,805	262,043	259,932	271,754
Total Part Time	68,301	71,637	70,556	73,231	80,147
Revenue and Expenses - Totals					
(Includes Inpatient and Outpatient)					
Total Net Revenue	$39,631,141,073	$39,425,199,072	$38,036,670,123	$36,298,364,734	$37,341,333,037
Total Expenses	36,701,651,997	36,231,662,045	36,228,704,518	34,698,028,587	35,232,988,561
COMMUNITY HEALTH INDICATORS PER 1000 POPULATION					
Total Population (in thousands)	18,554	18,368	18,271	18,146	17,989
Inpatient					
Beds	3.4	3.4	3.5	3.5	3.6
Admissions	130.7	135.4	138.8	142.6	149.8
Inpatient Days	716.8	741.2	764.8	796.9	822.1
Inpatient Surgeries	39.5	39.6	40.9	40.6	43.0
Births	11.2	12.1	12.8	13.5	14.1
Outpatient					
Emergency Outpatient Visits	513.4	518.7	527.1	526.7	530.7
Other Outpatient Visits	1,370.4	1,400.7	1,420.2	1,398.8	1,356.9
Total Outpatient Visits	1,883.8	1,919.4	1,947.3	1,925.5	1,887.6
Outpatient Surgeries	74.7	73.2	73.2	72.1	75.7
Expense per Capita (per person)	$1,989.3	$1,985.6	$1,995.9	$1,925.2	$1,971.6

U.S. Census Divisions

TABLE 5

U.S. CENSUS DIVISION 6: WEST NORTH CENTRAL

U.S. Registered Community Hospitals
(Nonfederal, short-term general and other special hospitals)

Overview 2007–2011

	2011	2010	2009	2008	2007
Total Community Hospitals					
in Census Division 6, West North Central . . .	**682**	**685**	**689**	**683**	**670**
Bed Size Category					
6-24	126	113	108	103	94
25-49	218	220	217	214	212
50-99	154	164	167	166	163
100-199	91	97	104	105	106
200-299	38	35	38	38	40
300-399	25	28	25	26	23
400-499	14	12	14	15	15
500 + ...	16	16	16	16	17
Location					
Hospitals Urban	220	223	224	220	178
Hospitals Rural	462	462	465	463	492
Control					
State and Local Government	236	235	237	236	241
Not for Profit	396	398	399	395	391
Investor owned	50	52	53	52	38
Physician Models					
Independent Practice Association	62	70	77	82	86
Group Practice without Walls	12	11	14	13	15
Open Physician-Hospital Organization	68	70	84	89	88
Closed Physician-Hospital Organization	26	23	27	26	30
Management Service Organization	20	17	19	25	28
Integrated Salary Model	330	317	339	315	305
Equity Model	6	2	5	6	6
Foundation	22	17	14	21	20
Insurance Products					
Health Maintenance Organization	56	59	56	59	62
Preferred Provider Organization	89	88	84	93	121
Indemnity Fee for Service	29	27	29	32	27
Managed Care Contracts					
Health Maintenance Organization	311	310	320	313	312
Preferred Provider Organization	442	446	469	471	471
Affiliations					
Hospitals in a System	352	348	347	339	326
Hospitals in a Network	287	277	282	280	279
Hospitals in a Group Purchasing Organization . .	557	552	573	570	571

U.S. Census Divisions

TABLE 5

U.S. CENSUS DIVISION 6: WEST NORTH CENTRAL

U.S. Registered Community Hospitals
(Nonfederal, short-term general and other special hospitals)

Utilization, Personnel, Revenue and Expenses, Community Health Indicators 2007–2011

	2011	2010	2009	2008	2007
TOTAL FACILITY (Includes Hospital and Nursing Home Units)					
Utilization - Inpatient					
Beds	67,559	68,830	70,039	70,208	70,058
Admissions	2,453,988	2,464,267	2,523,626	2,589,852	2,565,443
Inpatient Days	14,718,938	14,928,227	15,492,237	15,912,612	15,932,234
Average Length of Stay	6.0	6.1	6.1	6.1	6.2
Inpatient Surgeries	674,685	683,170	705,862	722,817	721,238
Births	264,259	264,621	274,101	279,320	281,227
Utilization - Outpatient					
Emergency Outpatient Visits	8,573,615	8,260,672	8,272,930	8,056,684	7,704,372
Other Outpatient Visits	49,766,340	50,003,264	48,365,884	45,865,406	43,815,430
Total Outpatient Visits	58,339,955	58,263,936	56,638,814	53,922,090	51,519,802
Outpatient Surgeries	1,352,232	1,322,974	1,367,598	1,420,972	1,413,357
Personnel					
Full Time RNs	75,384	73,425	70,664	67,029	64,883
Full Time LPNs	7,158	7,282	7,481	7,692	7,799
Part Time RNs	51,864	52,648	54,581	55,475	51,436
Part Time LPNs	4,132	4,485	4,775	5,225	5,731
Total Full Time	301,105	297,067	289,975	285,576	278,512
Total Part Time	160,171	164,985	169,233	171,973	161,850
Revenue - Inpatient					
Gross Inpatient Revenue	$74,583,373,377	$71,077,555,297	$68,351,872,323	$65,013,165,311	$59,939,612,338
Revenue - Outpatient					
Gross Outpatient Revenue	$68,953,101,651	$62,710,234,207	$58,193,971,919	$50,949,559,907	$45,736,849,741
Revenue and Expenses - Totals					
(Includes Inpatient and Outpatient)					
Total Gross Revenue	$143,536,475,028	$133,787,789,504	$126,545,844,242	$115,962,725,218	$105,676,462,079
Deductions from Revenue	89,596,077,363	82,115,750,561	76,480,891,243	67,883,978,998	61,925,172,023
Net Patient Revenue	53,940,397,665	51,672,038,943	50,064,952,999	48,078,746,220	43,751,290,056
Other Operating Revenue	2,870,841,462	2,830,841,723	2,646,149,834	2,675,404,595	2,616,805,771
Other Nonoperating Revenue	1,096,847,381	1,318,194,215	557,107,759	-524,235,863	1,412,620,373
Total Net Revenue	57,908,086,508	55,821,074,881	53,268,210,592	50,229,914,952	47,780,716,200
Total Expenses	54,026,689,854	51,771,367,599	50,238,229,445	48,227,547,446	44,256,405,517
HOSPITAL UNIT (Excludes Separate Nursing Home Units)					
Utilization - Inpatient					
Beds	58,568	59,661	59,833	58,879	58,121
Admissions	2,432,961	2,443,671	2,498,928	2,561,317	2,534,429
Inpatient Days	11,849,105	12,018,243	12,233,218	12,328,044	12,109,078
Average Length of Stay	4.9	4.9	4.9	4.8	4.8
Personnel					
Total Full Time	295,954	291,819	283,837	279,159	271,540
Total Part Time	155,670	160,316	164,037	166,260	155,511
Revenue and Expenses - Totals					
(Includes Inpatient and Outpatient)					
Total Net Revenue	$57,296,078,737	$55,268,629,929	$52,624,057,167	$49,501,040,808	$47,065,541,644
Total Expenses	53,536,656,669	51,251,683,260	49,653,268,189	47,573,291,977	43,615,288,526
COMMUNITY HEALTH INDICATORS PER 1000 POPULATION					
Total Population (in thousands)	20,640	20,451	20,336	20,206	20,060
Inpatient					
Beds	3.3	3.4	3.4	3.5	3.5
Admissions	118.9	120.5	124.1	128.2	127.9
Inpatient Days	713.1	729.9	761.8	787.5	794.2
Inpatient Surgeries	32.7	33.4	34.7	35.8	36.0
Births	12.8	12.9	13.5	13.8	14.0
Outpatient					
Emergency Outpatient Visits	415.4	403.9	406.8	398.7	384.1
Other Outpatient Visits	2,411.2	2,445.0	2,378.3	2,269.9	2,184.2
Total Outpatient Visits	2,826.6	2,848.9	2,785.1	2,668.6	2,568.2
Outpatient Surgeries	65.5	64.7	67.2	70.3	70.5
Expense per Capita (per person)	$2,617.6	$2,531.4	$2,470.4	$2,386.8	$2,206.1

U.S. Census Divisions

TABLE 5

U.S. CENSUS DIVISION 7: WEST SOUTH CENTRAL

U.S. Registered Community Hospitals
(Nonfederal, short-term general and other special hospitals)

Overview 2007–2011

	2011	2010	2009	2008	2007
Total Community Hospitals					
in Census Division 7, West South Central...	746	750	758	757	735
Bed Size Category					
6-24	114	119	112	112	105
25-49	226	220	223	219	213
50-99	144	146	147	151	147
100-199	109	115	124	124	118
200-299	62	61	61	61	65
300-399	37	35	35	37	39
400-499	20	20	22	21	20
500 + ...	34	34	34	32	28
Location					
Hospitals Urban.........................	431	436	440	442	404
Hospitals Rural	315	314	318	315	331
Control					
State and Local Government...............	210	221	230	225	226
Not for Profit	276	267	263	273	268
Investor owned	260	262	265	259	241
Physician Models					
Independent Practice Association	94	109	109	103	122
Group Practice without Walls...............	31	33	41	28	32
Open Physician-Hospital Organization	126	128	137	143	146
Closed Physician-Hospital Organization	32	30	31	32	28
Management Service Organization	93	94	99	92	93
Integrated Salary Model....................	211	181	168	155	142
Equity Model	10	16	17	19	14
Foundation..............................	47	43	44	50	49
Insurance Products					
Health Maintenance Organization	101	96	90	78	84
Preferred Provider Organization.............	116	118	105	93	116
Indemnity Fee for Service	34	36	30	32	30
Managed Care Contracts					
Health Maintenance Organization	457	449	458	453	445
Preferred Provider Organization.............	554	540	544	551	551
Affiliations					
Hospitals in a System.....................	436	434	457	454	432
Hospitals in a Network....................	193	184	175	177	181
Hospitals in a Group Purchasing Organization..	629	623	624	622	600

U.S. Census Divisions

TABLE 5

U.S. CENSUS DIVISION 7: WEST SOUTH CENTRAL

U.S. Registered Community Hospitals
(Nonfederal, short-term general and other special hospitals)

Utilization, Personnel, Revenue and Expenses, Community Health Indicators 2007–2011

	2011	2010	2009	2008	2007
TOTAL FACILITY (Includes Hospital and Nursing Home Units)					
Utilization - Inpatient					
Beds	96,825	97,399	98,807	97,720	94,072
Admissions	3,929,807	4,005,387	4,083,758	4,061,559	3,919,411
Inpatient Days	20,460,393	20,922,699	21,466,556	21,234,945	20,533,725
Average Length of Stay	5.2	5.2	5.3	5.2	5.2
Inpatient Surgeries	1,118,349	1,150,547	1,181,045	1,169,284	1,187,576
Births	503,256	528,045	561,702	546,219	536,959
Utilization - Outpatient					
Emergency Outpatient Visits	15,575,261	15,392,542	14,987,499	14,148,116	13,551,624
Other Outpatient Visits	44,066,578	45,924,148	44,027,580	42,236,693	39,885,211
Total Outpatient Visits	59,641,839	61,316,690	59,015,079	56,384,809	53,436,835
Outpatient Surgeries	1,683,472	1,707,264	1,671,570	1,642,752	1,624,911
Personnel					
Full Time RNs	121,426	123,112	120,752	110,558	107,131
Full Time LPNs	14,606	15,573	16,584	17,702	17,350
Part Time RNs	35,553	33,058	33,815	33,899	32,312
Part Time LPNs	3,347	3,961	4,411	4,592	4,559
Total Full Time	428,649	434,296	436,301	419,150	413,130
Total Part Time	103,538	99,628	101,491	102,483	96,722
Revenue - Inpatient					
Gross Inpatient Revenue	$146,271,380,775	$139,926,153,510	$132,565,357,014	$122,760,036,602	$109,628,591,480
Revenue - Outpatient					
Gross Outpatient Revenue	$104,883,587,404	$95,633,086,065	$84,978,216,080	$73,261,517,369	$63,422,381,320
Revenue and Expenses - Totals (Includes Inpatient and Outpatient)					
Total Gross Revenue	$251,154,968,179	$235,559,239,575	$217,543,573,094	$196,021,553,971	$173,050,972,800
Deductions from Revenue	184,194,250,743	169,768,881,745	154,142,249,102	136,945,981,599	118,940,845,500
Net Patient Revenue	66,960,717,436	65,790,357,830	63,401,323,992	59,075,572,372	54,110,127,300
Other Operating Revenue	5,893,843,564	5,622,273,906	5,328,857,978	4,942,957,894	4,713,837,579
Other Nonoperating Revenue	1,909,520,980	1,791,442,768	267,367,879	412,762,180	1,530,873,066
Total Net Revenue	74,764,081,980	73,204,074,504	68,997,549,849	64,431,292,446	60,354,837,945
Total Expenses	67,280,680,393	65,549,933,822	64,399,048,894	60,693,798,710	55,938,005,973
HOSPITAL UNIT (Excludes Separate Nursing Home Units)					
Utilization - Inpatient					
Beds	94,783	95,427	96,504	95,219	91,393
Admissions	3,916,503	3,991,294	4,068,586	4,044,358	3,902,159
Inpatient Days	19,861,338	20,336,517	20,737,974	20,585,465	19,711,788
Average Length of Stay	5.1	5.1	5.1	5.1	5.1
Personnel					
Total Full Time	427,100	432,842	433,900	416,608	410,704
Total Part Time	103,146	99,156	100,856	101,661	96,037
Revenue and Expenses - Totals (Includes Inpatient and Outpatient)					
Total Net Revenue	$74,607,353,353	$73,043,779,992	$68,839,731,724	$64,269,536,853	$60,143,040,802
Total Expenses	67,137,888,126	65,399,265,396	64,241,260,529	60,516,951,798	55,631,442,741
COMMUNITY HEALTH INDICATORS PER 1000 POPULATION					
Total Population (in thousands)	36,979	36,378	35,851	35,268	34,668
Inpatient					
Beds	2.6	2.7	2.8	2.8	2.7
Admissions	106.3	110.1	113.9	115.2	113.1
Inpatient Days	553.3	575.2	598.8	602.1	592.3
Inpatient Surgeries	30.2	31.6	32.9	33.2	34.3
Births	13.6	14.5	15.7	15.5	15.5
Outpatient					
Emergency Outpatient Visits	421.2	423.1	418.1	401.2	390.9
Other Outpatient Visits	1,191.7	1,262.4	1,228.1	1,197.6	1,150.5
Total Outpatient Visits	1,612.9	1,685.6	1,646.1	1,598.8	1,541.4
Outpatient Surgeries	45.5	46.9	46.6	46.6	46.9
Expense per Capita (per person)	$1,819.4	$1,801.9	$1,796.3	$1,721.0	$1,613.5

U.S. Census Divisions

TABLE 5

U.S. CENSUS DIVISION 8: MOUNTAIN

U.S. Registered Community Hospitals
(Nonfederal, short-term general and other special hospitals)

Overview 2007–2011

	2011	2010	2009	2008	2007
Total Community Hospitals					
in Census Division 8, Mountain............	**384**	**382**	**382**	**374**	**365**
Bed Size Category					
6-24.....................................	55	53	50	48	46
25-49....................................	99	98	96	94	90
50-99....................................	87	88	96	92	92
100-199..................................	63	66	61	66	66
200-299..................................	35	32	35	34	34
300-399..................................	20	21	21	17	15
400-499..................................	13	11	8	9	9
500 +....................................	12	13	15	14	13
Location					
Hospitals Urban..........................	191	189	189	183	156
Hospitals Rural..........................	193	193	193	191	209
Control					
State and Local Government...............	94	94	97	96	95
Not for Profit...........................	197	195	191	189	192
Investor owned..........................	93	93	94	89	78
Physician Models					
Independent Practice Association...........	41	42	48	46	48
Group Practice without Walls...............	13	8	9	8	10
Open Physician-Hospital Organization........	36	34	36	33	33
Closed Physician-Hospital Organization.......	15	14	16	16	17
Management Service Organization...........	24	27	26	22	24
Integrated Salary Model...................	140	125	130	122	120
Equity Model............................	5	5	5	6	6
Foundation..............................	12	13	11	14	14
Insurance Products					
Health Maintenance Organization............	57	54	53	53	55
Preferred Provider Organization.............	58	56	54	49	61
Indemnity Fee for Service.................	26	27	29	25	36
Managed Care Contracts					
Health Maintenance Organization............	141	147	153	156	155
Preferred Provider Organization.............	184	185	198	199	196
Affiliations					
Hospitals in a System.....................	229	230	232	225	211
Hospitals in a Network....................	110	112	111	110	107
Hospitals in a Group Purchasing Organization..	259	248	257	255	258

U.S. Census Divisions

TABLE 5

U.S. CENSUS DIVISION 8: MOUNTAIN

U.S. Registered Community Hospitals
(Nonfederal, short-term general and other special hospitals)

Utilization, Personnel, Revenue and Expenses, Community Health Indicators 2007–2011

	2011	2010	2009	2008	2007
TOTAL FACILITY (Includes Hospital and Nursing Home Units)					
Utilization - Inpatient					
Beds	47,119	46,872	47,028	46,293	44,564
Admissions	2,064,195	2,091,454	2,089,087	2,098,239	2,033,246
Inpatient Days	10,303,057	10,379,491	10,509,716	10,533,261	10,290,695
Average Length of Stay	5.0	5.0	5.0	5.0	5.1
Inpatient Surgeries	646,125	662,412	673,176	638,455	633,790
Births	268,969	278,694	300,722	314,340	313,570
Utilization - Outpatient					
Emergency Outpatient Visits	7,567,323	7,497,043	7,485,406	7,302,452	7,077,571
Other Outpatient Visits	31,476,244	29,432,803	28,867,801	28,396,866	26,578,776
Total Outpatient Visits	39,043,567	36,929,846	36,353,207	35,699,318	33,656,347
Outpatient Surgeries	996,441	982,327	962,734	936,167	856,886
Personnel					
Full Time RNs	64,271	66,717	64,343	62,485	57,336
Full Time LPNs	3,129	3,511	4,372	4,011	4,199
Part Time RNs	25,828	23,141	24,303	24,804	22,170
Part Time LPNs	1,197	1,170	1,401	1,594	1,768
Total Full Time	228,851	233,880	229,182	224,101	218,760
Total Part Time	76,297	68,863	73,288	75,630	68,111
Revenue - Inpatient					
Gross Inpatient Revenue	$77,570,487,787	$74,568,371,912	$69,773,749,237	$65,876,774,754	$58,788,545,403
Revenue - Outpatient					
Gross Outpatient Revenue	$59,010,644,319	$53,530,101,037	$47,901,898,628	$41,380,379,213	$35,716,383,231
Revenue and Expenses - Totals					
(Includes Inpatient and Outpatient)					
Total Gross Revenue	$136,581,132,106	$128,098,472,949	$117,675,647,865	$107,257,153,967	$94,504,928,634
Deductions from Revenue	94,240,727,395	86,894,343,376	78,561,440,721	70,987,810,766	61,088,641,713
Net Patient Revenue	42,340,404,711	41,204,129,573	39,114,207,144	36,269,343,201	33,416,286,921
Other Operating Revenue	1,885,009,958	1,804,886,179	1,641,533,021	1,612,417,661	1,585,270,393
Other Nonoperating Revenue	497,930,676	550,761,263	383,043,417	-20,098,533	870,215,218
Total Net Revenue	44,723,345,345	43,559,777,015	41,138,783,582	37,861,662,329	35,871,772,532
Total Expenses	40,362,478,873	38,771,182,258	37,489,628,683	35,816,821,042	32,708,537,125
HOSPITAL UNIT (Excludes Separate Nursing Home Units)					
Utilization - Inpatient					
Beds	43,922	43,563	43,572	42,780	40,648
Admissions	2,054,557	2,081,194	2,078,283	2,087,447	2,022,366
Inpatient Days	9,320,023	9,356,938	9,453,606	9,502,108	9,123,808
Average Length of Stay	4.5	4.5	4.5	4.6	4.5
Personnel					
Total Full Time	226,920	231,537	226,895	220,221	214,707
Total Part Time	75,224	67,617	72,075	74,179	66,557
Revenue and Expenses - Totals					
(Includes Inpatient and Outpatient)					
Total Net Revenue	$44,490,329,013	$43,323,260,876	$40,917,090,747	$37,657,242,332	$35,656,821,227
Total Expenses	40,156,890,139	38,565,221,584	37,287,396,355	35,628,245,086	32,520,257,859
COMMUNITY HEALTH INDICATORS PER 1000 POPULATION					
Total Population (in thousands)	22,373	22,379	22,123	21,793	21,385
Inpatient					
Beds	2.1	2.1	2.1	2.1	2.1
Admissions	92.3	93.5	94.4	96.3	95.1
Inpatient Days	460.5	463.8	475.1	483.3	481.2
Inpatient Surgeries	28.9	29.6	30.4	29.3	29.6
Births	12.0	12.5	13.6	14.4	14.7
Outpatient					
Emergency Outpatient Visits	338.2	335.0	338.4	335.1	331.0
Other Outpatient Visits	1,406.9	1,315.2	1,304.9	1,303.0	1,242.9
Total Outpatient Visits	1,745.1	1,650.2	1,643.2	1,638.1	1,573.9
Outpatient Surgeries	44.5	43.9	43.5	43.0	40.1
Expense per Capita (per person)	$1,804.0	$1,732.5	$1,694.6	$1,643.5	$1,529.5

TABLE 5

U.S. CENSUS DIVISION 9: PACIFIC

U.S. Registered Community Hospitals
(Nonfederal, short-term general and other special hospitals)

Overview 2007–2011

	2011	2010	2009	2008	2007
Total Community Hospitals					
in Census Division 9, Pacific	535	535	535	543	545
Bed Size Category					
6-24	42	41	39	36	35
25-49	97	97	98	97	95
50-99	73	70	73	82	85
100-199	133	139	139	139	145
200-299	86	84	87	92	89
300-399	55	55	57	53	54
400-499	31	31	27	27	24
500 + ...	18	18	15	17	18
Location					
Hospitals Urban...........................	414	413	413	420	406
Hospitals Rural	121	122	122	123	139
Control					
State and Local Government...............	133	135	135	141	139
Not for Profit	318	319	319	315	316
Investor owned	84	81	81	87	90
Physician Models					
Independent Practice Association	79	83	78	88	108
Group Practice without Walls................	24	24	24	22	20
Open Physician-Hospital Organization	22	20	19	22	26
Closed Physician-Hospital Organization	11	10	11	10	10
Management Service Organization	47	48	47	44	51
Integrated Salary Model....................	115	113	110	107	111
Equity Model	6	7	5	2	4
Foundation...............................	59	60	55	52	44
Insurance Products					
Health Maintenance Organization	64	55	64	64	69
Preferred Provider Organization..............	62	56	54	48	63
Indemnity Fee for Service	21	15	14	15	21
Managed Care Contracts					
Health Maintenance Organization	228	231	231	226	257
Preferred Provider Organization..............	252	259	270	263	287
Affiliations					
Hospitals in a System......................	336	330	324	328	329
Hospitals in a Network.....................	121	110	111	107	100
Hospitals in a Group Purchasing Organization..	315	310	352	333	346

U.S. Census Divisions

TABLE 5

U.S. CENSUS DIVISION 9: PACIFIC

U.S. Registered Community Hospitals
(Nonfederal, short-term general and other special hospitals)

Utilization, Personnel, Revenue and Expenses, Community Health Indicators 2007–2011

	2011	2010	2009	2008	2007
TOTAL FACILITY (Includes Hospital and Nursing Home Units)					
Utilization - Inpatient					
Beds	92,601	93,088	91,046	92,389	91,955
Admissions	4,471,783	4,501,591	4,514,874	4,557,658	4,365,002
Inpatient Days	22,232,780	22,640,225	22,791,572	23,454,079	22,401,234
Average Length of Stay.	5.0	5.0	5.0	5.1	5.1
Inpatient Surgeries.	1,192,531	1,241,853	1,252,243	1,260,249	1,299,136
Births.	629,315	632,032	645,081	676,180	662,060
Utilization - Outpatient					
Emergency Outpatient Visits.	15,480,506	15,128,224	15,055,923	14,473,721	14,319,461
Other Outpatient Visits.	62,797,927	61,596,946	57,529,665	58,052,120	54,654,796
Total Outpatient Visits	78,278,433	76,725,170	72,585,588	72,525,841	68,974,257
Outpatient Surgeries	1,846,317	1,835,447	1,833,478	1,886,717	1,811,593
Personnel					
Full Time RNs	136,326	134,508	130,132	126,718	114,266
Full Time LPNs	7,594	8,301	8,642	9,011	8,993
Part Time RNs.	72,866	71,284	70,581	72,526	75,566
Part Time LPNs	3,211	3,453	3,839	4,274	4,950
Total Full Time.	493,680	487,053	477,901	477,563	454,501
Total Part Time	199,030	193,703	191,891	201,710	211,443
Revenue - Inpatient					
Gross Inpatient Revenue.	$219,593,141,460	$211,874,242,966	$193,636,178,785	$181,416,247,444	$168,961,978,477
Revenue - Outpatient					
Gross Outpatient Revenue	$138,274,865,366	$124,558,809,024	$109,199,995,898	$98,528,236,224	$84,834,034,482
Revenue and Expenses - Totals					
(Includes Inpatient and Outpatient)					
Total Gross Revenue.	$357,868,006,826	$336,433,051,990	$302,836,174,683	$279,944,483,668	$253,796,012,959
Deductions from Revenue	253,322,749,612	239,252,607,338	212,570,073,192	194,777,375,687	175,398,585,106
Net Patient Revenue	104,545,257,214	97,180,444,652	90,266,101,491	85,167,107,981	78,397,427,853
Other Operating Revenue	5,990,186,797	6,027,711,222	5,590,026,520	5,041,401,269	4,653,195,596
Other Nonoperating Revenue	2,259,696,906	1,866,228,283	1,090,362,535	23,014,193	2,776,806,260
Total Net Revenue.	112,795,140,917	105,074,384,157	96,946,490,546	90,231,523,443	85,827,429,709
Total Expenses.	105,001,431,937	98,998,692,542	93,038,063,591	88,037,635,750	79,632,236,072
HOSPITAL UNIT (Excludes Separate Nursing Home Units)					
Utilization - Inpatient					
Beds	88,926	88,925	86,836	87,253	86,642
Admissions	4,450,403	4,478,851	4,489,343	4,527,176	4,330,186
Inpatient Days	21,093,072	21,344,190	21,533,040	21,897,397	20,880,648
Average Length of Stay.	4.7	4.8	4.8	4.8	4.8
Personnel					
Total Full Time.	490,810	483,548	473,892	473,367	449,821
Total Part Time	197,584	192,111	189,876	199,475	208,757
Revenue and Expenses - Totals					
(Includes Inpatient and Outpatient)					
Total Net Revenue.	$112,319,758,152	$104,531,350,858	$96,415,616,765	$89,624,997,242	$85,096,193,516
Total Expenses.	104,639,691,795	98,595,961,703	92,611,409,620	87,584,896,173	79,167,104,551
COMMUNITY HEALTH INDICATORS PER 1000 POPULATION					
Total Population (in thousands)	50,491	49,877	49,445	48,905	48,383
Inpatient					
Beds	1.8	1.9	1.8	1.9	1.9
Admissions	88.6	90.3	91.3	93.2	90.2
Inpatient Days	440.3	453.9	460.9	479.6	463.0
Inpatient Surgeries.	23.6	24.9	25.3	25.8	26.9
Births.	12.5	12.7	13.0	13.8	13.7
Outpatient					
Emergency Outpatient Visits.	306.6	303.3	304.5	296.0	296.0
Other Outpatient Visits.	1,243.7	1,235.0	1,163.5	1,187.0	1,129.6
Total Outpatient Visits	1,550.3	1,538.3	1,468.0	1,483.0	1,425.6
Outpatient Surgeries	36.6	36.8	37.1	38.6	37.4
Expense per Capita (per person).	$2,079.6	$1,984.8	$1,881.6	$1,800.2	$1,645.9

U.S. Census Divisions

TABLE 6

ALABAMA

U.S. Registered Community Hospitals
(Nonfederal, short-term general and other special hospitals)

Overview 2007–2011

	2011	2010	2009	2008	2007
Total Community Hospitals in Alabama	**102**	**105**	**108**	**109**	**109**
Bed Size Category					
6-24	9	7	7	8	6
25-49	23	27	27	25	25
50-99	21	22	24	27	26
100-199	24	28	28	25	29
200-299	12	9	9	11	11
300-399	6	6	7	7	6
400-499	3	3	3	3	2
500 + ...	4	3	3	3	4
Location					
Hospitals Urban	57	58	60	60	58
Hospitals Rural	45	47	48	49	51
Control					
State and Local Government	39	40	42	42	42
Not for Profit	24	24	26	27	27
Investor owned	39	41	40	40	40
Physician Models					
Independent Practice Association	4	7	8	8	7
Group Practice without Walls	0	1	2	2	3
Open Physician-Hospital Organization	7	7	3	3	5
Closed Physician-Hospital Organization	4	0	1	2	2
Management Service Organization	10	7	5	10	12
Integrated Salary Model	13	18	16	14	14
Equity Model	0	0	0	0	1
Foundation	5	7	5	5	6
Insurance Products					
Health Maintenance Organization	3	7	10	13	12
Preferred Provider Organization	12	8	9	10	8
Indemnity Fee for Service	1	1	1	3	2
Managed Care Contracts					
Health Maintenance Organization	35	37	36	35	32
Preferred Provider Organization	44	51	49	49	42
Affiliations					
Hospitals in a System	61	64	67	68	67
Hospitals in a Network	8	9	11	12	12
Hospitals in a Group Purchasing Organization ..	53	56	70	68	64

States

TABLE 6

ALABAMA

U.S. Registered Community Hospitals
(Nonfederal, short-term general and other special hospitals)

Utilization, Personnel, Revenue and Expenses, Community Health Indicators 2007–2011

	2011	2010	2009	2008	2007
TOTAL FACILITY (Includes Hospital and Nursing Home Units)					
Utilization - Inpatient					
Beds	15,387	15,086	15,290	15,250	15,682
Admissions	625,425	642,309	665,788	687,446	696,131
Inpatient Days	3,259,740	3,336,285	3,459,946	3,524,687	3,551,293
Average Length of Stay	5.2	5.2	5.2	5.1	5.1
Inpatient Surgeries	225,340	197,605	203,945	202,900	221,162
Births	56,038	58,287	62,819	62,436	62,617
Utilization - Outpatient					
Emergency Outpatient Visits	2,301,480	2,304,682	2,286,343	2,271,755	2,253,215
Other Outpatient Visits	6,428,214	6,496,039	6,905,010	6,746,766	5,934,478
Total Outpatient Visits	8,729,694	8,800,721	9,191,353	9,018,521	8,187,693
Outpatient Surgeries	410,937	372,359	380,226	364,648	365,487
Personnel					
Full Time RNs	19,179	19,033	18,906	17,930	17,077
Full Time LPNs	1,334	1,533	1,587	1,795	2,005
Part Time RNs	6,030	6,521	6,495	6,708	7,708
Part Time LPNs	407	544	584	755	885
Total Full Time	63,640	63,565	64,706	64,821	63,949
Total Part Time	16,258	17,485	17,181	18,103	20,423
Revenue - Inpatient					
Gross Inpatient Revenue	$20,721,285,712	$20,382,077,101	$19,226,829,885	$18,436,910,861	$17,301,065,902
Revenue - Outpatient					
Gross Outpatient Revenue	$16,116,899,016	$15,107,168,189	$13,746,107,465	$11,949,849,370	$10,302,085,003
Revenue and Expenses - Totals					
(Includes Inpatient and Outpatient)					
Total Gross Revenue	$36,838,184,728	$35,489,245,290	$32,972,937,350	$30,386,760,231	$27,603,150,905
Deductions from Revenue	28,275,034,462	26,885,327,851	24,887,051,667	22,550,588,921	19,968,905,297
Net Patient Revenue	8,563,150,266	8,603,917,439	8,085,885,683	7,836,171,310	7,634,245,608
Other Operating Revenue	419,270,245	398,593,891	476,168,844	499,586,864	522,333,646
Other Nonoperating Revenue	124,960,404	180,032,402	209,998,612	-56,405,573	268,802,396
Total Net Revenue	9,107,380,915	9,182,543,732	8,772,053,139	8,279,352,601	8,425,381,650
Total Expenses	8,285,877,588	8,334,444,846	8,276,604,492	8,288,702,647	7,960,186,498
HOSPITAL UNIT (Excludes Separate Nursing Home Units)					
Utilization - Inpatient					
Beds	14,953	14,569	14,861	14,824	15,042
Admissions	624,134	641,118	664,534	686,256	693,215
Inpatient Days	3,142,919	3,188,617	3,314,802	3,377,540	3,347,267
Average Length of Stay	5.0	5.0	5.0	4.9	4.8
Personnel					
Total Full Time	63,302	63,159	64,371	64,502	63,572
Total Part Time	16,224	17,373	17,120	18,073	20,305
Revenue and Expenses - Totals					
(Includes Inpatient and Outpatient)					
Total Net Revenue	$9,085,772,314	$9,160,325,136	$8,749,089,004	$8,258,544,123	$8,397,411,188
Total Expenses	8,272,890,643	8,308,793,595	8,249,699,883	8,268,150,713	7,937,260,895
COMMUNITY HEALTH INDICATORS PER 1000 POPULATION					
Total Population (in thousands)	4,803	4,730	4,709	4,677	4,638
Inpatient					
Beds	3.2	3.2	3.2	3.3	3.4
Admissions	130.2	135.8	141.4	147.0	150.1
Inpatient Days	678.7	705.4	734.8	753.5	765.7
Inpatient Surgeries	46.9	41.8	43.3	43.4	47.7
Births	11.7	12.3	13.3	13.3	13.5
Outpatient					
Emergency Outpatient Visits	479.2	487.3	485.6	485.7	485.8
Other Outpatient Visits	1,338.4	1,373.5	1,466.4	1,442.4	1,279.6
Total Outpatient Visits	1,817.6	1,860.8	1,952.0	1,928.1	1,765.4
Outpatient Surgeries	85.6	78.7	80.7	78.0	78.8
Expense per Capita (per person)	$1,725.2	$1,762.2	$1,757.7	$1,772.1	$1,716.3

States

TABLE 6

ALASKA

U.S. Registered Community Hospitals
(Nonfederal, short-term general and other special hospitals)

Overview 2007–2011

	2011	2010	2009	2008	2007
Total Community Hospitals in Alaska.........	23	22	22	22	22
Bed Size Category					
6-24	7	6	6	6	6
25-49	7	7	8	7	7
50-99	4	4	3	4	4
100-199	3	3	3	3	3
200-299	1	1	1	1	1
300-399	1	1	1	1	1
400-499	0	0	0	0	0
500 + ...	0	0	0	0	0
Location					
Hospitals Urban...........................	6	5	5	5	3
Hospitals Rural	17	17	17	17	19
Control					
State and Local Government................	7	7	6	7	7
Not for Profit	14	13	14	13	13
Investor owned	2	2	2	2	2
Physician Models					
Independent Practice Association	1	1	0	0	2
Group Practice without Walls................	0	0	0	0	0
Open Physician-Hospital Organization	2	2	2	2	3
Closed Physician-Hospital Organization	1	1	1	0	0
Management Service Organization	0	0	1	0	0
Integrated Salary Model	4	4	3	4	4
Equity Model	0	0	0	0	0
Foundation...............................	0	0	0	0	0
Insurance Products					
Health Maintenance Organization	0	0	0	0	0
Preferred Provider Organization..............	4	1	2	2	3
Indemnity Fee for Service	1	0	0	1	0
Managed Care Contracts					
Health Maintenance Organization	1	0	0	0	0
Preferred Provider Organization..............	7	5	7	8	9
Affiliations					
Hospitals in a System.....................	9	9	8	8	8
Hospitals in a Network	1	3	5	3	4
Hospitals in a Group Purchasing Organization..	8	8	12	11	11

States

TABLE 6

ALASKA

U.S. Registered Community Hospitals
(Nonfederal, short-term general and other special hospitals)

Utilization, Personnel, Revenue and Expenses, Community Health Indicators 2007–2011

	2011	2010	2009	2008	2007
TOTAL FACILITY (Includes Hospital and Nursing Home Units)					
Utilization - Inpatient					
Beds	1,556	1,543	1,532	1,553	1,554
Admissions	54,715	57,005	57,227	58,204	56,584
Inpatient Days	340,060	342,960	338,547	346,837	337,028
Average Length of Stay	6.2	6.0	5.9	6.0	6.0
Inpatient Surgeries	16,420	17,999	20,294	20,522	18,924
Births	9,196	8,919	9,358	8,882	9,047
Utilization - Outpatient					
Emergency Outpatient Visits	315,181	296,573	296,524	328,164	328,947
Other Outpatient Visits	1,450,455	1,486,369	1,470,894	1,365,178	1,455,616
Total Outpatient Visits	1,765,636	1,782,942	1,767,418	1,693,342	1,784,563
Outpatient Surgeries	43,714	47,417	50,469	43,567	44,193
Personnel					
Full Time RNs	2,456	2,238	2,348	2,090	2,091
Full Time LPNs	177	178	163	163	197
Part Time RNs	820	906	816	848	512
Part Time LPNs	35	28	27	48	45
Total Full Time	10,084	9,608	9,421	8,809	8,712
Total Part Time	2,177	2,584	2,125	2,435	1,661
Revenue - Inpatient					
Gross Inpatient Revenue	$2,510,713,374	$2,340,223,028	$1,920,419,380	$2,045,394,009	$1,688,213,313
Revenue - Outpatient					
Gross Outpatient Revenue	$2,540,116,099	$2,263,620,240	$1,956,296,065	$1,623,182,947	$1,379,909,276
Revenue and Expenses - Totals					
(Includes Inpatient and Outpatient)					
Total Gross Revenue	$5,050,829,473	$4,603,843,268	$3,876,715,445	$3,668,576,956	$3,068,122,589
Deductions from Revenue	3,205,558,785	2,836,623,088	2,198,399,661	2,054,343,109	1,623,832,318
Net Patient Revenue	1,845,270,688	1,767,220,180	1,678,315,784	1,614,233,847	1,444,290,271
Other Operating Revenue	216,227,533	146,570,128	65,784,620	66,832,290	78,687,582
Other Nonoperating Revenue	19,647,439	21,027,327	18,948,295	16,635,452	41,367,990
Total Net Revenue	2,081,145,660	1,934,817,635	1,763,048,699	1,697,701,589	1,564,345,843
Total Expenses	1,747,385,857	1,590,214,704	1,753,736,940	1,570,873,845	1,458,281,758
HOSPITAL UNIT (Excludes Separate Nursing Home Units)					
Utilization - Inpatient					
Beds	1,346	1,334	1,300	1,381	1,280
Admissions	54,498	56,797	56,918	58,081	56,310
Inpatient Days	270,835	275,518	263,515	293,939	252,315
Average Length of Stay	5.0	4.9	4.6	5.1	4.5
Personnel					
Total Full Time	9,855	9,428	9,174	8,712	8,469
Total Part Time	2,080	2,443	1,990	2,350	1,546
Revenue and Expenses - Totals					
(Includes Inpatient and Outpatient)					
Total Net Revenue	$2,048,187,683	$1,900,578,038	$1,724,497,539	$1,678,203,874	$1,502,363,012
Total Expenses	1,720,343,546	1,564,596,210	1,726,965,040	1,560,050,288	1,432,798,379
COMMUNITY HEALTH INDICATORS PER 1000 POPULATION					
Total Population (in thousands)	723	709	698	688	682
Inpatient					
Beds	2.2	2.2	2.2	2.3	2.3
Admissions	75.7	80.4	81.9	84.6	82.9
Inpatient Days	470.5	483.8	484.7	504.0	494.0
Inpatient Surgeries	22.7	25.4	29.1	29.8	27.7
Births	12.7	12.6	13.4	12.9	13.3
Outpatient					
Emergency Outpatient Visits	436.1	418.4	424.5	476.9	482.1
Other Outpatient Visits	2,006.9	2,096.8	2,105.9	1,983.9	2,133.4
Total Outpatient Visits	2,443.0	2,515.2	2,530.4	2,460.8	2,615.5
Outpatient Surgeries	60.5	66.9	72.3	63.3	64.8
Expense per Capita (per person)	$2,417.8	$2,243.3	$2,510.8	$2,282.8	$2,137.3

States

TABLE 6

ARIZONA

U.S. Registered Community Hospitals
(Nonfederal, short-term general and other special hospitals)

Overview 2007–2011

	2011	2010	2009	2008	2007
Total Community Hospitals in Arizona	**70**	**73**	**72**	**71**	**66**
Bed Size Category					
6-24	5	5	4	4	4
25-49	12	10	10	10	10
50-99	14	18	18	18	14
100-199	12	13	11	12	13
200-299	11	11	12	11	11
300-399	4	5	8	7	6
400-499	7	6	4	4	3
500 + ...	5	5	5	5	5
Location					
Hospitals Urban............................	56	58	58	57	50
Hospitals Rural	14	15	14	14	16
Control					
State and Local Government...............	4	5	7	4	4
Not for Profit	47	46	43	44	43
Investor owned	19	22	22	23	19
Physician Models					
Independent Practice Association	7	8	9	10	9
Group Practice without Walls................	3	1	1	2	3
Open Physician-Hospital Organization	5	6	6	5	7
Closed Physician-Hospital Organization	2	3	4	4	4
Management Service Organization	9	8	4	3	4
Integrated Salary Model....................	19	15	16	12	12
Equity Model	0	0	0	0	0
Foundation...............................	2	2	2	3	3
Insurance Products					
Health Maintenance Organization	10	9	8	10	11
Preferred Provider Organization..............	8	7	5	3	10
Indemnity Fee for Service	5	5	4	3	9
Managed Care Contracts					
Health Maintenance Organization	30	32	32	33	33
Preferred Provider Organization..............	31	31	33	31	33
Affiliations					
Hospitals in a System.....................	46	48	49	48	44
Hospitals in a Network	17	19	14	14	11
Hospitals in a Group Purchasing Organization..	40	45	41	43	39

States

TABLE 6

ARIZONA

U.S. Registered Community Hospitals
(Nonfederal, short-term general and other special hospitals)

Utilization, Personnel, Revenue and Expenses, Community Health Indicators 2007–2011

	2011	2010	2009	2008	2007
TOTAL FACILITY (Includes Hospital and Nursing Home Units)					
Utilization - Inpatient					
Beds	13,352	13,385	13,455	13,138	12,157
Admissions	700,855	711,901	705,371	716,136	675,216
Inpatient Days	3,106,331	3,160,244	3,203,551	3,235,063	3,041,795
Average Length of Stay	4.4	4.4	4.5	4.5	4.5
Inpatient Surgeries	239,277	247,886	249,404	225,735	209,707
Births	74,547	80,960	88,943	96,193	97,159
Utilization - Outpatient					
Emergency Outpatient Visits	2,189,955	2,240,946	2,137,007	2,172,149	2,122,695
Other Outpatient Visits	6,362,148	5,886,520	4,965,037	5,542,202	5,190,865
Total Outpatient Visits	8,552,103	8,127,466	7,102,044	7,714,351	7,313,560
Outpatient Surgeries	250,415	257,530	264,098	254,546	221,754
Personnel					
Full Time RNs	20,524	22,440	21,733	20,898	18,124
Full Time LPNs	649	807	1,428	957	920
Part Time RNs	5,929	5,419	6,207	6,462	6,140
Part Time LPNs	152	135	217	251	274
Total Full Time	67,996	71,092	68,218	65,668	64,015
Total Part Time	15,965	14,521	16,938	18,272	17,536
Revenue - Inpatient					
Gross Inpatient Revenue	$26,796,619,071	$26,745,329,251	$25,403,304,711	$23,681,284,471	$21,143,464,204
Revenue - Outpatient					
Gross Outpatient Revenue	$16,955,905,216	$15,678,580,294	$14,088,508,773	$12,097,995,360	$10,534,254,958
Revenue and Expenses - Totals					
(Includes Inpatient and Outpatient)					
Total Gross Revenue	$43,752,524,287	$42,423,909,545	$39,491,813,484	$35,779,279,831	$31,677,719,162
Deductions from Revenue	32,157,030,582	30,579,491,050	28,395,520,445	25,364,507,854	21,946,070,382
Net Patient Revenue	11,595,493,705	11,844,418,495	11,096,293,039	10,414,771,977	9,731,648,780
Other Operating Revenue	515,033,121	504,651,779	405,351,865	363,332,345	367,303,347
Other Nonoperating Revenue	82,344,006	65,552,870	146,545,191	-141,211,261	203,652,122
Total Net Revenue	12,192,870,832	12,414,623,144	11,648,190,095	10,636,893,061	10,302,604,249
Total Expenses	11,520,903,768	11,271,574,937	10,838,466,876	10,461,227,615	9,586,339,104
HOSPITAL UNIT (Excludes Separate Nursing Home Units)					
Utilization - Inpatient					
Beds	13,226	13,265	13,311	12,954	11,949
Admissions	698,689	709,606	703,074	713,487	672,878
Inpatient Days	3,063,786	3,120,611	3,154,344	3,189,855	2,981,340
Average Length of Stay	4.4	4.4	4.5	4.5	4.4
Personnel					
Total Full Time	67,911	70,791	68,133	63,940	62,623
Total Part Time	15,936	14,477	16,909	17,993	17,258
Revenue and Expenses - Totals					
(Includes Inpatient and Outpatient)					
Total Net Revenue	$12,154,799,416	$12,377,572,952	$11,622,780,339	$10,627,564,240	$10,291,634,189
Total Expenses	11,504,061,948	11,256,388,031	10,821,151,582	10,447,130,955	9,573,110,290
COMMUNITY HEALTH INDICATORS PER 1000 POPULATION					
Total Population (in thousands)	6,483	6,677	6,596	6,499	6,362
Inpatient					
Beds	2.1	2.0	2.0	2.0	1.9
Admissions	108.1	106.6	106.9	110.2	106.1
Inpatient Days	479.2	473.3	485.7	497.7	478.1
Inpatient Surgeries	36.9	37.1	37.8	34.7	33.0
Births	11.5	12.1	13.5	14.8	15.3
Outpatient					
Emergency Outpatient Visits	337.8	335.6	324.0	334.2	333.6
Other Outpatient Visits	981.4	881.7	752.8	852.7	815.9
Total Outpatient Visits	1,319.3	1,217.3	1,076.8	1,186.9	1,149.5
Outpatient Surgeries	38.6	38.6	40.0	39.2	34.9
Expense per Capita (per person)	$1,777.2	$1,688.2	$1,643.2	$1,609.6	$1,506.8

States

TABLE 6

ARKANSAS

U.S. Registered Community Hospitals
(Nonfederal, short-term general and other special hospitals)

Overview 2007–2011

	2011	2010	2009	2008	2007
Total Community Hospitals in Arkansas.......	84	85	86	86	84
Bed Size Category					
6-24	5	6	7	7	5
25-49	33	32	31	30	30
50-99	14	16	18	18	17
100-199	18	18	17	18	19
200-299	5	6	5	6	6
300-399	6	4	5	5	5
400-499	2	2	2	0	0
500 + ...	1	1	1	2	2
Location					
Hospitals Urban...........................	36	37	37	37	31
Hospitals Rural	48	48	49	49	53
Control					
State and Local Government................	11	14	15	13	14
Not for Profit	50	45	45	46	45
Investor owned	23	26	26	27	25
Physician Models					
Independent Practice Association	9	16	16	17	17
Group Practice without Walls...............	5	6	6	6	6
Open Physician-Hospital Organization	24	25	28	28	28
Closed Physician-Hospital Organization	5	6	6	4	3
Management Service Organization	10	10	10	10	12
Integrated Salary Model....................	18	21	20	18	16
Equity Model	0	1	2	2	2
Foundation................................	6	7	8	11	8
Insurance Products					
Health Maintenance Organization	14	14	14	15	14
Preferred Provider Organization..............	10	14	14	13	14
Indemnity Fee for Service	2	4	3	4	4
Managed Care Contracts					
Health Maintenance Organization	46	46	50	47	49
Preferred Provider Organization..............	64	62	66	65	68
Affiliations					
Hospitals in a System.....................	44	46	47	46	45
Hospitals in a Network.....................	26	26	28	29	27
Hospitals in a Group Purchasing Organization..	73	67	78	80	82

States

TABLE 6

ARKANSAS

U.S. Registered Community Hospitals
(Nonfederal, short-term general and other special hospitals)

Utilization, Personnel, Revenue and Expenses, Community Health Indicators 2007–2011

	2011	2010	2009	2008	2007
TOTAL FACILITY (Includes Hospital and Nursing Home Units)					
Utilization - Inpatient					
Beds	9,425	9,451	9,565	9,686	9,502
Admissions	363,516	370,401	380,478	376,158	366,452
Inpatient Days	1,882,912	1,908,843	1,957,556	1,989,969	1,908,909
Average Length of Stay	5.2	5.2	5.1	5.3	5.2
Inpatient Surgeries	102,964	104,912	101,681	102,681	116,019
Births	36,809	36,913	38,556	39,013	39,602
Utilization - Outpatient					
Emergency Outpatient Visits	1,391,537	1,376,649	1,355,032	1,301,330	1,294,119
Other Outpatient Visits	3,419,087	3,645,562	3,692,949	3,671,422	3,942,397
Total Outpatient Visits	4,810,624	5,022,211	5,047,981	4,972,752	5,236,516
Outpatient Surgeries	160,223	155,784	143,094	136,565	147,222
Personnel					
Full Time RNs	11,429	11,059	10,620	9,700	9,678
Full Time LPNs	1,897	1,890	2,080	2,455	2,313
Part Time RNs	3,700	4,068	4,030	3,596	3,478
Part Time LPNs	606	663	809	824	824
Total Full Time	39,108	38,553	38,571	38,480	37,480
Total Part Time	10,746	11,921	11,981	11,549	10,872
Revenue - Inpatient					
Gross Inpatient Revenue	$9,587,181,461	$9,211,448,957	$8,800,185,973	$8,250,771,568	$7,750,748,662
Revenue - Outpatient					
Gross Outpatient Revenue	$7,800,635,792	$7,084,460,315	$6,421,124,915	$5,568,220,057	$5,054,791,861
Revenue and Expenses - Totals					
(Includes Inpatient and Outpatient)					
Total Gross Revenue	$17,387,817,253	$16,295,909,272	$15,221,310,888	$13,818,991,625	$12,805,540,523
Deductions from Revenue	12,106,848,283	11,007,346,255	10,164,398,525	9,011,385,599	8,220,632,392
Net Patient Revenue	5,280,968,970	5,288,563,017	5,056,912,363	4,807,606,026	4,584,908,131
Other Operating Revenue	220,871,438	221,189,649	193,955,665	169,341,834	162,135,731
Other Nonoperating Revenue	52,395,249	69,605,801	73,678,302	31,674,701	56,666,788
Total Net Revenue	5,554,235,657	5,579,358,467	5,324,546,330	5,008,622,561	4,803,710,650
Total Expenses	5,236,539,234	5,246,234,974	5,161,176,256	4,921,858,438	4,585,732,810
HOSPITAL UNIT (Excludes Separate Nursing Home Units)					
Utilization - Inpatient					
Beds	9,041	9,228	9,132	9,250	9,067
Admissions	362,005	368,895	378,746	374,159	364,431
Inpatient Days	1,757,602	1,830,615	1,824,645	1,854,685	1,767,173
Average Length of Stay	4.9	5.0	4.8	5.0	4.8
Personnel					
Total Full Time	38,835	38,362	38,050	38,028	37,156
Total Part Time	10,639	11,881	11,767	11,398	10,768
Revenue and Expenses - Totals					
(Includes Inpatient and Outpatient)					
Total Net Revenue	$5,526,988,517	$5,558,657,844	$5,301,946,109	$4,986,288,187	$4,782,794,055
Total Expenses	5,219,018,613	5,234,362,445	5,141,870,990	4,902,909,300	4,567,507,045
COMMUNITY HEALTH INDICATORS PER 1000 POPULATION					
Total Population (in thousands)	2,938	2,910	2,889	2,868	2,842
Inpatient					
Beds	3.2	3.2	3.3	3.4	3.3
Admissions	123.7	127.3	131.7	131.2	128.9
Inpatient Days	640.9	655.9	677.5	693.9	671.6
Inpatient Surgeries	35.0	36.0	35.2	35.8	40.8
Births	12.5	12.7	13.3	13.6	13.9
Outpatient					
Emergency Outpatient Visits	473.6	473.0	469.0	453.8	455.3
Other Outpatient Visits	1,163.8	1,252.7	1,278.1	1,280.2	1,387.1
Total Outpatient Visits	1,637.4	1,725.7	1,747.0	1,734.0	1,842.4
Outpatient Surgeries	54.5	53.5	49.5	47.6	51.8
Expense per Capita (per person)	$1,782.4	$1,802.7	$1,786.2	$1,716.3	$1,613.4

States

TABLE 6

CALIFORNIA

U.S. Registered Community Hospitals
(Nonfederal, short-term general and other special hospitals)

Overview 2007–2011

	2011	2010	2009	2008	2007
Total Community Hospitals in California	**345**	**343**	**343**	**352**	**355**
Bed Size Category					
6-24	13	13	13	14	14
25-49	39	38	37	36	34
50-99	43	42	42	50	53
100-199	101	104	106	107	111
200-299	65	61	64	66	66
300-399	47	47	50	44	45
400-499	23	24	20	22	18
500 + ...	14	14	11	13	14
Location					
Hospitals Urban...........................	314	312	313	321	317
Hospitals Rural	31	31	30	31	38
Control					
State and Local Government................	69	69	69	71	71
Not for Profit	202	202	202	202	203
Investor owned	74	72	72	79	81
Physician Models					
Independent Practice Association	64	66	62	72	89
Group Practice without Walls...............	11	11	12	12	12
Open Physician-Hospital Organization	6	5	5	6	10
Closed Physician-Hospital Organization	5	6	7	7	4
Management Service Organization	30	28	26	27	33
Integrated Salary Model....................	24	24	25	30	32
Equity Model	3	3	0	1	4
Foundation...............................	51	50	40	39	39
Insurance Products					
Health Maintenance Organization	40	35	42	46	48
Preferred Provider Organization.............	24	22	22	19	27
Indemnity Fee for Service	16	11	9	10	15
Managed Care Contracts					
Health Maintenance Organization	147	156	157	154	179
Preferred Provider Organization.............	146	157	159	158	183
Affiliations					
Hospitals in a System.....................	230	226	225	231	235
Hospitals in a Network.....................	70	59	59	59	55
Hospitals in a Group Purchasing Organization..	185	182	210	206	206

States

TABLE 6

CALIFORNIA

U.S. Registered Community Hospitals
(Nonfederal, short-term general and other special hospitals)

Utilization, Personnel, Revenue and Expenses, Community Health Indicators 2007–2011

	2011	2010	2009	2008	2007
TOTAL FACILITY (Includes Hospital and Nursing Home Units)					
Utilization - Inpatient					
Beds	70,008	70,440	68,745	69,587	69,325
Admissions	3,393,166	3,423,820	3,433,319	3,460,688	3,276,372
Inpatient Days	17,090,593	17,443,427	17,582,055	18,044,888	17,154,514
Average Length of Stay	5.0	5.1	5.1	5.2	5.2
Inpatient Surgeries	858,118	907,650	899,439	904,722	951,529
Births	488,863	493,712	500,085	526,946	514,164
Utilization - Outpatient					
Emergency Outpatient Visits	11,073,272	10,945,256	10,554,310	10,068,613	10,006,018
Other Outpatient Visits	41,601,911	40,784,007	37,700,623	38,808,536	35,930,559
Total Outpatient Visits	52,675,183	51,729,263	48,254,933	48,877,149	45,936,577
Outpatient Surgeries	1,273,633	1,261,889	1,248,053	1,309,864	1,250,377
Personnel					
Full Time RNs	103,753	103,010	98,905	98,152	86,556
Full Time LPNs	6,227	6,817	7,145	7,531	7,494
Part Time RNs	50,209	48,553	48,356	49,205	54,152
Part Time LPNs	2,420	2,625	2,900	3,281	3,948
Total Full Time	365,577	358,559	353,440	356,834	338,268
Total Part Time	134,162	129,897	130,048	134,602	150,145
Revenue - Inpatient					
Gross Inpatient Revenue	$183,080,834,445	$176,241,777,468	$160,482,118,425	$150,337,219,745	$141,494,365,112
Revenue - Outpatient					
Gross Outpatient Revenue	$105,412,786,768	$93,211,672,697	$81,537,158,136	$74,357,000,289	$63,410,673,627
Revenue and Expenses - Totals					
(Includes Inpatient and Outpatient)					
Total Gross Revenue	$288,493,621,213	$269,453,450,165	$242,019,276,561	$224,694,220,034	$204,905,038,739
Deductions from Revenue	211,224,646,235	198,665,132,469	176,891,970,909	162,955,378,616	147,778,238,783
Net Patient Revenue	77,268,974,978	70,788,317,696	65,127,305,652	61,738,841,418	57,126,799,956
Other Operating Revenue	4,404,016,212	4,549,376,153	4,239,820,033	3,808,102,197	3,501,284,745
Other Nonoperating Revenue	1,779,948,031	1,405,680,400	900,886,474	139,168,261	2,141,531,027
Total Net Revenue	83,452,939,221	76,743,374,249	70,268,012,159	65,686,111,876	62,769,615,728
Total Expenses	77,265,358,490	72,279,546,582	67,532,620,386	64,441,142,995	58,050,140,085
HOSPITAL UNIT (Excludes Separate Nursing Home Units)					
Utilization - Inpatient					
Beds	67,306	67,288	65,699	65,773	65,169
Admissions	3,374,467	3,404,159	3,411,915	3,435,099	3,246,140
Inpatient Days	16,266,645	16,480,612	16,688,765	16,911,379	15,982,046
Average Length of Stay	4.8	4.8	4.9	4.9	4.9
Personnel					
Total Full Time	363,402	355,707	350,441	353,564	334,625
Total Part Time	133,098	128,661	128,548	132,907	147,999
Revenue and Expenses - Totals					
(Includes Inpatient and Outpatient)					
Total Net Revenue	$83,072,725,098	$76,308,938,222	$69,852,937,155	$65,179,794,371	$62,185,142,736
Total Expenses	77,001,174,879	71,979,685,381	67,204,581,934	64,094,102,118	57,679,563,342
COMMUNITY HEALTH INDICATORS PER 1000 POPULATION					
Total Population (in thousands)	37,692	37,267	36,962	36,580	36,226
Inpatient					
Beds	1.9	1.9	1.9	1.9	1.9
Admissions	90.0	91.9	92.9	94.6	90.4
Inpatient Days	453.4	468.1	475.7	493.3	473.5
Inpatient Surgeries	22.8	24.4	24.3	24.7	26.3
Births	13.0	13.2	13.5	14.4	14.2
Outpatient					
Emergency Outpatient Visits	293.8	293.7	285.5	275.2	276.2
Other Outpatient Visits	1,103.7	1,094.4	1,020.0	1,060.9	991.8
Total Outpatient Visits	1,397.5	1,388.1	1,305.5	1,336.2	1,268.1
Outpatient Surgeries	33.8	33.9	33.8	35.8	34.5
Expense per Capita (per person)	$2,049.9	$1,939.5	$1,827.1	$1,761.6	$1,602.4

States

TABLE **6**

COLORADO

U.S. Registered Community Hospitals
(Nonfederal, short-term general and other special hospitals)

Overview 2007–2011

	2011	2010	2009	2008	2007
Total Community Hospitals in Colorado.......	82	80	81	78	75
Bed Size Category					
6-24	11	11	13	10	10
25-49	23	21	19	21	18
50-99	17	16	18	16	17
100-199	12	14	11	13	12
200-299	7	6	10	9	9
300-399	8	8	5	4	4
400-499	3	2	3	3	4
500 + ...	1	2	2	2	1
Location					
Hospitals Urban...........................	44	43	43	41	38
Hospitals Rural	38	37	38	37	37
Control					
State and Local Government................	27	27	28	28	28
Not for Profit	38	37	37	37	37
Investor owned	17	16	16	13	10
Physician Models					
Independent Practice Association	11	10	9	9	7
Group Practice without Walls...............	3	2	1	1	2
Open Physician-Hospital Organization	13	13	12	12	8
Closed Physician-Hospital Organization	4	3	3	2	3
Management Service Organization	4	4	3	3	3
Integrated Salary Model....................	37	34	33	32	29
Equity Model.............................	2	2	1	2	3
Foundation...............................	2	4	1	2	2
Insurance Products					
Health Maintenance Organization	9	10	11	9	8
Preferred Provider Organization.............	9	10	10	9	10
Indemnity Fee for Service	1	2	3	3	4
Managed Care Contracts					
Health Maintenance Organization	40	46	47	48	40
Preferred Provider Organization.............	45	52	53	54	46
Affiliations					
Hospitals in a System.....................	46	46	46	44	41
Hospitals in a Network	27	27	24	25	23
Hospitals in a Group Purchasing Organization..	63	60	58	57	53

TABLE 6

COLORADO

U.S. Registered Community Hospitals
(Nonfederal, short-term general and other special hospitals)

Utilization, Personnel, Revenue and Expenses, Community Health Indicators 2007–2011

	2011	2010	2009	2008	2007
TOTAL FACILITY (Includes Hospital and Nursing Home Units)					
Utilization - Inpatient					
Beds	10,167	10,208	10,364	10,053	9,708
Admissions	432,887	449,369	445,291	442,161	425,959
Inpatient Days	2,170,349	2,234,925	2,237,893	2,210,340	2,169,902
Average Length of Stay	5.0	5.0	5.0	5.0	5.1
Inpatient Surgeries	137,218	141,751	143,822	141,724	139,125
Births	62,264	63,653	65,130	68,659	66,512
Utilization - Outpatient					
Emergency Outpatient Visits	1,730,788	1,677,353	1,725,417	1,621,056	1,548,319
Other Outpatient Visits	6,934,427	6,572,791	7,134,664	6,786,916	6,206,101
Total Outpatient Visits	8,665,215	8,250,144	8,860,081	8,407,972	7,754,420
Outpatient Surgeries	219,321	211,730	206,315	204,045	185,515
Personnel					
Full Time RNs	15,239	15,787	15,411	15,300	14,201
Full Time LPNs	472	551	684	775	823
Part Time RNs	6,449	5,235	5,377	5,123	3,543
Part Time LPNs	190	179	215	240	181
Total Full Time	63,370	55,072	54,311	53,002	53,751
Total Part Time	18,322	15,268	15,782	16,290	10,814
Revenue - Inpatient					
Gross Inpatient Revenue	$19,860,096,681	$19,013,208,766	$17,525,068,092	$16,296,307,033	$14,291,552,936
Revenue - Outpatient					
Gross Outpatient Revenue	$16,603,620,063	$14,766,810,304	$13,322,614,754	$11,343,750,441	$9,499,093,812
Revenue and Expenses - Totals					
(Includes Inpatient and Outpatient)					
Total Gross Revenue	$36,463,716,744	$33,780,019,070	$30,847,682,846	$27,640,117,474	$23,790,646,748
Deductions from Revenue	25,752,881,907	23,450,147,224	21,100,773,225	18,781,874,571	15,715,614,730
Net Patient Revenue	10,710,834,837	10,329,871,846	9,746,909,621	8,858,242,903	8,075,032,018
Other Operating Revenue	513,568,821	501,184,086	489,463,546	518,570,378	603,828,098
Other Nonoperating Revenue	143,185,607	196,854,806	146,646,198	-27,071,112	258,400,086
Total Net Revenue	11,367,589,265	11,027,910,738	10,383,019,365	9,349,742,169	8,937,260,202
Total Expenses	10,054,322,089	9,590,946,802	9,244,357,277	8,889,584,362	8,011,595,534
HOSPITAL UNIT (Excludes Separate Nursing Home Units)					
Utilization - Inpatient					
Beds	9,599	9,537	9,777	9,518	9,016
Admissions	430,676	447,782	443,718	441,061	424,899
Inpatient Days	1,995,737	2,026,168	2,056,115	2,076,120	1,986,909
Average Length of Stay	4.6	4.5	4.6	4.7	4.7
Personnel					
Total Full Time	52,935	54,554	53,795	52,602	53,421
Total Part Time	18,169	14,960	15,572	16,131	10,670
Revenue and Expenses - Totals					
(Includes Inpatient and Outpatient)					
Total Net Revenue	$11,330,471,189	$10,984,832,365	$10,343,931,411	$9,321,879,151	$8,905,534,902
Total Expenses	10,014,190,366	9,546,862,102	9,207,018,816	8,862,237,046	7,977,887,275
COMMUNITY HEALTH INDICATORS PER 1000 POPULATION					
Total Population (in thousands)	5,117	5,095	5,025	4,935	4,842
Inpatient					
Beds	2.0	2.0	2.1	2.0	2.0
Admissions	84.6	88.2	88.6	89.6	88.0
Inpatient Days	424.2	438.6	445.4	447.9	448.1
Inpatient Surgeries	26.8	27.8	28.6	28.7	28.7
Births	12.2	12.5	13.0	13.9	13.7
Outpatient					
Emergency Outpatient Visits	338.3	329.2	343.4	328.5	319.8
Other Outpatient Visits	1,355.2	1,290.0	1,419.9	1,375.2	1,281.7
Total Outpatient Visits	1,693.5	1,619.2	1,763.3	1,703.7	1,601.4
Outpatient Surgeries	42.9	41.6	41.1	41.3	38.3
Expense per Capita (per person)	$1,965.0	$1,882.3	$1,839.8	$1,801.3	$1,654.5

States

TABLE 6

CONNECTICUT

U.S. Registered Community Hospitals
(Nonfederal, short-term general and other special hospitals)

Overview 2007–2011

	2011	2010	2009	2008	2007
Total Community Hospitals in Connecticut	35	34	35	35	34
Bed Size Category					
6-24	0	0	0	0	0
25-49	2	1	1	1	1
50-99	8	8	8	8	8
100-199	12	10	12	12	11
200-299	4	5	3	4	5
300-399	5	5	6	5	5
400-499	1	2	2	2	1
500 + ...	3	3	3	3	3
Location					
Hospitals Urban..........................	30	29	30	30	28
Hospitals Rural	5	5	5	5	6
Control					
State and Local Government...............	1	1	1	1	1
Not for Profit............................	33	32	33	32	32
Investor owned	1	1	1	2	1
Physician Models					
Independent Practice Association	6	7	8	8	8
Group Practice without Walls...............	0	2	0	1	1
Open Physician-Hospital Organization	4	5	6	3	5
Closed Physician-Hospital Organization	3	2	2	2	2
Management Service Organization	4	5	4	3	4
Integrated Salary Model....................	17	17	15	18	13
Equity Model.............................	1	1	1	1	0
Foundation...............................	9	5	1	0	1
Insurance Products					
Health Maintenance Organization	0	2	2	3	2
Preferred Provider Organization.............	0	0	0	0	3
Indemnity Fee for Service	0	0	0	1	0
Managed Care Contracts					
Health Maintenance Organization	25	23	22	22	22
Preferred Provider Organization.............	25	22	23	22	23
Affiliations					
Hospitals in a System.....................	15	14	12	9	9
Hospitals in a Network....................	12	11	12	13	14
Hospitals in a Group Purchasing Organization..	27	28	28	28	29

TABLE 6

CONNECTICUT

U.S. Registered Community Hospitals
(Nonfederal, short-term general and other special hospitals)

Utilization, Personnel, Revenue and Expenses, Community Health Indicators 2007–2011

	2011	2010	2009	2008	2007
TOTAL FACILITY (Includes Hospital and Nursing Home Units)					
Utilization - Inpatient					
Beds	7,745	8,091	7,935	7,906	7,483
Admissions	402,838	406,718	407,710	400,632	396,895
Inpatient Days	2,110,564	2,290,323	2,345,878	2,296,558	2,128,239
Average Length of Stay	5.2	5.6	5.8	5.7	5.4
Inpatient Surgeries	103,828	108,070	109,334	107,611	111,119
Births	37,565	37,483	38,932	40,963	41,620
Utilization - Outpatient					
Emergency Outpatient Visits	1,643,282	1,661,088	1,607,670	1,524,545	1,461,985
Other Outpatient Visits	6,884,506	6,605,714	6,567,848	6,550,089	6,088,953
Total Outpatient Visits	8,527,788	8,266,802	8,175,518	8,074,634	7,550,938
Outpatient Surgeries	204,949	201,480	198,390	192,544	198,022
Personnel					
Full Time RNs	11,075	10,483	10,831	10,057	9,736
Full Time LPNs	258	264	311	348	363
Part Time RNs	7,107	6,609	6,512	6,883	7,422
Part Time LPNs	229	194	229	361	353
Total Full Time	44,784	43,689	44,091	42,558	41,918
Total Part Time	22,538	21,507	20,842	23,152	22,594
Revenue - Inpatient					
Gross Inpatient Revenue	$14,148,582,803	$13,295,787,334	$12,736,578,199	$11,484,375,092	$10,507,210,277
Revenue - Outpatient					
Gross Outpatient Revenue	$11,773,260,720	$10,537,030,956	$9,767,664,004	$8,402,315,796	$7,345,514,961
Revenue and Expenses - Totals					
(Includes Inpatient and Outpatient)					
Total Gross Revenue	$25,921,843,523	$23,832,818,290	$22,504,242,203	$19,886,690,888	$17,852,725,238
Deductions from Revenue	16,507,379,096	15,121,712,588	14,125,599,354	12,234,710,097	10,801,568,841
Net Patient Revenue	9,414,464,427	8,711,105,702	8,378,642,849	7,651,980,791	7,051,156,397
Other Operating Revenue	462,365,876	455,355,109	420,171,188	368,547,369	303,008,601
Other Nonoperating Revenue	57,595,778	115,215,987	-1,279,820	-125,823,097	157,150,928
Total Net Revenue	9,934,426,081	9,281,676,798	8,797,534,217	7,894,704,263	7,511,315,926
Total Expenses	9,561,576,935	8,928,296,028	8,565,211,235	7,906,958,696	7,221,249,850
HOSPITAL UNIT (Excludes Separate Nursing Home Units)					
Utilization - Inpatient					
Beds	7,468	7,676	7,648	7,237	7,196
Admissions	402,394	405,842	407,207	399,384	396,101
Inpatient Days	2,109,561	2,146,637	2,245,293	2,060,023	2,028,334
Average Length of Stay	5.2	5.3	5.5	5.2	5.1
Personnel					
Total Full Time	44,768	43,306	44,052	41,790	41,538
Total Part Time	22,521	21,256	20,826	22,313	22,178
Revenue and Expenses - Totals					
(Includes Inpatient and Outpatient)					
Total Net Revenue	$9,928,376,462	$9,235,623,435	$8,759,788,307	$7,822,208,146	$7,478,024,431
Total Expenses	9,556,797,059	8,888,242,578	8,530,306,215	7,846,566,914	7,189,144,542
COMMUNITY HEALTH INDICATORS PER 1000 POPULATION					
Total Population (in thousands)	3,581	3,527	3,518	3,503	3,489
Inpatient					
Beds	2.2	2.3	2.3	2.3	2.1
Admissions	112.5	115.3	115.9	114.4	113.8
Inpatient Days	589.4	649.4	666.8	655.6	610.0
Inpatient Surgeries	29.0	30.6	31.1	30.7	31.9
Births	10.5	10.6	11.1	11.7	11.9
Outpatient					
Emergency Outpatient Visits	458.9	471.0	456.9	435.2	419.1
Other Outpatient Visits	1,922.7	1,872.9	1,866.8	1,869.9	1,745.4
Total Outpatient Visits	2,381.6	2,343.9	2,323.7	2,305.1	2,164.4
Outpatient Surgeries	57.2	57.1	56.4	55.0	56.8
Expense per Capita (per person)	$2,670.3	$2,531.5	$2,434.5	$2,257.2	$2,069.9

States

TABLE 6

DELAWARE

U.S. Registered Community Hospitals
(Nonfederal, short-term general and other special hospitals)

Overview 2007–2011

	2011	2010	2009	2008	2007
Total Community Hospitals in Delaware.......	7	7	7	7	6
Bed Size Category					
6-24	0	0	0	0	0
25-49	1	1	1	1	0
50-99	0	0	0	0	0
100-199	2	2	2	3	1
200-299	2	2	2	1	3
300-399	1	1	1	1	1
400-499	0	0	0	0	0
500 + ...	1	1	1	1	1
Location					
Hospitals Urban...........................	5	5	5	5	4
Hospitals Rural	2	2	2	2	2
Control					
State and Local Government...............	0	0	0	0	0
Not for Profit	6	6	6	6	6
Investor owned	1	1	1	1	0
Physician Models					
Independent Practice Association	0	0	0	0	0
Group Practice without Walls................	0	0	0	0	0
Open Physician-Hospital Organization	0	0	0	0	1
Closed Physician-Hospital Organization	0	0	0	0	0
Management Service Organization	0	0	0	0	1
Integrated Salary Model....................	2	3	3	2	3
Equity Model	0	0	0	0	0
Foundation...............................	1	1	1	1	1
Insurance Products					
Health Maintenance Organization	0	1	1	0	0
Preferred Provider Organization..............	0	1	1	0	0
Indemnity Fee for Service	0	1	1	0	0
Managed Care Contracts					
Health Maintenance Organization	3	4	5	5	5
Preferred Provider Organization..............	3	4	5	5	5
Affiliations					
Hospitals in a System.....................	3	3	3	3	2
Hospitals in a Network	0	0	0	0	0
Hospitals in a Group Purchasing Organization..	5	6	6	6	5

TABLE 6

DELAWARE

U.S. Registered Community Hospitals
(Nonfederal, short-term general and other special hospitals)

Utilization, Personnel, Revenue and Expenses, Community Health Indicators 2007–2011

	2011	2010	2009	2008	2007
TOTAL FACILITY (Includes Hospital and Nursing Home Units)					
Utilization - Inpatient					
Beds	2,143	2,155	2,125	2,071	2,288
Admissions	100,288	101,735	102,153	103,726	107,037
Inpatient Days	578,466	580,261	597,993	613,049	671,628
Average Length of Stay	5.8	5.7	5.9	5.9	6.3
Inpatient Surgeries	31,852	28,828	29,930	30,845	32,039
Births	11,496	11,486	12,158	12,536	12,312
Utilization - Outpatient					
Emergency Outpatient Visits	417,689	406,652	392,660	363,979	343,713
Other Outpatient Visits	1,432,957	1,380,658	1,351,824	1,317,097	1,495,036
Total Outpatient Visits	1,850,646	1,787,310	1,744,484	1,681,076	1,838,749
Outpatient Surgeries	62,618	67,852	70,362	60,343	63,526
Personnel					
Full Time RNs	3,990	3,689	3,485	3,334	3,010
Full Time LPNs	171	126	135	164	179
Part Time RNs	1,927	2,195	2,486	2,326	2,021
Part Time LPNs	136	125	133	156	148
Total Full Time	14,456	13,885	13,707	13,954	12,707
Total Part Time	5,598	5,846	6,406	6,340	5,485
Revenue - Inpatient					
Gross Inpatient Revenue	$2,830,331,928	$2,671,560,601	$2,528,530,549	$2,385,974,140	$2,244,196,638
Revenue - Outpatient					
Gross Outpatient Revenue	$2,262,497,249	$2,026,156,087	$1,797,902,276	$1,569,559,056	$1,352,820,078
Revenue and Expenses - Totals					
(Includes Inpatient and Outpatient)					
Total Gross Revenue	$5,092,829,177	$4,697,716,688	$4,326,432,825	$3,955,533,196	$3,597,016,716
Deductions from Revenue	2,640,575,715	2,394,621,807	2,111,070,905	1,865,226,783	1,679,045,929
Net Patient Revenue	2,452,253,462	2,303,094,881	2,215,361,920	2,090,306,413	1,917,970,787
Other Operating Revenue	178,700,023	165,608,644	159,598,810	121,047,453	167,718,247
Other Nonoperating Revenue	171,781,254	77,555,669	-156,561,766	81,948,435	62,950,703
Total Net Revenue	2,802,734,739	2,546,259,194	2,218,398,964	2,293,302,301	2,148,639,737
Total Expenses	2,408,075,977	2,344,087,243	2,264,467,218	2,119,860,075	1,949,799,885
HOSPITAL UNIT (Excludes Separate Nursing Home Units)					
Utilization - Inpatient					
Beds	2,033	1,941	1,911	1,967	1,892
Admissions	99,921	101,130	101,502	103,438	105,462
Inpatient Days	540,146	509,077	525,133	577,278	538,981
Average Length of Stay	5.4	5.0	5.2	5.6	5.1
Personnel					
Total Full Time	14,301	13,670	13,553	13,883	12,391
Total Part Time	5,582	5,705	6,246	6,316	5,297
Revenue and Expenses - Totals					
(Includes Inpatient and Outpatient)					
Total Net Revenue	$2,791,771,225	$2,525,583,028	$2,197,822,141	$2,283,604,301	$2,109,958,350
Total Expenses	2,396,081,133	2,323,082,005	2,243,045,075	2,110,993,075	1,902,038,450
COMMUNITY HEALTH INDICATORS PER 1000 POPULATION					
Total Population (in thousands)	907	891	885	876	865
Inpatient					
Beds	2.4	2.4	2.4	2.4	2.6
Admissions	110.6	114.1	115.4	118.4	123.8
Inpatient Days	637.7	650.9	675.6	699.7	776.5
Inpatient Surgeries	35.1	32.3	33.8	35.2	37.0
Births	12.7	12.9	13.7	14.3	14.2
Outpatient					
Emergency Outpatient Visits	460.4	456.2	443.6	415.4	397.4
Other Outpatient Visits	1,579.7	1,548.8	1,527.3	1,503.2	1,728.6
Total Outpatient Visits	2,040.1	2,004.9	1,970.9	1,918.6	2,126.0
Outpatient Surgeries	69.0	76.1	79.5	68.9	73.4
Expense per Capita (per person)	$2,654.6	$2,629.5	$2,558.4	$2,419.3	$2,254.4

DISTRICT OF COLUMBIA

U.S. Registered Community Hospitals
(Nonfederal, short-term general and other special hospitals)

Overview 2007–2011

	2011	2010	2009	2008	2007
Total Community Hospitals in District of Columbia	11	11	10	10	10
Bed Size Category					
6-24	0	0	0	0	0
25-49	0	0	0	0	0
50-99	1	1	1	1	1
100-199	2	2	1	1	1
200-299	3	4	3	3	2
300-399	2	1	2	3	4
400-499	1	1	1	0	0
500 + ...	2	2	2	2	2
Location					
Hospitals Urban...........................	11	11	10	10	10
Hospitals Rural	0	0	0	0	0
Control					
State and Local Government................	1	1	0	0	0
Not for Profit	7	7	7	7	7
Investor owned	3	3	3	3	3
Physician Models					
Independent Practice Association	0	1	0	1	0
Group Practice without Walls................	1	0	1	1	1
Open Physician-Hospital Organization	0	0	0	0	1
Closed Physician-Hospital Organization	1	1	1	1	1
Management Service Organization	1	1	1	1	1
Integrated Salary Model....................	4	5	5	4	5
Equity Model..............................	0	0	0	0	0
Foundation................................	1	1	1	1	1
Insurance Products					
Health Maintenance Organization	4	2	3	3	4
Preferred Provider Organization..............	1	0	0	0	1
Indemnity Fee for Service	1	0	0	0	1
Managed Care Contracts					
Health Maintenance Organization	6	7	7	7	7
Preferred Provider Organization..............	6	6	7	7	5
Affiliations					
Hospitals in a System......................	8	9	7	7	7
Hospitals in a Network.....................	4	5	4	2	2
Hospitals in a Group Purchasing Organization..	7	8	8	8	7

TABLE 6

DISTRICT OF COLUMBIA

U.S. Registered Community Hospitals
(Nonfederal, short-term general and other special hospitals)

Utilization, Personnel, Revenue and Expenses, Community Health Indicators 2007–2011

	2011	2010	2009	2008	2007
TOTAL FACILITY (Includes Hospital and Nursing Home Units)					
Utilization - Inpatient					
Beds	3,635	3,458	3,452	3,358	3,418
Admissions	131,577	131,976	138,456	137,260	136,488
Inpatient Days	954,752	926,254	927,419	954,416	908,940
Average Length of Stay	7.3	7.0	6.7	7.0	6.7
Inpatient Surgeries	40,477	41,736	42,667	43,173	42,870
Births	13,792	13,814	14,507	14,901	14,871
Utilization - Outpatient					
Emergency Outpatient Visits	455,553	430,637	457,292	436,918	461,465
Other Outpatient Visits	1,994,547	1,888,245	1,954,514	1,919,145	1,905,247
Total Outpatient Visits	2,450,100	2,318,882	2,411,806	2,356,063	2,366,712
Outpatient Surgeries	62,767	58,907	62,497	65,742	59,336
Personnel					
Full Time RNs	5,435	5,458	5,222	4,447	4,357
Full Time LPNs	216	267	304	215	296
Part Time RNs	1,643	1,966	1,845	1,796	1,796
Part Time LPNs	32	46	35	38	46
Total Full Time	22,815	22,654	22,371	21,247	20,507
Total Part Time	4,525	5,259	4,666	4,463	4,946
Revenue - Inpatient					
Gross Inpatient Revenue	$6,334,158,623	$6,016,677,081	$5,895,449,855	$5,686,127,872	$5,672,805,649
Revenue - Outpatient					
Gross Outpatient Revenue	$3,932,470,181	$3,470,432,807	$3,108,162,999	$2,835,491,356	$2,666,461,627
Revenue and Expenses - Totals					
(Includes Inpatient and Outpatient)					
Total Gross Revenue	$10,266,628,804	$9,493,109,888	$9,003,612,854	$8,521,619,228	$8,339,267,276
Deductions from Revenue	6,617,584,769	5,971,324,649	5,592,219,614	5,300,645,413	5,229,606,649
Net Patient Revenue	3,649,044,035	3,521,785,239	3,411,393,240	3,220,973,815	3,109,660,627
Other Operating Revenue	277,637,308	205,891,415	214,814,678	192,446,948	187,903,112
Other Nonoperating Revenue	95,995,539	33,913,566	32,415,954	-139,712,361	67,564,569
Total Net Revenue	4,022,676,882	3,761,590,220	3,658,623,872	3,273,708,402	3,365,128,308
Total Expenses	3,766,313,652	3,582,285,072	3,585,829,997	3,392,800,661	3,224,779,035
HOSPITAL UNIT (Excludes Separate Nursing Home Units)					
Utilization - Inpatient					
Beds	3,470	3,161	3,157	3,061	3,123
Admissions	130,232	130,125	136,578	135,521	134,769
Inpatient Days	909,564	822,314	822,965	850,769	805,786
Average Length of Stay	7.0	6.3	6.0	6.3	6.0
Personnel					
Total Full Time	22,710	22,327	22,067	21,151	20,210
Total Part Time	4,500	5,181	4,595	4,437	4,882
Revenue and Expenses - Totals					
(Includes Inpatient and Outpatient)					
Total Net Revenue	$4,007,011,323	$3,726,836,744	$3,624,105,283	$3,244,092,304	$3,331,993,244
Total Expenses	3,750,371,864	3,552,676,361	3,556,839,618	3,363,055,134	3,196,280,439
COMMUNITY HEALTH INDICATORS PER 1000 POPULATION					
Total Population (in thousands)	618	611	600	590	586
Inpatient					
Beds	5.9	5.7	5.8	5.7	5.8
Admissions	212.9	216.1	230.9	232.6	232.8
Inpatient Days	1,544.9	1,517.0	1,546.6	1,617.5	1,550.0
Inpatient Surgeries	65.5	68.4	71.2	73.2	73.1
Births	22.3	22.6	24.2	25.3	25.4
Outpatient					
Emergency Outpatient Visits	737.1	705.3	762.6	740.4	786.9
Other Outpatient Visits	3,227.4	3,092.5	3,259.4	3,252.4	3,249.0
Total Outpatient Visits	3,964.6	3,797.8	4,022.0	3,992.8	4,035.9
Outpatient Surgeries	101.6	96.5	104.2	111.4	101.2
Expense per Capita (per person)	$6,094.4	$5,866.9	$5,979.8	$5,749.8	$5,499.2

States

TABLE 6

FLORIDA

U.S. Registered Community Hospitals
(Nonfederal, short-term general and other special hospitals)

Overview 2007–2011

	2011	2010	2009	2008	2007
Total Community Hospitals in Florida.........	213	210	210	211	200
Bed Size Category					
6-24	3	2	2	3	2
25-49	21	21	21	23	18
50-99	38	39	39	35	33
100-199	55	50	51	55	53
200-299	37	38	37	37	35
300-399	27	27	25	25	27
400-499	9	9	12	11	10
500 + ...	23	24	23	22	22
Location					
Hospitals Urban...........................	184	181	181	181	166
Hospitals Rural	29	29	29	30	34
Control					
State and Local Government................	26	27	25	25	26
Not for Profit	81	79	82	86	82
Investor owned	106	104	103	100	92
Physician Models					
Independent Practice Association	5	5	4	6	6
Group Practice without Walls................	9	7	9	3	3
Open Physician-Hospital Organization	24	19	19	12	9
Closed Physician-Hospital Organization	5	7	6	10	7
Management Service Organization	14	14	8	5	6
Integrated Salary Model....................	64	59	52	52	59
Equity Model.............................	1	1	0	0	1
Foundation...............................	3	4	4	2	5
Insurance Products					
Health Maintenance Organization	15	11	13	8	9
Preferred Provider Organization..............	18	16	17	10	8
Indemnity Fee for Service	7	5	6	5	5
Managed Care Contracts					
Health Maintenance Organization	111	98	88	81	98
Preferred Provider Organization..............	113	101	91	82	97
Affiliations					
Hospitals in a System......................	167	160	160	159	149
Hospitals in a Network	37	35	35	38	38
Hospitals in a Group Purchasing Organization..	101	106	116	118	123

States

TABLE 6

FLORIDA

U.S. Registered Community Hospitals
(Nonfederal, short-term general and other special hospitals)

Utilization, Personnel, Revenue and Expenses, Community Health Indicators 2007–2011

	2011	2010	2009	2008	2007
TOTAL FACILITY (Includes Hospital and Nursing Home Units)					
Utilization - Inpatient					
Beds	52,923	53,318	53,293	52,836	51,648
Admissions	2,508,311	2,452,089	2,452,546	2,396,691	2,387,525
Inpatient Days	12,365,513	12,191,209	12,261,161	12,192,327	12,351,368
Average Length of Stay	4.9	5.0	5.0	5.1	5.2
Inpatient Surgeries	614,726	650,557	655,203	659,237	660,217
Births	186,919	202,862	206,284	218,035	223,202
Utilization - Outpatient					
Emergency Outpatient Visits	7,580,718	7,559,853	7,477,209	7,161,108	7,085,930
Other Outpatient Visits	16,827,980	16,683,248	17,396,409	17,268,832	16,410,090
Total Outpatient Visits	24,408,698	24,243,101	24,873,618	24,429,940	23,496,020
Outpatient Surgeries	782,871	798,189	822,841	846,551	796,945
Personnel					
Full Time RNs	72,090	69,840	68,581	62,639	62,349
Full Time LPNs	3,595	4,111	4,470	4,563	5,159
Part Time RNs	16,461	16,844	17,495	20,188	18,904
Part Time LPNs	789	901	1,092	1,154	1,318
Total Full Time	234,893	232,349	229,515	220,165	220,065
Total Part Time	49,243	47,580	49,670	54,335	54,010
Revenue - Inpatient					
Gross Inpatient Revenue	$100,263,145,301	$98,439,589,940	$90,412,617,613	$80,168,815,722	$76,599,198,509
Revenue - Outpatient					
Gross Outpatient Revenue	$63,221,928,643	$58,858,434,042	$52,572,001,561	$44,224,777,407	$39,745,819,297
Revenue and Expenses - Totals					
(Includes Inpatient and Outpatient)					
Total Gross Revenue	$163,485,073,944	$157,298,023,982	$142,984,619,174	$124,393,593,129	$116,345,017,806
Deductions from Revenue	126,350,152,571	119,355,324,858	107,498,135,646	91,084,229,921	84,506,636,341
Net Patient Revenue	37,134,921,373	37,942,699,124	35,486,483,528	33,309,363,208	31,838,381,465
Other Operating Revenue	2,293,290,171	2,190,285,623	1,811,268,561	2,104,002,109	1,913,000,678
Other Nonoperating Revenue	613,632,452	562,284,781	483,113,737	64,179,556	592,244,508
Total Net Revenue	40,041,843,996	40,695,269,528	37,780,865,826	35,477,544,873	34,343,626,651
Total Expenses	36,908,772,722	36,318,160,204	34,922,141,446	33,117,894,364	31,504,674,840
HOSPITAL UNIT (Excludes Separate Nursing Home Units)					
Utilization - Inpatient					
Beds	52,055	52,415	52,361	51,863	50,444
Admissions	2,504,407	2,448,276	2,448,331	2,392,911	2,382,000
Inpatient Days	12,096,907	11,888,876	11,942,896	11,874,879	11,954,597
Average Length of Stay	4.8	4.9	4.9	5.0	5.0
Personnel					
Total Full Time	234,104	231,450	228,263	219,027	218,802
Total Part Time	49,111	47,423	49,227	54,203	53,792
Revenue and Expenses - Totals					
(Includes Inpatient and Outpatient)					
Total Net Revenue	$39,961,735,021	$40,594,960,399	$37,709,543,480	$35,402,114,525	$34,260,176,558
Total Expenses	36,803,286,544	36,197,864,998	34,839,959,163	33,027,271,463	31,421,178,984
COMMUNITY HEALTH INDICATORS PER 1000 POPULATION					
Total Population (in thousands)	19,058	18,678	18,538	18,424	18,278
Inpatient					
Beds	2.8	2.9	2.9	2.9	2.8
Admissions	131.6	131.3	132.3	130.1	130.6
Inpatient Days	648.9	652.7	661.4	661.8	675.8
Inpatient Surgeries	32.3	34.8	35.3	35.8	36.1
Births	9.8	10.9	11.1	11.8	12.2
Outpatient					
Emergency Outpatient Visits	397.8	404.7	403.3	388.7	387.7
Other Outpatient Visits	883.0	893.2	938.4	937.3	897.8
Total Outpatient Visits	1,280.8	1,297.9	1,341.8	1,326.0	1,285.5
Outpatient Surgeries	41.1	42.7	44.4	45.9	43.6
Expense per Capita (per person)	$1,936.7	$1,944.4	$1,883.8	$1,797.6	$1,723.6

States

TABLE **6**

GEORGIA

U.S. Registered Community Hospitals
(Nonfederal, short-term general and other special hospitals)

Overview 2007–2011

	2011	2010	2009	2008	2007
Total Community Hospitals in Georgia	153	154	152	153	147
Bed Size Category					
6-24	6	6	6	4	3
25-49	38	39	38	41	35
50-99	26	24	24	22	22
100-199	41	42	42	44	42
200-299	17	17	16	15	18
300-399	6	7	8	9	8
400-499	8	10	10	9	11
500 + ...	11	9	8	9	8
Location					
Hospitals Urban	88	89	87	87	64
Hospitals Rural	65	65	65	66	83
Control					
State and Local Government	49	52	53	56	57
Not for Profit	68	66	63	63	59
Investor owned	36	36	36	34	31
Physician Models					
Independent Practice Association	6	8	10	10	8
Group Practice without Walls	0	0	1	2	1
Open Physician-Hospital Organization	14	18	15	19	22
Closed Physician-Hospital Organization	16	17	16	15	17
Management Service Organization	9	8	7	8	8
Integrated Salary Model	39	41	37	35	34
Equity Model	4	5	5	6	4
Foundation	4	4	3	5	5
Insurance Products					
Health Maintenance Organization	8	9	12	10	6
Preferred Provider Organization	15	20	21	20	24
Indemnity Fee for Service	4	5	7	7	6
Managed Care Contracts					
Health Maintenance Organization	77	81	83	79	67
Preferred Provider Organization	83	94	95	89	83
Affiliations					
Hospitals in a System	80	81	79	81	74
Hospitals in a Network	41	40	39	42	42
Hospitals in a Group Purchasing Organization . .	95	104	105	100	92

TABLE 6

GEORGIA

U.S. Registered Community Hospitals
(Nonfederal, short-term general and other special hospitals)

Utilization, Personnel, Revenue and Expenses, Community Health Indicators 2007–2011

	2011	2010	2009	2008	2007
TOTAL FACILITY (Includes Hospital and Nursing Home Units)					
Utilization - Inpatient					
Beds	25,282	25,513	25,419	25,583	25,483
Admissions	956,503	961,391	956,870	959,375	963,583
Inpatient Days	6,094,960	6,138,828	6,059,475	6,172,510	6,278,894
Average Length of Stay	6.4	6.4	6.3	6.4	6.5
Inpatient Surgeries	265,074	265,789	267,788	269,766	277,885
Births	123,546	128,531	135,505	142,382	146,746
Utilization - Outpatient					
Emergency Outpatient Visits	4,035,426	4,095,951	4,081,812	3,843,244	3,747,532
Other Outpatient Visits	10,740,295	10,195,629	10,308,523	10,340,848	10,010,319
Total Outpatient Visits	14,775,721	14,291,580	14,390,335	14,184,092	13,757,851
Outpatient Surgeries	494,889	497,929	511,272	487,070	491,459
Personnel					
Full Time RNs	30,458	30,393	29,719	27,823	27,684
Full Time LPNs	3,119	3,276	3,506	3,651	3,738
Part Time RNs	10,000	10,469	11,965	11,963	13,312
Part Time LPNs	740	857	977	1,035	1,253
Total Full Time	110,421	112,040	111,451	108,871	107,711
Total Part Time	29,260	29,110	32,522	32,169	35,093
Revenue - Inpatient					
Gross Inpatient Revenue	$30,470,684,745	$28,768,523,466	$26,548,862,459	$25,139,478,750	$24,285,401,220
Revenue - Outpatient					
Gross Outpatient Revenue	$24,110,026,415	$22,700,713,568	$20,738,855,918	$18,392,697,423	$16,838,734,295
Revenue and Expenses - Totals					
(Includes Inpatient and Outpatient)					
Total Gross Revenue	$54,580,711,160	$51,469,237,034	$47,287,718,377	$43,532,176,173	$41,124,135,515
Deductions from Revenue	38,089,080,759	35,169,736,402	31,401,538,356	28,602,816,610	26,341,808,978
Net Patient Revenue	16,491,630,401	16,299,500,632	15,886,180,021	14,929,359,563	14,782,326,537
Other Operating Revenue	811,702,301	773,260,104	755,206,277	788,733,742	594,706,811
Other Nonoperating Revenue	228,081,442	324,122,628	128,720,872	-102,237,534	373,626,935
Total Net Revenue	17,531,414,144	17,396,883,364	16,770,107,170	15,615,855,771	15,750,660,283
Total Expenses	16,450,926,776	16,070,507,038	15,616,820,380	15,098,639,740	14,709,027,733
HOSPITAL UNIT (Excludes Separate Nursing Home Units)					
Utilization - Inpatient					
Beds	21,581	21,605	21,868	22,332	22,171
Admissions	949,217	953,677	949,070	953,328	957,240
Inpatient Days	4,924,671	4,826,637	4,890,754	5,113,980	5,168,328
Average Length of Stay	5.2	5.1	5.2	5.4	5.4
Personnel					
Total Full Time	107,993	109,514	108,900	106,600	105,488
Total Part Time	28,663	28,416	31,885	31,471	34,314
Revenue and Expenses - Totals					
(Includes Inpatient and Outpatient)					
Total Net Revenue	$17,334,774,424	$17,166,588,760	$16,591,803,789	$15,449,511,224	$15,588,075,384
Total Expenses	16,266,797,779	15,896,591,116	15,452,332,194	14,947,753,769	14,621,668,884
COMMUNITY HEALTH INDICATORS PER 1000 POPULATION					
Total Population (in thousands)	9,815	9,908	9,829	9,698	9,534
Inpatient					
Beds	2.6	2.6	2.6	2.6	2.7
Admissions	97.5	97.0	97.3	98.9	101.1
Inpatient Days	621.0	619.6	616.5	636.5	658.6
Inpatient Surgeries	27.0	26.8	27.2	27.8	29.1
Births	12.6	13.0	13.8	14.7	15.4
Outpatient					
Emergency Outpatient Visits	411.1	413.4	415.3	396.3	393.1
Other Outpatient Visits	1,094.3	1,029.0	1,048.8	1,066.3	1,050.0
Total Outpatient Visits	1,505.4	1,442.4	1,464.0	1,462.6	1,443.1
Outpatient Surgeries	50.4	50.3	52.0	50.2	51.5
Expense per Capita (per person)	$1,676.1	$1,622.8	$1,588.8	$1,556.9	$1,549.2

States

TABLE 6

HAWAII

U.S. Registered Community Hospitals
(Nonfederal, short-term general and other special hospitals)

Overview 2007–2011

	2011	2010	2009	2008	2007
Total Community Hospitals in Hawaii	23	26	25	25	23
Bed Size Category					
6-24	5	6	5	4	3
25-49	4	3	4	4	4
50-99	5	4	5	5	3
100-199	4	7	5	6	7
200-299	4	5	5	5	5
300-399	0	0	0	0	0
400-499	1	1	1	1	1
500 + ...	0	0	0	0	0
Location					
Hospitals Urban.	11	14	13	14	13
Hospitals Rural	12	12	12	11	10
Control					
State and Local Government	7	8	7	8	7
Not for Profit	16	18	18	17	16
Investor owned	0	0	0	0	0
Physician Models					
Independent Practice Association	2	2	1	1	0
Group Practice without Walls.	0	0	0	0	0
Open Physician-Hospital Organization	2	2	2	3	2
Closed Physician-Hospital Organization	2	1	1	1	1
Management Service Organization	0	0	0	0	0
Integrated Salary Model	7	7	5	4	4
Equity Model	0	0	0	0	0
Foundation.	0	0	2	1	1
Insurance Products					
Health Maintenance Organization	1	1	2	0	1
Preferred Provider Organization.	3	3	3	1	1
Indemnity Fee for Service	0	1	1	0	0
Managed Care Contracts					
Health Maintenance Organization	10	7	9	9	11
Preferred Provider Organization.	10	8	9	9	10
Affiliations					
Hospitals in a System.	18	21	20	21	18
Hospitals in a Network	2	2	3	1	1
Hospitals in a Group Purchasing Organization. .	13	15	14	13	12

TABLE 6

HAWAII

U.S. Registered Community Hospitals
(Nonfederal, short-term general and other special hospitals)

Utilization, Personnel, Revenue and Expenses, Community Health Indicators 2007–2011

	2011	2010	2009	2008	2007
TOTAL FACILITY (Includes Hospital and Nursing Home Units)					
Utilization - Inpatient					
Beds	2,562	3,148	2,966	3,087	2,920
Admissions	105,039	110,577	111,706	111,310	110,788
Inpatient Days	720,633	827,977	772,508	846,756	796,898
Average Length of Stay.	6.9	7.5	6.9	7.6	7.2
Inpatient Surgeries.	27,447	30,626	32,340	30,723	32,305
Births.	10,756	9,271	11,031	10,522	9,921
Utilization - Outpatient					
Emergency Outpatient Visits	366,276	365,903	383,778	361,068	339,004
Other Outpatient Visits.	1,639,876	1,828,179	1,773,550	1,658,064	1,538,987
Total Outpatient Visits	2,006,152	2,194,082	2,157,328	2,019,132	1,877,991
Outpatient Surgeries	55,968	58,602	61,508	59,191	57,484
Personnel					
Full Time RNs	3,637	3,858	3,860	3,776	3,724
Full Time LPNs	231	292	252	298	302
Part Time RNs.	722	974	1,136	1,254	1,052
Part Time LPNs	42	53	82	78	57
Total Full Time.	13,674	14,755	14,505	14,550	14,045
Total Part Time	2,369	3,083	3,514	3,712	3,186
Revenue - Inpatient					
Gross Inpatient Revenue.	$3,138,945,148	$3,433,349,265	$3,279,585,271	$3,209,458,842	$2,947,813,604
Revenue - Outpatient					
Gross Outpatient Revenue	$2,692,147,508	$2,820,300,482	$2,476,907,535	$2,484,934,032	$2,190,455,686
Revenue and Expenses - Totals					
(Includes Inpatient and Outpatient)					
Total Gross Revenue.	$5,831,092,656	$6,253,649,747	$5,756,492,806	$5,694,392,874	$5,138,269,290
Deductions from Revenue.	3,693,272,779	3,827,427,740	3,433,368,063	3,484,200,407	3,151,824,643
Net Patient Revenue	2,137,819,877	2,426,222,007	2,323,124,743	2,210,192,467	1,986,444,647
Other Operating Revenue	170,282,864	171,665,631	174,637,723	150,555,239	137,045,681
Other Nonoperating Revenue	43,411,366	48,234,523	40,300,553	21,263,753	67,676,101
Total Net Revenue.	2,351,514,107	2,646,122,161	2,538,063,010	2,382,011,459	2,191,166,429
Total Expenses.	2,391,952,134	2,611,062,195	2,576,059,889	2,321,587,503	2,144,699,750
HOSPITAL UNIT (Excludes Separate Nursing Home Units)					
Utilization - Inpatient					
Beds	2,203	2,688	2,635	2,589	2,706
Admissions	103,143	108,956	109,467	108,918	108,877
Inpatient Days	598,213	660,450	657,887	667,147	716,562
Average Length of Stay.	5.8	6.1	6.0	6.1	6.6
Personnel					
Total Full Time.	13,399	14,428	14,178	14,172	13,832
Total Part Time	2,318	3,047	3,446	3,610	3,146
Revenue and Expenses - Totals					
(Includes Inpatient and Outpatient)					
Total Net Revenue.	$2,318,674,997	$2,601,754,091	$2,512,905,897	$2,353,764,329	$2,164,235,821
Total Expenses.	2,347,459,882	2,561,364,433	2,550,665,438	2,275,182,714	2,126,689,282
COMMUNITY HEALTH INDICATORS PER 1000 POPULATION					
Total Population (in thousands)	1,375	1,300	1,295	1,287	1,277
Inpatient					
Beds	1.9	2.4	2.3	2.4	2.3
Admissions	76.4	85.1	86.2	86.5	86.8
Inpatient Days	524.2	636.9	596.4	657.7	624.1
Inpatient Surgeries.	20.0	23.6	25.0	23.9	25.3
Births.	7.8	7.1	8.5	8.2	7.8
Outpatient					
Emergency Outpatient Visits	266.4	281.4	296.3	280.4	265.5
Other Outpatient Visits.	1,192.8	1,406.2	1,369.3	1,287.8	1,205.3
Total Outpatient Visits	1,459.2	1,687.6	1,665.7	1,568.3	1,470.8
Outpatient Surgeries	40.7	45.1	47.5	46.0	45.0
Expense per Capita (per person).	$1,739.8	$2,008.4	$1,989.0	$1,803.2	$1,679.7

States

TABLE 6

IDAHO

U.S. Registered Community Hospitals
(Nonfederal, short-term general and other special hospitals)

Overview 2007–2011

	2011	2010	2009	2008	2007
Total Community Hospitals in Idaho	40	41	41	39	39
Bed Size Category					
6-24	12	11	11	11	10
25-49	11	12	11	10	10
50-99	8	9	10	9	9
100-199	4	5	5	5	6
200-299	2	1	1	2	2
300-399	2	2	2	1	1
400-499	0	0	0	0	0
500 + ...	1	1	1	1	1
Location					
Hospitals Urban.	14	15	15	14	7
Hospitals Rural	26	26	26	25	32
Control					
State and Local Government.	19	20	20	22	21
Not for Profit	17	16	16	14	15
Investor owned	4	5	5	3	3
Physician Models					
Independent Practice Association	5	5	5	7	9
Group Practice without Walls.	1	1	2	2	2
Open Physician-Hospital Organization	7	4	4	3	3
Closed Physician-Hospital Organization	2	2	3	4	5
Management Service Organization	1	3	4	4	5
Integrated Salary Model	12	13	13	11	10
Equity Model	0	0	0	1	1
Foundation.	1	1	1	1	2
Insurance Products					
Health Maintenance Organization	1	2	2	2	2
Preferred Provider Organization.	2	2	4	4	3
Indemnity Fee for Service	1	0	1	1	1
Managed Care Contracts					
Health Maintenance Organization	13	14	15	16	15
Preferred Provider Organization.	17	19	22	21	22
Affiliations					
Hospitals in a System.	20	23	23	22	19
Hospitals in a Network	11	13	15	15	19
Hospitals in a Group Purchasing Organization. .	25	25	28	26	30

States

TABLE 6

IDAHO

U.S. Registered Community Hospitals
(Nonfederal, short-term general and other special hospitals)

Utilization, Personnel, Revenue and Expenses, Community Health Indicators 2007–2011

	2011	2010	2009	2008	2007
TOTAL FACILITY (Includes Hospital and Nursing Home Units)					
Utilization - Inpatient					
Beds..........................	3,306	3,376	3,382	3,311	3,296
Admissions....................	128,742	131,375	129,645	135,697	133,895
Inpatient Days.................	605,718	628,840	627,077	643,039	654,818
Average Length of Stay...........	4.7	4.8	4.8	4.7	4.9
Inpatient Surgeries...............	39,858	39,614	40,358	41,234	42,964
Births........................	19,487	18,941	20,126	23,014	23,236
Utilization - Outpatient					
Emergency Outpatient Visits........	517,995	489,718	514,299	520,941	521,382
Other Outpatient Visits.............	3,516,106	2,672,240	2,558,653	2,419,470	2,346,680
Total Outpatient Visits.............	4,034,101	3,161,958	3,072,952	2,940,411	2,868,062
Outpatient Surgeries	84,221	73,409	68,339	70,154	65,946
Personnel					
Full Time RNs	4,334	4,103	3,898	3,739	3,634
Full Time LPNs	458	403	399	421	429
Part Time RNs.................	2,341	2,245	2,119	2,641	2,228
Part Time LPNs................	209	166	169	215	220
Total Full Time................	19,181	18,010	16,594	16,336	15,868
Total Part Time	8,019	7,175	6,408	7,728	7,213
Revenue - Inpatient					
Gross Inpatient Revenue...........	$3,108,970,857	$2,899,758,710	$2,707,480,791	$2,561,301,943	$2,248,997,324
Revenue - Outpatient					
Gross Outpatient Revenue	$3,623,818,467	$3,113,164,805	$2,775,500,660	$2,451,235,258	$2,086,866,647
Revenue and Expenses - Totals					
(Includes Inpatient and Outpatient)					
Total Gross Revenue..............	$6,732,789,324	$6,012,923,515	$5,482,981,451	$5,012,537,201	$4,335,863,971
Deductions from Revenue..........	3,621,413,551	3,190,452,073	2,796,704,816	2,484,822,454	1,983,781,556
Net Patient Revenue	3,111,375,773	2,822,471,442	2,686,276,635	2,527,714,747	2,352,082,415
Other Operating Revenue	103,709,342	96,182,670	83,202,052	90,838,094	82,800,813
Other Nonoperating Revenue	49,967,037	47,366,046	-11,931,355	15,092,420	77,705,507
Total Net Revenue................	3,265,052,152	2,966,020,158	2,757,547,332	2,633,645,261	2,512,588,735
Total Expenses..................	2,791,035,799	2,546,624,205	2,563,109,938	2,406,259,158	2,224,117,950
HOSPITAL UNIT (Excludes Separate Nursing Home Units)					
Utilization - Inpatient					
Beds..........................	2,950	3,027	3,013	3,004	2,895
Admissions....................	127,750	129,900	127,927	134,364	132,563
Inpatient Days.................	503,243	525,428	518,291	553,925	541,539
Average Length of Stay...........	3.9	4.0	4.1	4.1	4.1
Personnel					
Total Full Time..................	18,937	17,803	16,327	16,134	15,619
Total Part Time	7,878	7,040	6,227	7,599	7,060
Revenue and Expenses - Totals					
(Includes Inpatient and Outpatient)					
Total Net Revenue................	$3,240,672,233	$2,934,932,796	$2,730,768,774	$2,607,116,770	$2,485,446,404
Total Expenses..................	2,775,730,301	2,524,919,767	2,541,756,270	2,389,059,009	2,205,976,897
COMMUNITY HEALTH INDICATORS PER 1000 POPULATION					
Total Population (in thousands)	1,585	1,560	1,546	1,528	1,499
Inpatient					
Beds..........................	2.1	2.2	2.2	2.2	2.2
Admissions....................	81.2	84.2	83.9	88.8	89.3
Inpatient Days.................	382.2	403.2	405.7	421.0	436.8
Inpatient Surgeries...............	25.1	25.4	26.1	27.0	28.7
Births........................	12.3	12.1	13.0	15.1	15.5
Outpatient					
Emergency Outpatient Visits........	326.8	314.0	332.7	341.0	347.8
Other Outpatient Visits.............	2,218.4	1,713.2	1,655.2	1,583.9	1,565.2
Total Outpatient Visits.............	2,545.2	2,027.2	1,987.9	1,925.0	1,913.0
Outpatient Surgeries	53.1	47.1	44.2	45.9	44.0
Expense per Capita (per person).....	$1,760.9	$1,632.7	$1,658.1	$1,575.3	$1,483.5

States

TABLE 6

ILLINOIS

U.S. Registered Community Hospitals
(Nonfederal, short-term general and other special hospitals)

Overview 2007–2011

	2011	2010	2009	2008	2007
Total Community Hospitals in Illinois.........	188	189	189	191	190
Bed Size Category					
6-24......................................	11	10	8	6	3
25-49.....................................	36	32	31	33	34
50-99.....................................	31	36	37	34	32
100-199...................................	51	50	49	50	53
200-299...................................	24	25	29	30	34
300-399...................................	18	19	17	21	16
400-499...................................	9	9	10	9	10
500 +.....................................	8	8	8	8	8
Location					
Hospitals Urban..........................	124	125	125	127	119
Hospitals Rural	64	64	64	64	71
Control					
State and Local Government...............	24	26	26	26	27
Not for Profit	145	143	147	149	150
Investor owned	19	20	16	16	13
Physician Models					
Independent Practice Association	22	28	30	29	32
Group Practice without Walls...............	8	4	5	8	7
Open Physician-Hospital Organization	43	43	47	41	41
Closed Physician-Hospital Organization	11	13	11	8	10
Management Service Organization	21	22	27	24	26
Integrated Salary Model....................	59	62	64	61	57
Equity Model	3	2	4	3	3
Foundation...............................	8	13	6	7	7
Insurance Products					
Health Maintenance Organization	16	19	18	20	22
Preferred Provider Organization..............	17	17	16	18	22
Indemnity Fee for Service	7	7	7	10	7
Managed Care Contracts					
Health Maintenance Organization	114	123	127	120	120
Preferred Provider Organization..............	127	134	142	133	131
Affiliations					
Hospitals in a System.....................	113	108	104	105	103
Hospitals in a Network....................	43	47	47	45	44
Hospitals in a Group Purchasing Organization..	142	157	158	149	144

TABLE 6

ILLINOIS

U.S. Registered Community Hospitals
(Nonfederal, short-term general and other special hospitals)

Utilization, Personnel, Revenue and Expenses, Community Health Indicators 2007–2011

	2011	2010	2009	2008	2007
TOTAL FACILITY (Includes Hospital and Nursing Home Units)					
Utilization - Inpatient					
Beds	32,775	33,310	33,856	34,506	34,560
Admissions	1,511,770	1,542,958	1,557,816	1,610,844	1,606,241
Inpatient Days	7,398,797	7,552,956	7,769,059	8,069,859	8,107,743
Average Length of Stay	4.9	4.9	5.0	5.0	5.0
Inpatient Surgeries	386,166	403,226	399,042	406,437	412,696
Births	152,929	159,563	166,005	176,458	172,896
Utilization - Outpatient					
Emergency Outpatient Visits	5,414,964	5,366,010	5,312,763	5,123,091	5,068,338
Other Outpatient Visits	26,277,834	27,192,086	26,780,252	25,863,666	25,579,122
Total Outpatient Visits	31,692,798	32,558,096	32,093,015	30,986,757	30,647,460
Outpatient Surgeries	731,909	738,783	723,461	728,072	723,558
Personnel					
Full Time RNs	42,707	41,948	39,989	39,613	39,478
Full Time LPNs	1,730	1,769	1,882	2,142	2,308
Part Time RNs	23,563	23,493	24,237	23,785	22,555
Part Time LPNs	769	808	827	1,051	1,086
Total Full Time	163,470	163,519	162,002	164,936	165,962
Total Part Time	74,154	74,448	76,241	73,769	72,865
Revenue - Inpatient					
Gross Inpatient Revenue	$51,831,662,656	$50,630,716,983	$48,011,580,288	$45,587,537,606	$42,978,477,154
Revenue - Outpatient					
Gross Outpatient Revenue	$46,237,076,561	$41,884,636,238	$38,198,138,940	$34,572,195,642	$30,813,226,194
Revenue and Expenses - Totals					
(Includes Inpatient and Outpatient)					
Total Gross Revenue	$97,069,639,217	$92,515,353,221	$86,209,719,228	$80,159,733,248	$73,791,703,348
Deductions from Revenue	67,477,849,736	63,248,692,053	58,012,296,593	53,322,130,324	47,626,354,101
Net Patient Revenue	29,591,789,481	29,266,661,168	28,197,422,635	26,837,602,924	26,165,349,247
Other Operating Revenue	1,900,816,882	1,918,358,653	1,923,701,500	1,822,911,841	1,776,488,686
Other Nonoperating Revenue	1,093,755,704	712,723,108	-244,005,396	38,822,875	1,235,227,543
Total Net Revenue	32,586,362,067	31,897,742,929	29,877,118,739	28,699,337,640	29,177,065,476
Total Expenses	29,831,858,047	29,193,599,201	28,870,203,691	27,982,801,609	26,624,446,808
HOSPITAL UNIT (Excludes Separate Nursing Home Units)					
Utilization - Inpatient					
Beds	31,305	31,615	32,096	32,847	32,590
Admissions	1,497,436	1,526,371	1,540,936	1,597,722	1,593,560
Inpatient Days	7,012,553	7,117,426	7,294,792	7,595,924	7,592,769
Average Length of Stay	4.7	4.7	4.7	4.8	4.8
Personnel					
Total Full Time	162,704	162,567	160,793	163,669	159,417
Total Part Time	73,555	73,868	75,623	73,011	72,017
Revenue and Expenses - Totals					
(Includes Inpatient and Outpatient)					
Total Net Revenue	$32,474,980,131	$31,785,482,525	$29,750,884,315	$28,605,435,197	$29,063,650,445
Total Expenses	29,734,524,075	29,102,876,687	28,774,155,633	27,899,476,892	26,479,602,469
COMMUNITY HEALTH INDICATORS PER 1000 POPULATION					
Total Population (in thousands)	12,869	12,944	12,910	12,843	12,779
Inpatient					
Beds	2.5	2.6	2.6	2.7	2.7
Admissions	117.5	119.2	120.7	125.4	125.7
Inpatient Days	574.9	583.5	601.8	628.3	634.4
Inpatient Surgeries	30.0	31.2	30.9	31.6	32.3
Births	11.9	12.3	12.9	13.7	13.5
Outpatient					
Emergency Outpatient Visits	420.8	414.5	411.5	398.9	396.6
Other Outpatient Visits	2,041.9	2,100.7	2,074.3	2,013.8	2,001.6
Total Outpatient Visits	2,462.7	2,515.2	2,485.8	2,412.7	2,398.2
Outpatient Surgeries	56.9	57.1	56.0	56.7	56.6
Expense per Capita (per person)	$2,318.1	$2,255.3	$2,236.2	$2,178.8	$2,083.4

States

TABLE 6

INDIANA

U.S. Registered Community Hospitals
(Nonfederal, short-term general and other special hospitals)

Overview 2007–2011

	2011	2010	2009	2008	2007
Total Community Hospitals in Indiana	125	125	123	123	114
Bed Size Category					
6-24	5	5	5	6	5
25-49	40	41	41	40	37
50-99	30	28	27	28	23
100-199	23	21	23	20	18
200-299	13	16	14	16	18
300-399	5	5	4	4	3
400-499	3	3	2	2	3
500 + ...	6	6	7	7	7
Location					
Hospitals Urban...........................	85	85	83	83	70
Hospitals Rural	40	40	40	40	44
Control					
State and Local Government................	30	33	34	39	39
Not for Profit	71	67	64	59	56
Investor owned	24	25	25	25	19
Physician Models					
Independent Practice Association	3	6	9	8	6
Group Practice without Walls................	4	2	2	4	4
Open Physician-Hospital Organization	21	26	26	25	28
Closed Physician-Hospital Organization	7	8	9	9	11
Management Service Organization	8	9	9	9	13
Integrated Salary Model	53	55	53	49	48
Equity Model	3	2	3	2	1
Foundation	2	5	7	6	4
Insurance Products					
Health Maintenance Organization	27	29	26	26	30
Preferred Provider Organization..............	30	33	27	25	43
Indemnity Fee for Service	4	6	4	5	7
Managed Care Contracts					
Health Maintenance Organization	62	65	69	64	68
Preferred Provider Organization..............	71	77	84	80	82
Affiliations					
Hospitals in a System......................	87	85	82	79	70
Hospitals in a Network	45	46	44	42	41
Hospitals in a Group Purchasing Organization..	87	97	98	103	101

TABLE 6

TABLE 6

INDIANA

U.S. Registered Community Hospitals
(Nonfederal, short-term general and other special hospitals)

Utilization, Personnel, Revenue and Expenses, Community Health Indicators 2007–2011

	2011	2010	2009	2008	2007
TOTAL FACILITY (Includes Hospital and Nursing Home Units)					
Utilization - Inpatient					
Beds	17,467	17,759	17,298	17,612	17,055
Admissions	737,438	718,348	713,456	732,627	690,866
Inpatient Days	3,724,041	3,756,021	3,687,549	3,829,835	3,513,575
Average Length of Stay	5.0	5.2	5.2	5.2	5.1
Inpatient Surgeries	200,907	206,124	206,101	217,917	196,104
Births	76,049	77,124	78,371	82,040	82,852
Utilization - Outpatient					
Emergency Outpatient Visits	3,144,973	3,185,166	3,004,721	3,041,160	3,080,110
Other Outpatient Visits	15,367,982	15,543,606	14,446,277	13,981,154	13,641,278
Total Outpatient Visits	18,512,955	18,728,772	17,450,998	17,022,314	16,721,388
Outpatient Surgeries	429,164	423,827	430,435	433,467	420,587
Personnel					
Full Time RNs	23,243	22,345	21,653	20,417	17,979
Full Time LPNs	1,697	1,664	1,742	2,092	2,075
Part Time RNs	13,697	14,136	13,502	14,045	14,638
Part Time LPNs	768	874	995	1,275	1,040
Total Full Time	87,241	86,266	86,530	83,800	79,310
Total Part Time	39,619	41,019	40,675	43,202	42,633
Revenue - Inpatient					
Gross Inpatient Revenue	$23,724,867,721	$21,889,172,836	$19,297,952,821	$18,735,608,044	$16,424,208,617
Revenue - Outpatient					
Gross Outpatient Revenue	$23,279,155,929	$20,791,179,952	$18,451,255,529	$16,228,904,838	$14,405,730,848
Revenue and Expenses - Totals					
(Includes Inpatient and Outpatient)					
Total Gross Revenue	$47,004,023,650	$42,680,352,788	$37,749,208,350	$34,964,512,882	$30,830,019,465
Deductions from Revenue	30,555,814,094	26,936,969,969	22,765,297,520	20,658,195,492	17,923,123,410
Net Patient Revenue	16,448,209,556	15,743,382,819	14,983,910,830	14,306,317,390	12,906,896,055
Other Operating Revenue	1,117,137,691	881,745,072	769,461,090	837,647,729	847,569,677
Other Nonoperating Revenue	405,284,123	434,805,381	282,345,047	-665,292,556	543,156,760
Total Net Revenue	17,970,631,370	17,059,933,272	16,035,716,967	14,478,672,563	14,297,622,492
Total Expenses	16,082,098,784	15,349,922,777	14,724,925,283	14,654,457,324	13,178,097,122
HOSPITAL UNIT (Excludes Separate Nursing Home Units)					
Utilization - Inpatient					
Beds	16,942	17,208	16,879	16,911	16,295
Admissions	732,496	713,224	707,886	724,499	682,827
Inpatient Days	3,562,156	3,584,106	3,567,515	3,612,957	3,287,612
Average Length of Stay	4.9	5.0	5.0	5.0	4.8
Personnel					
Total Full Time	86,943	85,948	85,900	82,933	78,394
Total Part Time	39,255	40,630	40,280	42,676	42,129
Revenue and Expenses - Totals					
(Includes Inpatient and Outpatient)					
Total Net Revenue	$17,906,999,370	$17,017,380,655	$15,997,778,555	$14,424,793,981	$14,228,510,655
Total Expenses	16,032,853,104	15,311,258,669	14,696,533,580	14,603,238,942	13,123,516,451
COMMUNITY HEALTH INDICATORS PER 1000 POPULATION					
Total Population (in thousands)	6,517	6,445	6,423	6,388	6,346
Inpatient					
Beds	2.7	2.8	2.7	2.8	2.7
Admissions	113.2	111.5	111.1	114.7	108.9
Inpatient Days	571.4	582.8	574.1	599.5	553.7
Inpatient Surgeries	30.8	32.0	32.1	34.1	30.9
Births	11.7	12.0	12.2	12.8	13.1
Outpatient					
Emergency Outpatient Visits	482.6	494.2	467.8	476.1	485.4
Other Outpatient Visits	2,358.2	2,411.6	2,249.1	2,188.6	2,149.5
Total Outpatient Visits	2,840.8	2,905.8	2,716.9	2,664.6	2,634.9
Outpatient Surgeries	65.9	65.8	67.0	67.9	66.3
Expense per Capita (per person)	$2,467.7	$2,381.6	$2,292.5	$2,293.9	$2,076.6

States

TABLE 6

IOWA

U.S. Registered Community Hospitals
(Nonfederal, short-term general and other special hospitals)

Overview 2007–2011

	2011	2010	2009	2008	2007
Total Community Hospitals in Iowa............	118	118	118	118	117
Bed Size Category					
6-24	19	18	15	13	13
25-49	48	49	51	53	50
50-99	27	27	26	26	28
100-199	10	10	12	11	11
200-299	6	6	6	6	6
300-399	5	5	5	5	5
400-499	1	1	1	2	2
500 + ...	2	2	2	2	2
Location					
Hospitals Urban.........................	34	34	34	34	22
Hospitals Rural	84	84	84	84	95
Control					
State and Local Government...............	59	59	59	59	59
Not for Profit	57	57	58	58	58
Investor owned	2	2	1	1	0
Physician Models					
Independent Practice Association	12	13	13	15	15
Group Practice without Walls...............	5	4	3	3	3
Open Physician-Hospital Organization	18	20	24	27	26
Closed Physician-Hospital Organization	11	10	10	10	11
Management Service Organization	9	8	9	12	12
Integrated Salary Model....................	74	72	70	65	64
Equity Model	1	0	0	0	1
Foundation..............................	5	4	4	6	5
Insurance Products					
Health Maintenance Organization	8	8	9	9	13
Preferred Provider Organization.............	20	23	22	20	26
Indemnity Fee for Service	5	5	6	4	6
Managed Care Contracts					
Health Maintenance Organization	74	73	71	70	69
Preferred Provider Organization.............	94	99	98	97	97
Affiliations					
Hospitals in a System......................	64	66	64	64	63
Hospitals in a Network	77	73	72	70	70
Hospitals in a Group Purchasing Organization..	115	115	112	112	111

States

TABLE **6**

IOWA

U.S. Registered Community Hospitals
(Nonfederal, short-term general and other special hospitals)

Utilization, Personnel, Revenue and Expenses, Community Health Indicators 2007–2011

	2011	2010	2009	2008	2007
TOTAL FACILITY (Includes Hospital and Nursing Home Units)					
Utilization - Inpatient					
Beds	9,981	10,075	10,276	10,531	10,515
Admissions	340,412	341,744	354,534	373,330	368,272
Inpatient Days	2,058,730	2,058,304	2,185,446	2,248,874	2,266,094
Average Length of Stay	6.0	6.0	6.2	6.0	6.2
Inpatient Surgeries	83,333	87,343	92,154	101,343	100,151
Births	37,284	38,193	39,522	39,060	40,274
Utilization - Outpatient					
Emergency Outpatient Visits	1,273,985	1,223,271	1,230,737	1,226,568	1,165,305
Other Outpatient Visits	9,053,438	9,805,308	9,724,268	9,154,060	9,390,580
Total Outpatient Visits	10,327,423	11,028,579	10,955,005	10,380,628	10,555,885
Outpatient Surgeries	256,117	253,148	265,368	337,632	337,757
Personnel					
Full Time RNs	11,084	10,516	10,657	10,589	10,263
Full Time LPNs	788	775	814	902	915
Part Time RNs	6,843	6,988	7,147	7,573	7,388
Part Time LPNs	412	548	587	734	824
Total Full Time	44,535	43,589	43,659	45,177	44,058
Total Part Time	23,010	23,302	24,045	20,052	25,304
Revenue - Inpatient					
Gross Inpatient Revenue	$7,955,026,036	$7,478,207,382	$7,402,854,971	$7,173,320,596	$6,622,133,635
Revenue - Outpatient					
Gross Outpatient Revenue	$9,276,348,064	$8,615,345,555	$7,932,610,080	$7,008,785,229	$6,341,069,890
Revenue and Expenses - Totals					
(Includes Inpatient and Outpatient)					
Total Gross Revenue	$17,231,374,100	$16,093,552,937	$15,335,465,051	$14,182,105,825	$12,963,203,525
Deductions from Revenue	10,246,167,955	9,374,915,563	8,788,605,112	7,919,893,373	7,059,676,768
Net Patient Revenue	6,985,206,145	6,718,637,374	6,546,859,939	6,262,212,452	5,903,526,757
Other Operating Revenue	502,660,629	483,246,348	490,608,985	479,246,797	468,286,796
Other Nonoperating Revenue	223,831,009	236,093,511	9,177,812	-17,782,222	235,126,914
Total Net Revenue	7,711,697,783	7,437,977,233	7,046,646,736	6,723,677,027	6,606,940,467
Total Expenses	7,174,090,504	6,934,527,799	6,824,533,485	6,518,050,247	6,082,343,644
HOSPITAL UNIT (Excludes Separate Nursing Home Units)					
Utilization - Inpatient					
Beds	8,287	8,341	8,385	8,524	8,486
Admissions	336,335	337,483	348,765	365,727	360,207
Inpatient Days	1,533,884	1,521,829	1,602,497	1,616,630	1,626,922
Average Length of Stay	4.6	4.5	4.6	4.4	4.5
Personnel					
Total Full Time	43,792	42,836	42,865	44,290	43,130
Total Part Time	22,278	22,670	23,241	25,160	24,397
Revenue and Expenses - Totals					
(Includes Inpatient and Outpatient)					
Total Net Revenue	$7,624,566,231	$7,354,382,506	$6,945,244,251	$6,614,103,911	$6,497,382,484
Total Expenses	7,096,506,924	6,860,708,589	6,739,111,985	6,429,352,282	5,997,176,987
COMMUNITY HEALTH INDICATORS PER 1000 POPULATION					
Total Population (in thousands)	3,062	3,023	3,008	2,994	2,979
Inpatient					
Beds	3.3	3.3	3.4	3.5	3.5
Admissions	111.2	113.0	117.9	124.7	123.6
Inpatient Days	672.3	680.9	726.6	751.1	760.8
Inpatient Surgeries	27.2	28.9	30.6	33.8	33.6
Births	12.2	12.6	13.1	13.0	13.5
Outpatient					
Emergency Outpatient Visits	416.0	404.6	409.2	409.7	391.2
Other Outpatient Visits	2,956.4	3,243.5	3,233.0	3,057.5	3,152.6
Total Outpatient Visits	3,372.4	3,648.1	3,642.1	3,467.2	3,543.8
Outpatient Surgeries	83.6	83.7	88.2	112.8	113.4
Expense per Capita (per person)	$2,342.7	$2,293.9	$2,268.9	$2,177.0	$2,041.9

States

TABLE 6

KANSAS

U.S. Registered Community Hospitals
(Nonfederal, short-term general and other special hospitals)

Overview 2007–2011

	2011	2010	2009	2008	2007
Total Community Hospitals in Kansas	**132**	**130**	**133**	**132**	**128**
Bed Size Category					
6-24	20	19	18	15	14
25-49	50	49	50	51	51
50-99	38	37	40	39	38
100-199	14	16	15	17	14
200-299	5	4	5	5	6
300-399	2	2	2	2	2
400-499	0	0	0	0	0
500 + ...	3	3	3	3	3
Location					
Hospitals Urban........................	33	33	33	33	24
Hospitals Rural	99	97	100	99	104
Control					
State and Local Government...............	63	62	62	62	62
Not for Profit	53	51	54	53	55
Investor owned	16	17	17	17	11
Physician Models					
Independent Practice Association	15	13	14	14	13
Group Practice without Walls...............	3	2	2	3	2
Open Physician-Hospital Organization	12	11	14	15	15
Closed Physician-Hospital Organization	1	0	2	2	2
Management Service Organization	5	3	4	4	4
Integrated Salary Model....................	77	69	71	65	62
Equity Model	1	0	0	1	1
Foundation..............................	8	5	3	3	4
Insurance Products					
Health Maintenance Organization	1	1	2	5	6
Preferred Provider Organization..............	9	9	8	11	28
Indemnity Fee for Service	0	1	2	3	5
Managed Care Contracts					
Health Maintenance Organization	55	56	52	51	46
Preferred Provider Organization..............	110	109	111	112	107
Affiliations					
Hospitals in a System.....................	55	53	54	52	47
Hospitals in a Network....................	82	83	83	82	79
Hospitals in a Group Purchasing Organization..	129	128	126	126	124

States

TABLE **6**

KANSAS

U.S. Registered Community Hospitals
(Nonfederal, short-term general and other special hospitals)

Utilization, Personnel, Revenue and Expenses, Community Health Indicators 2007–2011

	2011	2010	2009	2008	2007
TOTAL FACILITY (Includes Hospital and Nursing Home Units)					
Utilization - Inpatient					
Beds	10,023	9,965	10,127	10,269	10,079
Admissions	302,351	304,769	315,820	328,279	325,355
Inpatient Days	1,923,661	1,960,261	2,014,165	2,079,667	2,025,564
Average Length of Stay	6.4	6.4	6.4	6.3	6.2
Inpatient Surgeries	76,828	79,305	79,857	82,907	84,061
Births	38,707	39,777	41,092	41,592	41,753
Utilization - Outpatient					
Emergency Outpatient Visits	1,041,234	1,019,521	1,042,407	1,028,706	1,003,181
Other Outpatient Visits	5,955,302	5,660,293	5,687,308	5,497,497	5,394,624
Total Outpatient Visits	6,996,536	6,679,814	6,729,715	6,526,203	6,397,805
Outpatient Surgeries	161,889	157,746	160,653	162,784	158,129
Personnel					
Full Time RNs	10,968	10,852	10,517	9,924	9,353
Full Time LPNs	1,014	1,056	1,132	1,104	1,085
Part Time RNs	4,533	4,535	4,550	4,448	4,483
Part Time LPNs	409	441	495	502	533
Total Full Time	39,286	38,881	38,833	38,038	36,715
Total Part Time	14,111	14,183	14,585	14,394	14,215
Revenue - Inpatient					
Gross Inpatient Revenue	$9,707,362,014	$9,158,840,266	$8,857,616,660	$8,347,025,856	$7,570,341,842
Revenue - Outpatient					
Gross Outpatient Revenue	$8,606,191,704	$7,804,133,580	$7,296,946,111	$6,341,227,760	$5,585,998,443
Revenue and Expenses - Totals					
(Includes Inpatient and Outpatient)					
Total Gross Revenue	$18,313,553,718	$16,962,973,846	$16,154,562,771	$14,688,253,616	$13,156,340,285
Deductions from Revenue	12,295,093,634	11,147,817,611	10,508,920,047	9,366,195,974	8,521,152,481
Net Patient Revenue	6,018,460,084	5,815,156,235	5,645,642,724	5,322,057,642	4,635,187,804
Other Operating Revenue	215,888,633	203,257,460	212,360,609	194,026,086	190,949,651
Other Nonoperating Revenue	66,106,732	128,773,371	25,755,861	33,604,548	143,977,328
Total Net Revenue	6,300,455,449	6,147,187,066	5,883,759,194	5,549,688,276	4,970,114,783
Total Expenses	5,963,380,431	5,759,373,331	5,603,169,760	5,330,135,811	4,536,195,594
HOSPITAL UNIT (Excludes Separate Nursing Home Units)					
Utilization - Inpatient					
Beds	8,495	8,338	8,418	8,435	8,287
Admissions	299,829	302,003	313,046	325,383	322,629
Inpatient Days	1,449,789	1,447,040	1,507,027	1,551,696	1,496,858
Average Length of Stay	4.8	4.8	4.8	4.8	4.6
Personnel					
Total Full Time	38,237	37,806	37,721	36,923	35,595
Total Part Time	13,543	13,660	13,972	13,775	13,608
Revenue and Expenses - Totals					
(Includes Inpatient and Outpatient)					
Total Net Revenue	$6,224,061,786	$6,068,771,082	$5,807,209,303	$5,472,326,781	$4,898,350,636
Total Expenses	5,897,756,162	5,694,269,627	5,536,264,786	5,262,852,507	4,478,090,750
COMMUNITY HEALTH INDICATORS PER 1000 POPULATION					
Total Population (in thousands)	2,871	2,841	2,819	2,797	2,776
Inpatient					
Beds	3.5	3.5	3.6	3.7	3.6
Admissions	105.3	107.3	112.0	117.4	117.2
Inpatient Days	670.0	690.0	714.6	743.4	729.8
Inpatient Surgeries	26.8	27.9	28.3	29.6	30.3
Births	13.5	14.0	14.6	14.9	15.0
Outpatient					
Emergency Outpatient Visits	362.6	358.8	369.8	367.7	361.4
Other Outpatient Visits	2,074.1	1,992.3	2,017.7	1,965.2	1,943.6
Total Outpatient Visits	2,436.8	2,351.1	2,387.5	2,333.0	2,305.0
Outpatient Surgeries	56.4	55.5	57.0	58.2	57.0
Expense per Capita (per person)	$2,076.9	$2,027.1	$1,987.8	$1,905.4	$1,634.3

States

TABLE 6

KENTUCKY

U.S. Registered Community Hospitals
(Nonfederal, short-term general and other special hospitals)

Overview 2007–2011

	2011	2010	2009	2008	2007
Total Community Hospitals in Kentucky.......	106	106	104	105	104
Bed Size Category					
6-24	3	1	1	1	1
25-49	34	34	33	34	32
50-99	22	24	24	23	24
100-199	25	24	23	22	19
200-299	7	8	8	10	14
300-399	10	10	9	9	8
400-499	1	3	3	3	3
500 + ...	4	2	3	3	3
Location					
Hospitals Urban...........................	43	43	42	41	34
Hospitals Rural	63	63	62	64	70
Control					
State and Local Government...............	12	11	11	14	12
Not for Profit	74	75	73	71	73
Investor owned	20	20	20	20	19
Physician Models					
Independent Practice Association	5	5	6	7	7
Group Practice without Walls...............	0	0	2	2	3
Open Physician-Hospital Organization	7	9	12	11	11
Closed Physician-Hospital Organization	2	3	4	5	5
Management Service Organization	8	8	3	2	3
Integrated Salary Model....................	42	43	38	39	38
Equity Model.............................	0	0	1	1	0
Foundation..............................	3	4	3	3	2
Insurance Products					
Health Maintenance Organization	7	10	5	4	9
Preferred Provider Organization.............	14	15	9	9	17
Indemnity Fee for Service	5	8	2	3	2
Managed Care Contracts					
Health Maintenance Organization	44	48	46	41	43
Preferred Provider Organization.............	53	59	57	60	63
Affiliations					
Hospitals in a System.....................	80	79	76	72	68
Hospitals in a Network	17	22	23	24	27
Hospitals in a Group Purchasing Organization..	71	80	77	82	83

States

TABLE 6

KENTUCKY

U.S. Registered Community Hospitals
(Nonfederal, short-term general and other special hospitals)

Utilization, Personnel, Revenue and Expenses, Community Health Indicators 2007–2011

	2011	2010	2009	2008	2007
TOTAL FACILITY (Includes Hospital and Nursing Home Units)					
Utilization - Inpatient					
Beds	14,182	14,238	14,124	14,180	14,423
Admissions	599,601	608,644	597,224	610,449	611,689
Inpatient Days	3,061,415	3,141,502	3,113,326	3,216,149	3,188,902
Average Length of Stay	5.1	5.2	5.2	5.3	5.2
Inpatient Surgeries	170,702	173,656	173,196	176,178	178,549
Births	49,657	53,630	50,085	54,872	56,096
Utilization - Outpatient					
Emergency Outpatient Visits	2,350,367	2,386,673	2,321,519	2,339,390	2,305,046
Other Outpatient Visits	8,182,293	8,050,866	7,798,087	7,319,408	7,219,771
Total Outpatient Visits	10,532,660	10,437,539	10,119,606	9,658,798	9,524,817
Outpatient Surgeries	400,593	385,960	372,057	385,428	376,310
Personnel					
Full Time RNs	17,989	17,666	16,592	16,222	15,410
Full Time LPNs	1,436	1,648	1,849	1,807	2,045
Part Time RNs	6,060	6,087	6,016	6,151	6,335
Part Time LPNs	343	397	419	445	539
Total Full Time	64,035	63,493	61,699	61,610	60,572
Total Part Time	18,453	18,309	18,144	18,576	18,836
Revenue - Inpatient					
Gross Inpatient Revenue	$16,313,648,119	$15,503,184,961	$14,536,872,535	$13,943,782,950	$13,031,881,310
Revenue - Outpatient					
Gross Outpatient Revenue	$15,995,475,627	$14,305,855,765	$12,460,315,729	$11,459,995,978	$10,354,782,898
Revenue and Expenses - Totals					
(Includes Inpatient and Outpatient)					
Total Gross Revenue	$32,309,123,746	$29,809,040,726	$26,997,188,264	$25,403,778,928	$23,386,664,208
Deductions from Revenue	22,051,533,008	19,784,508,926	17,477,244,235	16,462,600,038	14,766,322,595
Net Patient Revenue	10,257,590,738	10,024,531,800	9,519,944,029	8,941,178,890	8,620,341,613
Other Operating Revenue	383,110,150	338,831,936	353,366,856	309,734,161	282,137,777
Other Nonoperating Revenue	135,433,381	145,526,221	-11,001,226	-81,140,239	206,333,489
Total Net Revenue	10,776,134,269	10,508,889,957	9,862,309,659	9,169,772,812	9,108,812,879
Total Expenses	10,049,280,333	9,801,870,954	9,424,000,735	8,831,617,722	8,398,874,713
HOSPITAL UNIT (Excludes Separate Nursing Home Units)					
Utilization - Inpatient					
Beds	13,595	13,367	13,243	13,383	13,437
Admissions	592,962	602,635	591,112	603,967	604,725
Inpatient Days	2,886,190	2,889,658	2,843,189	2,975,158	2,886,705
Average Length of Stay	4.9	4.8	4.8	4.9	4.8
Personnel					
Total Full Time	63,514	62,730	60,717	60,776	59,665
Total Part Time	18,315	17,998	17,826	18,322	18,550
Revenue and Expenses - Totals					
(Includes Inpatient and Outpatient)					
Total Net Revenue	$10,690,507,752	$10,416,730,891	$9,778,913,020	$9,092,827,775	$9,023,023,649
Total Expenses	9,975,988,671	9,715,872,866	9,348,520,481	8,766,577,356	8,337,062,529
COMMUNITY HEALTH INDICATORS PER 1000 POPULATION					
Total Population (in thousands)	4,369	4,339	4,314	4,288	4,256
Inpatient					
Beds	3.2	3.3	3.3	3.3	3.4
Admissions	137.2	140.3	138.4	142.4	143.7
Inpatient Days	700.7	723.9	721.7	750.0	749.2
Inpatient Surgeries	39.1	40.0	40.1	41.1	41.9
Births	11.4	12.4	11.6	12.8	13.2
Outpatient					
Emergency Outpatient Visits	537.9	550.0	538.1	545.6	541.6
Other Outpatient Visits	1,872.7	1,855.3	1,807.6	1,707.0	1,696.3
Total Outpatient Visits	2,410.6	2,405.3	2,345.7	2,252.6	2,237.8
Outpatient Surgeries	91.7	88.9	86.2	89.9	88.4
Expense per Capita (per person)	$2,299.9	$2,258.8	$2,184.5	$2,059.6	$1,973.3

States

TABLE 6

LOUISIANA

U.S. Registered Community Hospitals
(Nonfederal, short-term general and other special hospitals)

Overview 2007–2011

	2011	2010	2009	2008	2007
Total Community Hospitals in Louisiana	**127**	**126**	**128**	**130**	**129**
Bed Size Category					
6-24	18	18	16	19	16
25-49	40	40	39	37	39
50-99	24	22	24	22	24
100-199	19	21	26	28	28
200-299	12	12	10	9	9
300-399	8	6	5	7	6
400-499	2	3	3	5	5
500 + ...	4	4	5	3	2
Location					
Hospitals Urban...........................	77	76	77	80	79
Hospitals Rural	50	50	51	50	50
Control					
State and Local Government................	48	50	54	50	50
Not for Profit	39	38	35	38	38
Investor owned	40	38	39	42	41
Physician Models					
Independent Practice Association	7	7	9	8	9
Group Practice without Walls................	7	6	5	4	5
Open Physician-Hospital Organization	12	12	14	14	14
Closed Physician-Hospital Organization	6	5	7	8	5
Management Service Organization	5	4	4	8	3
Integrated Salary Model....................	30	29	27	24	22
Equity Model	0	2	2	4	2
Foundation...............................	3	1	2	4	3
Insurance Products					
Health Maintenance Organization	9	8	7	9	5
Preferred Provider Organization..............	11	10	8	6	7
Indemnity Fee for Service	2	2	1	2	2
Managed Care Contracts					
Health Maintenance Organization	45	47	47	51	50
Preferred Provider Organization..............	57	57	55	61	58
Affiliations					
Hospitals in a System.....................	60	57	64	70	70
Hospitals in a Network	22	22	22	24	20
Hospitals in a Group Purchasing Organization..	66	71	71	72	63

States

TABLE 6

LOUISIANA

U.S. Registered Community Hospitals
(Nonfederal, short-term general and other special hospitals)

Utilization, Personnel, Revenue and Expenses, Community Health Indicators 2007–2011

	2011	2010	2009	2008	2007
TOTAL FACILITY (Includes Hospital and Nursing Home Units)					
Utilization - Inpatient					
Beds	15,342	15,421	15,857	16,007	15,516
Admissions	607,413	625,489	639,450	636,767	630,873
Inpatient Days	3,257,484	3,341,419	3,517,185	3,378,368	3,448,099
Average Length of Stay	5.4	5.3	5.5	5.3	5.5
Inpatient Surgeries	171,534	174,853	180,909	184,754	187,991
Births	54,963	61,525	71,711	67,081	69,359
Utilization - Outpatient					
Emergency Outpatient Visits	2,446,704	2,514,006	2,450,514	2,381,889	2,194,465
Other Outpatient Visits	7,096,563	9,840,934	9,922,624	8,779,479	8,233,730
Total Outpatient Visits	9,543,267	12,354,940	12,373,138	11,161,368	10,428,195
Outpatient Surgeries	277,370	283,987	279,065	278,141	288,118
Personnel					
Full Time RNs	18,529	18,458	18,666	17,187	16,261
Full Time LPNs	2,819	2,884	2,803	3,034	2,675
Part Time RNs	5,250	4,899	5,230	5,039	4,942
Part Time LPNs	594	628	686	773	616
Total Full Time	70,360	71,458	73,220	70,862	69,031
Total Part Time	15,769	15,447	16,165	15,367	14,004
Revenue - Inpatient					
Gross Inpatient Revenue	$17,640,121,901	$17,480,238,475	$16,516,892,572	$15,609,477,577	$14,226,935,015
Revenue - Outpatient					
Gross Outpatient Revenue	$14,296,885,978	$13,195,535,770	$11,720,385,666	$10,443,222,809	$8,622,281,370
Revenue and Expenses - Totals					
(Includes Inpatient and Outpatient)					
Total Gross Revenue	$31,937,007,959	$30,675,774,245	$28,237,278,238	$26,052,700,386	$22,849,216,385
Deductions from Revenue	22,487,315,530	21,158,064,386	19,280,756,846	17,411,142,732	15,075,589,108
Net Patient Revenue	9,449,692,429	9,517,709,859	8,956,521,392	8,641,557,654	7,773,627,277
Other Operating Revenue	727,155,809	672,891,456	549,360,404	521,425,542	530,981,708
Other Nonoperating Revenue	297,471,661	498,721,170	-74,290,469	33,327,586	276,902,027
Total Net Revenue	10,474,319,899	10,689,322,485	9,431,591,327	9,196,310,782	8,581,511,012
Total Expenses	9,705,109,556	9,593,366,678	9,451,348,220	9,014,212,755	8,192,722,277
HOSPITAL UNIT (Excludes Separate Nursing Home Units)					
Utilization - Inpatient					
Beds	14,874	14,721	15,199	15,323	14,832
Admissions	606,108	623,661	638,013	634,313	629,620
Inpatient Days	3,126,298	3,134,514	3,306,229	3,273,703	3,236,493
Average Length of Stay	5.2	5.0	5.2	5.2	5.1
Personnel					
Total Full Time	69,994	70,950	72,664	70,017	68,659
Total Part Time	15,644	15,241	15,946	15,147	13,879
Revenue and Expenses - Totals					
(Includes Inpatient and Outpatient)					
Total Net Revenue	$10,452,759,116	$10,655,165,063	$9,395,699,394	$9,161,979,219	$8,548,109,513
Total Expenses	9,680,765,455	9,556,204,131	9,410,102,839	8,973,038,466	8,161,833,462
COMMUNITY HEALTH INDICATORS PER 1000 POPULATION					
Total Population (in thousands)	4,575	4,529	4,492	4,452	4,376
Inpatient					
Beds	3.4	3.4	3.5	3.6	3.5
Admissions	132.8	138.1	142.4	143.0	144.2
Inpatient Days	712.0	737.7	783.0	758.9	787.9
Inpatient Surgeries	37.5	38.6	40.3	41.5	43.0
Births	12.0	13.6	16.0	15.1	15.8
Outpatient					
Emergency Outpatient Visits	534.8	555.0	545.5	535.1	501.5
Other Outpatient Visits	1,551.2	2,172.7	2,208.9	1,972.2	1,881.5
Total Outpatient Visits	2,086.0	2,727.7	2,754.4	2,507.3	2,383.0
Outpatient Surgeries	60.6	62.7	62.1	62.5	65.8
Expense per Capita (per person)	$2,121.4	$2,118.0	$2,104.0	$2,025.0	$1,872.1

States

TABLE **6**

MAINE

U.S. Registered Community Hospitals
(Nonfederal, short-term general and other special hospitals)

Overview 2007–2011

	2011	2010	2009	2008	2007
Total Community Hospitals in Maine..........	37	37	37	37	37
Bed Size Category					
6-24	2	2	2	2	2
25-49	16	15	16	16	16
50-99	9	10	9	9	9
100-199	7	7	7	7	7
200-299	1	1	1	1	1
300-399	1	1	1	1	1
400-499	0	0	0	0	0
500 + ...	1	1	1	1	1
Location					
Hospitals Urban..........................	15	15	15	15	8
Hospitals Rural	22	22	22	22	29
Control					
State and Local Government...............	2	2	2	2	2
Not for Profit	34	34	34	34	34
Investor owned	1	1	1	1	1
Physician Models					
Independent Practice Association	3	4	4	3	4
Group Practice without Walls...............	4	4	4	2	2
Open Physician-Hospital Organization	10	10	10	12	12
Closed Physician-Hospital Organization	3	4	1	0	0
Management Service Organization	4	5	5	5	4
Integrated Salary Model...................	24	24	23	20	21
Equity Model	1	1	1	1	1
Foundation..............................	1	1	1	0	0
Insurance Products					
Health Maintenance Organization	4	5	3	5	4
Preferred Provider Organization..............	4	4	3	4	5
Indemnity Fee for Service	2	3	2	2	3
Managed Care Contracts					
Health Maintenance Organization	25	23	20	21	22
Preferred Provider Organization..............	26	26	22	20	17
Affiliations					
Hospitals in a System.....................	20	20	12	14	15
Hospitals in a Network	19	18	18	17	18
Hospitals in a Group Purchasing Organization..	33	33	32	31	34

States

TABLE 6

MAINE

U.S. Registered Community Hospitals
(Nonfederal, short-term general and other special hospitals)

Utilization, Personnel, Revenue and Expenses, Community Health Indicators 2007–2011

	2011	2010	2009	2008	2007
TOTAL FACILITY (Includes Hospital and Nursing Home Units)					
Utilization - Inpatient					
Beds	3,557	3,571	3,583	3,504	3,509
Admissions	144,718	145,806	150,199	148,635	151,877
Inpatient Days	814,216	808,166	822,849	845,428	839,900
Average Length of Stay	5.6	5.5	5.5	5.7	5.5
Inpatient Surgeries	39,585	42,190	43,395	44,812	43,205
Births	12,434	12,874	13,146	13,489	13,707
Utilization - Outpatient					
Emergency Outpatient Visits	765,481	790,243	792,592	780,874	718,242
Other Outpatient Visits	5,388,213	5,174,906	4,967,837	4,312,504	3,982,761
Total Outpatient Visits	6,153,694	5,965,149	5,760,429	5,093,378	4,701,003
Outpatient Surgeries	123,494	137,762	115,503	130,708	128,931
Personnel					
Full Time RNs	4,999	4,813	4,909	4,707	4,702
Full Time LPNs	204	248	262	234	222
Part Time RNs	3,429	3,658	3,232	3,384	3,571
Part Time LPNs	132	116	153	159	143
Total Full Time	23,480	22,775	23,628	23,172	22,259
Total Part Time	12,998	12,597	10,590	11,058	11,809
Revenue - Inpatient					
Gross Inpatient Revenue	$3,332,670,956	$3,184,130,431	$3,177,081,239	$3,043,869,279	$2,773,541,415
Revenue - Outpatient					
Gross Outpatient Revenue	$4,713,427,286	$4,265,543,968	$3,904,796,010	$3,446,970,975	$3,066,834,815
Revenue and Expenses - Totals					
(Includes Inpatient and Outpatient)					
Total Gross Revenue	$8,046,098,242	$7,449,674,399	$7,081,877,249	$6,490,840,254	$5,840,376,230
Deductions from Revenue	3,940,954,482	3,559,422,414	3,352,561,094	2,989,235,436	2,569,231,346
Net Patient Revenue	4,105,143,760	3,890,251,985	3,729,316,155	3,501,604,818	3,271,144,884
Other Operating Revenue	195,118,835	106,225,360	98,806,755	93,262,738	95,971,646
Other Nonoperating Revenue	40,642,341	36,578,921	24,828,817	13,684,134	74,855,385
Total Net Revenue	4,340,904,936	4,033,056,266	3,852,951,727	3,608,551,690	3,441,971,915
Total Expenses	4,160,648,639	4,238,756,324	3,725,426,220	3,516,496,379	3,265,842,064
HOSPITAL UNIT (Excludes Separate Nursing Home Units)					
Utilization - Inpatient					
Beds	3,135	3,185	3,189	3,108	3,090
Admissions	143,500	144,564	148,985	147,524	150,702
Inpatient Days	669,361	673,425	685,582	712,754	709,283
Average Length of Stay	4.7	4.7	4.6	4.8	4.7
Personnel					
Total Full Time	23,121	22,465	23,103	22,480	21,683
Total Part Time	12,682	12,310	10,299	10,596	11,516
Revenue and Expenses - Totals					
(Includes Inpatient and Outpatient)					
Total Net Revenue	$4,305,024,694	$4,000,528,653	$3,820,585,488	$3,580,910,825	$3,413,422,605
Total Expenses	4,127,705,413	4,208,922,953	3,694,875,984	3,486,675,727	3,236,639,252
COMMUNITY HEALTH INDICATORS PER 1000 POPULATION					
Total Population (in thousands)	1,328	1,313	1,318	1,320	1,317
Inpatient					
Beds	2.7	2.7	2.7	2.7	2.7
Admissions	109.0	111.1	113.9	112.6	115.3
Inpatient Days	613.0	615.5	624.2	640.6	637.6
Inpatient Surgeries	29.8	32.1	32.9	34.0	32.8
Births	9.4	9.8	10.0	10.2	10.4
Outpatient					
Emergency Outpatient Visits	576.3	601.9	601.2	591.7	545.2
Other Outpatient Visits	4,056.8	3,941.5	3,768.4	3,267.8	3,023.4
Total Outpatient Visits	4,633.1	4,543.4	4,369.6	3,859.5	3,568.6
Outpatient Surgeries	93.0	104.9	87.6	99.0	97.9
Expense per Capita (per person)	$3,132.6	$3,228.4	$2,825.9	$2,664.6	$2,479.2

States

TABLE 6

MARYLAND

U.S. Registered Community Hospitals
(Nonfederal, short-term general and other special hospitals)

Overview 2007–2011

	2011	2010	2009	2008	2007
Total Community Hospitals in Maryland.......	48	47	49	50	49
Bed Size Category					
6-24	0	0	0	0	0
25-49	3	2	2	2	3
50-99	6	6	6	6	5
100-199	14	13	13	13	13
200-299	9	11	15	15	14
300-399	8	9	6	8	8
400-499	5	4	5	3	3
500 + ...	3	2	2	3	3
Location					
Hospitals Urban...........................	42	41	43	44	40
Hospitals Rural	6	6	6	6	9
Control					
State and Local Government...............	0	0	0	0	0
Not for Profit............................	46	45	47	48	47
Investor owned	2	2	2	2	2
Physician Models					
Independent Practice Association	8	7	5	3	3
Group Practice without Walls................	2	3	3	3	4
Open Physician-Hospital Organization	5	6	4	4	5
Closed Physician-Hospital Organization	4	1	2	2	3
Management Service Organization	11	10	7	6	6
Integrated Salary Model....................	29	30	29	27	25
Equity Model	4	3	3	4	3
Foundation...............................	6	6	4	5	2
Insurance Products					
Health Maintenance Organization	16	16	14	12	10
Preferred Provider Organization..............	6	5	5	5	6
Indemnity Fee for Service	2	2	2	2	3
Managed Care Contracts					
Health Maintenance Organization	30	32	34	36	36
Preferred Provider Organization..............	29	29	32	33	34
Affiliations					
Hospitals in a System......................	32	30	33	32	30
Hospitals in a Network.....................	16	17	17	15	13
Hospitals in a Group Purchasing Organization..	43	42	42	44	45

States

TABLE 6

MARYLAND

U.S. Registered Community Hospitals
(Nonfederal, short-term general and other special hospitals)

Utilization, Personnel, Revenue and Expenses, Community Health Indicators 2007–2011

	2011	2010	2009	2008	2007
TOTAL FACILITY (Includes Hospital and Nursing Home Units)					
Utilization - Inpatient					
Beds	11,887	11,682	11,887	12,018	11,743
Admissions	683,678	707,549	715,496	711,267	698,057
Inpatient Days	3,147,613	3,160,045	3,252,959	3,298,930	3,243,033
Average Length of Stay	4.6	4.5	4.5	4.6	4.6
Inpatient Surgeries	195,892	195,577	201,144	196,641	195,341
Births	68,727	69,042	70,210	73,595	72,022
Utilization - Outpatient					
Emergency Outpatient Visits	2,469,637	2,460,678	2,429,724	2,282,417	2,285,417
Other Outpatient Visits	6,301,934	5,912,927	5,864,175	5,800,698	5,016,402
Total Outpatient Visits	8,771,571	8,373,605	8,293,899	8,083,115	7,301,819
Outpatient Surgeries	363,469	352,770	354,443	355,489	350,768
Personnel					
Full Time RNs	18,228	17,338	16,670	16,216	15,333
Full Time LPNs	453	429	472	554	592
Part Time RNs	8,618	8,448	9,291	8,857	8,651
Part Time LPNs	188	185	236	271	257
Total Full Time	72,370	68,011	66,942	66,471	63,954
Total Part Time	27,470	26,604	28,595	27,048	25,034
Revenue - Inpatient					
Gross Inpatient Revenue	$10,026,767,506	$9,444,745,728	$9,330,184,751	$8,955,048,928	$8,470,935,614
Revenue - Outpatient					
Gross Outpatient Revenue	$6,952,785,504	$5,942,458,212	$5,482,610,364	$4,920,676,123	$4,305,767,399
Revenue and Expenses - Totals					
(Includes Inpatient and Outpatient)					
Total Gross Revenue	$16,979,553,090	$15,387,203,940	$14,812,795,115	$13,875,725,051	$12,776,703,013
Deductions from Revenue	4,223,063,054	3,358,927,214	3,011,679,371	2,596,608,560	2,295,774,013
Net Patient Revenue	12,756,490,036	12,028,276,726	11,801,115,744	11,279,116,491	10,480,929,000
Other Operating Revenue	520,917,847	481,101,758	477,892,272	462,807,673	432,880,309
Other Nonoperating Revenue	289,518,580	134,850,598	-253,477,709	-106,798,785	189,549,902
Total Net Revenue	13,566,926,463	12,644,229,082	12,025,530,307	11,635,125,379	11,103,359,211
Total Expenses	12,730,746,066	12,132,497,694	11,898,147,143	11,389,973,159	10,520,002,176
HOSPITAL UNIT (Excludes Separate Nursing Home Units)					
Utilization - Inpatient					
Beds	11,310	11,113	11,318	11,272	10,986
Admissions	677,236	700,707	708,844	704,669	690,355
Inpatient Days	2,995,832	2,998,068	3,079,527	3,104,039	3,007,468
Average Length of Stay	4.4	4.3	4.3	4.4	4.4
Personnel					
Total Full Time	71,903	67,425	66,271	65,813	63,276
Total Part Time	27,194	26,242	28,247	26,682	24,731
Revenue and Expenses - Totals					
(Includes Inpatient and Outpatient)					
Total Net Revenue	$13,476,477,632	$12,543,530,248	$11,912,050,531	$11,517,892,326	$10,987,997,184
Total Expenses	12,629,434,037	12,026,632,893	11,787,009,932	11,280,192,702	10,409,152,064
COMMUNITY HEALTH INDICATORS PER 1000 POPULATION					
Total Population (in thousands)	5,828	5,737	5,699	5,659	5,634
Inpatient					
Beds	2.0	2.0	2.1	2.1	2.1
Admissions	117.3	123.3	125.5	125.7	123.9
Inpatient Days	540.1	550.8	570.7	583.0	575.6
Inpatient Surgeries	33.6	34.1	35.3	34.8	34.7
Births	11.8	12.0	12.3	13.0	12.8
Outpatient					
Emergency Outpatient Visits	423.7	428.9	426.3	403.3	405.6
Other Outpatient Visits	1,081.3	1,030.6	1,028.9	1,025.1	890.3
Total Outpatient Visits	1,505.0	1,459.5	1,455.2	1,428.5	1,296.0
Outpatient Surgeries	62.4	61.5	62.2	62.8	62.3
Expense per Capita (per person)	$2,184.3	$2,114.7	$2,087.6	$2,012.8	$1,867.2

States

TABLE 6

MASSACHUSETTS

U.S. Registered Community Hospitals
(Nonfederal, short-term general and other special hospitals)

Overview 2007–2011

	2011	2010	2009	2008	2007
Total Community Hospitals in Massachusetts..	79	79	78	75	78
Bed Size Category					
6-24	5	6	6	6	5
25-49	8	8	8	7	7
50-99	13	10	12	11	14
100-199	24	29	25	22	23
200-299	15	12	11	11	11
300-399	7	6	8	9	8
400-499	1	1	1	2	3
500 + ...	6	7	7	7	7
Location					
Hospitals Urban.........................	77	77	76	73	67
Hospitals Rural	2	2	2	2	11
Control					
State and Local Government...............	1	1	2	2	3
Not for Profit...........................	65	67	68	65	67
Investor owned	13	11	8	8	8
Physician Models					
Independent Practice Association	20	26	22	21	25
Group Practice without Walls...............	2	3	2	2	2
Open Physician-Hospital Organization	20	19	17	15	15
Closed Physician-Hospital Organization	5	7	7	6	10
Management Service Organization	11	12	9	10	10
Integrated Salary Model....................	32	35	32	30	30
Equity Model............................	2	2	4	4	4
Foundation..............................	4	5	6	4	7
Insurance Products					
Health Maintenance Organization	11	9	8	6	11
Preferred Provider Organization..............	8	5	5	3	9
Indemnity Fee for Service	5	3	2	1	6
Managed Care Contracts					
Health Maintenance Organization	56	59	52	48	53
Preferred Provider Organization..............	51	55	51	45	52
Affiliations					
Hospitals in a System......................	46	43	41	39	39
Hospitals in a Network	27	25	20	22	24
Hospitals in a Group Purchasing Organization..	55	62	55	58	60

States

TABLE 6

MASSACHUSETTS

U.S. Registered Community Hospitals
(Nonfederal, short-term general and other special hospitals)

Utilization, Personnel, Revenue and Expenses, Community Health Indicators 2007–2011

	2011	2010	2009	2008	2007
TOTAL FACILITY (Includes Hospital and Nursing Home Units)					
Utilization - Inpatient					
Beds	15,865	15,694	15,483	15,710	16,496
Admissions	838,080	823,246	819,625	808,489	842,417
Inpatient Days	4,168,038	4,164,008	4,187,076	4,190,441	4,391,528
Average Length of Stay.	5.0	5.1	5.1	5.2	5.2
Inpatient Surgeries.	205,653	209,277	213,059	216,569	229,481
Births.	72,707	72,306	73,363	77,002	77,250
Utilization - Outpatient					
Emergency Outpatient Visits	3,092,821	3,153,290	3,116,535	3,119,580	3,187,172
Other Outpatient Visits.	19,206,984	18,597,755	18,237,800	17,340,178	16,393,033
Total Outpatient Visits	22,299,805	21,751,045	21,354,335	20,459,758	19,580,205
Outpatient Surgeries	418,519	471,811	446,779	451,925	462,064
Personnel					
Full Time RNs	21,636	20,665	20,920	20,635	20,433
Full Time LPNs	827	797	825	857	935
Part Time RNs.	23,007	22,332	21,508	21,666	21,460
Part Time LPNs	686	707	745	814	905
Total Full Time	114,923	112,453	112,122	108,893	106,269
Total Part Time	60,016	67,465	64,002	64,047	64,052
Revenue - Inpatient					
Gross Inpatient Revenue.	$23,543,488,752	$22,838,917,130	$22,083,175,335	$21,768,649,075	$21,032,291,099
Revenue - Outpatient					
Gross Outpatient Revenue	$26,601,731,821	$26,120,785,816	$24,897,792,185	$22,264,309,254	$20,101,218,739
Revenue and Expenses - Totals					
(Includes Inpatient and Outpatient)					
Total Gross Revenue.	$50,145,220,573	$48,959,702,946	$46,980,967,520	$44,032,958,329	$41,133,509,838
Deductions from Revenue	29,585,822,724	28,469,292,992	27,289,257,271	25,449,205,856	23,579,085,229
Net Patient Revenue	20,559,397,849	20,490,409,954	19,691,710,249	18,583,752,473	17,554,424,609
Other Operating Revenue	3,539,011,217	3,161,300,000	3,056,380,254	2,794,111,079	2,603,492,463
Other Nonoperating Revenue	59,227,576	180,218,312	-134,832,543	-71,544,749	710,404,019
Total Net Revenue.	24,157,636,642	23,831,928,266	22,613,257,960	21,306,318,803	20,868,321,091
Total Expenses.	23,068,835,920	22,819,002,547	22,049,297,978	20,772,347,640	19,480,349,556
HOSPITAL UNIT (Excludes Separate Nursing Home Units)					
Utilization - Inpatient					
Beds	15,836	15,569	15,374	15,586	16,311
Admissions	837,325	820,368	817,254	805,960	837,201
Inpatient Days	4,158,948	4,125,806	4,153,746	4,156,756	4,324,089
Average Length of Stay.	5.0	5.0	5.1	5.2	5.2
Personnel					
Total Full Time.	114,916	112,401	112,051	108,805	106,159
Total Part Time	69,898	67,389	64,777	63,855	64,470
Revenue and Expenses - Totals					
(Includes Inpatient and Outpatient)					
Total Net Revenue.	$24,152,583,333	$23,814,188,986	$22,595,437,262	$21,279,253,160	$20,834,366,846
Total Expenses.	23,064,002,066	22,805,667,399	22,031,539,336	20,753,005,237	19,457,179,959
COMMUNITY HEALTH INDICATORS PER 1000 POPULATION					
Total Population (in thousands)	6,588	6,631	6,594	6,544	6,499
Inpatient					
Beds	2.4	2.4	2.3	2.4	2.5
Admissions	127.2	124.1	124.3	123.6	129.6
Inpatient Days	632.7	627.9	635.0	640.4	675.7
Inpatient Surgeries.	31.2	31.6	32.3	33.1	35.3
Births.	11.0	10.9	11.1	11.8	11.9
Outpatient					
Emergency Outpatient Visits	469.5	475.5	472.7	476.7	490.4
Other Outpatient Visits.	2,915.7	2,804.5	2,766.0	2,649.9	2,522.3
Total Outpatient Visits	3,385.2	3,280.1	3,238.7	3,126.7	3,012.7
Outpatient Surgeries	63.5	71.1	67.8	69.1	71.1
Expense per Capita (per person).	$3,501.9	$3,441.1	$3,344.1	$3,174.5	$2,997.3

States

TABLE **6**

MICHIGAN

U.S. Registered Community Hospitals
(Nonfederal, short-term general and other special hospitals)

Overview 2007–2011

	2011	2010	2009	2008	2007
Total Community Hospitals in Michigan.......	153	156	158	153	143
Bed Size Category					
6-24	12	12	11	9	8
25-49	45	44	42	40	30
50-99	30	35	38	39	42
100-199	19	18	21	20	18
200-299	18	18	17	15	15
300-399	14	15	14	14	13
400-499	5	3	4	6	7
500 + ...	10	11	11	10	10
Location					
Hospitals Urban...........................	95	97	99	94	85
Hospitals Rural	58	59	59	59	58
Control					
State and Local Government...............	14	14	15	15	16
Not for Profit	119	125	126	123	123
Investor owned	20	17	17	15	4
Physician Models					
Independent Practice Association	18	15	15	13	13
Group Practice without Walls...............	9	9	5	5	4
Open Physician-Hospital Organization	45	39	41	41	40
Closed Physician-Hospital Organization	15	17	13	14	17
Management Service Organization	18	19	15	12	15
Integrated Salary Model....................	83	86	88	85	81
Equity Model	1	0	0	0	2
Foundation...............................	8	8	9	7	7
Insurance Products					
Health Maintenance Organization	39	41	44	40	42
Preferred Provider Organization..............	39	41	45	42	49
Indemnity Fee for Service	14	13	17	16	15
Managed Care Contracts					
Health Maintenance Organization	106	114	120	117	110
Preferred Provider Organization..............	110	119	124	123	116
Affiliations					
Hospitals in a System.....................	96	96	96	89	79
Hospitals in a Network....................	65	70	72	71	66
Hospitals in a Group Purchasing Organization..	121	127	130	132	128

States

TABLE 6

MICHIGAN

U.S. Registered Community Hospitals
(Nonfederal, short-term general and other special hospitals)

Utilization, Personnel, Revenue and Expenses, Community Health Indicators 2007–2011

	2011	2010	2009	2008	2007
TOTAL FACILITY (Includes Hospital and Nursing Home Units)					
Utilization - Inpatient					
Beds	25,351	25,623	25,863	25,272	25,396
Admissions	1,191,236	1,207,546	1,219,893	1,221,970	1,204,263
Inpatient Days	6,173,528	6,214,588	6,332,816	6,350,025	6,275,096
Average Length of Stay	5.2	5.1	5.2	5.2	5.2
Inpatient Surgeries	342,090	355,358	359,169	370,118	347,370
Births	107,031	111,192	113,883	118,965	122,072
Utilization - Outpatient					
Emergency Outpatient Visits	4,675,863	4,550,617	4,538,588	4,428,070	4,468,623
Other Outpatient Visits	26,307,833	25,699,720	24,759,189	23,570,226	23,417,840
Total Outpatient Visits	30,983,696	30,250,337	29,297,777	27,998,296	27,886,463
Outpatient Surgeries	656,318	704,866	694,079	707,236	726,158
Personnel					
Full Time RNs	37,356	36,166	34,530	33,536	32,510
Full Time LPNs	1,255	1,377	1,591	1,770	1,772
Part Time RNs	18,736	18,803	18,878	18,989	19,064
Part Time LPNs	810	916	949	1,156	1,151
Total Full Time	140,100	144,577	141,897	139,918	139,154
Total Part Time	63,510	64,909	65,113	65,331	63,156
Revenue - Inpatient					
Gross Inpatient Revenue	$33,127,653,060	$32,307,141,469	$31,376,243,717	$29,869,338,749	$27,912,729,445
Revenue - Outpatient					
Gross Outpatient Revenue	$31,983,063,304	$30,177,541,390	$28,205,271,055	$26,487,242,565	$24,527,347,942
Revenue and Expenses - Totals					
(Includes Inpatient and Outpatient)					
Total Gross Revenue	$65,110,716,364	$62,484,682,859	$59,581,514,772	$56,356,581,314	$52,440,077,387
Deductions from Revenue	40,060,740,730	38,000,334,594	35,829,939,127	33,607,413,797	31,030,821,925
Net Patient Revenue	25,049,975,634	24,484,348,265	23,751,575,645	22,749,167,517	21,409,255,462
Other Operating Revenue	1,133,933,341	1,105,518,315	1,092,750,061	1,094,570,561	1,094,719,240
Other Nonoperating Revenue	626,908,309	555,064,648	-550,883,455	-268,360,656	919,654,570
Total Net Revenue	26,810,817,284	26,144,931,228	24,293,442,251	23,575,377,422	23,423,629,272
Total Expenses	25,328,136,970	24,872,817,460	24,366,675,781	23,392,920,738	21,728,603,773
HOSPITAL UNIT (Excludes Separate Nursing Home Units)					
Utilization - Inpatient					
Beds	24,256	24,243	24,499	23,838	23,682
Admissions	1,187,933	1,203,343	1,215,211	1,217,600	1,199,366
Inpatient Days	5,802,388	5,761,918	5,877,775	5,868,107	5,699,371
Average Length of Stay	4.9	4.8	4.8	4.8	4.8
Personnel					
Total Full Time	142,322	143,514	140,743	138,950	138,010
Total Part Time	62,695	64,019	64,048	64,550	62,250
Revenue and Expenses - Totals					
(Includes Inpatient and Outpatient)					
Total Net Revenue	$26,702,789,590	$26,022,486,264	$24,172,162,834	$23,455,611,994	$23,302,680,432
Total Expenses	25,261,120,163	24,753,757,439	24,287,466,409	23,316,518,420	21,640,135,083
COMMUNITY HEALTH INDICATORS PER 1000 POPULATION					
Total Population (in thousands)	9,876	9,931	9,970	10,002	10,051
Inpatient					
Beds	2.6	2.6	2.6	2.5	2.5
Admissions	120.6	121.6	122.4	122.2	119.8
Inpatient Days	625.1	625.8	635.2	634.8	624.3
Inpatient Surgeries	34.6	35.8	36.0	37.0	34.6
Births	10.8	11.2	11.4	11.9	12.1
Outpatient					
Emergency Outpatient Visits	473.4	458.2	455.2	442.7	444.6
Other Outpatient Visits	2,663.8	2,587.8	2,483.4	2,356.4	2,329.9
Total Outpatient Visits	3,137.2	3,046.0	2,938.7	2,799.1	2,774.5
Outpatient Surgeries	66.5	71.0	69.6	70.7	72.2
Expense per Capita (per person)	$2,564.6	$2,504.5	$2,444.1	$2,338.7	$2,161.9

States

TABLE 6

MINNESOTA

U.S. Registered Community Hospitals
(Nonfederal, short-term general and other special hospitals)

Overview 2007–2011

	2011	2010	2009	2008	2007
Total Community Hospitals in Minnesota......	132	133	132	130	131
Bed Size Category					
6-24	23	19	19	17	18
25-49	29	29	26	25	25
50-99	34	38	37	37	36
100-199	29	30	34	35	36
200-299	4	5	4	4	4
300-399	6	5	4	4	3
400-499	4	4	5	5	6
500 + ...	3	3	3	3	3
Location					
Hospitals Urban..........................	51	51	50	49	46
Hospitals Rural	81	82	82	81	85
Control					
State and Local Government...............	38	36	38	37	40
Not for Profit	93	96	93	93	91
Investor owned	1	1	1	0	0
Physician Models					
Independent Practice Association	10	18	20	20	25
Group Practice without Walls................	2	3	4	2	4
Open Physician-Hospital Organization	8	9	10	11	9
Closed Physician-Hospital Organization	3	3	3	3	5
Management Service Organization	1	1	1	2	1
Integrated Salary Model	52	49	52	47	44
Equity Model	1	0	1	1	1
Foundation...............................	2	1	1	2	1
Insurance Products					
Health Maintenance Organization	15	14	11	9	8
Preferred Provider Organization..............	16	15	13	14	12
Indemnity Fee for Service	6	6	3	4	1
Managed Care Contracts					
Health Maintenance Organization	47	46	54	51	53
Preferred Provider Organization..............	53	52	57	55	58
Affiliations					
Hospitals in a System.....................	78	77	73	69	70
Hospitals in a Network	29	27	22	24	25
Hospitals in a Group Purchasing Organization..	90	90	93	91	92

States

TABLE 6

MINNESOTA

U.S. Registered Community Hospitals
(Nonfederal, short-term general and other special hospitals)

Utilization, Personnel, Revenue and Expenses, Community Health Indicators 2007–2011

	2011	2010	2009	2008	2007
TOTAL FACILITY (Includes Hospital and Nursing Home Units)					
Utilization - Inpatient					
Beds	14,985	15,346	15,589	15,621	15,809
Admissions	596,199	591,919	623,504	640,976	635,133
Inpatient Days	3,592,914	3,596,879	3,726,573	3,873,690	3,929,879
Average Length of Stay	6.0	6.1	6.0	6.0	6.2
Inpatient Surgeries	178,802	177,600	186,593	186,775	186,218
Births	64,004	62,885	67,064	69,360	70,789
Utilization - Outpatient					
Emergency Outpatient Visits	1,928,364	1,832,257	1,873,419	1,772,982	1,727,682
Other Outpatient Visits	8,863,642	9,232,626	8,906,635	8,233,087	8,125,800
Total Outpatient Visits	10,792,006	11,064,883	10,780,054	10,006,069	9,853,482
Outpatient Surgeries	315,819	303,839	311,336	294,628	299,076
Personnel					
Full Time RNs	11,275	11,163	9,976	9,744	9,704
Full Time LPNs	1,491	1,467	1,361	1,365	1,429
Part Time RNs	20,434	21,198	22,208	22,355	20,379
Part Time LPNs	1,716	1,767	1,862	2,031	2,206
Total Full Time	58,426	56,863	51,952	51,432	50,937
Total Part Time	58,167	62,186	64,411	64,764	58,808
Revenue - Inpatient					
Gross Inpatient Revenue	$19,485,000,173	$18,410,175,974	$17,936,453,916	$17,008,252,322	$15,698,619,417
Revenue - Outpatient					
Gross Outpatient Revenue	$16,843,850,432	$15,401,043,442	$13,869,730,845	$12,005,677,625	$11,064,301,671
Revenue and Expenses - Totals					
(Includes Inpatient and Outpatient)					
Total Gross Revenue	$36,328,850,605	$33,811,219,416	$31,806,184,761	$29,013,929,947	$26,762,921,088
Deductions from Revenue	21,780,756,415	20,208,906,364	18,729,750,687	16,742,727,027	15,261,878,579
Net Patient Revenue	14,548,094,190	13,602,313,052	13,076,434,074	12,271,202,920	11,501,042,509
Other Operating Revenue	673,017,078	627,863,165	654,722,103	615,406,723	596,121,525
Other Nonoperating Revenue	265,096,109	222,331,201	35,427,093	-172,569,600	316,210,452
Total Net Revenue	15,486,207,377	14,452,507,418	13,766,583,270	12,714,040,043	12,413,374,486
Total Expenses	14,474,689,902	13,507,569,053	12,894,812,345	12,401,406,555	11,693,354,628
HOSPITAL UNIT (Excludes Separate Nursing Home Units)					
Utilization - Inpatient					
Beds	12,651	13,128	13,443	12,837	12,895
Admissions	592,372	588,566	620,484	637,183	631,175
Inpatient Days	2,813,323	2,835,161	2,987,272	2,943,441	2,927,784
Average Length of Stay	4.7	4.8	4.8	4.6	4.6
Personnel					
Total Full Time	57,414	55,794	51,026	50,078	49,542
Total Part Time	56,546	60,461	62,837	62,661	56,612
Revenue and Expenses - Totals					
(Includes Inpatient and Outpatient)					
Total Net Revenue	$15,260,507,840	$14,309,968,863	$13,627,368,247	$12,531,828,490	$12,245,206,091
Total Expenses	14,318,110,391	13,362,374,519	12,751,881,151	12,221,469,706	11,521,791,897
COMMUNITY HEALTH INDICATORS PER 1000 POPULATION					
Total Population (in thousands)	5,345	5,290	5,266	5,231	5,191
Inpatient					
Beds	2.8	2.9	3.0	3.0	3.0
Admissions	111.5	111.9	118.4	122.5	122.3
Inpatient Days	672.2	679.9	707.6	740.6	757.0
Inpatient Surgeries	33.5	33.6	35.4	35.7	35.9
Births	12.0	11.9	12.7	13.3	13.6
Outpatient					
Emergency Outpatient Visits	360.8	346.3	355.7	339.0	332.8
Other Outpatient Visits	1,658.3	1,745.2	1,691.3	1,574.0	1,565.3
Total Outpatient Visits	2,019.1	2,091.5	2,047.0	1,913.0	1,898.1
Outpatient Surgeries	59.1	57.4	59.1	56.3	57.6
Expense per Capita (per person)	$2,708.2	$2,553.2	$2,448.6	$2,370.9	$2,252.5

States

TABLE 6

MISSISSIPPI

U.S. Registered Community Hospitals
(Nonfederal, short-term general and other special hospitals)

Overview 2007–2011

	2011	2010	2009	2008	2007
Total Community Hospitals in Mississippi	99	96	97	98	95
Bed Size Category					
6-24	3	2	2	2	2
25-49	32	32	32	31	30
50-99	23	22	24	25	25
100-199	24	23	23	23	22
200-299	8	6	5	6	4
300-399	2	3	3	3	4
400-499	3	3	3	3	3
500 + ...	4	5	5	5	5
Location					
Hospitals Urban............................	29	29	28	29	19
Hospitals Rural	70	67	69	69	76
Control					
State and Local Government................	40	41	40	41	42
Not for Profit	29	27	28	30	29
Investor owned	30	28	29	27	24
Physician Models					
Independent Practice Association	5	5	5	6	6
Group Practice without Walls................	2	2	3	2	2
Open Physician-Hospital Organization	18	16	15	16	18
Closed Physician-Hospital Organization	1	2	3	5	2
Management Service Organization	11	8	8	7	7
Integrated Salary Model....................	27	22	22	22	16
Equity Model	1	1	2	1	0
Foundation...............................	10	7	8	6	7
Insurance Products					
Health Maintenance Organization	7	7	6	8	7
Preferred Provider Organization..............	37	35	36	38	40
Indemnity Fee for Service	9	9	10	12	9
Managed Care Contracts					
Health Maintenance Organization	18	14	15	14	8
Preferred Provider Organization..............	38	33	30	37	26
Affiliations					
Hospitals in a System......................	48	45	43	42	39
Hospitals in a Network.....................	28	29	30	30	31
Hospitals in a Group Purchasing Organization..	0	0	0	1	10

States

TABLE 6

MISSISSIPPI

U.S. Registered Community Hospitals
(Nonfederal, short-term general and other special hospitals)

Utilization, Personnel, Revenue and Expenses, Community Health Indicators 2007–2011

	2011	2010	2009	2008	2007
TOTAL FACILITY (Includes Hospital and Nursing Home Units)					
Utilization - Inpatient					
Beds	12,867	12,925	12,879	13,094	12,712
Admissions	393,566	402,947	412,912	430,680	417,929
Inpatient Days	2,513,957	2,557,704	2,600,075	2,807,964	2,675,307
Average Length of Stay	6.4	6.3	6.3	6.5	6.4
Inpatient Surgeries	102,170	107,497	114,231	113,847	115,564
Births	38,046	39,044	41,266	43,775	44,650
Utilization - Outpatient					
Emergency Outpatient Visits	1,761,207	1,705,959	1,720,780	1,694,645	1,736,141
Other Outpatient Visits	3,015,093	2,880,177	2,964,042	3,320,962	2,688,325
Total Outpatient Visits	4,776,300	4,586,136	4,684,822	5,015,607	4,424,466
Outpatient Surgeries	169,856	174,969	172,105	173,799	176,076
Personnel					
Full Time RNs	12,842	12,176	11,847	11,143	10,987
Full Time LPNs	1,475	1,570	1,651	1,726	1,799
Part Time RNs	3,346	3,489	3,543	3,757	3,670
Part Time LPNs	290	344	423	487	502
Total Full Time	48,461	46,910	46,451	46,424	45,895
Total Part Time	10,875	11,258	11,656	12,158	11,902
Revenue - Inpatient					
Gross Inpatient Revenue	$10,947,704,087	$10,614,195,531	$11,045,652,557	$11,036,455,713	$9,436,579,499
Revenue - Outpatient					
Gross Outpatient Revenue	$9,159,843,292	$8,108,639,171	$8,571,533,053	$7,520,162,560	$6,352,192,000
Revenue and Expenses - Totals					
(Includes Inpatient and Outpatient)					
Total Gross Revenue	$20,107,547,379	$18,722,834,702	$19,617,185,610	$18,556,618,273	$15,788,771,499
Deductions from Revenue	14,441,074,648	13,026,769,588	13,518,559,893	12,632,981,913	10,466,830,159
Net Patient Revenue	5,666,472,731	5,696,065,114	6,098,625,717	5,923,636,360	5,321,941,340
Other Operating Revenue	284,527,695	332,166,296	279,046,585	319,430,782	335,839,429
Other Nonoperating Revenue	62,903,487	101,837,598	76,839,630	36,224,687	126,182,224
Total Net Revenue	6,013,903,913	6,130,069,008	6,454,511,932	6,279,291,829	5,783,962,993
Total Expenses	5,804,948,349	5,635,912,981	6,071,620,664	5,817,368,267	5,702,007,832
HOSPITAL UNIT (Excludes Separate Nursing Home Units)					
Utilization - Inpatient					
Beds	11,142	11,260	11,196	11,401	11,013
Admissions	392,650	402,148	412,159	429,960	417,221
Inpatient Days	1,948,010	2,004,002	2,048,068	2,233,999	2,088,193
Average Length of Stay	5.0	5.0	5.0	5.2	5.0
Personnel					
Total Full Time	47,168	45,658	45,069	45,125	44,537
Total Part Time	10,502	10,899	11,336	11,832	11,547
Revenue and Expenses - Totals					
(Includes Inpatient and Outpatient)					
Total Net Revenue	$5,924,570,004	$6,056,564,286	$6,377,178,448	$6,211,348,322	$5,699,630,012
Total Expenses	5,744,275,169	5,576,805,214	6,011,102,605	5,767,228,058	5,640,280,980
COMMUNITY HEALTH INDICATORS PER 1000 POPULATION					
Total Population (in thousands)	2,979	2,960	2,952	2,940	2,922
Inpatient					
Beds	4.3	4.4	4.4	4.5	4.4
Admissions	132.1	136.1	139.9	146.5	143.0
Inpatient Days	844.0	864.0	880.8	955.0	915.7
Inpatient Surgeries	34.3	36.3	38.7	38.7	39.6
Births	12.8	13.2	14.0	14.9	15.3
Outpatient					
Emergency Outpatient Visits	591.3	576.2	582.9	576.4	594.2
Other Outpatient Visits	1,012.3	972.9	1,004.1	1,129.5	920.1
Total Outpatient Visits	1,603.6	1,549.1	1,587.0	1,705.9	1,514.3
Outpatient Surgeries	57.0	59.1	58.3	59.1	60.3
Expense per Capita (per person)	$1,948.9	$1,903.7	$2,056.8	$1,978.6	$1,951.6

States

TABLE **6**

MISSOURI

U.S. Registered Community Hospitals
(Nonfederal, short-term general and other special hospitals)

Overview 2007–2011

	2011	2010	2009	2008	2007
Total Community Hospitals in Missouri	120	122	125	123	117
Bed Size Category					
6-24	8	7	8	8	5
25-49	40	41	39	38	36
50-99	19	21	22	19	17
100-199	21	22	24	26	27
200-299	12	11	12	12	15
300-399	9	11	9	9	7
400-499	5	3	5	5	4
500 + ...	6	6	6	6	6
Location					
Hospitals Urban...........................	67	69	72	70	58
Hospitals Rural	53	53	53	53	59
Control					
State and Local Government...............	35	35	35	35	35
Not for Profit	63	64	64	62	61
Investor owned	22	23	26	26	21
Physician Models					
Independent Practice Association	6	8	8	10	13
Group Practice without Walls...............	0	0	0	0	0
Open Physician-Hospital Organization	15	14	15	14	14
Closed Physician-Hospital Organization	7	8	8	8	7
Management Service Organization	0	1	1	2	4
Integrated Salary Model....................	66	67	69	66	65
Equity Model	1	1	1	1	0
Foundation...............................	2	4	2	3	3
Insurance Products					
Health Maintenance Organization	16	16	15	16	16
Preferred Provider Organization..............	14	14	13	14	14
Indemnity Fee for Service	5	4	4	5	5
Managed Care Contracts					
Health Maintenance Organization	93	95	99	97	99
Preferred Provider Organization..............	101	103	107	106	107
Affiliations					
Hospitals in a System.....................	70	72	73	72	66
Hospitals in a Network....................	36	37	38	38	40
Hospitals in a Group Purchasing Organization..	116	114	115	115	114

TABLE **6**

MISSOURI

U.S. Registered Community Hospitals
(Nonfederal, short-term general and other special hospitals)

Utilization, Personnel, Revenue and Expenses, Community Health Indicators 2007–2011

	2011	2010	2009	2008	2007
TOTAL FACILITY (Includes Hospital and Nursing Home Units)					
Utilization - Inpatient					
Beds	18,749	18,745	19,101	18,968	18,454
Admissions	815,640	821,322	825,090	841,118	833,114
Inpatient Days	4,172,415	4,196,865	4,256,929	4,396,779	4,310,130
Average Length of Stay.	5.1	5.1	5.2	5.2	5.2
Inpatient Surgeries	210,625	213,685	219,835	222,378	220,098
Births.	73,779	74,903	77,799	80,282	79,940
Utilization - Outpatient					
Emergency Outpatient Visits	2,952,675	2,871,884	2,894,040	2,860,410	2,677,716
Other Outpatient Visits.	17,251,450	16,929,041	16,319,944	15,968,175	14,297,938
Total Outpatient Visits	20,204,125	19,800,925	19,213,984	18,828,585	16,975,654
Outpatient Surgeries	370,574	374,120	382,232	377,592	378,013
Personnel					
Full Time RNs	27,023	26,334	25,768	24,084	23,139
Full Time LPNs	2,407	2,398	2,508	2,711	2,719
Part Time RNs.	11,436	11,453	12,399	12,367	11,264
Part Time LPNs	654	719	826	837	922
Total Full Time	101,030	100,265	98,635	96,722	93,628
Total Part Time	35,841	36,219	37,004	36,336	34,771
Revenue - Inpatient					
Gross Inpatient Revenue.	$25,816,258,642	$24,578,843,364	$23,360,022,165	$22,713,673,771	$20,986,021,738
Revenue - Outpatient					
Gross Outpatient Revenue	$23,228,488,113	$20,597,557,308	$19,480,819,585	$17,415,385,697	$15,502,302,919
Revenue and Expenses - Totals					
(Includes Inpatient and Outpatient)					
Total Gross Revenue.	$49,044,746,755	$45,176,400,672	$42,840,841,750	$40,129,059,468	$36,488,324,657
Deductions from Revenue	32,241,337,674	28,944,744,487	27,014,970,190	24,102,018,264	22,479,673,810
Net Patient Revenue	16,803,409,081	16,231,656,185	15,825,871,560	16,027,041,204	14,008,650,847
Other Operating Revenue	999,246,088	1,085,534,981	875,169,162	985,155,809	969,705,284
Other Nonoperating Revenue	214,485,919	529,984,875	522,159,166	-360,477,386	443,559,855
Total Net Revenue	18,017,141,088	17,847,176,041	17,223,199,888	16,651,719,627	15,421,915,986
Total Expenses.	17,172,219,045	16,521,828,978	16,235,293,324	15,824,162,545	14,391,329,687
HOSPITAL UNIT (Excludes Separate Nursing Home Units)					
Utilization - Inpatient					
Beds	17,772	17,754	18,188	17,970	17,293
Admissions	809,450	816,764	818,739	834,653	824,907
Inpatient Days	3,892,314	3,946,461	3,999,089	4,109,631	3,971,643
Average Length of Stay.	4.8	4.8	4.9	4.9	4.8
Personnel					
Total Full Time.	100,248	99,631	97,598	96,023	92,704
Total Part Time	35,394	35,866	36,601	35,963	34,258
Revenue and Expenses - Totals					
(Includes Inpatient and Outpatient)					
Total Net Revenue.	$17,938,622,213	$17,771,368,041	$17,122,754,301	$16,539,007,342	$15,292,838,772
Total Expenses.	17,109,487,583	16,444,776,729	16,149,196,359	15,727,570,466	14,270,140,082
COMMUNITY HEALTH INDICATORS PER 1000 POPULATION					
Total Population (in thousands)	6,011	6,012	5,988	5,956	5,910
Inpatient					
Beds	3.1	3.1	3.2	3.2	3.1
Admissions	135.7	136.6	137.8	141.2	141.0
Inpatient Days	694.2	698.1	711.0	738.2	729.3
Inpatient Surgeries	35.0	35.5	36.7	37.3	37.2
Births.	12.3	12.5	13.0	13.5	13.5
Outpatient					
Emergency Outpatient Visits	491.2	477.7	483.3	480.2	453.1
Other Outpatient Visits.	2,870.1	2,816.0	2,725.6	2,680.9	2,419.4
Total Outpatient Visits	3,361.4	3,293.7	3,209.0	3,161.1	2,872.4
Outpatient Surgeries	61.7	62.2	63.8	63.4	64.0
Expense per Capita (per person).	$2,856.9	$2,748.3	$2,711.5	$2,656.7	$2,435.2

States

TABLE 6

MONTANA

U.S. Registered Community Hospitals
(Nonfederal, short-term general and other special hospitals)

Overview 2007–2011

	2011	2010	2009	2008	2007
Total Community Hospitals in Montana	**48**	**48**	**48**	**48**	**52**
Bed Size Category					
6-24	11	10	8	9	9
25-49	12	15	16	14	15
50-99	14	12	13	15	17
100-199	8	8	8	7	8
200-299	1	1	1	1	1
300-399	1	1	1	1	1
400-499	1	1	0	1	1
500 + ...	0	0	1	0	0
Location					
Hospitals Urban...........................	6	6	6	5	3
Hospitals Rural	42	42	42	43	49
Control					
State and Local Government................	10	8	7	8	9
Not for Profit	37	39	40	39	42
Investor owned	1	1	1	1	1
Physician Models					
Independent Practice Association	5	7	9	9	10
Group Practice without Walls...............	4	3	3	3	3
Open Physician-Hospital Organization	4	5	5	6	7
Closed Physician-Hospital Organization	1	1	1	2	2
Management Service Organization	5	6	7	6	6
Integrated Salary Model....................	29	27	28	29	30
Equity Model	1	2	2	2	1
Foundation...............................	6	4	3	5	5
Insurance Products					
Health Maintenance Organization	4	4	4	4	5
Preferred Provider Organization..............	7	8	8	9	9
Indemnity Fee for Service	5	6	6	4	6
Managed Care Contracts					
Health Maintenance Organization	9	11	11	13	14
Preferred Provider Organization..............	25	22	25	27	31
Affiliations					
Hospitals in a System.....................	12	12	12	11	11
Hospitals in a Network....................	23	22	22	24	24
Hospitals in a Group Purchasing Organization..	41	39	44	47	48

TABLE 6

MONTANA

U.S. Registered Community Hospitals
(Nonfederal, short-term general and other special hospitals)

Utilization, Personnel, Revenue and Expenses, Community Health Indicators 2007–2011

	2011	2010	2009	2008	2007
TOTAL FACILITY (Includes Hospital and Nursing Home Units)					
Utilization - Inpatient					
Beds	3,626	3,692	3,820	3,765	4,002
Admissions	94,966	97,453	101,327	103,840	106,860
Inpatient Days	828,778	848,356	869,897	903,981	957,251
Average Length of Stay	8.7	8.7	8.6	8.7	9.0
Inpatient Surgeries	28,395	29,136	30,167	30,697	32,021
Births	10,254	10,217	10,432	10,708	10,714
Utilization - Outpatient					
Emergency Outpatient Visits	369,610	357,543	357,066	346,670	354,943
Other Outpatient Visits	3,173,110	3,146,841	2,973,218	2,807,604	2,680,087
Total Outpatient Visits	3,542,720	3,504,384	3,330,284	3,154,274	3,035,030
Outpatient Surgeries	47,582	48,043	45,364	45,012	43,987
Personnel					
Full Time RNs	2,860	2,946	2,843	2,496	2,654
Full Time LPNs	454	478	508	497	530
Part Time RNs	2,088	1,930	2,067	1,936	1,847
Part Time LPNs	256	257	283	328	330
Total Full Time	14,304	14,816	14,621	13,974	14,098
Total Part Time	7,502	7,138	7,470	7,358	7,091
Revenue - Inpatient					
Gross Inpatient Revenue	$2,102,143,134	$2,049,917,318	$2,001,422,796	$1,868,192,302	$1,749,392,120
Revenue - Outpatient					
Gross Outpatient Revenue	$2,622,907,633	$2,452,151,901	$2,187,645,447	$1,879,526,779	$1,692,878,144
Revenue and Expenses - Totals					
(Includes Inpatient and Outpatient)					
Total Gross Revenue	$4,725,050,767	$4,502,069,219	$4,189,068,243	$3,747,719,081	$3,442,270,264
Deductions from Revenue	2,261,961,105	2,145,913,313	1,939,387,748	1,670,030,190	1,497,426,748
Net Patient Revenue	2,463,089,662	2,356,155,906	2,249,680,495	2,077,688,891	1,944,843,516
Other Operating Revenue	98,796,127	93,578,995	90,423,031	80,597,184	82,175,840
Other Nonoperating Revenue	56,310,483	64,235,515	-5,428,277	16,554,468	73,552,521
Total Net Revenue	2,618,196,272	2,513,970,416	2,334,675,249	2,174,840,543	2,100,571,877
Total Expenses	2,485,931,042	2,379,151,295	2,263,313,965	2,077,753,777	1,933,325,734
HOSPITAL UNIT (Excludes Separate Nursing Home Units)					
Utilization - Inpatient					
Beds	2,347	2,398	2,421	2,292	2,426
Admissions	92,852	95,238	99,163	101,233	103,637
Inpatient Days	430,418	442,106	435,087	440,713	465,512
Average Length of Stay	4.6	4.6	4.4	4.4	4.5
Personnel					
Total Full Time	13,628	14,038	13,813	12,999	13,047
Total Part Time	7,007	6,602	6,946	6,770	6,498
Revenue and Expenses - Totals					
(Includes Inpatient and Outpatient)					
Total Net Revenue	$2,538,770,978	$2,441,209,709	$2,259,366,824	$2,092,696,080	$2,015,682,825
Total Expenses	2,403,184,670	2,306,425,879	2,191,842,514	2,002,337,963	1,859,283,771
COMMUNITY HEALTH INDICATORS PER 1000 POPULATION					
Total Population (in thousands)	998	980	975	968	957
Inpatient					
Beds	3.6	3.8	3.9	3.9	4.2
Admissions	95.1	99.4	103.9	107.3	111.6
Inpatient Days	830.3	865.5	892.2	933.8	1,000.0
Inpatient Surgeries	28.4	29.7	30.9	31.7	33.5
Births	10.3	10.4	10.7	11.1	11.2
Outpatient					
Emergency Outpatient Visits	370.3	364.8	366.2	358.1	370.8
Other Outpatient Visits	3,178.8	3,210.6	3,049.5	2,900.3	2,799.9
Total Outpatient Visits	3,549.1	3,575.3	3,415.7	3,258.4	3,170.7
Outpatient Surgeries	47.7	49.0	46.5	46.5	46.0
Expense per Capita (per person)	$2,490.4	$2,427.3	$2,321.4	$2,146.4	$2,019.7

States

TABLE 6

NEBRASKA

U.S. Registered Community Hospitals
(Nonfederal, short-term general and other special hospitals)

Overview 2007–2011

	2011	2010	2009	2008	2007
Total Community Hospitals in Nebraska.......	**86**	**88**	**87**	**86**	**85**
Bed Size Category					
6-24	24	23	22	21	18
25-49	25	23	22	23	26
50-99	19	23	22	23	22
100-199	8	9	10	7	8
200-299	6	4	6	7	4
300-399	2	4	4	4	5
400-499	1	1	0	0	1
500 + ...	1	1	1	1	1
Location					
Hospitals Urban..........................	16	17	16	16	14
Hospitals Rural	70	71	71	70	71
Control					
State and Local Government...............	37	39	40	38	40
Not for Profit	46	46	45	46	43
Investor owned	3	3	2	2	2
Physician Models					
Independent Practice Association	6	6	6	8	6
Group Practice without Walls...............	0	1	2	2	3
Open Physician-Hospital Organization	10	12	13	13	13
Closed Physician-Hospital Organization	1	0	1	0	0
Management Service Organization	2	3	2	3	3
Integrated Salary Model....................	26	27	33	32	31
Equity Model	0	0	0	0	0
Foundation...............................	1	0	1	2	2
Insurance Products					
Health Maintenance Organization	3	3	2	3	4
Preferred Provider Organization..............	12	11	13	14	19
Indemnity Fee for Service	4	3	3	4	4
Managed Care Contracts					
Health Maintenance Organization	15	16	17	19	21
Preferred Provider Organization..............	43	43	50	53	53
Affiliations					
Hospitals in a System......................	29	26	28	29	28
Hospitals in a Network	32	28	33	36	38
Hospitals in a Group Purchasing Organization..	44	47	54	56	57

States

TABLE 6

NEBRASKA

U.S. Registered Community Hospitals
(Nonfederal, short-term general and other special hospitals)

Utilization, Personnel, Revenue and Expenses, Community Health Indicators 2007–2011

	2011	2010	2009	2008	2007
TOTAL FACILITY (Includes Hospital and Nursing Home Units)					
Utilization - Inpatient					
Beds	6,592	7,246	7,442	7,264	7,468
Admissions	203,394	208,949	209,750	214,808	214,628
Inpatient Days	1,313,451	1,461,558	1,552,206	1,562,960	1,619,546
Average Length of Stay.	6.5	7.0	7.4	7.3	7.5
Inpatient Surgeries.	65,592	65,316	67,275	71,248	68,537
Births.	25,778	24,575	26,224	26,802	26,659
Utilization - Outpatient					
Emergency Outpatient Visits	716,718	700,818	688,519	639,756	630,134
Other Outpatient Visits.	4,239,738	3,870,823	3,969,589	3,987,333	3,569,670
Total Outpatient Visits	4,956,456	4,571,641	4,658,108	4,627,089	4,199,804
Outpatient Surgeries	118,596	112,213	120,310	130,440	133,820
Personnel					
Full Time RNs	7,863	8,038	7,653	7,104	6,962
Full Time LPNs	687	856	876	913	906
Part Time RNs.	4,182	4,286	4,111	4,477	4,018
Part Time LPNs	393	489	512	530	550
Total Full Time	27,779	29,024	28,451	27,407	27,636
Total Part Time	13,543	14,502	13,922	15,212	13,899
Revenue - Inpatient					
Gross Inpatient Revenue.	$6,329,607,253	$6,579,976,131	$6,240,788,042	$5,994,545,329	$5,595,875,292
Revenue - Outpatient					
Gross Outpatient Revenue	$5,571,277,484	$5,335,861,059	$4,923,545,533	$4,349,628,655	$3,960,071,473
Revenue and Expenses - Totals					
(Includes Inpatient and Outpatient)					
Total Gross Revenue.	$11,900,884,737	$11,915,837,190	$11,164,333,575	$10,344,173,984	$9,555,946,765
Deductions from Revenue	7,094,550,376	7,060,882,109	6,451,826,044	5,885,164,745	5,361,837,259
Net Patient Revenue.	4,806,334,361	4,854,955,081	4,712,507,531	4,459,009,239	4,194,109,506
Other Operating Revenue	243,522,454	211,231,348	209,020,415	210,752,208	186,903,385
Other Nonoperating Revenue	203,146,705	132,518,504	-28,338,616	-24,908,037	165,706,153
Total Net Revenue.	5,253,003,520	5,198,704,933	4,893,189,330	4,644,853,410	4,546,719,044
Total Expenses.	4,659,397,050	4,710,906,183	4,471,302,656	4,380,337,731	4,013,619,694
HOSPITAL UNIT (Excludes Separate Nursing Home Units)					
Utilization - Inpatient					
Beds	5,817	6,168	6,102	5,793	5,929
Admissions	201,622	206,235	206,131	211,021	211,109
Inpatient Days	1,082,517	1,128,398	1,144,790	1,117,877	1,157,386
Average Length of Stay.	5.4	5.5	5.6	5.3	5.5
Personnel					
Total Full Time.	27,230	28,177	27,569	26,467	26,664
Total Part Time	13,178	13,927	13,239	14,524	13,150
Revenue and Expenses - Totals					
(Includes Inpatient and Outpatient)					
Total Net Revenue.	$5,207,994,214	$5,123,202,118	$4,790,650,335	$4,527,469,170	$4,444,144,173
Total Expenses.	4,613,479,154	4,634,581,746	4,379,557,407	4,274,392,152	3,932,011,095
COMMUNITY HEALTH INDICATORS PER 1000 POPULATION					
Total Population (in thousands)	1,843	1,811	1,797	1,782	1,770
Inpatient					
Beds	3.6	4.0	4.1	4.1	4.2
Admissions	110.4	115.4	116.7	120.5	121.3
Inpatient Days	712.8	807.0	864.0	877.1	915.0
Inpatient Surgeries.	35.6	36.1	37.4	40.0	38.7
Births.	14.0	13.6	14.6	15.0	15.1
Outpatient					
Emergency Outpatient Visits	389.0	387.0	383.2	359.0	356.0
Other Outpatient Visits.	2,300.9	2,137.3	2,209.5	2,237.6	2,016.9
Total Outpatient Visits	2,689.9	2,524.3	2,592.7	2,596.6	2,372.9
Outpatient Surgeries	64.4	62.0	67.0	73.2	75.6
Expense per Capita (per person).	$2,528.7	$2,601.2	$2,488.7	$2,458.2	$2,267.7

States

TABLE **6**

NEVADA

U.S. Registered Community Hospitals
(Nonfederal, short-term general and other special hospitals)

Overview 2007–2011

	2011	2010	2009	2008	2007
Total Community Hospitals in Nevada	38	36	35	35	33
Bed Size Category					
6-24	4	4	4	4	3
25-49	6	6	6	6	6
50-99	12	12	11	11	10
100-199	7	6	6	6	6
200-299	4	3	3	3	3
300-399	2	2	2	2	2
400-499	0	0	0	0	0
500 + ...	3	3	3	3	3
Location					
Hospitals Urban............................	27	25	24	24	23
Hospitals Rural	11	11	11	11	10
Control					
State and Local Government................	6	6	6	6	6
Not for Profit	13	13	13	13	13
Investor owned	19	17	16	16	14
Physician Models					
Independent Practice Association	4	2	3	3	3
Group Practice without Walls................	0	0	0	0	0
Open Physician-Hospital Organization	1	1	1	0	1
Closed Physician-Hospital Organization	2	2	2	1	1
Management Service Organization	2	2	4	3	2
Integrated Salary Model....................	7	2	3	4	3
Equity Model	1	0	0	0	0
Foundation...............................	0	0	0	0	0
Insurance Products					
Health Maintenance Organization	7	7	5	4	4
Preferred Provider Organization..............	7	7	6	5	4
Indemnity Fee for Service	3	4	3	3	3
Managed Care Contracts					
Health Maintenance Organization	20	13	12	11	13
Preferred Provider Organization..............	21	15	15	14	13
Affiliations					
Hospitals in a System......................	27	25	24	24	22
Hospitals in a Network	6	5	5	5	6
Hospitals in a Group Purchasing Organization..	22	16	18	18	17

TABLE 6

NEVADA

U.S. Registered Community Hospitals
(Nonfederal, short-term general and other special hospitals)

Utilization, Personnel, Revenue and Expenses, Community Health Indicators 2007–2011

	2011	2010	2009	2008	2007
TOTAL FACILITY (Includes Hospital and Nursing Home Units)					
Utilization - Inpatient					
Beds	5,507	5,192	5,119	5,144	5,051
Admissions	249,805	241,296	245,866	247,232	244,187
Inpatient Days	1,359,447	1,296,929	1,311,084	1,300,514	1,275,671
Average Length of Stay	5.4	5.4	5.3	5.3	5.2
Inpatient Surgeries	63,902	69,928	72,737	68,365	71,526
Births	21,822	24,844	30,373	29,248	30,441
Utilization - Outpatient					
Emergency Outpatient Visits	820,812	820,675	820,980	780,500	751,845
Other Outpatient Visits	1,859,971	1,849,263	1,988,669	2,135,809	1,903,945
Total Outpatient Visits	2,680,783	2,669,938	2,809,649	2,916,309	2,655,790
Outpatient Surgeries	98,155	103,406	104,340	100,526	90,820
Personnel					
Full Time RNs	6,582	6,436	6,357	6,457	6,112
Full Time LPNs	351	406	404	452	445
Part Time RNs	2,011	1,439	1,340	1,521	1,617
Part Time LPNs	85	68	74	83	88
Total Full Time	20,545	20,948	20,386	21,672	20,043
Total Part Time	5,300	3,779	3,630	3,766	4,061
Revenue - Inpatient					
Gross Inpatient Revenue	$11,616,603,674	$10,608,864,288	$10,439,117,032	$10,133,945,714	$9,157,234,146
Revenue - Outpatient					
Gross Outpatient Revenue	$6,466,989,068	$5,826,489,194	$5,312,533,278	$4,647,890,751	$3,939,962,372
Revenue and Expenses - Totals					
(Includes Inpatient and Outpatient)					
Total Gross Revenue	$18,083,592,742	$16,435,353,482	$15,751,650,310	$14,781,836,465	$13,097,196,518
Deductions from Revenue	14,019,540,936	12,559,876,799	11,866,367,378	10,926,597,214	9,514,175,359
Net Patient Revenue	4,064,051,806	3,875,476,683	3,885,282,932	3,855,239,251	3,583,021,159
Other Operating Revenue	107,770,969	97,417,940	98,119,383	94,718,637	93,358,804
Other Nonoperating Revenue	75,853,300	93,314,155	73,065,405	49,631,516	86,652,018
Total Net Revenue	4,247,676,075	4,066,208,778	4,056,467,720	3,999,589,404	3,763,031,981
Total Expenses	4,070,512,098	3,940,182,337	3,957,622,058	3,912,575,991	3,536,781,905
HOSPITAL UNIT (Excludes Separate Nursing Home Units)					
Utilization - Inpatient					
Beds	5,443	5,174	5,076	5,119	5,026
Admissions	249,708	241,287	245,844	247,208	244,175
Inpatient Days	1,341,532	1,291,351	1,298,643	1,293,475	1,267,602
Average Length of Stay	5.4	5.4	5.3	5.2	5.2
Personnel					
Total Full Time	20,517	20,939	20,368	21,651	20,025
Total Part Time	5,312	3,779	3,630	3,763	4,056
Revenue and Expenses - Totals					
(Includes Inpatient and Outpatient)					
Total Net Revenue	$4,243,197,676	$4,065,636,650	$4,053,142,416	$3,997,480,744	$3,760,531,168
Total Expenses	4,067,942,062	3,939,711,041	3,956,074,612	3,911,278,159	3,535,439,430
COMMUNITY HEALTH INDICATORS PER 1000 POPULATION					
Total Population (in thousands)	2,723	2,655	2,643	2,616	2,568
Inpatient					
Beds	2.0	2.0	1.9	2.0	2.0
Admissions	91.7	90.9	93.0	94.5	95.1
Inpatient Days	499.2	488.5	496.0	497.2	496.8
Inpatient Surgeries	23.5	26.3	27.5	26.1	27.9
Births	8.0	9.4	11.5	11.2	11.9
Outpatient					
Emergency Outpatient Visits	301.4	309.1	310.6	298.4	292.8
Other Outpatient Visits	683.0	696.6	752.4	816.5	741.5
Total Outpatient Visits	984.4	1,005.7	1,063.0	1,114.9	1,034.3
Outpatient Surgeries	36.0	39.0	39.5	38.4	35.4
Expense per Capita (per person)	$1,494.7	$1,484.2	$1,497.3	$1,495.8	$1,377.4

States

TABLE 6

NEW HAMPSHIRE

U.S. Registered Community Hospitals
(Nonfederal, short-term general and other special hospitals)

Overview 2007–2011

	2011	2010	2009	2008	2007
Total Community Hospitals in New Hampshire	28	28	28	28	28
Bed Size Category					
6-24	1	1	1	1	1
25-49	10	9	9	8	8
50-99	6	7	7	9	9
100-199	7	7	7	6	6
200-299	3	3	3	3	3
300-399	1	1	1	1	1
400-499	0	0	0	0	0
500 +	0	0	0	0	0
Location					
Hospitals Urban	11	11	11	11	10
Hospitals Rural	17	17	17	17	18
Control					
State and Local Government	0	0	0	0	0
Not for Profit	24	24	24	24	24
Investor owned	4	4	4	4	4
Physician Models					
Independent Practice Association	2	2	2	2	3
Group Practice without Walls	2	2	2	2	2
Open Physician-Hospital Organization	5	9	10	10	10
Closed Physician-Hospital Organization	0	0	0	1	2
Management Service Organization	0	0	1	0	2
Integrated Salary Model	20	17	16	16	16
Equity Model	0	0	0	0	0
Foundation	0	0	0	1	1
Insurance Products					
Health Maintenance Organization	0	0	0	0	0
Preferred Provider Organization	0	0	0	1	0
Indemnity Fee for Service	0	0	0	0	0
Managed Care Contracts					
Health Maintenance Organization	20	23	26	25	25
Preferred Provider Organization	19	21	25	24	24
Affiliations					
Hospitals in a System	6	6	6	6	6
Hospitals in a Network	11	10	11	11	12
Hospitals in a Group Purchasing Organization	25	26	27	26	27

States

TABLE 6

NEW HAMPSHIRE

U.S. Registered Community Hospitals
(Nonfederal, short-term general and other special hospitals)

Utilization, Personnel, Revenue and Expenses, Community Health Indicators 2007–2011

	2011	2010	2009	2008	2007
TOTAL FACILITY (Includes Hospital and Nursing Home Units)					
Utilization - Inpatient					
Beds	2,840	2,851	2,863	2,858	2,841
Admissions	122,341	119,971	122,959	124,184	121,747
Inpatient Days	634,954	624,399	655,015	664,659	659,511
Average Length of Stay	5.2	5.2	5.3	5.4	5.4
Inpatient Surgeries	34,281	33,622	33,041	35,022	34,217
Births	12,649	12,630	13,261	13,636	13,995
Utilization - Outpatient					
Emergency Outpatient Visits	677,358	667,605	627,769	623,814	619,714
Other Outpatient Visits	4,318,549	4,109,910	4,097,077	3,844,709	3,479,378
Total Outpatient Visits	4,995,907	4,777,515	4,724,846	4,468,523	4,099,092
Outpatient Surgeries	91,348	92,450	91,495	91,320	85,548
Personnel					
Full Time RNs	4,282	4,298	4,191	4,181	4,070
Full Time LPNs	276	278	250	223	199
Part Time RNs	3,128	3,008	3,017	3,102	2,604
Part Time LPNs	126	139	176	156	151
Total Full Time	21,846	22,066	21,046	20,853	19,705
Total Part Time	10,000	10,151	10,294	10,452	9,465
Revenue - Inpatient					
Gross Inpatient Revenue	$4,150,081,268	$3,890,334,236	$3,730,906,874	$3,458,246,012	$3,409,556,142
Revenue - Outpatient					
Gross Outpatient Revenue	$5,916,747,273	$5,494,839,267	$4,960,506,458	$4,446,890,786	$3,772,204,893
Revenue and Expenses - Totals					
(Includes Inpatient and Outpatient)					
Total Gross Revenue	$10,066,828,541	$9,385,173,503	$8,691,413,332	$7,905,136,798	$7,181,761,035
Deductions from Revenue	5,928,255,856	5,410,431,600	4,934,553,834	4,413,714,285	3,943,723,858
Net Patient Revenue	4,138,572,685	3,974,741,903	3,756,859,498	3,491,422,513	3,238,037,177
Other Operating Revenue	129,629,985	106,982,372	93,662,673	87,274,249	83,643,504
Other Nonoperating Revenue	296,520	52,157,491	-52,943,319	-67,525,945	99,299,362
Total Net Revenue	4,268,499,190	4,133,881,766	3,797,578,852	3,511,170,817	3,420,980,043
Total Expenses	3,948,270,249	3,781,620,257	3,539,365,267	3,330,628,143	3,070,122,158
HOSPITAL UNIT (Excludes Separate Nursing Home Units)					
Utilization - Inpatient					
Beds	2,710	2,721	2,683	2,678	2,661
Admissions	121,996	119,391	122,334	123,622	121,196
Inpatient Days	593,304	577,175	602,460	605,089	600,484
Average Length of Stay	4.9	4.8	4.9	4.9	5.0
Personnel					
Total Full Time	21,766	22,003	20,963	20,767	19,612
Total Part Time	9,960	10,110	10,246	10,380	9,388
Revenue and Expenses - Totals					
(Includes Inpatient and Outpatient)					
Total Net Revenue	$4,256,119,678	$4,120,469,030	$3,781,637,703	$3,496,911,705	$3,407,280,709
Total Expenses	3,938,257,684	3,770,403,066	3,528,118,615	3,319,098,045	3,059,851,657
COMMUNITY HEALTH INDICATORS PER 1000 POPULATION					
Total Population (in thousands)	1,318	1,324	1,325	1,322	1,317
Inpatient					
Beds	2.2	2.2	2.2	2.2	2.2
Admissions	92.8	90.6	92.8	93.9	92.4
Inpatient Days	481.7	471.8	494.5	502.8	500.6
Inpatient Surgeries	26.0	25.4	24.9	26.5	26.0
Births	9.6	9.5	10.0	10.3	10.6
Outpatient					
Emergency Outpatient Visits	513.9	504.4	473.9	471.9	470.4
Other Outpatient Visits	3,276.1	3,105.3	3,093.1	2,908.5	2,641.2
Total Outpatient Visits	3,790.0	3,609.7	3,567.1	3,380.5	3,111.6
Outpatient Surgeries	69.3	69.9	69.1	69.1	64.9
Expense per Capita (per person)	$2,995.2	$2,857.2	$2,672.1	$2,519.6	$2,330.5

States

TABLE 6

NEW JERSEY

U.S. Registered Community Hospitals
(Nonfederal, short-term general and other special hospitals)

Overview 2007–2011

	2011	2010	2009	2008	2007
Total Community Hospitals in New Jersey.....	73	73	74	73	73
Bed Size Category					
6-24	0	0	0	0	0
25-49	1	2	3	3	0
50-99	7	6	5	4	6
100-199	18	16	19	19	18
200-299	21	20	16	16	17
300-399	10	11	12	13	14
400-499	9	9	11	11	12
500 + ...	7	9	8	7	6
Location					
Hospitals Urban...........................	73	73	74	73	73
Hospitals Rural	0	0	0	0	0
Control					
State and Local Government................	2	3	3	4	3
Not for Profit	61	62	64	61	65
Investor owned	10	8	7	8	5
Physician Models					
Independent Practice Association	10	12	14	16	17
Group Practice without Walls................	1	3	3	2	2
Open Physician-Hospital Organization	3	4	7	10	6
Closed Physician-Hospital Organization	2	2	4	2	2
Management Service Organization	13	12	13	12	10
Integrated Salary Model.....................	25	23	22	17	19
Equity Model	0	0	2	0	1
Foundation...............................	7	4	3	3	1
Insurance Products					
Health Maintenance Organization	7	6	3	4	7
Preferred Provider Organization..............	7	7	5	6	12
Indemnity Fee for Service	2	3	4	3	5
Managed Care Contracts					
Health Maintenance Organization	48	53	53	52	48
Preferred Provider Organization..............	47	53	54	53	49
Affiliations					
Hospitals in a System......................	42	42	43	42	41
Hospitals in a Network.....................	29	26	28	33	29
Hospitals in a Group Purchasing Organization..	53	54	55	61	52

TABLE 6

NEW JERSEY

U.S. Registered Community Hospitals
(Nonfederal, short-term general and other special hospitals)

Utilization, Personnel, Revenue and Expenses, Community Health Indicators 2007–2011

	2011	2010	2009	2008	2007
TOTAL FACILITY (Includes Hospital and Nursing Home Units)					
Utilization - Inpatient					
Beds	20,396	21,096	21,054	20,867	21,544
Admissions	1,050,828	1,067,267	1,094,810	1,086,445	1,084,226
Inpatient Days	5,344,077	5,433,359	5,565,763	5,595,966	5,613,126
Average Length of Stay.	5.1	5.1	5.1	5.2	5.2
Inpatient Surgeries.	243,218	254,003	250,689	255,641	266,546
Births.	101,362	100,677	105,841	107,580	107,824
Utilization - Outpatient					
Emergency Outpatient Visits	3,474,457	3,360,970	3,484,463	3,350,786	3,175,910
Other Outpatient Visits.	12,350,842	12,619,644	14,948,039	14,789,129	14,013,705
Total Outpatient Visits	15,825,299	15,980,614	18,432,502	18,139,915	17,189,615
Outpatient Surgeries	381,281	378,695	385,028	378,011	379,519
Personnel					
Full Time RNs	27,286	26,849	27,096	26,330	27,020
Full Time LPNs	881	976	948	988	1,239
Part Time RNs.	14,084	12,933	11,792	11,559	12,682
Part Time LPNs	321	342	313	341	446
Total Full Time.	100,956	101,574	102,243	100,758	106,135
Total Part Time	43,164	39,829	37,722	37,240	39,675
Revenue - Inpatient					
Gross Inpatient Revenue.	$56,915,377,319	$53,676,558,488	$53,769,546,685	$55,005,071,849	$49,634,356,051
Revenue - Outpatient					
Gross Outpatient Revenue	$27,132,937,292	$25,954,408,517	$23,718,074,694	$21,188,946,872	$18,690,116,226
Revenue and Expenses - Totals					
(Includes Inpatient and Outpatient)					
Total Gross Revenue.	$84,048,314,611	$79,630,967,005	$77,487,621,379	$76,194,018,721	$68,324,472,277
Deductions from Revenue	66,316,458,143	62,268,213,291	60,433,181,540	60,144,230,629	53,091,395,932
Net Patient Revenue	17,731,856,468	17,362,753,714	17,054,439,839	16,049,788,092	15,233,076,345
Other Operating Revenue	1,039,183,060	991,173,520	937,712,136	843,164,744	994,975,114
Other Nonoperating Revenue	157,790,540	355,140,452	506,772,443	-674,159,972	387,392,141
Total Net Revenue.	18,928,830,068	18,709,067,686	18,498,924,418	16,218,792,864	16,615,443,600
Total Expenses.	18,237,577,704	17,953,893,599	17,724,384,287	17,087,597,199	16,016,305,676
HOSPITAL UNIT (Excludes Separate Nursing Home Units)					
Utilization - Inpatient					
Beds	19,853	20,533	20,583	20,358	21,151
Admissions	1,046,456	1,061,552	1,091,384	1,082,467	1,080,885
Inpatient Days	5,168,493	5,258,495	5,408,363	5,429,164	5,482,670
Average Length of Stay.	4.9	5.0	5.0	5.0	5.1
Personnel					
Total Full Time.	100,398	100,902	101,537	99,958	105,444
Total Part Time	42,916	39,482	37,475	36,951	39,453
Revenue and Expenses - Totals					
(Includes Inpatient and Outpatient)					
Total Net Revenue.	$18,869,785,791	$18,584,183,240	$18,453,887,888	$16,159,968,959	$16,577,766,424
Total Expenses.	18,187,967,013	17,859,249,404	17,680,544,335	17,039,861,968	15,991,283,969
COMMUNITY HEALTH INDICATORS PER 1000 POPULATION					
Total Population (in thousands)	8,821	8,733	8,708	8,663	8,636
Inpatient					
Beds	2.3	2.4	2.4	2.4	2.5
Admissions	119.1	122.2	125.7	125.4	125.5
Inpatient Days	605.8	622.2	639.2	645.9	650.0
Inpatient Surgeries.	27.6	29.1	28.8	29.5	30.9
Births.	11.5	11.5	12.2	12.4	12.5
Outpatient					
Emergency Outpatient Visits	393.9	384.9	400.2	386.8	367.8
Other Outpatient Visits.	1,400.1	1,445.1	1,716.6	1,707.1	1,622.7
Total Outpatient Visits	1,794.0	1,830.0	2,116.8	2,093.9	1,990.5
Outpatient Surgeries	43.2	43.4	44.2	43.6	43.9
Expense per Capita (per person).	$2,067.5	$2,055.9	$2,035.5	$1,972.4	$1,854.6

States

TABLE 6

NEW MEXICO

U.S. Registered Community Hospitals
(Nonfederal, short-term general and other special hospitals)

Overview 2007–2011

	2011	2010	2009	2008	2007
Total Community Hospitals in New Mexico	36	36	37	36	35
Bed Size Category					
6-24	4	4	4	4	4
25-49	8	8	8	9	9
50-99	12	12	14	10	10
100-199	7	8	8	10	9
200-299	3	2	1	1	1
300-399	0	0	0	0	0
400-499	0	0	0	0	0
500 + ...	2	2	2	2	2
Location					
Hospitals Urban...........................	14	14	15	14	13
Hospitals Rural	22	22	22	22	22
Control					
State and Local Government................	6	6	7	7	7
Not for Profit	15	16	14	14	15
Investor owned	15	14	16	15	13
Physician Models					
Independent Practice Association	3	4	4	3	5
Group Practice without Walls................	0	0	1	0	0
Open Physician-Hospital Organization	4	3	4	4	4
Closed Physician-Hospital Organization	0	0	0	1	0
Management Service Organization	0	0	0	1	2
Integrated Salary Model....................	9	11	13	10	11
Equity Model	0	0	1	1	1
Foundation...............................	0	1	2	2	2
Insurance Products					
Health Maintenance Organization	7	6	7	7	8
Preferred Provider Organization..............	7	6	7	6	5
Indemnity Fee for Service	4	5	5	4	4
Managed Care Contracts					
Health Maintenance Organization	13	14	19	17	21
Preferred Provider Organization..............	13	15	19	19	22
Affiliations					
Hospitals in a System.....................	28	28	30	28	26
Hospitals in a Network.....................	11	11	10	7	6
Hospitals in a Group Purchasing Organization..	22	20	26	22	25

States

TABLE 6

NEW MEXICO

U.S. Registered Community Hospitals
(Nonfederal, short-term general and other special hospitals)

Utilization, Personnel, Revenue and Expenses, Community Health Indicators 2007–2011

	2011	2010	2009	2008	2007
TOTAL FACILITY (Includes Hospital and Nursing Home Units)					
Utilization - Inpatient					
Beds	4,068	3,975	3,913	3,935	3,695
Admissions	175,112	186,092	183,116	174,169	170,081
Inpatient Days	861,109	831,384	844,787	809,916	764,458
Average Length of Stay	4.9	4.5	4.6	4.7	4.5
Inpatient Surgeries	53,331	49,435	51,319	48,698	52,350
Births	21,537	23,767	26,224	24,127	24,530
Utilization - Outpatient					
Emergency Outpatient Visits	854,871	844,650	829,138	770,475	650,026
Other Outpatient Visits	3,740,262	3,795,337	3,814,530	3,481,084	3,458,967
Total Outpatient Visits	4,595,133	4,639,987	4,643,668	4,251,559	4,108,993
Outpatient Surgeries	93,352	92,079	92,936	84,596	85,918
Personnel					
Full Time RNs	5,549	6,022	5,579	5,151	4,690
Full Time LPNs	292	391	455	401	415
Part Time RNs	2,092	2,065	2,213	1,997	2,025
Part Time LPNs	72	124	145	143	220
Total Full Time	19,318	20,493	21,568	19,610	18,112
Total Part Time	5,387	5,559	6,609	5,789	5,808
Revenue - Inpatient					
Gross Inpatient Revenue	$5,955,197,886	$5,597,578,195	$5,011,641,495	$4,955,498,423	$4,068,780,483
Revenue - Outpatient					
Gross Outpatient Revenue	$5,493,320,827	$5,288,644,232	$4,601,410,841	$4,098,164,016	$3,553,788,776
Revenue and Expenses - Totals					
(Includes Inpatient and Outpatient)					
Total Gross Revenue	$11,448,518,713	$10,886,222,427	$9,613,052,336	$9,053,662,439	$7,622,569,259
Deductions from Revenue	7,609,704,329	6,965,889,535	5,938,985,924	5,863,897,074	4,772,970,882
Net Patient Revenue	3,838,814,384	3,920,332,892	3,674,066,412	3,189,765,365	2,849,598,377
Other Operating Revenue	211,597,602	193,738,359	179,587,865	201,317,481	147,824,626
Other Nonoperating Revenue	53,311,105	32,566,260	22,192,097	25,179,087	67,325,548
Total Net Revenue	4,103,723,091	4,146,637,511	3,875,846,374	3,416,261,933	3,064,748,551
Total Expenses	3,713,540,269	3,540,766,412	3,378,281,656	3,078,569,624	2,857,121,542
HOSPITAL UNIT (Excludes Separate Nursing Home Units)					
Utilization - Inpatient					
Beds	4,068	3,928	3,863	3,838	3,582
Admissions	175,112	186,058	182,956	173,883	169,533
Inpatient Days	861,109	818,802	841,637	788,033	736,788
Average Length of Stay	4.9	4.4	4.6	4.5	4.3
Personnel					
Total Full Time	19,318	20,450	21,545	19,566	18,009
Total Part Time	5,387	5,554	6,606	5,778	5,765
Revenue and Expenses - Totals					
(Includes Inpatient and Outpatient)					
Total Net Revenue	$4,103,723,091	$4,145,724,111	$3,872,546,211	$3,409,480,468	$3,054,320,532
Total Expenses	3,713,540,269	3,537,873,415	3,375,982,169	3,074,660,998	2,852,899,697
COMMUNITY HEALTH INDICATORS PER 1000 POPULATION					
Total Population (in thousands)	2,082	2,034	2,010	1,987	1,969
Inpatient					
Beds	2.0	2.0	1.9	2.0	1.9
Admissions	84.1	91.5	91.1	87.7	86.4
Inpatient Days	413.6	408.8	420.4	407.7	388.3
Inpatient Surgeries	25.6	24.3	25.5	24.5	26.6
Births	10.3	11.7	13.0	12.1	12.5
Outpatient					
Emergency Outpatient Visits	410.6	415.3	412.6	387.8	330.2
Other Outpatient Visits	1,796.3	1,866.1	1,898.1	1,752.1	1,757.0
Total Outpatient Visits	2,206.8	2,281.4	2,310.7	2,139.9	2,087.1
Outpatient Surgeries	44.8	45.3	46.2	42.6	43.6
Expense per Capita (per person)	$1,783.4	$1,740.9	$1,681.0	$1,549.5	$1,451.3

States

TABLE 6

NEW YORK

U.S. Registered Community Hospitals
(Nonfederal, short-term general and other special hospitals)

Overview 2007–2011

	2011	2010	2009	2008	2007
Total Community Hospitals in New York	182	185	189	194	202
Bed Size Category					
6-24	6	5	4	5	6
25-49	7	7	7	9	8
50-99	19	18	19	19	21
100-199	41	40	45	47	48
200-299	36	44	40	38	41
300-399	26	25	28	29	31
400-499	14	13	15	14	14
500 + ...	33	33	31	33	33
Location					
Hospitals Urban..........................	145	147	150	154	166
Hospitals Rural	37	38	39	40	36
Control					
State and Local Government...............	26	25	25	26	26
Not for Profit	156	160	164	167	174
Investor owned	0	0	0	1	2
Physician Models					
Independent Practice Association	35	35	32	38	43
Group Practice without Walls...............	5	6	4	5	5
Open Physician-Hospital Organization	14	12	9	13	18
Closed Physician-Hospital Organization	10	10	10	9	11
Management Service Organization	15	18	15	13	16
Integrated Salary Model....................	77	74	63	56	56
Equity Model	2	0	0	4	3
Foundation...............................	3	2	3	2	6
Insurance Products					
Health Maintenance Organization	48	45	39	50	42
Preferred Provider Organization.............	21	30	22	30	23
Indemnity Fee for Service	10	22	12	15	14
Managed Care Contracts					
Health Maintenance Organization	116	116	111	115	119
Preferred Provider Organization.............	111	109	101	105	105
Affiliations					
Hospitals in a System.....................	84	82	80	73	76
Hospitals in a Network	83	82	76	73	74
Hospitals in a Group Purchasing Organization..	134	128	116	116	125

TABLE 6

NEW YORK

U.S. Registered Community Hospitals
(Nonfederal, short-term general and other special hospitals)

Utilization, Personnel, Revenue and Expenses, Community Health Indicators 2007–2011

	2011	2010	2009	2008	2007
TOTAL FACILITY (Includes Hospital and Nursing Home Units)					
Utilization - Inpatient					
Beds	58,080	59,510	60,400	61,237	62,367
Admissions	2,491,403	2,509,980	2,533,577	2,528,191	2,540,711
Inpatient Days	16,924,697	17,226,868	17,474,823	17,973,047	18,344,398
Average Length of Stay	6.8	6.9	6.9	7.1	7.2
Inpatient Surgeries	615,656	683,336	653,545	660,660	679,506
Births	239,622	238,062	238,647	242,326	247,523
Utilization - Outpatient					
Emergency Outpatient Visits	8,432,260	8,063,821	8,542,392	8,114,078	8,193,513
Other Outpatient Visits	45,578,620	45,586,391	45,702,429	44,455,562	44,944,035
Total Outpatient Visits	54,010,880	53,650,212	54,244,821	52,569,640	53,137,548
Outpatient Surgeries	1,335,088	1,369,360	1,369,632	1,340,449	1,362,222
Personnel					
Full Time RNs	81,500	79,270	79,073	76,900	76,438
Full Time LPNs	5,403	5,095	5,781	5,964	6,184
Part Time RNs	23,368	24,090	21,651	22,118	22,590
Part Time LPNs	1,427	1,492	1,442	1,561	1,696
Total Full Time	350,923	333,121	344,168	340,045	335,364
Total Part Time	85,040	80,711	76,142	74,972	75,084
Revenue - Inpatient					
Gross Inpatient Revenue	$86,312,444,902	$83,446,219,992	$79,742,230,648	$76,153,885,959	$73,373,569,851
Revenue - Outpatient					
Gross Outpatient Revenue	$56,035,192,523	$52,554,490,709	$48,142,548,531	$43,198,790,671	$38,929,448,202
Revenue and Expenses - Totals					
(Includes Inpatient and Outpatient)					
Total Gross Revenue	$142,347,637,425	$136,000,710,701	$127,884,779,179	$119,352,676,630	$112,303,018,053
Deductions from Revenue	87,498,353,474	83,151,232,467	77,411,417,932	71,744,138,399	66,207,959,482
Net Patient Revenue	54,849,283,951	52,849,478,234	50,473,361,247	47,608,538,231	46,095,058,571
Other Operating Revenue	4,212,820,400	4,222,330,075	3,824,228,913	3,624,584,884	3,905,891,729
Other Nonoperating Revenue	541,024,602	925,916,282	1,020,046,507	-31,698,081	1,052,459,422
Total Net Revenue	59,603,128,953	57,997,724,591	55,317,636,667	51,201,425,034	51,053,409,722
Total Expenses	58,543,388,525	56,081,000,844	54,164,979,905	52,930,511,542	50,122,518,825
HOSPITAL UNIT (Excludes Separate Nursing Home Units)					
Utilization - Inpatient					
Beds	51,072	53,436	54,708	55,922	56,413
Admissions	2,471,603	2,494,952	2,518,427	2,514,606	2,525,283
Inpatient Days	14,460,605	15,107,729	15,475,231	16,133,356	16,221,721
Average Length of Stay	5.9	6.1	6.1	6.4	6.4
Personnel					
Total Full Time	346,182	329,655	339,060	334,474	330,451
Total Part Time	82,889	78,770	73,758	72,541	72,893
Revenue and Expenses - Totals					
(Includes Inpatient and Outpatient)					
Total Net Revenue	$58,992,643,837	$57,401,240,974	$54,761,298,914	$50,719,366,889	$50,534,703,285
Total Expenses	57,946,106,911	55,490,108,946	53,587,952,457	52,469,154,258	49,634,461,793
COMMUNITY HEALTH INDICATORS PER 1000 POPULATION					
Total Population (in thousands)	19,465	19,578	19,541	19,468	19,423
Inpatient					
Beds	3.0	3.0	3.1	3.1	3.2
Admissions	128.0	128.2	129.7	129.9	130.8
Inpatient Days	869.5	879.9	894.2	923.2	944.5
Inpatient Surgeries	31.6	34.9	33.4	33.9	35.0
Births	12.3	12.2	12.2	12.4	12.7
Outpatient					
Emergency Outpatient Visits	433.2	411.9	437.1	416.8	421.9
Other Outpatient Visits	2,341.5	2,328.5	2,338.7	2,283.5	2,314.0
Total Outpatient Visits	2,774.7	2,740.4	2,775.9	2,700.3	2,735.8
Outpatient Surgeries	68.6	69.9	70.1	68.9	70.1
Expense per Capita (per person)	$3,007.6	$2,864.5	$2,771.8	$2,718.9	$2,580.6

States

TABLE 6

NORTH CAROLINA

U.S. Registered Community Hospitals
(Nonfederal, short-term general and other special hospitals)

Overview 2007–2011

	2011	2010	2009	2008	2007
Total Community Hospitals in North Carolina..	117	117	115	116	113
Bed Size Category					
6-24	3	4	4	4	4
25-49	20	19	18	16	14
50-99	28	25	20	22	19
100-199	31	35	39	40	40
200-299	13	13	13	12	14
300-399	8	6	6	7	7
400-499	1	2	2	2	2
500 + ...	13	13	13	13	13
Location					
Hospitals Urban............................	59	59	58	58	52
Hospitals Rural	58	58	57	58	61
Control					
State and Local Government................	30	32	32	32	32
Not for Profit	75	73	74	74	75
Investor owned	12	12	9	10	6
Physician Models					
Independent Practice Association	10	10	11	11	13
Group Practice without Walls...............	1	2	3	2	2
Open Physician-Hospital Organization	9	10	11	10	11
Closed Physician-Hospital Organization	6	6	7	6	7
Management Service Organization	12	12	14	16	13
Integrated Salary Model....................	57	54	50	57	48
Equity Model	2	4	5	3	2
Foundation...............................	2	3	2	5	4
Insurance Products					
Health Maintenance Organization	6	7	4	7	9
Preferred Provider Organization.............	16	14	10	10	20
Indemnity Fee for Service	6	5	2	2	3
Managed Care Contracts					
Health Maintenance Organization	71	70	71	80	78
Preferred Provider Organization.............	77	75	80	89	88
Affiliations					
Hospitals in a System.....................	90	78	70	69	60
Hospitals in a Network....................	43	41	39	41	40
Hospitals in a Group Purchasing Organization..	94	90	90	102	102

States

TABLE 6

NORTH CAROLINA

U.S. Registered Community Hospitals
(Nonfederal, short-term general and other special hospitals)

Utilization, Personnel, Revenue and Expenses, Community Health Indicators 2007–2011

	2011	2010	2009	2008	2007
TOTAL FACILITY (Includes Hospital and Nursing Home Units)					
Utilization - Inpatient					
Beds	23,136	23,012	22,830	23,140	23,158
Admissions	1,035,400	1,038,337	1,034,112	1,041,918	1,027,909
Inpatient Days	5,830,425	5,852,967	5,788,671	6,019,401	6,069,660
Average Length of Stay.	5.6	5.6	5.6	5.8	5.9
Inpatient Surgeries.	287,065	293,323	296,668	292,208	292,262
Births.	115,013	117,422	122,588	126,934	125,276
Utilization - Outpatient					
Emergency Outpatient Visits	4,448,191	4,259,853	4,249,375	4,166,718	4,068,389
Other Outpatient Visits.	14,180,481	14,026,042	14,071,173	13,566,350	13,699,957
Total Outpatient Visits	18,628,672	18,285,895	18,320,548	17,733,068	17,768,346
Outpatient Surgeries	551,009	558,068	561,072	561,677	548,944
Personnel					
Full Time RNs	37,691	37,461	36,051	33,527	32,542
Full Time LPNs	1,457	1,585	1,567	1,847	1,867
Part Time RNs.	13,740	13,790	13,892	15,014	13,391
Part Time LPNs	433	509	560	717	765
Total Full Time.	134,652	130,456	128,117	127,114	124,066
Total Part Time	36,793	35,766	37,093	39,645	36,185
Revenue - Inpatient					
Gross Inpatient Revenue.	$30,029,780,874	$28,197,730,702	$25,877,825,356	$23,694,080,318	$22,069,980,664
Revenue - Outpatient					
Gross Outpatient Revenue	$27,738,748,951	$24,683,456,547	$22,124,796,442	$19,809,416,116	$17,851,201,525
Revenue and Expenses - Totals					
(Includes Inpatient and Outpatient)					
Total Gross Revenue.	$57,768,529,825	$52,881,187,249	$48,002,621,798	$43,503,496,434	$39,921,182,189
Deductions from Revenue.	37,629,541,786	33,708,237,290	29,458,448,362	26,008,781,838	23,217,172,845
Net Patient Revenue	20,138,988,039	19,172,949,959	18,544,173,436	17,494,714,596	16,704,009,344
Other Operating Revenue	1,235,529,371	1,122,729,376	1,094,994,175	988,309,628	844,581,143
Other Nonoperating Revenue	273,053,042	492,730,856	213,265,535	-560,668,606	571,143,345
Total Net Revenue.	21,647,570,452	20,788,410,191	19,852,433,146	17,922,355,618	18,119,733,832
Total Expenses.	20,062,914,117	18,847,920,294	18,590,518,185	17,662,604,664	16,635,094,264
HOSPITAL UNIT (Excludes Separate Nursing Home Units)					
Utilization - Inpatient					
Beds	21,041	20,841	20,811	20,496	20,302
Admissions	1,027,691	1,030,472	1,026,457	1,031,609	1,016,854
Inpatient Days	5,171,227	5,150,233	5,133,526	5,128,782	5,093,680
Average Length of Stay.	5.0	5.0	5.0	5.0	5.0
Personnel					
Total Full Time.	133,321	128,958	126,542	125,088	121,526
Total Part Time	36,217	35,100	36,425	38,721	35,164
Revenue and Expenses - Totals					
(Includes Inpatient and Outpatient)					
Total Net Revenue.	$21,508,952,533	$20,648,909,546	$19,725,156,052	$17,753,404,722	$17,925,776,886
Total Expenses.	19,925,373,321	18,715,167,064	18,471,921,787	17,488,022,607	16,444,335,265
COMMUNITY HEALTH INDICATORS PER 1000 POPULATION					
Total Population (in thousands)	9,656	9,459	9,381	9,247	9,064
Inpatient					
Beds	2.4	2.4	2.4	2.5	2.6
Admissions	107.2	109.8	110.2	112.7	113.4
Inpatient Days	603.8	618.8	617.1	650.9	669.6
Inpatient Surgeries.	29.7	31.0	31.6	31.6	32.2
Births.	11.9	12.4	13.1	13.7	13.8
Outpatient					
Emergency Outpatient Visits	460.6	450.4	453.0	450.6	448.8
Other Outpatient Visits.	1,468.5	1,482.8	1,500.0	1,467.1	1,511.5
Total Outpatient Visits	1,929.2	1,933.2	1,953.0	1,917.7	1,960.3
Outpatient Surgeries	57.1	59.0	59.8	60.7	60.6
Expense per Capita (per person).	$2,077.7	$1,992.6	$1,981.7	$1,910.1	$1,835.3

States

TABLE **6**

NORTH DAKOTA

U.S. Registered Community Hospitals
(Nonfederal, short-term general and other special hospitals)

Overview 2007–2011

	2011	2010	2009	2008	2007
Total Community Hospitals in North Dakota ...	41	41	41	41	41
Bed Size Category					
6-24	13	10	10	11	11
25-49	14	15	15	12	11
50-99	7	8	9	11	12
100-199	2	3	2	2	2
200-299	3	3	3	3	3
300-399	0	0	0	0	0
400-499	1	1	1	1	1
500 + ...	1	1	1	1	1
Location					
Hospitals Urban...........................	8	8	8	7	6
Hospitals Rural	33	33	33	34	35
Control					
State and Local Government................	0	0	0	0	0
Not for Profit	39	39	39	39	40
Investor owned	2	2	2	2	1
Physician Models					
Independent Practice Association	3	4	4	4	4
Group Practice without Walls................	0	0	0	0	0
Open Physician-Hospital Organization	1	1	2	3	3
Closed Physician-Hospital Organization	0	0	0	0	1
Management Service Organization	0	0	0	0	1
Integrated Salary Model....................	8	10	16	15	14
Equity Model	0	0	1	1	1
Foundation...............................	1	1	2	4	3
Insurance Products					
Health Maintenance Organization	0	1	0	0	0
Preferred Provider Organization..............	5	5	5	7	4
Indemnity Fee for Service	1	2	2	4	1
Managed Care Contracts					
Health Maintenance Organization	2	1	3	1	2
Preferred Provider Organization..............	11	13	17	16	17
Affiliations					
Hospitals in a System......................	19	17	17	15	16
Hospitals in a Network.....................	7	8	12	8	7
Hospitals in a Group Purchasing Organization..	17	19	28	25	29

States

TABLE 6

NORTH DAKOTA

U.S. Registered Community Hospitals
(Nonfederal, short-term general and other special hospitals)

Utilization, Personnel, Revenue and Expenses, Community Health Indicators 2007–2011

	2011	2010	2009	2008	2007
TOTAL FACILITY (Includes Hospital and Nursing Home Units)					
Utilization - Inpatient					
Beds	3,145	3,345	3,362	3,442	3,488
Admissions	94,125	94,436	92,593	89,225	89,010
Inpatient Days	701,723	718,950	751,653	744,876	772,643
Average Length of Stay	7.5	7.6	8.1	8.3	8.7
Inpatient Surgeries	28,285	29,558	27,732	26,451	28,861
Births	12,731	12,851	10,552	9,966	9,687
Utilization - Outpatient					
Emergency Outpatient Visits	408,870	353,557	303,190	289,070	274,223
Other Outpatient Visits	2,540,152	2,722,180	2,059,310	1,406,490	1,474,224
Total Outpatient Visits	2,949,022	3,075,737	2,362,500	1,695,560	1,748,447
Outpatient Surgeries	59,702	54,165	56,128	46,734	45,328
Personnel					
Full Time RNs	3,103	2,889	2,497	2,424	2,356
Full Time LPNs	501	514	599	512	556
Part Time RNs	2,485	2,452	2,163	2,002	2,030
Part Time LPNs	404	392	361	460	566
Total Full Time	14,000	13,902	13,328	12,312	12,036
Total Part Time	8,536	8,187	7,909	7,148	7,666
Revenue - Inpatient					
Gross Inpatient Revenue	$2,320,300,120	$2,002,135,268	$2,019,340,609	$1,483,180,662	$1,414,871,895
Revenue - Outpatient					
Gross Outpatient Revenue	$2,783,603,262	$2,551,094,052	$2,583,127,227	$1,953,610,192	$1,687,925,226
Revenue and Expenses - Totals					
(Includes Inpatient and Outpatient)					
Total Gross Revenue	$5,103,903,382	$4,643,229,320	$4,602,467,836	$3,436,790,854	$3,102,797,121
Deductions from Revenue	2,807,521,605	2,493,872,027	2,518,310,749	1,680,883,923	1,444,698,089
Net Patient Revenue	2,296,381,777	2,149,357,293	2,084,157,087	1,755,906,931	1,658,099,032
Other Operating Revenue	107,145,231	96,921,743	91,082,749	87,201,376	83,258,147
Other Nonoperating Revenue	22,983,677	33,585,013	13,376,054	-13,097,663	43,988,926
Total Net Revenue	2,426,510,685	2,279,864,049	2,188,615,890	1,830,010,644	1,785,346,105
Total Expenses	2,229,494,218	2,142,846,297	2,133,367,717	1,853,693,024	1,748,248,300
HOSPITAL UNIT (Excludes Separate Nursing Home Units)					
Utilization - Inpatient					
Beds	2,944	3,063	2,569	2,649	2,610
Admissions	92,902	92,796	90,862	86,795	86,408
Inpatient Days	633,852	634,164	485,393	479,593	472,732
Average Length of Stay	6.8	6.8	5.3	5.5	5.5
Personnel					
Total Full Time	14,472	13,822	12,820	11,728	11,350
Total Part Time	8,439	8,048	7,540	6,808	7,147
Revenue and Expenses - Totals					
(Includes Inpatient and Outpatient)					
Total Net Revenue	$2,414,246,674	$2,258,523,169	$2,145,215,671	$1,780,423,431	$1,729,923,488
Total Expenses	2,223,176,123	2,126,714,369	2,094,921,706	1,809,203,400	1,702,249,310
COMMUNITY HEALTH INDICATORS PER 1000 POPULATION					
Total Population (in thousands)	684	654	647	641	638
Inpatient					
Beds	4.6	5.1	5.2	5.4	5.5
Admissions	137.6	144.4	143.1	139.1	139.5
Inpatient Days	1,026.0	1,099.7	1,162.0	1,161.3	1,210.7
Inpatient Surgeries	41.4	45.2	42.9	41.2	45.2
Births	18.6	19.7	16.3	15.5	15.2
Outpatient					
Emergency Outpatient Visits	597.8	540.8	468.7	450.7	429.7
Other Outpatient Visits	3,714.0	4,163.8	3,183.6	2,192.8	2,310.0
Total Outpatient Visits	4,311.9	4,704.6	3,652.3	2,643.4	2,739.6
Outpatient Surgeries	87.3	82.8	86.8	72.9	71.0
Expense per Capita (per person)	$3,259.8	$3,277.6	$3,298.1	$2,890.0	$2,739.3

States

TABLE 6

OHIO

U.S. Registered Community Hospitals
(Nonfederal, short-term general and other special hospitals)

Overview 2007–2011

	2011	2010	2009	2008	2007
Total Community Hospitals in Ohio..........	183	183	183	181	171
Bed Size Category					
6-24	2	3	4	4	3
25-49	47	44	45	44	37
50-99	33	33	32	29	26
100-199	40	41	43	45	47
200-299	27	28	25	25	24
300-399	12	12	11	11	12
400-499	9	9	11	10	11
500 + ...	13	13	12	13	11
Location					
Hospitals Urban...........................	128	128	128	126	121
Hospitals Rural	55	55	55	55	50
Control					
State and Local Government...............	19	21	22	21	23
Not for Profit	138	138	138	139	137
Investor owned	26	24	23	21	11
Physician Models					
Independent Practice Association	15	15	19	25	27
Group Practice without Walls................	6	7	8	9	11
Open Physician-Hospital Organization	50	52	46	41	41
Closed Physician-Hospital Organization	15	9	10	13	25
Management Service Organization	33	35	39	49	39
Integrated Salary Model	70	71	64	68	65
Equity Model	8	9	7	8	6
Foundation..............................	29	31	28	27	24
Insurance Products					
Health Maintenance Organization	33	36	32	31	35
Preferred Provider Organization..............	39	43	44	34	45
Indemnity Fee for Service	14	16	15	11	26
Managed Care Contracts					
Health Maintenance Organization	114	113	120	112	110
Preferred Provider Organization..............	119	120	129	120	120
Affiliations					
Hospitals in a System......................	118	114	111	107	99
Hospitals in a Network.....................	76	77	77	74	70
Hospitals in a Group Purchasing Organization..	135	133	143	141	139

TABLE 6

OHIO

U.S. Registered Community Hospitals
(Nonfederal, short-term general and other special hospitals)

Utilization, Personnel, Revenue and Expenses, Community Health Indicators 2007–2011

	2011	2010	2009	2008	2007
TOTAL FACILITY (Includes Hospital and Nursing Home Units)					
Utilization - Inpatient					
Beds	33,828	34,316	33,994	33,860	32,866
Admissions	1,504,603	1,516,501	1,531,076	1,547,720	1,542,176
Inpatient Days	7,434,042	7,598,267	7,744,235	7,814,849	7,753,839
Average Length of Stay	4.9	5.0	5.1	5.0	5.0
Inpatient Surgeries	393,731	405,507	407,777	413,959	416,220
Births	128,695	133,946	141,295	143,941	146,861
Utilization - Outpatient					
Emergency Outpatient Visits	6,506,331	6,383,429	6,207,290	6,023,705	5,918,218
Other Outpatient Visits	29,390,397	29,375,819	28,033,655	26,868,157	27,167,211
Total Outpatient Visits	35,896,728	35,759,248	34,240,945	32,891,862	33,085,429
Outpatient Surgeries	803,825	817,556	800,882	787,850	763,623
Personnel					
Full Time RNs	52,672	51,255	48,681	45,914	44,637
Full Time LPNs	3,790	3,309	3,580	3,769	4,022
Part Time RNs	26,034	25,325	24,409	24,600	23,100
Part Time LPNs	1,788	1,808	1,859	2,080	2,113
Total Full Time	203,689	198,795	198,906	194,709	185,526
Total Part Time	78,003	76,929	75,934	76,454	69,946
Revenue - Inpatient					
Gross Inpatient Revenue	$51,716,805,929	$49,069,396,749	$45,306,391,429	$41,893,875,454	$38,144,462,997
Revenue - Outpatient					
Gross Outpatient Revenue	$47,899,777,396	$44,283,440,488	$40,277,248,420	$35,108,967,663	$30,960,953,256
Revenue and Expenses - Totals (Includes Inpatient and Outpatient)					
Total Gross Revenue	$99,616,583,325	$93,352,837,237	$85,583,639,849	$77,002,843,117	$69,105,416,253
Deductions from Revenue	67,235,879,337	61,559,545,620	55,069,727,140	48,579,748,500	42,732,933,128
Net Patient Revenue	32,380,703,988	31,793,291,617	30,513,912,709	28,423,094,617	26,372,483,125
Other Operating Revenue	2,439,029,875	2,302,711,954	2,204,346,362	1,902,066,455	1,781,044,376
Other Nonoperating Revenue	66,768,231	824,057,575	899,809,957	-1,531,882,065	696,280,084
Total Net Revenue	34,886,502,094	34,920,061,146	33,618,069,028	28,793,279,007	28,849,807,585
Total Expenses	32,605,625,518	32,374,139,783	30,929,648,514	29,074,986,966	26,781,375,793
HOSPITAL UNIT (Excludes Separate Nursing Home Units)					
Utilization - Inpatient					
Beds	32,734	33,157	32,613	32,422	31,350
Admissions	1,492,180	1,503,171	1,517,223	1,532,848	1,526,090
Inpatient Days	7,086,115	7,219,041	7,292,581	7,365,607	7,283,480
Average Length of Stay	4.7	4.8	4.8	4.8	4.8
Personnel					
Total Full Time	202,974	197,828	197,669	193,511	184,300
Total Part Time	77,530	76,311	75,222	75,671	69,255
Revenue and Expenses - Totals (Includes Inpatient and Outpatient)					
Total Net Revenue	$34,777,592,693	$34,807,563,235	$33,478,190,434	$28,664,373,342	$28,691,701,961
Total Expenses	32,496,965,573	32,265,651,508	30,795,620,302	28,951,022,330	26,629,876,388
COMMUNITY HEALTH INDICATORS PER 1000 POPULATION					
Total Population (in thousands)	11,545	11,532	11,543	11,528	11,521
Inpatient					
Beds	2.9	3.0	2.9	2.9	2.9
Admissions	130.3	131.5	132.6	134.3	133.9
Inpatient Days	643.9	658.9	670.9	677.9	673.0
Inpatient Surgeries	34.1	35.2	35.3	35.9	36.1
Births	11.1	11.6	12.2	12.5	12.7
Outpatient					
Emergency Outpatient Visits	563.6	553.5	537.8	522.5	513.7
Other Outpatient Visits	2,545.7	2,547.3	2,428.7	2,330.7	2,358.1
Total Outpatient Visits	3,109.3	3,100.8	2,966.5	2,853.2	2,871.8
Outpatient Surgeries	69.6	70.9	69.4	68.3	66.3
Expense per Capita (per person)	$2,824.2	$2,807.3	$2,679.6	$2,522.1	$2,324.6

States

TABLE 6

OKLAHOMA

U.S. Registered Community Hospitals
(Nonfederal, short-term general and other special hospitals)

Overview 2007–2011

	2011	2010	2009	2008	2007
Total Community Hospitals in Oklahoma......	115	113	116	115	113
Bed Size Category					
6-24.....................................	21	22	20	23	24
25-49....................................	44	41	42	41	38
50-99....................................	24	22	26	24	25
100-199..................................	14	15	15	14	12
200-299..................................	2	2	3	2	4
300-399..................................	4	5	4	5	4
400-499..................................	1	1	1	2	2
500 +....................................	5	5	5	4	4
Location					
Hospitals Urban..........................	49	48	49	50	44
Hospitals Rural	66	65	67	65	69
Control					
State and Local Government...............	41	44	45	45	45
Not for Profit	38	36	36	37	35
Investor owned	36	33	35	33	33
Physician Models					
Independent Practice Association	16	14	15	11	16
Group Practice without Walls................	4	6	6	4	7
Open Physician-Hospital Organization	11	9	11	11	16
Closed Physician-Hospital Organization	1	0	0	3	3
Management Service Organization	7	7	11	11	13
Integrated Salary Model....................	49	34	26	22	17
Equity Model.............................	1	0	0	1	1
Foundation...............................	1	0	1	1	0
Insurance Products					
Health Maintenance Organization	13	8	7	5	9
Preferred Provider Organization..............	16	10	8	8	12
Indemnity Fee for Service	8	4	4	3	3
Managed Care Contracts					
Health Maintenance Organization	48	38	38	41	41
Preferred Provider Organization..............	76	63	62	64	68
Affiliations					
Hospitals in a System......................	60	53	60	57	58
Hospitals in a Network.....................	30	22	19	20	25
Hospitals in a Group Purchasing Organization..	91	87	89	85	86

States

TABLE 6

OKLAHOMA

U.S. Registered Community Hospitals
(Nonfederal, short-term general and other special hospitals)

Utilization, Personnel, Revenue and Expenses, Community Health Indicators 2007–2011

	2011	2010	2009	2008	2007
TOTAL FACILITY (Includes Hospital and Nursing Home Units)					
Utilization - Inpatient					
Beds	11,303	11,170	11,316	10,988	10,862
Admissions	424,190	429,096	442,394	462,954	453,977
Inpatient Days	2,257,353	2,340,946	2,401,771	2,436,253	2,359,878
Average Length of Stay	5.3	5.5	5.4	5.3	5.2
Inpatient Surgeries	107,010	109,345	117,362	117,982	115,503
Births	46,583	48,569	53,456	49,851	49,623
Utilization - Outpatient					
Emergency Outpatient Visits	1,847,389	1,762,821	1,743,802	1,645,625	1,618,741
Other Outpatient Visits	4,175,877	3,895,891	3,827,100	3,785,996	3,654,371
Total Outpatient Visits	6,023,266	5,658,712	5,570,902	5,431,621	5,273,112
Outpatient Surgeries	211,753	206,440	200,043	198,007	197,718
Personnel					
Full Time RNs	11,500	11,105	10,929	10,585	10,229
Full Time LPNs	1,612	1,686	1,903	1,986	2,275
Part Time RNs	4,046	3,984	3,654	3,684	3,523
Part Time LPNs	464	567	500	508	650
Total Full Time	44,647	43,629	43,977	43,201	43,508
Total Part Time	13,085	13,056	12,159	12,279	12,348
Revenue - Inpatient					
Gross Inpatient Revenue	$13,445,502,051	$12,758,064,725	$12,064,230,137	$11,758,611,895	$10,320,519,778
Revenue - Outpatient					
Gross Outpatient Revenue	$10,390,808,413	$9,221,121,763	$8,258,194,596	$7,423,183,911	$6,214,687,591
Revenue and Expenses - Totals					
(Includes Inpatient and Outpatient)					
Total Gross Revenue	$23,836,310,464	$21,979,186,488	$20,322,424,733	$19,181,795,806	$16,535,207,369
Deductions from Revenue	16,779,981,602	15,258,319,649	13,635,382,267	12,656,733,800	10,641,812,711
Net Patient Revenue	7,056,328,862	6,720,866,839	6,687,042,466	6,525,062,006	5,893,394,658
Other Operating Revenue	269,741,536	235,730,490	201,195,524	211,578,156	234,090,824
Other Nonoperating Revenue	185,667,771	102,371,200	-36,278,624	37,213,785	137,588,524
Total Net Revenue	7,511,738,169	7,058,968,529	6,851,959,366	6,773,853,947	6,265,074,006
Total Expenses	6,782,884,227	6,484,581,837	6,376,319,309	6,361,690,040	5,731,142,311
HOSPITAL UNIT (Excludes Separate Nursing Home Units)					
Utilization - Inpatient					
Beds	11,033	10,981	11,013	10,699	10,542
Admissions	423,362	427,982	440,886	461,577	452,687
Inpatient Days	2,183,306	2,280,666	2,277,293	2,339,600	2,256,043
Average Length of Stay	5.2	5.3	5.2	5.1	5.0
Personnel					
Total Full Time	44,486	43,532	43,684	42,916	43,203
Total Part Time	13,026	12,983	12,110	12,202	12,267
Revenue and Expenses - Totals					
(Includes Inpatient and Outpatient)					
Total Net Revenue	$7,501,813,546	$7,049,646,928	$6,836,200,847	$6,759,273,857	$6,249,707,579
Total Expenses	6,772,484,570	6,475,775,258	6,361,745,192	6,348,305,959	5,658,213,009
COMMUNITY HEALTH INDICATORS PER 1000 POPULATION					
Total Population (in thousands)	3,792	3,724	3,687	3,644	3,612
Inpatient					
Beds	3.0	3.0	3.1	3.0	3.0
Admissions	111.9	115.2	120.0	127.0	125.7
Inpatient Days	595.4	628.5	651.4	668.6	653.3
Inpatient Surgeries	28.2	29.4	31.8	32.4	32.0
Births	12.3	13.0	14.5	13.7	13.7
Outpatient					
Emergency Outpatient Visits	487.2	473.3	473.0	451.6	448.1
Other Outpatient Visits	1,101.4	1,046.0	1,038.0	1,039.0	1,011.7
Total Outpatient Visits	1,588.6	1,519.3	1,510.9	1,490.6	1,459.8
Outpatient Surgeries	55.8	55.4	54.3	54.3	54.7
Expense per Capita (per person)	$1,789.0	$1,741.1	$1,729.4	$1,745.8	$1,586.6

States

TABLE 6

OREGON

U.S. Registered Community Hospitals
(Nonfederal, short-term general and other special hospitals)

Overview 2007–2011

	2011	2010	2009	2008	2007
Total Community Hospitals in Oregon	59	58	58	58	58
Bed Size Category					
6-24	9	9	8	8	7
25-49	20	20	19	19	20
50-99	10	10	12	11	11
100-199	9	9	9	9	9
200-299	4	4	4	5	4
300-399	2	1	1	0	1
400-499	3	3	3	4	4
500 + ...	2	2	2	2	2
Location					
Hospitals Urban.	30	29	29	29	26
Hospitals Rural	29	29	29	29	32
Control					
State and Local Government.	12	12	12	13	13
Not for Profit	45	44	44	43	43
Investor owned	2	2	2	2	2
Physician Models					
Independent Practice Association	11	12	13	13	13
Group Practice without Walls.	9	9	8	8	7
Open Physician-Hospital Organization	6	6	6	6	6
Closed Physician-Hospital Organization	2	2	2	2	3
Management Service Organization	13	14	14	14	14
Integrated Salary Model.	40	39	35	35	36
Equity Model	0	0	1	1	0
Foundation.	4	5	6	5	3
Insurance Products					
Health Maintenance Organization	16	15	15	14	16
Preferred Provider Organization.	17	19	15	14	21
Indemnity Fee for Service	3	3	3	3	5
Managed Care Contracts					
Health Maintenance Organization	35	34	29	30	34
Preferred Provider Organization.	52	51	51	51	47
Affiliations					
Hospitals in a System.	40	39	39	37	37
Hospitals in a Network	28	27	25	25	24
Hospitals in a Group Purchasing Organization. .	58	57	56	56	57

States

TABLE 6

OREGON

U.S. Registered Community Hospitals
(Nonfederal, short-term general and other special hospitals)

Utilization, Personnel, Revenue and Expenses, Community Health Indicators 2007–2011

	2011	2010	2009	2008	2007
TOTAL FACILITY (Includes Hospital and Nursing Home Units)					
Utilization - Inpatient					
Beds	6,805	6,420	6,481	6,814	6,841
Admissions	342,649	321,334	323,733	348,600	347,089
Inpatient Days	1,468,277	1,387,082	1,437,561	1,551,894	1,534,999
Average Length of Stay	4.3	4.3	4.4	4.5	4.4
Inpatient Surgeries	123,292	114,683	114,337	120,048	119,933
Births	43,262	41,914	43,940	47,273	48,230
Utilization - Outpatient					
Emergency Outpatient Visits	1,404,165	1,229,539	1,312,068	1,330,142	1,301,629
Other Outpatient Visits	7,969,367	7,982,714	7,587,931	7,228,022	6,877,816
Total Outpatient Visits	9,373,532	9,212,253	8,899,999	8,558,164	8,179,445
Outpatient Surgeries	211,379	205,542	207,341	210,333	213,159
Personnel					
Full Time RNs	10,359	9,293	9,230	9,498	9,248
Full Time LPNs	185	189	212	214	179
Part Time RNs	7,692	7,003	7,068	7,753	7,217
Part Time LPNs	154	131	165	171	212
Total Full Time	39,278	35,968	35,768	37,581	36,209
Total Part Time	20,655	18,954	19,325	20,437	19,627
Revenue - Inpatient					
Gross Inpatient Revenue	$9,510,397,093	$8,342,718,826	$7,965,180,365	$7,942,127,860	$7,305,555,599
Revenue - Outpatient					
Gross Outpatient Revenue	$8,564,788,044	$7,669,159,468	$7,028,661,629	$6,403,379,909	$5,753,564,088
Revenue and Expenses - Totals					
(Includes Inpatient and Outpatient)					
Total Gross Revenue	$18,075,185,137	$16,011,878,294	$14,993,841,994	$14,345,507,769	$13,059,119,687
Deductions from Revenue	9,586,390,414	8,389,072,711	7,773,324,462	7,249,042,014	6,506,212,357
Net Patient Revenue	8,488,794,723	7,622,805,583	7,220,517,532	7,096,465,755	6,552,907,330
Other Operating Revenue	357,481,939	356,073,198	354,503,423	351,902,221	303,815,392
Other Nonoperating Revenue	115,998,119	164,944,836	-58,115,473	-55,685,102	238,442,802
Total Net Revenue	8,962,274,781	8,143,823,617	7,516,905,482	7,392,682,874	7,095,165,524
Total Expenses	8,726,772,182	7,875,937,042	7,402,240,332	7,376,298,400	6,704,406,099
HOSPITAL UNIT (Excludes Separate Nursing Home Units)					
Utilization - Inpatient					
Beds	6,618	6,233	6,228	6,551	6,577
Admissions	342,499	321,153	323,516	348,313	346,747
Inpatient Days	1,426,510	1,338,597	1,373,086	1,485,018	1,464,066
Average Length of Stay	4.2	4.2	4.2	4.3	4.2
Personnel					
Total Full Time	39,186	35,872	35,629	37,436	36,068
Total Part Time	20,579	18,863	19,243	20,381	19,561
Revenue and Expenses - Totals					
(Includes Inpatient and Outpatient)					
Total Net Revenue	$8,952,622,279	$8,133,821,379	$7,504,259,729	$7,380,524,478	$7,083,566,291
Total Expenses	8,718,381,099	7,866,577,239	7,391,642,279	7,366,061,834	6,693,285,719
COMMUNITY HEALTH INDICATORS PER 1000 POPULATION					
Total Population (in thousands)	3,872	3,856	3,826	3,783	3,733
Inpatient					
Beds	1.8	1.7	1.7	1.8	1.8
Admissions	88.5	83.3	84.6	92.1	93.0
Inpatient Days	379.2	359.8	375.8	410.2	411.2
Inpatient Surgeries	31.8	29.7	29.9	31.7	32.1
Births	11.2	10.9	11.5	12.5	12.9
Outpatient					
Emergency Outpatient Visits	362.7	318.9	343.0	351.6	348.7
Other Outpatient Visits	2,058.3	2,070.5	1,983.4	1,910.7	1,842.5
Total Outpatient Visits	2,420.9	2,389.4	2,326.4	2,262.3	2,191.1
Outpatient Surgeries	54.6	53.3	54.2	55.6	57.1
Expense per Capita (per person)	$2,253.9	$2,042.8	$1,934.9	$1,949.9	$1,796.0

States

TABLE 6

PENNSYLVANIA

U.S. Registered Community Hospitals
(Nonfederal, short-term general and other special hospitals)

Overview 2007–2011

	2011	2010	2009	2008	2007
Total Community Hospitals in Pennsylvania ...	194	196	194	201	187
Bed Size Category					
6-24	3	3	3	2	2
25-49	28	29	29	29	21
50-99	40	42	40	42	33
100-199	47	46	47	49	53
200-299	34	34	37	41	40
300-399	18	17	13	14	12
400-499	10	11	10	9	12
500 + ...	14	14	15	15	14
Location					
Hospitals Urban...........................	146	147	145	152	143
Hospitals Rural	48	49	49	49	44
Control					
State and Local Government................	2	2	2	3	2
Not for Profit	145	151	153	160	158
Investor owned	47	43	39	38	27
Physician Models					
Independent Practice Association	8	7	8	9	9
Group Practice without Walls................	6	8	13	13	12
Open Physician-Hospital Organization	22	24	25	32	31
Closed Physician-Hospital Organization	3	3	4	4	5
Management Service Organization	19	21	26	27	25
Integrated Salary Model....................	73	75	73	69	75
Equity Model	1	2	3	2	2
Foundation...............................	8	8	6	6	5
Insurance Products					
Health Maintenance Organization	35	29	24	29	29
Preferred Provider Organization..............	41	42	39	44	41
Indemnity Fee for Service	19	17	12	15	12
Managed Care Contracts					
Health Maintenance Organization	120	117	115	116	122
Preferred Provider Organization..............	116	115	109	112	117
Affiliations					
Hospitals in a System.....................	128	118	112	116	101
Hospitals in a Network....................	51	49	47	48	49
Hospitals in a Group Purchasing Organization..	134	139	134	131	138

TABLE 6

PENNSYLVANIA

U.S. Registered Community Hospitals
(Nonfederal, short-term general and other special hospitals)

Utilization, Personnel, Revenue and Expenses, Community Health Indicators 2007–2011

	2011	2010	2009	2008	2007
TOTAL FACILITY (Includes Hospital and Nursing Home Units)					
Utilization - Inpatient					
Beds	39,676	39,889	39,212	40,407	39,728
Admissions	1,766,191	1,809,935	1,841,550	1,901,417	1,880,382
Inpatient Days	9,659,186	9,769,701	9,865,210	10,353,793	10,257,605
Average Length of Stay	5.5	5.4	5.4	5.4	5.5
Inpatient Surgeries	526,338	534,919	540,046	558,918	549,182
Births	132,967	134,404	137,478	143,674	143,281
Utilization - Outpatient					
Emergency Outpatient Visits	6,221,333	6,120,131	6,009,572	6,006,841	5,771,876
Other Outpatient Visits	31,681,366	32,432,398	31,882,222	32,449,554	31,012,536
Total Outpatient Visits	37,902,699	38,552,529	37,891,794	38,456,395	36,784,412
Outpatient Surgeries	895,861	914,558	917,586	948,852	931,789
Personnel					
Full Time RNs	54,899	53,217	51,430	51,379	49,838
Full Time LPNs	3,115	3,406	3,769	4,183	4,225
Part Time RNs	25,473	24,947	25,315	25,909	26,044
Part Time LPNs	1,311	1,558	1,737	2,013	2,050
Total Full Time	211,563	207,153	203,289	211,389	204,480
Total Part Time	73,672	72,508	74,386	75,418	75,971
Revenue - Inpatient					
Gross Inpatient Revenue	$81,435,847,151	$77,752,923,156	$73,916,497,474	$72,947,964,529	$68,794,426,900
Revenue - Outpatient					
Gross Outpatient Revenue	$58,909,827,289	$52,558,766,166	$47,748,195,221	$43,951,207,740	$39,611,381,052
Revenue and Expenses - Totals					
(Includes Inpatient and Outpatient)					
Total Gross Revenue	$140,345,674,440	$130,311,689,322	$121,664,692,695	$116,899,172,269	$108,405,807,952
Deductions from Revenue	104,430,760,108	96,372,359,561	89,109,854,967	85,447,182,883	78,990,384,684
Net Patient Revenue	35,914,914,332	33,939,329,761	32,554,837,728	31,451,989,386	29,415,423,268
Other Operating Revenue	1,762,852,582	1,560,413,652	1,478,517,269	1,437,920,156	1,437,490,621
Other Nonoperating Revenue	671,813,569	355,838,893	-446,883,805	183,327,965	696,634,527
Total Net Revenue	38,349,580,483	35,855,582,306	33,586,471,192	33,073,237,507	31,549,548,416
Total Expenses	35,246,467,258	33,929,583,373	32,711,950,307	31,323,216,832	28,750,837,150
HOSPITAL UNIT (Excludes Separate Nursing Home Units)					
Utilization - Inpatient					
Beds	37,995	38,271	37,446	38,441	37,762
Admissions	1,748,683	1,793,060	1,822,836	1,880,413	1,859,317
Inpatient Days	9,116,795	9,324,956	9,383,976	9,836,158	9,655,775
Average Length of Stay	5.2	5.2	5.1	5.2	5.2
Personnel					
Total Full Time	210,543	205,956	201,932	209,962	202,951
Total Part Time	73,114	71,746	73,493	74,556	75,053
Revenue and Expenses - Totals					
(Includes Inpatient and Outpatient)					
Total Net Revenue	$38,167,896,294	$35,657,261,435	$33,390,355,912	$32,864,948,434	$31,356,583,352
Total Expenses	35,082,553,586	33,767,820,668	32,546,735,654	31,124,814,383	28,586,982,718
COMMUNITY HEALTH INDICATORS PER 1000 POPULATION					
Total Population (in thousands)	12,743	12,633	12,605	12,566	12,523
Inpatient					
Beds	3.1	3.2	3.1	3.2	3.2
Admissions	138.6	143.3	146.1	151.3	150.2
Inpatient Days	758.0	773.4	782.7	823.9	819.1
Inpatient Surgeries	41.3	42.3	42.8	44.5	43.9
Births	10.4	10.6	10.9	11.4	11.4
Outpatient					
Emergency Outpatient Visits	488.2	484.5	476.8	478.0	460.9
Other Outpatient Visits	2,486.2	2,567.3	2,529.4	2,582.3	2,476.5
Total Outpatient Visits	2,974.4	3,051.8	3,006.1	3,060.3	2,937.5
Outpatient Surgeries	70.3	72.4	72.8	75.5	74.4
Expense per Capita (per person)	$2,766.0	$2,685.8	$2,595.2	$2,492.6	$2,295.9

States

TABLE 6

RHODE ISLAND

U.S. Registered Community Hospitals
(Nonfederal, short-term general and other special hospitals)

Overview 2007–2011

	2011	2010	2009	2008	2007
Total Community Hospitals in Rhode Island ...	11	11	11	11	11
Bed Size Category					
6-24	0	0	0	0	0
25-49	0	0	0	0	0
50-99	1	1	1	1	1
100-199	5	5	5	6	6
200-299	3	3	3	2	2
300-399	1	1	1	1	1
400-499	0	0	0	0	0
500 + ...	1	1	1	1	1
Location					
Hospitals Urban...........................	11	11	11	11	10
Hospitals Rural	0	0	0	0	1
Control					
State and Local Government................	0	0	0	0	0
Not for Profit	11	11	11	11	11
Investor owned	0	0	0	0	0
Physician Models					
Independent Practice Association	5	5	4	6	6
Group Practice without Walls................	1	0	0	0	0
Open Physician-Hospital Organization	5	6	6	7	7
Closed Physician-Hospital Organization	0	0	1	1	1
Management Service Organization	2	2	2	2	2
Integrated Salary Model....................	5	6	5	5	5
Equity Model.............................	0	0	0	0	0
Foundation...............................	2	2	2	3	3
Insurance Products					
Health Maintenance Organization	1	1	1	2	2
Preferred Provider Organization..............	1	0	0	1	2
Indemnity Fee for Service	0	0	0	0	1
Managed Care Contracts					
Health Maintenance Organization	6	7	7	9	10
Preferred Provider Organization..............	7	7	7	10	9
Affiliations					
Hospitals in a System......................	5	5	5	5	5
Hospitals in a Network.....................	6	6	3	1	1
Hospitals in a Group Purchasing Organization..	7	7	7	9	10

TABLE 6

RHODE ISLAND

U.S. Registered Community Hospitals
(Nonfederal, short-term general and other special hospitals)

Utilization, Personnel, Revenue and Expenses, Community Health Indicators 2007–2011

	2011	2010	2009	2008	2007
TOTAL FACILITY (Includes Hospital and Nursing Home Units)					
Utilization - Inpatient					
Beds	2,468	2,479	2,512	2,463	2,449
Admissions	120,407	123,188	126,761	127,413	128,519
Inpatient Days	611,837	621,614	654,695	666,745	672,831
Average Length of Stay.	5.1	5.0	5.2	5.2	5.2
Inpatient Surgeries.	32,737	32,612	39,752	38,970	37,084
Births.	11,249	11,492	11,815	12,785	13,305
Utilization - Outpatient					
Emergency Outpatient Visits	542,625	495,149	502,224	494,817	485,624
Other Outpatient Visits.	1,699,025	2,127,266	2,131,290	2,139,409	2,082,179
Total Outpatient Visits	2,241,650	2,622,415	2,633,514	2,634,226	2,567,803
Outpatient Surgeries	67,432	66,930	79,583	82,597	91,082
Personnel					
Full Time RNs	2,426	2,251	2,255	2,301	2,269
Full Time LPNs	70	58	87	92	119
Part Time RNs	2,737	2,771	2,705	3,147	2,840
Part Time LPNs	60	54	95	118	149
Total Full Time.	12,810	12,686	12,928	12,908	12,810
Total Part Time	7,800	8,001	7,707	8,873	8,459
Revenue - Inpatient					
Gross Inpatient Revenue.	$3,763,721,393	$3,623,363,473	$3,585,072,822	$3,383,235,261	$3,157,359,726
Revenue - Outpatient					
Gross Outpatient Revenue	$3,841,600,497	$3,560,931,543	$3,292,773,520	$3,067,731,603	$2,874,889,949
Revenue and Expenses - Totals					
(Includes Inpatient and Outpatient)					
Total Gross Revenue.	$7,605,321,890	$7,184,295,016	$6,877,846,342	$6,450,966,864	$6,032,249,675
Deductions from Revenue	4,867,608,639	4,555,181,118	4,297,920,625	4,018,043,505	3,748,195,534
Net Patient Revenue	2,737,713,251	2,629,113,898	2,579,925,717	2,432,923,359	2,284,054,141
Other Operating Revenue	257,774,487	265,788,290	241,675,005	247,620,663	241,675,507
Other Nonoperating Revenue	10,927,762	6,408,073	6,908,048	6,024,220	26,894,546
Total Net Revenue.	3,006,415,500	2,901,310,261	2,828,508,770	2,686,568,242	2,552,624,194
Total Expenses.	3,021,867,827	2,883,693,916	2,812,067,020	2,649,565,524	2,504,792,635
HOSPITAL UNIT (Excludes Separate Nursing Home Units)					
Utilization - Inpatient					
Beds	2,468	2,479	2,512	2,439	2,425
Admissions	120,407	123,188	126,761	127,095	127,928
Inpatient Days	611,837	621,614	654,695	662,377	665,265
Average Length of Stay.	5.1	5.0	5.2	5.2	5.2
Personnel					
Total Full Time.	12,810	12,686	12,928	12,846	12,799
Total Part Time	7,800	8,001	7,707	8,790	8,451
Revenue and Expenses - Totals					
(Includes Inpatient and Outpatient)					
Total Net Revenue.	$3,006,415,500	$2,901,310,261	$2,828,508,770	$2,679,872,351	$2,549,240,364
Total Expenses.	3,021,867,827	2,883,693,916	2,812,067,020	2,643,600,577	2,501,997,062
COMMUNITY HEALTH INDICATORS PER 1000 POPULATION					
Total Population (in thousands)	1,051	1,057	1,053	1,054	1,055
Inpatient					
Beds	2.3	2.3	2.4	2.3	2.3
Admissions	114.5	116.6	120.4	120.9	121.8
Inpatient Days	582.0	588.2	621.6	632.9	637.7
Inpatient Surgeries.	31.1	30.9	37.7	37.0	35.2
Births.	10.7	10.9	11.2	12.1	12.6
Outpatient					
Emergency Outpatient Visits	516.1	468.5	476.9	469.7	460.3
Other Outpatient Visits.	1,616.1	2,012.8	2,023.6	2,030.8	1,973.6
Total Outpatient Visits	2,132.3	2,481.3	2,500.5	2,500.4	2,433.9
Outpatient Surgeries	64.1	63.3	75.6	78.4	86.3
Expense per Capita (per person).	$2,874.4	$2,728.5	$2,670.0	$2,515.0	$2,374.2

States

TABLE 6

SOUTH CAROLINA

U.S. Registered Community Hospitals
(Nonfederal, short-term general and other special hospitals)

Overview 2007–2011

	2011	2010	2009	2008	2007
Total Community Hospitals in South Carolina	66	67	70	69	67
Bed Size Category					
6-24	2	1	2	0	1
25-49	17	19	18	18	16
50-99	11	10	13	12	11
100-199	14	13	13	14	14
200-299	8	9	10	12	14
300-399	6	7	7	7	5
400-499	3	3	2	1	2
500 +	5	5	5	5	4
Location					
Hospitals Urban	41	42	45	44	39
Hospitals Rural	25	25	25	25	28
Control					
State and Local Government	19	17	20	20	19
Not for Profit	23	24	25	25	23
Investor owned	24	26	25	24	25
Physician Models					
Independent Practice Association	6	5	5	6	3
Group Practice without Walls	1	1	1	3	0
Open Physician-Hospital Organization	4	4	7	8	7
Closed Physician-Hospital Organization	2	1	0	1	1
Management Service Organization	0	2	1	0	1
Integrated Salary Model	20	19	15	14	13
Equity Model	1	0	0	0	0
Foundation	0	0	0	0	0
Insurance Products					
Health Maintenance Organization	6	7	7	2	2
Preferred Provider Organization	9	10	10	5	7
Indemnity Fee for Service	1	6	6	1	1
Managed Care Contracts					
Health Maintenance Organization	43	39	45	37	33
Preferred Provider Organization	43	38	46	36	36
Affiliations					
Hospitals in a System	44	44	47	45	43
Hospitals in a Network	12	12	12	15	16
Hospitals in a Group Purchasing Organization	60	59	58	52	1

States

TABLE 6

SOUTH CAROLINA

U.S. Registered Community Hospitals
(Nonfederal, short-term general and other special hospitals)

Utilization, Personnel, Revenue and Expenses, Community Health Indicators 2007–2011

	2011	2010	2009	2008	2007
TOTAL FACILITY (Includes Hospital and Nursing Home Units)					
Utilization - Inpatient					
Beds	12,253	12,495	12,483	12,498	12,032
Admissions	508,652	522,793	528,204	528,872	518,994
Inpatient Days	2,878,860	3,002,541	2,960,134	2,962,830	3,006,247
Average Length of Stay	5.7	5.7	5.6	5.6	5.8
Inpatient Surgeries	194,171	194,895	205,119	196,304	190,349
Births	53,530	54,894	57,559	56,068	56,616
Utilization - Outpatient					
Emergency Outpatient Visits	1,687,578	1,453,696	2,171,925	1,954,264	1,890,731
Other Outpatient Visits	4,732,533	4,922,633	4,147,745	3,969,951	4,151,591
Total Outpatient Visits	6,420,111	6,376,329	6,319,670	5,924,215	6,042,322
Outpatient Surgeries	298,549	289,794	300,093	294,280	280,735
Personnel					
Full Time RNs	17,357	17,476	17,451	16,203	15,120
Full Time LPNs	947	1,062	1,170	1,292	1,363
Part Time RNs	4,897	5,184	5,246	5,834	5,826
Part Time LPNs	280	347	395	510	514
Total Full Time	58,183	58,567	58,933	58,372	54,571
Total Part Time	13,721	14,343	14,332	16,302	16,040
Revenue - Inpatient					
Gross Inpatient Revenue	$19,216,509,155	$18,371,422,174	$17,448,319,308	$16,743,319,395	$14,774,254,035
Revenue - Outpatient					
Gross Outpatient Revenue	$14,306,685,453	$12,660,946,189	$11,900,471,047	$10,266,244,867	$8,994,634,785
Revenue and Expenses - Totals					
(Includes Inpatient and Outpatient)					
Total Gross Revenue	$33,523,194,608	$31,032,368,363	$29,348,790,355	$27,009,564,262	$23,768,888,820
Deductions from Revenue	23,252,635,242	21,049,743,519	19,883,727,173	18,082,987,646	15,526,589,717
Net Patient Revenue	10,270,559,366	9,982,624,844	9,465,063,182	8,926,576,616	8,242,299,103
Other Operating Revenue	243,603,622	249,339,525	236,614,730	262,341,118	224,352,076
Other Nonoperating Revenue	141,294,623	210,607,769	190,176,135	85,822,937	161,793,047
Total Net Revenue	10,655,457,611	10,442,572,138	9,891,854,047	9,274,740,671	8,628,444,226
Total Expenses	9,707,103,556	9,349,824,264	9,264,970,348	8,890,465,525	7,888,982,140
HOSPITAL UNIT (Excludes Separate Nursing Home Units)					
Utilization - Inpatient					
Beds	11,479	11,611	11,739	11,728	11,080
Admissions	504,604	518,130	524,147	524,838	514,618
Inpatient Days	2,632,449	2,729,473	2,685,104	2,750,321	2,686,337
Average Length of Stay	5.2	5.3	5.1	5.2	5.2
Personnel					
Total Full Time	57,533	57,811	58,169	57,714	53,761
Total Part Time	13,382	14,118	13,998	16,043	15,737
Revenue and Expenses - Totals					
(Includes Inpatient and Outpatient)					
Total Net Revenue	$10,577,543,806	$10,354,825,713	$9,821,499,987	$9,217,872,804	$8,562,824,215
Total Expenses	9,635,628,294	9,272,925,368	9,204,773,809	8,842,007,632	7,826,701,269
COMMUNITY HEALTH INDICATORS PER 1000 POPULATION					
Total Population (in thousands)	4,679	4,597	4,561	4,503	4,424
Inpatient					
Beds	2.6	2.7	2.7	2.8	2.7
Admissions	108.7	113.7	115.8	117.4	117.3
Inpatient Days	615.2	653.2	649.0	657.9	679.5
Inpatient Surgeries	41.5	42.4	45.0	43.6	43.0
Births	11.4	11.9	12.6	12.5	12.8
Outpatient					
Emergency Outpatient Visits	360.7	316.2	476.2	434.0	427.4
Other Outpatient Visits	1,011.4	1,070.8	909.3	881.6	938.4
Total Outpatient Visits	1,372.0	1,387.1	1,385.5	1,315.5	1,365.7
Outpatient Surgeries	63.8	63.0	65.8	65.3	63.5
Expense per Capita (per person)	$2,074.5	$2,033.9	$2,031.2	$1,974.2	$1,783.1

States

TABLE 6

SOUTH DAKOTA

U.S. Registered Community Hospitals
(Nonfederal, short-term general and other special hospitals)

Overview 2007–2011

	2011	2010	2009	2008	2007
Total Community Hospitals in South Dakota...	53	53	53	53	51
Bed Size Category					
6-24	19	17	16	18	15
25-49	12	14	14	12	13
50-99	10	10	11	11	10
100-199	7	7	7	7	8
200-299	2	2	2	1	2
300-399	1	1	1	2	1
400-499	2	2	2	2	1
500 + ...	0	0	0	0	1
Location					
Hospitals Urban...........................	11	11	11	11	8
Hospitals Rural	42	42	42	42	43
Control					
State and Local Government...............	4	4	3	5	5
Not for Profit	45	45	46	44	43
Investor owned	4	4	4	4	3
Physician Models					
Independent Practice Association	10	8	12	11	10
Group Practice without Walls................	2	1	3	3	3
Open Physician-Hospital Organization	4	3	6	6	8
Closed Physician-Hospital Organization	3	2	3	3	4
Management Service Organization	3	1	2	2	3
Integrated Salary Model....................	27	23	28	25	25
Equity Model	2	1	2	2	2
Foundation................................	3	2	1	1	2
Insurance Products					
Health Maintenance Organization	13	16	17	17	15
Preferred Provider Organization..............	13	11	10	13	18
Indemnity Fee for Service	8	6	9	8	5
Managed Care Contracts					
Health Maintenance Organization	25	23	24	24	22
Preferred Provider Organization..............	30	27	29	32	32
Affiliations					
Hospitals in a System......................	37	37	38	38	36
Hospitals in a Network	24	21	22	22	20
Hospitals in a Group Purchasing Organization..	46	39	45	45	44

States

TABLE 6

SOUTH DAKOTA

U.S. Registered Community Hospitals
(Nonfederal, short-term general and other special hospitals)

Utilization, Personnel, Revenue and Expenses, Community Health Indicators 2007–2011

	2011	2010	2009	2008	2007
TOTAL FACILITY (Includes Hospital and Nursing Home Units)					
Utilization - Inpatient					
Beds	4,084	4,108	4,142	4,113	4,245
Admissions	101,867	101,128	102,335	102,116	99,931
Inpatient Days	956,044	935,410	1,005,265	1,005,766	1,008,378
Average Length of Stay	9.4	9.2	9.8	9.8	10.1
Inpatient Surgeries	31,220	30,363	32,416	31,715	33,312
Births	11,976	11,437	11,848	12,258	12,125
Utilization - Outpatient					
Emergency Outpatient Visits	251,769	259,364	240,618	239,192	226,131
Other Outpatient Visits	1,862,618	1,782,993	1,698,830	1,618,764	1,562,594
Total Outpatient Visits	2,114,387	2,042,357	1,939,448	1,857,956	1,788,725
Outpatient Surgeries	69,535	67,743	71,571	71,162	61,234
Personnel					
Full Time RNs	4,068	3,633	3,596	3,160	3,106
Full Time LPNs	270	216	191	185	189
Part Time RNs	1,951	1,736	2,003	2,253	1,874
Part Time LPNs	144	129	132	131	130
Total Full Time	15,443	14,483	15,119	14,488	13,502
Total Part Time	6,954	6,316	7,357	8,067	7,187
Revenue - Inpatient					
Gross Inpatient Revenue	$2,969,819,139	$2,779,376,912	$2,534,795,960	$2,293,166,775	$2,051,748,519
Revenue - Outpatient					
Gross Outpatient Revenue	$2,643,342,592	$2,405,199,211	$2,107,192,538	$1,875,244,749	$1,595,180,119
Revenue and Expenses - Totals					
(Includes Inpatient and Outpatient)					
Total Gross Revenue	$5,613,161,731	$5,184,576,123	$4,641,988,498	$4,168,411,524	$3,646,928,638
Deductions from Revenue	3,130,649,704	2,884,612,400	2,468,508,414	2,187,095,692	1,796,255,037
Net Patient Revenue	2,482,512,027	2,299,963,723	2,173,480,084	1,981,315,832	1,850,673,601
Other Operating Revenue	129,361,349	122,786,678	113,185,811	103,615,596	121,580,983
Other Nonoperating Revenue	101,197,230	34,907,740	-20,449,611	30,994,497	64,050,745
Total Net Revenue	2,713,070,606	2,457,658,141	2,266,216,284	2,115,925,925	2,036,305,329
Total Expenses	2,353,418,704	2,194,315,958	2,075,750,158	1,919,761,533	1,791,313,970
HOSPITAL UNIT (Excludes Separate Nursing Home Units)					
Utilization - Inpatient					
Beds	2,602	2,869	2,728	2,671	2,621
Admissions	100,451	99,824	100,901	100,555	97,994
Inpatient Days	443,426	505,190	507,150	509,176	455,753
Average Length of Stay	4.4	5.1	5.0	5.1	4.7
Personnel					
Total Full Time	14,561	13,753	14,238	13,650	12,555
Total Part Time	6,292	5,684	6,607	7,369	6,339
Revenue and Expenses - Totals					
(Includes Inpatient and Outpatient)					
Total Net Revenue	$2,626,079,779	$2,382,414,150	$2,185,615,059	$2,035,881,683	$1,957,696,000
Total Expenses	2,278,140,332	2,128,257,681	2,002,334,795	1,848,451,464	1,713,828,405
COMMUNITY HEALTH INDICATORS PER 1000 POPULATION					
Total Population (in thousands)	824	820	812	805	797
Inpatient					
Beds	5.0	5.0	5.1	5.1	5.3
Admissions	123.6	123.3	126.0	126.9	125.4
Inpatient Days	1,160.1	1,140.6	1,237.4	1,250.1	1,265.2
Inpatient Surgeries	37.9	37.0	39.9	39.4	41.8
Births	14.5	13.9	14.6	15.2	15.2
Outpatient					
Emergency Outpatient Visits	305.5	316.3	296.2	297.3	283.7
Other Outpatient Visits	2,260.2	2,174.2	2,091.2	2,012.1	1,960.5
Total Outpatient Visits	2,565.7	2,490.4	2,387.4	2,309.4	2,244.2
Outpatient Surgeries	84.4	82.6	88.1	88.5	76.8
Expense per Capita (per person)	$2,855.8	$2,675.7	$2,555.1	$2,386.2	$2,247.5

States

TABLE 6

TENNESSEE

U.S. Registered Community Hospitals
(Nonfederal, short-term general and other special hospitals)

Overview 2007–2011

	2011	2010	2009	2008	2007
Total Community Hospitals in Tennessee	133	134	137	137	133
Bed Size Category					
6-24	7	6	6	7	7
25-49	36	35	36	36	28
50-99	32	32	32	32	34
100-199	26	29	30	29	33
200-299	13	12	13	12	12
300-399	7	6	7	7	5
400-499	3	5	6	5	6
500 + ...	9	9	7	9	8
Location					
Hospitals Urban..........................	78	78	81	81	67
Hospitals Rural	55	56	56	56	66
Control					
State and Local Government................	21	20	22	22	22
Not for Profit	50	56	59	60	61
Investor owned	62	58	56	55	50
Physician Models					
Independent Practice Association	17	19	17	14	16
Group Practice without Walls................	5	4	3	4	4
Open Physician-Hospital Organization	11	11	11	19	21
Closed Physician-Hospital Organization	3	3	3	5	5
Management Service Organization	17	16	18	15	17
Integrated Salary Model.....................	29	31	26	19	16
Equity Model	0	0	0	0	0
Foundation...............................	3	4	7	8	6
Insurance Products					
Health Maintenance Organization	8	8	5	14	16
Preferred Provider Organization..............	17	17	16	26	25
Indemnity Fee for Service	3	3	2	10	14
Managed Care Contracts					
Health Maintenance Organization	68	66	67	86	77
Preferred Provider Organization..............	69	72	75	87	80
Affiliations					
Hospitals in a System......................	105	101	103	104	101
Hospitals in a Network	38	41	41	45	38
Hospitals in a Group Purchasing Organization..	70	69	77	89	85

States

TABLE 6

TENNESSEE

U.S. Registered Community Hospitals
(Nonfederal, short-term general and other special hospitals)

Utilization, Personnel, Revenue and Expenses, Community Health Indicators 2007–2011

	2011	2010	2009	2008	2007
TOTAL FACILITY (Includes Hospital and Nursing Home Units)					
Utilization - Inpatient					
Beds	20,042	20,830	20,959	21,102	21,688
Admissions	805,805	832,554	859,191	859,344	969,763
Inpatient Days	4,465,285	4,579,402	4,799,858	4,911,215	5,372,297
Average Length of Stay	5.5	5.5	5.6	5.7	5.5
Inpatient Surgeries	234,368	249,367	255,557	243,820	258,348
Births	64,202	70,685	79,804	83,978	90,042
Utilization - Outpatient					
Emergency Outpatient Visits	3,113,164	3,130,660	3,301,872	3,251,592	3,253,035
Other Outpatient Visits	7,799,873	8,299,669	8,281,474	7,995,403	8,565,760
Total Outpatient Visits	10,913,037	11,430,329	11,583,346	11,246,995	11,818,795
Outpatient Surgeries	405,105	411,688	413,202	385,344	443,649
Personnel					
Full Time RNs	25,298	24,475	25,846	24,727	27,626
Full Time LPNs	2,503	2,706	2,938	3,286	3,744
Part Time RNs	9,124	9,222	8,514	8,891	10,578
Part Time LPNs	652	767	742	881	1,028
Total Full Time	89,424	88,145	93,028	90,902	105,326
Total Part Time	23,382	25,539	24,476	25,311	30,136
Revenue - Inpatient					
Gross Inpatient Revenue	$27,704,113,354	$26,846,357,974	$25,367,667,093	$24,012,198,547	$24,331,008,568
Revenue - Outpatient					
Gross Outpatient Revenue	$20,574,396,531	$19,276,589,146	$17,453,642,146	$15,732,131,119	$16,507,650,360
Revenue and Expenses - Totals					
(Includes Inpatient and Outpatient)					
Total Gross Revenue	$48,278,509,885	$46,122,947,120	$42,821,309,239	$39,744,329,666	$40,838,658,928
Deductions from Revenue	34,865,417,816	32,931,211,533	29,947,998,235	27,469,500,901	27,397,484,207
Net Patient Revenue	13,413,092,069	13,191,735,587	12,873,311,004	12,274,828,765	13,441,174,721
Other Operating Revenue	445,637,920	409,743,303	432,326,528	496,258,779	523,978,490
Other Nonoperating Revenue	158,051,242	268,674,837	-81,972,728	81,614,397	363,631,353
Total Net Revenue	14,016,781,231	13,870,153,727	13,223,664,804	12,852,701,941	14,328,784,564
Total Expenses	12,769,264,645	12,699,265,618	12,694,504,650	11,996,245,958	13,405,461,053
HOSPITAL UNIT (Excludes Separate Nursing Home Units)					
Utilization - Inpatient					
Beds	19,080	19,750	19,682	19,467	20,088
Admissions	797,947	825,283	850,278	849,060	958,480
Inpatient Days	4,182,726	4,244,905	4,400,598	4,396,275	4,889,474
Average Length of Stay	5.2	5.1	5.2	5.2	5.1
Personnel					
Total Full Time	88,534	87,258	91,886	89,529	103,980
Total Part Time	23,260	25,367	24,274	25,004	29,745
Revenue and Expenses - Totals					
(Includes Inpatient and Outpatient)					
Total Net Revenue	$13,930,291,003	$13,791,578,759	$13,131,489,651	$12,735,644,514	$14,221,268,188
Total Expenses	12,708,497,514	12,630,190,370	12,619,381,549	11,896,072,460	13,318,384,157
COMMUNITY HEALTH INDICATORS PER 1000 POPULATION					
Total Population (in thousands)	6,403	6,338	6,296	6,240	6,173
Inpatient					
Beds	3.1	3.3	3.3	3.4	3.5
Admissions	125.8	131.4	136.5	137.7	157.1
Inpatient Days	697.3	722.5	762.3	787.0	870.3
Inpatient Surgeries	36.6	39.3	40.6	39.1	41.9
Births	10.0	11.2	12.7	13.5	14.6
Outpatient					
Emergency Outpatient Visits	486.2	493.9	524.4	521.1	527.0
Other Outpatient Visits	1,218.1	1,309.5	1,315.3	1,281.2	1,387.6
Total Outpatient Visits	1,704.3	1,803.4	1,839.7	1,802.3	1,914.6
Outpatient Surgeries	63.3	65.0	65.6	61.7	71.9
Expense per Capita (per person)	$1,994.2	$2,003.6	$2,016.2	$1,922.3	$2,171.7

States

TABLE 6

TEXAS

U.S. Registered Community Hospitals
(Nonfederal, short-term general and other special hospitals)

Overview 2007–2011

	2011	2010	2009	2008	2007
Total Community Hospitals in Texas..........	**420**	**426**	**428**	**426**	**409**
Bed Size Category					
6-24	70	73	69	63	60
25-49	109	107	111	111	106
50-99	82	86	79	87	81
100-199	58	61	66	64	59
200-299	43	41	43	44	46
300-399	19	20	21	20	24
400-499	15	14	16	14	13
500 + ...	24	24	23	23	20
Location					
Hospitals Urban...........................	269	275	277	275	250
Hospitals Rural	151	151	151	151	159
Control					
State and Local Government................	110	113	116	117	117
Not for Profit	149	148	147	152	150
Investor owned	161	165	165	157	142
Physician Models					
Independent Practice Association	62	72	69	67	80
Group Practice without Walls...............	15	15	24	14	14
Open Physician-Hospital Organization	79	82	84	90	88
Closed Physician-Hospital Organization	20	19	18	17	17
Management Service Organization	71	73	74	63	65
Integrated Salary Model	114	97	95	91	87
Equity Model	9	13	13	12	9
Foundation...............................	37	35	33	34	38
Insurance Products					
Health Maintenance Organization	65	66	62	49	56
Preferred Provider Organization..............	79	84	75	66	83
Indemnity Fee for Service	22	26	22	23	21
Managed Care Contracts					
Health Maintenance Organization	318	318	323	314	305
Preferred Provider Organization..............	357	358	361	361	357
Affiliations					
Hospitals in a System.....................	272	278	286	281	259
Hospitals in a Network	115	114	106	104	109
Hospitals in a Group Purchasing Organization..	399	398	386	385	369

TABLE 6

TEXAS

U.S. Registered Community Hospitals
(Nonfederal, short-term general and other special hospitals)

Utilization, Personnel, Revenue and Expenses, Community Health Indicators 2007–2011

	2011	2010	2009	2008	2007
TOTAL FACILITY (Includes Hospital and Nursing Home Units)					
Utilization - Inpatient					
Beds	60,755	61,357	62,069	61,039	58,192
Admissions	2,534,688	2,580,401	2,621,436	2,585,680	2,468,109
Inpatient Days	13,062,644	13,331,491	13,590,044	13,430,355	12,816,839
Average Length of Stay............	5.2	5.2	5.2	5.2	5.2
Inpatient Surgeries................	736,841	761,437	781,093	763,867	768,063
Births.........................	364,901	381,038	397,979	390,274	378,375
Utilization - Outpatient					
Emergency Outpatient Visits........	9,889,631	9,739,066	9,438,151	8,819,272	8,444,299
Other Outpatient Visits............	29,375,051	28,541,761	26,584,907	25,999,796	24,054,713
Total Outpatient Visits	39,264,682	38,280,827	36,023,058	34,819,068	32,499,012
Outpatient Surgeries	1,034,126	1,061,053	1,049,368	1,030,039	991,853
Personnel					
Full Time RNs	79,968	82,490	80,537	73,086	70,963
Full Time LPNs	8,278	9,113	9,798	10,227	10,087
Part Time RNs	22,557	20,107	20,901	21,580	20,369
Part Time LPNs.................	1,683	2,103	2,416	2,487	2,469
Total Full Time.................	274,534	280,656	280,633	266,604	263,105
Total Part Time	63,938	59,204	61,186	63,288	59,498
Revenue - Inpatient					
Gross Inpatient Revenue...........	$105,598,575,282	$100,476,401,353	$95,184,048,332	$87,141,175,562	$77,330,388,025
Revenue - Outpatient					
Gross Outpatient Revenue	$72,395,257,221	$66,131,968,217	$58,578,510,903	$49,826,890,592	$43,530,620,498
Revenue and Expenses - Totals					
(Includes Inpatient and Outpatient)					
Total Gross Revenue..............	$177,993,832,503	$166,608,369,570	$153,762,559,235	$136,968,066,154	$120,861,008,523
Deductions from Revenue..........	132,820,105,328	122,345,151,455	111,061,711,464	97,866,719,468	85,002,811,289
Net Patient Revenue	45,173,727,175	44,263,218,115	42,700,847,771	39,101,346,686	35,858,197,234
Other Operating Revenue	4,676,074,781	4,492,462,311	4,384,346,385	4,040,612,362	3,786,629,316
Other Nonoperating Revenue	1,373,986,299	1,120,744,597	304,258,670	310,546,108	1,059,715,727
Total Net Revenue...............	51,223,788,255	49,876,425,023	47,389,452,826	43,452,505,156	40,704,542,277
Total Expenses..................	45,556,147,376	44,225,750,333	43,410,205,109	40,396,037,477	37,428,408,575
HOSPITAL UNIT (Excludes Separate Nursing Home Units)					
Utilization - Inpatient					
Beds	59,835	60,497	61,160	59,947	56,952
Admissions	2,525,028	2,570,756	2,610,941	2,574,309	2,455,421
Inpatient Days	12,794,132	13,090,722	13,329,807	13,117,477	12,452,079
Average Length of Stay............	5.1	5.1	5.1	5.1	5.1
Personnel					
Total Full Time..................	273,785	279,998	279,502	265,647	261,686
Total Part Time	63,837	59,051	61,033	62,914	59,123
Revenue and Expenses - Totals					
(Includes Inpatient and Outpatient)					
Total Net Revenue...............	$51,125,792,174	$49,780,310,157	$47,305,885,374	$43,361,995,590	$40,562,429,655
Total Expenses..................	45,465,619,488	44,132,923,562	43,327,541,508	40,292,698,073	37,243,889,225
COMMUNITY HEALTH INDICATORS PER 1000 POPULATION					
Total Population (in thousands)	25,675	25,213	24,782	24,304	23,838
Inpatient					
Beds	2.4	2.4	2.5	2.5	2.4
Admissions	98.7	102.3	105.8	106.4	103.5
Inpatient Days	508.8	528.7	548.4	552.6	537.7
Inpatient Surgeries................	28.7	30.2	31.5	31.4	32.2
Births.........................	14.2	15.1	16.1	16.1	15.9
Outpatient					
Emergency Outpatient Visits........	385.2	386.3	380.8	362.9	354.2
Other Outpatient Visits............	1,144.1	1,132.0	1,072.7	1,069.8	1,009.1
Total Outpatient Visits	1,529.3	1,518.3	1,453.6	1,432.6	1,363.3
Outpatient Surgeries	40.3	42.1	42.3	42.4	41.6
Expense per Capita (per person).....	$1,774.4	$1,754.1	$1,751.7	$1,662.1	$1,570.1

States

TABLE 6

UTAH

U.S. Registered Community Hospitals
(Nonfederal, short-term general and other special hospitals)

Overview 2007–2011

	2011	2010	2009	2008	2007
Total Community Hospitals in Utah............	46	44	44	43	41
Bed Size Category					
6-24	8	8	6	6	6
25-49	16	15	15	14	12
50-99	4	3	6	6	8
100-199	9	8	8	9	8
200-299	4	5	4	4	4
300-399	3	3	3	2	1
400-499	2	2	1	1	1
500 + ...	0	0	1	1	1
Location					
Hospitals Urban..........................	28	26	26	26	20
Hospitals Rural	18	18	18	17	21
Control					
State and Local Government................	6	6	6	5	4
Not for Profit	25	23	23	23	22
Investor owned	15	15	15	15	15
Physician Models					
Independent Practice Association	4	4	6	2	2
Group Practice without Walls................	2	1	1	0	0
Open Physician-Hospital Organization	1	1	3	2	2
Closed Physician-Hospital Organization	3	2	2	1	1
Management Service Organization	2	2	2	1	1
Integrated Salary Model	18	13	13	13	14
Equity Model	1	1	1	0	0
Foundation...............................	1	1	2	1	0
Insurance Products					
Health Maintenance Organization	17	15	15	16	16
Preferred Provider Organization..............	15	13	13	12	15
Indemnity Fee for Service	7	5	7	7	9
Managed Care Contracts					
Health Maintenance Organization	12	14	13	14	15
Preferred Provider Organization..............	18	17	17	19	17
Affiliations					
Hospitals in a System......................	38	36	36	37	36
Hospitals in a Network.....................	11	11	16	15	14
Hospitals in a Group Purchasing Organization..	25	22	21	19	23

States

TABLE 6

UTAH

U.S. Registered Community Hospitals
(Nonfederal, short-term general and other special hospitals)

Utilization, Personnel, Revenue and Expenses, Community Health Indicators 2007–2011

	2011	2010	2009	2008	2007
TOTAL FACILITY (Includes Hospital and Nursing Home Units)					
Utilization - Inpatient					
Beds	5,135	5,086	4,973	4,874	4,584
Admissions.....................	236,131	224,264	226,239	226,376	223,971
Inpatient Days	993,098	979,963	1,003,710	1,015,945	1,003,917
Average Length of Stay...........	4.2	4.4	4.4	4.5	4.5
Inpatient Surgeries...............	71,272	70,503	71,568	67,840	71,541
Births........................	52,695	49,392	52,189	55,088	53,731
Utilization - Outpatient					
Emergency Outpatient Visits........	855,152	834,897	865,286	856,277	900,975
Other Outpatient Visits............	4,999,514	4,642,827	4,609,086	4,449,171	4,062,804
Total Outpatient Visits	5,854,666	5,477,724	5,474,372	5,305,448	4,963,779
Outpatient Surgeries	174,376	166,870	155,162	152,105	138,824
Personnel					
Full Time RNs	7,462	7,303	6,961	6,780	6,318
Full Time LPNs	337	358	367	378	500
Part Time RNs..................	4,362	4,353	4,454	4,620	4,170
Part Time LPNs	181	187	222	277	380
Total Full Time.................	26,733	26,111	26,390	26,648	25,903
Total Part Time	13,696	13,418	14,135	14,535	13,269
Revenue - Inpatient					
Gross Inpatient Revenue...........	$7,051,376,726	$6,581,097,114	$5,718,543,491	$5,428,255,474	$5,250,442,289
Revenue - Outpatient					
Gross Outpatient Revenue	$6,027,847,868	$5,300,499,527	$4,667,222,276	$4,060,507,024	$3,704,805,862
Revenue and Expenses - Totals					
(Includes Inpatient and Outpatient)					
Total Gross Revenue..............	$13,079,224,594	$11,881,596,641	$10,385,765,767	$9,488,762,498	$8,955,248,151
Deductions from Revenue..........	7,638,050,195	6,906,546,426	5,568,409,487	5,093,986,033	4,961,871,950
Net Patient Revenue	5,441,174,399	4,975,050,215	4,817,356,280	4,394,776,465	3,993,376,201
Other Operating Revenue	265,484,132	243,975,154	228,925,055	207,762,710	158,758,359
Other Nonoperating Revenue	10,166,250	31,741,257	12,752,174	20,119,824	39,067,658
Total Net Revenue................	5,716,824,781	5,250,766,626	5,059,033,509	4,622,658,999	4,191,202,218
Total Expenses..................	4,679,558,728	4,470,510,613	4,263,844,434	4,041,481,901	3,710,391,899
HOSPITAL UNIT (Excludes Separate Nursing Home Units)					
Utilization - Inpatient					
Beds	5,008	4,931	4,808	4,720	4,431
Admissions.....................	235,615	223,117	224,928	225,065	223,089
Inpatient Days	954,737	935,962	961,475	976,402	960,104
Average Length of Stay...........	4.1	4.2	4.3	4.3	4.3
Personnel					
Total Full Time..................	26,670	26,037	26,296	26,562	25,822
Total Part Time	13,647	13,364	14,068	14,449	13,158
Revenue and Expenses - Totals					
(Includes Inpatient and Outpatient)					
Total Net Revenue................	$5,708,620,280	$5,239,992,029	$5,050,316,084	$4,612,854,633	$4,183,929,529
Total Expenses..................	4,672,187,702	4,461,414,330	4,255,351,046	4,034,303,806	3,704,812,297
COMMUNITY HEALTH INDICATORS PER 1000 POPULATION					
Total Population (in thousands)	2,817	2,831	2,785	2,727	2,664
Inpatient					
Beds	1.8	1.8	1.8	1.8	1.7
Admissions.....................	83.8	79.2	81.2	83.0	84.1
Inpatient Days	352.5	346.2	360.5	372.5	376.9
Inpatient Surgeries...............	25.3	24.9	25.7	24.9	26.9
Births........................	18.7	17.4	18.7	20.2	20.2
Outpatient					
Emergency Outpatient Visits........	303.5	294.9	310.7	314.0	338.2
Other Outpatient Visits............	1,774.6	1,640.1	1,655.2	1,631.3	1,525.2
Total Outpatient Visits	2,078.2	1,935.1	1,966.0	1,945.3	1,863.4
Outpatient Surgeries	61.9	58.9	55.7	55.8	52.1
Expense per Capita (per person).....	$1,661.1	$1,579.3	$1,531.2	$1,481.8	$1,392.9

States

TABLE **6**

VERMONT

U.S. Registered Community Hospitals
(Nonfederal, short-term general and other special hospitals)

Overview 2007–2011

	2011	2010	2009	2008	2007
Total Community Hospitals in Vermont	14	14	14	14	14
Bed Size Category					
6-24	2	1	1	1	0
25-49	6	6	6	6	7
50-99	3	4	4	4	4
100-199	1	1	1	1	1
200-299	1	1	1	1	1
300-399	0	0	0	0	0
400-499	1	1	1	1	1
500 + ...	0	0	0	0	0
Location					
Hospitals Urban.	2	2	2	2	2
Hospitals Rural	12	12	12	12	12
Control					
State and Local Government.	0	0	0	0	0
Not for Profit	14	14	14	14	14
Investor owned	0	0	0	0	0
Physician Models					
Independent Practice Association	0	0	0	0	0
Group Practice without Walls.	0	0	0	0	0
Open Physician-Hospital Organization	3	3	2	3	2
Closed Physician-Hospital Organization	1	1	1	1	1
Management Service Organization	0	0	0	0	1
Integrated Salary Model	7	8	7	9	7
Equity Model	0	0	0	0	0
Foundation.	0	0	0	0	0
Insurance Products					
Health Maintenance Organization	2	2	3	3	3
Preferred Provider Organization.	1	0	0	0	2
Indemnity Fee for Service	1	0	0	0	2
Managed Care Contracts					
Health Maintenance Organization	5	6	6	7	7
Preferred Provider Organization.	5	5	4	6	6
Affiliations					
Hospitals in a System.	1	1	1	1	1
Hospitals in a Network	5	5	5	5	5
Hospitals in a Group Purchasing Organization. .	10	10	10	12	11

States

TABLE 6

VERMONT

U.S. Registered Community Hospitals
(Nonfederal, short-term general and other special hospitals)

Utilization, Personnel, Revenue and Expenses, Community Health Indicators 2007–2011

	2011	2010	2009	2008	2007
TOTAL FACILITY (Includes Hospital and Nursing Home Units)					
Utilization - Inpatient					
Beds	1,218	1,288	1,296	1,302	1,362
Admissions	48,941	49,449	50,922	51,301	49,892
Inpatient Days	310,510	305,289	321,741	328,506	337,004
Average Length of Stay	6.3	6.2	6.3	6.4	6.8
Inpatient Surgeries	13,258	13,950	15,557	14,160	14,224
Births	12,755	5,604	5,829	5,982	5,981
Utilization - Outpatient					
Emergency Outpatient Visits	296,666	352,808	357,793	304,717	259,661
Other Outpatient Visits	2,788,192	2,999,812	2,997,816	3,001,378	2,514,148
Total Outpatient Visits	3,084,858	3,352,620	3,355,609	3,306,095	2,773,809
Outpatient Surgeries	48,381	48,158	48,673	47,401	44,800
Personnel					
Full Time RNs	1,720	1,748	1,671	1,690	1,551
Full Time LPNs	159	166	163	218	214
Part Time RNs	1,595	1,311	1,262	1,239	1,211
Part Time LPNs	128	149	110	160	162
Total Full Time	9,724	9,629	9,738	9,611	9,373
Total Part Time	4,930	4,078	3,920	3,763	3,624
Revenue - Inpatient					
Gross Inpatient Revenue	$1,055,321,773	$1,154,115,173	$1,055,165,310	$903,264,654	$906,951,930
Revenue - Outpatient					
Gross Outpatient Revenue	$2,665,042,545	$2,538,622,333	$2,313,816,425	$2,017,330,510	$1,784,747,426
Revenue and Expenses - Totals					
(Includes Inpatient and Outpatient)					
Total Gross Revenue	$3,720,364,318	$3,692,737,506	$3,368,981,735	$2,920,595,164	$2,691,699,356
Deductions from Revenue	1,901,314,973	1,982,861,871	1,719,852,956	1,383,550,785	1,256,738,757
Net Patient Revenue	1,819,049,345	1,709,875,635	1,649,128,779	1,537,044,379	1,434,960,599
Other Operating Revenue	57,250,217	56,110,764	51,534,989	46,804,137	45,513,360
Other Nonoperating Revenue	18,547,865	35,893,255	-10,009,965	-27,559,443	38,665,452
Total Net Revenue	1,894,847,427	1,801,879,654	1,690,653,803	1,556,289,073	1,519,139,411
Total Expenses	1,776,728,126	1,714,899,646	1,660,403,783	1,558,572,905	1,451,986,474
HOSPITAL UNIT (Excludes Separate Nursing Home Units)					
Utilization - Inpatient					
Beds	1,010	1,080	1,118	1,061	1,106
Admissions	48,523	49,078	50,549	51,001	49,396
Inpatient Days	241,161	233,003	259,463	245,411	249,628
Average Length of Stay	5.0	4.7	5.1	4.8	5.1
Personnel					
Total Full Time	9,591	9,493	9,397	9,218	8,963
Total Part Time	4,811	3,963	3,708	3,538	3,409
Revenue and Expenses - Totals					
(Includes Inpatient and Outpatient)					
Total Net Revenue	$1,876,507,339	$1,783,366,299	$1,669,557,556	$1,536,579,410	$1,494,392,921
Total Expenses	1,759,323,094	1,697,709,912	1,635,099,616	1,540,919,362	1,434,525,067
COMMUNITY HEALTH INDICATORS PER 1000 POPULATION					
Total Population (in thousands)	626	622	622	621	620
Inpatient					
Beds	1.9	2.1	2.1	2.1	2.2
Admissions	78.1	79.4	81.9	82.6	80.4
Inpatient Days	495.7	490.5	517.5	529.0	543.2
Inpatient Surgeries	21.2	22.4	25.0	22.8	22.9
Births	20.4	9.0	9.4	9.6	9.6
Outpatient					
Emergency Outpatient Visits	473.6	566.8	575.5	490.6	418.5
Other Outpatient Visits	4,450.9	4,819.5	4,821.5	4,832.8	4,052.1
Total Outpatient Visits	4,924.5	5,386.3	5,397.0	5,323.4	4,470.6
Outpatient Surgeries	77.2	77.4	78.3	76.3	72.2
Expense per Capita (per person)	$2,836.3	$2,755.2	$2,670.5	$2,509.6	$2,340.2

States

TABLE 6

VIRGINIA

U.S. Registered Community Hospitals
(Nonfederal, short-term general and other special hospitals)

Overview 2007–2011

	2011	2010	2009	2008	2007
Total Community Hospitals in Virginia	89	89	90	90	87
Bed Size Category					
6-24	5	5	3	4	4
25-49	15	14	15	15	13
50-99	15	15	17	16	15
100-199	23	25	27	25	25
200-299	13	12	11	13	15
300-399	6	6	5	5	3
400-499	5	5	5	4	4
500 + ...	7	7	7	8	8
Location					
Hospitals Urban..........................	59	59	60	60	52
Hospitals Rural	30	30	30	30	35
Control					
State and Local Government...............	4	4	4	4	4
Not for Profit	65	64	66	65	64
Investor owned	20	21	20	21	19
Physician Models					
Independent Practice Association	12	13	12	11	12
Group Practice without Walls...............	9	10	8	10	11
Open Physician-Hospital Organization	8	9	7	13	11
Closed Physician-Hospital Organization	2	2	1	1	2
Management Service Organization	17	18	15	10	9
Integrated Salary Model....................	47	51	40	39	37
Equity Model	8	8	7	7	7
Foundation...............................	2	1	1	2	2
Insurance Products					
Health Maintenance Organization	18	15	13	17	19
Preferred Provider Organization..............	20	18	12	18	22
Indemnity Fee for Service	9	2	1	5	14
Managed Care Contracts					
Health Maintenance Organization	59	55	48	50	56
Preferred Provider Organization..............	61	59	54	56	60
Affiliations					
Hospitals in a System......................	73	70	69	60	55
Hospitals in a Network.....................	44	44	37	38	45
Hospitals in a Group Purchasing Organization..	65	70	57	60	63

TABLE 6

VIRGINIA

U.S. Registered Community Hospitals
(Nonfederal, short-term general and other special hospitals)

Utilization, Personnel, Revenue and Expenses, Community Health Indicators 2007–2011

	2011	2010	2009	2008	2007
TOTAL FACILITY (Includes Hospital and Nursing Home Units)					
Utilization - Inpatient					
Beds	17,797	17,747	17,538	17,648	16,895
Admissions	788,441	776,678	793,145	795,578	787,319
Inpatient Days	4,391,769	4,310,430	4,375,451	4,452,740	4,354,340
Average Length of Stay	5.6	5.5	5.5	5.6	5.5
Inpatient Surgeries	210,890	223,354	234,981	235,678	229,376
Births	98,141	99,623	96,209	98,991	98,733
Utilization - Outpatient					
Emergency Outpatient Visits	3,407,824	3,256,956	3,199,466	3,091,131	3,040,762
Other Outpatient Visits	10,710,596	10,524,980	10,959,387	10,223,288	9,892,129
Total Outpatient Visits	14,118,420	13,781,936	14,158,853	13,314,419	12,932,891
Outpatient Surgeries	446,691	439,146	448,650	463,342	463,212
Personnel					
Full Time RNs	24,546	24,035	23,711	23,382	22,863
Full Time LPNs	2,062	2,226	2,231	2,460	2,445
Part Time RNs	11,202	11,030	10,025	10,075	9,823
Part Time LPNs	614	703	684	861	777
Total Full Time	83,312	82,310	82,332	83,178	80,744
Total Part Time	29,682	30,091	28,083	28,749	27,126
Revenue - Inpatient					
Gross Inpatient Revenue	$25,657,236,400	$24,373,894,322	$22,941,847,825	$22,555,481,294	$21,113,593,014
Revenue - Outpatient					
Gross Outpatient Revenue	$22,821,731,869	$21,205,056,723	$18,818,269,487	$17,042,951,627	$15,015,219,220
Revenue and Expenses - Totals					
(Includes Inpatient and Outpatient)					
Total Gross Revenue	$48,478,968,269	$45,578,951,045	$41,760,117,312	$39,598,432,921	$36,128,812,234
Deductions from Revenue	32,415,072,411	30,139,978,214	26,616,556,088	25,464,931,182	23,062,020,224
Net Patient Revenue	16,063,895,858	15,438,972,831	15,143,561,224	14,133,501,739	13,066,792,010
Other Operating Revenue	538,832,905	425,128,846	422,020,787	404,136,415	356,732,830
Other Nonoperating Revenue	170,711,732	253,492,718	10,537,285	-269,241,513	393,479,251
Total Net Revenue	16,773,440,495	16,117,594,395	15,576,119,296	14,268,396,641	13,817,004,091
Total Expenses	15,341,349,476	14,709,796,266	14,456,123,508	13,800,772,246	12,626,089,380
HOSPITAL UNIT (Excludes Separate Nursing Home Units)					
Utilization - Inpatient					
Beds	16,091	16,163	16,422	16,478	16,097
Admissions	781,788	770,195	788,427	790,203	782,324
Inpatient Days	3,823,198	3,775,706	3,995,348	4,052,958	3,977,976
Average Length of Stay	4.9	4.9	5.1	5.1	5.1
Personnel					
Total Full Time	82,422	81,441	81,316	82,241	79,956
Total Part Time	29,292	29,637	27,710	28,385	26,940
Revenue and Expenses - Totals					
(Includes Inpatient and Outpatient)					
Total Net Revenue	$16,629,452,446	$15,986,427,239	$15,479,330,448	$14,180,093,186	$13,715,806,678
Total Expenses	15,208,955,950	14,592,391,811	14,367,593,188	13,713,829,141	12,526,340,640
COMMUNITY HEALTH INDICATORS PER 1000 POPULATION					
Total Population (in thousands)	8,097	7,952	7,883	7,795	7,720
Inpatient					
Beds	2.2	2.2	2.2	2.3	2.2
Admissions	97.4	97.7	100.6	102.1	102.0
Inpatient Days	542.4	542.0	555.1	571.2	564.1
Inpatient Surgeries	26.0	28.1	29.8	30.2	29.7
Births	12.1	12.5	12.2	12.7	12.8
Outpatient					
Emergency Outpatient Visits	420.9	409.6	405.9	396.5	393.9
Other Outpatient Visits	1,322.9	1,323.5	1,390.3	1,311.4	1,281.4
Total Outpatient Visits	1,743.7	1,733.1	1,796.2	1,708.0	1,675.3
Outpatient Surgeries	55.2	55.2	56.9	59.4	60.0
Expense per Capita (per person)	$1,894.8	$1,849.8	$1,833.9	$1,770.4	$1,635.6

States

TABLE 6

WASHINGTON

U.S. Registered Community Hospitals
(Nonfederal, short-term general and other special hospitals)

Overview 2007–2011

	2011	2010	2009	2008	2007
Total Community Hospitals in Washington	85	86	87	86	87
Bed Size Category					
6-24	8	7	7	4	5
25-49	27	29	30	31	30
50-99	11	10	11	12	14
100-199	16	16	16	14	15
200-299	12	13	13	15	13
300-399	5	6	5	8	7
400-499	4	3	3	0	1
500 + ...	2	2	2	2	2
Location					
Hospitals Urban...........................	53	53	53	51	47
Hospitals Rural	32	33	34	35	40
Control					
State and Local Government................	38	39	41	42	41
Not for Profit	41	42	41	40	41
Investor owned	6	5	5	4	5
Physician Models					
Independent Practice Association	1	2	2	2	4
Group Practice without Walls...............	4	4	4	2	1
Open Physician-Hospital Organization	6	5	4	5	5
Closed Physician-Hospital Organization	1	0	0	0	2
Management Service Organization	4	6	6	3	4
Integrated Salary Model	40	39	42	34	35
Equity Model	3	4	4	0	0
Foundation...............................	4	5	7	7	1
Insurance Products					
Health Maintenance Organization	7	4	5	4	4
Preferred Provider Organization..............	14	11	12	12	11
Indemnity Fee for Service	1	0	1	1	1
Managed Care Contracts					
Health Maintenance Organization	35	34	36	33	33
Preferred Provider Organization..............	37	38	44	37	38
Affiliations					
Hospitals in a System......................	39	35	32	31	31
Hospitals in a Network	20	19	19	19	16
Hospitals in a Group Purchasing Organization..	51	48	60	47	60

States

TABLE 6

WASHINGTON

U.S. Registered Community Hospitals
(Nonfederal, short-term general and other special hospitals)

Utilization, Personnel, Revenue and Expenses, Community Health Indicators 2007–2011

	2011	2010	2009	2008	2007
TOTAL FACILITY (Includes Hospital and Nursing Home Units)					
Utilization - Inpatient					
Beds	11,670	11,537	11,322	11,348	11,315
Admissions	576,214	588,855	588,889	578,856	574,169
Inpatient Days	2,613,217	2,638,779	2,660,901	2,663,704	2,577,795
Average Length of Stay	4.5	4.5	4.5	4.6	4.5
Inpatient Surgeries	167,254	170,895	185,833	184,234	176,445
Births	77,238	78,216	80,667	82,557	80,698
Utilization - Outpatient					
Emergency Outpatient Visits	2,321,612	2,290,953	2,509,243	2,385,734	2,343,863
Other Outpatient Visits	10,136,318	9,515,677	8,996,667	8,992,320	8,851,818
Total Outpatient Visits	12,457,930	11,806,630	11,505,910	11,378,054	11,195,681
Outpatient Surgeries	261,623	261,997	266,107	263,762	246,380
Personnel					
Full Time RNs	16,121	16,109	15,789	13,202	12,647
Full Time LPNs	774	825	870	805	821
Part Time RNs	13,423	13,848	13,205	13,466	12,633
Part Time LPNs	560	616	665	696	688
Total Full Time	65,087	68,163	61,767	59,789	57,267
Total Part Time	39,667	39,185	36,879	40,524	36,824
Revenue - Inpatient					
Gross Inpatient Revenue	$21,352,251,400	$21,516,174,379	$19,988,875,344	$17,882,046,988	$15,526,030,849
Revenue - Outpatient					
Gross Outpatient Revenue	$19,065,026,947	$18,594,056,137	$16,200,972,533	$13,659,739,047	$12,099,431,805
Revenue and Expenses - Totals					
(Includes Inpatient and Outpatient)					
Total Gross Revenue	$40,417,278,347	$40,110,230,516	$36,189,847,877	$31,541,786,035	$27,625,462,654
Deductions from Revenue	25,612,881,399	25,534,351,330	22,273,010,097	19,034,411,541	16,338,477,005
Net Patient Revenue	14,804,396,948	14,575,879,186	13,916,837,780	12,507,374,494	11,286,985,649
Other Operating Revenue	842,178,249	804,026,112	755,280,721	664,009,322	632,362,196
Other Nonoperating Revenue	300,691,951	226,341,197	188,342,686	-98,368,171	287,788,340
Total Net Revenue	15,947,267,148	15,606,246,495	14,860,461,187	13,073,015,645	12,207,136,185
Total Expenses	14,869,963,274	14,641,932,019	13,773,406,044	12,327,733,007	11,274,708,380
HOSPITAL UNIT (Excludes Separate Nursing Home Units)					
Utilization - Inpatient					
Beds	11,453	11,382	10,974	10,959	10,910
Admissions	575,796	587,786	587,527	576,765	572,112
Inpatient Days	2,530,869	2,589,013	2,549,787	2,539,914	2,465,659
Average Length of Stay	4.4	4.4	4.3	4.4	4.3
Personnel					
Total Full Time	64,968	68,113	64,470	59,483	56,827
Total Part Time	39,509	39,097	36,649	40,227	36,505
Revenue and Expenses - Totals					
(Includes Inpatient and Outpatient)					
Total Net Revenue	$15,927,548,095	$15,586,259,128	$14,821,016,445	$13,032,710,190	$12,160,885,656
Total Expenses	14,852,332,389	14,623,738,440	13,737,554,929	12,289,499,219	11,234,767,829
COMMUNITY HEALTH INDICATORS PER 1000 POPULATION					
Total Population (in thousands)	6,830	6,746	6,664	6,566	6,465
Inpatient					
Beds	1.7	1.7	1.7	1.7	1.8
Admissions	84.4	87.3	88.4	88.2	88.8
Inpatient Days	382.6	391.2	399.3	405.7	398.7
Inpatient Surgeries	24.5	25.3	27.9	28.1	27.3
Births	11.3	11.6	12.1	12.6	12.5
Outpatient					
Emergency Outpatient Visits	339.9	339.6	376.5	363.3	362.5
Other Outpatient Visits	1,484.1	1,410.5	1,350.0	1,369.5	1,369.2
Total Outpatient Visits	1,824.0	1,750.1	1,726.5	1,732.9	1,731.7
Outpatient Surgeries	38.3	38.8	39.9	40.2	38.1
Expense per Capita (per person)	$2,177.1	$2,170.4	$2,066.8	$1,877.5	$1,744.0

TABLE 6

WEST VIRGINIA

U.S. Registered Community Hospitals
(Nonfederal, short-term general and other special hospitals)

Overview 2007–2011

	2011	2010	2009	2008	2007
Total Community Hospitals in West Virginia ...	55	56	56	56	56
Bed Size Category					
6-24	3	3	3	3	3
25-49	15	14	14	13	13
50-99	13	13	13	14	14
100-199	11	14	14	14	14
200-299	8	9	8	8	7
300-399	2	1	2	2	3
400-499	1	0	0	0	1
500 + ...	2	2	2	2	1
Location					
Hospitals Urban...........................	26	27	27	27	20
Hospitals Rural	29	29	29	29	36
Control					
State and Local Government...............	8	8	10	10	10
Not for Profit	33	34	32	32	31
Investor owned	14	14	14	14	15
Physician Models					
Independent Practice Association	2	3	4	4	6
Group Practice without Walls..............	0	0	0	0	2
Open Physician-Hospital Organization	14	13	14	14	14
Closed Physician-Hospital Organization	1	3	3	3	2
Management Service Organization	2	2	3	5	5
Integrated Salary Model....................	25	25	25	25	25
Equity Model	0	0	0	0	1
Foundation...............................	0	0	0	0	0
Insurance Products					
Health Maintenance Organization	5	6	5	3	5
Preferred Provider Organization..............	10	10	9	7	9
Indemnity Fee for Service	2	3	2	2	4
Managed Care Contracts					
Health Maintenance Organization	28	31	31	27	27
Preferred Provider Organization..............	40	42	42	38	38
Affiliations					
Hospitals in a System.....................	30	29	25	23	23
Hospitals in a Network....................	21	21	22	20	23
Hospitals in a Group Purchasing Organization..	52	53	53	52	52

TABLE 6

WEST VIRGINIA

U.S. Registered Community Hospitals
(Nonfederal, short-term general and other special hospitals)

Utilization, Personnel, Revenue and Expenses, Community Health Indicators 2007–2011

	2011	2010	2009	2008	2007
TOTAL FACILITY (Includes Hospital and Nursing Home Units)					
Utilization - Inpatient					
Beds	7,365	7,298	7,408	7,470	7,436
Admissions	282,194	278,221	280,252	283,673	286,892
Inpatient Days	1,632,308	1,612,811	1,648,197	1,665,076	1,656,614
Average Length of Stay	5.8	5.8	5.9	5.9	5.8
Inpatient Surgeries	82,491	83,992	80,776	79,916	77,775
Births	20,639	20,487	21,010	20,856	21,296
Utilization - Outpatient					
Emergency Outpatient Visits	1,216,780	1,207,918	1,221,485	1,183,158	1,171,507
Other Outpatient Visits	5,544,015	5,446,482	5,463,158	5,431,951	5,283,575
Total Outpatient Visits	6,760,795	6,654,400	6,684,643	6,615,109	6,455,082
Outpatient Surgeries	222,505	212,434	215,853	212,489	207,785
Personnel					
Full Time RNs	8,593	8,532	8,282	8,084	7,949
Full Time LPNs	1,099	1,217	1,298	1,387	1,416
Part Time RNs	3,252	3,395	3,447	3,392	3,460
Part Time LPNs	396	419	403	435	392
Total Full Time	33,119	33,349	32,751	32,463	31,879
Total Part Time	9,903	10,143	10,082	10,211	10,145
Revenue - Inpatient					
Gross Inpatient Revenue	$6,028,967,872	$5,597,580,327	$5,174,519,813	$4,927,056,831	$4,544,128,430
Revenue - Outpatient					
Gross Outpatient Revenue	$5,824,592,215	$5,444,045,714	$5,161,162,251	$4,531,051,911	$4,100,750,655
Revenue and Expenses - Totals					
(Includes Inpatient and Outpatient)					
Total Gross Revenue	$11,853,560,087	$11,041,626,041	$10,335,682,064	$9,458,108,742	$8,644,879,085
Deductions from Revenue	7,049,221,237	6,386,501,669	5,787,332,486	5,198,077,289	4,577,611,437
Net Patient Revenue	4,804,338,850	4,655,124,372	4,548,349,578	4,260,031,453	4,067,267,648
Other Operating Revenue	133,361,426	126,269,003	168,034,621	71,741,101	125,951,483
Other Nonoperating Revenue	-338,296	63,579,778	54,115,339	-125,408,354	100,086,468
Total Net Revenue	4,937,361,980	4,844,973,153	4,770,499,538	4,206,364,200	4,293,305,599
Total Expenses	4,724,080,410	4,689,352,987	4,584,221,488	4,289,258,433	4,018,748,717
HOSPITAL UNIT (Excludes Separate Nursing Home Units)					
Utilization - Inpatient					
Beds	6,554	6,454	6,575	6,587	6,553
Admissions	277,659	272,471	274,341	277,157	280,751
Inpatient Days	1,378,567	1,340,666	1,371,913	1,381,747	1,375,020
Average Length of Stay	5.0	4.9	5.0	5.0	4.9
Personnel					
Total Full Time	32,566	32,752	32,152	31,838	31,203
Total Part Time	9,508	9,781	9,787	9,825	9,763
Revenue and Expenses - Totals					
(Includes Inpatient and Outpatient)					
Total Net Revenue	$4,873,165,838	$4,774,505,282	$4,700,079,381	$4,123,228,602	$4,225,397,482
Total Expenses	4,670,781,412	4,637,567,799	4,529,683,828	4,229,627,238	3,964,906,237
COMMUNITY HEALTH INDICATORS PER 1000 POPULATION					
Total Population (in thousands)	1,855	1,826	1,820	1,815	1,811
Inpatient					
Beds	4.0	4.0	4.1	4.1	4.1
Admissions	152.1	152.4	154.0	156.3	158.4
Inpatient Days	879.8	883.5	905.7	917.5	914.7
Inpatient Surgeries	44.5	46.0	44.4	44.0	42.9
Births	11.1	11.2	11.5	11.5	11.8
Outpatient					
Emergency Outpatient Visits	655.8	661.7	671.2	651.9	646.8
Other Outpatient Visits	2,988.1	2,983.5	3,002.1	2,993.0	2,917.2
Total Outpatient Visits	3,643.9	3,645.2	3,673.3	3,644.9	3,564.0
Outpatient Surgeries	119.9	116.4	118.6	117.1	114.7
Expense per Capita (per person)	$2,546.2	$2,568.8	$2,519.1	$2,363.4	$2,218.8

States

TABLE 6

WISCONSIN

U.S. Registered Community Hospitals
(Nonfederal, short-term general and other special hospitals)

Overview 2007–2011

	2011	2010	2009	2008	2007
Total Community Hospitals in Wisconsin......	125	124	126	126	124
Bed Size Category					
6-24	15	13	12	12	12
25-49	36	37	37	36	33
50-99	31	31	32	32	27
100-199	22	21	25	24	33
200-299	11	13	11	13	10
300-399	7	5	6	6	6
400-499	1	2	2	2	2
500 + ...	2	2	1	1	1
Location					
Hospitals Urban...........................	69	68	69	69	61
Hospitals Rural	56	56	57	57	63
Control					
State and Local Government...............	2	2	2	2	2
Not for Profit	119	117	118	119	117
Investor owned	4	5	6	5	5
Physician Models					
Independent Practice Association	11	9	13	13	10
Group Practice without Walls................	3	3	3	2	1
Open Physician-Hospital Organization	4	4	3	3	6
Closed Physician-Hospital Organization	4	4	2	3	4
Management Service Organization	2	2	3	2	1
Integrated Salary Model....................	56	38	34	32	30
Equity Model.............................	6	9	12	17	3
Foundation...............................	2	2	2	2	2
Insurance Products					
Health Maintenance Organization	36	20	23	23	25
Preferred Provider Organization..............	36	31	35	36	38
Indemnity Fee for Service	15	15	16	15	16
Managed Care Contracts					
Health Maintenance Organization	118	116	116	116	83
Preferred Provider Organization..............	120	118	118	120	86
Affiliations					
Hospitals in a System.....................	72	72	74	72	70
Hospitals in a Network....................	43	37	36	39	31
Hospitals in a Group Purchasing Organization..	123	118	116	118	86

States

TABLE 6

WISCONSIN

U.S. Registered Community Hospitals
(Nonfederal, short-term general and other special hospitals)

Utilization, Personnel, Revenue and Expenses, Community Health Indicators 2007–2011

	2011	2010	2009	2008	2007
TOTAL FACILITY (Includes Hospital and Nursing Home Units)					
Utilization - Inpatient					
Beds	13,134	13,520	13,637	13,707	13,981
Admissions	573,077	588,592	609,329	617,295	613,356
Inpatient Days	2,873,295	2,966,909	3,125,349	3,172,566	3,168,542
Average Length of Stay	5.0	5.0	5.1	5.1	5.2
Inpatient Surgeries	214,111	228,469	256,942	233,044	239,199
Births	66,783	67,843	70,129	69,465	70,500
Utilization - Outpatient					
Emergency Outpatient Visits	2,130,925	2,160,341	2,080,601	2,066,654	2,106,402
Other Outpatient Visits	13,379,041	12,444,617	12,847,067	12,136,773	10,966,003
Total Outpatient Visits	15,509,966	14,604,958	14,927,668	14,203,427	13,072,405
Outpatient Surgeries	531,355	522,864	535,955	491,040	497,452
Personnel					
Full Time RNs	15,048	14,476	14,345	14,522	13,480
Full Time LPNs	622	673	711	707	711
Part Time RNs	14,982	15,552	16,139	15,398	15,499
Part Time LPNs	706	794	908	927	1,028
Total Full Time	63,544	63,254	63,168	63,883	61,173
Total Part Time	46,533	48,472	51,235	47,517	47,796
Revenue - Inpatient					
Gross Inpatient Revenue	$16,185,500,212	$15,357,857,584	$15,634,706,846	$13,612,135,956	$12,925,578,410
Revenue - Outpatient					
Gross Outpatient Revenue	$18,798,615,788	$16,468,660,136	$14,805,407,754	$13,162,259,140	$11,746,652,525
Revenue and Expenses - Totals					
(Includes Inpatient and Outpatient)					
Total Gross Revenue	$34,984,116,000	$31,826,517,720	$30,440,114,600	$26,774,395,096	$24,672,230,935
Deductions from Revenue	19,455,297,266	16,996,231,064	16,618,465,592	13,709,265,312	12,424,903,890
Net Patient Revenue	15,528,818,734	14,830,286,656	13,821,649,008	13,065,129,784	12,247,327,045
Other Operating Revenue	644,957,778	630,341,533	716,584,248	643,332,317	473,238,179
Other Nonoperating Revenue	288,307,316	285,539,514	-26,443,242	-30,738,485	294,160,363
Total Net Revenue	16,462,083,828	15,746,167,703	14,511,790,014	13,677,723,616	13,014,725,587
Total Expenses	14,997,010,589	14,230,620,575	13,496,778,176	12,923,890,000	11,916,247,096
HOSPITAL UNIT (Excludes Separate Nursing Home Units)					
Utilization - Inpatient					
Beds	11,814	12,092	12,049	12,067	12,337
Admissions	570,650	586,022	606,542	614,395	610,759
Inpatient Days	2,453,855	2,511,474	2,597,929	2,629,527	2,622,596
Average Length of Stay	4.3	4.3	4.3	4.3	4.3
Personnel					
Total Full Time	62,919	62,460	62,376	63,068	60,418
Total Part Time	45,754	47,543	50,255	46,533	46,827
Revenue and Expenses - Totals					
(Includes Inpatient and Outpatient)					
Total Net Revenue	$16,360,856,116	$15,640,069,501	$14,399,372,197	$13,576,550,948	$12,892,939,703
Total Expenses	14,902,736,502	14,124,128,291	13,393,867,097	12,830,682,268	11,827,708,589
COMMUNITY HEALTH INDICATORS PER 1000 POPULATION					
Total Population (in thousands)	5,712	5,669	5,655	5,628	5,602
Inpatient					
Beds	2.3	2.4	2.4	2.4	2.5
Admissions	100.3	103.8	107.8	109.7	109.5
Inpatient Days	503.0	523.4	552.7	563.8	565.7
Inpatient Surgeries	37.5	40.3	45.4	41.4	42.7
Births	11.7	12.0	12.4	12.3	12.6
Outpatient					
Emergency Outpatient Visits	373.1	381.1	367.9	367.2	376.0
Other Outpatient Visits	2,342.4	2,195.4	2,271.9	2,156.6	1,957.7
Total Outpatient Visits	2,715.4	2,576.5	2,639.8	2,523.9	2,333.7
Outpatient Surgeries	93.0	92.2	94.8	87.3	88.8
Expense per Capita (per person)	$2,625.6	$2,510.5	$2,386.8	$2,296.5	$2,127.3

States

TABLE 6

WYOMING

U.S. Registered Community Hospitals
(Nonfederal, short-term general and other special hospitals)

Overview 2007–2011

	2011	2010	2009	2008	2007
Total Community Hospitals in Wyoming.......	24	24	24	24	24
Bed Size Category					
6-24	0	0	0	0	0
25-49	11	11	11	10	10
50-99	6	6	6	7	7
100-199	4	4	4	4	4
200-299	3	3	3	3	3
300-399	0	0	0	0	0
400-499	0	0	0	0	0
500 + ...	0	0	0	0	0
Location					
Hospitals Urban..........................	2	2	2	2	2
Hospitals Rural	22	22	22	22	22
Control					
State and Local Government...............	16	16	16	16	16
Not for Profit	5	5	5	5	5
Investor owned	3	3	3	3	3
Physician Models					
Independent Practice Association	2	2	3	3	3
Group Practice without Walls...............	0	0	0	0	0
Open Physician-Hospital Organization	1	1	1	1	1
Closed Physician-Hospital Organization	1	1	1	1	1
Management Service Organization	1	2	2	1	1
Integrated Salary Model	9	10	11	11	11
Equity Model	0	0	0	0	0
Foundation...............................	0	0	0	0	0
Insurance Products					
Health Maintenance Organization	2	1	1	1	1
Preferred Provider Organization..............	3	3	1	1	5
Indemnity Fee for Service	0	0	0	0	0
Managed Care Contracts					
Health Maintenance Organization	4	3	4	4	4
Preferred Provider Organization..............	14	14	14	14	12
Affiliations					
Hospitals in a System.....................	12	12	12	11	12
Hospitals in a Network	4	4	5	5	4
Hospitals in a Group Purchasing Organization..	21	21	21	23	23

States

TABLE 6

WYOMING

U.S. Registered Community Hospitals
(Nonfederal, short-term general and other special hospitals)

Utilization, Personnel, Revenue and Expenses, Community Health Indicators 2007–2011

	2011	2010	2009	2008	2007
TOTAL FACILITY (Includes Hospital and Nursing Home Units)					
Utilization - Inpatient					
Beds	1,958	1,958	2,002	2,073	2,071
Admissions	45,697	49,704	52,232	52,628	53,077
Inpatient Days	378,227	398,850	411,717	414,463	422,883
Average Length of Stay	8.3	8.0	7.9	7.9	8.0
Inpatient Surgeries	12,872	14,159	13,801	14,162	14,556
Births	6,363	6,920	7,305	7,303	7,247
Utilization - Outpatient					
Emergency Outpatient Visits	228,140	231,261	236,213	234,384	227,386
Other Outpatient Visits	890,706	866,984	823,944	774,610	729,327
Total Outpatient Visits	1,118,846	1,098,245	1,060,157	1,008,994	956,713
Outpatient Surgeries	29,019	29,260	26,180	25,183	24,122
Personnel					
Full Time RNs	1,721	1,680	1,561	1,664	1,603
Full Time LPNs	116	117	127	130	137
Part Time RNs	556	455	526	504	600
Part Time LPNs	52	54	76	57	69
Total Full Time	7,404	7,338	7,094	7,291	6,670
Total Part Time	2,067	2,005	2,310	1,892	2,319
Revenue - Inpatient					
Gross Inpatient Revenue	$1,079,479,758	$1,072,618,270	$967,170,829	$951,929,394	$878,681,901
Revenue - Outpatient					
Gross Outpatient Revenue	$1,216,235,177	$1,103,760,780	$946,462,599	$801,309,584	$704,732,660
Revenue and Expenses - Totals					
(Includes Inpatient and Outpatient)					
Total Gross Revenue	$2,295,714,935	$2,176,379,050	$1,913,633,428	$1,753,238,978	$1,583,414,561
Deductions from Revenue	1,180,144,790	1,096,026,956	955,291,698	802,095,376	696,730,106
Net Patient Revenue	1,115,570,145	1,080,352,094	958,341,730	951,143,602	886,684,455
Other Operating Revenue	69,049,844	74,157,196	66,460,224	55,280,832	49,220,506
Other Nonoperating Revenue	26,792,888	19,130,354	-798,016	21,606,525	63,859,758
Total Net Revenue	1,211,412,877	1,173,639,644	1,024,003,938	1,020,030,959	999,764,719
Total Expenses	1,046,675,080	1,031,425,657	980,632,479	949,368,614	848,863,457
HOSPITAL UNIT (Excludes Separate Nursing Home Units)					
Utilization - Inpatient					
Beds	1,281	1,303	1,303	1,335	1,323
Admissions	44,155	48,206	50,673	51,146	51,592
Inpatient Days	169,461	196,510	188,014	183,585	184,014
Average Length of Stay	3.8	4.1	3.7	3.6	3.6
Personnel					
Total Full Time	7,004	6,925	6,618	6,767	6,141
Total Part Time	1,888	1,841	2,117	1,696	2,092
Revenue and Expenses - Totals					
(Includes Inpatient and Outpatient)					
Total Net Revenue	$1,170,074,150	$1,133,360,264	$984,238,688	$988,170,246	$959,741,678
Total Expenses	1,006,052,821	991,627,019	938,219,346	907,237,150	810,848,202
COMMUNITY HEALTH INDICATORS PER 1000 POPULATION					
Total Population (in thousands)	568	548	544	533	523
Inpatient					
Beds	3.4	3.6	3.7	3.9	4.0
Admissions	80.4	90.8	96.0	98.7	101.4
Inpatient Days	665.7	728.3	756.5	777.6	807.9
Inpatient Surgeries	22.7	25.9	25.4	26.6	27.8
Births	11.2	12.6	13.4	13.7	13.8
Outpatient					
Emergency Outpatient Visits	401.5	422.3	434.0	439.8	434.4
Other Outpatient Visits	1,567.7	1,583.1	1,513.9	1,453.4	1,393.4
Total Outpatient Visits	1,969.3	2,005.4	1,947.9	1,893.1	1,827.8
Outpatient Surgeries	51.1	53.4	48.1	47.2	46.1
Expense per Capita (per person)	$1,842.2	$1,883.4	$1,801.7	$1,781.2	$1,621.8

Table 7

Facilities and Services

Table		Page

| **7** | Facilities and Services in the U. S. Census Divisions and States for 2011 | 155 |

The facilities and services presented in Table 7 are listed below in alphabetical order by major heading (where applicable).

Table 7

2011 Facilities and Services in the U.S. Census Divisions and States

These data include only hospital-based facilities and services as reported by responding hospitals in Section C of the 2011 AHA Annual Survey, beginning on page 215. All hospitals are represented with Community Hospitals listed separately under United States. No estimates have been made for nonresponding hospitals. Definitions of facilities and services are listed in the Glossary, page 201.

CLASSIFICATION	HOSPITALS REPORTING	ADULT DAY CARE PROGRAM Number	Percent	AIRBORNE INFECTION ISOLATION ROOM Number	Percent	ALCOHOL/DRUG ABUSE OR DEPENDENCY INPATIENT CARE UNITS Number	Percent	ALCOHOL/DRUG ABUSE OR DEPENDENCY OUTPATIENT SERVICES Number	Percent	ALZHEIMER CENTER Number	Percent	AMBULANCE SERVICE Number	Percent	AMBULATORY SURGERY CENTER Number	Percent	ARTHRITIS TREATMENT CENTER Number	Percent	ASSISTED LIVING Number	Percent
UNITED STATES	4,782	227	4.7	3,625	75.8	464	9.7	702	14.7	199	4.2	755	15.8	1,235	25.8	278	5.8	200	4.2
COMMUNITY HOSPITALS	4,082	194	4.8	3,308	81.0	324	7.9	537	13.2	180	4.4	733	18.0	1,174	28.8	266	6.5	179	4.4
CENSUS DIVISION 1, NEW ENGLAND	201	15	7.5	151	75.1	22	10.9	56	27.9	16	8.0	29	14.4	78	38.8	17	8.5	7	3.5
Connecticut	31	2	6.5	24	77.4	5	16.1	12	38.7	4	12.9	4	12.9	19	61.3	3	9.7	0	0.0
Maine	39	2	5.1	29	74.4	7	17.9	13	33.3	4	10.3	8	20.5	13	33.3	0	0.0	3	7.7
Massachusetts	80	5	6.3	57	71.3	7	8.8	23	28.8	5	6.3	9	11.3	28	35.0	10	12.5	0	0.0
New Hampshire	27	5	18.5	25	92.6	0	0.0	2	7.4	1	3.7	6	22.2	6	22.2	2	7.4	2	7.4
Rhode Island	10	0	0.0	7	70.0	2	20.0	4	40.0	1	10.0	1	10.0	6	60.0	0	0.0	1	10.0
Vermont	14	1	7.1	9	64.3	1	7.1	2	14.3	1	7.1	1	7.1	6	42.9	2	14.3	1	7.1
CENSUS DIVISION 2, MIDDLE ATLANTIC	396	38	9.6	312	78.8	74	18.7	112	28.3	30	7.6	77	19.4	180	45.5	62	15.7	14	3.5
New Jersey	69	10	14.5	52	75.4	11	15.9	23	33.3	8	11.6	21	30.4	23	33.3	9	13.0	4	5.8
New York	165	22	13.3	130	78.8	51	30.9	67	40.6	11	6.7	30	18.2	108	65.5	35	21.2	2	1.2
Pennsylvania	162	6	3.7	130	80.2	12	7.4	22	13.6	11	6.8	25	16.0	49	30.2	18	11.1	8	4.9
CENSUS DIVISION 3, SOUTH ATLANTIC	707	24	3.4	558	78.9	72	10.2	106	15.0	30	4.2	103	14.6	180	25.5	42	5.9	22	3.1
Delaware	8	2	25.0	5	62.5	0	0.0	1	12.5	1	12.5	2	25.0	4	50.0	0	0.0	0	0.0
District of Columbia	10	0	0.0	8	80.0	1	10.0	4	40.0	3	30.0	2	20.0	5	50.0	2	20.0	1	10.0
Florida	176	3	1.7	138	78.4	16	9.1	13	7.4	7	4.0	16	9.1	53	30.1	7	4.0	1	0.6
Georgia	120	2	1.7	91	75.8	14	11.7	17	14.2	5	4.2	24	20.0	22	18.3	4	3.3	5	4.2
Maryland	54	5	9.3	45	83.3	6	11.1	17	31.5	4	7.4	3	5.6	21	38.9	8	14.8	6	11.1
North Carolina	115	4	3.5	97	84.3	12	10.4	18	15.7	4	3.5	25	21.7	40	34.8	9	7.8	4	3.5
South Carolina	82	2	2.4	62	75.6	14	17.1	11	13.4	3	3.7	13	15.9	8	9.8	3	3.7	0	0.0
Virginia	83	5	6.0	69	83.1	8	9.6	20	24.1	3	3.6	12	14.5	21	25.3	6	7.2	5	6.0
West Virginia	59	1	1.7	43	72.9	1	1.7	5	8.5	0	0.0	6	10.2	6	10.2	3	5.1	0	0.0
CENSUS DIVISION 4, EAST NORTH CENTRAL	726	43	5.9	594	81.8	104	14.3	156	21.5	53	7.3	116	16.0	207	28.5	64	8.8	32	4.4
Illinois	164	14	8.5	139	84.8	22	13.4	39	23.8	9	5.5	25	15.2	36	22.0	13	7.9	2	1.2
Indiana	122	4	3.3	92	75.4	14	11.5	22	18.0	2	1.6	30	24.6	40	32.8	4	3.3	4	3.3
Michigan	134	5	3.7	113	84.3	14	10.4	27	20.1	6	4.5	19	14.2	33	24.6	13	9.7	5	3.7
Ohio	160	9	5.6	135	84.4	17	10.6	32	20.0	10	6.3	27	16.9	54	33.8	16	10.0	6	3.8
Wisconsin	146	11	7.5	115	78.8	37	25.3	36	24.7	26	17.8	15	10.3	44	30.1	18	12.3	15	10.3
CENSUS DIVISION 5, EAST SOUTH CENTRAL	376	6	1.6	262	69.7	34	9.0	34	9.0	6	1.6	50	13.3	64	17.0	7	1.9	8	2.1
Alabama	95	1	1.1	70	73.7	6	6.3	8	8.4	2	2.1	10	10.5	22	23.2	2	2.1	1	1.1
Kentucky	86	3	3.5	72	83.7	6	7.0	9	10.5	1	1.2	11	12.8	16	18.6	3	3.5	2	2.3
Mississippi	110	0	0.0	54	49.1	15	13.6	8	7.3	2	1.8	17	15.5	9	8.2	0	0.0	3	2.7
Tennessee	85	2	2.4	66	77.6	7	8.2	9	10.6	1	1.2	12	14.1	17	20.0	2	2.4	2	2.4
CENSUS DIVISION 6, WEST NORTH CENTRAL	658	36	5.5	463	70.4	58	8.8	75	11.4	25	3.8	167	25.4	120	18.2	23	3.5	64	9.7
Iowa	126	3	2.4	69	55.1	12	9.5	17	13.5	3	2.4	57	45.2	24	19.0	3	2.4	10	7.9
Kansas	153	8	5.2	102	66.7	3	2.0	6	3.9	3	2.0	23	15.0	14	9.2	2	1.3	12	7.8
Minnesota	100	14	14.0	73	73.0	10	10.0	18	18.0	7	7.0	34	34.0	29	29.0	4	4.0	15	15.0
Missouri	150	1	0.7	119	79.3	25	16.7	21	14.0	4	2.7	28	18.7	23	15.3	9	6.0	2	1.3
Nebraska	55	2	3.6	37	67.3	4	7.3	6	10.9	4	7.3	9	16.4	13	23.6	1	1.8	8	14.5
North Dakota	24	2	8.3	19	79.2	4	16.7	3	12.5	0	0.0	4	16.7	6	25.0	3	12.5	1	4.2
South Dakota	50	6	12.0	31	62.0	0	0.0	4	8.0	4	8.0	12	24.0	11	22.0	1	2.0	16	32.0
CENSUS DIVISION 7, WEST SOUTH CENTRAL	888	12	1.4	675	76.0	42	4.7	54	5.1	7	0.8	99	11.1	146	16.4	19	2.1	20	2.3
Arkansas	93	3	3.2	69	74.2	3	3.2	4	4.3	1	1.1	13	14.0	16	17.2	2	2.2	2	2.2
Louisiana	97	3	3.1	71	73.2	5	5.2	4	4.1	1	1.0	8	8.2	27	27.8	6	6.2	3	3.1
Oklahoma	127	2	1.6	94	74.0	2	1.6	8	6.3	1	0.8	13	10.2	23	18.1	2	1.6	3	2.4
Texas	571	4	0.7	441	77.2	32	5.6	38	6.7	4	0.7	65	11.4	80	14.0	9	1.6	12	2.1
CENSUS DIVISION 8, MOUNTAIN	354	26	7.3	252	71.2	26	7.3	47	13.3	13	3.7	70	19.8	99	28.0	16	4.5	20	5.6
Arizona	64	2	3.1	47	73.4	4	6.3	13	20.3	2	3.1	5	7.8	19	29.7	3	4.7	1	1.6
Colorado	70	3	4.3	59	84.3	5	7.1	9	12.9	2	2.9	16	22.9	20	28.6	3	4.3	3	4.3
Idaho	35	6	17.1	23	65.7	3	8.6	5	14.3	0	0.0	11	31.4	15	42.9	3	8.6	3	8.6
Montana	57	14	24.6	37	64.9	3	5.3	4	7.0	3	5.3	13	22.8	12	21.1	1	1.8	5	9.3
Nevada	36	0	0.0	18	50.0	1	2.8	4	11.1	0	0.0	3	8.3	6	16.7	0	0.0	1	2.8
New Mexico	33	0	0.0	22	66.7	4	12.1	4	12.1	0	0.0	6	18.2	12	36.4	3	9.1	3	9.1
Utah	35	1	2.9	28	80.0	3	8.6	4	11.4	2	5.7	6	17.1	11	31.4	3	8.6	0	0.0
Wyoming	24	0	0.0	18	75.0	3	12.5	4	16.7	4	16.7	10	41.7	4	16.7	0	0.0	2	8.3
CENSUS DIVISION 9, PACIFIC	476	27	5.7	358	75.2	32	6.7	62	13.0	19	4.0	44	9.2	161	33.8	28	5.9	13	2.7
Alaska	14	0	0.0	9	64.3	3	21.4	4	28.6	0	0.0	1	7.1	1	7.1	0	0.0	0	0.0
California	307	21	6.8	230	74.9	21	6.8	41	13.4	17	5.5	24	7.8	108	35.2	19	6.2	3	1.0
Hawaii	17	0	0.0	12	70.6	0	0.0	0	0.0	0	0.0	0	0.0	4	23.5	1	5.9	0	0.0
Oregon	59	2	3.4	53	89.8	1	1.7	5	6.5	1	1.7	7	11.9	14	23.7	3	5.1	2	3.4
Washington	79	4	5.1	54	68.4	7	8.9	11	13.9	1	1.3	12	15.2	34	43.0	5	6.3	8	10.1

Table 7 (Continued)

These data include only hospital-based facilities and services as reported by responding hospitals in Section C of the 2011 AHA Annual Survey, beginning on page 215. All hospitals are represented with Community Hospitals listed separately under United States. No estimates have been made for nonresponding hospitals. Definitions of facilities and services are listed in the Glossary, page 201.

CLASSIFICATION	HOSPITALS REPORTING	AUXILIARY		BARIATRIC/ WEIGHT CONTROL SERVICES		BIRTHING/ LDR/ LDRP ROOM		BLOOD DONOR CENTER		BREAST CANCER SCREENING		BURN CARE UNITS		CASE MANAGEMENT		CHAPLAINCY/ PASTORAL CARE SERVICES		CHEMOTHERAPY	
		Number	Percent	Number	Percent	Number	Percent	Number	Percent	Number	Percent	Number	Percent	Number	Percent	Number	Percent	Number	Percent
UNITED STATES	4,782	2,776	58.1	1,185	24.8	2,592	54.2	318	6.6	3,322	69.5	173	3.6	4,064	85.4	3,135	65.6	2,461	51.5
COMMUNITY HOSPITALS	4,082	2,700	66.1	1,108	27.1	2,557	62.6	309	7.6	3,240	79.4	165	4.0	3,618	88.6	2,848	69.8	2,382	58.4
CENSUS DIVISION 1, NEW ENGLAND	201	116	57.7	64	31.8	130	64.7	32	15.9	158	78.6	10	5.0	191	95.0	164	81.6	149	74.1
Connecticut	31	17	54.8	16	51.6	24	77.4	5	16.1	24	77.4	1	3.2	30	96.8	29	93.5	25	80.6
Maine	39	25	64.1	7	17.9	29	74.4	0	0.0	34	87.2	2	5.1	38	97.4	29	74.4	27	69.2
Massachusetts	80	40	50.0	29	36.3	44	55.0	22	27.5	59	73.8	4	5.0	74	92.5	65	81.3	58	72.5
New Hampshire	27	18	66.7	6	22.2	19	70.4	4	14.8	22	81.5	1	3.7	26	96.3	22	81.5	20	74.1
Rhode Island	10	6	60.0	4	40.0	4	40.0	0	0.0	8	80.0	1	10.0	10	100.0	9	90.0	9	90.0
Vermont	14	10	71.4	2	14.3	10	71.4	1	7.1	11	78.6	1	7.1	13	92.9	10	71.4	10	71.4
CENSUS DIVISION 2, MIDDLE ATLANTIC	396	267	67.4	171	43.2	235	59.3	66	16.7	316	79.8	25	6.3	367	92.7	314	79.3	268	67.7
New Jersey	69	52	75.4	39	56.5	45	65.2	12	17.4	51	73.9	5	7.2	64	92.8	57	82.6	51	73.9
New York	165	111	67.3	73	44.2	107	64.8	38	23.0	142	86.1	13	7.9	157	95.2	139	84.2	121	73.3
Pennsylvania	162	104	64.2	59	36.4	83	51.2	16	9.9	123	75.9	7	4.3	146	90.1	118	72.8	96	59.3
CENSUS DIVISION 3, SOUTH ATLANTIC	707	443	62.7	185	26.2	386	54.6	55	7.8	530	75.0	21	3.0	635	89.8	540	76.4	383	54.2
Delaware	8	6	75.0	4	50.0	4	50.0	0	0.0	6	75.0		0.0	7	87.5	8	100.0	6	75.0
District of Columbia	10	3	30.0	5	50.0	6	60.0	3	30.0	6	60.0	1	10.0	9	90.0	9	90.0	6	60.0
Florida	176	100	56.8	51	29.0	85	48.3	13	7.4	127	72.2	6	3.4	165	93.8	131	74.4	105	59.7
Georgia	120	82	68.3	27	22.5	64	53.3	5	4.2	94	78.3	3	2.5	106	88.3	86	71.7	51	42.5
Maryland	54	43	79.6	17	31.5	32	59.3	13	24.1	37	68.5	2	3.7	49	90.7	48	88.9	43	79.6
North Carolina	115	71	61.7	34	29.6	76	66.1	7	6.1	89	77.4	3	2.6	104	90.4	94	81.7	70	60.9
South Carolina	82	45	54.9	15	18.3	44	53.7	5	6.1	58	70.7	2	2.4	71	86.6	53	64.6	30	36.6
Virginia	83	56	67.5	25	30.1	47	56.6	9	10.8	68	81.9	3	3.6	73	88.0	70	84.3	50	60.2
West Virginia	59	37	62.7	7	11.9	28	47.5	0	0.0	47	79.7	1	1.7	51	86.4	41	69.5	22	37.3
CENSUS DIVISION 4, EAST NORTH CENTRAL	726	464	63.9	199	27.4	456	62.8	39	5.4	593	81.7	37	5.1	648	89.3	545	75.1	462	63.6
Illinois	164	112	68.3	50	30.5	102	62.2	11	6.7	140	85.4	8	4.9	150	91.5	133	81.1	112	68.3
Indiana	122	62	50.8	28	23.0	83	68.0	4	3.3	97	79.5	3	2.5	112	91.8	98	80.3	70	57.4
Michigan	134	99	73.9	47	35.1	77	57.5	7	5.2	114	85.1	7	5.2	119	88.8	99	73.9	94	70.1
Ohio	160	108	67.5	42	26.3	97	60.6	13	8.1	133	83.1	11	6.9	145	90.6	129	80.6	115	71.9
Wisconsin	146	83	56.8	32	21.9	97	66.4	4	2.7	109	74.7	8	5.5	122	83.6	86	58.9	71	48.6
CENSUS DIVISION 5, EAST SOUTH CENTRAL	376	174	46.3	71	18.9	173	46.0	11	2.9	260	69.1	12	3.2	305	81.1	228	60.6	129	34.3
Alabama	95	50	52.6	26	27.4	47	49.5	4	4.2	70	73.7	5	5.3	82	86.3	57	60.0	37	38.9
Kentucky	86	57	66.3	24	27.9	41	47.7	3	3.5	70	81.4	4	4.7	79	91.9	70	81.4	40	46.5
Mississippi	110	31	28.2	8	7.3	44	40.0	1	0.9	57	51.8	1	0.9	67	60.9	34	30.9	20	18.2
Tennessee	85	36	42.4	13	15.3	41	48.2	3	3.5	63	74.1	2	2.4	77	90.6	67	78.8	32	37.6
CENSUS DIVISION 6, WEST NORTH CENTRAL	658	427	64.9	119	18.1	356	54.1	21	3.2	462	70.2	27	4.1	474	72.0	345	52.4	356	54.1
Iowa	126	110	87.3	15	11.9	79	62.7	3	2.4	113	89.7	6	4.8	101	80.2	55	43.7	86	68.3
Kansas	153	78	51.0	23	15.0	70	45.8	1	0.7	77	50.3	4	2.6	89	58.2	69	45.1	51	33.3
Minnesota	100	73	73.0	24	24.0	71	71.0	4	4.0	84	84.0	4	4.0	73	73.0	57	57.0	71	71.0
Missouri	150	99	66.0	30	20.0	72	48.0	8	5.3	105	70.0	8	5.3	129	86.0	104	69.3	71	47.3
Nebraska	55	28	50.9	13	23.6	35	63.6	2	3.6	41	74.5	3	5.5	39	70.9	26	47.3	37	67.3
North Dakota	24	17	70.8	6	33.3	9	37.5	1	4.2	13	54.2	2	8.3	17	70.8	16	66.7	12	50.0
South Dakota	50	22	44.0	6	12.0	20	40.0	2	4.0	29	58.0	0	0.0	26	52.0	18	36.0	28	56.0
CENSUS DIVISION 7, WEST SOUTH CENTRAL	888	421	47.4	170	19.1	359	40.4	30	3.4	433	48.8	19	2.1	759	85.5	456	51.4	254	28.6
Arkansas	93	56	60.2	13	14.0	40	43.0	3	3.2	52	55.9	1	1.1	79	84.9	41	44.1	33	35.5
Louisiana	97	44	45.4	22	22.7	45	46.4	7	7.2	65	67.0	4	4.1	90	92.8	50	51.5	41	42.3
Oklahoma	127	62	48.8	17	13.4	51	40.2	4	3.1	64	50.4	2	1.6	104	81.9	72	56.7	33	26.0
Texas	571	259	45.4	118	20.7	223	39.1	16	2.8	252	44.1	12	2.1	486	85.1	293	51.3	147	25.7
CENSUS DIVISION 8, MOUNTAIN	354	199	56.2	78	22.0	207	58.5	20	5.6	240	67.8	7	2.0	288	81.4	199	56.2	172	48.6
Arizona	64	37	57.8	18	28.1	34	53.1	4	6.3	40	62.5	1	1.6	61	95.3	46	71.9	33	51.6
Colorado	70	47	67.1	24	34.3	48	68.6	11	15.7	56	80.0	1	1.4	59	84.3	48	68.6	49	70.0
Idaho	35	25	71.4	11	31.4	22	62.9	0	0.0	24	68.6	1	2.9	26	74.3	19	54.3	15	42.9
Montana	57	32	56.1	5	8.8	26	45.6	0	0.0	36	63.2	0	0.0	34	59.6	23	40.4	20	35.1
Nevada	36	9	25.0	7	19.4	14	38.9	2	5.6	18	50.0	1	2.8	31	86.1	15	41.7	14	38.9
New Mexico	33	20	60.6	1	3.0	20	60.6	1	3.0	21	63.6	2	6.1	29	87.9	22	66.7	11	33.3
Utah	35	13	37.1	10	28.6	25	71.4	2	5.7	26	74.3	1	2.9	28	80.0	13	37.1	18	51.4
Wyoming	24	16	66.7	2	8.3	18	75.0	0	0.0	19	79.2	0	0.0	20	83.3	13	54.2	12	50.0
CENSUS DIVISION 9, PACIFIC	476	265	55.7	128	26.9	290	60.9	44	9.2	330	69.3	15	3.2	417	87.6	344	72.3	288	60.5
Alaska	14	6	42.9	2	14.3	9	64.3	0	0.0	8	57.1	1	7.1	12	85.7	9	64.3	10	71.4
California	307	163	53.1	85	27.7	176	57.3	43	14.0	204	66.4	10	3.3	272	88.6	219	71.3	186	60.6
Hawaii	17	6	35.3	5	29.4	7	41.2	0	0.0	11	64.7	1	5.9	13	76.5	6	35.3	11	64.7
Oregon	59	47	79.7	16	27.1	51	86.4	0	0.0	52	88.1	1	1.7	51	86.4	48	81.4	37	62.7
Washington	79	43	54.4	20	25.3	47	59.5	1	1.3	55	69.6	2	2.5	69	87.3	62	78.5	44	55.7

Table 7 (Continued)

These data include only hospital-based facilities and services as reported by responding hospitals in Section C of the 2011 AHA Annual Survey, beginning on page 215. All hospitals are represented with Community Hospitals listed separately under United States. No estimates have been made for nonresponding hospitals. Definitions of facilities and services are listed in the Glossary, page 201.

CLASSIFICATION	HOSPITALS REPORTING	CHILDREN'S WELLNESS PROGRAM		CHIROPRACTIC SERVICES		COMMUNITY OUTREACH		COMPLEMENTARY AND ALTERNATIVE MEDICINE SERVICES		COMPUTER ASSISTED ORTHOPEDIC SURGERY (CAOS)		CRISIS PREVENTION		DENTAL SERVICES		ENABLING SERVICES		ENROLLMENT ASSISTANCE SERVICES		EXTRACORPOREAL SHOCK WAVE LITHOTRIPTER (ESWL)	
		Number	Percent	Number	Percent	Number	Percent	Number	Percent	Number	Percent	Number	Percent	Number	Percent	Number	Percent	Number	Percent	Number	Percent
UNITED STATES	4,782	917	19.2	119	2.5	3,190	66.7	902	18.9	674	14.1	1,008	21.1	1,025	21.4	1,144	23.9	2,425	50.7	1,267	26.5
COMMUNITY HOSPITALS	4,082	886	21.7	89	2.2	2,965	72.6	853	20.9	656	16.1	877	21.5	877	21.5	1,063	26.0	2,254	55.2	1,212	29.7
CENSUS DIVISION 1, NEW ENGLAND	201	67	33.3	8	4.0	138	68.6	85	42.3	34	16.9	72	35.8	49	24.4	74	36.8	152	75.6	107	53.2
Connecticut	31	13	41.9	1	3.2	28	90.3	22	71.0	7	22.6	19	61.3	11	35.5	13	41.9	24	77.4	18	58.1
Maine	39	12	30.8	1	2.5	32	82.1	14	35.9	4	10.3	8	20.5	4	10.3	11	28.2	24	61.5	17	43.6
Massachusetts	80	25	31.3	4	5.0	66	82.5	27	33.8	14	17.5	28	35.0	11	18.8	30	37.5	66	82.5	45	56.3
New Hampshire	27	12	44.4	1	3.7	23	85.2	15	55.6	6	22.2	11	40.7	11	40.7	12	44.4	22	81.5	14	51.9
Rhode Island	10	2	20.0	0	0.0	10	100.0	3	30.0	2	20.0	4	40.0	4	40.0	3	30.0	8	80.0	7	70.0
Vermont	14	3	21.4	1	7.1	9	64.3	4	28.6	1	7.1	2	14.3	4	26.6	5	35.7	8	57.1	6	42.9
CENSUS DIVISION 2, MIDDLE ATLANTIC	396	139	35.1	18	4.5	308	77.8	118	29.8	86	21.7	164	41.4	155	35.1	144	36.4	255	64.4	140	35.4
New Jersey	69	30	43.5	3	4.3	51	73.5	22	31.9	16	23.2	40	58.0	22	26.0	29	42.0	42	60.9	21	30.4
New York	165	65	39.4	13	7.9	140	84.8	61	37.0	36	21.8	80	48.5	85	52.1	58	35.2	113	68.5	60	36.4
Pennsylvania	162	44	27.2	2	1.2	117	72.2	35	21.6	34	21.0	44	27.2	43	30.2	57	35.2	100	61.7	59	36.4
CENSUS DIVISION 3, SOUTH ATLANTIC	707	114	16.1	9	1.3	506	71.6	128	13.1	125	17.7	155	21.9	163	23.1	195	27.6	401	56.7	229	32.4
Delaware	8	5	62.5	0	0.0	5	62.5	3	37.5	1	12.5	3	37.5	4	50.0	2	25.0	6	75.0	3	37.5
District of Columbia	10	4	40.0	0	0.0	8	80.0	4	40.0	3	30.0	4	40.0	5	50.0	5	50.0	6	60.0	3	20.0
Florida	176	16	9.1	2	1.1	120	68.2	25	14.2	37	21.0	27	15.3	24	13.6	36	20.5	93	52.8	78	44.3
Georgia	120	8	6.7	2	1.7	77	64.2	11	9.2	22	18.3	24	20.0	20	16.7	30	25.0	71	59.2	30	25.0
Maryland	54	17	31.5	1	1.9	41	75.9	23	42.6	14	25.9	24	42.6	22	40.7	27	50.0	40	74.1	27	50.0
North Carolina	115	21	18.3	2	1.7	87	75.7	22	9.1	15	13.0	24	20.9	32	27.8	37	32.2	59	51.3	40	18.3
South Carolina	82	16	19.5	0	0.0	65	79.3	8	4.9	8	9.8	8	9.8	17	20.7	11	13.4	36	43.9	21	22.0
Virginia	83	15	18.1	1	1.2	63	75.9	28	33.7	22	26.5	31	37.3	27	32.5	36	43.4	61	73.5	34	41.0
West Virginia	59	12	20.3	1	1.7	40	67.8	8	13.6	3	5.1	11	18.6	12	20.3	11	18.6	29	49.2	16	27.1
CENSUS DIVISION 4, EAST NORTH CENTRAL	726	191	26.3	28	3.9	552	73.0	236	32.5	125	17.2	207	28.5	177	24.4	257	35.4	441	60.7	217	29.9
Illinois	164	48	29.3	8	4.9	125	73.2	44	26.8	31	18.9	58	35.4	42	26.2	53	32.3	94	57.3	42	25.6
Indiana	122	33	27.0	1	0.8	100	82.0	33	27.0	10	8.2	29	23.8	20	16.4	27	22.1	80	65.6	31	25.4
Michigan	134	48	35.8	6	4.5	107	79.9	52	38.8	23	17.2	44	32.8	35	26.1	65	48.5	94	70.1	48	35.8
Ohio	160	38	23.8	11	6.9	130	81.3	48	30.0	37	23.1	42	26.3	52	32.5	62	38.8	99	61.9	60	37.5
Wisconsin	146	24	16.4	2	1.4	90	61.6	59	40.4	24	16.4	34	23.3	27	18.5	50	34.2	74	50.7	36	24.7
CENSUS DIVISION 5, EAST SOUTH CENTRAL	376	44	11.7	5	1.3	234	62.2	19	5.1	35	9.3	44	11.7	76	20.2	52	13.8	143	38.0	86	22.9
Alabama	95	11	11.6	2	2.1	54	56.8	4	4.2	10	10.5	10	10.5	10	7.4	9	9.5	43	45.3	23	26.3
Kentucky	86	13	15.1	1	1.2	61	70.9	10	11.6	12	14.0	11	12.8	18	20.9	22	25.6	49	57.0	21	24.4
Mississippi	110	12	10.9	2	1.8	66	60.0	3	2.7	6	5.5	9	8.2	32	29.1	5	4.5	15	13.6	15	15.5
Tennessee	85	8	9.4	0	0.0	55	62.4	2	2.4	7	8.2	14	16.5	19	22.4	16	18.8	36	42.4	23	27.1
CENSUS DIVISION 6, WEST NORTH CENTRAL	658	112	17.0	18	2.7	415	63.1	101	15.3	52	7.9	120	18.2	120	18.2	126	19.1	270	41.0	110	16.7
Iowa	126	26	20.6	2	1.6	96	76.2	28	22.2	12	9.5	30	23.8	23	18.3	32	25.4	65	51.6	15	11.9
Kansas	153	13	8.5	2	1.3	57	37.3	8	5.2	5	3.3	7	4.6	14	9.2	13	8.5	45	29.4	22	14.4
Minnesota	100	22	22.0	5	5.0	72	72.0	26	26.0	10	10.0	24	24.0	18	18.0	17	17.0	42	42.0	25	25.3
Missouri	150	28	18.7	6	4.0	98	65.3	26	17.3	13	8.7	36	24.0	47	31.5	46	30.7	71	47.3	27	18.0
Nebraska	55	11	20.0	0	0.0	41	74.5	6	10.9	9	16.4	13	23.6	9	16.4	9	16.4	24	43.6	10	18.2
North Dakota	24	6	25.0	2	8.3	16	56.7	3	12.5	2	8.3	4	16.7	4	16.7	6	25.0	12	50.0	3	12.5
South Dakota	50	6	12.0	1	2.0	35	70.0	4	8.0	1	2.0	6	12.0	5	10.0	3	6.0	11	22.0	4	8.0
CENSUS DIVISION 7, WEST SOUTH CENTRAL	888	104	11.7	7	0.8	418	47.1	49	5.5	87	9.8	79	8.9	127	14.3	119	13.4	337	38.0	170	19.1
Arkansas	93	8	8.6	1	1.1	52	55.9	3	3.2	4	4.3	11	11.8	9	9.7	9	9.7	37	39.8	15	16.1
Louisiana	97	22	22.7	1	1.0	49	50.5	7	7.2	14	14.4	17	17.5	14	14.4	13	13.4	48	49.5	18	18.6
Oklahoma	127	13	10.2	1	0.8	58	45.7	5	3.9	8	6.3	7	5.5	20	15.7	11	8.7	40	31.5	24	18.9
Texas	571	61	10.7	4	0.7	259	45.4	34	6.0	61	10.7	44	7.7	84	14.7	86	15.1	212	37.1	113	19.8
CENSUS DIVISION 8, MOUNTAIN	354	65	18.4	8	2.3	232	65.5	66	18.6	48	13.6	72	20.3	68	19.2	66	18.6	172	48.6	67	19.1
Arizona	64	16	25.0	1	1.6	41	64.1	19	29.7	15	23.4	16	25.0	16	25.0	17	26.6	34	53.1	19	29.7
Colorado	70	8	11.4	3	4.3	52	74.3	21	30.0	13	18.6	13	18.6	13	18.6	15	21.4	40	57.1	13	18.6
Idaho	35	7	20.0	1	2.9	25	71.4	6	17.1	7	20.0	5	14.3	8	22.9	5	14.3	17	48.6	4	11.4
Montana	57	12	21.1	2	3.5	34	59.5	9	15.8	5	8.8	10	17.5	4	7.0	7	12.3	32	56.1	7	12.3
Nevada	36	6	16.7	0	0.0	17	47.2	0	0.0	1	2.8	6	16.7	5	13.9	7	19.4	11	30.6	2	5.6
New Mexico	33	5	15.2	0	0.0	23	69.7	2	6.1	2	6.1	3	9.1	6	18.2	4	12.1	13	39.4	9	27.3
Utah	35	8	22.9	1	2.9	26	74.3	6	17.1	5	14.3	13	37.1	13	37.1	10	28.6	21	60.0	9	25.7
Wyoming	24	3	12.5	0	0.0	14	58.3	3	12.5	0	0.0	6	25.0	3	12.5	1	4.2	4	16.7	4	16.7
CENSUS DIVISION 9, PACIFIC	476	81	17.0	18	3.8	357	75.0	100	21.0	82	17.2	95	20.0	90	18.9	111	23.3	254	53.4	141	29.6
Alaska	14	2	14.3	0	0.0	10	71.4	1	7.1	1	7.1	4	28.6	2	14.3	1	7.1	7	50.0	5	35.7
California	307	52	16.9	13	4.2	227	73.9	63	20.5	47	15.3	54	17.6	66	21.5	67	21.8	152	49.5	93	30.3
Hawaii	17	1	5.9	0	0.0	9	52.9	2	11.8	2	11.8	2	11.8	4	23.5	2	11.8	6	35.3	4	23.5
Oregon	59	12	20.3	2	3.4	54	91.5	16	27.1	19	32.2	10	16.9	4	6.8	19	32.2	45	76.3	19	32.2
Washington	79	14	17.7	3	3.8	57	72.2	18	22.3	13	16.5	25	31.6	14	17.7	22	27.8	44	55.7	20	25.3

Table 7 (Continued)

These data include only hospital-based facilities and services as reported by responding hospitals in Section C of the 2011 AHA Annual Survey, beginning on page 215. All hospitals are represented with Community Hospitals listed separately under United States. No estimates have been made for nonresponding hospitals. Definitions of facilities and services are listed in the Glossary, page 201.

CLASSIFICATION	HOSPITALS REPORTING	FERTILITY CLINIC Number	Percent	FITNESS CENTER Number	Percent	FREESTANDING OUTPATIENT CARE CENTER Number	Percent	GENETIC TESTING/COUNSELING Number	Percent	GERIATRIC SERVICES Number	Percent	HEALTH FAIR Number	Percent	COMMUNITY HEALTH EDUCATION Number	Percent	HEALTH RESEARCH Number	Percent	HEALTH SCREENINGS Number	Percent	HEMODIALYSIS Number	Percent	HIV/AIDS SERVICES Number	Percent
UNITED STATES	4,782	238	5.0	1,333	27.9	1,449	30.3	653	13.7	1,821	38.1	3,460	72.4	3,432	71.8	1,073	22.4	3,550	74.2	1,476	30.9	1,096	22.9
COMMUNITY HOSPITALS	4,082	234	5.7	1,244	30.5	1,342	32.9	636	15.6	1,659	40.6	3,269	80.1	3,197	78.3	983	24.1	3,342	81.9	1,381	33.8	1,012	24.8
CENSUS DIVISION 1, NEW ENGLAND	201	24	11.9	53	26.4	90	44.8	53	26.4	94	46.8	161	80.1	171	85.1	74	36.8	172	85.6	68	33.8	86	42.8
Connecticut	31	5	16.1	10	32.3	19	61.3	14	45.2	16	51.6	24	77.4	27	87.1	19	61.3	26	83.9	12	38.7	18	58.1
Maine	39	2	5.1	13	33.3	16	41.0	7	17.9	13	33.3	30	76.9	32	82.1	10	25.6	34	87.2	7	17.9	14	35.9
Massachusetts	80	11	13.8	11	13.8	32	40.0	22	27.5	36	45.0	64	80.0	65	81.3	27	33.8	67	83.8	36	45.0	34	42.5
New Hampshire	27	3	11.1	10	37.0	12	44.4	5	18.5	15	55.6	26	96.3	25	92.6	7	25.9	24	88.9	3	11.1	12	44.4
Rhode Island	10	1	10.0	4	40.0	7	70.0	3	30.0	9	90.0	9	90.0	10	100.0	7	70.0	10	100.0	7	70.0	5	50.0
Vermont	14	2	14.3	5	35.7	4	28.6	2	14.3	5	35.7	8	57.1	12	85.7	4	28.6	11	78.6	3	21.4	3	21.4
CENSUS DIVISION 2, MIDDLE ATLANTIC	396	45	11.4	116	29.3	204	51.5	123	31.1	229	57.8	315	79.5	318	80.3	152	38.4	330	83.3	202	51.0	181	45.7
New Jersey	69	6	8.7	20	29.0	29	42.0	30	43.5	45	65.2	50	72.5	53	76.8	32	46.4	56	81.2	43	62.3	36	52.2
New York	165	28	17.0	49	29.7	104	63.0	61	37.0	101	61.2	141	85.5	145	87.9	71	43.0	143	86.7	107	64.8	88	53.3
Pennsylvania	162	11	6.8	47	29.0	71	43.8	32	19.8	83	51.2	124	76.5	120	74.1	49	30.2	131	80.9	52	32.1	57	35.2
CENSUS DIVISION 3, SOUTH ATLANTIC	707	33	4.7	202	28.6	258	36.5	103	14.6	266	37.6	550	77.8	528	74.7	177	25.0	553	78.2	281	39.7	211	29.8
Delaware	8	0	0.0	4	50.0	5	62.5	4	50.0	3	37.5	4	50.0	6	75.0	5	62.5	6	75.0	5	62.5	5	62.5
District of Columbia	10	1	10.0	2	20.0	4	40.0	5	50.0	4	40.0	6	60.0	7	70.0	6	60.0	6	60.0	6	60.0	6	60.0
Florida	176	8	4.5	55	31.3	63	35.8	29	16.5	69	39.2	131	74.4	133	75.6	51	29.0	134	76.1	87	49.4	46	26.1
Georgia	120	3	2.5	31	25.8	44	36.7	9	7.5	40	33.3	86	71.7	82	68.3	27	22.5	91	75.8	42	35.0	32	26.7
Maryland	54	6	11.1	13	24.1	24	44.4	21	38.9	31	57.4	45	83.3	42	77.8	25	46.3	46	85.2	35	64.8	25	46.3
North Carolina	115	6	5.2	39	33.9	41	35.7	12	10.4	42	36.5	94	81.7	94	81.7	25	21.7	96	83.5	37	32.2	29	25.2
South Carolina	82	2	2.4	20	24.4	24	29.3	5	6.1	34	41.5	63	76.8	58	70.7	13	15.9	58	70.7	28	34.1	27	32.9
Virginia	83	5	6.0	20	24.1	37	44.6	14	16.9	28	33.7	69	83.1	62	74.7	19	22.9	66	79.5	27	32.5	31	37.3
West Virginia	59	2	3.4	18	30.5	16	27.1	4	6.8	15	25.4	52	88.1	44	74.6	6	10.2	50	84.7	14	23.7	10	16.9
CENSUS DIVISION 4, EAST NORTH CENTRAL	726	44	6.1	260	35.8	279	38.4	115	15.8	363	50.0	578	79.6	611	84.2	224	30.9	603	83.1	228	31.4	174	24.0
Illinois	164	11	6.7	52	31.7	64	39.0	26	15.9	86	52.4	138	84.1	138	84.1	55	33.5	142	86.6	46	28.0	47	28.7
Indiana	122	6	4.9	39	32.0	41	33.6	15	12.3	45	36.9	103	84.4	102	83.6	32	26.2	104	85.2	27	22.1	20	16.4
Michigan	134	11	8.2	47	35.1	63	47.0	25	18.7	70	52.2	109	81.3	112	83.6	55	41.0	119	88.8	52	38.8	49	36.6
Ohio	160	11	6.9	64	40.0	65	40.6	28	17.5	61	38.1	136	85.0	140	87.5	58	36.3	140	87.5	73	45.6	51	31.9
Wisconsin	146	5	3.4	58	39.7	46	31.5	21	14.4	101	69.2	92	63.0	119	81.5	24	16.4	98	67.1	30	20.5	7	4.8
CENSUS DIVISION 5, EAST SOUTH CENTRAL	376	8	2.1	94	25.0	76	20.2	26	6.9	111	29.5	250	66.5	227	60.4	49	13.0	246	65.4	93	24.7	62	16.5
Alabama	95	3	3.2	28	29.5	20	21.1	5	5.3	31	32.6	70	73.7	61	64.2	14	14.7	71	74.7	33	34.7	12	12.6
Kentucky	86	2	2.3	18	20.9	24	27.9	8	9.3	26	30.2	73	84.9	70	81.4	17	19.8	72	83.7	20	23.3	11	12.8
Mississippi	110	2	1.8	31	28.2	8	7.3	3	2.7	23	20.9	49	44.5	45	40.9	4	3.6	42	38.2	12	10.9	20	20.0
Tennessee	85	1	1.2	17	20.0	24	28.2	10	11.8	31	36.5	58	68.2	51	60.0	14	16.5	61	71.8	28	32.9	17	20.0
CENSUS DIVISION 6, WEST NORTH CENTRAL	658	31	4.7	234	35.6	104	15.8	57	8.7	245	37.2	469	71.3	472	71.7	94	14.3	512	77.8	138	21.0	116	17.6
Iowa	126	3	2.4	47	37.3	17	13.5	7	5.6	54	42.9	107	84.9	103	81.7	16	12.7	119	94.4	25	19.8	17	13.5
Kansas	153	2	1.3	41	26.8	9	5.9	10	6.5	42	27.5	81	52.9	75	49.0	10	6.5	86	56.2	16	10.5	17	11.1
Minnesota	100	7	7.0	37	37.0	22	22.0	14	14.0	47	47.0	75	75.0	86	86.0	16	16.0	82	82.0	18	18.0	19	19.0
Missouri	150	10	6.7	57	38.0	41	27.3	18	12.0	54	36.0	109	72.7	106	70.7	30	20.0	117	78.0	48	32.0	36	24.0
Nebraska	55	4	7.3	22	40.0	10	18.2	4	7.3	20	36.4	43	78.2	44	80.0	10	18.2	44	80.0	13	23.6	10	18.2
North Dakota	24	4	16.7	12	50.0	2	8.3	2	8.3	11	45.8	16	66.7	19	79.2	6	25.0	18	75.0	8	33.3	5	20.8
South Dakota	50	1	2.0	18	36.0	3	6.0	2	4.0	17	34.0	38	76.0	39	78.0	6	12.0	46	92.0	4	8.0	4	8.0
CENSUS DIVISION 7, WEST SOUTH CENTRAL	888	17	1.9	180	20.3	175	19.7	56	6.3	246	27.7	542	61.0	494	55.6	103	11.6	526	59.2	194	21.8	104	11.7
Arkansas	93	0	0.0	18	19.4	15	16.1	4	4.3	27	29.0	66	71.0	54	58.1	8	8.6	66	71.0	16	17.2	12	12.9
Louisiana	97	2	2.1	19	19.6	29	29.9	10	10.3	37	38.1	63	64.9	57	58.8	20	20.6	57	58.8	29	29.9	23	23.7
Oklahoma	127	3	2.4	17	13.4	17	13.4	6	4.7	29	22.8	75	59.1	76	59.8	15	11.8	74	58.3	21	16.5	12	9.4
Texas	571	12	2.1	126	22.1	114	20.0	36	6.3	153	26.8	338	59.2	307	53.8	60	10.5	329	57.6	128	22.4	57	10.0
CENSUS DIVISION 8, MOUNTAIN	354	11	3.1	94	26.6	95	26.8	42	11.9	108	30.5	267	75.4	259	73.2	63	17.8	266	75.1	100	28.2	60	16.9
Arizona	64	3	4.7	22	34.4	25	39.1	7	10.9	20	31.3	43	67.2	50	78.1	20	31.3	50	78.1	32	50.0	15	23.4
Colorado	70	2	2.9	28	40.0	20	28.6	5	7.1	18	25.7	54	77.1	58	82.9	17	24.3	54	77.1	20	28.6	17	24.3
Idaho	35	1	2.9	9	25.7	9	25.7	5	14.3	10	28.6	30	85.7	28	80.0	4	11.4	26	74.3	7	20.0	4	11.4
Montana	57	1	1.8	7	12.3	15	26.3	3	5.3	19	33.3	46	80.7	39	68.4	6	10.5	48	84.2	13	22.8	9	15.8
Nevada	36	0	0.0	2	5.6	2	5.6	1	2.8	7	19.4	21	58.3	19	52.8	5	13.9	16	44.4	10	27.8	4	11.1
New Mexico	33	0	0.0	8	24.2	7	21.2	0	0.0	13	39.4	24	72.7	29	87.9	1	3.0	24	72.7	6	18.2	7	21.2
Utah	35	4	11.4	8	22.9	15	42.9	6	17.1	13	37.1	30	85.7	18	51.4	10	28.6	28	80.0	13	37.1	7	20.0
Wyoming	24	0	0.0	4	16.7	2	8.3	0	0.0	8	33.3	19	79.2	18	75.0	0	0.0	20	83.3	7	29.2	2	8.3
CENSUS DIVISION 9, PACIFIC	476	25	5.3	100	21.0	168	35.3	78	16.4	159	33.4	328	68.9	352	73.9	137	28.8	342	71.8	172	36.1	102	21.4
Alaska	14	0	0.0	4	28.6	1	7.1	2	14.3	3	21.4	9	64.3	12	85.7	4	28.6	11	78.6	1	7.1	1	7.1
California	307	20	6.5	60	19.5	114	37.1	54	17.6	109	35.5	204	66.4	213	69.4	95	30.9	207	67.4	128	41.7	75	24.4
Hawaii	17	0	0.0	1	5.9	3	17.6	2	11.8	4	23.5	9	52.9	10	58.8	3	17.6	11	64.7	4	23.5	3	17.6
Oregon	59	1	1.7	21	35.6	21	35.6	4	6.8	20	33.9	49	83.1	53	89.8	12	20.3	51	86.4	17	28.8	11	18.6
Washington	79	4	5.1	14	17.7	29	36.7	16	20.3	23	29.1	57	72.2	64	81.0	23	29.1	62	78.5	22	27.8	12	15.2

Table 7 (Continued)

These data include only hospital-based facilities and services as reported by responding hospitals in Section C of the 2011 AHA Annual Survey, beginning on page 215. All hospitals are represented with Community Hospitals listed separately under United States. No estimates have been made for nonresponding hospitals. Definitions of facilities and services are listed in the Glossary, page 201.

CLASSIFICATION	HOSPITALS REPORTING	HOME HEALTH SERVICES Number	Percent	HOSPICE Number	Percent	HOSPITAL-BASED OUTPATIENT CARE CENTER SERVICES Number	Percent	IMMUNIZATION PROGRAM Number	Percent	INDIGENT CARE CLINIC Number	Percent	LINGUISTIC/ TRANSLATION SERVICES Number	Percent	MEALS ON WHEELS Number	Percent	MOBILE HEALTH SERVICES Number	Percent	NEONATAL INTERMEDIATE CARE UNITS Number	Percent	NEUROLOGICAL SERVICES Number	Percent	NUTRITION PROGRAMS CENTER Number	Percent
UNITED STATES	4,782	1,303	27.2	971	20.3	3,430	71.7	1,801	37.7	734	15.3	2,608	54.5	430	9.0	496	10.4	704	14.7	2,287	47.8	3,515	73.5
COMMUNITY HOSPITALS	4,082	1,240	30.4	913	22.4	3,179	77.9	1,661	40.7	703	17.2	2,406	58.9	418	10.2	465	11.4	696	17.1	2,137	52.4	3,180	77.9
CENSUS DIVISION 1, NEW ENGLAND	201	44	21.9	56	27.9	170	84.6	112	55.7	50	24.9	139	69.2	7	3.5	24	11.9	29	14.4	137	68.2	184	91.5
Connecticut	31	8	25.8	16	51.6	27	87.1	16	51.6	13	41.9	20	64.5	0	0.0	6	19.4	5	16.1	26	83.9	27	87.1
Maine	39	7	17.9	6	15.4	31	79.5	27	69.2	9	23.1	20	51.3	3	7.7	3	7.7	4	10.3	18	46.2	37	94.9
Massachusetts	80	20	25.0	20	25.0	68	85.0	40	50.0	13	16.3	65	81.3	2	2.5	9	11.3	14	17.5	56	70.0	72	90.0
New Hampshire	27	5	18.5	7	25.9	24	88.9	14	51.9	7	25.9	17	63.0	1	3.7	4	14.8	3	11.1	20	74.1	27	100.0
Rhode Island	10	2	20.0	2	20.0	9	90.0	8	80.0	5	50.0	9	90.0	0	0.0	1	10.0	2	20.0	9	90.0	10	100.0
Vermont	14	2	14.3	5	35.7	11	78.6	7	50.0	3	21.4	8	57.1	1	7.1	1	7.1	1	7.1	8	57.1	11	78.6
CENSUS DIVISION 2, MIDDLE ATLANTIC	396	112	28.3	105	26.5	321	81.1	215	54.3	146	36.9	266	67.2	39	9.8	67	16.9	117	29.5	289	73.0	330	83.3
New Jersey	69	14	20.3	17	24.6	53	76.8	34	49.3	41	59.4	54	78.3	11	15.9	16	23.2	42	60.9	56	81.2	57	82.6
New York	165	44	26.7	46	27.9	141	85.5	102	61.8	67	40.6	123	74.5	16	9.7	40	24.2	52	31.5	131	79.4	141	85.5
Pennsylvania	162	54	33.3	42	25.9	127	78.4	79	48.3	38	23.5	89	54.9	12	7.4	11	6.8	23	14.2	102	63.0	132	81.5
CENSUS DIVISION 3, SOUTH ATLANTIC	707	164	23.2	125	17.7	517	73.1	240	33.9	111	15.7	382	54.0	29	4.1	95	13.4	140	19.8	402	56.9	538	76.1
Delaware	8	4	50.0	1	12.5	5	62.5	6	75.0	2	25.0	7	87.5	0	0.0	0	0.0	1	12.5	6	75.0	7	87.5
District of Columbia	10	1	10.0	0	0.0	9	90.0	7	70.0	4	40.0	8	80.0	0	0.0	4	40.0	4	40.0	8	80.0	9	90.0
Florida	176	35	19.9	20	11.4	122	69.3	46	26.1	27	15.3	93	52.8	1	0.6	19	10.8	24	13.6	120	68.2	125	71.0
Georgia	120	16	13.3	19	15.8	81	67.5	30	25.0	14	11.7	64	53.3	2	1.7	13	10.8	29	24.2	54	45.0	88	73.3
Maryland	54	11	20.4	15	27.8	43	79.6	31	57.4	20	37.0	37	68.5	5	9.3	11	20.4	5	9.3	41	75.9	46	85.2
North Carolina	115	34	29.6	23	20.0	92	80.0	39	33.9	20	17.4	64	55.7	4	3.5	18	15.7	35	30.4	60	52.2	89	77.4
South Carolina	82	15	18.3	8	9.8	60	73.2	21	25.6	5	6.1	37	45.1	4	4.9	9	11.0	27	32.9	36	43.9	62	75.6
Virginia	83	33	39.8	32	38.6	62	74.7	28	33.7	14	16.9	52	62.7	9	10.8	18	21.7	13	15.7	49	59.0	66	79.5
West Virginia	59	15	25.4	7	11.9	43	72.9	32	54.2	6	10.2	20	33.9	4	6.8	3	5.1	2	3.4	28	47.5	46	78.0
CENSUS DIVISION 4, EAST NORTH CENTRAL	726	229	31.5	190	26.2	573	78.9	325	44.8	151	20.8	457	62.9	130	17.9	88	12.1	88	12.1	412	56.7	622	85.7
Illinois	164	55	33.5	47	28.7	129	78.7	66	40.2	31	18.9	100	61.0	26	15.9	14	8.5	30	18.3	99	60.4	132	80.5
Indiana	122	41	33.6	34	27.9	90	73.8	43	35.2	21	17.2	76	62.3	27	22.1	16	13.1	18	14.8	64	52.5	101	82.8
Michigan	134	43	32.1	46	34.3	112	83.6	79	59.0	35	26.1	90	67.2	12	9.0	14	10.4	11	8.2	83	61.9	116	86.6
Ohio	160	60	37.5	45	28.1	130	81.3	74	46.3	46	28.8	106	66.3	24	15.0	24	15.0	29	18.1	105	65.6	143	89.4
Wisconsin	146	30	20.5	18	12.3	112	76.7	63	43.2	18	12.3	85	58.2	41	28.1	20	13.7	0	0.0	61	41.8	130	89.0
CENSUS DIVISION 5, EAST SOUTH CENTRAL	376	86	22.9	37	9.8	216	57.4	73	19.4	24	6.4	158	42.0	10	2.7	27	7.2	65	17.3	142	37.8	212	56.4
Alabama	95	28	29.5	6	6.3	65	68.4	18	18.9	6	6.3	46	48.4	4	4.2	5	5.3	9	9.5	43	45.3	53	55.8
Kentucky	86	30	34.9	12	14.0	67	77.9	16	18.6	9	10.5	47	54.7	4	4.7	13	15.1	16	18.6	39	45.3	60	69.8
Mississippi	110	10	9.1	7	6.4	34	30.9	22	20.0	5	4.5	22	20.0	1	0.9	3	2.7	30	27.3	22	20.0	38	34.5
Tennessee	85	18	21.2	12	14.1	50	58.8	17	20.0	4	4.7	43	50.6	1	1.2	6	7.1	10	11.8	38	44.7	61	71.8
CENSUS DIVISION 6, WEST NORTH CENTRAL	858	262	39.8	180	27.4	499	75.8	266	40.4	51	5.9	315	47.9	117	17.8	63	9.6	73	11.1	201	30.5	465	70.7
Iowa	126	61	48.4	53	42.1	110	87.3	64	50.8	12	9.5	73	57.9	33	26.2	12	9.5	11	8.7	36	28.6	112	88.9
Kansas	153	48	31.4	16	10.5	109	71.2	35	22.9	4	2.6	54	35.3	33	21.6	5	3.3	11	7.2	27	17.6	79	51.6
Minnesota	100	41	41.0	43	43.0	81	81.0	43	43.0	8	8.0	52	52.0	18	18.0	11	11.0	10	10.0	30	30.0	77	77.0
Missouri	150	56	37.3	31	20.7	109	72.7	65	43.3	18	12.0	86	57.3	17	11.3	21	14.0	29	19.3	74	49.3	118	78.7
Nebraska	55	25	45.5	17	30.9	40	72.7	22	40.0	3	5.5	29	52.7	7	12.7	2	3.6	5	9.1	20	36.4	39	70.9
North Dakota	24	10	41.7	8	33.3	16	66.7	10	41.7	3	12.5	8	33.3	2	8.3	3	12.5	5	20.8	6	25.0	15	62.5
South Dakota	50	21	42.0	12	24.0	34	68.0	27	54.0	3	6.0	13	26.0	7	14.0	9	18.0	2	4.0	8	16.0	25	50.0
CENSUS DIVISION 7, WEST SOUTH CENTRAL	888	184	20.7	80	9.0	546	61.5	240	27.0	72	8.1	394	44.4	43	4.8	52	5.9	90	10.1	313	35.2	562	63.3
Arkansas	93	40	43.0	10	10.8	63	67.7	14	15.1	14	15.1	40	43.0	5	5.4	7	7.5	8	8.6	27	29.0	62	66.7
Louisiana	97	14	14.4	6	5.2	59	60.8	16	16.5	3	3.1	34	35.1	2	2.1	2	2.1	9	9.3	38	39.2	69	71.1
Oklahoma	127	38	29.9	15	11.8	67	52.8	42	33.0	7	5.5	53	41.7	17	13.4	6	4.7	5	3.9	34	26.8	60	47.2
Texas	571	92	16.1	49	3.6	357	62.5	160	28.0	48	8.4	267	46.8	19	3.3	32	5.6	68	11.9	214	37.5	371	65.0
CENSUS DIVISION 8, MOUNTAIN	354	90	25.4	87	24.6	244	68.9	124	35.0	42	11.9	194	54.8	32	9.0	25	7.1	46	13.0	139	39.3	257	72.6
Arizona	64	17	26.6	17	25.6	45	70.3	21	32.8	10	15.6	44	68.8	8	12.5	7	10.9	12	18.8	34	53.1	50	78.1
Colorado	70	17	24.3	12	17.1	55	78.6	20	28.6	8	11.4	45	64.3	8	11.4	5	7.1	10	14.3	35	50.0	57	81.4
Idaho	35	7	20.0	10	23.6	26	74.3	14	40.0	6	17.1	22	62.9	3	8.6	4	11.4	0	0.0	10	28.6	23	65.7
Montana	57	18	31.6	21	36.8	42	73.7	27	47.4	6	10.5	17	29.8	10	17.5	4	7.0	2	3.5	14	24.6	41	71.9
Nevada	36	5	13.9	3	3.3	16	44.4	10	27.8	4	11.1	17	47.2	0	0.0	1	2.8	5	13.9	10	36.1	20	55.6
New Mexico	33	9	27.3	7	21.2	19	57.6	11	33.3	1	3.0	17	51.5	1	3.0	0	0.0	6	18.2	10	30.3	20	60.6
Utah	35	9	25.7	10	23.6	26	74.3	13	37.1	5	14.3	21	60.0	1	2.9	2	5.7	8	22.9	16	45.7	29	82.9
Wyoming	24	8	33.3	7	29.2	15	62.5	8	33.3	2	8.3	11	45.8	1	4.2	2	8.3	3	12.5	7	29.2	17	70.8
CENSUS DIVISION 9, PACIFIC	476	132	27.7	111	23.3	344	72.3	206	43.3	87	18.3	303	63.7	23	4.8	55	11.6	56	11.8	252	52.9	345	72.5
Alaska	14	6	42.9	3	21.4	9	64.3	5	35.7	2	14.3	9	64.3	0	0.0	0	0.0	2	14.3	5	35.7	10	71.4
California	307	74	24.1	56	21.5	214	69.7	132	43.0	61	19.9	196	63.8	18	5.9	35	11.4	32	10.4	178	58.0	210	68.4
Hawaii	17	6	35.3	2	11.8	8	47.1	3	17.6	1	5.9	8	47.1	1	5.9	2	11.8	1	5.9	8	47.1	13	73.5
Oregon	59	28	47.5	25	42.4	53	89.8	24	40.7	12	20.3	42	71.2	1	1.7	7	11.9	5	8.5	23	39.0	54	91.5
Washington	79	18	22.8	15	19.0	60	75.9	42	53.2	11	13.9	48	60.8	3	3.8	11	13.9	16	20.3	38	48.1	58	73.4

Table 7 (Continued)

These data include only hospital-based facilities and services as reported by responding hospitals in Section C of the 2011 AHA Annual Survey, beginning on page 215. All hospitals are represented with Community Hospitals listed separately under United States. No estimates have been made for nonresponding hospitals. Definitions of facilities and services are listed in the Glossary, page 201.

CLASSIFICATION	HOSPITALS REPORTING	OBSTETRICS INPATIENT CARE UNITS Number	Percent	OCCUPATIONAL HEALTH SERVICES Number	Percent	ONCOLOGY SERVICES Number	Percent	ORTHOPEDIC SERVICES Number	Percent	OTHER SPECIAL CARE UNITS Number	Percent	OUTPATIENT SURGERY Number	Percent	PAIN MANAGEMENT PROGRAM Number	Percent	PALLIATIVE CARE PROGRAM Number	Percent	PALLIATIVE CARE INPATIENT UNIT Number	Percent	PATIENT CONTROLLED ANALGESIA (PCA) Number	Percent	PATIENT EDUCATION CENTER Number	Percent
UNITED STATES	4,782	2,362	49.4	2,995	62.6	2,462	51.5	3,287	68.7	734	15.3	3,844	80.4	2,444	51.1	1,585	33.1	466	9.7	3,181	66.5	2,583	54.0
COMMUNITY HOSPITALS	4,082	2,178	53.4	2,784	68.2	2,378	58.3	3,082	75.5	695	17.0	3,624	88.8	2,249	55.1	1,485	36.4	407	10.0	2,963	72.6	2,351	57.6
CENSUS DIVISION 1, NEW ENGLAND	201	140	69.7	158	78.6	149	74.1	171	85.1	21	10.4	171	85.1	140	69.7	95	47.3	30	14.9	163	81.1	136	67.7
Connecticut	31	20	64.5	20	64.5	25	80.6	24	77.4	9	29.0	26	83.9	24	77.4	19	61.3	5	16.1	26	83.9	20	64.5
Maine	39	30	76.9	27	69.2	26	66.7	36	92.3	3	7.7	35	89.7	23	59.0	20	51.3	6	15.4	32	82.1	25	64.1
Massachusetts	80	49	61.3	65	81.3	59	73.8	67	83.8	4	5.0	64	80.0	61	76.3	26	32.5	9	11.3	62	77.5	56	70.0
New Hampshire	27	22	81.5	26	96.3	20	74.1	25	92.6	5	18.5	24	88.9	17	63.0	16	59.3	7	25.9	24	88.9	19	70.4
Rhode Island	10	8	80.0	8	80.0	9	90.0	8	80.0	0	0.0	10	100.0	8	80.0	5	50.0	1	10.0	8	80.0	9	90.0
Vermont	14	11	78.6	12	85.7	10	71.4	11	78.6	0	0.0	12	85.7	7	50.0	9	64.3	2	14.3	11	78.6	7	50.0
CENSUS DIVISION 2, MIDDLE ATLANTIC	396	269	67.9	291	73.5	284	71.7	324	81.8	81	20.5	339	85.6	284	71.7	207	52.3	76	19.2	291	73.5	259	65.4
New Jersey	69	38	55.1	43	62.3	52	75.4	52	75.4	12	17.4	57	82.6	53	76.8	40	58.0	15	21.7	46	66.7	47	68.1
New York	165	127	77.0	129	78.2	129	78.2	141	85.5	38	23.0	150	90.9	120	72.7	102	61.8	42	25.5	127	77.0	108	65.5
Pennsylvania	162	104	64.2	119	73.5	103	63.6	130	80.2	31	19.1	132	81.5	111	68.5	65	40.1	19	11.7	118	72.8	104	64.2
CENSUS DIVISION 3, SOUTH ATLANTIC	707	382	54.0	479	67.8	390	55.2	531	75.1	134	19.0	568	80.3	384	54.3	255	36.1	59	8.3	499	70.6	413	58.4
Delaware	8	7	87.5	5	62.5	6	75.0	6	75.0	2	25.0	6	75.0	4	50.0	4	50.0	0	0.0	6	75.0	6	75.0
District of Columbia	10	5	50.0	8	80.0	6	60.0	7	70.0	3	30.0	7	70.0	7	70.0	7	70.0	1	10.0	7	70.0	8	80.0
Florida	176	83	47.2	113	64.2	110	62.5	135	76.7	42	23.9	145	82.4	93	52.8	61	34.7	18	10.2	126	71.6	93	52.8
Georgia	120	54	45.0	74	61.7	55	45.8	82	68.3	16	13.3	94	78.3	58	48.3	27	22.5	9	7.5	70	58.3	63	52.5
Maryland	54	36	66.7	45	83.3	43	79.6	46	85.2	15	27.8	45	83.3	43	79.6	34	63.0	7	13.0	45	83.3	35	64.8
North Carolina	115	75	65.2	83	72.2	68	59.1	93	80.9	27	23.5	100	87.0	82	71.3	41	35.7	11	9.6	91	79.1	67	58.3
South Carolina	82	40	48.8	55	67.1	30	36.6	59	72.0	15	18.3	58	70.7	33	40.2	22	26.8	2	2.4	54	65.9	54	65.9
Virginia	83	48	57.8	64	77.1	51	61.4	65	78.3	12	14.5	69	83.1	48	57.8	41	49.4	8	9.6	67	80.7	53	63.9
West Virginia	59	34	57.6	32	54.2	22	37.3	38	64.4	2	3.4	44	74.6	16	27.1	18	30.5	3	5.1	33	55.9	34	57.6
CENSUS DIVISION 4, EAST NORTH CENTRAL	726	460	63.4	510	70.2	477	65.7	570	78.5	205	28.2	646	89.0	463	63.8	280	38.6	86	11.8	562	77.4	506	69.7
Illinois	164	91	55.5	107	65.2	111	67.7	127	77.4	21	12.8	147	89.6	108	65.9	63	38.4	13	7.9	132	80.5	98	59.8
Indiana	122	93	76.2	85	69.7	97	58.2	97	79.5	21	17.2	106	86.9	64	52.5	38	31.1	10	8.2	93	76.2	75	61.5
Michigan	134	94	70.1	104	77.6	93	69.4	111	82.8	28	20.9	120	89.6	79	59.0	59	44.0	18	13.4	109	81.3	90	67.2
Ohio	160	108	67.5	120	75.0	119	74.4	142	88.8	28	17.5	149	93.1	119	74.4	63	39.4	31	19.4	132	82.5	111	69.4
Wisconsin	146	74	50.7	94	64.4	83	56.8	93	63.7	107	73.3	124	84.9	93	63.7	57	39.0	14	9.6	96	65.8	132	90.4
CENSUS DIVISION 5, EAST SOUTH CENTRAL	376	150	39.9	181	48.1	145	38.6	205	54.5	51	13.6	286	76.1	143	38.0	65	17.3	21	5.6	189	50.3	177	47.1
Alabama	95	36	37.9	46	48.4	41	43.2	61	64.2	10	10.5	78	82.1	40	42.1	17	17.9	7	7.4	51	53.7	51	53.7
Kentucky	86	50	58.1	49	57.0	41	47.7	58	67.4	11	12.8	72	83.7	45	52.3	24	27.9	6	7.0	59	68.6	49	57.0
Mississippi	110	27	24.5	34	30.9	29	26.4	34	30.9	16	14.5	69	62.7	30	27.3	7	6.4	1	0.9	31	28.2	45	40.9
Tennessee	85	37	43.5	52	61.2	34	40.0	52	61.2	14	16.5	67	78.8	28	32.9	17	20.0	7	8.2	48	56.5	39	45.9
CENSUS DIVISION 6, WEST NORTH CENTRAL	658	309	47.0	435	66.1	296	45.0	395	60.0	75	11.4	556	84.5	284	43.2	194	29.5	55	8.4	412	62.6	318	48.3
Iowa	126	81	64.3	92	73.0	77	61.1	93	73.8	11	8.7	118	93.7	61	48.4	35	27.8	6	4.8	91	72.2	91	72.2
Kansas	153	47	30.7	79	51.6	39	25.5	67	43.8	10	6.5	121	79.1	55	35.9	28	18.3	6	3.9	78	51.0	50	51.0
Minnesota	100	51	51.0	80	80.0	51	51.0	66	66.0	11	11.0	96	96.0	44	44.0	41	41.0	15	15.0	70	70.0	50	50.0
Missouri	150	79	52.7	102	68.0	72	48.0	101	67.3	27	18.0	111	74.0	72	48.0	51	34.0	14	9.3	107	71.3	89	59.3
Nebraska	55	25	45.5	39	70.9	31	56.4	39	70.9	8	14.5	50	90.9	27	49.1	18	32.7	6	10.9	33	60.0	33	60.0
North Dakota	24	12	50.0	10	41.7	10	41.7	9	37.5	3	12.5	20	83.3	9	37.5	9	37.5	5	20.8	13	54.2	10	41.7
South Dakota	50	14	28.0	33	66.0	16	32.0	20	40.0	5	10.0	40	80.0	16	32.0	12	24.0	3	6.0	20	40.0	21	42.0
CENSUS DIVISION 7, WEST SOUTH CENTRAL	888	282	31.8	423	47.6	269	30.3	488	55.0	88	9.9	589	66.3	315	35.5	152	17.1	36	4.1	512	57.7	363	40.9
Arkansas	93	36	38.7	48	51.6	33	35.5	52	55.9	4	4.3	66	71.0	23	24.7	13	14.0	3	3.2	53	57.0	35	37.6
Louisiana	97	46	47.4	52	53.6	43	44.3	57	58.8	8	8.2	72	74.2	31	32.0	22	22.7	2	2.1	58	59.8	41	42.3
Oklahoma	127	49	38.6	49	38.6	30	23.6	66	52.0	12	9.4	91	71.7	45	35.4	21	16.5	11	8.7	65	51.2	40	31.5
Texas	571	151	26.4	274	48.0	163	28.5	313	54.8	64	11.2	360	63.0	216	37.8	96	16.8	20	3.5	336	58.8	247	43.3
CENSUS DIVISION 8, MOUNTAIN	354	169	47.7	204	57.6	165	46.6	240	67.8	25	7.1	278	78.5	175	49.4	106	29.9	36	10.2	223	63.0	160	45.2
Arizona	64	35	54.7	35	54.7	34	53.1	49	76.6	3	4.7	53	82.8	34	53.1	25	39.1	10	15.6	43	67.2	31	48.4
Colorado	70	36	51.4	48	68.6	46	65.7	56	80.0	13	18.6	64	91.4	38	54.3	29	41.4	5	7.1	54	77.1	33	47.1
Idaho	35	17	48.6	23	65.7	11	31.4	27	77.1	1	2.9	30	85.7	18	51.4	8	22.9	4	11.4	23	65.7	19	54.3
Montana	57	26	45.6	31	54.4	19	33.3	23	40.4	1	1.8	36	63.2	25	43.9	15	26.3	5	8.8	27	47.4	23	40.4
Nevada	36	12	33.3	20	55.6	13	36.1	23	63.9	1	2.8	21	58.3	15	41.7	7	19.4	3	8.3	19	52.8	11	30.6
New Mexico	33	15	45.5	12	36.4	14	42.4	17	51.5	1	3.0	24	72.7	10	30.3	6	18.2	4	12.1	20	60.6	11	33.3
Utah	35	13	37.1	21	60.0	18	51.4	24	68.6	4	11.4	30	85.7	22	62.9	10	28.6	3	8.6	23	65.7	21	60.0
Wyoming	24	15	62.5	14	58.3	10	41.7	17	70.8	1	4.2	20	83.3	13	54.2	6	25.0	2	8.3	14	58.3	11	45.8
CENSUS DIVISION 9, PACIFIC	476	201	42.2	314	66.0	287	60.3	363	76.3	54	11.3	411	86.3	256	53.8	231	48.5	67	14.1	330	69.3	251	52.7
Alaska	14	8	57.1	6	42.9	5	35.7	9	64.3	4	28.6	10	71.4	4	28.6	3	21.4	1	7.1	11	78.6	6	42.9
California	307	101	32.9	202	65.8	194	63.2	236	76.9	34	11.1	264	86.0	174	56.7	150	48.9	45	14.7	204	66.4	161	52.4
Hawaii	17	9	52.9	14	82.4	9	52.9	12	70.6	3	17.6	12	70.6	6	35.3	7	41.2	1	5.9	10	58.8	7	41.2
Oregon	59	43	72.9	37	62.7	35	59.3	48	81.4	5	8.5	56	94.9	32	54.2	31	52.5	9	15.3	50	84.7	33	55.9
Washington	79	40	50.6	55	69.6	44	55.7	58	73.4	14	17.7	69	87.3	40	50.6	40	50.6	11	13.9	55	69.6	44	55.7

Table 7 (Continued)

These data include only hospital-based facilities and services as reported by responding hospitals in Section C of the 2011 AHA Annual Survey, beginning on page 215. All hospitals are represented with Community Hospitals listed separately under United States. No estimates have been made for nonresponding hospitals. Definitions of facilities and services are listed in the Glossary, page 201.

CLASSIFICATION	HOSPITALS REPORTING	PATIENT REPRESENTATIVE SERVICES No.	%	PHYSICAL REHAB. INPATIENT CARE UNITS No.	%	PRIMARY CARE DEPARTMENT No.	%	PSYCHIATRIC INPATIENT CARE UNITS No.	%	RETIREMENT HOUSING No.	%	ROBOTIC SURGERY No.	%	RURAL HEALTH CLINIC No.	%	SLEEP CENTER No.	%	SOCIAL WORK SERVICES No.	%	SPORTS MEDICINE No.	%	SUPPORT GROUPS No.	%
UNITED STATES	4,782	3,144	65.7	1,401	29.3	1,825	33.2	1,618	33.8	153	3.2	975	20.4	967	20.2	2,227	46.6	4,013	83.9	1,813	37.9	2,960	61.9
COMMUNITY HOSPITALS	4,082	2,828	69.3	1,307	32.0	1,707	41.8	1,253	30.9	150	3.7	945	23.2	894	21.9	2,139	52.4	3,514	86.1	1,756	43.0	2,716	66.5
CENSUS DIVISION 1, NEW ENGLAND	201	158	78.6	43	21.4	118	58.7	105	52.2	7	3.5	50	24.9	29	14.4	117	58.2	192	95.5	109	54.2	173	86.1
Connecticut	31	24	77.4	7	22.6	19	61.3	23	74.2	2	6.5	17	54.8	0	0.0	23	74.2	28	90.3	16	51.6	28	90.3
Maine	39	28	71.8	12	30.8	30	76.9	14	35.9	3	7.7	3	7.7	15	38.5	22	56.4	38	97.4	16	41.0	35	89.7
Massachusetts	80	65	81.3	11	13.8	35	43.8	46	57.5	0	0.0	20	25.0	3	3.8	45	56.3	76	95.0	45	56.3	69	86.3
New Hampshire	27	23	85.2	7	25.9	19	70.4	9	33.3	1	3.7	6	22.2	5	18.5	16	59.3	27	100.0	20	74.1	23	85.2
Rhode Island	10	8	80.0	3	30.0	8	80.0	8	80.0	0	0.0	3	30.0	1	10.0	6	60.0	10	100.0	4	40.0	10	100.0
Vermont	14	10	71.4	3	21.4	7	50.0	5	35.7	1	7.1	1	7.1	5	35.7	5	35.7	13	92.9	8	57.1	8	57.1
CENSUS DIVISION 2, MIDDLE ATLANTIC	396	306	77.3	156	39.4	222	56.1	232	58.6	7	1.8	126	31.8	33	8.3	224	56.6	371	93.7	189	47.7	315	79.5
New Jersey	69	59	85.5	22	31.9	43	62.3	44	63.8	2	2.9	30	43.5	2	2.9	44	63.8	66	95.7	26	37.7	51	73.9
New York	165	137	83.0	68	41.2	116	70.3	104	63.0	2	1.2	51	30.9	19	11.5	82	49.7	155	93.9	88	53.3	136	82.4
Pennsylvania	162	110	67.9	66	40.7	63	38.9	84	51.9	3	1.9	45	27.3	12	7.4	98	60.5	150	92.6	75	46.3	128	79.0
CENSUS DIVISION 3, SOUTH ATLANTIC	707	495	70.0	215	30.4	252	35.6	251	35.5	7	1.0	183	25.9	90	12.7	370	52.3	597	84.4	287	40.6	458	64.8
Delaware	8	7	87.5	3	37.5	4	50.0	4	37.5	0	0.0	2	25.0	0	0.0	5	62.5	8	100.0	3	37.5	7	87.5
District of Columbia	10	9	90.0	4	40.0	5	50.0	5	30.0	0	0.0	4	40.0	0	0.0	6	60.0	10	100.0	7	70.0	7	70.0
Florida	176	111	63.1	42	23.9	58	33.0	50	28.4	5	2.0	61	34.7	14	8.0	79	44.9	129	73.3	78	44.3	113	64.2
Georgia	120	79	65.8	29	24.2	37	30.8	35	29.2	5	4.2	27	22.5	19	15.8	64	53.3	95	79.2	37	30.8	60	50.0
Maryland	54	45	83.3	15	27.8	26	48.1	33	51.1	1	1.9	18	33.3	1	1.9	37	68.5	51	94.4	25	46.3	46	85.2
North Carolina	115	85	73.9	32	27.8	43	37.4	46	40.0	0	3.0	36	31.3	15	13.0	70	60.9	102	88.7	49	42.6	78	67.8
South Carolina	82	55	67.1	57	69.5	21	25.6	26	31.7	1	1.2	12	14.6	17	20.7	36	43.9	73	89.0	28	34.1	49	59.8
Virginia	83	64	77.1	24	28.9	33	39.8	35	42.2	1	1.2	18	21.7	8	9.6	44	53.0	75	90.4	40	48.2	62	74.7
West Virginia	59	40	67.8	9	15.3	25	42.4	15	25.4	1	1.0	5	8.5	16	27.1	29	49.2	54	91.5	20	33.9	36	61.0
CENSUS DIVISION 4, EAST NORTH CENTRAL	726	558	76.9	262	36.1	352	48.5	276	38.0	29	4.0	175	24.1	129	17.8	451	62.1	664	91.5	387	53.3	565	77.8
Illinois	154	124	75.6	49	29.9	73	44.5	65	39.6	9	3.5	44	26.8	42	25.6	108	65.9	148	90.2	83	50.6	138	84.1
Indiana	122	92	75.4	43	35.2	50	41.0	44	36.1	3	2.5	21	17.2	11	9.0	80	65.6	103	84.4	54	44.3	96	78.7
Michigan	134	105	78.4	47	35.1	86	64.2	55	41.0	3	2.2	42	31.3	41	30.6	90	67.2	126	94.0	84	62.7	115	85.8
Ohio	160	128	80.0	55	34.4	80	55.0	70	43.8	6	3.8	42	26.3	11	6.9	105	65.6	150	93.8	90	56.3	121	75.6
Wisconsin	146	109	74.7	68	46.6	63	42.2	42	28.8	8	5.5	26	17.8	24	16.4	68	46.6	137	93.8	76	52.1	95	65.1
CENSUS DIVISION 5, EAST SOUTH CENTRAL	376	225	59.8	113	30.1	101	26.9	142	37.8	5	1.3	72	19.1	68	18.1	162	43.1	301	80.1	115	30.6	187	49.7
Alabama	95	49	51.6	18	18.9	20	21.1	38	40.0	5	2.1	22	23.2	11	11.6	47	49.5	68	71.6	36	37.9	49	51.6
Kentucky	86	60	69.8	23	26.7	36	41.9	32	37.2	2	2.9	16	18.6	28	32.6	51	59.3	74	86.0	26	30.2	55	64.0
Mississippi	110	60	54.5	48	43.6	23	20.9	43	39.1	1	1.2	15	13.6	26	23.6	22	20.0	95	86.4	21	19.1	38	34.5
Tennessee	85	56	65.9	24	28.2	22	25.9	29	34.1	1	1.2	19	22.4	3	3.5	42	49.4	64	75.3	32	37.6	45	52.9
CENSUS DIVISION 6, WEST NORTH CENTRAL	658	374	56.8	199	30.2	271	41.2	177	26.9	67	10.2	70	10.6	262	39.8	308	46.8	535	81.3	272	41.3	400	60.8
Iowa	126	71	56.3	30	23.8	64	50.8	38	30.2	18	14.3	13	10.3	44	34.9	69	54.8	109	86.5	58	46.0	99	78.6
Kansas	153	66	43.1	28	18.3	52	34.0	26	17.0	12	7.8	10	6.5	68	44.4	39	25.5	107	69.9	42	27.5	58	37.9
Minnesota	100	61	61.0	27	27.0	40	40.0	29	29.0	12	12.0	12	12.0	27	27.0	55	55.0	90	90.0	46	46.0	75	75.0
Missouri	150	111	74.0	35	56.7	59	39.3	61	40.7	2	1.3	22	14.7	60	40.0	87	58.0	133	88.7	71	47.3	93	62.0
Nebraska	55	29	52.7	12	21.8	24	43.6	10	18.2	3	3.6	9	16.4	27	49.1	31	56.4	46	83.6	23	41.8	35	63.6
North Dakota	24	15	62.5	7	29.2	12	50.0	8	33.3	3	12.5	2	8.3	12	50.0	8	33.3	19	79.2	13	54.2	14	58.3
South Dakota	50	21	42.0	10	20.0	20	40.0	5	10.0	13	26.0	2	4.0	24	48.0	19	38.0	31	62.0	19	38.0	26	52.0
CENSUS DIVISION 7, WEST SOUTH CENTRAL	888	500	56.3	222	25.0	185	20.8	215	24.2	14	1.6	113	12.7	173	19.5	291	32.8	659	74.2	206	23.2	371	41.8
Arkansas	93	51	54.8	24	25.8	20	21.5	35	37.6	3	3.2	13	14.0	20	21.5	41	44.1	67	72.0	23	24.7	43	46.2
Louisiana	97	53	54.6	33	34.0	29	29.9	38	39.2	3	3.1	15	15.5	18	18.6	27	27.8	73	75.3	23	23.7	44	45.4
Oklahoma	127	63	49.6	34	26.8	25	19.7	34	26.8	3	2.4	11	8.7	21	16.5	58	45.7	82	64.6	33	26.0	41	32.3
Texas	571	333	58.3	131	22.9	111	19.4	108	18.9	5	0.9	74	13.0	114	20.0	165	28.9	437	76.5	127	22.2	243	42.6
CENSUS DIVISION 8, MOUNTAIN	354	221	62.4	83	23.4	145	41.0	83	23.4	9	2.5	70	19.8	102	28.8	155	43.8	279	78.8	121	34.2	184	52.0
Arizona	64	43	67.2	17	26.6	23	31.3	23	29.7	9	9.0	20	31.3	14	21.9	19	29.7	54	84.4	17	26.6	38	59.4
Colorado	70	51	72.9	20	28.6	39	55.7	11	15.7	0	0.4	20	28.6	26	37.1	46	65.7	55	78.6	35	50.0	44	62.9
Idaho	35	24	68.6	7	20.0	15	45.7	11	22.9	0	0.0	7	20.0	16	45.7	18	51.4	28	80.0	14	40.0	17	48.6
Montana	57	29	50.9	9	15.8	31	54.4	8	14.0	1	1.5	8	14.0	32	56.1	19	33.3	44	77.2	24	42.1	26	45.6
Nevada	36	15	41.7	8	22.2	4	11.1	11	30.6	0	0.8	5	13.9	3	8.3	6	16.7	26	72.2	5	13.9	13	36.1
New Mexico	33	18	54.5	8	24.2	11	33.3	8	24.2	0	0.0	3	9.1	3	9.1	10	30.3	22	66.7	2	6.1	16	48.5
Utah	35	26	74.3	11	31.4	11	37.1	12	34.3	0	0.0	6	17.1	3	8.6	22	62.9	28	80.0	17	48.6	18	51.4
Wyoming	24	15	62.5	3	12.5	11	45.8	6	25.0	3	1.2	1	4.2	5	20.8	15	62.5	22	91.7	7	29.2	12	50.0
CENSUS DIVISION 9, PACIFIC	476	307	64.5	108	22.7	179	37.6	137	28.8	8	1.7	116	24.4	81	17.0	149	31.3	415	87.2	127	26.7	307	64.5
Alaska	14	9	64.3	2	14.3	3	21.4	5	42.9	0	0.0	2	14.3	1	7.1	9	64.3	12	85.7	2	14.3	7	50.0
California	367	190	61.9	76	24.3	97	31.6	88	28.7	4	0.3	79	25.7	43	14.0	68	22.1	275	89.6	69	22.5	189	61.6
Hawaii	17	7	41.2	1	5.3	6	35.3	5	35.3	2	1.7	2	5.9	2	11.8	4	23.5	15	88.2	5	29.4	9	52.9
Oregon	59	44	74.6	10	16.9	31	52.5	15	25.4	1	1.7	13	22.0	13	22.0	30	50.8	48	81.4	23	39.0	53	89.8
Washington	79	57	72.2	19	24.1	42	53.2	22	27.8	3	2.8	21	26.6	22	27.8	38	48.1	65	82.3	28	35.4	49	62.0

Table 7 (Continued)

These data include only hospital-based facilities and services as reported by responding hospitals in Section C of the 2011 AHA Annual Survey, beginning on page 215. All hospitals are represented with Community Hospitals listed separately under United States. No estimates have been made for nonresponding hospitals. Definitions of facilities and services are listed in the Glossary, page 201.

CLASSIFICATION	HOSPITALS REPORTING	SWING BED SERVICES Number	Percent	TEEN OUTREACH SERVICES Number	Percent	TOBACCO TREATMENT/ CESSATION PROGRAM Number	Percent	TRANSPORTATION TO HEALTH FACILITIES Number	Percent	URGENT CARE CENTER Number	Percent	VIRTUAL COLONOSCOPY Number	Percent	VOLUNTEER SERVICES DEPARTMENT Number	Percent	WOMEN'S HEALTH SERVICES Number	Percent	WOUND MANAGEMENT SERVICES Number	Percent
UNITED STATES	4,782	1,481	31.0	605	12.7	2,340	48.9	1,116	23.3	1,043	21.8	772	16.1	3,542	74.1	2,289	47.9	3,062	64.0
COMMUNITY HOSPITALS	4,082	1,433	35.1	579	14.2	2,148	52.7	967	23.7	983	24.1	743	18.2	3,298	80.8	2,183	53.5	2,828	69.3
CENSUS DIVISION 1, NEW ENGLAND	201	47	23.4	52	25.9	144	72.7	65	32.3	70	34.8	45	22.4	185	92.0	145	72.1	150	74.6
Connecticut	31	5	16.1	5	16.1	22	68.8	5	16.1	16	51.6	14	45.2	27	87.1	19	61.3	26	83.9
Maine	39	12	30.8	7	17.9	30	75.0	11	28.2	12	30.8	7	17.9	35	89.7	31	79.5	30	76.9
Massachusetts	80	7	8.8	21	26.3	48	64.9	34	42.5	28	35.0	18	22.5	73	91.3	55	68.8	57	71.3
New Hampshire	27	15	55.6	8	29.6	22	78.6	8	29.6	9	33.3	4	14.8	27	100.0	24	88.9	19	70.4
Rhode Island	10	1	10.0	2	20.0	10	83.3	3	30.0	3	30.0	1	10.0	10	100.0	8	80.0	8	80.0
Vermont	14	7	50.0	1	7.1	12	100.0	4	28.6	2	14.3	1	7.1	13	92.9	8	57.1	10	71.4
CENSUS DIVISION 2, MIDDLE ATLANTIC	396	60	15.2	105	26.5	277	66.9	135	34.1	96	24.2	96	24.2	355	89.6	267	67.4	294	74.2
New Jersey	69	7	10.1	26	37.7	42	57.5	40	58.0	16	23.2	14	20.3	59	85.5	51	73.9	58	84.1
New York	165	24	14.5	42	25.5	126	75.0	52	31.5	48	29.1	51	30.9	155	93.9	125	75.8	124	75.2
Pennsylvania	162	29	17.9	37	22.8	109	63.0	43	26.5	32	19.8	31	19.1	141	87.0	91	56.2	112	69.1
CENSUS DIVISION 3, SOUTH ATLANTIC	707	137	19.4	89	12.6	380	53.1	159	22.5	151	21.4	127	18.0	587	83.0	381	53.9	471	66.6
Delaware	8	0	0.0	3	37.5	7	63.6	5	62.5	1	12.5	1	12.5	7	87.5	6	75.0	7	87.5
District of Columbia	10	2	20.0	4	40.0	6	50.0	4	40.0	3	30.0	3	30.0	9	90.0	7	70.0	8	80.0
Florida	176	16	9.1	16	9.1	77	48.1	33	18.8	38	21.6	26	14.8	145	82.4	92	52.3	125	71.0
Georgia	120	37	30.8	13	10.8	56	43.8	24	20.0	23	19.2	12	10.0	90	75.0	59	49.2	73	60.8
Maryland	54	2	3.7	15	27.8	39	67.2	18	33.3	18	33.3	15	27.8	49	90.7	33	61.1	41	75.9
North Carolina	115	27	23.5	13	11.3	68	59.1	34	29.6	33	28.7	29	25.2	102	88.7	62	53.9	77	67.0
South Carolina	82	9	11.0	10	12.2	38	48.1	13	15.9	9	11.0	11	13.4	63	76.8	45	54.9	51	62.2
Virginia	83	20	24.1	10	12.0	52	58.4	19	22.9	14	16.9	20	24.1	76	91.6	46	55.4	58	69.9
West Virginia	59	24	40.7	5	8.5	37	58.7	9	15.3	12	20.3	10	16.9	46	78.0	31	52.5	31	52.5
CENSUS DIVISION 4, EAST NORTH CENTRAL	726	206	28.4	119	16.4	443	61.4	199	27.4	285	39.3	154	21.2	617	85.0	409	56.3	498	68.6
Illinois	164	52	31.7	28	17.1	97	56.1	46	28.0	51	31.1	47	28.7	136	82.9	91	55.5	111	67.7
Indiana	122	37	30.3	22	18.0	84	77.8	25	20.5	42	34.4	22	18.0	102	83.6	69	56.6	77	63.1
Michigan	134	26	19.4	26	19.4	98	66.7	38	28.4	52	38.8	28	20.9	123	91.8	84	62.7	99	73.9
Ohio	160	38	23.8	27	16.9	111	73.0	57	35.6	56	35.0	30	18.8	150	93.8	100	62.5	112	70.0
Wisconsin	146	53	36.3	16	11.0	53	37.6	33	22.6	84	57.5	27	18.5	106	72.6	65	44.5	99	67.8
CENSUS DIVISION 5, EAST SOUTH CENTRAL	376	137	36.4	34	9.0	162	38.7	56	14.9	43	11.4	40	10.6	264	70.2	148	39.4	173	46.0
Alabama	95	34	23.2	8	8.4	40	33.3	12	12.6	12	12.6	12	12.6	67	70.5	37	38.9	43	45.3
Kentucky	86	34	39.5	7	8.1	60	61.2	15	17.4	13	15.1	13	15.1	72	83.7	46	53.5	49	57.0
Mississippi	110	55	50.0	10	9.1	22	20.0	17	15.5	10	9.1	9	8.2	60	54.5	29	26.4	32	29.1
Tennessee	85	26	30.6	9	10.6	40	44.0	12	14.1	8	9.4	11	12.9	65	76.5	36	42.4	49	57.6
CENSUS DIVISION 6, WEST NORTH CENTRAL	658	394	59.9	57	8.7	307	47.3	164	24.9	118	17.9	85	12.9	431	65.5	238	36.2	397	60.3
Iowa	126	90	71.4	17	13.5	81	64.8	26	20.6	16	17.5	15	11.9	98	77.8	49	38.9	85	67.5
Kansas	153	100	65.4	6	3.9	44	28.8	34	22.2	16	10.5	19	12.4	75	49.0	41	26.8	83	54.2
Minnesota	100	57	57.0	11	11.0	52	51.0	23	23.0	35	35.0	18	18.0	74	74.0	38	38.0	60	60.0
Missouri	150	52	34.7	15	10.0	79	53.0	53	35.3	33	22.0	18	12.0	107	71.3	69	46.0	97	64.7
Nebraska	55	35	63.6	6	10.9	26	50.0	12	21.8	5	5.5	10	18.2	36	65.5	22	40.0	33	60.0
North Dakota	24	16	66.7	0	0.0	10	41.7	7	29.2	5	20.8	3	12.5	16	66.7	9	37.5	11	45.8
South Dakota	50	44	88.0	2	4.0	15	34.1	9	18.0	4	8.0	2	4.0	25	50.0	10	20.0	28	56.0
CENSUS DIVISION 7, WEST SOUTH CENTRAL	888	246	27.7	47	5.3	273	30.9	131	14.8	88	9.9	91	10.2	477	53.7	291	32.8	522	58.8
Arkansas	93	37	39.8	6	6.5	34	37.4	18	19.4	9	9.7	7	7.5	56	60.2	30	32.3	50	53.8
Louisiana	97	22	22.7	9	9.3	45	44.1	19	19.6	15	15.5	7	7.2	53	54.6	41	42.3	57	58.8
Oklahoma	127	55	43.3	4	3.1	41	33.3	20	15.7	15	11.8	13	10.2	75	59.1	40	31.5	67	52.8
Texas	571	132	23.1	28	4.9	153	27.0	74	13.0	49	8.6	64	11.2	293	51.3	180	31.5	348	60.9
CENSUS DIVISION 8, MOUNTAIN	354	149	42.1	42	11.9	161	48.1	80	22.6	82	23.2	57	16.1	250	70.6	170	48.0	225	63.6
Arizona	64	14	21.9	10	15.6	36	61.0	17	26.6	18	28.1	17	26.6	50	78.1	34	53.1	47	73.4
Colorado	70	29	41.4	8	11.4	32	45.1	11	15.7	12	17.1	9	12.9	55	78.6	42	60.0	56	80.0
Idaho	35	18	51.4	7	20.0	16	53.3	10	28.6	9	25.7	4	11.4	29	82.9	15	42.9	21	60.0
Montana	57	44	77.2	4	7.0	21	39.6	25	43.9	18	31.6	14	24.6	37	64.9	21	36.8	29	50.9
Nevada	36	6	16.7	1	2.8	10	37.0	2	5.6	5	13.9	2	5.6	17	47.2	13	36.1	19	52.8
New Mexico	33	7	21.2	3	9.1	18	50.0	4	12.1	6	18.2	2	6.1	16	48.5	14	42.4	20	60.6
Utah	35	12	34.3	6	17.1	14	43.8	6	17.1	7	20.0	4	11.4	28	80.0	20	57.1	22	62.9
Wyoming	24	19	79.2	3	12.5	14	51.9	5	20.8	7	29.2	5	20.8	18	75.0	11	45.8	11	45.8
CENSUS DIVISION 9, PACIFIC	476	105	22.1	60	12.6	193	43.1	127	26.7	110	23.1	77	16.2	376	79.0	240	50.4	332	69.7
Alaska	14	6	42.9	2	14.3	8	61.5	3	21.4	2	14.3	2	14.3	9	64.3	5	35.7	10	71.4
California	307	43	14.0	37	12.1	90	33.1	90	29.3	67	21.8	47	15.3	240	78.2	141	45.9	206	67.1
Hawaii	17	5	29.4	2	11.8	9	45.0	4	23.5	2	11.8	2	11.8	14	82.4	10	58.8	13	76.5
Oregon	59	28	47.5	6	10.2	44	72.1	17	28.8	16	27.1	14	23.7	53	89.8	39	66.1	51	86.4
Washington	79	23	29.1	13	16.5	38	54.3	13	16.5	23	29.1	12	15.2	60	75.9	45	57.0	52	65.8

Table 7 (Continued)

These data include only hospital-based facilities and services as reported by responding hospitals in Section C of the 2011 AHA Annual Survey, beginning on page 215. All hospitals are represented with Community Hospitals listed separately under United States. No estimates have been made for nonresponding hospitals. Definitions of facilities and services are listed in the Glossary, page 201.

CLASSIFICATION	HOSPITALS REPORTING	GENERAL MEDICAL SURGICAL CARE ADULT UNITS Number	Percent	PEDIATRIC UNITS Number	Percent	INTENSIVE CARE UNITS CARDIAC UNITS Number	Percent	MEDICAL SURGICAL UNITS Number	Percent	NEONATAL UNITS Number	Percent	OTHER UNITS Number	Percent	PEDIATRIC UNITS Number	Percent	ACUTE LONG-TERM CARE UNITS Number	Percent	LONG-TERM CARE UNITS SKILLED NURSING CARE UNITS Number	Percent	INTERMEDIATE NURSING CARE UNITS Number	Percent	OTHER LONG-TERM CARE UNITS Number	Percent
UNITED STATES	4,782	4,054	84.8	2,023	42.4	1,334	27.9	3,021	63.2	964	20.2	535	11.2	413	8.7	344	7.2	1,145	23.9	370	7.7	230	4.8
COMMUNITY HOSPITALS	4,082	3,791	92.9	1,980	48.5	1,297	31.8	2,887	70.7	949	23.2	517	12.7	412	10.1	216	5.3	1,050	25.7	330	8.1	192	4.7
CENSUS DIVISION 1, NEW ENGLAND	201	169	84.1	109	54.2	53	26.4	156	77.6	36	17.9	13	6.5	16	8.0	11	5.5	35	17.4	20	10.0	7	3.5
Connecticut	31	26	83.9	18	58.1	11	35.5	25	80.6	14	45.2	1	3.2	3	9.7	1	3.2	1	3.2	3	10.0	0	0.0
Maine	39	35	89.7	20	51.3	6	15.4	32	82.1	4	10.3	4	10.3	3	7.7	3	7.7	12	30.8	9	23.1	5	12.8
Massachusetts	80	62	77.5	47	58.8	25	31.3	57	71.3	14	17.5	4	5.0	6	7.5	6	7.5	8	10.0	7	8.8	2	2.5
New Hampshire	27	24	88.9	15	55.6	6	22.2	22	81.5	2	7.4	2	7.4	2	7.4	1	3.7	9	33.3	7	25.9	0	0.0
Rhode Island	10	9	90.0	4	40.0	3	30.0	8	80.0	1	10.0	2	20.0	1	10.0	0	0.0	1	10.0	1	10.0	0	0.0
Vermont	14	13	92.9	5	35.7	3	14.3	12	85.7	1	7.1	0	0.0	1	7.1	0	0.0	5	35.7	1	7.1	0	0.0
CENSUS DIVISION 2, MIDDLE ATLANTIC	396	342	86.4	202	51.0	183	46.2	306	77.3	121	30.6	52	13.1	58	14.6	18	4.5	105	26.5	10	2.5	20	5.1
New Jersey	69	57	82.6	43	62.3	33	47.8	57	82.5	23	33.3	8	11.6	17	24.6	4	5.8	14	20.3	5	7.2	5	7.2
New York	165	155	93.9	94	57.0	92	55.8	137	83.0	58	35.2	24	14.5	35	20.0	9	5.5	51	30.9	5	2.4	12	7.3
Pennsylvania	162	130	80.2	65	40.1	58	35.8	112	69.1	40	24.7	20	12.3	6	4.9	5	3.1	40	24.7	1	0.6	3	1.9
CENSUS DIVISION 3, SOUTH ATLANTIC	707	592	83.7	304	43.0	224	31.7	508	71.9	151	21.4	98	13.9	65	9.2	65	9.2	182	25.7	62	8.8	41	5.8
Delaware	8	5	62.5	5	62.5	5	62.5	5	62.5	3	37.5	1	12.5	3	37.5	1	12.5	2	25.0	1	12.5	0	0.0
District of Columbia	10	6	60.0	4	40.0	5	50.0	6	60.0	5	50.0	1	10.0	3	20.0	1	10.0	1	10.0	1	10.0	0	0.0
Florida	176	148	84.1	61	34.7	71	40.3	139	79.0	46	26.1	21	11.9	23	13.1	11	6.3	16	9.1	10	5.7	3	1.7
Georgia	120	102	85.0	39	32.5	27	22.5	73	60.8	26	21.7	12	10.0	5	4.2	10	8.3	33	27.5	11	9.2	6	5.0
Maryland	54	45	83.3	33	61.1	20	37.0	45	83.3	16	29.6	6	11.1	4	7.4	4	7.4	14	25.9	1	1.9	2	3.7
North Carolina	115	103	89.6	53	46.1	31	27.0	87	75.7	23	20.0	15	13.0	12	10.4	7	6.1	37	32.2	12	10.4	1	0.9
South Carolina	82	64	78.0	50	61.0	25	30.5	55	67.0	9	11.0	29	35.4	6	7.3	26	31.7	38	46.3	9	11.0	24	29.3
Virginia	83	69	83.1	34	41.0	24	28.9	65	78.3	19	22.9	9	10.8	7	8.4	3	3.6	17	20.5	9	10.8	2	2.4
West Virginia	59	50	84.7	25	42.4	16	27.1	33	55.9	4	6.8	4	6.8	3	5.1	2	3.4	24	40.7	8	13.6	2	3.4
CENSUS DIVISION 4, EAST NORTH CENTRAL	726	642	88.4	381	52.5	235	32.4	494	68.0	132	18.2	137	18.9	76	10.5	42	5.8	155	21.3	48	6.6	42	5.8
Illinois	164	148	90.2	92	56.1	42	25.6	115	70.1	30	18.3	13	7.9	19	11.6	9	5.5	49	29.9	8	4.9	12	7.3
Indiana	122	105	86.1	61	50.0	26	23.0	81	66.4	22	18.0	11	9.0	9	7.4	3	2.5	19	15.6	12	9.8	4	3.3
Michigan	134	120	89.6	66	49.3	46	34.3	96	71.6	21	15.7	19	14.2	9	6.7	7	5.2	25	18.7	6	4.5	4	3.0
Ohio	160	145	90.6	63	39.4	55	34.4	127	79.4	31	19.4	20	12.5	13	8.1	10	6.3	38	23.8	14	8.8	12	7.5
Wisconsin	146	124	84.9	99	67.8	64	43.8	75	51.4	28	19.2	74	50.7	26	17.8	13	8.9	24	16.4	8	5.5	8	5.5
CENSUS DIVISION 5, EAST SOUTH CENTRAL	376	332	88.3	161	42.8	109	29.0	267	71.0	62	16.5	79	21.0	29	7.7	16	4.3	78	20.7	16	4.3	28	7.4
Alabama	95	85	89.5	33	34.7	27	28.4	63	66.3	16	16.8	15	15.8	6	6.3	5	5.3	8	8.4	7	7.4	3	3.2
Kentucky	86	74	86.0	32	37.2	23	26.7	54	62.8	16	18.6	9	10.5	5	5.8	8	9.3	26	30.2	3	3.5	5	5.8
Mississippi	110	104	94.5	69	62.7	39	35.5	100	90.9	15	13.6	43	39.1	10	9.1	0	0.0	26	23.6	6	0.0	19	17.3
Tennessee	85	69	81.2	27	31.8	20	23.5	50	58.8	15	17.6	12	14.1	8	9.4	3	3.5	18	21.2	6	7.1	1	1.2
CENSUS DIVISION 6, WEST NORTH CENTRAL	658	593	90.1	290	44.1	141	21.4	324	49.2	87	13.2	47	7.1	48	7.3	41	6.2	277	42.1	129	19.6	56	8.5
Iowa	126	119	94.4	65	51.6	24	19.0	72	57.1	19	15.1	8	6.3	11	8.7	8	6.3	56	44.4	42	33.3	16	12.7
Kansas	153	136	88.9	46	30.1	14	9.2	53	34.6	14	11.8	9	5.9	14	9.3	8	5.2	65	42.5	44	28.8	15	9.8
Minnesota	100	95	95.0	49	49.0	28	28.0	58	58.0	10	10.0	7	5.7	8	8.0	4	4.0	45	45.0	7	7.0	9	9.0
Missouri	150	119	79.3	79	52.7	43	28.7	84	56.0	20	13.3	18	12.0	8	5.3	14	9.3	43	28.7	14	9.3	9	6.0
Nebraska	55	52	94.5	19	34.5	15	27.3	24	43.6	14	25.5	3	5.5	5	9.1	2	3.6	27	49.1	6	10.9	5	9.1
North Dakota	24	23	95.8	11	45.8	11	45.8	13	54.2	7	29.2	2	8.3	5	20.8	3	12.5	11	45.8	5	20.8	2	8.3
South Dakota	50	49	98.0	21	42.0	10	20.0	20	40.0	3	6.0	4	8.0	3	6.0	2	4.0	30	60.0	11	22.0	7	14.0
CENSUS DIVISION 7, WEST SOUTH CENTRAL	888	653	73.5	260	29.3	148	16.7	412	46.4	155	17.5	49	5.5	53	6.0	110	12.4	100	11.3	23	2.6	12	1.4
Arkansas	93	71	76.3	25	26.9	26	28.0	42	45.2	11	11.8	4	4.3	7	6.3	9	9.7	15	16.1	4	2.2	2	2.2
Louisiana	97	76	78.4	44	45.4	21	21.6	57	58.6	28	28.9	9	9.3	12	12.4	10	10.3	23	23.7	4	4.1	2	2.1
Oklahoma	127	105	82.7	37	29.1	21	15.7	51	40.2	12	9.4	7	5.5	4	3.1	11	8.7	24	18.9	4	3.1	2	1.6
Texas	571	401	70.2	154	27.0	81	14.2	262	45.9	104	18.2	29	5.1	35	6.1	80	14.0	38	6.7	13	2.3	7	1.2
CENSUS DIVISION 8, MOUNTAIN	354	314	88.7	145	41.0	72	20.3	205	57.9	73	20.6	21	5.9	29	8.2	21	5.9	97	27.4	35	9.9	16	4.5
Arizona	64	57	89.1	22	34.4	24	37.5	45	70.3	12	18.8	3	4.7	7	10.9	7	10.9	7	10.9	3	4.7	1	1.6
Colorado	70	66	94.3	31	44.3	10	14.3	48	68.6	25	35.7	4	5.7	6	8.6	1	1.4	13	18.6	5	7.1	4	5.7
Idaho	35	32	91.4	13	37.1	7	20.0	16	45.7	7	20.0	2	5.7	2	5.7	3	8.6	13	37.1	4	11.4	1	2.9
Montana	57	55	96.5	23	40.4	10	17.5	23	40.4	6	10.5	2	3.5	4	7.0	2	3.5	35	61.4	10	17.5	4	7.0
Nevada	36	23	63.9	8	22.2	6	16.7	18	50.0	6	16.7	4	11.1	4	11.1	5	13.9	1	2.8	1	2.8	0	0.0
New Mexico	33	28	84.8	17	51.5	4	12.1	21	63.6	6	18.2	2	6.1	2	6.1	3	9.1	6	18.2	4	12.1	2	6.1
Utah	35	30	85.7	22	62.9	11	31.4	18	51.4	12	34.3	2	5.7	3	8.6	1	2.9	10	28.6	5	14.3	0	0.0
Wyoming	24	23	95.8	9	37.5	0	0.0	16	66.7	1	4.2	2	8.3	1	4.2	2	8.3	12	50.0	3	12.5	4	16.7
CENSUS DIVISION 9, PACIFIC	476	417	87.6	176	37.0	169	35.5	349	73.3	147	30.9	39	8.2	44	9.2	20	4.2	116	24.4	27	5.7	8	1.7
Alaska	14	12	85.7	3	21.4	2	14.3	8	57.1	2	14.3	2	14.3	2	14.3	0	0.0	6	42.9	3	21.4	2	14.3
California	307	265	86.3	114	37.1	123	40.1	231	75.2	118	38.4	24	7.8	34	11.1	14	4.6	83	27.0	8	2.6	2	1.6
Hawaii	17	13	76.5	3	17.6	6	35.3	11	64.7	1	5.9	0	0.0	0	0.0	2	11.8	5	29.4	4	23.5	1	5.9
Oregon	59	58	98.3	22	37.3	17	28.8	49	83.1	8	13.6	3	5.1	2	3.4	3	5.1	10	16.9	10	16.9	3	5.9
Washington	79	69	87.3	34	43.0	21	26.6	50	63.3	18	22.8	10	12.7	6	7.6	3	3.8	12	15.2	2	2.5	0	0.0

Table 7 (Continued)

These data include only hospital-based facilities and services as reported by responding hospitals in Section C of the 2011 AHA Annual Survey, beginning on page 215. All hospitals are represented with Community Hospitals listed separately under United States. No estimates have been made for nonresponding hospitals. Definitions of facilities and services are listed in the Glossary; page 201.

CARDIOLOGY AND CARDIAC SERVICES

Classification	Hospitals Reporting	Adult Cardiology Services No.	%	Pediatric Cardiology Services No.	%	Adult Diagnostic Catheterization No.	%	Pediatric Diagnostic Catheterization No.	%	Adult Interventional Cardiac Catheterization No.	%	Pediatric Interventional Cardiac Catheterization No.	%	Adult Cardiac Surgery No.	%	Pediatric Cardiac Surgery No.	%	Adult Cardiac Electro-Physiology No.	%	Pediatric Cardiac Electro-Physiology No.	%	Cardiac Rehabilitation No.	%
UNITED STATES	4,782	2,254	47.1	403	8.4	1,805	37.7	201	4.2	1,521	31.8	188	3.9	1,132	23.7	176	3.7	1,293	27.0	194	4.1	2,459	51.4
COMMUNITY HOSPITALS	4,082	2,150	52.7	396	9.7	1,735	42.5	198	4.9	1,462	35.8	187	4.6	1,090	26.7	175	4.3	1,242	30.4	190	4.7	2,387	58.5
CENSUS DIVISION 1, NEW ENGLAND	201	128	63.7	18	9.0	77	38.3	10	5.0	57	28.4	10	5.0	41	20.4	10	5.0	62	30.8	11	5.5	135	67.2
Connecticut	31	23	74.2	4	12.9	15	48.4	3	9.7	14	45.2	3	9.7	12	38.7	3	9.7	13	41.9	5	16.1	23	74.2
Maine	39	19	48.7	4	10.3	11	28.2	1	2.6	5	12.8	1	2.6	4	10.3	1	2.6	7	17.9	2	5.1	29	74.4
Massachusetts	80	57	71.3	7	8.8	35	43.8	2	2.5	26	32.5	2	2.5	19	23.8	4	5.0	27	33.8	3	3.8	48	60.0
New Hampshire	27	16	59.3	1	3.7	9	33.3	2	7.4	7	25.9	1	3.7	3	11.1	1	3.7	8	29.6	1	3.7	20	74.1
Rhode Island	10	6	60.0	1	10.0	4	40.0	1	10.0	3	30.0	1	10.0	1	10.0	0	0.0	4	40.0	0	0.0	6	60.0
Vermont	14	7	50.0	1	7.1	3	21.4	1	7.1	2	14.3	2	14.3	2	14.3	1	7.1	3	21.4	0	0.0	9	64.3
CENSUS DIVISION 2, MIDDLE ATLANTIC	396	275	69.4	76	19.2	199	50.3	23	5.8	164	41.4	23	5.8	113	28.5	20	5.1	141	35.6	24	6.1	235	59.3
New Jersey	69	51	73.9	21	30.4	48	69.6	2	2.9	37	53.6	3	4.3	18	26.1	2	2.9	24	34.8	4	5.8	44	63.8
New York	165	121	73.3	38	23.0	73	44.2	15	9.1	59	35.8	14	8.5	39	23.6	11	6.7	60	36.4	13	7.9	89	53.9
Pennsylvania	162	103	63.6	17	10.5	78	48.1	6	3.7	68	42.0	6	3.7	56	34.6	7	4.3	57	35.2	7	4.3	102	63.0
CENSUS DIVISION 3, SOUTH ATLANTIC	707	393	55.6	62	8.8	341	48.2	28	4.0	259	36.6	26	3.7	170	24.0	25	3.5	241	34.1	28	4.0	371	52.5
Delaware	8	5	62.5	1	12.5	4	50.0	1	12.5	4	50.0	1	12.5	3	37.5	1	12.5	2	25.0	1	12.5	5	62.5
District of Columbia	10	5	50.0	1	10.0	4	40.0	1	10.0	4	40.0	1	10.0	3	30.0	1	10.0	4	40.0	1	10.0	5	50.0
Florida	176	117	66.5	19	10.8	104	59.1	10	5.7	90	51.1	8	4.5	65	36.9	9	5.1	77	43.8	9	5.1	76	43.2
Georgia	120	50	41.7	5	4.2	48	40.0	1	0.8	39	32.5	1	0.8	18	15.0	1	0.8	36	30.0	1	0.8	49	40.8
Maryland	54	39	72.2	7	13.0	36	66.7	3	5.6	25	46.3	3	5.6	10	18.5	2	3.7	31	57.4	4	7.4	34	63.0
North Carolina	115	69	60.0	11	9.6	54	47.0	5	4.3	33	28.7	6	5.2	26	22.6	5	4.3	37	32.2	5	4.3	75	65.2
South Carolina	82	35	42.7	4	4.9	32	39.0	1	1.2	19	23.2	1	1.2	19	23.2	1	1.2	15	18.3	3	3.7	39	47.6
Virginia	83	50	60.2	11	13.3	32	45.8	4	4.8	35	42.2	4	4.8	20	24.1	4	4.8	32	38.6	3	3.6	58	69.9
West Virginia	59	23	39.0	3	5.1	21	35.6	2	3.4	10	16.9	1	1.7	6	10.2	1	1.7	7	11.9	1	1.7	30	50.8
CENSUS DIVISION 4, EAST NORTH CENTRAL	726	403	55.5	66	9.1	330	45.5	28	3.9	279	38.4	28	3.9	219	30.2	29	4.0	254	35.0	33	4.5	511	70.4
Illinois	164	104	63.4	27	16.5	86	52.4	8	4.9	81	49.4	8	4.9	59	36.0	9	5.5	67	40.9	11	6.7	127	77.4
Indiana	122	55	45.1	8	6.6	49	40.2	3	3.3	45	36.9	4	3.3	34	27.9	4	3.3	32	26.2	4	3.3	81	66.4
Michigan	134	79	59.0	11	8.2	61	45.5	3	2.2	46	34.3	3	2.2	36	26.9	3	2.2	55	41.0	4	3.0	90	67.2
Ohio	160	106	66.3	13	8.1	86	53.8	8	5.0	64	40.0	8	5.0	58	36.3	7	4.4	62	38.8	7	4.4	105	65.6
Wisconsin	146	59	40.4	7	4.8	48	32.9	5	3.4	43	29.5	5	3.4	32	21.9	6	4.1	38	26.0	7	4.8	108	74.0
CENSUS DIVISION 5, EAST SOUTH CENTRAL	376	139	37.0	19	5.1	119	31.6	11	2.9	92	24.5	11	2.9	73	19.4	10	2.7	68	18.1	12	3.2	133	35.4
Alabama	95	36	37.9	5	5.3	36	37.9	3	3.2	32	33.7	2	2.1	25	26.3	2	2.1	26	27.4	2	2.1	37	38.9
Kentucky	86	43	50.0	3	3.5	34	39.5	2	2.3	25	29.1	2	2.3	19	22.1	2	2.3	15	17.4	2	2.3	44	51.2
Mississippi	110	23	20.9	5	4.5	14	12.7	1	0.9	10	9.1	2	1.8	11	10.0	1	0.9	9	8.2	4	3.6	19	17.3
Tennessee	85	37	43.5	6	7.1	35	41.2	5	5.9	25	29.4	5	5.9	18	21.2	5	5.9	18	21.2	4	4.7	33	38.8
CENSUS DIVISION 6, WEST NORTH CENTRAL	658	217	33.0	37	5.6	149	22.6	16	2.4	143	21.7	15	2.3	94	14.3	15	2.3	113	17.2	18	2.7	457	69.5
Iowa	126	42	33.3	4	3.2	26	20.6	2	1.6	26	20.6	2	1.6	12	9.5	2	1.6	24	19.0	2	1.6	107	84.9
Kansas	153	36	23.5	7	4.6	25	16.3	2	1.3	24	15.7	2	1.3	17	11.1	1	0.7	16	10.5	3	2.0	74	48.4
Minnesota	100	35	35.0	8	8.0	19	19.0	2	2.0	17	17.0	2	2.0	14	14.0	2	2.0	17	17.0	4	4.0	83	83.0
Missouri	150	71	47.3	9	6.0	55	36.7	4	2.7	52	34.7	4	2.7	35	23.3	5	3.3	39	26.0	4	2.7	89	59.3
Nebraska	55	18	32.7	4	7.3	13	23.6	2	3.6	13	23.6	2	3.6	8	14.5	2	3.6	11	20.0	3	5.5	42	76.4
North Dakota	24	7	29.2	2	8.3	5	20.8	2	8.3	5	20.8	2	8.3	5	20.8	2	8.3	4	16.7	1	4.2	20	83.3
South Dakota	50	8	16.0	3	6.0	6	12.0	2	4.0	6	12.0	1	2.0	3	6.0	1	2.0	2	4.0	1	2.0	42	84.0
CENSUS DIVISION 7, WEST SOUTH CENTRAL	888	312	35.1	44	5.0	266	30.0	29	3.3	235	26.5	26	2.9	196	22.1	23	2.6	177	19.9	20	2.3	280	31.5
Arkansas	93	30	32.3	3	3.2	26	28.0	1	1.1	23	24.7	1	1.1	18	19.4	1	1.1	12	12.9	1	1.1	35	37.6
Louisiana	97	51	52.6	11	11.3	40	41.2	7	7.2	36	37.1	7	7.2	29	29.9	5	5.2	27	27.8	5	5.2	36	37.1
Oklahoma	127	40	31.5	3	2.4	31	24.4	2	1.6	26	20.5	2	1.6	19	15.0	2	1.6	15	11.8	2	1.6	32	25.2
Texas	571	191	33.5	27	4.7	169	29.6	19	3.3	150	26.3	16	2.8	130	22.8	15	2.6	123	21.5	12	2.1	177	31.0
CENSUS DIVISION 8, MOUNTAIN	354	139	39.3	28	7.9	115	32.5	19	5.4	110	31.1	17	4.8	76	21.5	14	4.0	79	22.3	17	4.8	156	44.1
Arizona	64	36	56.3	6	9.4	31	48.4	4	6.3	31	48.4	2	3.1	22	34.4	3	4.7	23	35.9	5	7.8	29	45.3
Colorado	70	36	51.4	7	10.0	34	48.6	3	4.3	33	47.1	3	4.3	20	28.6	2	2.9	20	28.6	3	4.3	42	60.0
Idaho	35	11	31.4	4	11.4	9	25.7	2	5.7	8	22.9	2	5.7	5	14.3	1	2.9	4	11.4	1	2.9	10	28.6
Montana	57	12	21.1	2	3.5	8	14.0	1	1.8	8	14.0	1	1.8	6	10.5	1	1.8	7	12.3	1	1.8	28	49.1
Nevada	36	14	38.9	3	8.3	13	36.1	4	11.1	12	33.3	4	11.1	8	22.2	2	5.6	11	30.6	4	11.1	10	27.8
New Mexico	33	10	30.3	2	6.1	7	21.2	2	6.1	5	15.2	2	6.1	4	12.1	2	6.1	6	18.2	2	6.1	9	27.3
Utah	35	17	48.6	4	11.4	11	31.4	3	8.6	11	31.4	3	8.6	8	22.9	3	8.6	6	17.1	1	2.9	14	40.0
Wyoming	24	3	12.5	0	0.0	2	8.3	0	0.0	2	8.3	0	0.0	3	12.5	0	0.0	2	8.3	0	0.0	14	58.3
CENSUS DIVISION 9, PACIFIC	476	248	52.1	53	11.1	209	43.9	37	7.8	182	38.2	32	6.7	150	31.5	30	6.3	158	33.2	31	6.5	181	38.0
Alaska	14	3	21.4	2	14.3	3	21.4	1	7.1	3	21.4	1	7.1	1	7.1	0	0.0	2	14.3	1	7.1	5	35.7
California	307	172	56.0	36	11.7	143	46.6	24	7.8	123	40.1	21	6.8	110	35.8	21	6.8	112	36.5	19	6.2	114	37.1
Hawaii	17	8	47.1	1	5.9	7	41.2	2	11.8	6	35.3	1	5.9	6	29.4	0	0.0	6	35.3	1	5.9	2	11.8
Oregon	59	28	47.5	7	11.9	23	39.0	5	8.5	20	33.9	5	8.5	15	25.4	4	6.8	17	28.8	5	8.5	27	45.8
Washington	79	37	46.8	7	8.9	33	41.8	5	6.3	30	38.0	4	5.1	19	24.1	5	6.3	21	26.6	5	6.3	33	41.8

Table 7 (Continued)

These data include only hospital-based facilities and services as reported by responding hospitals in Section C of the 2011 AHA Annual Survey, beginning on page 215. All hospitals are represented with Community Hospitals listed separately under United States. No estimates have been made for nonresponding hospitals. Definitions of facilities and services are listed in the Glossary, page 201.

CLASSIFICATION	HOSPITALS REPORTING	EMERGENCY DEPARTMENT Number	Percent	PEDIATRIC EMERGENCY DEPARTMENT Number	Percent	FREESTANDING/SATELLITE EMERGENCY DEPARTMENT Number	Percent	TRAUMA CENTER (CERTIFIED) Number	Percent	ENDOSCOPIC ULTRASOUND Number	Percent	ABLATION OF BARRETT'S ESOPHAGUS Number	Percent	ESOPHAGEAL IMPEDANCE STUDY Number	Percent	ENDOSCOPIC RETROGRADE CHOLANGIO-PANCREATOGRAPHY Number	Percent	OPTICAL COLONOSCOPY Number	Percent
UNITED STATES	4,782	3,981	83.2	594	12.4	307	6.4	1,653	34.6	1,474	30.8	1,022	21.4	985	20.6	1,941	40.6	2,774	58.0
COMMUNITY HOSPITALS	4,082	3,745	91.7	565	13.8	291	7.1	1,617	39.6	1,410	34.5	979	24.0	943	23.1	1,871	45.8	2,632	64.2
CENSUS DIVISION 1, NEW ENGLAND	201	168	83.6	32	15.9	17	8.5	63	31.5	76	37.8	55	27.4	57	28.4	107	53.2	138	68.7
Connecticut	31	25	80.6	5	16.1	4	12.9	11	35.5	17	54.8	15	48.4	14	45.2	23	74.2	22	71.0
Maine	39	35	89.7	5	12.8	3	7.1	14	35.8	11	28.2	8	20.5	10	25.6	10	25.6	29	74.4
Massachusetts	80	61	76.3	12	15.0	3	3.8	19	23.8	28	35.0	18	22.5	22	27.5	43	53.8	49	61.3
New Hampshire	27	24	88.9	6	22.2	7	25.9	14	51.9	11	40.7	8	29.6	6	22.2	15	55.6	18	66.7
Rhode Island	10	10	100.0	2	20.0	0	0.0	1	10.0	6	60.0	4	40.0	3	30.0	8	80.0	9	90.0
Vermont	14	13	92.9	2	14.3	0	0.0	4	28.6	3	21.4	2	14.3	2	14.3	8	57.1	11	78.6
CENSUS DIVISION 2, MIDDLE ATLANTIC	396	330	83.3	82	20.7	31	7.8	116	29.3	174	43.9	107	27.0	104	26.3	246	62.1	254	64.1
New Jersey	69	58	84.1	27	39.1	9	13.0	12	17.4	39	56.5	31	44.9	25	36.2	49	71.0	43	62.3
New York	165	147	89.1	38	23.0	10	6.1	70	42.4	82	49.7	47	28.5	40	24.2	106	64.2	112	67.9
Pennsylvania	162	125	77.2	17	10.5	12	7.4	34	21.0	53	32.7	29	17.9	39	24.1	91	56.2	99	61.1
CENSUS DIVISION 3, SOUTH ATLANTIC	707	576	81.5	97	13.7	46	6.5	153	21.6	243	34.4	173	24.5	190	26.9	351	49.6	445	62.9
Delaware	8	6	75.0	2	25.0	1	12.5	5	62.5	2	25.0	4	50.0	3	37.5	5	62.5	3	37.5
District of Columbia	10	7	70.0	3	30.0	1	10.0	4	40.0	7	70.0	4	40.0	5	50.0	3	30.0	5	50.0
Florida	176	143	81.3	34	19.3	13	7.4	28	15.9	72	40.9	54	30.7	47	26.7	108	61.4	123	69.9
Georgia	120	99	82.5	11	9.2	1	0.8	15	12.5	36	30.0	21	17.5	27	22.5	49	40.8	69	57.5
Maryland	54	43	79.6	13	24.1	6	11.1	10	18.5	28	51.9	14	25.9	16	29.6	33	61.1	36	66.7
North Carolina	115	100	87.0	10	8.7	9	7.8	19	16.5	38	33.0	30	26.1	36	31.3	56	48.7	85	73.9
South Carolina	82	59	72.0	2	2.4	3	3.7	20	24.4	21	25.6	17	20.7	15	18.3	29	35.4	35	42.7
Virginia	83	70	84.3	19	22.9	2	2.4	23	27.7	27	32.5	20	24.1	29	34.9	47	56.6	56	67.5
West Virginia	59	49	83.1	3	5.1	0	0.0	29	49.2	12	20.3	9	15.3	12	20.3	21	35.6	33	55.9
CENSUS DIVISION 4, EAST NORTH CENTRAL	726	632	87.1	106	14.6	74	10.2	262	36.1	259	35.7	194	26.7	185	25.5	335	46.1	468	53.1
Illinois	164	153	93.3	30	18.3	13	7.9	66	40.2	59	36.0	48	29.3	44	26.8	94	57.3	115	70.7
Indiana	122	97	79.5	3	2.5	5	4.1	15	12.3	43	35.2	32	26.2	25	20.5	50	41.0	72	59.0
Michigan	134	117	87.3	16	11.9	15	11.2	42	31.3	55	41.0	27	20.1	28	20.9	61	45.5	94	70.1
Ohio	160	142	88.8	21	13.1	31	19.4	43	26.9	65	40.6	51	31.9	48	30.0	82	51.3	100	62.5
Wisconsin	146	123	84.2	36	24.7	10	6.8	96	65.8	37	25.3	36	24.7	40	27.4	48	32.9	73	52.1
CENSUS DIVISION 5, EAST SOUTH CENTRAL	376	312	83.0	30	8.0	34	9.0	145	38.6	77	20.5	63	16.8	67	17.8	116	30.9	175	46.5
Alabama	95	85	89.5	10	10.5	4	4.2	37	38.9	18	18.9	17	17.9	16	16.8	33	34.7	50	52.6
Kentucky	86	73	84.9	3	3.5	8	9.3	19	22.1	27	31.4	17	19.8	19	22.1	37	43.0	46	53.5
Mississippi	110	87	79.1	8	7.3	21	19.1	76	69.1	8	7.3	9	8.2	13	11.8	18	16.4	34	30.9
Tennessee	85	67	78.8	9	10.6	1	1.2	13	15.3	24	28.2	20	23.5	19	22.4	28	32.9	28	32.9
CENSUS DIVISION 6, WEST NORTH CENTRAL	658	574	87.2	63	9.6	25	3.8	258	39.2	130	19.8	82	12.5	90	13.7	155	23.6	381	57.9
Iowa	126	119	94.4	13	10.3	4	3.2	90	71.4	29	23.0	11	8.7	18	14.3	23	18.3	80	63.5
Kansas	153	126	82.4	7	4.6	3	2.0	13	8.5	16	10.5	14	9.2	13	8.5	23	15.0	85	55.6
Minnesota	100	93	93.0	8	8.0	2	2.0	65	65.0	27	27.0	15	15.0	16	16.0	29	38.0	58	58.0
Missouri	150	115	76.7	20	13.3	8	5.3	30	20.0	31	20.7	27	18.0	22	14.7	57	38.0	77	51.3
Nebraska	55	50	90.9	7	12.7	4	7.3	28	50.9	18	32.7	10	18.2	11	20.0	13	23.6	36	65.5
North Dakota	24	23	95.8	2	8.3	3	12.5	13	54.2	3	12.5	3	12.5	5	20.8	5	20.8	15	62.5
South Dakota	50	48	96.0	6	12.0	1	2.0	19	38.0	6	12.0	2	4.0	5	10.0	5	10.0	30	60.0
CENSUS DIVISION 7, WEST SOUTH CENTRAL	888	681	76.7	83	9.3	44	5.0	335	37.7	201	22.6	139	15.7	108	12.2	273	30.7	428	48.2
Arkansas	93	72	77.4	9	9.7	6	6.5	38	40.9	20	21.5	11	11.8	12	12.9	20	21.5	45	48.4
Louisiana	97	71	73.2	9	9.3	2	2.1	19	19.6	29	29.9	19	19.6	20	20.6	39	40.2	55	56.7
Oklahoma	127	114	89.3	15	11.8	3	2.4	41	32.3	21	16.5	18	14.2	12	9.4	34	26.8	66	52.0
Texas	571	424	74.3	54	9.5	33	5.8	237	41.5	131	22.9	91	15.9	64	11.2	180	31.5	262	45.9
CENSUS DIVISION 8, MOUNTAIN	354	304	85.9	49	13.8	23	6.5	148	41.8	109	30.8	71	20.1	80	22.6	119	33.6	208	58.8
Arizona	64	55	85.9	13	20.3	6	9.4	22	34.4	31	48.4	23	35.9	20	31.3	34	53.1	36	56.3
Colorado	70	65	92.9	8	11.4	7	10.0	50	71.4	23	32.9	16	22.9	20	28.6	34	48.6	50	71.4
Idaho	35	31	88.6	4	11.4	0	0.0	5	14.3	11	31.4	7	20.0	5	14.3	9	25.7	22	62.9
Montana	57	52	91.2	8	14.0	0	0.0	27	47.4	8	14.0	4	7.0	6	10.5	7	12.3	32	56.6
Nevada	36	23	63.9	4	11.1	1	2.8	4	11.1	8	22.2	6	16.7	5	13.9	10	27.8	17	47.2
New Mexico	33	26	78.8	3	9.1	3	9.1	6	18.2	6	18.2	4	12.1	4	12.1	8	24.2	18	54.5
Utah	35	30	85.7	7	20.0	3	8.6	17	48.6	13	37.1	9	25.7	15	42.9	14	40.0	25	71.4
Wyoming	24	22	91.7	3	12.5	2	8.3	17	70.8	7	29.2	2	8.3	5	20.8	3	12.5	14	58.3
CENSUS DIVISION 9, PACIFIC	476	404	84.9	52	10.9	13	2.7	173	36.3	205	43.1	138	29.0	104	21.8	239	50.2	287	60.3
Alaska	14	12	85.7	1	7.1	0	0.0	3	21.4	4	28.6	4	28.6	0	0.0	3	21.4	9	64.3
California	307	249	81.1	32	10.4	6	2.0	72	23.5	134	43.6	98	31.9	74	24.1	176	57.3	179	58.3
Hawaii	17	13	76.5	2	11.8	0	0.0	3	17.6	9	29.4	3	17.6	2	11.8	7	41.2	6	35.3
Oregon	59	58	98.3	7	11.9	2	3.4	42	71.2	28	47.5	19	32.2	9	15.3	20	33.9	46	78.0
Washington	79	72	91.1	10	12.7	5	6.3	53	67.1	34	43.0	17	21.5	19	24.1	33	41.8	47	59.5

Facilities and Services

Table 7 (Continued)

These data include only hospital-based facilities and services as reported by responding hospitals in Section C of the 2011 AHA Annual Survey, beginning on page 215. All hospitals are represented with Community Hospitals listed separately under United States. No estimates have been made for nonresponding hospitals. Definitions of facilities and services are listed in the Glossary, page 201.

CLASSIFICATION	HOSPITALS REPORTING	PHYSICAL REHABILITATION SERVICES — ASSISTIVE TECHNOLOGY CENTER Number	Percent	ELECTRO-DIAGNOSTIC SERVICES Number	Percent	PHYSICAL REHABILITATION OUTPATIENT SERVICES Number	Percent	PROSTHETIC ORTHOTIC SERVICES Number	Percent	ROBOT ASSISTED WALKING THERAPY Number	Percent	SIMULATED REHABILITATION ENVIRONMENT Number	Percent	PSYCHIATRIC SERVICES — CHILD/ADOLESCENT SERVICES Number	Percent	CONSULTATION/ LIAISON SERVICES Number	Percent	EDUCATION SERVICES Number	Percent	EMERGENCY SERVICES Number	Percent	GERIATRIC SERVICES Number	Percent
UNITED STATES	4,782	770	16.1	1,064	22.3	3,456	72.3	811	17.0	177	3.7	1,142	23.9	844	17.6	1,520	31.8	1,153	24.1	1,567	32.8	1,427	29.8
COMMUNITY HOSPITALS	4,082	667	16.3	1,000	24.5	3,274	80.2	714	17.5	159	3.9	1,059	25.9	634	15.5	1,286	31.5	900	22.0	1,374	33.7	1,168	28.6
CENSUS DIVISION 1, NEW ENGLAND	201	40	19.9	56	27.9	172	85.6	51	25.4	10	5.0	56	27.9	62	30.8	108	53.7	78	38.8	102	50.7	86	42.8
Connecticut	31	8	25.8	12	38.7	25	80.6	12	38.7	3	9.7	13	41.9	15	48.4	23	74.2	17	54.8	25	80.6	17	54.8
Maine	39	5	12.8	6	15.4	34	87.2	6	15.4	1	2.6	10	25.6	10	25.6	14	35.9	10	25.6	11	28.2	10	25.6
Massachusetts	80	19	23.8	25	31.3	69	86.3	19	23.8	4	5.0	18	22.5	24	30.0	46	57.5	33	41.3	41	51.3	38	47.5
New Hampshire	27	4	14.8	6	22.2	25	92.6	7	25.9	1	3.7	7	25.9	8	29.6	13	48.1	8	29.6	12	44.4	10	37.0
Rhode Island	10	1	10.0	5	50.0	7	70.0	2	20.0	0	0.0	3	30.0	2	20.0	6	60.0	6	60.0	8	80.0	8	80.0
Vermont	14	3	21.4	2	14.3	12	85.7	5	35.7	1	7.1	5	35.7	3	21.4	6	42.9	4	28.6	5	35.7	3	21.4
CENSUS DIVISION 2, MIDDLE ATLANTIC	396	102	25.8	184	46.5	323	81.6	117	29.5	26	6.6	135	34.1	129	32.6	231	58.3	157	39.6	219	55.3	200	50.5
New Jersey	69	18	26.1	35	50.7	54	78.3	18	26.1	5	7.2	22	31.9	30	43.5	48	69.6	31	44.9	47	68.1	36	52.2
New York	165	44	26.7	75	45.5	142	86.1	63	38.2	10	6.1	55	33.3	60	36.4	106	64.2	73	44.2	98	59.4	91	55.2
Pennsylvania	162	40	24.7	74	45.7	127	78.4	36	22.2	11	6.8	58	35.8	39	24.1	77	47.5	53	32.7	74	45.7	73	45.1
CENSUS DIVISION 3, SOUTH ATLANTIC	707	115	16.3	173	24.5	491	69.4	132	18.7	35	5.0	191	27.0	121	17.1	231	32.7	175	24.8	260	36.8	211	29.8
Delaware	8	2	25.0	2	25.0	6	75.0	4	50.0	0	0.0	1	12.5	2	25.0	4	50.0	3	37.5	2	25.0	3	37.5
District of Columbia	10	2	20.0	4	40.0	8	80.0	4	40.0	2	20.0	4	40.0	4	40.0	8	80.0	5	50.0	8	80.0	5	50.0
Florida	176	40	22.7	39	22.2	138	78.4	31	17.6	11	6.3	51	29.0	26	14.8	49	27.8	29	16.5	56	31.8	45	25.6
Georgia	120	10	8.3	15	12.5	86	71.7	17	14.2	1	0.8	26	21.7	13	10.8	33	27.5	25	20.8	30	25.0	30	25.0
Maryland	54	15	27.8	26	48.1	41	75.9	20	37.0	3	5.6	21	38.9	18	33.3	33	61.1	24	44.4	38	70.4	30	55.6
North Carolina	115	24	20.9	35	30.4	96	83.5	22	19.1	7	6.1	39	33.9	17	14.8	37	32.2	34	29.6	46	40.0	38	33.0
South Carolina	82	5	6.1	9	11.0	8	9.8	4	4.9	5	6.1	13	15.9	13	15.9	21	25.6	16	19.5	22	26.8	21	25.6
Virginia	83	13	15.7	31	37.3	67	80.7	23	27.7	3	3.6	26	31.3	16	19.3	32	38.6	24	28.9	44	53.0	26	31.3
West Virginia	59	4	6.8	12	20.3	41	69.5	7	11.9	3	5.1	10	16.9	12	20.3	14	23.7	15	25.4	14	23.7	13	22.0
CENSUS DIVISION 4, EAST NORTH CENTRAL	726	117	16.1	221	30.4	598	82.4	163	22.5	25	3.4	254	35.0	159	21.9	299	41.2	238	32.8	280	38.6	256	35.3
Illinois	164	24	14.6	56	34.1	140	85.4	34	20.7	7	4.3	62	37.8	47	28.7	69	42.1	60	36.6	68	41.5	69	42.1
Indiana	122	16	13.1	23	18.9	96	78.7	21	17.2	1	0.8	32	26.2	23	18.9	36	29.5	31	25.4	36	29.5	35	28.7
Michigan	134	28	20.9	54	40.3	112	83.6	31	23.1	8	6.0	53	39.6	26	19.4	67	50.0	52	38.8	64	47.8	49	36.6
Ohio	160	31	19.4	62	38.8	132	82.5	41	25.6	6	3.8	59	36.9	27	16.9	69	43.1	53	33.1	65	40.6	56	35.0
Wisconsin	146	18	12.3	26	17.8	118	80.8	36	24.7	3	2.1	48	32.9	36	24.7	58	39.7	42	28.8	47	32.2	47	32.2
CENSUS DIVISION 5, EAST SOUTH CENTRAL	376	35	9.3	55	14.6	254	67.6	34	9.0	18	4.8	61	16.2	37	9.8	81	21.5	63	16.8	86	22.9	123	32.7
Alabama	95	7	7.4	11	11.6	66	69.5	12	12.6	7	7.4	14	14.7	10	10.5	21	22.1	15	15.8	24	25.3	32	33.7
Kentucky	86	7	8.1	15	17.4	63	73.3	6	7.0	4	4.7	13	15.1	8	9.3	24	27.9	18	20.9	26	30.2	23	26.7
Mississippi	110	10	9.1	11	10.0	60	54.5	7	6.4	3	2.7	15	13.6	9	8.2	18	16.4	15	13.6	16	14.5	41	37.3
Tennessee	85	11	12.9	18	21.2	65	76.5	9	10.6	4	4.7	19	22.4	10	11.8	18	21.2	15	17.6	20	23.5	27	31.8
CENSUS DIVISION 6, WEST NORTH CENTRAL	658	83	12.6	118	17.9	518	78.7	101	15.3	13	2.0	126	19.1	104	15.8	163	24.8	136	20.7	181	27.5	159	24.2
Iowa	126	21	16.7	22	17.5	103	81.7	14	11.1	0	0.0	27	21.4	27	21.4	35	27.8	33	26.2	44	34.9	33	26.2
Kansas	153	13	8.5	12	7.8	114	74.5	12	7.8	2	1.3	19	12.4	8	5.2	16	10.5	14	9.2	24	15.7	29	17.0
Minnesota	100	15	15.0	19	19.0	89	89.0	15	15.0	4	4.0	19	19.0	23	23.0	37	37.0	29	29.0	33	33.0	35	35.0
Missouri	150	14	9.3	30	20.0	109	72.7	34	22.7	4	2.7	40	26.7	30	20.0	55	36.7	42	28.0	56	37.3	48	32.0
Nebraska	55	7	12.7	14	25.5	44	80.0	13	23.6	1	1.8	10	18.2	7	12.7	9	16.4	6	14.5	9	16.4	9	14.5
North Dakota	24	9	37.5	10	41.7	19	79.2	5	20.8	2	8.3	4	16.7	6	25.0	6	25.0	6	25.0	7	29.2	5	20.8
South Dakota	50	4	8.0	11	22.0	40	80.0	8	16.0	0	0.0	7	14.0	3	6.0	5	10.0	4	8.0	8	16.0	4	8.0
CENSUS DIVISION 7, WEST SOUTH CENTRAL	888	140	15.8	85	9.6	526	59.2	81	9.1	28	3.2	167	18.8	91	10.2	164	18.5	130	14.6	168	18.9	203	22.9
Arkansas	93	16	17.2	8	8.6	58	62.4	8	8.6	3	3.2	12	12.9	15	16.1	23	24.7	16	17.2	22	23.7	26	28.0
Louisiana	97	10	10.3	10	10.3	53	54.6	9	9.3	1	1.0	26	26.8	9	9.3	21	21.6	19	19.6	26	26.8	31	32.0
Oklahoma	127	15	11.8	13	10.2	83	65.4	13	10.2	1	0.8	21	16.5	10	7.9	24	18.9	17	13.4	29	22.8	26	20.5
Texas	571	99	17.3	54	9.5	332	58.1	51	8.9	23	4.0	108	18.9	57	10.0	96	16.8	78	13.7	91	15.9	120	21.0
CENSUS DIVISION 8, MOUNTAIN	354	63	17.8	58	16.4	244	68.9	47	13.3	10	2.8	59	16.7	58	16.4	87	24.6	69	19.5	114	32.2	85	24.0
Arizona	64	12	18.8	16	25.0	42	65.6	10	15.6	3	4.7	12	18.8	10	15.6	23	35.9	18	28.1	21	32.8	21	32.8
Colorado	70	13	18.6	16	22.9	57	81.4	12	17.1	3	4.3	17	24.3	10	14.3	14	20.0	12	17.1	21	30.0	12	17.1
Idaho	35	4	11.4	3	8.6	24	68.6	3	8.6	0	0.0	7	20.0	5	14.3	9	25.7	8	22.9	9	25.7	5	14.3
Montana	57	8	14.0	7	12.3	43	75.4	5	8.8	0	0.0	6	10.5	6	10.5	13	22.8	8	14.0	19	33.3	11	19.3
Nevada	36	6	16.7	3	8.3	19	52.8	1	2.8	2	5.6	3	8.3	2	5.6	4	11.1	6	18.2	10	27.8	10	27.8
New Mexico	33	8	24.2	5	15.2	23	69.7	3	9.1	2	6.1	6	18.2	10	30.3	9	27.3	9	25.7	10	30.3	11	33.3
Utah	35	10	28.6	8	22.9	22	62.9	10	28.6	0	0.0	5	14.3	6	17.1	10	28.6	6	17.1	15	42.9	8	22.9
Wyoming	24	2	8.3	0	0.0	14	58.3	3	12.5	0	0.0	3	12.5	4	16.7	5	20.8	4	16.7	9	37.5	7	29.2
CENSUS DIVISION 9, PACIFIC	476	75	15.8	114	23.9	330	69.3	85	17.9	12	2.5	93	19.5	83	17.4	156	32.8	107	22.5	157	33.0	104	21.8
Alaska	14	1	7.1	2	14.3	12	85.7	3	21.4	0	0.0	1	7.1	7	50.0	7	50.0	5	35.7	8	57.1	2	14.3
California	307	47	15.3	71	23.1	203	66.1	50	16.3	7	2.3	61	19.9	47	15.3	98	31.9	66	21.5	91	29.6	72	23.5
Hawaii	17	2	11.8	1	5.9	12	70.6	4	23.5	1	5.9	4	23.5	3	17.6	4	23.5	5	29.4	5	29.4	5	29.4
Oregon	59	12	20.3	16	27.1	49	83.1	8	13.6	2	3.4	6	10.2	9	15.3	21	35.6	11	18.6	24	40.7	8	13.6
Washington	79	13	16.5	24	30.4	54	68.4	20	25.3	2	2.5	21	26.6	17	21.5	26	32.9	20	25.3	29	36.7	17	21.5

Table 7 (Continued)

These data include only hospital-based facilities and services as reported by responding hospitals in Section C of the 2011 AHA Annual Survey, beginning on page 215. All hospitals are represented with Community Hospitals listed separately under United States. No estimates have been made for nonresponding hospitals. Definitions of facilities and services are listed in the Glossary, page 201.

CLASSIFICATION	HOSPITALS REPORTING	PSYCHIATRIC SERVICES — OUTPATIENT SERVICES Number	Percent	PARTIAL HOSPITALIZATION PROGRAM Number	Percent	RESIDENTIAL TREATMENT Number	Percent	RADIOLOGY, DIAGNOSTIC — CT SCANNER Number	Percent	DIAGNOSTIC RADIOISOTOPE FACILITY Number	Percent	ELECTRON BEAM COMPUTED TOMOGRAPHY (EBCT) Number	Percent	FULL-FIELD DIGITAL MAMMOGRAPHY (FFDM) Number	Percent	MAGNETIC RESONANCE IMAGING (MRI) Number	Percent	INTRAOPERATIVE MAGNETIC IMAGING Number	Percent	MULTI-SLICE SPIRAL COMPUTED TOMOGRAPHY (<64 SLICE CT) Number	Percent
UNITED STATES	4,782	1,305	27.3	749	15.7	278	5.8	3,961	83.2	2,689	56.2	337	7.0	2,343	49.0	3,073	64.3	228	4.8	2,821	59.0
COMMUNITY HOSPITALS	4,082	1,051	25.7	577	14.1	148	3.6	3,742	91.7	2,594	63.5	320	7.8	2,282	55.9	2,911	71.3	214	5.2	2,697	66.1
CENSUS DIVISION 1, NEW ENGLAND	201	103	51.2	67	33.3	8	4.0	172	85.6	140	69.7	10	5.0	128	63.7	133	66.2	11	5.5	126	62.7
Connecticut	31	22	71.0	15	48.4	3	9.7	26	83.9	22	71.0	6	19.4	21	67.7	23	74.2	5	16.1	24	77.4
Maine	39	14	35.9	7	17.9	0	0.0	35	89.7	30	76.9	0	0.0	22	56.4	25	64.1	2	5.1	21	53.8
Massachusetts	80	39	48.8	27	33.8	3	3.8	65	81.3	58	72.5	4	5.0	52	65.0	51	63.8	4	5.0	49	61.3
New Hampshire	27	11	40.7	8	29.6	1	3.7	24	88.9	13	48.1	0	0.0	18	66.7	14	51.9	0	0.0	17	63.0
Rhode Island	10	9	90.0	7	70.0	0	0.0	9	90.0	8	80.0	0	0.0	8	80.0	9	90.0	0	0.0	9	90.0
Vermont	14	8	57.1	3	21.4	1	7.1	13	92.9	9	64.3	0	0.0	7	50.0	11	78.6	0	0.0	6	42.9
CENSUS DIVISION 2, MIDDLE ATLANTIC	396	161	40.7	91	23.0	45	11.4	342	86.4	290	73.2	14	3.6	253	63.9	300	75.8	22	5.6	256	64.6
New Jersey	69	34	49.3	30	43.5	12	17.4	57	82.6	53	76.8	6	8.8	47	68.1	54	78.3	8	11.6	48	69.6
New York	165	85	51.5	37	22.4	23	13.9	153	92.7	123	74.5	5	3.3	112	67.9	131	79.4	8	4.8	107	64.8
Pennsylvania	162	42	25.9	24	14.8	10	6.2	132	81.5	114	70.4	3	1.7	94	58.0	115	71.0	6	3.7	101	62.3
CENSUS DIVISION 3, SOUTH ATLANTIC	707	178	25.2	118	16.7	44	6.2	588	83.2	459	64.9	58	8.2	386	54.6	505	71.4	23	3.3	468	66.2
Delaware	8	4	50.0	1	12.5	1	12.5	6	75.0	5	62.5	2	25.0	4	50.0	6	75.0	0	0.0	4	50.0
District of Columbia	10	5	50.0	4	40.0	0	0.0	7	70.0	7	70.0	1	10.0	5	50.0	7	70.0	1	10.0	7	70.0
Florida	176	34	19.3	20	11.4	7	4.0	151	85.8	120	68.2	22	12.5	102	58.0	139	79.0	9	5.1	125	71.0
Georgia	120	27	22.5	22	18.3	6	5.0	105	87.5	71	59.2	4	3.3	65	54.2	88	73.3	4	3.3	75	62.5
Maryland	54	29	53.7	25	46.3	5	9.3	45	83.3	40	74.1	6	11.1	27	50.0	38	70.4	2	3.7	41	75.9
North Carolina	115	31	27.0	12	10.4	9	7.8	97	84.3	78	67.8	8	7.0	64	55.7	88	76.5	4	3.5	79	68.7
South Carolina	82	17	20.7	10	12.2	4	4.9	59	72.0	46	56.1	5	6.1	41	50.0	47	57.3	1	1.2	48	58.5
Virginia	83	24	28.9	18	21.7	10	12.0	70	84.3	55	66.3	8	9.6	52	62.7	61	73.5	2	2.4	56	67.5
West Virginia	59	7	11.9	6	10.2	2	3.4	48	81.4	37	62.7	2	3.4	26	44.1	31	52.5	0	0.0	33	55.9
CENSUS DIVISION 4, EAST NORTH CENTRAL	726	255	35.1	158	21.8	47	6.5	646	89.0	508	70.0	68	9.4	444	61.2	520	71.6	52	7.2	464	63.9
Illinois	164	70	42.7	46	28.0	13	7.9	152	92.7	111	67.7	10	6.1	108	65.9	116	70.7	6	3.7	112	68.3
Indiana	122	33	27.0	24	19.7	9	7.4	104	85.2	77	63.1	10	8.2	70	57.4	97	79.5	4	3.3	77	63.1
Michigan	134	50	37.3	24	17.9	5	3.7	118	88.1	100	74.6	11	8.2	87	64.9	86	64.2	6	4.5	89	66.4
Ohio	160	55	34.4	37	23.1	13	8.1	150	93.8	120	75.0	21	13.1	103	64.4	136	85.0	11	6.9	113	70.6
Wisconsin	146	47	32.2	27	18.5	7	4.8	122	83.6	100	68.5	16	11.0	76	52.1	85	58.2	25	17.1	73	50.0
CENSUS DIVISION 5, EAST SOUTH CENTRAL	376	65	17.3	36	9.6	20	5.3	312	83.0	206	54.8	23	6.1	148	39.4	237	63.0	19	5.1	204	54.3
Alabama	95	20	21.1	11	11.6	4	4.2	84	88.4	60	63.2	6	6.3	54	37.9	66	69.5	4	4.2	57	60.0
Kentucky	86	14	16.3	7	8.1	5	5.8	74	86.0	48	55.8	3	3.5	47	54.7	64	74.4	7	8.1	55	64.0
Mississippi	110	15	13.6	7	6.4	4	3.6	86	78.2	56	50.9	10	9.1	25	22.7	52	47.3	5	4.5	42	38.2
Tennessee	85	16	18.8	11	12.9	7	8.2	68	80.0	42	49.4	4	4.7	40	47.1	55	64.7	3	3.5	50	58.8
CENSUS DIVISION 6, WEST NORTH CENTRAL	658	163	24.8	68	10.3	30	4.6	565	85.9	252	38.3	23	3.5	277	42.1	369	56.1	16	2.4	384	58.4
Iowa	126	32	25.4	14	11.1	4	3.2	117	92.9	47	37.3	4	3.2	54	50.8	72	57.1	2	1.6	86	68.3
Kansas	153	15	9.8	7	4.6	5	3.3	122	79.7	51	33.3	3	2.0	37	24.2	56	36.6	3	2.0	74	48.4
Minnesota	100	38	38.0	15	15.0	7	7.0	93	93.0	41	41.0	5	5.0	52	52.0	67	67.0	5	5.0	57	57.0
Missouri	150	51	34.0	18	12.0	10	6.7	120	80.0	71	47.3	6	4.0	51	40.7	111	74.0	3	2.0	87	58.0
Nebraska	55	14	25.5	7	12.7	4	7.3	49	89.1	22	40.0	4	7.3	33	60.0	32	58.2	2	3.6	35	63.6
North Dakota	24	9	37.5	5	20.8	0	0.0	21	87.5	8	33.3	1	4.2	11	45.8	13	54.2	1	4.2	18	75.0
South Dakota	50	4	8.0	2	4.0	0	0.0	43	86.0	12	24.0	0	0.0	19	38.0	18	36.0	0	0.0	27	54.0
CENSUS DIVISION 7, WEST SOUTH CENTRAL	888	160	18.0	80	9.0	36	4.1	642	72.3	355	40.0	34	3.8	296	33.3	458	51.6	35	3.9	417	47.0
Arkansas	93	24	25.8	9	9.7	9	9.7	71	76.3	39	41.9	2	2.2	32	34.4	55	59.1	3	3.2	46	49.5
Louisiana	97	27	27.8	14	14.4	2	2.1	74	76.3	47	48.5	2	2.0	50	51.5	55	56.7	2	2.1	47	48.5
Oklahoma	127	24	18.9	8	6.3	11	8.7	101	79.5	46	36.2	13	10.3	50	39.4	69	54.3	5	3.9	58	45.7
Texas	571	85	14.9	49	8.6	14	2.5	396	69.4	223	39.1	19	3.3	164	28.7	279	48.9	25	4.4	266	46.6
CENSUS DIVISION 8, MOUNTAIN	354	87	24.6	52	14.7	22	6.2	300	84.7	172	48.6	24	6.8	170	48.0	228	64.4	23	6.5	206	58.2
Arizona	64	24	37.5	12	18.8	3	4.7	56	87.5	38	59.4	7	10.9	29	45.3	51	79.7	8	12.5	42	65.6
Colorado	70	15	21.4	6	8.6	3	4.3	66	94.3	43	61.4	4	5.7	40	57.1	55	78.6	6	8.6	48	68.6
Idaho	35	7	20.0	4	11.4	3	8.6	33	94.3	14	40.0	2	5.7	14	40.0	21	60.0	2	5.7	24	68.6
Montana	57	10	17.5	8	14.0	3	5.3	44	77.2	19	33.3	0	0.0	26	45.6	23	40.4	0	0.0	26	45.6
Nevada	36	9	25.0	5	13.9	3	8.3	23	63.9	17	47.2	2	5.6	12	33.3	21	58.3	3	8.3	15	41.7
New Mexico	33	9	27.3	3	9.1	2	6.1	26	78.8	13	39.4	2	6.1	12	36.4	17	51.5	2	6.1	19	57.6
Utah	35	8	22.9	9	25.7	3	8.6	29	82.9	18	51.4	6	17.1	24	68.6	24	68.6	2	5.7	20	57.1
Wyoming	24	5	20.8	5	20.8	2	8.3	23	95.8	10	41.7	1	4.2	13	54.2	16	66.7	0	0.0	12	50.0
CENSUS DIVISION 9, PACIFIC	476	133	27.9	79	16.6	23	5.5	414	87.0	307	64.5	43	9.0	241	50.6	323	67.9	27	5.7	296	62.2
Alaska	14	7	50.0	5	35.7	2	14.3	12	85.7	6	42.9	0	0.0	7	50.0	10	71.4	0	0.0	9	64.3
California	307	85	27.7	50	16.3	12	3.9	261	85.0	203	66.1	32	10.4	142	46.3	207	67.4	18	5.9	181	59.0
Hawaii	17	4	23.5	3	17.6	1	5.9	12	70.6	10	58.8	1	5.9	10	58.8	10	58.8	0	0.0	6	35.3
Oregon	59	13	22.0	7	11.9	3	5.1	58	98.3	40	67.8	4	6.5	40	67.8	43	72.9	6	10.2	48	81.4
Washington	79	24	30.4	14	17.7	8	10.1	71	89.9	48	60.8	5	6.3	42	53.2	53	67.1	3	3.8	52	65.8

Table 7 (Continued)

These data include only hospital-based facilities and services as reported by responding hospitals in Section C of the 2011 AHA Annual Survey, beginning on page 215. All hospitals are represented with Community Hospitals listed separately under United States. No estimates have been made for nonresponding hospitals. Definitions of facilities and services are listed in the Glossary, page 201.

Columns under RADIOLOGY, DIAGNOSTIC: Multi-Slice Spiral Computed Tomography (64+ Slice CT), Positron Emission Tomography (PET), Positron Emission Tomography/CT (PET/CT), Single Photon Emission Computerized Tomography (SPECT), Ultrasound. Columns under RADIOLOGY, THERAPEUTIC: Image-Guided Radiation Therapy (IGRT), Intensity-Modulated Radiation Therapy (IMRT), Proton Beam Therapy, Shaped Beam Radiation System, Stereotactic Radiosurgery.

CLASSIFICATION	HOSPITALS REPORTING	MULTI-SLICE SPIRAL CT (64+) No.	%	PET No.	%	PET/CT No.	%	SPECT No.	%	ULTRASOUND No.	%	IGRT No.	%	IMRT No.	%	PROTON BEAM No.	%	SHAPED BEAM No.	%	STEREOTACTIC No.	%
UNITED STATES	4,782	1,991	41.6	743	15.5	955	20.0	1,742	36.4	3,859	80.7	917	19.2	1,087	22.7	102	2.1	851	17.8	814	17.0
COMMUNITY HOSPITALS	4,082	1,900	46.5	709	17.4	915	22.4	1,695	41.5	3,628	88.9	890	21.8	1,059	25.9	93	2.3	833	20.4	795	19.5
CENSUS DIVISION 1, NEW ENGLAND	201	105	52.2	38	18.9	51	25.4	107	53.2	181	90.0	54	26.9	61	30.3	4	2.0	53	26.4	49	24.4
Connecticut	31	17	54.8	13	41.9	17	54.8	20	64.5	28	90.3	18	58.1	18	58.1	2	6.5	15	48.4	13	41.9
Maine	39	18	46.2	3	7.7	5	12.8	19	48.7	34	87.2	4	10.3	6	15.4		0.0	5	12.8	4	10.3
Massachusetts	80	45	56.3	13	16.3	20	25.0	42	52.5	73	91.3	25	31.3	29	36.3	2	2.5	27	33.8	25	31.3
New Hampshire	27	13	48.1	4	14.8	5	18.5	14	51.9	24	88.9	5	18.5	6	22.2		0.0	4	14.8	4	14.8
Rhode Island	10	5	50.0	1	10.0	1	10.0	6	60.0	9	90.0	1	10.0	1	10.0		0.0	1	10.0	2	20.0
Vermont	14	7	50.0	4	28.6	3	21.4	6	42.9	13	92.9	1	7.1	1	7.1		0.0	1	7.1	1	7.1
CENSUS DIVISION 2, MIDDLE ATLANTIC	396	225	56.8	87	22.0	115	29.0	207	52.3	345	87.1	127	32.1	161	40.7	11	2.8	120	30.3	106	26.8
New Jersey	69	36	52.2	18	26.1	24	34.8	37	53.6	58	84.1	30	43.5	37	53.6	1	1.4	32	46.4	20	29.0
New York	165	99	60.0	38	23.0	45	27.3	81	49.1	156	94.5	49	29.7	63	38.2	7	4.2	42	25.5	40	24.2
Pennsylvania	162	90	55.6	31	19.1	46	28.4	89	54.9	131	80.9	48	29.6	61	37.7	3	1.9	46	28.4	46	28.4
CENSUS DIVISION 3, SOUTH ATLANTIC	707	329	46.5	129	18.2	167	23.6	309	43.7	592	83.7	170	24.0	197	27.9	9	1.3	159	22.5	147	20.8
Delaware	8	5	62.5	2	25.0	4	50.0	4	50.0	6	75.0	3	37.5	4	50.0		0.0	3	37.5	3	37.5
District of Columbia	10	5	50.0	3	30.0	4	40.0	5	50.0	8	80.0	4	40.0	4	40.0		0.0	5	50.0	4	40.0
Florida	176	89	50.6	38	21.6	50	28.4	67	38.1	150	85.2	42	23.9	45	25.6	3	1.7	38	21.6	50	28.4
Georgia	120	43	35.8	22	18.3	24	20.0	35	29.2	105	87.5	24	20.0	26	21.7	1	0.8	24	20.0	29	24.2
Maryland	54	36	66.7	13	24.1	14	25.9	34	63.0	45	83.3	19	35.2	21	38.9	1	1.9	16	29.6	13	24.1
North Carolina	115	54	47.0	20	17.4	30	26.1	66	57.4	99	86.1	35	30.4	40	34.8	4	3.5	32	27.8	20	17.4
South Carolina	82	29	35.4	4	4.9	8	9.8	25	30.5	61	74.4	7	8.5	14	17.1		0.0	9	11.0	6	7.3
Virginia	83	45	54.2	16	19.3	23	27.7	50	60.2	70	84.3	28	33.7	33	39.8		0.0	23	27.7	16	19.3
West Virginia	59	23	39.0	11	18.6	10	16.9	23	39.0	48	81.4	8	13.6	10	16.9		0.0	9	15.3	6	10.2
CENSUS DIVISION 4, EAST NORTH CENTRAL	726	384	52.9	172	23.7	211	29.1	347	47.8	628	86.5	194	26.7	218	30.0	20	2.8	173	23.8	145	20.0
Illinois	164	106	64.6	29	17.7	38	23.2	72	43.9	146	89.0	44	26.8	55	33.5	3	1.8	40	24.4	30	18.3
Indiana	122	49	40.2	24	19.7	32	26.2	47	38.5	103	84.4	33	27.0	39	32.0	4	3.3	29	23.8	20	16.4
Michigan	134	84	62.7	29	21.6	40	29.9	67	50.0	121	90.3	39	29.1	43	32.1	2	1.5	37	27.6	36	26.9
Ohio	160	84	52.5	54	33.8	58	36.3	95	59.4	146	91.3	42	26.3	43	26.9	6	3.8	36	22.5	35	21.9
Wisconsin	146	61	41.8	36	24.7	43	29.5	66	45.2	112	76.7	36	24.7	38	26.0	5	3.4	31	21.2	24	16.4
CENSUS DIVISION 5, EAST SOUTH CENTRAL	376	118	31.4	55	14.6	64	17.0	130	34.6	305	81.1	50	13.3	63	16.8	11	2.9	46	12.2	53	14.1
Alabama	95	35	36.8	15	15.8	20	21.1	32	33.7	80	84.2	15	15.8	16	16.8	2	2.1	11	11.6	14	14.7
Kentucky	86	34	39.5	11	12.8	16	18.6	36	41.9	75	87.2	11	12.8	16	18.6	2	2.3	10	11.6	17	19.8
Mississippi	110	23	20.9	15	13.6	11	10.0	32	29.1	82	74.5	10	9.1	9	8.2	2	1.8	8	7.3	10	9.1
Tennessee	85	26	30.6	14	16.5	17	20.0	30	35.3	68	80.0	14	16.5	22	25.9	5	5.9	17	20.0	12	14.1
CENSUS DIVISION 6, WEST NORTH CENTRAL	658	185	28.1	67	10.2	98	14.9	172	26.1	514	78.1	91	13.8	106	16.1	13	2.0	78	11.9	74	11.2
Iowa	126	34	27.0	11	8.7	14	11.1	37	29.4	115	91.3	10	8.7	13	10.3	4	2.6	12	9.5	12	9.5
Kansas	153	28	18.3	6	3.9	11	7.2	26	17.0	99	64.7	10	6.5	14	9.2	3	3.0	12	7.8	7	4.6
Minnesota	100	40	40.0	12	12.0	17	17.0	26	26.0	85	85.0	16	16.0	19	19.0	3	2.0	12	12.0	13	13.0
Missouri	150	52	34.7	20	13.3	34	22.7	53	35.3	120	80.0	32	21.3	38	25.3	1	1.8	23	15.3	24	16.0
Nebraska	55	19	34.5	11	20.0	15	27.3	17	30.9	42	76.4	13	23.6	11	20.0	1	4.2	11	20.0	11	20.0
North Dakota	24	5	20.8	2	8.3	3	12.5	6	25.0	16	66.7	3	12.5	3	12.5		0.0	1	4.2	3	12.5
South Dakota	50	7	14.0	5	10.0	4	8.0	7	14.0	37	74.0	6	12.0	8	16.0	1	2.0	7	14.0	4	8.0
CENSUS DIVISION 7, WEST SOUTH CENTRAL	888	280	31.5	62	7.0	90	10.1	198	22.3	597	67.2	79	8.9	97	10.9	9	1.0	72	8.1	100	11.3
Arkansas	93	28	30.1	8	8.6	9	9.7	20	21.5	69	74.2	8	8.6	7	7.5	2	2.2	4	4.3	11	11.8
Louisiana	97	39	40.2	6	6.2	15	15.5	23	23.7	73	75.3	16	16.5	17	17.5	2	2.1	14	14.4	18	18.6
Oklahoma	127	37	29.1	12	9.4	18	14.2	24	18.9	91	71.7	20	15.7	20	15.7		0.0	18	14.2	14	11.0
Texas	571	176	30.8	36	6.3	48	8.4	131	22.9	364	63.7	35	6.1	53	9.3	5	0.9	36	6.3	57	10.0
CENSUS DIVISION 8, MOUNTAIN	354	151	42.7	51	14.4	56	15.8	91	25.7	289	81.6	49	13.8	59	16.7	11	3.1	49	13.8	47	13.3
Arizona	64	33	51.6	16	25.0	17	26.6	23	35.9	54	84.4	7	10.9	12	18.8	3	4.7	10	15.6	9	14.1
Colorado	70	40	57.1	11	15.7	13	18.6	22	31.4	64	91.4	13	18.6	16	22.9	1	2.9	15	21.4	16	22.9
Idaho	35	11	31.4	3	8.6	3	8.6	7	20.0	30	85.7	5	14.3	5	14.3	1	3.5	4	11.4	2	5.7
Montana	57	17	29.8	6	10.5	6	10.5	12	21.1	40	70.2	7	12.3	7	12.3		0.0	5	8.8	5	8.8
Nevada	36	11	30.6	1	2.8	1	2.8	6	16.7	23	63.9	3	8.3	3	8.3	1	3.0	2	5.6	5	13.9
New Mexico	33	15	45.5	5	15.2	6	18.2	8	24.2	25	75.8	3	9.1	5	15.2	1	3.0	5	15.2	4	12.1
Utah	35	16	45.7	7	20.0	10	28.6	9	25.7	30	85.7	7	20.0	7	20.0	1	2.9	6	17.1	4	11.4
Wyoming	24	8	33.3	2	8.3		0.0	4	16.7	23	95.8	4	16.7	4	16.7		0.0	2	8.3	2	8.3
CENSUS DIVISION 9, PACIFIC	476	214	45.0	82	17.2	103	21.6	181	38.0	408	85.7	103	21.6	125	26.3	14	2.9	101	21.2	93	19.5
Alaska	14	5	35.7	1	7.1		0.0	2	14.3	11	78.6		0.0	2	14.3		0.0	1	7.1	1	7.1
California	307	146	47.6	56	18.2	68	22.1	122	39.7	262	85.3	65	21.2	81	26.4	10	3.3	64	20.8	65	21.2
Hawaii	17	8	47.1	1	5.9	3	17.6	2	11.8	12	70.6	1	5.9	3	17.6		0.0	1	5.9	3	17.6
Oregon	59	23	39.0	8	13.6	10	16.9	31	52.5	58	98.3	14	23.7	15	25.4	3	5.1	14	23.7	10	16.9
Washington	79	32	40.5	17	21.5	22	27.8	24	30.4	65	82.3	23	29.1	24	30.4	1	1.3	21	26.6	14	17.7

Table 7 (Continued)

These data include only hospital-based facilities and services as reported by responding hospitals in Section C of the 2011 AHA Annual Survey, beginning on page 215. All hospitals are represented with Community Hospitals listed separately under United States. No estimates have been made for nonresponding hospitals. Definitions of facilities and services are listed in the Glossary, page 201.

CLASSIFICATION	HOSPITALS REPORTING	BONE MARROW Number	BONE MARROW Percent	TRANSPLANT HEART Number	HEART Percent	KIDNEY Number	KIDNEY Percent	LIVER Number	LIVER Percent	LUNG Number	LUNG Percent	TISSUE Number	TISSUE Percent	OTHER Number	OTHER Percent
UNITED STATES	4,782	204	4.3	134	2.8	223		129	2.7	74	1.5	339	7.1	241	5.0
COMMUNITY HOSPITALS	4,082	200	4.9	129	3.2	220		127	3.1	72	1.8	324	7.9	234	5.7
CENSUS DIVISION 1, NEW ENGLAND	201	15	7.5	7	3.5	17		8	4.0	4	2.0	20	10.0	16	8.0
Connecticut	31	1	3.2	2	6.5	3		2	6.5	0	0.0	4	12.9	4	12.9
Maine	39	1	2.6	0	0.0	1		0	0.0	0	0.0	0	0.0	1	2.6
Massachusetts	80	9	11.3	4	5.0	9		5	6.3	3	3.8	11	13.8	7	8.8
New Hampshire	27	1	3.7	0	0.0	1		0	0.0	0	0.0	1	3.7	1	3.7
Rhode Island	10	2	20.0	1	10.0	2		1	10.0	1	10.0	2	20.0	2	20.0
Vermont	14	1	7.1	0	0.0	1		0	0.0	0	0.0	2	14.3	1	7.1
CENSUS DIVISION 2, MIDDLE ATLANTIC	396	29	7.3	16	4.0	34		19	4.8	8	2.0	42	10.6	43	10.9
New Jersey	69	2	2.9	2	2.9	5		2	2.9	1	1.4	4	5.8	5	7.2
New York	165	13	7.9	5	3.0	13		6	3.6	1	0.6	19	11.5	19	11.5
Pennsylvania	162	14	8.6	9	5.6	16		11	6.8	6	3.7	19	11.7	19	11.7
CENSUS DIVISION 3, SOUTH ATLANTIC	707	38	5.4	25	3.5	30		19	2.7	13	1.8	57	8.1	41	5.8
Delaware	8	2	25.0	1	12.5	2		1	12.5	0	0.0	0	0.0	0	0.0
District of Columbia	10	2	20.0	2	20.0	2		1	10.0	0	0.0	3	30.0	3	30.0
Florida	176	11	6.3	8	4.5	7		6	3.4	4	2.3	14	8.0	6	3.4
Georgia	120	5	4.2	3	2.5	4		3	2.5	2	1.7	8	6.7	5	4.2
Maryland	54	3	5.6	2	3.7	2		2	3.7	2	3.7	5	9.3	6	11.1
North Carolina	115	5	4.3	4	3.5	5		3	2.6	2	1.7	5	4.3	9	7.8
South Carolina	82	4	4.9	1	1.2			1	1.2	1	1.2	7	8.5	4	4.9
Virginia	83	5	6.0	4	4.8	6		2	2.4	2	2.4	11	13.3	7	8.4
West Virginia	59	1	1.7	0	0.0	1		0	0.0	0	0.0	4	6.8	1	1.7
CENSUS DIVISION 4, EAST NORTH CENTRAL	726	34	4.7	23	3.2	30		22	3.0	14	1.9	70	9.6	29	4.0
Illinois	164	10	6.1	5	3.7	6		6	3.7	2	1.2	18	11.0	10	3.1
Indiana	122	3	2.5	2	1.6	2		1	0.8	1	0.8	8	6.6	3	3.0
Michigan	134	8	6.0	6	4.5	10		6	4.5	4	3.0	20	14.9	8	6.0
Ohio	160	8	5.0	5	3.1	8		5	3.1	3	1.9	18	11.3	6	3.8
Wisconsin	146	5	3.4	4	2.7	4		4	2.7	4	2.7	6	4.1	5	3.4
CENSUS DIVISION 5, EAST SOUTH CENTRAL	376	11	2.9	7	1.9	11		5	1.3	4	1.1	19	5.1	13	3.5
Alabama	95	2	2.1	1	1.1	1		1	1.1	1	1.1	4	4.2	3	3.2
Kentucky	86	4	4.7	3	3.5	3		2	2.3	2	2.3	4	4.7	3	3.5
Mississippi	110	1	0.9	1	0.9	1		0	0.0	0	0.0	1	0.9	1	0.9
Tennessee	85	4	4.7	2	2.4	6		2	2.4	1	1.2	10	11.8	6	7.1
CENSUS DIVISION 6, WEST NORTH CENTRAL	658	16	2.4	8	1.2	22		10	1.5	4	0.6	27	4.1	23	3.5
Iowa	126	1	0.8	0	0.0	2		1	0.8	0	0.8	3	2.4	5	4.0
Kansas	153	2	1.3	0	0.0	2		1	0.7	0	0.0	2	1.3	3	2.0
Minnesota	100	3	3.0	2	2.0	3		2	1.0	1	1.0	5	5.0	2	2.0
Missouri	150	6	4.0	4	2.7	8		6	4.0	2	1.3	11	7.3	9	6.0
Nebraska	55	3	5.5	1	1.8	2		1	1.8	1	0.0	3	5.5	2	3.6
North Dakota	24	0	0.0	0	0.0			0	0.0	0	0.0	0	0.0	1	4.2
South Dakota	50	1	2.0	0	0.0	2		0	0.0	0	0.0	3	6.0	1	2.0
CENSUS DIVISION 7, WEST SOUTH CENTRAL	888	20	2.3	18	2.0	34		19	2.1	11	1.2	36	4.1	28	3.2
Arkansas	93	3	3.2	2	2.2	3		1	1.1	0	0.0	2	2.2	1	1.1
Louisiana	97	3	3.1	2	2.1	3		2	2.1	1	1.0	8	8.2	5	5.2
Oklahoma	127	2	1.6	1	0.8	5		2	1.6	1	0.8	4	3.1	2	1.6
Texas	571	12	2.1	13	2.3	23		14	2.5	9	1.6	22	3.9	20	3.5
CENSUS DIVISION 8, MOUNTAIN	354	14	4.0	11	3.1	15		10	2.8	6	1.7	23	6.5	14	4.0
Arizona	64	3	4.7	3	4.7	4		3	4.7	2	3.1	6	9.4	4	6.3
Colorado	70	4	5.7	3	4.3	4		3	4.3	2	2.9	6	8.6	3	4.3
Idaho	35	1	2.9	0	0.0	0		0	0.0	0	0.0	2	5.7	1	2.9
Montana	57	2	3.5	1	1.8	1		1	1.8	-	1.8	3	5.3	1	1.8
Nevada	36	0	0.0	0	0.0	1		0	0.0	1	0.0	1	2.8	0	0.0
New Mexico	33	1	3.0	0	0.0	2		0	0.0	0	0.0	0	0.0	2	6.1
Utah	35	3	8.6	4	11.4	3		3	8.6	1	2.9	5	14.3	3	8.6
Wyoming	24	0	0.0	0	0.0	0		0	0.0	0	0.0	0	0.0	0	0.0
CENSUS DIVISION 9, PACIFIC	476	27	5.7	19	4.0	27		17	3.6	10	2.1	45	9.5	34	7.1
Alaska	14	0	0.0	0	0.0	0		0	0.0	0	0.0	0	0.0	1	7.1
California	307	18	5.9	13	4.2	19		12	3.9	8	2.6	34	11.1	23	7.5
Hawaii	17	1	5.9	0	0.0	2		0	0.0	0	0.0	0	0.0	2	11.8
Oregon	59	2	3.4	2	3.4	6		1	1.7	0	1.7	4	6.8	4	6.8
Washington	79	6	7.6	4	5.1			4	5.1	2	2.5	7	8.9	4	5.1

Table 8

MSAs

Metropolitan Statistical Areas

Metropolitan Statistical Areas (MSAs) definitions announced by the U.S. Office of Management and Budget (OMB) effective June 6, 2003 were added with the 2006 edition.

According to the OMB, an MSA is a geographical designation that represents an integrated social and economic unit with a large population nucleus. Under these standards, an area qualifies for recognition as an MSA if there is a city within the area of at least 50,000 with a total metropolitan population of at least 100,000. MSAs are defined as entire counties. In addition to the county containing the main city, an MSA also includes additional counties having strong economic and social ties to the central county. Such counties must have a specified level of commuting to the central counties and must meet certain standards regarding metropolitan character, such as population density.

When an MSA encompasses two or more central cities, up to three cities may be specified in the MSA title. They will be listed in order of population size. When a single central city exists, the MSA is named for that particular city. A MSA may extend beyond a single state.

An MSA containing a single core with a population of 2.5 million or more may be subdivided to form smaller groupings of counties referred to as Metropolitan Divisions. Where they exist the Metropolitan Divisions are shown in this table rather than the entire MSA.

TABLE 8

U.S. CENSUS DIVISION 1, NEW ENGLAND

U.S. Community Hospitals
(Nonfederal, short-term general and other special hospitals)

2011 Utilization, Personnel and Finances

CLASSIFICATION	Hospitals	Beds	Admissions	Inpatient Days	Adjusted Patient Days	Average Daily Census	Adjusted Average Daily Census	Average Stay (days)	Surgical Operations	NEWBORNS Bassinets	NEWBORNS Births	OUTPATIENT VISITS Emergency	OUTPATIENT VISITS Total
UNITED STATES	4,973	797,403	34,843,085	187,072,013	358,286,020	512,944	982,377	5.4	26,907,712	56,290	3,730,342	129,461,658	656,078,942
Nonmetropolitan	1,984	133,716	4,192,377	26,166,177	70,109,403	71,710	192,165	6.2	4,127,991	10,856	454,761	23,737,253	123,877,956
Metropolitan	2,989	663,687	30,650,708	160,905,836	288,176,617	441,234	790,212	5.2	22,779,721	45,434	3,275,581	105,724,405	532,200,986
CENSUS DIVISION 1, NEW ENGLAND	204	33,693	1,677,325	8,650,119	19,803,424	23,705	54,255	5.2	1,383,465	2,419	159,359	7,018,233	47,303,702
Nonmetropolitan	58	3,819	150,490	898,970	2,854,751	2,460	7,818	6.0	175,302	382	21,231	1,001,363	7,906,533
Metropolitan	146	29,874	1,526,835	7,751,149	16,948,673	21,245	46,437	5.1	1,208,163	2,037	138,128	6,016,870	39,397,169
Connecticut	35	7,745	402,838	2,110,564	3,982,592	5,784	10,913	5.2	308,777	486	37,565	1,643,282	8,527,788
Nonmetropolitan	5	391	21,056	91,933	230,217	252	630	4.4	19,453	43	2,208	133,176	753,091
Metropolitan	30	7,354	381,782	2,018,631	3,752,375	5,532	10,283	5.3	289,324	443	35,357	1,510,106	7,774,697
Bridgeport-Stamford-Norwalk	6	1,915	92,790	492,180	935,335	1,348	2,563	5.3	64,534	165	11,345	361,629	1,940,685
Hartford-West Hartford-East Hartford	12	2,706	134,242	702,633	1,308,801	1,927	3,587	5.2	114,952	127	12,297	577,680	3,422,004
New Haven-Milford	10	2,297	129,977	708,131	1,234,884	1,940	3,384	5.4	89,211	119	9,236	423,424	1,698,734
Norwich-New London	2	436	24,773	115,687	273,355	317	749	4.7	20,627	32	2,479	147,373	713,274
Maine	37	3,557	144,718	814,216	2,144,100	2,232	5,875	5.6	163,079	292	12,434	765,481	6,153,694
Nonmetropolitan	22	1,303	44,364	291,624	940,499	799	2,575	6.6	52,323	133	4,175	357,056	2,612,136
Metropolitan	15	2,254	100,354	522,592	1,203,601	1,433	3,300	5.2	110,756	159	8,259	408,425	3,541,558
Bangor	4	483	27,128	125,725	258,810	345	711	4.6	29,439	20	1,696	80,873	588,575
Lewiston-Auburn	2	361	16,361	74,380	185,881	204	509	4.5	10,598	35	1,427	80,648	1,126,573
Portland-South Portland-Biddeford.	9	1,410	56,865	322,487	758,910	884	2,080	5.7	70,719	104	5,136	246,904	1,826,410
Massachusetts	79	15,865	838,080	4,168,038	9,554,851	11,424	26,176	5.0	624,172	1,112	72,707	3,092,821	22,299,805
Nonmetropolitan	2	44	1,921	6,992	49,995	19	137	3.6	2,693	10	238	23,300	140,115
Metropolitan	77	15,821	836,159	4,161,046	9,504,856	11,405	26,039	5.0	621,479	1,102	72,469	3,069,521	22,159,690
Barnstable Town	3	414	23,291	104,839	251,239	286	689	4.5	13,968	18	1,305	127,477	907,054
Boston-Cambridge-Quincy.	47	10,458	566,812	2,812,283	6,495,441	7,707	17,794	5.0	418,946	728	49,208	1,752,921	14,173,878
Pittsfield.	3	338	15,577	76,448	209,660	210	574	4.9	16,095	26	1,110	88,751	620,333
Providence-New Bedford-Fall River	4	1,174	63,514	298,139	647,141	817	1,773	4.7	41,068	69	4,683	294,593	1,514,382
Springfield	11	1,849	77,603	443,913	915,862	1,218	2,509	5.7	59,189	114	7,390	386,781	2,370,497
Worcester.	9	1,588	89,362	425,424	985,513	1,167	2,700	4.8	72,213	147	8,773	418,998	2,573,546
New Hampshire	28	2,840	122,341	634,954	1,778,453	1,738	4,872	5.2	125,629	272	12,649	677,358	4,995,907
Nonmetropolitan	17	1,302	55,653	316,027	972,864	864	2,665	5.7	64,177	117	4,638	270,452	2,740,632
Metropolitan	11	1,538	66,688	318,927	805,589	874	2,207	4.8	61,452	155	8,011	406,906	2,255,275
Manchester-Nashua	5	847	38,691	182,544	480,913	500	1,317	4.7	31,096	96	5,285	187,669	1,281,154
Rockingham County-Strafford County	6	691	27,997	136,383	324,676	374	890	4.9	30,356	59	2,726	219,237	974,121
Rhode Island.	11	2,468	120,407	611,837	1,245,104	1,677	3,411	5.1	100,169	147	11,249	542,625	2,241,650
Metropolitan	11	2,468	120,407	611,837	1,245,104	1,677	3,411	5.1	100,169	147	11,249	542,625	2,241,650
Providence-New Bedford-Fall River	11	2,468	120,407	611,837	1,245,104	1,677	3,411	5.1	100,169	147	11,249	542,625	2,241,650
Vermont	14	1,218	48,941	310,510	1,098,324	850	3,008	6.3	61,639	110	12,755	296,666	3,084,858
Nonmetropolitan	12	779	27,496	192,394	661,176	526	1,811	7.0	36,656	79	9,972	217,379	1,660,559
Metropolitan	2	439	21,445	118,116	437,148	324	1,197	5.5	24,983	31	2,783	79,287	1,424,299
Burlington-South Burlington	2	439	21,445	118,116	437,148	324	1,197	5.5	24,983	31	2,783	79,287	1,424,299

MSAs

TABLE 8

U.S. CENSUS DIVISION 1, NEW ENGLAND

U.S. Community Hospitals
(Nonfederal, short-term general and other special hospitals)

2011 Utilization, Personnel and Finances

FULL-TIME EQUIVALENT PERSONNEL					FULL-TIME EQUIV. TRAINEES			EXPENSES						
								LABOR				TOTAL		
Physicians and Dentists	Registered Nurses	Licensed Practical Nurses	Other Salaried Personnel	Total Personnel	Medical and Dental Residents	Other Trainees	Total Trainees	Payroll (in thousands)	Employee Benefits (in thousands)	Total (in thousands)	Percent of Total	Amount (in thousands)	Adjusted per Admission	Adjusted per Inpatient Day
111,741	1,313,626	85,820	3,138,428	4,649,615	99,458	8,198	107,656	$283,964,687	$76,727,241	$360,691,957	51.4	$702,091,034	$10,532.52	$1,959.58
14,153	157,107	25,812	467,855	664,927	1,988	339	2,327	34,086,208	9,249,087	43,335,308	53.7	80,718,425	7,197.79	1,151.32
97,588	1,156,519	60,008	2,670,573	3,984,688	97,470	7,859	105,329	249,878,479	67,478,154	317,356,649	51.1	621,372,609	11,207.00	2,156.22
12,431	66,638	2,475	200,347	281,891	8,287	1,480	9,767	18,903,672	5,077,437	23,981,110	52.7	45,537,928	11,636.95	2,299.50
1,704	7,475	553	24,994	34,726	423	14	437	2,296,185	640,429	2,936,612	57.1	5,147,420	10,640.97	1,803.11
10,727	59,163	1,922	175,353	247,165	7,864	1,466	9,330	16,607,487	4,437,008	21,044,498	52.1	40,390,508	11,777.44	2,383.11
1,149	14,628	374	38,226	54,377	1,449	228	1,677	4,028,938	1,183,479	5,212,418	54.5	9,561,577	12,320.89	2,400.84
53	580	46	1,908	2,587	2	1	3	212,330	62,605	274,935	57.1	481,232	8,965.00	2,090.34
1,096	14,048	328	36,318	51,790	1,447	227	1,674	3,816,608	1,120,874	4,937,483	54.4	9,080,345	12,570.26	2,419.89
252	2,817	40	8,142	11,251	393	12	405	931,265	286,349	1,217,615	54.8	2,220,058	12,434.86	2,373.54
589	4,867	103	14,555	20,114	125	163	288	1,455,785	427,999	1,883,784	56.0	3,364,290	13,225.87	2,570.51
206	5,807	157	11,282	17,452	929	27	956	1,178,345	340,421	1,518,766	51.0	2,976,433	12,898.39	2,410.29
49	557	28	2,339	2,973	0	25	25	251,213	66,105	317,318	61.1	519,564	8,851.17	1,900.69
1,500	6,715	270	21,191	29,676	298	5	303	1,843,328	469,036	2,312,363	55.6	4,160,649	10,921.25	1,940.51
513	2,489	122	8,509	11,633	5	2	7	665,943	166,041	831,985	57.0	1,458,538	9,709.35	1,550.81
987	4,226	148	12,682	18,043	293	3	290	1,177,385	302,994	1,480,378	54.8	2,702,110	11,710.22	2,245.02
255	1,190	33	2,670	4,148	27	2	29	283,967	70,336	354,302	51.4	689,748	11,997.92	2,665.08
191	721	48	2,500	3,460	20	0	20	204,274	41,475	245,750	55.2	445,344	10,944.80	2,395.86
541	2,315	67	7,512	10,436	246	1	247	689,140	191,184	880,326	56.2	1,567,018	11,820.39	2,064.83
7,176	33,140	1,173	102,197	143,686	5,032	1,161	6,193	9,151,801	2,292,461	11,444,266	49.6	23,068,836	11,586.88	2,414.36
24	87	12	323	446	0	0	0	41,804	9,133	50,936	57.5	88,659	6,249.75	1,773.36
7,152	33,053	1,161	101,874	143,240	5,032	1,101	6,193	9,109,997	2,283,328	11,393,330	49.6	22,980,177	11,625.18	2,417.73
54	541	11	1,708	2,314	0	0	0	216,449	70,281	286,730	53.9	531,588	9,250.64	2,115.87
5,651	23,615	737	72,847	102,850	4,099	1,079	5,178	6,648,951	1,627,903	8,276,917	48.1	17,194,748	12,779.47	2,647.20
88	623	51	1,881	2,643	78	7	85	191,352	50,801	242,154	59.2	400,180	9,401.01	1,951.68
70	1,017	00	5,076	7,131	6	2	8	480,190	131,007	611,197	59.0	1,036,264	7,375.86	1,601.30
564	3,433	122	9,948	14,067	343	4	347	705,572	160,708	866,280	52.8	1,640,858	9,511.78	1,791.60
725	2,924	172	10,414	14,235	506	69	575	867,484	242,568	1,110,052	51.2	2,167,530	9,976.30	2,199.39
1,122	5,845	338	19,118	26,423	415	8	423	1,708,237	514,945	2,223,181	56.3	3,948,270	11,493.77	2,220.06
791	3,144	224	9,984	14,143	407	8	415	976,349	288,713	1,265,002	56.6	2,235,452	13,135.88	2,297.80
331	2,701	114	9,134	12,280	8	0	8	731,888	226,232	958,119	55.9	1,712,819	9,881.55	2,126.17
267	1,475	52	5,441	7,235	3	0	3	407,788	133,970	541,757	57.5	941,458	9,107.21	1,957.65
64	1,226	62	3,693	5,045	5	0	5	324,100	92,262	416,362	54.0	771,361	11,025.74	2,375.79
656	3,795	99	11,372	15,922	786	3	789	1,321,532	380,726	1,702,258	56.3	3,021,868	12,257.56	2,427.00
656	3,795	99	11,372	15,922	786	3	789	1,321,532	380,726	1,702,258	56.3	3,021,868	12,257.56	2,427.00
656	3,795	99	11,372	15,922	786	3	789	1,321,532	380,726	1,702,258	56.3	3,021,868	12,257.56	2,427.00
828	2,515	221	8,243	11,807	307	75	382	849,836	236,789	1,086,624	61.2	1,776,728	10,140.39	1,617.67
323	1,175	149	4,270	5,917	9	3	12	399,759	113,937	513,694	58.1	883,538	9,254.42	1,336.31
505	1,340	72	3,973	5,890	298	72	370	450,077	122,852	572,930	64.1	893,190	11,201.14	2,043.22
505	1,340	72	3,973	5,890	298	72	370	450,077	122,852	572,930	64.1	893,190	11,201.14	2,043.22

MSAs

TABLE 8

U.S. CENSUS DIVISION 2, MIDDLE ATLANTIC

U.S. Community Hospitals
(Nonfederal, short-term general and other special hospitals)

2011 Utilization, Personnel and Finances

MSAs

CLASSIFICATION	Hospitals	Beds	Admissions	Inpatient Days	Adjusted Patient Days	Average Daily Census	Adjusted Average Daily Census	Average Stay (days)	Surgical Operations	NEWBORNS Bassinets	NEWBORNS Births	OUTPATIENT VISITS Emergency	OUTPATIENT VISITS Total
UNITED STATES	4,973	797,403	34,843,085	187,072,013	358,286,020	512,944	982,377	5.4	26,907,712	56,290	3,730,342	129,461,658	656,078,942
Nonmetropolitan	1,984	133,716	4,192,377	26,166,177	70,109,403	71,710	192,165	6.2	4,127,991	10,856	454,761	23,737,253	123,877,956
Metropolitan	2,989	663,687	30,650,708	160,905,836	288,176,617	441,234	790,212	5.2	22,779,721	45,434	3,275,581	105,724,405	532,200,986
CENSUS DIVISION 2, MIDDLE ATLANTIC.	449	118,152	5,308,422	31,927,960	56,130,387	87,515	153,823	6.0	3,997,442	6,461	473,951	18,128,050	107,738,878
Nonmetropolitan	85	10,648	355,348	2,525,068	6,465,013	6,920	17,713	7.1	366,882	666	28,365	1,846,827	12,778,630
Metropolitan	364	107,504	4,953,074	29,402,892	49,665,374	80,595	136,110	5.9	3,630,560	5,795	445,586	16,281,223	94,960,248
New Jersey	73	20,396	1,050,828	5,344,077	8,185,752	14,644	22,430	5.1	624,499	1,412	101,362	3,474,457	15,825,299
Metropolitan	73	20,396	1,050,828	5,344,077	8,185,752	14,644	22,430	5.1	624,499	1,412	101,362	3,474,457	15,825,299
Allentown-Bethlehem-Easton	2	251	11,789	49,025	104,821	134	287	4.2	16,814	12	802	43,521	195,168
Atlantic City	3	824	41,861	198,158	248,295	543	680	4.7	17,060	56	3,751	147,664	447,205
Camden	10	2,913	146,901	713,580	1,066,924	1,956	2,923	4.9	78,702	145	12,754	574,234	1,511,393
Edison	17	4,964	253,179	1,331,027	1,999,162	3,648	5,479	5.3	141,824	401	25,518	796,926	2,697,908
New York-White Plains-Wayne . . .	12	3,906	236,902	1,050,355	1,599,884	2,878	4,384	4.4	133,609	307	23,375	660,836	5,044,654
Newark-Union	18	5,494	262,282	1,506,453	2,301,469	4,128	6,307	5.7	162,464	336	26,047	877,547	3,893,191
Ocean City	1	180	9,705	35,832	62,149	98	170	3.7	4,318	16	537	46,658	150,865
Trenton-Ewing	6	1,301	60,168	323,985	561,868	887	1,539	5.4	47,580	91	5,385	200,730	1,462,103
Vineland-Millville-Bridgeton	2	365	18,523	96,498	170,357	265	467	5.2	14,684	24	2,046	84,661	305,360
Wilmington	2	198	9,518	39,164	70,823	107	194	4.1	7,444	24	1,147	41,680	117,452
New York	182	58,080	2,491,403	16,924,697	29,961,118	46,369	82,086	6.8	1,950,744	3,154	239,622	8,432,260	54,010,880
Nonmetropolitan	37	4,945	150,660	1,281,072	3,411,831	3,509	9,347	8.5	167,579	293	13,576	705,167	5,719,112
Metropolitan	145	53,135	2,340,743	15,643,625	26,549,287	42,860	72,739	6.7	1,783,165	2,861	226,046	7,727,093	48,291,768
Albany-Schenectady-Troy	9	2,508	109,085	702,513	1,389,917	1,924	3,809	6.4	90,953	87	8,957	340,812	2,530,247
Binghamton	2	614	26,864	143,846	375,862	394	1,029	5.4	34,898	46	2,772	102,934	1,806,570
Buffalo-Niagara Falls	11	4,739	155,874	1,435,961	2,399,449	3,934	6,573	9.2	158,468	215	12,374	509,630	2,930,059
Elmira	2	456	16,079	117,609	277,337	323	760	7.3	11,385	20	1,518	63,898	486,116
Glens Falls	1	300	17,136	81,309	139,444	223	382	4.7	15,387	22	1,390	53,213	764,338
Ithaca	1	190	6,325	29,425	91,469	81	251	4.7	6,734	19	836	31,843	253,390
Kingston	3	295	14,720	79,531	120,801	218	331	5.4	6,857	20	521	47,990	310,412
Nassau-Suffolk	24	8,901	413,917	2,768,556	4,355,648	7,586	11,934	6.7	320,364	473	36,198	1,118,822	5,700,395
New York-White Plains-Wayne . . .	63	27,580	1,266,355	8,224,855	13,400,270	22,534	36,715	6.5	866,365	1,456	130,336	4,216,229	23,241,895
Poughkeepsie-Newburgh-Middle-town	7	1,518	70,971	382,572	622,261	1,048	1,704	5.4	51,711	97	6,887	260,213	973,219
Rochester	11	3,088	126,365	899,070	1,853,828	2,463	5,078	7.1	120,235	203	12,648	628,632	6,042,180
Syracuse	6	1,970	80,216	519,628	917,774	1,423	2,514	6.5	69,109	131	7,886	226,603	1,991,699
Utica-Rome	5	976	36,836	258,750	605,227	709	1,659	7.0	30,699	72	3,723	126,274	1,261,248
Pennsylvania	194	39,676	1,766,191	9,659,186	17,983,517	26,502	49,307	5.5	1,422,199	1,895	132,967	6,221,333	37,902,699
Nonmetropolitan	48	5,703	204,688	1,243,996	3,053,182	3,411	8,366	6.1	199,303	373	14,789	1,141,660	7,059,518
Metropolitan	146	33,973	1,561,503	8,415,190	14,930,335	23,091	40,941	5.4	1,222,896	1,522	118,178	5,079,673	30,843,181
Allentown-Bethlehem-Easton	9	2,283	114,369	621,486	1,142,666	1,702	3,131	5.4	68,850	86	8,378	381,739	1,909,757
Altoona	4	583	23,402	124,559	250,049	341	685	5.3	24,159	30	1,670	87,781	558,834
Erie	7	1,223	43,777	240,232	413,252	658	1,132	5.5	32,886	51	3,525	147,044	607,615
Harrisburg-Carlisle	9	1,796	79,847	424,934	746,900	1,182	2,063	5.3	70,551	74	7,221	286,184	1,544,149
Johnstown	3	594	26,451	151,894	280,245	416	767	5.7	26,169	14	1,293	80,278	541,755
Lancaster	4	1,046	48,924	242,157	448,034	664	1,227	4.9	51,072	63	5,093	187,699	1,877,022
Lebanon	1	158	8,983	42,460	92,993	116	255	4.7	9,271	19	884	53,789	268,138
Philadelphia	45	12,487	621,527	3,240,611	5,320,013	8,879	14,577	5.2	448,227	631	49,804	1,835,158	9,656,110
Pittsburgh	36	8,980	387,472	2,215,875	3,895,968	6,089	10,693	5.7	339,502	304	22,210	1,160,360	7,990,527
Reading	3	951	40,718	221,378	409,304	607	1,122	5.4	25,707	56	4,295	168,172	1,389,667
Scranton--Wilkes-Barre	13	1,834	79,061	413,851	817,288	1,134	2,238	5.2	51,062	65	6,135	327,352	2,052,602
State College	2	278	12,930	61,515	114,462	169	314	4.8	10,549	5	1,291	49,899	241,063
Williamsport	3	405	13,549	103,805	275,652	285	756	7.7	20,996	22	1,092	79,867	284,555
York-Hanover	4	820	40,190	205,565	446,691	562	1,224	5.1	23,204	73	3,974	148,375	1,270,131
Youngstown-Warren-Boardman . .	3	535	20,303	104,868	276,818	287	757	5.2	20,691	29	1,313	85,976	651,256

TABLE 8

U.S. CENSUS DIVISION 2, MIDDLE ATLANTIC

U.S. Community Hospitals
(Nonfederal, short-term general and other special hospitals)

2011 Utilization, Personnel and Finances

FULL-TIME EQUIVALENT PERSONNEL					FULL-TIME EQUIV. TRAINEES			EXPENSES						
								LABOR				TOTAL		
Physicians and Dentists	Registered Nurses	Licensed Practical Nurses	Other Salaried Personnel	Total Personnel	Medical and Dental Residents	Other Trainees	Total Trainees	Payroll (in thousands)	Employee Benefits (in thousands)	Total (in thousands)	Percent of Total	Amount (in thousands)	Adjusted per Admission	Adjusted per Inpatient Day
111,741	1,313,626	85,820	3,138,428	4,649,615	99,458	8,198	107,656	$283,964,687	$76,727,241	$360,691,957	51.4	$702,091,034	$10,532.52	$1,959.58
14,153	157,107	25,812	467,855	664,927	1,988	339	2,327	34,086,208	9,249,087	43,335,308	53.7	80,718,425	7,197.79	1,151.32
97,588	1,156,519	60,008	2,670,573	3,984,688	97,470	7,859	105,329	249,878,479	67,478,154	317,356,649	51.1	621,372,609	11,207.00	2,156.22
25,037	195,142	10,917	504,687	735,783	27,445	1,151	28,596	47,408,891	13,592,987	61,001,881	54.5	112,027,433	12,018.53	1,995.84
1,404	11,988	2,018	38,160	53,570	626	21	647	2,772,578	762,633	3,535,212	53.3	6,634,637	7,213.45	1,026.24
23,633	183,154	8,899	466,527	682,213	26,819	1,130	27,949	44,636,313	12,830,354	57,466,669	54.5	105,392,797	12,544.57	2,122.06
2,079	34,323	1,038	82,003	120,043	2,437	61	2,408	7,017,765	1,063,739	9,001,507	54.2	18,237,578	11,295.93	2,227.97
2,679	34,323	1,038	82,003	120,043	2,437	61	2,498	7,917,765	1,963,739	9,881,507	54.2	18,237,578	11,295.93	2,227.97
26	436	31	1,255	1,748	21	0	21	84,687	21,982	106,670	51.3	207,816	8,270.65	1,982.58
86	1,652	26	3,420	5,184	41	1	42	358,548	100,101	458,648	54.7	838,158	16,216.98	3,375.65
593	4,286	119	10,623	15,621	298	0	298	950,489	256,126	1,206,615	49.5	2,437,647	11,194.55	2,284.74
349	8,579	271	18,734	27,933	419	9	428	1,781,839	450,447	2,232,286	52.7	4,239,766	11,182.70	2,120.77
697	7,182	158	18,380	26,417	421	17	438	1,815,548	405,101	2,220,650	55.2	4,023,596	11,110.12	2,514.93
717	9,232	261	21,904	32,114	1,093	28	1,121	2,230,062	541,313	2,771,376	57.4	4,830,863	11,960.28	2,099.03
0	232	3	634	869	0	2	2	47,918	17,654	65,573	60.7	108,095	6,421.60	1,739.28
207	2,016	89	5,481	7,793	102	4	106	464,339	114,170	578,509	51.6	1,122,042	10,509.36	1,996.99
0	456	50	1,055	1,561	39	0	39	133,647	42,845	176,493	57.4	307,587	9,060.54	1,805.54
4	252	30	517	803	3	0	3	50,687	14,001	64,687	53.0	122,007	7,067.67	1,722.71
15,047	93,186	6,114	262,100	376,447	16,489	505	16,994	26,100,546	7,952,736	34,053,280	58.2	58,543,389	13,311.02	1,953.98
735	4,750	996	17,249	23,730	86	4	90	1,307,017	330,466	1,637,481	59.1	2,770,499	6,791.34	812.03
14,312	88,436	5,118	244,851	352,717	16,403	501	16,904	24,793,530	7,622,271	32,415,799	58.1	55,772,890	13,977.58	2,100.73
375	3,699	266	10,618	14,958	229	17	246	870,234	173,794	1,044,027	51.3	2,034,174	9,647.63	1,463.52
142	1,327	112	3,299	4,880	80	8	88	271,893	70,259	342,153	52.2	655,601	8,893.12	1,744.26
439	6,514	300	15,338	22,591	316	91	407	1,409,531	524,567	1,934,097	57.1	3,389,444	13,006.76	1,412.59
50	694	67	1,769	2,500	23	2	25	155,651	47,671	203,322	66.3	306,821	7,617.01	1,100.01
56	750	33	1,682	2,521	27	3	30	138,285	37,899	176,184	60.5	291,370	9,914.59	2,089.51
9	300	4	757	1,070	0	0	0	55,120	19,965	75,085	43.9	171,195	8,706.91	1,871.62
3	484	31	1,124	1,642	5	1	6	79,999	20,616	100,616	50.0	201,352	9,112.61	1,666.81
3,828	15,956	599	49,100	69,483	3,304	33	3,337	4,346,804	1,228,117	5,574,920	59.3	9,393,689	14,406.44	2,156.67
8,195	45,900	2,425	129,233	185,753	11,320	289	11,609	14,706,929	4,658,873	19,365,804	58.9	32,899,614	15,758.53	2,455.15
99	2,318	74	4,712	7,203	36	4	40	476,946	160,581	637,526	51.7	1,232,446	10,695.16	1,980.59
904	6,013	574	15,672	23,163	644	9	653	1,255,253	341,579	1,596,832	57.0	2,799,147	10,567.85	1,600.03
112	3,060	446	7,484	11,102	388	42	430	735,480	248,556	984,037	56.7	1,734,022	12,907.23	1,890.25
100	1,421	187	4,063	5,771	31	2	33	291,402	89,794	381,196	57.5	663,211	8,364.89	1,095.80
7,311	67,633	3,765	160,584	239,293	8,519	585	9,104	13,390,580	3,676,512	17,067,094	48.4	35,246,467	10,653.03	1,959.93
669	7,238	1,022	20,911	29,840	540	17	557	1,465,561	432,167	1,897,731	40.1	3,864,138	7,549.90	1,205.61
6,642	60,395	2,743	139,673	209,453	7,979	568	8,547	11,925,018	3,244,345	15,169,363	40.3	31,382,329	11,220.90	2,101.92
566	4,508	139	9,649	14,862	449	72	521	783,211	226,996	1,010,207	49.7	2,031,372	10,130.83	1,777.75
33	879	84	1,785	2,781	23	0	23	159,740	47,473	207,212	53.2	389,812	7,793.44	1,558.94
123	1,837	77	3,496	5,533	80	16	96	266,979	78,551	345,530	45.9	752,478	9,955.91	1,820.87
794	3,403	284	9,512	13,993	872	115	987	722,137	192,246	914,382	51.8	1,765,634	12,617.44	2,363.95
17	989	95	2,504	3,605	82	0	82	158,669	45,825	204,494	50.6	404,522	8,187.54	1,443.46
177	1,911	156	5,466	7,710	51	3	54	438,017	146,178	584,196	53.9	1,084,684	11,795.18	2,420.99
23	245	26	914	1,208	0	0	0	54,538	17,379	71,918	45.6	157,562	8,008.64	1,694.34
3,182	24,336	569	53,357	81,444	4,723	269	4,992	5,527,996	1,430,969	6,958,964	50.1	13,891,328	13,448.31	2,611.15
1,343	15,159	545	34,043	51,090	1,316	81	1,397	2,348,474	610,596	2,959,072	42.6	6,950,614	9,873.10	1,784.05
250	1,471	140	4,652	6,513	90	0	90	346,080	115,264	461,344	53.9	855,806	11,260.61	2,090.88
43	2,441	298	6,335	9,117	75	10	85	450,008	113,030	563,038	43.6	1,292,020	8,120.45	1,580.86
3	401	22	977	1,403	0	0	0	103,273	27,691	130,964	51.8	252,651	10,050.16	2,207.29
8	523	103	1,114	1,748	28	0	28	97,971	26,957	124,927	48.5	257,584	8,528.41	934.45
54	1,615	141	4,046	5,856	182	0	182	348,521	125,850	474,371	49.7	955,376	10,768.32	2,138.78
26	677	64	1,823	2,590	8	2	10	119,404	39,340	158,744	46.6	340,886	6,362.55	1,231.45

MSAs

TABLE 8   U.S. CENSUS DIVISION 3, SOUTH ATLANTIC

U.S. Community Hospitals
(Nonfederal, short-term general and other special hospitals)

2011 Utilization, Personnel and Finances

MSAs

CLASSIFICATION	Hospitals	Beds	Admissions	Inpatient Days	Adjusted Patient Days	Average Daily Census	Adjusted Average Daily Census	Average Stay (days)	Surgical Operations	NEWBORNS Bassinets	NEWBORNS Births	OUTPATIENT VISITS Emergency	OUTPATIENT VISITS Total
UNITED STATES	4,973	797,403	34,843,085	187,072,013	358,286,020	512,944	982,377	5.4	26,907,712	56,290	3,730,342	129,461,658	656,078,942
Nonmetropolitan	1,984	133,716	4,192,377	26,166,177	70,109,403	71,710	192,165	6.2	4,127,991	10,856	454,761	23,737,253	123,877,956
Metropolitan	2,989	663,687	30,650,708	160,905,836	288,176,617	441,234	790,212	5.2	22,779,721	45,434	3,275,581	105,724,405	532,200,986
CENSUS DIVISION 3, SOUTH ATLANTIC.	759	156,421	6,995,044	37,874,666	69,881,716	103,789	191,532	5.4	5,208,006	10,343	691,803	25,719,396	98,184,734
Nonmetropolitan	244	24,041	831,301	5,146,103	12,123,800	14,099	33,233	6.2	741,532	1,801	76,987	4,644,532	17,375,990
Metropolitan	515	132,380	6,163,743	32,728,563	57,757,916	89,690	158,299	5.3	4,466,474	8,542	614,816	21,074,864	80,808,744
Delaware	7	2,143	100,288	578,466	1,073,859	1,585	2,942	5.8	94,470	85	11,496	417,689	1,850,646
Nonmetropolitan	2	404	13,945	94,471	223,150	259	611	6.8	15,471	24	1,691	86,129	567,746
Metropolitan	5	1,739	86,343	483,995	850,709	1,326	2,331	5.6	78,999	61	9,805	331,560	1,282,900
Dover	1	310	17,524	90,699	189,883	248	520	5.2	13,117	12	2,322	77,309	463,646
Wilmington	4	1,429	68,819	393,296	660,826	1,078	1,811	5.7	65,882	49	7,483	254,251	819,254
District of Columbia	11	3,635	131,577	954,752	1,578,564	2,615	4,324	7.3	103,244	195	13,792	455,553	2,450,100
Metropolitan	11	3,635	131,577	954,752	1,578,564	2,615	4,324	7.3	103,244	195	13,792	455,553	2,450,100
Washington-Arlington-Alexandria. .	11	3,635	131,577	954,752	1,578,564	2,615	4,324	7.3	103,244	195	13,792	455,553	2,450,100
Florida	213	52,923	2,508,311	12,365,513	20,406,222	33,902	55,979	4.9	1,397,597	2,782	186,919	7,580,718	24,408,698
Nonmetropolitan	29	1,946	108,685	411,347	863,122	1,129	2,378	3.8	61,749	97	5,637	427,286	1,500,505
Metropolitan	184	50,977	2,399,626	11,954,166	19,543,100	32,773	53,601	5.0	1,335,848	2,685	181,282	7,153,432	22,908,193
Cape Coral-Fort Myers	4	1,563	79,285	412,300	729,848	1,129	2,000	5.2	41,814	129	6,403	163,080	1,423,389
Deltona-Daytona Beach-Ormond Beach	5	1,421	56,791	265,172	485,080	726	1,329	4.7	37,615	59	4,096	301,304	755,608
Fort Lauderdale-Pompano Beach-Deerfield Beach	19	5,526	248,654	1,205,544	1,981,622	3,303	5,429	4.8	119,560	246	20,121	869,890	2,237,460
Fort Walton Beach-Crestview-Destin	3	424	21,908	92,989	151,725	255	416	4.2	12,803	32	1,519	80,723	202,419
Gainesville	3	1,332	66,694	373,196	550,283	1,023	1,508	5.6	52,047	38	5,753	97,687	889,521
Jacksonville	14	3,929	183,569	977,089	1,586,048	2,677	4,347	5.3	132,744	294	14,774	606,318	1,757,921
Lakeland	5	1,704	74,001	327,197	574,270	895	1,574	4.4	38,069	51	5,079	273,429	616,716
Miami-Miami Beach-Kendall	26	7,587	325,848	1,761,997	2,764,953	4,854	7,628	5.4	152,494	273	20,066	941,225	2,869,400
Naples-Marco Island	2	751	34,730	157,903	241,320	432	661	4.5	14,136	36	3,033	108,232	345,948
North Port-Bradenton-Sarasota. . .	8	1,855	78,083	370,912	615,847	1,015	1,686	4.8	45,462	59	5,199	273,708	946,673
Ocala	3	721	38,296	168,116	273,529	461	750	4.4	19,868	26	2,668	139,819	258,962
Orlando-Kissimmee	11	5,528	299,728	1,484,679	2,352,247	4,067	6,445	5.0	164,879	459	27,731	953,480	2,340,927
Palm Bay-Melbourne-Titusville . . .	6	1,318	59,425	303,338	534,779	831	1,465	5.1	33,939	100	5,022	169,642	717,372
Palm Coast.	1	99	6,270	25,326	55,923	69	153	4.0	4,521	0	0	38,893	144,639
Panama City-Lynn Haven	4	554	28,852	143,800	251,349	394	689	5.0	18,577	28	2,525	114,318	312,136
Pensacola-Ferry Pass-Brent	7	1,435	67,859	318,414	584,567	873	1,602	4.7	43,012	69	4,771	291,204	1,098,009
Port St. Lucie-Fort Pierce	3	876	46,655	211,993	347,261	581	951	4.5	26,018	50	1,818	142,099	233,155
Punta Gorda	3	636	28,205	138,815	212,184	381	582	4.9	20,839	8	1,143	68,253	150,991
Sebastian-Vero Beach	3	425	20,828	100,524	165,033	276	452	4.8	12,329	22	1,140	67,602	196,458
Tallahassee	4	792	40,307	204,997	370,321	562	1,014	5.1	23,345	62	4,688	104,261	518,531
Tampa-St. Petersburg-Clearwater .	36	8,770	407,906	2,038,924	3,258,192	5,584	8,928	5.0	232,269	463	28,851	896,552	3,494,585
West Palm Beach-Boca Raton-Boynton Beach	14	3,731	185,732	870,941	1,456,699	2,385	3,992	4.7	89,508	181	14,882	451,713	1,397,373
Georgia	153	25,282	956,503	6,094,960	12,155,641	16,701	33,299	6.4	759,963	1,927	123,546	4,035,426	14,775,721
Nonmetropolitan	65	6,276	146,880	1,424,291	3,474,955	3,905	9,519	9.7	152,462	387	17,898	920,034	3,193,162
Metropolitan	88	19,006	809,623	4,670,669	8,680,686	12,796	23,780	5.8	607,501	1,540	105,648	3,115,392	11,582,559
Albany.	3	567	22,399	121,072	275,765	332	755	5.4	16,840	42	2,814	105,850	785,194
Athens-Clarke County	2	524	27,278	120,968	243,748	331	668	4.4	23,841	44	3,998	107,863	342,980
Atlanta-Sandy Springs-Marietta . .	44	9,906	446,578	2,587,671	4,775,626	7,090	13,084	5.8	315,425	862	64,765	1,634,045	5,976,406
Augusta-Richmond County	8	1,608	63,060	365,738	620,213	1,002	1,698	5.8	74,107	124	6,616	270,749	1,087,166
Brunswick.	1	510	11,848	127,973	255,637	351	700	10.8	7,556	20	1,322	55,705	181,527
Chattanooga	2	198	6,342	64,871	140,102	178	384	10.2	6,858	15	742	24,638	100,917
Columbus.	5	1,131	37,541	216,600	424,157	593	1,162	5.8	25,703	31	4,354	143,611	366,284
Dalton	2	249	10,330	40,763	80,431	111	221	3.9	4,671	40	1,876	80,260	255,160
Gainesville	1	513	27,361	117,824	188,517	323	516	4.3	17,936	63	3,432	101,758	324,482
Hinesville-Fort Stewart	1	133	2,249	6,989	24,089	19	66	3.1	400	6	400	28,000	30,000
Macon	6	1,106	46,268	270,457	441,007	742	1,208	5.8	33,366	96	3,479	114,947	512,651
Rome	3	578	26,825	135,677	243,646	371	667	5.1	20,073	30	2,374	107,263	322,539
Savannah	5	1,215	50,846	323,881	608,864	887	1,668	6.4	40,385	71	5,659	185,794	772,016
Valdosta	3	492	14,843	98,412	201,148	269	551	6.6	10,703	62	1,634	72,669	257,473
Warner Robins	2	276	15,855	71,773	157,736	197	432	4.5	9,637	34	2,183	82,240	267,764

TABLE **8**

U.S. CENSUS DIVISION 3, SOUTH ATLANTIC

U.S. Community Hospitals
(Nonfederal, short-term general and other special hospitals)

2011 Utilization, Personnel and Finances

Physicians and Dentists	Registered Nurses	Licensed Practical Nurses	Other Salaried Personnel	Total Personnel	Medical and Dental Residents	Other Trainees	Total Trainees	Payroll (in thousands)	Employee Benefits (in thousands)	Total (in thousands)	Percent of Total	Amount (in thousands)	Adjusted per Admission	Adjusted per Inpatient Day
111,741	1,313,626	85,820	3,138,428	4,649,615	99,458	8,198	107,656	$283,964,687	$76,727,241	$360,691,957	51.4	$702,091,034	$10,532.52	$1,959.58
14,153	157,107	25,812	467,855	664,927	1,988	339	2,327	34,086,208	9,249,087	43,335,308	53.7	80,718,425	7,197.79	1,151.32
97,588	1,156,519	60,008	2,670,573	3,984,688	97,470	7,859	105,329	249,878,479	67,478,154	317,356,649	51.1	621,372,609	11,207.00	2,156.22
14,797	254,253	14,911	566,489	850,450	16,162	716	16,878	48,645,056	11,997,332	60,642,384	49.7	122,100,283	9,516.15	1,747.24
1,560	27,759	4,136	76,013	100,468	210	47	263	5,255,706	1,364,671	6,620,377	52.1	12,712,896	6,539.14	1,048.59
13,237	226,494	10,775	490,476	740,982	15,946	669	16,615	43,389,350	10,632,661	54,022,007	49.4	109,387,386	10,047.77	1,893.89
436	4,953	239	11,354	16,982	271	3	274	1,050,076	330,635	1,380,712	57.3	2,408,076	13,202.97	2,242.45
48	717	16	1,586	2,367	0	0	0	130,635	48,827	179,462	51.2	350,210	11,364.91	1,569.39
388	4,236	223	9,768	14,615	271	3	274	919,440	281,809	1,201,250	58.4	2,057,866	13,576.64	2,419.00
39	714	51	1,874	2,678	0	0	0	156,981	51,410	208,391	56.4	369,193	10,063.31	1,944.32
349	3,522	172	7,894	11,937	271	3	274	762,459	230,399	992,859	58.8	1,688,674	14,698.56	2,555.40
1,559	6,257	232	15,739	23,787	1,266	24	1,290	1,684,797	337,049	2,021,845	53.7	3,766,314	17,473.12	2,385.91
1,559	6,257	232	15,739	23,787	1,266	24	1,290	1,684,797	337,049	2,021,845	53.7	3,766,314	17,473.12	2,385.91
1,559	6,257	232	15,739	23,787	1,266	24	1,290	1,684,797	337,049	2,021,845	53.7	3,766,314	17,473.12	2,385.91
3,900	80,324	3,984	165,840	254,053	5,223	244	5,467	14,805,504	3,584,826	18,390,330	49.8	36,908,773	8,805.45	1,808.70
144	2,551	318	6,535	9,548	15	5	20	478,556	122,586	601,144	51.4	1,169,561	5,102.79	1,355.04
3,761	77,773	3,666	159,305	244,505	5,208	239	5,447	14,326,947	3,462,240	17,789,186	49.8	35,739,212	9,019.63	1,828.74
256	2,770	172	6,705	9,903	528	34	562	591,469	178,583	770,052	55.5	1,388,470	9,825.94	1,899.67
155	1,915	149	4,736	6,955	51	4	55	358,112	98,658	456,770	57.4	795,661	7,593.13	1,640.27
480	7,506	226	13,732	21,944	291	44	335	1,453,334	288,888	1,742,221	53.9	3,234,213	7,787.79	1,632.10
10	509	41	959	1,519	13	0	13	73,248	16,301	89,549	46.6	192,291	5,301.36	1,267.37
14	2,460	80	5,738	8,292	598	17	615	467,546	120,089	587,635	48.2	1,218,120	12,360.80	2,213.62
458	6,411	208	12,046	19,123	538	55	593	985,917	318,499	1,304,415	46.2	2,820,516	9,233.30	1,778.33
24	2,531	105	5,594	8,344	5	0	5	386,707	90,133	476,840	52.5	908,776	6,994.24	1,582.49
514	11,728	580	24,354	37,176	1,438	5	1,443	2,415,575	531,193	2,946,768	52.3	5,630,541	10,869.20	2,036.38
5	1,127	57	2,039	3,228	0	0	0	178,128	33,430	211,558	51.8	408,340	7,691.03	1,692.11
20	2,293	173	4,849	7,335	37	0	37	404,424	103,363	507,786	51.1	993,961	7,604.38	1,613.97
20	1,247	58	2,300	3,625	14	1	15	188,012	38,556	226,567	49.7	455,926	7,276.19	1,666.83
526	12,252	393	24,540	37,711	476	4	480	1,920,365	469,540	2,389,904	45.6	5,239,229	11,075.99	2,227.33
91	1,595	75	3,533	5,294	27	16	43	374,463	90,147	464,611	53.0	876,361	8,239.26	1,638.73
14	159	18	471	662	1	0	1	35,666	10,362	46,029	46.5	99,031	7,152.86	1,770.85
38	737	85	1,549	2,409	0	0	0	141,366	28,521	169,888	44.9	378,479	7,083.78	1,505.79
51	1,758	81	3,554	5,444	63	4	67	309,591	70,197	379,788	41.7	910,895	7,248.94	1,558.24
19	1,147	35	1,908	3,109	21	2	23	228,320	59,393	287,714	50.0	575,898	7,530.34	1,658.40
11	780	50	1,492	2,333	15	0	15	120,774	27,237	148,010	44.0	336,034	7,758.80	1,583.69
44	535	27	1,312	1,918	0	0	0	107,170	24,222	131,392	51.4	255,653	7,530.07	1,549.10
77	1,357	123	2,858	4,415	37	0	37	228,794	55,485	284,279	52.5	541,947	7,445.86	1,463.45
842	12,572	584	26,611	40,600	967	51	1,018	2,461,368	607,368	3,068,735	49.6	6,184,296	9,411.77	1,898.08
92	4,384	256	8,425	13,157	88	2	90	896,599	202,074	1,098,675	47.8	2,296,574	7394.97	1576.56
1,505	35,457	3,482	83,336	123,780	1,176	95	1,271	6,545,166	1,654,553	8,199,721	49.8	16,450,927	9,021.09	1,353.36
322	5,391	1,408	16,015	23,136	40	7	47	1,032,450	256,001	1,288,451	52.1	2,471,636	6,860.15	711.27
1,183	30,066	2,074	67,321	100,644	1,136	88	1,224	5,512,716	1,398,551	6,911,270	49.4	13,979,291	9,553.14	1,610.39
4	969	142	2,620	3,735	18	0	18	166,080	59,706	225,787	42.4	532,860	10,396.87	1,932.30
24	949	36	2,564	3,573	6	1	7	193,356	54,895	248,251	56.2	441,359	8,029.97	1,810.72
680	16,509	933	35,936	54,058	659	71	730	2,994,657	729,318	3,723,974	49.5	7,522,041	9,497.07	1,575.09
21	2,601	246	5,138	8,006	5	0	5	466,596	113,195	579,792	48.7	1,191,153	11,215.60	1,920.55
47	355	51	1,023	1,476	0	0	0	99,787	28,888	128,675	54.3	236,881	10,008.92	926.63
25	248	34	701	1,008	13	2	15	47,251	14,783	62,035	57.7	107,521	7,892.64	767.45
67	1,288	74	2,827	4,256	58	3	61	234,896	56,870	291,766	47.0	620,944	8,263.50	1,463.95
10	308	48	928	1,294	0	0	0	82,893	22,342	105,235	52.5	200,549	9,689.75	2,493.43
92	715	25	1,712	2,544	113	6	119	188,361	50,902	239,262	47.9	499,393	11,407.65	2,649.06
0	73	27	362	462	0	0	0	17,795	3,000	21,005	52.2	40,427	5,215.04	1,678.23
11	1,800	104	4,129	6,044	118	0	118	314,710	81,130	395,840	49.1	805,532	10,851.25	1,826.57
73	924	100	2,107	3,204	32	1	33	179,947	49,330	229,277	51.4	445,657	9,015.74	1,829.12
114	1,932	69	4,200	6,315	114	4	118	344,142	72,709	416,851	49.0	851,480	9,852.59	1,398.47
13	787	86	1,672	2,558	0	0	0	94,793	37,737	132,530	48.7	271,939	9,308.18	1,351.93
2	608	99	1,402	2,111	0	0	0	87,453	23,446	110,899	52.4	211,554	6,061.91	1,341.19

Table continues

MSAs

TABLE 8

U.S. CENSUS DIVISION 3, SOUTH ATLANTIC CONTINUED

U.S. Community Hospitals
(Nonfederal, short-term general and other special hospitals)

2011 Utilization, Personnel and Finances

CLASSIFICATION	Hospitals	Beds	Admissions	Inpatient Days	Adjusted Patient Days	Average Daily Census	Adjusted Average Daily Census	Average Stay (days)	Surgical Operations	NEWBORNS Bassinets	NEWBORNS Births	OUTPATIENT VISITS Emergency	OUTPATIENT VISITS Total
Maryland	48	11,887	683,678	3,147,613	5,376,690	8,624	14,734	4.6	559,361	948	68,727	2,469,637	8,771,571
Nonmetropolitan	6	426	29,990	105,083	221,711	288	608	3.5	38,649	50	2,730	193,659	925,283
Metropolitan	42	11,461	653,688	3,042,530	5,154,979	8,336	14,126	4.7	520,712	898	65,997	2,275,978	7,846,288
Baltimore-Towson	22	7,169	405,583	1,902,261	3,160,639	5,212	8,660	4.7	346,066	453	34,795	1,347,110	4,842,891
Bethesda-Gaithersburg-Frederick	7	1,727	116,389	500,105	873,514	1,370	2,394	4.3	69,841	224	18,575	291,527	1,047,996
Cumberland	1	373	15,626	98,022	183,876	269	504	6.3	11,154	20	1,011	55,183	503,866
Hagerstown-Martinsburg	1	278	16,206	70,046	128,682	192	353	4.3	8,462	41	1,948	72,575	198,508
Salisbury	3	546	25,989	142,886	266,001	391	729	5.5	18,077	28	2,035	91,474	532,270
Washington-Arlington-Alexandria	7	1,249	66,863	302,835	485,099	830	1,329	4.5	59,632	120	6,965	371,638	554,048
Wilmington	1	119	7,032	26,375	57,168	72	157	3.8	7,480	12	668	46,471	166,709
North Carolina	117	23,136	1,035,400	5,830,425	11,815,696	15,972	32,376	5.6	838,074	1,689	115,013	4,448,191	18,628,672
Nonmetropolitan	58	6,555	249,651	1,388,528	3,239,917	3,803	8,878	5.6	206,169	577	25,116	1,517,300	5,321,597
Metropolitan	59	16,581	785,749	4,441,897	8,575,779	12,169	23,498	5.7	631,905	1,112	89,897	2,930,891	13,307,075
Asheville	6	1,260	57,470	299,488	548,401	821	1,503	5.2	53,951	58	5,318	178,266	1,235,321
Burlington	1	218	12,247	50,814	128,583	139	352	4.1	7,872	21	1,227	54,155	122,091
Charlotte-Gastonia-Concord	12	3,523	177,311	932,601	1,852,110	2,553	5,076	5.3	137,440	305	23,762	723,472	2,983,692
Durham	6	1,979	94,941	591,476	1,137,688	1,621	3,118	6.2	81,370	61	8,643	232,901	2,221,109
Fayetteville	1	666	33,968	214,258	346,395	587	949	6.3	16,205	48	4,741	127,603	543,201
Goldsboro	1	274	11,674	53,349	116,917	146	320	4.6	12,680	30	1,506	55,902	149,578
Greensboro-High Point	5	1,745	76,411	436,848	876,248	1,197	2,401	5.7	47,505	111	8,800	323,774	1,225,214
Greenville	1	847	44,352	251,762	352,370	690	965	5.7	19,885	42	3,592	111,418	373,359
Hickory-Lenoir-Morganton	5	985	34,853	238,285	531,296	653	1,456	6.8	30,252	62	3,422	172,537	592,908
Jacksonville	1	144	9,603	35,951	88,241	98	242	3.7	6,396	23	2,128	62,666	130,981
Raleigh-Cary	6	1,864	92,619	510,514	1,076,342	1,400	2,949	5.5	97,507	144	14,452	394,460	2,125,399
Rocky Mount	3	447	17,303	93,813	177,374	257	486	5.4	11,366	34	1,656	86,132	230,369
Wilmington	4	919	41,451	228,849	487,547	626	1,336	5.5	34,048	48	4,367	171,387	508,614
Winston-Salem	7	1,710	81,546	503,889	856,267	1,381	2,345	6.2	75,428	125	6,283	236,218	865,239
South Carolina	66	12,253	508,652	2,878,860	5,161,554	7,884	14,142	5.7	492,720	884	53,530	1,687,578	6,420,111
Nonmetropolitan	25	2,890	102,426	563,149	1,171,501	1,540	3,210	5.5	94,450	235	9,899	425,383	1,186,744
Metropolitan	41	9,363	406,226	2,315,711	3,990,053	6,344	10,932	5.7	398,270	649	43,631	1,262,195	5,233,367
Anderson	2	427	20,448	105,686	170,543	290	467	5.2	16,281	28	1,985	61,953	676,473
Augusta-Richmond County	2	281	12,898	64,190	106,086	176	291	5.0	10,944	18	1,122	57,856	154,463
Charleston-North Charleston	6	1,822	83,849	449,792	777,608	1,231	2,130	5.4	79,183	125	9,211	230,231	1,491,864
Charlotte-Gastonia-Concord	2	327	15,906	81,243	122,931	223	337	5.1	15,238	37	1,922	67,208	164,075
Columbia	7	2,162	88,217	532,354	905,210	1,457	2,481	6.0	72,324	131	9,651	249,891	773,341
Florence	6	1,258	44,846	282,580	462,207	774	1,266	6.3	55,565	64	3,486	73,672	199,679
Greenville	10	1,457	69,622	372,026	663,786	1,021	1,819	5.3	76,483	111	8,565	256,074	902,264
Myrtle Beach-Conway-North Myrtle Beach	3	674	27,227	171,114	348,176	469	954	6.3	24,047	54	2,678	114,476	243,655
Spartanburg	2	695	34,365	184,758	303,482	506	831	5.4	37,197	57	3,727	93,747	495,698
Sumter	1	260	8,848	71,968	130,024	197	356	8.1	11,008	24	1,284	57,087	131,855
Virginia	89	17,797	788,441	4,391,769	8,723,335	12,035	23,901	5.6	657,581	1,341	98,141	3,407,824	14,118,420
Nonmetropolitan	30	2,787	89,407	592,162	1,354,159	1,622	3,711	6.6	84,778	170	7,146	528,931	2,166,029
Metropolitan	59	15,010	699,034	3,799,607	7,369,176	10,413	20,190	5.4	572,803	1,171	90,995	2,878,893	11,952,391
Blacksburg-Christiansburg-Radford	4	328	15,667	62,910	143,681	172	394	4.0	18,924	32	1,603	90,002	230,757
Charlottesville	3	759	39,944	213,734	404,146	586	1,107	5.4	72,484	42	3,357	109,664	2,088,897
Danville	1	290	9,128	45,373	81,975	124	225	5.0	5,761	20	1,394	20,571	100,067
Harrisonburg	1	238	14,686	55,398	146,991	152	403	3.8	18,056	28	1,688	72,699	357,412
Kingsport-Bristol-Bristol	1	100	6,222	21,866	62,058	60	170	3.5	7,106	12	687	38,575	136,952
Lynchburg	2	1,205	33,885	334,220	597,134	916	1,636	9.9	17,371	39	2,611	113,801	508,303
Richmond	14	3,542	152,396	829,716	1,467,247	2,275	4,019	5.4	119,313	196	15,668	510,765	1,684,165
Roanoke	3	1,177	58,372	337,353	571,626	924	1,566	5.8	39,674	52	5,336	232,667	592,981
Virginia Beach-Norfolk-Newport News	15	3,318	160,523	871,678	1,900,965	2,390	5,208	5.4	129,797	287	19,774	845,458	3,557,915
Washington-Arlington-Alexandria	14	3,594	183,210	910,505	1,791,886	2,494	4,910	5.0	133,215	417	36,554	778,239	2,324,971
Winchester	1	459	25,001	116,854	201,467	320	552	4.7	11,102	46	2,323	66,452	369,971
West Virginia	55	7,365	282,194	1,632,308	3,590,155	4,471	9,835	5.8	304,996	492	20,639	1,216,780	6,760,795
Nonmetropolitan	29	2,757	90,317	567,072	1,575,285	1,553	4,318	6.3	87,804	261	6,870	545,810	2,514,924
Metropolitan	26	4,608	191,877	1,065,236	2,014,870	2,918	5,517	5.6	217,192	231	13,769	670,970	4,245,871
Charleston	7	1,326	54,603	301,294	579,630	826	1,587	5.5	90,322	69	3,895	151,220	974,158
Cumberland	1	25	804	3,369	14,967	9	41	4.2	1,443	0	0	13,394	55,577
Hagerstown-Martinsburg	2	212	8,496	43,284	109,295	118	299	5.1	8,684	21	914	54,354	226,993
Huntington-Ashland	3	730	43,503	191,395	342,571	524	938	4.4	30,400	55	2,903	124,669	732,704
Morgantown	4	789	37,954	223,473	336,155	612	921	5.9	34,110	14	2,398	84,635	816,396
Parkersburg-Marietta-Vienna	2	485	17,120	92,226	161,174	253	441	5.4	17,478	23	1,542	76,696	353,543
Washington-Arlington-Alexandria	1	25	1,793	5,436	20,227	15	55	3.0	3,017	8	294	28,448	72,361
Weirton-Steubenville	1	238	6,651	38,811	70,120	106	192	5.8	6,570	21	289	40,599	197,491
Wheeling	4	734	20,513	152,839	316,023	419	866	7.5	24,904	20	1,534	87,878	778,739
Winchester	1	44	440	13,109	64,708	36	177	29.8	264	0	0	9,077	37,909

TABLE 8

U.S. CENSUS DIVISION 3, SOUTH ATLANTIC CONTINUED

U.S. Community Hospitals
(Nonfederal, short-term general and other special hospitals)

2011 Utilization, Personnel and Finances

FULL-TIME EQUIVALENT PERSONNEL					FULL-TIME EQUIV. TRAINEES			EXPENSES						
								LABOR				TOTAL		
Physicians and Dentists	Registered Nurses	Licensed Practical Nurses	Other Salaried Personnel	Total Personnel	Medical and Dental Residents	Other Trainees	Total Trainees	Payroll (in thousands)	Employee Benefits (in thousands)	Total (in thousands)	Percent of Total	Amount (in thousands)	Adjusted per Admission	Adjusted per Inpatient Day
2,612	22,527	541	58,685	84,365	1,678	66	1,744	5,099,431	1,225,749	6,325,179	49.7	12,730,746	10,793.68	2,367.77
56	860	26	2,710	3,652	0	11	11	204,798	52,717	257,515	52.9	486,726	7,666.19	2,195.32
2,556	21,667	515	55,975	80,713	1,678	55	1,733	4,894,632	1,173,032	6,067,664	49.6	12,244,020	10,971.61	2,375.18
2,230	14,961	242	38,750	56,183	1,612	44	1,656	3,346,952	796,739	4,143,691	48.7	8,505,934	12,408.36	2,691.21
119	2,717	77	7,043	9,956	26	5	31	692,202	167,460	859,662	52.0	1,653,851	8,273.27	1,893.33
34	476	19	1,307	1,836	0	0	0	100,384	34,938	135,322	46.9	288,558	9,844.35	1,569.30
6	593	19	1,218	1,836	0	0	0	111,849	27,921	139,770	54.3	257,607	8,652.64	2,001.88
52	769	74	2,138	3,033	1	1	2	167,939	43,425	211,364	49.3	428,312	9,189.66	1,610.19
81	1,941	77	4,883	6,982	39	2	41	421,685	92,859	514,543	52.4	982,885	8,964.98	2,026.15
34	210	7	636	887	0	3	3	53,622	9,690	63,312	49.9	126,875	8,324.01	2,219.33
1,779	44,562	1,673	102,112	150,126	2,777	146	2,923	8,187,068	2,082,518	10,269,589	51.2	20,062,914	9,504.45	1,697.99
416	9,072	747	24,429	34,664	19	3	22	1,633,271	413,185	2,046,459	54.1	3,779,798	6,393.17	1,166.63
1,363	35,490	926	77,683	115,462	2,758	143	2,901	6,553,797	1,669,333	8,223,130	50.5	16,283,116	10,714.87	1,898.73
111	2,549	63	5,920	8,643	0	8	8	463,626	116,850	580,477	52.7	1,101,843	10,063.13	2,009.19
24	441	4	1,388	1,857	0	0	0	81,656	21,327	102,983	50.1	205,533	6,632.03	1,598.45
362	7,694	157	16,120	24,333	299	15	314	1,455,776	358,990	1,814,767	46.1	3,936,261	11,015.20	2,125.28
54	5,872	83	11,988	17,997	1,306	42	1,348	1,128,060	275,146	1,403,206	49.3	2,849,118	15,638.34	2,504.31
141	1,204	131	3,125	4,601	2	0	2	287,887	63,368	351,255	65.0	540,795	9,847.50	1,561.21
0	506	9	999	1,514	0	0	0	73,915	21,583	95,497	55.8	171,051	6,685.88	1,463.02
317	3,210	129	7,488	11,144	75	1	76	534,595	175,842	710,437	56.2	1,264,270	8,398.17	1,442.82
0	1,833	10	5,173	7,016	352	20	372	322,520	104,940	427,460	48.2	887,515	14,297.23	2,518.70
101	1,232	31	3,056	4,420	9	1	10	259,775	64,615	324,390	52.4	619,230	8,330.37	1,165.51
0	940	20	757	1,117	0	0	0	61,073	14,129	66,111	70.7	91,490	3,070.00	1,006.11
239	4,585	51	8,808	13,683	0	10	10	846,551	180,642	1,027,192	53.4	1,924,303	9,826.40	1,787.82
3	817	36	1,485	2,341	0	0	0	121,652	33,695	155,346	55.1	282,042	8,077.51	1,590.10
5	1,443	40	3,323	4,811	63	0	63	267,608	73,537	341,146	47.6	716,216	9,045.30	1,469.02
6	3,764	162	8,053	11,985	652	46	698	658,203	164,661	822,863	48.6	1,693,509	12,209.52	1,977.78
1,101	19,006	1,009	41,782	63,778	1,261	3	1,264	3,502,977	907,873	4,410,646	45.4	9,707,104	10,558.49	1,880.66
169	3,352	370	8,732	12,623	51	1	52	655,192	178,782	833,973	48.4	1,722,121	8,070.26	1,470.01
932	16,454	719	33,050	51,155	1,210	2	1,212	2,847,785	728,891	3,576,673	44.8	7,984,983	11,310.59	2,001.22
89	789	56	2,468	3,402	44	0	44	160,144	39,665	199,810	47.0	425,269	12,479.65	2,493.62
21	354	20	651	1,046	0	0	0	56,250	12,097	68,346	44.5	153,417	7,236.97	1,446.15
15	4,013	116	7,024	11,168	643	0	643	677,224	175,422	852,647	44.3	1,926,629	13,109.71	2,477.64
0	362	9	686	1,057	0	0	0	76,319	16,369	92,688	44.5	208,253	8,342.46	1,694.06
80	3,871	184	8,013	12,148	240	0	240	663,744	167,206	830,950	46.1	1,802,583	12,037.61	1,991.34
48	1,734	139	3,433	5,354	23	0	23	267,171	67,283	334,453	41.9	798,372	10,396.15	1,727.30
546	2,693	60	5,467	8,766	184	1	185	451,367	118,134	569,498	41.5	1,373,565	10,582.41	2,069.29
18	910	88	1,740	2,756	0	0	0	154,446	37,659	192,106	47.6	403,717	8,088.09	1,159.52
85	1,395	27	2,719	4,226	61	0	61	262,337	73,664	336,001	48.1	698,714	12,359.18	2,302.32
30	333	20	849	1,232	15	1	16	78,782	21,392	100,174	51.5	194,463	12,164.59	1,495.59
1,335	30,149	2,369	62,348	96,201	1,852	105	1,957	5,951,008	1,349,668	7,300,674	47.6	15,341,349	9,624.31	1,758.66
146	3,011	567	7,741	11,465	25	18	43	569,552	135,496	705,048	50.2	1,403,100	6,406.24	1,036.14
1,189	27,138	1,802	54,607	84,736	1,827	87	1,914	5,381,456	1,214,173	6,595,626	47.3	13,938,249	10,136.92	1,891.43
8	553	50	1,112	1,723	2	0	2	95,325	21,582	116,906	43.7	267,786	7,506.68	1,863.75
57	2,184	154	4,594	6,989	744	6	750	449,395	102,646	552,041	46.8	1,180,199	14,732.78	2,920.23
27	295	17	743	1,082	13	1	14	54,305	14,746	69,050	51.5	134,044	8,127.82	1,635.18
64	595	73	1,540	2,272	0	0	0	131,338	31,176	162,514	49.7	327,145	8,395.45	2,225.62
0	228	37	450	715	0	0	0	33,816	6,392	40,209	45.1	89,057	5,043.18	1,435.07
100	903	189	3,346	4,538	19	6	25	265,082	68,017	333,100	56.9	585,624	9,947.23	980.72
176	6,499	466	11,618	18,759	723	53	776	1,183,929	299,992	1,483,921	47.9	3,100,315	11,404.51	2,113.02
382	2,320	149	4,627	7,478	215	1	216	518,586	104,816	623,402	49.5	1,260,116	12,424.98	2,204.44
101	5,880	417	12,522	18,920	3	13	16	1,182,517	266,977	1,449,494	45.8	3,164,018	8,961.57	1,664.43
244	7,009	181	12,166	19,600	108	7	115	1,323,643	264,243	1,587,883	46.5	3,417,789	9,552.47	1,907.37
30	672	69	1,889	2,660	0	0	0	143,520	33,586	177,106	43.0	412,156	9,561.90	2,045.78
565	10,218	1,302	25,293	37,378	658	30	688	1,819,030	524,660	2,343,688	49.6	4,724,080	7,694.21	1,315.84
259	2,805	684	8,265	12,013	66	2	68	551,251	157,076	708,325	53.3	1,329,744	5,617.99	844.13
306	7,413	618	17,028	25,365	592	28	620	1,267,779	367,584	1,635,363	48.2	3,394,336	8,996.74	1,684.64
122	2,397	189	5,063	7,771	174	0	174	373,863	112,759	486,623	49.2	989,725	9,110.81	1,707.51
0	43	9	141	193	0	0	0	6,901	1,656	8,556	43.0	19,906	5,572.83	1,330.00
4	281	19	616	920	0	0	0	56,139	14,863	71,001	50.5	140,618	7,344.49	1,286.59
29	1,333	137	2,820	4,319	0	0	0	236,774	90,275	327,049	48.4	675,364	8,474.25	1,971.46
38	1,624	90	3,782	5,534	336	19	355	287,328	78,022	365,350	45.0	811,355	13,560.55	2,413.63
11	523	45	1,368	1,947	14	7	21	87,109	21,341	108,450	44.2	245,404	7,883.20	1,522.60
0	83	7	204	294	0	0	0	16,773	3,805	20,577	54.4	37,822	5,668.70	1,869.86
19	224	13	548	804	9	2	11	37,003	10,048	47,051	51.5	91,337	7,601.26	1,302.58
79	889	100	2,363	3,431	59	0	59	159,684	33,410	193,095	52.8	365,779	6,721.78	1,157.44
4	16	9	123	152	0	0	0	6,206	1,405	7,611	44.7	17,026	7,839.07	263.13

MSAs

TABLE 8

U.S. CENSUS DIVISION 4, EAST NORTH CENTRAL

U.S. Community Hospitals
(Nonfederal, short-term general and other special hospitals)

2011 Utilization, Personnel and Finances

CLASSIFICATION	Hospitals	Beds	Admissions	Inpatient Days	Adjusted Patient Days	Average Daily Census	Adjusted Average Daily Census	Average Stay (days)	Surgical Operations	NEWBORNS Bassinets	Births	OUTPATIENT VISITS Emergency	Total
UNITED STATES	4,973	797,403	34,843,085	187,072,013	358,286,020	512,944	982,377	5.4	26,907,712	56,290	3,730,342	129,461,658	656,078,942
Nonmetropolitan	1,984	133,716	4,192,377	26,166,177	70,109,403	71,710	192,165	6.2	4,127,991	10,856	454,761	23,737,253	123,877,956
Metropolitan	2,989	663,687	30,650,708	160,905,836	288,176,617	441,234	790,212	5.2	22,779,721	45,434	3,275,581	105,724,405	532,200,986
CENSUS DIVISION 4, EAST NORTH CENTRAL.	774	122,555	5,518,124	27,603,703	57,894,130	75,641	158,654	5.0	4,689,576	9,569	531,487	21,873,056	132,596,143
Nonmetropolitan	273	17,898	649,752	3,370,403	11,029,918	9,228	30,212	5.2	710,495	1,799	68,733	4,111,779	23,706,050
Metropolitan	501	104,657	4,868,372	24,233,300	46,864,212	66,413	128,442	5.0	3,979,081	7,770	462,754	17,761,277	108,890,093
Illinois	188	32,775	1,511,770	7,398,797	14,733,742	20,280	40,391	4.9	1,118,075	2,626	152,929	5,414,964	31,692,798
Nonmetropolitan	64	4,018	150,747	729,791	2,192,597	1,997	6,001	4.8	149,971	310	13,014	877,955	5,001,147
Metropolitan	124	28,757	1,361,023	6,669,006	12,541,145	18,283	34,390	4.9	968,104	2,316	139,915	4,537,009	26,691,651
Bloomington-Normal	2	349	16,126	59,367	114,737	163	314	3.7	10,917	39	2,275	64,269	501,943
Champaign-Urbana.	4	577	27,710	139,300	278,172	382	762	5.0	22,129	66	3,587	107,568	656,887
Chicago-Naperville-Joliet	77	20,308	985,247	4,850,066	8,738,647	13,300	23,974	4.9	643,585	1,573	102,047	3,025,490	18,037,421
Danville	2	226	7,292	51,926	163,850	142	449	7.1	3,763	26	679	44,566	222,410
Davenport-Moline-Rock Island . . .	5	544	23,314	112,848	282,049	310	772	4.8	17,931	73	2,300	107,780	635,108
Decatur	2	408	19,086	81,547	226,665	223	621	4.3	16,469	36	1,620	80,393	462,118
Kankakee-Bradley.	2	468	19,097	87,462	190,896	239	523	4.6	17,692	34	1,431	74,688	546,990
Lake County-Kenosha County . . .	5	908	54,117	210,794	420,556	577	1,152	3.9	41,780	107	6,785	196,303	757,076
Peoria	6	1,187	57,297	290,428	549,648	795	1,507	5.1	64,045	81	4,107	251,673	1,702,132
Rockford	4	903	43,037	214,122	366,792	586	1,004	5.0	39,484	83	4,513	162,463	1,114,973
Springfield	2	901	43,982	224,895	390,675	616	1,070	5.1	32,862	54	3,612	124,945	734,474
St. Louis	13	1,978	64,718	346,251	818,458	950	2,242	5.4	57,447	144	6,959	296,871	1,320,119
Indiana.	125	17,467	737,438	3,724,041	7,943,049	10,201	21,765	5.0	630,071	1,386	76,049	3,144,973	18,512,955
Nonmetropolitan	40	2,260	88,059	419,758	1,440,501	1,147	3,949	4.8	107,334	288	11,825	680,084	3,525,050
Metropolitan	85	15,207	649,379	3,304,283	6,502,548	9,054	17,816	5.1	522,737	1,098	64,224	2,464,889	14,987,905
Anderson	2	210	8,080	43,078	133,193	118	365	5.3	15,533	12	465	54,550	290,590
Bloomington	2	318	14,059	59,787	130,804	163	359	4.3	8,378	19	2,039	66,884	780,539
Cincinnati-Middletown	1	78	4,275	16,810	44,168	46	121	3.9	6,117	11	531	19,535	137,790
Columbus.	1	198	8,990	36,144	83,331	99	228	4.0	11,147	20	1,158	41,824	234,514
Elkhart-Goshen	2	427	18,178	68,644	130,320	188	358	3.8	13,452	51	2,219	86,927	565,592
Evansville.	7	1,290	50,571	285,383	572,314	782	1,569	5.6	36,521	62	4,547	169,046	981,648
Fort Wayne.	9	1,626	63,050	343,369	647,445	940	1,773	5.4	75,523	124	7,099	207,527	1,026,234
Gary	11	2,532	106,568	586,348	1,038,427	1,606	2,844	5.5	68,738	204	8,177	417,943	1,851,085
Indianapolis	26	5,045	212,134	1,118,263	2,256,115	3,065	6,181	5.3	160,931	320	22,625	806,204	6,151,302
Kokomo.	4	344	12,846	63,162	150,256	173	412	4.9	14,908	35	1,226	58,223	354,742
Lafayette	3	473	21,016	98,347	214,925	270	589	4.7	15,267	35	2,031	105,544	451,417
Louisville	6	557	34,338	154,976	309,129	424	847	4.5	28,653	38	2,857	118,558	662,024
Michigan City-La Porte.	2	375	13,959	69,582	144,366	191	396	5.0	11,159	35	1,402	52,273	258,228
Muncie	1	347	18,425	84,736	140,612	232	385	4.6	5,957	24	1,726	59,269	306,231
South Bend-Mishawaka	3	763	35,795	155,791	252,571	428	692	4.4	21,512	59	3,720	91,074	347,272
Terre Haute	5	624	27,095	119,863	254,572	329	697	4.4	28,941	49	2,402	109,508	588,697
Michigan.	153	25,351	1,191,236	6,173,528	12,808,679	16,912	35,094	5.2	998,408	1,705	107,031	4,675,863	30,983,696
Nonmetropolitan	58	4,150	143,234	824,891	2,700,167	2,260	7,399	5.8	171,166	349	14,008	842,795	5,729,103
Metropolitan	95	21,201	1,048,002	5,348,637	10,108,512	14,652	27,695	5.1	827,242	1,356	93,023	3,833,068	25,254,593
Ann Arbor	5	1,611	82,832	447,611	863,651	1,226	2,365	5.4	75,944	52	7,315	179,987	3,010,858
Battle Creek	3	322	14,648	63,947	174,531	176	478	4.4	10,504	26	1,607	66,995	377,151
Bay City.	2	364	16,986	87,966	137,131	241	376	5.2	10,680	14	937	44,380	363,195
Detroit-Livonia-Dearborn.	20	5,328	261,322	1,352,196	2,542,397	3,704	6,966	5.2	181,464	315	20,951	1,031,835	5,364,366
Flint	4	1,190	61,900	312,291	543,942	856	1,490	5.0	46,048	89	5,548	223,585	1,464,525
Grand Rapids-Wyoming	8	1,857	94,152	449,904	856,166	1,232	2,345	4.8	90,360	152	11,948	353,631	3,037,568
Holland-Grand Haven	3	226	10,169	37,460	87,789	103	241	3.7	9,489	52	1,205	113,185	556,347
Jackson.	2	349	20,722	92,428	187,872	253	515	4.5	11,404	17	1,740	74,973	512,185
Kalamazoo-Portage.	5	848	44,714	204,118	393,333	559	1,078	4.6	34,727	70	5,131	189,853	1,229,372
Lansing-East Lansing	6	1,062	50,654	244,116	513,863	669	1,408	4.8	45,407	41	5,465	206,999	1,230,387
Monroe	1	169	9,605	39,571	92,218	108	253	4.1	8,686	13	794	46,123	176,432
Muskegon-Norton Shores	4	452	19,750	83,466	230,892	228	632	4.2	21,333	26	2,180	105,623	887,765
Niles-Benton Harbor	3	509	18,107	132,392	262,987	362	720	7.3	13,442	35	1,845	80,168	358,539
Saginaw-Saginaw Township North . .	4	1,112	42,385	312,333	464,382	856	1,272	7.4	19,169	31	928	140,365	697,894
South Bend-Mishawaka	1	25	830	2,953	13,393	8	37	3.6	831	0	0	9,077	108,145
Warren-Farmington Hills-Troy . . .	24	5,777	299,226	1,485,885	2,743,965	4,071	7,519	5.0	247,754	423	25,429	966,289	5,879,864

MSAs

TABLE 8

U.S. CENSUS DIVISION 4, EAST NORTH CENTRAL

U.S. Community Hospitals
(Nonfederal, short-term general and other special hospitals)

2011 Utilization, Personnel and Finances

Physicians and Dentists	Registered Nurses	Licensed Practical Nurses	Other Salaried Personnel	Total Personnel	Medical and Dental Residents	Other Trainees	Total Trainees	Payroll (in thousands)	Employee Benefits (in thousands)	Total (in thousands)	Percent of Total	Amount (in thousands)	Adjusted per Admission	Adjusted per Inpatient Day
111,741	1,313,626	85,820	3,138,428	4,649,615	99,458	8,198	107,656	$283,964,687	$76,727,241	$360,691,957	51.4	$702,091,034	$10,532.52	$1,959.58
14,153	157,107	25,812	467,855	664,927	1,988	339	2,327	34,086,208	9,249,087	43,335,308	53.7	80,710,425	7,197.79	1,151.32
97,588	1,156,519	60,008	2,670,573	3,984,688	97,470	7,859	105,329	249,878,479	67,478,154	317,356,649	51.1	621,372,609	11,207.00	2,156.22
20,792	219,526	11,504	537,635	789,457	20,552	2,042	22,594	47,284,972	12,972,533	60,257,516	50.7	118,844,738	10,331.66	2,052.79
2,541	26,605	3,097	81,192	113,435	202	109	311	6,111,688	1,830,729	7,942,120	53.2	14,929,125	7,351.14	1,353.51
18,251	192,921	8,407	456,443	676,022	20,350	1,933	22,283	41,173,284	11,141,803	52,315,096	50.3	103,915,613	10,970.69	2,217.38
5,156	54,489	2,110	132,537	194,292	6,044	218	6,262	11,742,935	3,339,629	15,082,561	50.6	29,831,858	9,961.57	2,024.73
484	5,879	785	17,191	24,339	49	5	54	1,222,633	393,295	1,615,926	52.9	3,056,219	7,022.61	1,393.88
4,672	48,610	1,325	115,346	169,953	5,995	213	6,208	10,520,302	2,946,334	13,466,635	50.3	26,775,639	10,401.29	2,135.02
148	557	11	1,261	1,977	15	4	19	123,611	31,764	155,374	51.5	301,783	9,684.02	2,630.22
18	1,143	36	2,039	3,236	27	1	28	169,552	47,034	216,587	43.4	498,693	9,872.18	1,792.75
3,823	35,472	751	81,891	121,937	5,406	157	5,563	7,812,276	2,165,218	9,977,493	51.1	19,534,471	10,804.56	2,235.41
4	195	26	666	891	0	1	1	43,392	13,176	56,568	47.7	118,634	6,545.32	724.04
32	751	29	2,022	2,834	0	0	0	145,361	40,965	186,326	46.4	401,136	7,278.69	1,422.22
73	538	89	2,292	2,902	15	0	15	151,497	38,787	190,284	48.2	394,903	7,335.02	1,742.23
40	653	23	1,522	2,238	0	0	8	128,048	31,755	159,803	47.2	338,849	8,141.50	1,775.05
58	1,549	61	3,515	5,183	17	2	19	349,638	89,878	439,517	45.7	961,450	9,174.40	2,206.14
282	2,323	72	6,046	8,723	219	17	236	524,186	142,551	666,736	50.2	1,326,854	12,204.88	2,414.01
95	1,682	33	4,181	5,991	0	25	25	362,064	109,136	471,199	52.2	902,272	11,998.78	2,459.90
1	1,522	81	4,448	6,052	259	0	259	309,550	100,867	419,417	43.1	972,601	12,727.21	2,489.54
90	2,225	113	5,463	7,899	29	6	35	401,128	126,202	527,331	51.5	1,023,993	6,783.70	1,251.13
2,003	30,087	2,075	71,450	105,615	1,151	288	1,439	6,217,086	1,724,940	7,942,032	49.4	16,082,099	10,040.91	2,024.68
405	3,868	560	11,714	16,607	8	39	47	879,080	254,317	1,133,399	54.4	2,084,093	6,782.41	1,446.78
1,538	26,219	1,515	59,736	89,008	1,143	249	1,392	5,338,005	1,470,623	6,808,633	48.6	13,998,006	10,814.46	2,152.70
17	301	34	1,088	1,440	0	0	0	80,700	25,950	106,650	52.2	204,263	8,062.17	1,533.59
13	672	41	1,810	2,536	0	0	0	131,721	41,709	173,430	56.3	307,911	9,860.73	2,353.99
5	129	25	504	663	0	0	0	32,628	11,311	43,938	64.5	68,133	6,065.96	1,542.58
0	293	25	940	1,258	0	0	0	69,850	24,384	94,233	49.6	189,972	9,165.44	2,279.73
48	713	30	1,385	2,176	5	2	7	145,389	54,867	200,255	52.9	378,377	10,901.72	2,903.44
131	1,050	81	4,450	6,515	21	19	40	362,241	107,260	469,500	48.6	966,072	9,877.84	1,688.01
33	2,421	131	4,583	7,168	27	2	29	361,108	96,780	457,890	43.1	1,062,092	9,148.63	1,640.44
191	3,447	184	7,889	11,711	97	10	107	721,082	189,919	911,002	49.4	1,844,247	9,745.44	1,776.00
596	10,765	525	22,793	34,679	838	208	1,046	2,241,896	605,703	2,847,601	47.5	5,996,517	13,525.77	2,657.89
41	515	40	1,606	2,202	15	1	16	123,071	33,515	156,586	54.5	287,081	9,260.07	1,910.61
195	995	74	2,314	3,578	21	3	24	261,821	66,039	327,860	51.7	633,888	14,135.40	2,949.35
63	1,033	84	2,926	4,106	0	0	0	192,441	46,055	238,496	61.3	388,888	5,481.77	1,258.01
76	441	21	1,612	2,150	4	1	5	124,812	38,708	163,521	52.1	314,027	10,885.19	2,175.21
59	643	36	1,504	2,242	45	1	46	97,660	27,675	125,335	41.8	299,831	9,806.41	2,132.33
31	1,051	31	2,313	3,426	40	1	41	220,914	59,340	280,254	51.6	543,903	9,184.13	2,153.46
39	947	153	2,019	3,158	30	1	31	170,673	41,408	212,082	41.4	512,806	8,656.56	2,014.38
4,600	46,728	1,664	115,823	168,815	6,011	114	6,125	10,290,402	2,633,201	12,923,608	51.0	25,328,137	10,269.42	1,977.42
654	5,785	698	19,074	26,211	79	11	90	1,405,662	404,950	1,810,613	52.5	3,450,170	7,880.86	1,277.76
3,946	40,943	966	96,749	142,604	5,932	103	6,035	8,884,740	2,228,251	11,112,995	50.8	21,877,967	10,784.90	2,164.31
214	5,329	96	12,113	17,752	1,418	1	1,419	1,085,222	336,557	1,421,780	51.6	2,756,485	17,050.39	3,191.66
46	533	14	1,559	2,152	0	0	0	130,811	36,946	167,757	50.7	331,119	8,404.04	1,897.19
27	429	63	1,292	1,811	14	9	23	110,282	27,053	137,335	55.7	246,632	9,011.35	1,798.51
1,433	9,862	116	22,527	33,938	2,229	23	2,252	2,351,856	529,193	2,881,051	51.1	5,639,257	11,457.08	2,218.09
94	2,475	51	4,646	7,266	284	0	284	487,194	149,437	636,631	56.1	1,135,597	10,519.37	2,087.72
174	3,535	108	9,529	13,346	77	1	78	770,873	215,906	986,782	46.6	2,118,764	11,722.91	2,474.71
39	511	55	1,415	2,020	9	3	12	100,567	26,432	126,998	52.2	243,373	10,072.97	2,772.25
59	733	65	2,396	3,253	0	0	0	184,001	39,466	223,467	56.9	392,697	8,726.20	2,090.23
216	1,492	27	4,287	6,022	0	1	1	422,400	110,308	532,708	51.3	1,037,889	11,795.81	2,638.70
222	2,088	34	5,031	7,375	229	1	230	500,675	123,577	624,252	55.1	1,133,481	9,953.12	2,205.80
13	337	22	1,014	1,386	0	0	0	65,803	16,264	82,067	54.2	151,512	6,768.77	1,642.98
110	668	12	2,281	3,071	24	0	24	186,532	58,668	245,199	52.4	467,911	8,414.45	2,026.53
95	621	42	2,392	3,150	3	0	3	133,543	40,021	173,563	50.0	341,387	8,954.72	1,298.11
154	1,610	96	6,076	8,076	149	25	174	297,117	77,793	374,911	50.1	748,572	10,791.62	1,611.97
9	42	0	172	223	0	0	0	13,692	4,247	17,939	62.0	28,937	7,687.83	2,160.61
1,041	10,678	166	21,878	33,763	1,496	39	1,535	2,044,172	436,382	2,480,555	48.6	5,104,355	9,133.23	1,860.21

Table continues

MSAs

TABLE 8

U.S. CENSUS DIVISION 4, EAST NORTH CENTRAL CONTINUED

U.S. Community Hospitals
(Nonfederal, short-term general and other special hospitals)

2011 Utilization, Personnel and Finances

CLASSIFICATION	Hospitals	Beds	Admissions	Inpatient Days	Adjusted Patient Days	Average Daily Census	Adjusted Average Daily Census	Average Stay (days)	Surgical Operations	NEWBORNS Bassinets	NEWBORNS Births	OUTPATIENT VISITS Emergency	OUTPATIENT VISITS Total
Ohio	183	33,828	1,504,603	7,434,042	15,022,464	20,376	41,167	4.9	1,197,556	2,605	128,695	6,506,331	35,896,728
Nonmetropolitan	55	4,366	168,767	687,405	1,983,433	1,884	5,430	4.1	168,484	547	18,477	1,163,475	5,577,073
Metropolitan	128	29,462	1,335,836	6,746,637	13,039,031	18,492	35,737	5.1	1,029,072	2,058	110,218	5,342,856	30,319,655
Akron	8	1,863	92,244	458,389	943,553	1,256	2,584	5.0	60,006	102	7,195	395,068	2,374,470
Canton-Massillon	5	1,287	50,620	298,264	617,302	817	1,690	5.9	42,898	111	4,450	227,419	1,390,555
Cincinnati-Middletown	20	4,565	214,596	1,032,214	1,811,433	2,828	4,963	4.8	159,480	415	20,899	809,428	3,344,827
Cleveland-Elyria-Mentor	30	7,658	337,274	1,874,401	3,806,087	5,143	10,443	5.6	295,764	392	22,738	1,115,460	9,401,879
Columbus	19	5,112	252,209	1,157,513	2,151,523	3,171	5,895	4.6	185,007	401	26,259	1,036,819	5,479,579
Dayton	10	2,736	115,344	582,661	1,065,473	1,597	2,919	5.1	100,214	172	10,565	484,521	2,089,200
Lima	5	720	29,606	127,826	254,387	350	696	4.3	18,976	63	2,390	115,594	726,484
Mansfield	2	301	13,501	64,049	113,637	175	311	4.7	4,774	32	1,017	51,576	270,402
Parkersburg-Marietta-Vienna	2	177	8,874	39,562	80,768	108	221	4.5	9,589	16	295	51,047	240,955
Sandusky	1	236	8,318	40,794	100,860	112	276	4.9	14,362	15	704	47,834	276,788
Springfield	1	254	14,465	61,951	118,248	170	324	4.3	8,086	31	1,340	73,800	319,041
Toledo	13	2,450	108,704	544,765	1,107,591	1,493	3,035	5.0	83,910	161	8,326	436,489	2,726,117
Weirton-Steubenville	1	319	10,837	65,636	154,584	180	424	6.1	5,562	18	552	47,092	248,217
Wheeling	3	263	6,538	44,963	116,299	123	319	6.9	7,197	10	291	45,501	248,244
Youngstown-Warren-Boardman	8	1,521	72,706	353,649	597,286	969	1,637	4.9	33,247	119	3,197	405,208	1,182,897
Wisconsin	125	13,134	573,077	2,873,295	7,386,196	7,872	20,237	5.0	745,466	1,247	66,783	2,130,925	15,509,966
Nonmetropolitan	56	3,104	98,945	708,558	2,713,220	1,940	7,433	7.2	113,540	305	11,409	547,470	3,873,677
Metropolitan	69	10,030	474,132	2,164,737	4,672,976	5,932	12,804	4.6	631,926	942	55,374	1,583,455	11,636,289
Appleton	4	393	17,896	74,370	188,675	204	517	4.2	33,091	55	2,501	73,187	329,183
Duluth	1	25	579	4,556	45,312	12	124	7.9	3,556	0	0	13,599	47,301
Eau Claire	5	580	25,263	122,722	268,134	337	735	4.9	19,036	40	2,399	71,238	435,151
Fond du Lac	3	217	8,119	32,930	126,539	91	346	4.1	15,544	15	1,013	41,677	740,427
Green Bay	5	747	31,437	136,713	327,584	376	897	4.3	58,503	97	4,580	127,453	1,131,447
Janesville	3	267	14,430	61,007	151,813	167	416	4.2	12,457	21	1,762	78,210	1,372,791
La Crosse	2	412	20,356	80,706	172,317	221	472	4.0	24,735	42	2,311	35,629	309,660
Lake County-Kenosha County	3	488	24,087	97,624	227,860	267	624	4.1	23,201	66	2,992	157,333	961,828
Madison	7	1,459	71,571	368,313	792,400	1,008	2,172	5.1	138,625	90	7,667	190,921	1,493,021
Milwaukee-Waukesha-West Allis	22	3,971	192,409	899,916	1,715,875	2,466	4,704	4.7	222,255	333	21,102	575,547	3,597,185
Minneapolis-St. Paul-Bloomington	4	98	4,865	14,744	53,618	40	146	3.0	6,929	20	1,026	25,897	120,790
Oshkosh-Neenah	4	422	18,339	73,238	161,479	201	442	4.0	31,843	63	2,680	55,168	291,478
Racine	2	421	18,517	99,557	240,153	273	658	5.4	12,923	47	2,084	68,048	529,735
Sheboygan	2	208	7,778	27,177	72,403	74	198	3.5	15,625	28	1,308	27,646	152,567
Wausau	2	322	18,486	71,164	128,814	195	353	3.8	13,603	25	1,949	41,902	123,725

TABLE 8

U.S. CENSUS DIVISION 4, EAST NORTH CENTRAL CONTINUED

U.S. Community Hospitals
(Nonfederal, short-term general and other special hospitals)

2011 Utilization, Personnel and Finances

FULL-TIME EQUIVALENT PERSONNEL					FULL-TIME EQUIV. TRAINEES			EXPENSES						
								LABOR				TOTAL		
Physicians and Dentists	Registered Nurses	Licensed Practical Nurses	Other Salaried Personnel	Total Personnel	Medical and Dental Residents	Other Trainees	Total Trainees	Payroll (in thousands)	Employee Benefits (in thousands)	Total (in thousands)	Percent of Total	Amount (in thousands)	Adjusted per Admission	Adjusted per Inpatient Day
8,303	65,689	4,684	156,704	235,380	6,559	750	7,309	13,638,521	3,684,774	17,323,302	53.1	32,605,626	10,580.07	2,170.46
578	7,046	750	19,054	27,428	66	11	77	1,392,450	412,971	1,805,424	52.2	3,460,226	6,921.68	1,744.56
7,725	58,643	3,934	137,650	207,952	6,493	739	7,232	12,246,071	3,271,803	15,517,878	53.2	29,145,400	11,288.42	2,235.24
553	3,882	375	9,845	14,655	489	56	545	824,385	219,082	1,043,468	54.4	1,917,954	10,084.94	2,032.69
120	2,259	189	5,386	7,954	68	3	71	361,974	96,980	458,954	53.9	862,163	8,178.01	1,380.45
1,219	9,117	326	23,770	34,432	1,033	331	1,364	2,037,909	557,310	2,595,219	51.8	5,013,419	13,085.32	2,767.65
2,850	15,864	1,877	39,900	60,491	2,516	284	2,800	4,030,131	1,082,249	5,112,380	60.4	8,466,220	12,437.30	2,224.39
2,611	10,896	178	23,657	37,342	1,289	11	1,300	2,050,311	531,366	2,581,676	48.6	5,317,275	11,059.45	2,471.40
78	5,278	143	11,665	17,164	424	2	426	949,182	249,302	1,198,486	52.0	2,306,109	10,728.13	2,164.40
12	1,243	76	2,422	3,753	0	0	0	183,181	58,899	242,080	48.2	501,748	8,256.64	1,972.38
2	495	79	1,272	1,848	0	0	0	115,713	30,985	146,697	51.1	287,347	12,074.40	2,528.64
25	333	38	899	1,295	6	1	7	87,892	24,255	112,146	51.8	216,430	11,942.96	2,679.65
4	396	64	1,072	1,536	15	1	16	77,160	19,358	96,518	49.7	194,318	9,448.49	1,926.61
0	420	33	814	1,267	0	0	0	71,716	19,730	91,446	44.6	205,046	7,426.53	1,734.04
124	4,936	275	9,821	15,156	511	40	551	903,795	242,268	1,146,065	47.7	2,404,060	11,300.31	2,170.53
29	452	21	1,103	1,605	0	0	0	74,150	23,435	97,585	54.1	180,385	7,067.54	1,166.90
22	280	54	723	1,079	1	0	1	43,141	12,599	55,741	55.8	99,961	5,814.40	859.52
76	2,792	206	5,301	8,375	141	10	151	435,431	103,985	539,417	45.6	1,182,967	9,508.73	1,080.57
730	22,533	971	61,121	85,355	787	672	1,459	5,396,029	1,589,989	6,986,013	46.6	14,997,019	11,039.75	2,030.41
660	1,007	601	14,150	10,858	8	45	45	1,211,803	365,196	1,577,058	54.8	2,878,417	8,208.08	1,060.89
370	18,506	667	46,962	66,505	787	629	1,416	4,184,167	1,224,793	5,408,955	44.6	12,118,601	12,025.11	2,593.34
30	593	58	1,603	2,284	0	21	21	158,857	46,284	205,140	51.6	397,813	8,803.33	2,108.46
5	39	6	150	200	0	0	0	17,139	4,578	21,717	63.2	34,340	5,962.80	757.85
10	987	23	2,512	3,532	0	3	3	202,229	63,646	265,875	51.2	510,070	10,017.00	1,935.12
30	376	49	1,065	1,520	0	0	0	110,176	31,421	141,597	43.9	322,299	10,350.66	2,547.03
11	1,363	117	3,948	5,439	1	26	27	343,121	106,105	449,225	49.0	917,017	11,908.54	2,799.33
68	692	38	2,566	3,364	20	0	20	177,000	57,071	234,000	41.5	503,431	15,763.83	3,711.35
20	994	58	2,024	3,096	18	0	18	167,541	64,729	232,269	44.7	519,172	11,904.61	3,012.89
34	997	45	2,679	3,755	14	22	36	229,290	65,929	295,219	51.7	570,810	10,048.60	2,505.09
100	2,888	69	7,932	10,989	548	76	624	747,892	273,696	1,021,588	53.2	1,919,191	14,457.72	2,422.00
53	7,193	94	16,062	23,402	186	369	555	1,518,838	364,305	1,883,233	38.6	4,883,877	13,092.73	2,846.29
1	204	9	656	870	0	0	0	51,593	12,366	63,958	46.1	138,884	7,815.21	2,590.25
7	619	25	1,420	2,071	0	26	26	134,344	39,992	174,335	46.9	372,065	9,034.43	2,304.11
0	704	56	2,107	2,867	0	27	27	144,568	40,585	185,153	46.1	401,729	8,904.95	1,672.80
0	218	3	605	820	0	49	49	47,855	16,711	64,567	40.1	160,852	7,767.26	2,221.62
1	639	17	1,633	2,290	0	10	10	133,714	37,286	170,999	42.9	398,251	12,027.03	3,091.68

MSAs

TABLE 8

U.S. CENSUS DIVISION 5, EAST SOUTH CENTRAL

U.S. Community Hospitals
(Nonfederal, short-term general and other special hospitals)

2011 Utilization, Personnel and Finances

CLASSIFICATION	Hospitals	Beds	Admissions	Inpatient Days	Adjusted Patient Days	Average Daily Census	Adjusted Average Daily Census	Average Stay (days)	Surgical Operations	NEWBORNS Bassinets	NEWBORNS Births	OUTPATIENT VISITS Emergency	OUTPATIENT VISITS Total
UNITED STATES	4,973	797,403	34,843,085	187,072,013	358,286,020	512,944	982,377	5.4	26,907,712	56,290	3,730,342	129,461,658	656,078,942
Nonmetropolitan	1,984	133,716	4,192,377	26,166,177	70,109,403	71,710	192,165	6.2	4,127,991	10,856	454,761	23,737,253	123,877,956
Metropolitan	2,989	663,687	30,650,708	160,905,836	288,176,617	441,234	790,212	5.2	22,779,721	45,434	3,275,581	105,724,405	532,200,986
CENSUS DIVISION 5, EAST SOUTH CENTRAL	440	62,478	2,424,397	13,300,397	25,657,347	36,597	70,586	5.5	2,119,071	4,235	207,943	9,526,218	34,951,691
Nonmetropolitan	233	20,538	636,492	3,802,270	8,723,158	10,422	23,930	6.0	595,413	1,405	53,675	3,324,323	11,345,351
Metropolitan	207	41,940	1,787,905	9,498,127	16,934,189	26,175	46,656	5.3	1,523,658	2,830	154,268	6,201,895	23,606,340
Alabama	102	15,387	625,425	3,259,740	6,066,630	8,931	16,616	5.2	636,277	1,349	56,038	2,301,480	8,729,694
Nonmetropolitan	45	3,190	110,967	533,812	1,273,328	1,460	3,487	4.8	127,745	263	9,712	616,466	2,255,383
Metropolitan	57	12,197	514,458	2,725,928	4,793,302	7,471	13,129	5.3	508,532	1,086	46,326	1,685,014	6,474,311
Anniston-Oxford	3	420	19,944	87,020	169,535	238	464	4.4	11,757	38	1,651	78,186	199,947
Auburn-Opelika	1	377	14,835	100,323	219,033	275	600	6.8	12,875	38	1,648	44,987	117,475
Birmingham-Hoover	17	4,614	183,431	1,027,997	1,682,205	2,817	4,609	5.6	227,753	396	13,979	535,578	2,738,621
Columbus	1	48	1,033	14,344	14,877	39	41	13.9	0	0	0	0	3,854
Decatur	3	360	13,956	60,467	139,041	166	380	4.3	10,069	23	690	70,586	212,950
Dothan	4	861	32,503	163,858	328,686	449	900	5.0	30,394	57	3,554	103,124	299,293
Florence-Muscle Shoals	3	574	20,041	94,103	199,342	258	546	4.7	17,910	46	1,909	87,709	212,327
Gadsden	3	588	20,300	119,619	197,059	328	540	5.9	26,960	32	1,136	78,827	205,863
Huntsville	4	1,155	57,704	277,984	536,755	762	1,471	4.8	65,916	100	6,498	198,163	918,124
Mobile	6	1,453	67,447	367,114	610,267	1,007	1,671	5.4	52,112	187	6,465	184,011	671,055
Montgomery	8	1,106	49,345	244,957	420,299	672	1,151	5.0	34,053	112	5,603	176,474	416,134
Tuscaloosa	4	641	33,919	168,142	276,203	460	756	5.0	18,733	57	3,193	127,369	478,668
Kentucky	106	14,182	599,601	3,061,415	6,324,009	8,385	17,329	5.1	571,295	924	49,657	2,350,367	10,532,660
Nonmetropolitan	63	5,732	216,582	1,073,268	2,464,648	2,939	6,754	5.0	200,999	414	16,195	1,028,975	4,108,299
Metropolitan	43	8,450	383,019	1,988,147	3,859,361	5,446	10,575	5.2	370,296	510	33,462	1,321,392	6,424,361
Bowling Green	3	564	22,092	112,854	202,975	309	556	5.1	17,967	19	2,324	71,699	157,043
Cincinnati-Middletown	5	930	47,531	224,429	448,988	615	1,230	4.7	30,350	50	4,460	207,098	1,142,135
Clarksville	2	164	7,251	33,781	77,186	92	211	4.7	4,045	18	564	32,057	164,536
Elizabethtown	2	308	13,698	66,190	159,604	181	437	4.8	8,904	26	1,551	52,019	296,302
Evansville	1	192	5,435	26,277	64,088	72	176	4.8	4,023	12	675	28,248	254,883
Huntington-Ashland	2	763	30,845	182,512	441,050	500	1,209	5.9	64,786	25	1,524	106,182	904,260
Lexington-Fayette	14	2,089	90,918	496,056	899,779	1,358	2,466	5.5	72,714	160	6,672	232,815	1,388,896
Louisville	13	3,068	146,900	760,081	1,386,988	2,083	3,800	5.2	148,129	170	13,887	528,231	1,576,664
Owensboro	1	372	18,349	85,967	178,703	236	490	4.7	19,378	30	1,805	63,043	539,642
Mississippi	99	12,867	393,566	2,513,957	4,978,626	6,894	13,666	6.4	272,026	755	38,046	1,761,207	4,776,300
Nonmetropolitan	70	7,479	181,377	1,402,361	3,012,059	3,850	8,279	7.7	133,674	449	17,971	956,228	2,480,925
Metropolitan	29	5,388	212,189	1,111,596	1,966,567	3,044	5,387	5.2	138,352	306	20,075	804,979	2,295,375
Gulfport-Biloxi	6	906	29,683	152,746	283,117	419	776	5.1	26,317	66	2,860	167,455	657,819
Hattiesburg	3	756	36,163	179,361	281,299	491	771	5.0	18,134	28	3,849	111,210	215,791
Jackson	15	2,953	107,679	610,109	1,093,513	1,670	2,995	5.7	76,759	156	9,678	329,911	813,265
Memphis	3	344	18,446	84,398	152,966	231	419	4.6	6,053	24	2,043	71,623	124,664
Pascagoula	2	429	20,218	84,982	155,672	233	426	4.2	11,089	32	1,645	124,780	483,836
Tennessee	133	20,042	805,805	4,465,285	8,288,082	12,387	22,975	5.5	639,473	1,207	64,202	3,113,164	10,913,037
Nonmetropolitan	55	4,137	127,566	792,829	1,973,123	2,173	5,410	6.2	132,995	279	9,797	722,654	2,500,744
Metropolitan	78	15,905	678,239	3,672,456	6,314,959	10,214	17,565	5.4	506,478	928	54,405	2,390,510	8,412,293
Chattanooga	6	1,530	68,894	382,893	623,526	1,050	1,708	5.6	60,320	63	7,023	257,042	823,464
Clarksville	1	247	11,885	45,952	70,135	126	192	3.9	8,393	30	355	61,616	150,423
Cleveland	2	233	10,274	43,081	72,551	118	199	4.2	7,982	22	1,030	53,473	123,938
Jackson	2	739	33,515	176,692	340,012	484	932	5.3	28,268	47	3,087	94,255	208,261
Johnson City	5	837	36,162	201,896	352,841	555	971	5.6	24,197	49	2,684	105,785	409,636
Kingsport-Bristol-Bristol	6	1,015	45,025	213,344	388,931	584	1,067	4.7	26,779	66	2,715	191,395	513,233
Knoxville	11	2,387	96,985	533,123	962,393	1,612	2,896	5.5	75,772	153	8,946	380,048	1,248,336
Memphis	15	3,614	145,891	893,240	1,408,649	2,448	3,860	6.1	86,674	186	16,526	523,029	1,157,474
Morristown	3	332	10,173	45,303	85,453	123	234	4.5	13,086	29	621	55,555	200,294
Nashville-Davidson--Murfreesboro	27	4,971	219,435	1,136,932	2,010,468	3,114	5,506	5.2	175,007	283	11,418	668,312	3,577,234

MSAs

TABLE 8

U.S. CENSUS DIVISION 5, EAST SOUTH CENTRAL

U.S. Community Hospitals
(Nonfederal, short-term general and other special hospitals)

2011 Utilization, Personnel and Finances

FULL-TIME EQUIVALENT PERSONNEL					FULL-TIME EQUIV. TRAINEES			EXPENSES						
								LABOR				TOTAL		
Physicians and Dentists	Registered Nurses	Licensed Practical Nurses	Other Salaried Personnel	Total Personnel	Medical and Dental Residents	Other Trainees	Total Trainees	Payroll (in thousands)	Employee Benefits (in thousands)	Total (in thousands)	Percent of Total	Amount (in thousands)	Adjusted per Admission	Adjusted per Inpatient Day
111,741	1,313,626	85,820	3,138,428	4,649,615	99,458	8,198	107,656	$283,964,687	$76,727,241	$360,691,957	51.4	$702,091,034	$10,532.52	$1,959.58
14,153	157,107	25,812	467,855	664,927	1,988	339	2,327	34,086,208	9,249,087	43,335,308	53.7	80,718,425	7,197.79	1,151.32
97,588	1,156,519	60,008	2,670,573	3,984,688	97,470	7,859	105,329	249,878,479	67,478,154	317,356,649	51.1	621,372,609	11,207.00	2,156.22
5,840	87,586	7,581	194,433	295,440	4,335	285	4,620	14,725,093	3,770,774	18,495,876	50.1	36,909,371	7,803.89	1,438.55
1,316	21,506	3,373	57,814	84,009	195	34	229	3,665,934	947,018	4,612,957	54.0	8,536,450	5,722.81	978.60
4,524	66,080	4,208	136,619	211,431	4,140	251	4,391	11,059,159	2,823,756	13,882,919	48.9	28,372,921	8,762.59	1,675.48
771	22,196	1,539	45,761	70,267	1,453	49	1,502	3,337,793	822,961	4,160,757	50.2	8,285,878	6,945.16	1,365.81
156	3,356	503	8,704	12,719	23	4	27	473,102	118,725	591,826	54.6	1,083,641	4,056.95	851.03
615	18,840	1,036	37,057	57,548	1,430	45	1,475	2,864,692	704,236	3,568,931	49.6	7,202,237	7,778.32	1,502.56
14	550	63	1,110	1,737	0	0	0	72,788	16,694	89,481	56.1	159,488	4,129.89	940.74
22	572	47	1,741	2,382	0	0	0	87,683	22,987	110,670	48.3	229,364	7,081.54	1,047.17
158	7,212	243	13,242	20,855	886	13	899	1,206,514	287,856	1,494,371	46.2	3,237,350	10,518.70	1,924.47
0	26	4	107	137	0	0	0	6,515	1,281	7,796	64.6	12,061	11,261.52	810.72
19	360	27	1,025	1,431	2	0	2	62,356	13,701	76,057	60.7	125,243	3,973.70	900.76
74	1,142	80	2,378	3,674	136	3	139	185,693	36,397	222,090	60.7	365,917	5,465.12	1,113.27
37	588	50	1,349	2,024	14	1	15	86,346	26,434	112,779	55.2	204,343	4,787.68	1,025.09
5	677	11	1,016	1,741	0	0	0	62,920	18,361	101,271	41.7	211,593	6,946.42	1,174.70
133	2,537	153	4,617	7,440	4	0	4	335,637	110,628	446,265	52.1	856,893	7,402.32	1,596.43
110	2,306	81	4,950	7,447	360	6	366	337,934	89,971	427,906	50.0	856,307	7,561.61	1,403.17
27	1,636	104	3,021	4,788	20	1	21	206,861	40,688	247,551	42.8	578,031	6,720.83	1,375.29
16	1,234	140	2,502	3,892	0	21	21	193,446	39,248	232,694	67.3	345,736	6,108.74	1,251.75
1,041	21,019	1,603	48,784	72,447	781	36	817	3,780,873	1,035,858	4,816,732	47.9	10,049,280	7,867.09	1,589.07
540	6,914	868	18,131	26,453	92	15	107	1,257,910	349,073	1,606,991	53.2	3,019,388	5,833.35	1,225.08
501	14,105	735	30,653	45,994	689	21	710	2,522,956	686,786	3,209,741	45.7	7,029,892	9,253.79	1,821.52
1	737	28	1,444	2,210	0	0	0	117,851	31,704	149,555	48.7	307,206	7,730.41	1,513.52
36	1,300	73	3,681	5,090	23	2	25	326,462	100,160	426,622	54.9	776,849	7,961.56	1,730.22
20	239	25	706	990	5	1	6	44,402	11,525	55,927	52.5	106,466	6,563.08	1,379.35
30	443	8	1,177	1,658	0	0	0	77,673	20,656	90,329	51.5	191,002	5,666.87	1,196.72
25	228	28	711	992	7	9	16	36,336	15,453	51,789	56.4	91,889	6,931.87	1,433.79
178	1,039	256	2,973	4,446	9	3	12	218,918	66,939	285,857	47.3	604,647	7,796.06	1,370.93
97	9,400	134	8,283	11,994	606	4	610	673,184	174,116	847,300	45.4	1,867,456	10,997.45	2,075.46
111	5,930	155	9,863	16,059	39	2	41	912,208	228,696	1,140,903	41.2	2,769,479	10,119.78	1,996.76
3	709	28	1,815	2,555	0	0	0	115,923	37,536	153,459	48.7	314,898	8,255.73	1,762.13
1,212	14,513	1,616	35,954	53,295	564	47	611	2,588,592	636,061	3,224,656	55.6	5,804,948	7,623.30	1,165.97
399	6,601	1,147	18,557	26,704	42	11	53	1,206,539	295,343	1,501,883	54.8	2,742,385	7,118.53	910.47
813	7,912	469	17,397	26,591	522	36	558	1,382,054	340,718	1,722,773	56.3	3,062,564	8,140.18	1,557.31
142	1,281	91	2,782	4,296	0	0	0	237,551	51,907	289,458	66.1	437,964	7,811.31	1,546.94
40	995	98	2,444	3,577	0	0	0	180,371	42,730	223,101	51.0	437,057	7,749.93	1,553.71
544	4,197	213	9,029	13,983	517	19	536	754,114	183,892	938,006	55.6	1,686,300	8,745.27	1,542.15
1	652	39	1,143	1,835	0	17	17	77,851	20,186	98,038	50.9	192,743	5,766.08	1,260.04
88	787	28	1,999	2,900	5	0	5	132,166	42,004	174,170	56.5	308,439	8,223.51	1,981.34
2,816	29,858	2,823	63,934	99,431	1,537	153	1,690	5,017,834	1,275,894	6,293,731	49.3	12,769,265	8,525.28	1,540.68
221	4,635	855	12,422	18,133	38	4	42	728,377	183,877	912,257	53.9	1,691,036	5,256.68	857.04
2,595	25,223	1,968	51,512	81,298	1,499	149	1,648	4,289,458	1,092,017	5,381,474	48.6	11,078,228	9,419.32	1,754.28
171	2,511	206	5,611	8,499	192	6	198	485,287	119,498	604,784	52.6	1,149,560	10,074.85	1,843.64
6	384	22	638	1,050	13	1	14	47,615	10,852	58,467	47.2	123,999	6,835.69	1,768.01
3	297	28	613	941	0	1	1	45,163	10,459	55,622	47.6	116,841	6,786.38	1,610.47
22	1,176	154	3,125	4,477	4	0	4	212,538	54,116	266,654	53.3	499,960	7,798.10	1,470.42
4	1,248	120	2,002	3,374	0	0	0	175,316	37,242	212,558	49.3	431,227	6,998.63	1,222.16
5	1,320	67	2,937	4,329	6	29	35	196,876	71,492	268,368	42.8	627,407	7,562.85	1,613.16
101	4,108	346	8,026	12,581	3	22	25	613,738	153,903	767,640	48.9	1,569,619	8,966.69	1,630.95
86	5,602	278	10,789	16,755	304	78	382	910,985	213,262	1,124,246	49.0	2,293,358	9,746.32	1,628.06
16	341	33	811	1,201	5	0	5	52,591	12,710	65,302	50.0	130,509	6,827.59	1,527.27
2,181	8,236	714	16,960	28,091	972	12	984	1,549,348	408,483	1,957,833	47.3	4,135,747	10,645.40	2,057.11

MSAs

TABLE 8

U.S. CENSUS DIVISION 6, WEST NORTH CENTRAL

U.S. Community Hospitals
(Nonfederal, short-term general and other special hospitals)

2011 Utilization, Personnel and Finances

CLASSIFICATION	Hospitals	Beds	Admissions	Inpatient Days	Adjusted Patient Days	Average Daily Census	Adjusted Average Daily Census	Average Stay (days)	Surgical Operations	NEWBORNS Bassinets	NEWBORNS Births	OUTPATIENT VISITS Emergency	OUTPATIENT VISITS Total
UNITED STATES	4,973	797,403	34,843,085	187,072,013	358,286,020	512,944	982,377	5.4	26,907,712	56,290	3,730,342	129,461,658	656,078,942
Nonmetropolitan	1,984	133,716	4,192,377	26,166,177	70,109,403	71,710	192,165	6.2	4,127,991	10,856	454,761	23,737,253	123,877,956
Metropolitan	2,989	663,687	30,650,708	160,905,836	288,176,617	441,234	790,212	5.2	22,779,721	45,434	3,275,581	105,724,405	532,200,986
CENSUS DIVISION 6, WEST NORTH CENTRAL	682	67,559	2,453,988	14,718,938	32,998,686	40,344	90,448	6.0	2,026,917	4,756	264,259	8,573,615	58,339,955
Nonmetropolitan	462	25,490	571,775	5,020,361	14,215,370	13,775	38,986	8.8	600,142	1,926	71,069	2,856,705	22,335,336
Metropolitan	220	42,069	1,882,213	9,698,577	18,783,316	26,569	51,462	5.2	1,426,775	2,830	193,190	5,716,910	36,004,619
Iowa	118	9,981	340,412	2,058,730	5,416,492	5,638	14,833	6.0	339,450	730	37,284	1,273,985	10,327,423
Nonmetropolitan	84	4,325	100,974	805,098	2,750,387	2,203	7,531	8.0	129,936	328	10,254	517,765	4,852,362
Metropolitan	34	5,656	239,438	1,253,632	2,666,105	3,435	7,302	5.2	209,514	402	27,030	756,220	5,475,061
Ames	2	274	10,222	66,213	144,364	181	396	6.5	9,540	17	1,164	27,837	178,090
Cedar Rapids	4	771	28,860	165,701	453,515	454	1,242	5.7	31,800	54	3,357	111,187	856,124
Davenport-Moline-Rock Island . . .	3	489	23,018	100,285	177,337	275	485	4.4	12,861	33	2,832	93,897	221,231
Des Moines	8	1,406	66,576	336,968	654,632	923	1,792	5.1	40,203	118	8,937	189,880	927,675
Dubuque	3	416	13,625	72,438	141,507	198	388	5.3	13,495	34	1,548	53,291	139,988
Iowa City	3	994	40,003	250,966	488,989	688	1,339	6.3	32,624	54	3,215	86,014	1,447,709
Omaha-Council Bluffs	3	293	14,063	57,715	117,090	158	321	4.1	13,327	22	934	56,113	239,566
Sioux City	2	398	20,673	94,278	153,614	259	421	4.6	11,602	32	2,469	60,888	336,092
Waterloo-Cedar Falls.	6	615	22,398	109,068	335,057	299	918	4.9	44,062	38	2,574	77,113	1,128,586
Kansas.	132	10,023	302,351	1,923,661	4,485,012	5,265	12,288	6.4	238,717	708	38,707	1,041,234	6,996,536
Nonmetropolitan	99	4,863	95,883	899,735	2,626,873	2,460	7,196	9.4	95,909	347	11,187	387,719	3,362,686
Metropolitan	33	5,160	206,468	1,023,926	1,858,139	2,805	5,092	5.0	142,808	361	27,520	653,515	3,633,850
Kansas City	14	2,298	98,438	477,108	873,240	1,307	2,392	4.8	75,365	181	13,336	278,453	1,826,197
Lawrence	1	152	6,655	23,133	89,958	63	246	3.5	4,505	13	1,086	36,244	193,499
Topeka	6	829	31,826	163,227	328,654	447	900	5.1	18,362	39	3,057	98,003	706,817
Wichita	12	1,881	69,549	360,458	566,287	988	1,554	5.2	44,576	128	10,041	240,815	907,337
Minnesota	132	14,985	596,199	3,592,914	7,930,127	9,842	21,726	6.0	494,621	1,238	64,004	1,928,364	10,792,006
Nonmetropolitan	81	5,001	107,305	1,105,285	3,193,292	3,027	8,746	10.3	128,018	400	17,181	554,855	3,948,403
Metropolitan	51	9,984	488,894	2,487,629	4,736,835	6,815	12,980	5.1	366,603	838	46,823	1,373,509	6,843,603
Duluth	10	1,307	42,052	288,418	797,925	790	2,186	6.9	40,849	97	3,892	125,261	482,354
Grand Forks	2	127	1,668	24,928	102,345	68	280	14.9	3,972	6	377	14,322	128,098
Minneapolis-St. Paul-Bloomington .	31	6,508	346,349	1,587,093	2,766,757	4,348	7,582	4.6	276,906	653	38,450	1,045,649	5,008,380
Rochester.	4	1,338	71,079	411,573	705,407	1,128	1,933	5.8	30,214	51	1,303	125,681	734,154
St. Cloud	4	704	27,746	175,617	364,401	481	999	6.3	14,662	31	2,801	62,596	490,617
Missouri	120	18,749	815,640	4,172,415	8,593,333	11,432	23,545	5.1	581,199	1,162	73,779	2,952,675	20,204,125
Nonmetropolitan	53	3,713	134,438	620,594	1,726,398	1,705	4,731	4.6	107,200	342	13,925	714,413	5,180,891
Metropolitan	67	15,036	681,202	3,551,821	6,866,935	9,727	18,814	5.2	473,999	820	59,854	2,238,262	15,023,234
Columbia	4	989	44,556	227,146	395,205	622	1,082	5.1	39,216	66	4,769	107,761	1,033,003
Jefferson City	3	284	16,935	63,031	140,173	172	384	3.7	11,191	30	1,521	74,054	679,425
Joplin	4	741	35,549	176,297	333,104	483	913	5.0	23,088	58	3,279	165,483	962,451
Kansas City	21	3,511	149,752	808,763	1,661,407	2,215	4,552	5.4	103,452	188	14,176	612,945	3,455,587
Springfield	5	1,400	68,464	350,705	793,565	961	2,174	5.1	61,325	83	6,846	252,995	2,439,308
St. Joseph	2	393	19,424	87,779	166,600	241	457	4.5	10,061	20	1,712	57,133	959,823
St. Louis	28	7,718	346,522	1,838,100	3,376,881	5,033	9,252	5.3	225,666	375	27,551	967,891	5,493,637
Nebraska	86	6,592	203,394	1,313,451	2,887,358	3,628	7,962	6.5	184,188	516	25,778	716,718	4,956,456
Nonmetropolitan	70	3,443	73,979	653,675	1,720,781	1,818	4,766	8.8	75,803	301	8,402	336,481	2,536,401
Metropolitan	16	3,149	129,415	659,776	1,166,577	1,810	3,196	5.1	108,385	215	17,376	380,237	2,420,055
Lincoln	3	642	36,362	156,469	268,482	429	735	4.3	22,848	63	5,031	104,123	350,095
Omaha-Council Bluffs	13	2,507	93,053	503,307	898,095	1,381	2,461	5.4	85,537	152	12,345	276,114	2,069,960
North Dakota.	41	3,145	94,125	701,723	1,622,922	1,920	4,445	7.5	87,987	168	12,731	408,870	2,949,022
Nonmetropolitan	33	1,664	25,644	367,495	841,576	1,005	2,304	14.3	29,976	65	5,443	224,779	1,237,618
Metropolitan	8	1,481	68,481	334,228	781,346	915	2,141	4.9	58,011	103	7,288	184,091	1,711,404
Bismarck	3	540	21,681	102,959	236,942	282	649	4.7	17,411	27	2,159	46,215	695,820
Fargo	3	604	32,445	149,599	312,788	410	857	4.6	29,451	53	3,611	69,081	403,289
Grand Forks	2	337	14,355	81,670	231,616	223	635	5.7	11,149	23	1,518	68,795	612,295
South Dakota.	53	4,084	101,867	956,044	2,063,442	2,619	5,649	9.4	100,755	234	11,976	251,769	2,114,387
Nonmetropolitan	42	2,481	33,552	568,479	1,356,063	1,557	3,712	16.9	33,300	143	4,677	120,693	1,216,975
Metropolitan	11	1,603	68,315	387,565	707,379	1,062	1,937	5.7	67,455	91	7,299	131,076	897,412
Rapid City	3	509	18,756	133,630	216,752	366	594	7.1	10,500	52	2,231	58,230	197,427
Sioux Falls	8	1,094	49,559	253,935	490,627	696	1,343	5.1	56,955	39	5,068	72,846	699,985

 AHA Hospital Statistics © 2012 Health Forum LLC, an affiliate of the American Hospital Association

TABLE 8

U.S. CENSUS DIVISION 6, WEST NORTH CENTRAL

U.S. Community Hospitals
(Nonfederal, short-term general and other special hospitals)

2011 Utilization, Personnel and Finances

FULL-TIME EQUIVALENT PERSONNEL					FULL-TIME EQUIV. TRAINEES			EXPENSES						
								LABOR				TOTAL		
Physicians and Dentists	Registered Nurses	Licensed Practical Nurses	Other Salaried Personnel	Total Personnel	Medical and Dental Residents	Other Trainees	Total Trainees	Payroll (in thousands)	Employee Benefits (in thousands)	Total (in thousands)	Percent of Total	Amount (in thousands)	Adjusted per Admission	Adjusted per Inpatient Day
111,741	1,313,626	85,820	3,138,428	4,649,615	99,458	8,198	107,656	$283,964,687	$76,727,241	$360,691,957	51.4	$702,091,034	$10,532.52	$1,959.58
14,153	157,107	25,812	467,855	664,927	1,988	339	2,327	34,086,208	9,249,087	43,335,308	53.7	80,718,425	7,197.79	1,151.32
97,588	1,156,519	60,008	2,670,573	3,984,688	97,470	7,859	105,329	249,878,479	67,478,154	317,356,649	51.1	621,372,609	11,207.00	2,156.22
9,285	101,321	9,231	257,588	377,425	3,305	455	3,760	21,871,219	5,718,563	27,589,784	51.1	54,026,600	10,230.10	1,037.24
2,694	26,198	4,974	80,122	113,988	184	42	226	5,720,699	1,505,529	7,226,227	53.7	13,449,987	8,102.16	946.16
6,591	75,123	4,257	177,466	263,437	3,121	413	3,534	16,150,520	4,213,034	20,363,557	50.2	40,576,703	11,205.63	2,100.25
1,061	14,500	992	38,762	55,321	699	24	723	3,000,504	703,570	3,704,074	51.6	7,174,091	8,496.52	1,324.49
429	5,318	644	15,058	21,449	22	0	22	1,032,030	281,647	1,313,675	53.7	2,444,717	7,116.54	888.86
632	9,188	348	23,704	33,872	677	24	701	1,871,504	518,897	2,390,399	50.5	4,729,373	9,443.07	1,773.89
3	331	12	883	1,229	0	0	0	64,980	17,829	82,809	50.6	163,651	8,292.83	1,133.60
52	1,223	84	3,355	4,714	0	0	0	216,563	64,884	281,446	51.5	546,902	7,651.87	1,205.92
8	703	5	1,338	2,054	10	0	10	111,449	30,785	142,234	39.0	364,658	8,591.50	2,056.30
205	2,430	30	6,843	9,508	168	5	173	557,507	133,289	690,797	54.2	1,274,025	9,695.78	1,946.17
10	555	11	1,104	1,680	0	0	0	77,426	22,338	99,763	42.9	232,766	8,534.04	1,644.91
140	2,062	25	5,152	7,379	496	15	511	427,683	149,091	576,774	51.8	1,114,234	14,693.84	2,278.65
19	457	25	898	1,399	0	4	4	74,102	21,034	95,136	47.0	202,366	7,088.38	1,728.30
63	663	35	1,562	2,323	0	0	0	127,962	29,794	157,756	50.3	313,613	9,321.23	2,041.56
132	764	121	2,509	3,586	3	0	3	213,832	49,853	263,684	51.0	517,158	7,337.66	1,543.49
943	13,232	1,218	30,796	46,189	7	145	152	2,532,766	609,856	3,142,624	52.7	5,963,380	9,025.54	1,329.62
331	4,244	689	13,079	18,343	2	0	2	880,644	205,983	1,086,630	55.7	1,951,058	7,535.51	742.73
612	8,988	529	17,717	27,846	5	145	150	1,652,122	403,873	2,055,994	51.2	4,012,323	9,985.67	2,159.32
207	4,659	88	8,537	13,491	0	129	129	798,464	206,664	1,005,127	47.9	2,100,577	10,742.82	2,405.50
37	300	23	779	1,139	0	0	0	64,988	13,626	78,614	50.0	157,168	6,073.17	1,747.12
269	1,301	324	3,403	5,297	0	3	3	352,807	81,239	434,047	59.5	728,897	10,608.31	2,217.82
99	2,728	94	4,008	7,919	5	13	18	435,863	102,344	538,206	52.5	1,025,682	9,183.62	1,811.24
3,133	21,507	2,358	59,800	86,798	610	96	706	6,176,419	1,677,530	7,853,951	54.3	14,474,690	11,759.87	1,825.28
732	4,599	1,350	15,958	22,639	13	3	16	1,332,649	349,417	1,682,065	54.9	3,064,417	9,266.65	959.64
2,401	16,908	1,008	43,842	64,159	507	93	690	4,843,770	1,328,114	6,171,886	54.1	11,410,273	12,675.80	2,408.84
595	1,606	216	6,221	8,638	7	1	8	602,146	163,471	765,618	62.7	1,220,965	11,116.55	1,530.17
9	152	46	506	713	1	0	1	25,912	6,431	32,343	56.9	56,841	10,502.79	555.39
1,594	12,119	471	29,730	43,914	453	73	526	3,430,636	931,948	4,362,585	53.2	8,194,356	13,323.68	2,961.72
177	1,860	103	4,178	6,318	122	19	141	535,562	145,842	681,403	50.8	1,340,026	11,129.97	1,899.65
26	1,171	172	3,207	4,576	14	0	14	249,514	80,422	329,937	55.2	598,086	12,083.27	1,641.28
2,464	32,740	2,736	79,042	116,982	1,812	156	1,968	6,434,649	1,685,933	8,120,583	47.3	17,172,219	10,204.56	1,908.32
676	5,201	1,193	15,799	22,869	42	24	66	1,119,167	312,043	1,431,208	51.3	2,789,461	7,464.94	1,615.77
1,788	27,539	1,543	63,243	94,113	1,770	132	1,902	5,315,482	1,373,890	6,689,375	46.5	14,382,758	10,986.56	2,094.49
46	1,765	265	4,990	7,066	369	0	369	350,495	100,383	450,877	44.0	1,024,205	13,099.93	2,591.58
89	570	123	1,419	2,201	9	0	9	123,663	33,795	157,458	49.3	319,402	8,277.23	2,278.63
148	1,269	71	3,281	4,769	23	0	23	274,430	51,233	325,664	52.4	622,016	9,094.87	1,867.33
420	6,619	308	14,297	21,644	200	132	332	1,356,370	320,563	1,676,933	49.8	3,366,174	12,025.57	2,026.10
275	3,013	274	9,665	13,227	22	0	22	621,913	184,403	806,315	45.2	1,783,209	11,263.25	2,247.09
126	569	143	2,073	2,911	0	0	0	204,719	48,523	253,242	55.8	453,939	11,960.88	2,724.73
684	13,734	359	27,518	42,295	1,147	0	1,147	2,383,892	634,990	3,018,886	44.3	6,813,813	10,518.91	2,017.78
422	9,953	887	23,223	34,485	53	9	62	1,755,135	484,666	2,239,800	48.1	4,659,397	11,122.51	1,613.72
240	3,564	666	10,479	14,949	19	5	24	713,763	196,441	910,204	52.0	1,749,370	9,010.36	1,016.61
182	6,389	221	12,744	19,536	34	4	38	1,041,371	288,225	1,329,596	45.7	2,910,027	12,946.98	2,494.50
3	1,421	76	2,690	4,190	0	3	3	228,548	83,050	311,598	47.7	653,493	10,737.47	2,434.03
179	4,968	145	10,054	15,346	34	1	35	812,823	205,175	1,017,998	45.1	2,256,534	13,767.41	2,512.58
742	4,343	702	12,974	18,761	105	9	114	1,016,692	221,114	1,237,807	55.5	2,229,494	9,549.14	1,373.75
152	1,569	212	4,642	6,575	85	9	94	274,262	70,482	344,746	52.5	656,284	9,240.44	779.83
590	2,774	490	8,332	12,186	20	0	20	742,430	150,632	893,061	56.8	1,573,211	9,684.10	2,013.46
213	997	175	3,131	4,516	0	0	0	276,417	43,372	319,789	58.0	551,328	11,004.11	2,326.85
191	1,284	275	2,856	4,606	0	0	0	251,966	59,948	311,913	48.4	644,476	9,136.18	2,060.42
186	493	40	2,345	3,064	20	0	20	214,047	47,313	261,359	59.0	377,107	8,026.73	1,629.45
520	5,040	338	12,991	18,889	19	16	35	1,052,024	238,920	1,290,945	54.9	2,353,419	11,205.42	1,140.53
134	1,703	220	5,107	7,164	1	1	2	368,183	89,516	457,699	57.6	794,681	9,023.70	586.02
386	3,337	118	7,884	11,725	18	15	33	683,841	149,404	833,246	53.5	1,558,737	12,780.83	2,203.54
59	821	49	1,920	2,849	18	0	18	157,059	23,323	180,382	49.7	362,819	11,926.60	1,673.89
327	2,516	69	5,964	8,876	0	15	15	526,782	126,081	652,864	54.6	1,195,919	13,064.72	2,437.53

MSAs

TABLE **8**

U.S. CENSUS DIVISION 7, WEST SOUTH CENTRAL

U.S. Community Hospitals
(Nonfederal, short-term general and other special hospitals)

2011 Utilization, Personnel and Finances

MSAs

CLASSIFICATION	Hospitals	Beds	Admissions	Inpatient Days	Adjusted Patient Days	Average Daily Census	Adjusted Average Daily Census	Average Stay (days)	Surgical Operations	NEWBORNS Bassinets	NEWBORNS Births	OUTPATIENT VISITS Emergency	OUTPATIENT VISITS Total
UNITED STATES	4,973	797,403	34,843,085	187,072,013	358,286,020	512,944	982,377	5.4	26,907,712	56,290	3,730,342	129,461,658	656,078,942
Nonmetropolitan	1,984	133,716	4,192,377	26,166,177	70,109,403	71,710	192,165	6.2	4,127,991	10,856	454,761	23,737,253	123,877,956
Metropolitan	2,989	663,687	30,650,708	160,905,836	288,176,617	441,234	790,212	5.2	22,779,721	45,434	3,275,581	105,724,405	532,200,986
CENSUS DIVISION 7, WEST SOUTH CENTRAL	746	96,825	3,929,807	20,460,393	36,898,591	56,076	101,149	5.2	2,801,821	7,332	503,256	15,575,261	59,641,839
Nonmetropolitan	315	16,301	554,353	2,546,118	6,405,579	6,978	17,564	4.6	426,647	1,390	60,083	3,109,182	12,355,524
Metropolitan	431	80,524	3,375,454	17,914,275	30,493,012	49,098	83,585	5.3	2,375,174	5,942	443,173	12,466,079	47,286,315
Arkansas	84	9,425	363,516	1,882,912	3,608,998	5,157	9,887	5.2	263,187	638	36,809	1,391,537	4,810,624
Nonmetropolitan	48	3,168	105,350	532,234	1,302,619	1,458	3,568	5.1	70,829	241	9,978	518,176	1,848,183
Metropolitan	36	6,257	258,166	1,350,678	2,306,379	3,699	6,319	5.2	192,358	397	26,831	873,361	2,962,441
Fayetteville-Springdale-Rogers	6	920	42,449	182,867	316,853	501	868	4.3	39,839	92	6,349	163,753	381,822
Fort Smith	7	944	33,782	187,410	313,850	514	861	5.5	26,845	50	3,458	137,627	354,601
Hot Springs	3	489	17,580	98,090	168,356	269	461	5.6	17,146	24	1,645	60,748	214,853
Jonesboro	3	542	26,216	128,334	233,157	352	639	4.9	16,790	32	2,029	74,744	277,784
Little Rock-North Little Rock	15	2,887	123,599	677,505	1,125,452	1,854	3,083	5.5	83,989	151	11,580	363,607	1,517,446
Memphis	1	142	3,811	17,555	35,127	48	96	4.6	2,825	12	731	19,489	41,434
Pine Bluff	1	333	10,729	58,917	113,584	161	311	5.5	4,924	36	1,039	53,393	174,501
Louisiana	127	15,342	607,413	3,257,484	6,211,006	8,925	17,020	5.4	448,904	1,009	54,963	2,446,704	9,543,267
Nonmetropolitan	50	3,057	109,295	553,082	1,266,819	1,515	3,473	5.1	98,791	217	10,336	513,774	1,881,522
Metropolitan	77	12,285	498,118	2,704,402	4,944,187	7,410	13,547	5.4	350,113	792	44,627	1,932,930	7,661,745
Alexandria	6	797	32,755	185,204	333,601	508	914	5.7	17,208	63	2,617	139,384	416,057
Baton Rouge	13	2,296	88,107	545,713	1,044,274	1,494	2,861	6.2	62,864	129	9,791	335,117	1,395,765
Houma-Bayou Cane-Thibodaux . . .	5	508	25,568	118,151	271,523	325	744	4.6	18,889	63	3,274	145,159	521,587
Lafayette	7	919	36,882	196,761	357,284	539	978	5.3	23,314	55	2,152	147,247	494,310
Lake Charles	8	806	27,362	142,004	295,792	390	810	5.2	23,888	54	3,221	130,335	461,029
Monroe	9	867	35,172	187,460	334,219	514	918	5.3	22,855	62	2,706	119,456	490,259
New Orleans-Metairie-Kenner . . .	19	3,935	162,746	877,615	1,538,662	2,403	4,215	5.4	108,947	248	14,081	667,016	2,596,075
Shreveport-Bossier City	10	2,157	89,526	451,494	768,832	1,237	2,107	5.0	72,148	118	6,785	249,216	1,286,663
Oklahoma	115	11,303	424,190	2,257,353	4,313,332	6,193	11,845	5.3	318,763	794	46,583	1,847,389	6,023,266
Nonmetropolitan	66	3,642	123,419	566,531	1,388,596	1,556	3,816	4.6	98,596	337	13,244	679,950	2,373,820
Metropolitan	49	7,661	300,771	1,690,822	2,924,736	4,637	8,029	5.6	220,167	457	33,339	1,167,439	3,649,446
Fort Smith	2	110	3,628	13,637	36,468	37	100	3.8	2,118	11	136	32,774	49,826
Lawton	2	558	15,670	128,251	250,378	352	686	8.2	11,532	32	1,740	68,758	196,680
Oklahoma City	22	4,034	152,013	891,126	1,515,224	2,444	4,167	5.9	120,723	249	18,148	670,323	2,086,485
Tulsa	23	2,959	129,460	657,808	1,122,666	1,804	3,076	5.1	85,794	165	13,315	395,584	1,316,455
Texas	420	60,755	2,534,688	13,062,644	22,765,255	35,801	62,397	5.2	1,770,967	4,891	364,901	9,889,631	39,264,682
Nonmetropolitan	151	6,434	216,289	894,271	2,447,545	2,449	6,707	4.1	158,431	595	26,525	1,397,282	6,251,999
Metropolitan	269	54,321	2,318,399	12,168,373	20,317,710	33,352	55,690	5.2	1,612,536	4,296	338,376	8,492,349	33,012,683
Abilene	5	652	23,358	122,322	219,271	336	600	5.2	19,461	46	2,719	90,373	389,454
Amarillo	4	963	41,029	199,503	297,767	546	816	4.9	22,568	54	4,759	108,020	399,942
Austin-Round Rock	22	2,842	126,641	635,370	1,044,359	1,741	2,863	5.0	104,325	255	21,062	578,499	1,991,854
Beaumont-Port Arthur	8	1,230	49,918	250,574	434,444	687	1,192	5.0	31,725	78	4,894	225,388	590,789
Brownsville-Harlingen	3	870	40,272	190,180	286,150	521	784	4.7	21,807	92	6,138	113,781	207,112
College Station-Bryan	4	459	23,975	95,573	178,661	261	489	4.0	18,991	68	3,705	99,792	433,892
Corpus Christi	6	1,557	58,009	319,812	493,949	875	1,353	5.5	38,647	102	6,644	221,761	554,883
Dallas-Plano-Irving	50	9,098	383,529	2,040,269	3,342,346	5,608	9,180	5.3	242,482	746	58,294	151,0481	5,019,674
El Paso	6	1,711	81,938	390,120	617,997	1,070	1,694	4.8	54,358	168	15,764	287,219	1,232,205
Fort Worth-Arlington	26	4,877	217,206	1,131,410	1,799,659	3,098	4,931	5.2	128,313	401	33,040	936,677	2,729,450
Houston-Sugar Land-Baytown . . .	59	13,988	571,537	3,188,000	5,489,160	8,731	15,037	5.6	394,011	1,187	91,668	1,785,720	9,182,639
Killeen-Temple-Fort Hood	4	840	41,474	198,913	472,082	545	1,293	4.8	35,805	54	4,882	171,873	1,520,157
Laredo	2	509	25,974	120,351	198,543	329	544	4.6	23,189	63	5,990	80,372	263,377
Longview	5	640	28,442	140,371	244,586	384	670	4.9	25,223	59	3,729	140,792	293,373
Lubbock	6	1,213	57,101	269,520	429,412	739	1,177	4.7	37,517	58	5,028	172,375	708,646
McAllen-Edinburg-Mission	7	2,156	94,316	443,318	687,985	1,215	1,884	4.7	96,768	206	17,195	204,770	512,924
Midland	4	400	15,473	83,318	146,440	229	402	5.4	13,410	35	1,938	67,938	181,983
Odessa	3	536	21,136	111,724	174,798	306	479	5.3	12,222	39	3,618	72,609	320,764
San Angelo	2	409	17,355	81,935	168,653	225	462	4.7	21,070	36	1,987	80,097	195,083
San Antonio	19	5,264	239,341	1,217,687	1,962,739	3,337	5,378	5.1	160,757	347	29,628	908,413	4,015,449
Sherman-Denison	2	466	17,438	92,158	154,575	252	424	5.3	10,558	35	1,328	66,004	116,295
Texarkana TX-Texarkana AR	5	628	24,729	135,441	214,673	371	587	5.5	12,337	31	2,711	108,358	300,974
Tyler	6	1,117	49,100	286,725	480,713	786	1,317	5.8	33,324	41	3,373	150,299	957,639
Victoria	4	566	19,909	95,485	171,720	261	470	4.8	20,510	34	2,110	79,769	206,140
Waco	2	907	30,800	243,555	465,009	667	1,274	7.9	15,559	41	3,992	135,810	483,606
Wichita Falls	5	423	18,399	84,739	142,019	232	390	4.6	17,599	20	2,180	95,159	204,379

TABLE 8

U.S. CENSUS DIVISION 7, WEST SOUTH CENTRAL

U.S. Community Hospitals
(Nonfederal, short-term general and other special hospitals)

2011 Utilization, Personnel and Finances

	FULL-TIME EQUIVALENT PERSONNEL				FULL-TIME EQUIV. TRAINEES			EXPENSES						
								LABOR				TOTAL		
Physicians and Dentists	Registered Nurses	Licensed Practical Nurses	Other Salaried Personnel	Total Personnel	Medical and Dental Residents	Other Trainees	Total Trainees	Payroll (in thousands)	Employee Benefits (in thousands)	Total (in thousands)	Percent of Total	Amount (in thousands)	Adjusted per Admission	Adjusted per Inpatient Day
111,741	1,313,626	85,820	3,138,428	4,649,615	99,458	8,198	107,656	$283,964,687	$76,727,241	$360,691,957	51.4	$702,091,034	$10,532.52	$1,959.58
14,153	157,107	25,812	467,855	664,927	1,988	339	2,327	34,086,208	9,249,087	43,335,308	53.7	80,718,425	7,197.79	1,151.32
97,588	1,156,519	60,008	2,670,573	3,984,688	97,470	7,859	105,329	249,878,479	67,478,154	317,356,649	51.1	621,372,609	11,207.00	2,156.22
5,682	139,201	16,273	312,892	474,048	5,300	1,073	6,373	26,768,516	6,292,574	33,061,096	49.1	67,280,080	9,169.77	1,823.39
908	16,670	5,492	49,474	72,544	93	39	132	3,321,437	801,335	4,122,775	52.8	7,811,304	5,497.12	1,219.45
4,774	122,531	10,781	263,418	401,504	5,207	1,034	6,241	23,447,079	5,491,239	28,938,321	48.7	59,469,376	10,051.88	1,950.26
486	13,278	2,200	28,498	44,462	6	14	20	2,066,954	470,251	2,537,208	48.5	5,236,539	7,287.06	1,450.97
137	3,293	1,074	8,701	10,205	0	3	3	570,180	132,413	702,597	54.4	1,291,260	4,885.16	991.20
349	9,985	1,126	19,737	31,197	6	11	17	1,496,774	337,837	1,834,611	46.5	3,945,279	8,684.59	1,710.59
81	1,524	136	2,808	4,549	0	0	0	203,135	40,170	243,305	44.9	541,655	6,988.02	1,709.48
143	945	227	2,273	3,588	0	0	0	156,775	44,463	201,238	43.2	466,129	7,909.08	1,485.20
32	670	195	1,703	2,600	0	0	0	94,989	22,180	117,169	48.8	239,886	7,800.17	1,424.88
16	877	120	1,603	2,616	0	0	0	110,589	28,054	138,642	43.6	318,336	6,668.81	1,365.33
51	5,345	360	9,976	15,732	3	6	9	836,426	182,698	1,019,125	47.4	2,151,392	10,194.34	1,911.58
13	159	12	424	608	3	0	3	22,024	5,862	27,885	51.6	54,060	7,088.85	1,538.97
13	465	76	950	1,504	0	5	5	72,837	14,410	87,247	50.2	173,821	8,403.63	1,530.33
1,915	21,154	3,114	50,720	76,903	1,307	38	1,345	3,884,504	924,394	4,808,899	49.6	9,705,110	8,193.97	1,562.57
810	2,708	937	9,552	14,124	20	5	33	638,368	157,879	796,246	55.2	1,441,766	5,549.03	1,138.10
1,666	17,768	2,177	41,168	62,779	1,279	33	1,312	3,246,136	766,515	4,012,653	48.6	8,263,344	8,937.23	1,671.33
12	1,045	124	2,382	3,563	1	0	1	168,158	42,023	210,182	45.6	461,405	8,076.54	1,383.10
632	3,106	400	8,139	12,277	293	1	294	639,959	144,974	784,933	50.3	1,561,381	8,864.03	1,495.18
44	881	96	2,608	3,629	19	10	29	174,494	45,683	220,176	49.1	448,461	7,595.75	1,651.65
104	1,261	235	2,980	4,580	72	0	72	244,054	61,383	305,437	46.5	657,508	9,596.28	1,840.30
61	947	195	2,490	3,693	0	0	0	172,968	47,179	220,147	48.8	451,050	7,855.82	1,524.89
32	950	195	2,707	3,884	8	0	8	196,335	49,854	246,189	48.3	509,565	8,171.61	1,524.64
250	6,637	686	13,041	20,620	414	9	423	1,193,772	265,266	1,459,039	46.5	3,136,487	10,808.61	2,038.45
525	2,941	246	6,821	10,533	472	13	485	456,397	110,153	566,550	54.6	1,037,486	6,745.47	1,349.43
669	13,525	1,844	34,791	50,829	280	80	360	2,622,232	635,673	3,257,907	48.0	6,782,884	7,946.05	1,572.54
310	3,637	975	10,640	15,562	25	14	39	735,301	178,060	913,362	52.0	1,755,307	5,641.57	1,264.09
359	9,888	869	24,151	35,287	255	66	321	1,886,931	457,614	2,344,545	46.6	5,027,578	9,267.78	1,718.99
2	63	38	301	404	0	0	0	13,144	2,922	16,067	57.7	27,856	2,692.48	763.86
81	336	132	1,149	1,698	0	13	13	111,748	20,745	132,493	48.2	275,046	9,085.83	1,098.52
252	5,377	360	12,595	18,504	103	53	156	1,046,018	264,736	1,310,753	45.8	2,860,425	10,597.31	1,887.79
24	4,112	339	10,106	14,581	152	0	152	716,021	169,211	885,232	47.5	1,864,250	8,037.60	1,660.56
2,612	91,244	9,115	198,883	301,854	3,707	941	4,648	18,194,826	4,262,256	22,457,082	49.3	45,556,147	9,945.49	2,001.13
212	6,354	2,506	20,521	29,593	40	17	57	1,377,587	332,984	1,710,570	51.5	3,322,972	5,673.53	1,357.68
2,400	84,890	6,609	178,362	272,261	3,667	924	4,591	16,817,238	3,929,272	20,746,512	49.1	42,233,176	10,571.81	2,078.64
3	825	204	1,851	2,883	0	18	18	141,017	30,681	171,698	53.2	322,669	7,691.94	1,471.55
41	1,329	101	2,899	4,370	0	1	1	185,041	38,909	223,950	43.1	520,203	8,328.84	1,747.01
218	5,495	255	9,933	15,901	200	43	243	974,094	190,851	1,164,945	50.2	2,318,908	10,502.49	2,220.41
2	1,590	210	2,599	4,401	0	0	0	254,021	59,958	313,979	43.6	720,116	7,984.87	1,657.56
0	952	134	1,549	2,635	0	0	0	150,008	37,250	187,258	37.3	502,514	8,322.66	1,756.12
35	739	117	1,671	2,562	0	0	0	139,777	35,603	175,380	47.5	369,309	8,145.69	2,067.10
46	1,925	142	4,511	6,624	126	7	133	366,429	87,481	453,909	47.9	947,599	10,391.71	1,918.41
370	15,683	568	30,142	46,763	1,382	3	1,385	3,148,218	691,577	3,839,797	48.9	7,849,587	12,067.17	2,348.53
10	2,401	113	4,606	7,130	0	0	0	413,930	86,744	500,675	45.2	1,107,123	8,397.29	1,791.47
25	7,999	621	15,756	24,401	240	0	240	1,531,767	374,899	1,906,667	47.3	4,033,644	11,236.47	2,241.34
906	23,449	1,232	52,041	77,628	912	813	1,725	5,510,394	1,389,279	6,899,674	52.6	13,105,936	12,774.45	2,387.60
521	1,650	208	5,130	7,509	403	0	403	347,184	78,010	425,195	51.3	829,354	8,377.65	1,756.80
0	605	46	1,358	2,009	0	0	0	89,203	19,616	108,819	44.0	247,288	5,736.22	1,245.52
0	992	47	1,788	2,827	0	0	0	148,173	29,606	177,779	45.7	388,914	7,520.48	1,590.09
0	2,130	189	3,808	6,127	0	0	0	313,753	83,749	397,502	55.8	712,434	7,695.33	1,659.09
0	2,604	204	5,086	7,894	0	4	4	409,900	85,632	495,532	50.5	982,129	6,576.82	1,427.54
2	490	51	1,280	1,823	0	0	0	109,119	24,520	133,639	52.0	256,901	8,563.09	1,754.31
0	740	98	1,418	2,256	0	0	0	122,962	40,591	163,553	56.9	287,342	8,498.46	1,643.85
0	568	127	1,448	2,143	0	0	0	104,597	24,854	129,451	49.9	259,265	7,267.21	1,537.27
82	7,684	866	16,025	24,657	375	30	405	1,384,614	287,227	1,671,840	43.1	3,883,326	9,870.36	1,978.52
0	555	61	1,123	1,739	0	0	0	93,009	24,429	117,438	51.8	226,931	7,839.53	1,468.10
0	859	174	1,703	2,736	0	0	0	120,868	30,405	151,273	41.6	363,471	8,671.62	1,603.14
81	1,640	378	5,601	7,700	29	3	32	351,645	90,310	441,955	44.5	992,322	11,481.76	2,064.27
14	586	115	1,407	2,122	0	2	2	112,398	27,287	139,685	53.5	261,262	7,043.25	1,521.44
44	819	228	2,192	3,283	0	0	0	173,166	37,085	210,252	47.5	442,864	7,400.64	952.38
0	581	120	1,437	2,138	0	0	0	121,951	22,716	144,667	47.9	301,764	9,162.14	2,124.82

MSAs

TABLE 8

U.S. CENSUS DIVISION 8, MOUNTAIN

U.S. Community Hospitals
(Nonfederal, short-term general and other special hospitals)

2011 Utilization, Personnel and Finances

MSAs

CLASSIFICATION	Hospitals	Beds	Admissions	Inpatient Days	Adjusted Patient Days	Average Daily Census	Adjusted Average Daily Census	Average Stay (days)	Surgical Operations	NEWBORNS Bassinets	Births	OUTPATIENT VISITS Emergency	Total
UNITED STATES	4,973	797,403	34,843,085	187,072,013	358,286,020	512,944	982,377	5.4	26,907,712	56,290	3,730,342	129,461,658	656,078,942
Nonmetropolitan	1,984	133,716	4,192,377	26,166,177	70,109,403	71,710	192,165	6.2	4,127,991	10,856	454,761	23,737,253	123,877,956
Metropolitan.	2,989	663,687	30,650,708	160,905,836	288,176,617	441,234	790,212	5.2	22,779,721	45,434	3,275,581	105,724,405	532,200,986
CENSUS DIVISION 8, MOUNTAIN . . .	384	47,119	2,064,195	10,303,057	20,135,596	28,229	55,160	5.0	1,642,566	4,111	268,969	7,567,323	39,043,567
Nonmetropolitan	193	9,456	249,733	1,750,859	5,190,429	4,796	14,215	7.0	280,441	906	41,024	1,534,366	8,469,986
Metropolitan.	191	37,663	1,814,462	8,552,198	14,945,167	23,433	40,945	4.7	1,362,125	3,205	227,945	6,032,957	30,573,581
Arizona.	70	13,352	700,855	3,106,331	5,250,533	8,510	14,388	4.4	489,692	1,006	74,547	2,189,955	8,552,103
Nonmetropolitan	14	570	30,088	113,733	387,537	309	1,064	3.8	24,127	55	4,208	156,386	610,471
Metropolitan.	56	12,782	670,767	2,992,598	4,862,996	8,201	13,324	4.5	465,565	951	70,339	2,033,569	7,941,632
Flagstaff.	3	366	17,893	77,013	163,752	211	449	4.3	13,168	43	2,004	77,291	635,950
Lake Havasu City-Kingman.	4	527	26,878	116,374	219,907	320	602	4.3	17,130	33	2,893	121,532	542,523
Phoenix-Mesa-Scottsdale	33	8,482	464,811	2,051,343	3,246,086	5,621	8,893	4.4	321,442	693	47,462	1,274,981	4,876,516
Prescott.	3	316	15,534	53,673	109,616	146	300	3.5	10,110	11	1,535	97,406	237,876
Tucson	11	2,717	128,459	617,250	973,573	1,692	2,669	4.8	92,569	152	12,972	390,542	1,475,328
Yuma	2	374	17,192	76,945	150,062	211	411	4.5	11,146	19	3,473	71,817	173,439
Colorado.	82	10,167	432,887	2,170,349	4,423,149	5,946	12,117	5.0	356,539	960	62,264	1,730,788	8,665,215
Nonmetropolitan	38	1,541	39,918	261,381	948,702	716	2,597	6.5	46,332	160	6,243	268,242	1,701,685
Metropolitan.	44	8,626	392,969	1,908,968	3,474,447	5,230	9,520	4.9	310,207	800	56,021	1,462,546	6,963,530
Boulder	4	634	33,977	135,407	259,504	371	711	4.0	24,239	94	6,673	116,430	690,121
Colorado Springs	5	1,054	49,647	224,097	442,457	614	1,212	4.5	39,535	86	7,207	224,266	853,708
Denver-Aurora.	24	5,015	226,886	1,145,585	2,010,367	3,140	5,510	5.0	178,589	463	32,009	790,899	3,274,704
Fort Collins-Loveland.	4	563	29,309	119,924	242,472	328	664	4.1	21,256	53	3,855	106,310	840,428
Grand Junction	3	490	14,677	98,977	191,051	271	523	6.7	13,237	32	2,190	56,967	530,563
Greeley	2	298	16,215	74,595	121,030	204	331	4.6	14,218	38	2,026	51,395	510,738
Pueblo.	2	572	22,258	110,383	207,566	302	569	5.0	19,133	34	2,061	116,279	263,268
Idaho.	40	3,306	128,742	605,718	1,447,607	1,660	3,964	4.7	124,079	298	19,487	517,995	4,034,101
Nonmetropolitan	26	1,063	31,651	187,746	577,981	516	1,582	5.9	40,784	128	6,395	171,862	1,323,993
Metropolitan.	14	2,243	97,091	417,972	869,626	1,144	2,382	4.3	83,295	170	13,092	346,133	2,710,108
Boise City-Nampa.	7	1,267	58,853	224,530	481,815	614	1,319	3.8	49,981	107	8,112	220,277	2,151,703
Coeur d'Alene.	1	246	13,408	58,201	114,295	159	313	4.3	6,508	18	1,510	23,417	70,696
Idaho Falls.	2	319	11,303	61,996	99,170	170	272	5.5	12,394	10	1,508	37,388	171,647
Lewiston	1	136	4,881	23,125	47,123	63	129	4.7	3,441	15	303	26,987	134,670
Logan	1	65	397	12,745	36,763	35	101	32.1	847	5	97	954	4,961
Pocatello	2	210	8,249	37,375	90,460	103	248	4.5	10,124	15	1,562	37,110	176,431
Montana.	48	3,626	94,966	828,778	1,980,100	2,269	5,423	8.7	75,977	214	10,254	369,610	3,542,720
Nonmetropolitan	42	2,313	42,597	506,064	1,267,715	1,386	3,471	11.9	37,457	135	4,577	215,041	1,464,906
Metropolitan.	6	1,313	52,369	322,714	712,385	883	1,952	6.2	38,520	79	5,677	154,569	2,077,814
Billings	3	604	26,361	153,591	377,016	420	1,033	5.8	19,754	34	2,675	71,926	1,458,002
Great Falls.	1	438	12,637	107,416	219,014	294	600	8.5	7,981	24	1,489	36,744	335,652
Missoula	2	271	13,371	61,707	116,355	169	319	4.6	10,785	21	1,513	45,899	284,160
Nevada	38	5,507	249,805	1,359,447	2,192,978	3,727	6,006	5.4	162,057	284	21,822	820,812	2,680,783
Nonmetropolitan	11	383	10,098	67,929	189,052	187	517	6.7	14,501	26	1,345	91,237	449,841
Metropolitan.	27	5,124	239,707	1,291,518	2,003,926	3,540	5,489	5.4	147,556	258	20,477	729,575	2,230,942
Carson City	1	184	10,157	44,976	79,696	123	218	4.4	4,944	12	832	25,253	193,376
Las Vegas-Paradise	19	3,702	181,669	994,641	1,490,574	2,726	4,083	5.5	104,670	179	13,969	533,693	1,488,604
Reno-Sparks.	7	1,238	47,881	251,901	433,656	691	1,188	5.3	37,942	67	5,676	170,629	548,962
New Mexico.	36	4,068	175,112	861,109	1,797,411	2,361	4,926	4.9	146,683	501	21,537	854,871	4,595,133
Nonmetropolitan	22	1,435	51,340	212,743	546,031	584	1,497	4.1	56,232	165	7,856	380,595	1,399,919
Metropolitan.	14	2,633	123,772	648,366	1,251,380	1,777	3,429	5.2	90,451	336	13,681	474,276	3,195,214
Albuquerque	9	1,834	83,946	470,193	915,986	1,289	2,510	5.6	60,665	244	9,154	261,406	2,246,637
Farmington.	1	198	10,566	45,330	86,567	124	237	4.3	6,208	22	1,268	47,573	208,713
Las Cruces.	3	406	19,692	90,758	163,067	249	447	4.6	18,621	46	2,383	71,297	270,787
Santa Fe	1	195	9,568	42,085	85,760	115	235	4.4	4,957	24	876	94,000	469,077

TABLE 8

U.S. CENSUS DIVISION 8, MOUNTAIN

U.S. Community Hospitals
(Nonfederal, short-term general and other special hospitals)

2011 Utilization, Personnel and Finances

Physicians and Dentists	Registered Nurses	Licensed Practical Nurses	Other Salaried Personnel	Total Personnel	Medical and Dental Residents	Other Trainees	Total Trainees	Payroll (in thousands)	Employee Benefits (in thousands)	Total (in thousands)	Percent of Total	Amount (in thousands)	Adjusted per Admission	Adjusted per Inpatient Day
111,741	1,313,626	85,820	3,138,428	4,649,615	99,458	8,198	107,656	$283,964,687	$76,727,241	$360,691,957	51.4	$702,091,034	$10,532.52	$1,959.58
14,153	157,107	25,812	467,855	664,927	1,988	339	2,327	34,086,208	9,249,087	43,335,308	53.7	80,718,425	7,197.79	1,151.32
97,588	1,156,519	60,008	2,670,573	3,984,688	97,470	7,859	105,329	249,878,479	67,478,154	317,356,649	51.1	621,372,609	11,207.00	2,156.22
5,416	77,180	3,729	177,710	264,035	2,615	350	2,965	16,208,568	4,135,109	20,343,673	50.4	40,362,479	10,302.05	2,004.53
1,217	10,202	1,282	33,237	45,038	24	12	36	2,525,675	629,913	3,155,580	53.8	5,862,483	8,012.63	1,129.48
4,199	66,978	2,447	144,473	218,097	2,591	338	2,929	13,682,893	3,505,196	17,188,084	49.8	34,499,996	10,827.76	2,308.44
1,559	23,487	725	48,944	74,715	1,168	93	1,261	4,601,517	1,105,831	5,707,347	49.5	11,520,904	9,616.38	2,194.24
86	829	85	2,855	3,855	3	4	7	217,099	52,024	269,122	53.3	504,859	5,102.84	1,302.74
1,473	22,658	640	46,089	70,860	1,165	89	1,254	4,384,418	1,053,807	5,438,225	49.4	11,016,045	10,022.67	2,265.28
23	785	14	1,770	2,592	0	17	17	191,921	49,698	241,619	53.1	455,231	11,111.05	2,780.00
64	853	69	2,286	3,272	10	16	26	179,807	49,506	229,312	52.1	439,932	8,693.28	2,000.54
1,306	15,463	417	30,563	47,749	1,105	55	1,160	2,972,007	741,624	3,713,631	49.1	7,564,013	10,244.41	2,330.20
22	626	2	1,470	2,120	0	1	1	143,903	38,097	182,000	56.8	320,306	10,087.74	2,922.07
50	4,282	120	8,614	13,066	50	0	50	779,131	139,129	918,260	47.5	1,935,146	9,506.33	1,987.67
8	649	18	1,386	2,061	0	0	0	117,649	35,753	153,403	50.9	301,416	8,900.52	2,008.61
1,293	18,459	571	41,538	61,861	554	115	669	4,038,771	994,026	5,032,798	50.1	10,054,322	11,986.40	2,273.11
237	1,077	240	6,820	9,274	1	1	2	533,264	138,305	671,650	53.1	1,264,850	10,626.04	1,333.24
1,056	16,482	331	34,718	52,587	553	114	667	3,505,507	855,631	4,361,139	49.6	8,789,472	12,211.20	2,529.75
70	1,312	28	3,340	4,750	4	0	4	288,801	67,362	356,163	50.7	702,364	10,799.45	2,706.56
87	1,776	50	4,023	5,936	57	8	65	382,797	104,601	487,399	44.1	1,106,396	11,254.50	2,500.57
683	10,143	157	20,038	31,021	395	104	499	2,174,664	518,854	2,693,518	51.1	5,268,749	13,080.44	2,620.79
51	1,306	25	2,211	3,593	20	0	20	238,423	66,414	304,836	50.2	607,112	10,842.64	2,503.84
70	607	36	1,591	2,304	26	2	28	147,366	35,982	183,348	45.7	400,785	14,288.24	2,097.79
38	572	8	1,449	2,067	32	0	32	125,623	29,286	154,909	45.6	339,624	12,295.86	2,806.11
57	766	27	2,066	2,916	19	0	19	147,834	33,132	180,966	49.7	364,441	8,680.47	1,755.78
699	5,505	563	16,403	23,170	13	7	20	1,175,720	298,650	1,474,370	52.8	2,791,036	9,440.53	1,928.03
156	1,422	279	5,071	6,928	0	1	1	323,159	80,669	403,830	53.1	760,572	7,903.36	1,315.91
543	4,083	284	11,332	16,242	13	6	19	852,561	217,981	1,070,540	52.7	2,030,464	10,182.36	2,334.87
455	2,639	136	8,081	11,311	9	6	15	566,339	145,109	711,446	53.2	1,338,549	10,648.17	2,778.14
22	389	12	1,253	1,676	0	0	0	93,782	25,294	119,075	52.8	225,475	8,563.11	1,972.75
3	500	49	633	1,185	0	0	0	65,792	17,441	83,233	46.9	177,621	9,549.51	1,791.07
15	209	16	528	768	4	0	4	50,064	13,325	63,389	51.6	122,887	12,355.40	2,607.79
4	45	9	149	207	0	0	0	6,723	1,921	8,644	67.6	12,780	11,161.95	347.64
44	301	62	688	1,095	0	0	0	69,861	14,892	84,753	55.3	153,151	8,661.89	1,693.02
761	3,904	579	12,807	18,051	2	5	7	1,059,227	247,590	1,306,816	52.6	2,485,931	10,949.02	1,255.46
296	1,851	215	6,479	8,841	2	2	4	473,915	115,330	589,245	54.9	1,074,261	9,403.79	847.40
465	2,053	364	6,328	9,210	0	3	3	585,311	132,260	717,571	50.8	1,411,670	12,513.81	1,981.61
313	995	204	3,310	4,822	0	0	0	341,328	72,447	413,775	55.0	752,919	12,180.98	1,997.05
53	535	68	1,442	2,098	0	0	0	126,177	27,318	153,495	49.5	309,960	12,029.82	1,415.25
99	523	92	1,576	2,290	0	3	3	117,806	32,495	150,301	43.1	348,791	13,823.37	2,997.65
180	7,590	395	14,963	23,128	80	4	84	1,593,052	447,989	2,041,039	50.1	4,070,512	9,988.18	1,856.16
42	416	45	1,244	1,747	1	1	2	102,843	26,916	129,760	54.8	236,839	8,132.10	1,252.77
138	7,174	350	13,719	21,381	79	3	82	1,490,208	421,073	1,911,279	49.9	3,833,673	10,131.03	1,913.08
1	347	7	718	1,073	0	0	0	70,176	16,739	86,915	48.2	180,367	10,021.48	2,263.18
100	5,296	287	9,923	15,606	62	2	64	1,093,592	316,461	1,410,411	51.9	2,717,851	9,854.46	1,823.36
37	1,531	56	3,078	4,702	17	1	18	326,080	87,873	413,953	44.3	935,455	11,055.82	2,157.14
492	6,593	328	14,495	21,908	58	47	105	1,561,053	358,057	1,919,109	51.7	3,713,540	9,988.84	2,066.05
181	1,775	157	4,705	6,818	15	2	17	427,626	97,481	525,107	51.9	1,011,478	7,382.67	1,852.42
311	4,818	171	9,790	15,090	43	45	88	1,133,427	260,576	1,394,002	51.6	2,702,062	11,509.79	2,159.27
212	3,502	119	6,773	10,606	15	44	59	815,733	180,064	995,798	51.3	1,942,500	12,160.84	2,120.67
69	437	3	1,132	1,641	0	0	0	111,843	30,872	142,715	61.0	233,945	11,594.07	2,702.48
5	570	24	1,068	1,667	21	0	21	103,463	22,389	125,851	45.9	274,297	7,758.81	1,682.11
25	309	25	817	1,176	7	1	8	102,387	27,251	129,638	51.6	251,320	12,890.18	2,930.50

Table continues

MSAs

TABLE 8

U.S. CENSUS DIVISION 8, MOUNTAIN CONTINUED

U.S. Community Hospitals
(Nonfederal, short-term general and other special hospitals)

2011 Utilization, Personnel and Finances

MSAs

CLASSIFICATION	Hospitals	Beds	Admissions	Inpatient Days	Adjusted Patient Days	Average Daily Census	Adjusted Average Daily Census	Average Stay (days)	Surgical Operations	NEWBORNS Bassinets	NEWBORNS Births	OUTPATIENT VISITS Emergency	OUTPATIENT VISITS Total
Utah	46	5,135	236,131	993,098	2,088,900	2,720	5,721	4.2	245,648	678	52,695	855,152	5,854,666
Nonmetropolitan	18	622	17,062	105,171	457,500	287	1,253	6.2	29,579	107	6,275	95,852	630,387
Metropolitan	28	4,513	219,069	887,927	1,631,400	2,433	4,468	4.1	216,069	571	46,420	759,300	5,224,279
Logan	2	150	7,972	23,179	54,127	63	148	2.9	9,163	34	2,578	33,300	333,802
Ogden-Clearfield	4	794	37,338	139,200	244,760	382	670	3.7	26,794	103	7,802	133,189	525,818
Provo-Orem	6	729	36,802	141,347	254,590	388	697	3.8	35,510	133	11,327	123,470	696,472
Salt Lake City	15	2,579	122,566	532,197	982,256	1,458	2,691	4.3	133,078	285	22,472	428,049	3,213,299
St. George	1	261	14,391	52,004	95,667	142	262	3.6	11,524	16	2,241	41,292	454,888
Wyoming	24	1,958	45,697	378,227	954,918	1,036	2,615	8.3	41,891	170	6,363	228,140	1,118,846
Nonmetropolitan	22	1,529	26,979	296,092	815,911	811	2,234	11.0	31,429	130	4,125	155,151	888,784
Metropolitan	2	429	18,718	82,135	139,007	225	381	4.4	10,462	40	2,238	72,989	230,062
Casper	1	207	8,423	35,260	54,320	97	149	4.2	5,056	24	1,041	33,740	80,463
Cheyenne	1	222	10,295	46,875	84,687	128	232	4.6	5,406	16	1,197	39,249	149,599

TABLE 8

U.S. CENSUS DIVISION 8, MOUNTAIN CONTINUED

U.S. Community Hospitals
(Nonfederal, short-term general and other special hospitals)

2011 Utilization, Personnel and Finances

FULL-TIME EQUIVALENT PERSONNEL					FULL-TIME EQUIV. TRAINEES			EXPENSES						
								LABOR				TOTAL		
Physicians and Dentists	Registered Nurses	Licensed Practical Nurses	Other Salaried Personnel	Total Personnel	Medical and Dental Residents	Other Trainees	Total Trainees	Payroll (in thousands)	Employee Benefits (in thousands)	Total (in thousands)	Percent of Total	Amount (in thousands)	Adjusted per Admission	Adjusted per Inpatient Day
259	9,641	425	22,442	32,767	739	77	816	1,697,176	550,483	2,247,658	48.0	4,679,559	9,904.86	2,240.20
56	621	135	2,064	2,876	1	1	2	129,179	35,449	164,628	49.8	330,880	5,331.26	723.23
203	9,020	290	20,378	29,891	738	76	814	1,567,997	515,034	2,083,030	47.9	4,348,679	10,596.53	2,665.61
0	252	14	681	947	0	0	0	41,557	16,298	57,855	47.4	121,938	6,498.84	2,252.81
29	1,271	96	2,556	3,952	26	0	26	208,750	63,808	272,558	47.5	573,720	8,751.07	2,344.01
25	1,419	44	3,160	4,648	40	8	48	222,143	76,719	298,862	48.4	617,889	9,016.59	2,127.00
149	5,597	135	12,647	18,528	672	68	740	1,003,866	323,859	1,327,724	48.3	2,746,507	11,886.45	2,796.12
0	481	1	1,334	1,816	0	0	0	91,682	34,350	126,031	43.7	288,625	10,902.21	3,016.08
173	2,001	143	6,118	8,435	1	2	3	402,050	132,402	614,530	58.7	1,046,675	9,818.26	1,096.09
163	1,311	126	3,999	5,599	1	0	1	318,589	83,648	402,238	59.3	678,743	9,046.41	831.88
10	690	17	2,119	2,836	0	2	2	163,464	48,834	212,298	57.7	367,932	11,652.27	2,646.86
0	320	6	811	1,137	0	2	2	68,203	23,432	91,636	50.8	180,239	13,890.19	3,318.10
10	370	11	1,308	1,699	0	0	0	95,261	25,401	120,662	64.3	187,693	10,091.03	2,216.31

MSAs

TABLE **8**

U.S. CENSUS DIVISION 9, PACIFIC

U.S. Community Hospitals
(Nonfederal, short-term general and other special hospitals)

2011 Utilization, Personnel and Finances

MSAs

CLASSIFICATION	Hospitals	Beds	Admissions	Inpatient Days	Adjusted Patient Days	Average Daily Census	Adjusted Average Daily Census	Average Stay (days)	Surgical Operations	NEWBORNS Bassinets	Births	OUTPATIENT VISITS Emergency	Total
UNITED STATES	4,973	797,403	34,843,085	187,072,013	358,286,020	512,944	982,377	5.4	26,907,712	56,290	3,730,342	129,461,658	656,078,942
Nonmetropolitan	1,984	133,716	4,192,377	26,166,177	70,109,403	71,710	192,165	6.2	4,127,991	10,856	454,761	23,737,253	123,877,956
Metropolitan	2,989	663,687	30,650,708	160,905,836	288,176,617	441,234	790,212	5.2	22,779,721	45,434	3,275,581	105,724,405	532,200,986
CENSUS DIVISION 9, PACIFIC	535	92,601	4,471,783	22,232,780	38,886,143	61,048	106,770	5.0	3,038,848	7,064	629,315	15,480,506	78,278,433
Nonmetropolitan	121	5,525	193,133	1,106,025	3,101,385	3,032	8,494	5.7	231,137	581	33,594	1,308,176	7,604,556
Metropolitan	414	87,076	4,278,650	21,126,755	35,784,758	58,016	98,276	4.9	2,807,711	6,483	595,721	14,172,330	70,673,877
Alaska	23	1,556	54,715	340,060	817,834	933	2,241	6.2	60,134	166	9,196	315,181	1,765,636
Nonmetropolitan	17	571	12,303	107,685	346,230	296	949	8.8	21,085	62	2,838	101,727	598,848
Metropolitan	6	985	42,412	232,375	471,604	637	1,292	5.5	39,049	104	6,358	213,454	1,166,788
Anchorage	5	768	36,744	183,141	357,177	502	979	5.0	33,232	88	5,257	175,899	864,535
Fairbanks	1	217	5,668	49,234	114,427	135	313	8.7	5,817	16	1,101	37,555	302,253
California	345	70,008	3,393,166	17,090,593	28,551,485	46,826	78,223	5.0	2,131,751	5,098	488,863	11,073,272	52,675,183
Nonmetropolitan	31	1,373	52,458	291,170	779,345	798	2,134	5.6	62,360	127	10,231	421,394	2,485,481
Metropolitan	314	68,635	3,340,708	16,799,423	27,772,140	46,028	76,089	5.0	2,069,391	4,971	478,632	10,651,878	50,189,702
Bakersfield	8	1,431	75,947	341,196	592,027	935	1,623	4.5	39,708	91	13,042	185,791	617,358
Chico	4	529	30,586	135,164	270,995	369	743	4.4	17,080	43	3,403	146,149	836,815
El Centro	2	272	12,990	45,287	95,619	124	262	3.5	9,489	25	3,384	73,426	225,414
Fresno	8	1,627	93,945	446,715	724,866	1,224	1,986	4.8	45,524	93	14,203	246,984	1,594,160
Hanford-Corcoran	3	163	11,233	45,969	112,574	125	309	4.1	9,623	20	958	74,714	337,023
Los Angeles-Long Beach-Glendale	91	21,079	1,031,315	5,227,028	8,294,965	14,323	22,724	5.1	563,575	1,527	136,181	2,544,772	12,958,541
Madera	3	478	18,928	112,088	185,168	308	507	5.9	18,379	10	1,790	115,027	397,612
Merced	2	232	13,694	58,394	107,124	160	293	4.3	8,242	38	2,811	73,617	207,029
Modesto	4	1,362	53,558	330,341	494,813	904	1,356	6.2	34,012	74	8,081	212,603	369,979
Napa	2	290	14,000	64,456	106,006	177	291	4.6	13,108	12	1,123	32,820	303,842
Oakland-Fremont-Hayward	19	4,609	216,275	1,102,691	1,867,163	3,023	5,116	5.1	115,367	322	25,052	772,372	3,810,897
Oxnard-Thousand Oaks-Ventura . .	6	1,148	65,528	299,337	555,948	820	1,523	4.6	34,265	100	9,791	227,576	1,065,290
Redding	3	517	22,944	117,109	190,958	321	523	5.1	10,934	23	2,109	73,515	205,703
Riverside-San Bernardino-Ontario .	33	6,730	347,338	1,630,743	2,739,850	4,469	7,507	4.7	213,698	523	53,750	1,177,426	3,615,983
Sacramento—Arden-Arcade—Roseville	15	3,612	175,856	893,267	1,468,605	2,448	4,022	5.1	133,457	294	21,443	630,734	2,995,077
Salinas	4	716	33,616	166,903	281,966	458	773	5.0	18,322	81	7,094	160,234	620,323
San Diego-Carlsbad-San Marcos .	21	5,474	287,826	1,454,185	2,270,515	3,985	6,221	5.1	199,680	380	41,326	826,146	3,251,080
San Francisco-San Mateo-Redwood City	18	4,838	169,991	1,159,711	2,106,200	3,177	5,770	6.8	133,866	204	19,707	735,224	5,369,488
San Jose-Sunnyvale-Santa Clara .	11	3,244	160,494	795,261	1,311,314	2,177	3,595	5.0	112,783	347	30,005	583,793	4,114,708
San Luis Obispo-Paso Robles . . .	4	465	19,311	77,050	112,607	211	308	4.0	12,259	37	2,846	91,782	268,280
Santa Ana-Anaheim-Irvine	24	5,472	262,843	1,238,060	2,010,497	3,391	5,507	4.7	193,992	345	41,898	753,423	3,213,368
Santa Cruz-Watsonville	3	410	20,014	90,965	176,580	249	484	4.5	13,580	47	3,695	41,569	311,438
Santa Rosa-Petaluma	7	668	34,223	147,535	280,649	404	769	4.3	25,423	43	4,685	91,586	480,386
Stockton	7	1,118	61,685	261,810	502,622	717	1,377	4.2	32,945	102	10,171	286,390	1,316,642
Vallejo-Fairfield	3	507	24,424	108,916	195,626	299	535	4.5	14,019	45	4,217	104,914	341,448
Visalia-Porterville	3	683	37,531	208,504	331,036	571	908	5.6	16,892	53	7,460	203,403	771,855
Yuba City	1	212	11,834	50,875	72,689	139	199	4.3	3,566	16	2,134	53,002	147,992
Hawaii	23	2,562	105,039	720,633	1,403,259	1,973	3,845	6.9	83,415	202	10,756	366,276	2,006,152
Nonmetropolitan	12	876	29,024	226,290	539,283	619	1,477	7.8	26,757	72	4,480	109,518	352,733
Metropolitan	11	1,686	76,015	494,343	863,976	1,354	2,368	6.5	56,658	130	6,276	256,758	1,653,419
Honolulu	11	1,686	76,015	494,343	863,976	1,354	2,368	6.5	56,658	130	6,276	256,758	1,653,419
Oregon	59	6,805	342,649	1,468,277	2,941,566	4,024	8,061	4.3	334,671	663	43,262	1,404,165	9,373,532
Nonmetropolitan	29	1,345	57,384	234,146	691,708	643	1,895	4.1	61,790	167	8,059	378,375	2,365,073
Metropolitan	30	5,460	285,265	1,234,131	2,249,858	3,381	6,166	4.3	272,881	496	35,203	1,025,790	7,008,459
Bend	2	309	16,967	65,268	110,199	179	302	3.8	18,160	33	1,990	54,211	237,702
Corvallis	1	165	9,626	42,319	78,515	116	215	4.4	10,873	20	1,063	23,213	181,258
Eugene-Springfield	5	629	36,925	145,619	245,582	399	674	3.9	23,512	50	3,538	124,557	381,241
Medford	3	456	22,378	94,708	160,126	260	438	4.2	21,721	34	2,416	76,726	708,941
Portland-Vancouver-Beaverton . . .	15	3,348	171,589	772,219	1,431,927	2,116	3,924	4.5	180,064	300	21,168	604,462	4,729,067
Salem	4	553	27,780	113,998	223,509	311	613	4.1	18,551	59	5,028	142,621	770,250

TABLE 8

U.S. CENSUS DIVISION 9, PACIFIC

U.S. Community Hospitals
(Nonfederal, short-term general and other special hospitals)

2011 Utilization, Personnel and Finances

MSAs

FULL-TIME EQUIVALENT PERSONNEL					FULL-TIME EQUIV. TRAINEES			EXPENSES						
								LABOR				TOTAL		
Physicians and Dentists	Registered Nurses	Licensed Practical Nurses	Other Salaried Personnel	Total Personnel	Medical and Dental Residents	Other Trainees	Total Trainees	Payroll (in thousands)	Employee Benefits (in thousands)	Total (in thousands)	Percent of Total	Amount (in thousands)	Adjusted per Admission	Adjusted per Inpatient Day
111,741	1,313,626	85,820	3,138,428	4,649,615	99,458	8,198	107,656	$283,964,687	$76,727,241	$360,691,957	51.4	$702,091,034	$10,532.52	$1,959.58
14,153	157,107	25,812	467,855	664,927	1,988	339	2,327	34,086,208	9,249,087	43,335,308	53.7	80,718,425	7,197.79	1,151.32
97,588	1,156,519	60,008	2,670,573	3,984,688	97,470	7,859	105,329	249,878,479	67,478,154	317,356,649	51.1	621,372,609	11,207.00	2,156.22
12,461	172,779	9,199	386,647	581,086	11,457	646	12,103	42,148,700	13,169,932	55,318,637	52.7	105,001,432	13,418.36	2,700.23
809	8,704	887	26,849	37,249	25	21	46	2,416,306	766,830	3,183,130	56.5	5,634,123	10,600.04	1,816.65
11,652	164,075	8,312	359,798	543,837	11,432	625	12,057	39,732,393	12,403,102	52,135,498	52.5	99,367,308	13,623.74	2,776.81
164	2,868	193	7,867	11,092	51	11	62	695,531	202,387	897,916	51.4	1,747,386	14,270.32	2,136.60
99	924	118	3,280	4,421	4	9	13	269,957	88,114	358,069	56.7	631,639	15,569.89	1,824.33
65	1,944	75	4,587	6,671	47	2	49	425,574	114,273	539,847	48.4	1,115,747	13,626.44	2,365.85
58	1,659	69	3,774	5,560	47	2	49	342,873	89,944	432,816	48.0	902,190	13,130.79	2,525.89
7	285	6	813	1,111	0	0	0	82,702	24,329	107,031	50.1	213,556	16,211.68	1,866.31
8,266	128,863	7,434	278,765	423,328	8,816	509	9,325	30,875,802	9,825,940	40,701,744	52.7	77,265,358	13,614.66	2,706.18
72	2,371	292	6,602	9,337	0	5	5	633,499	215,225	848,724	54.2	1,565,314	11,589.08	2,008.50
8,194	126,492	7,142	272,163	413,991	8,816	504	9,320	30,242,303	9,610,715	39,853,020	52.6	75,700,045	13,664.04	2,725.75
161	2,107	145	5,072	7,485	160	3	163	505,095	167,925	673,019	56.5	1,191,689	9,553.92	2,012.90
67	1,007	109	2,758	3,941	20	4	24	273,715	90,242	363,956	54.9	662,682	11,243.71	2,445.36
20	392	41	1,036	1,489	11	2	13	82,717	24,791	107,508	51.5	185,328	6,755.91	1,938.19
88	3,004	310	4,309	9,190	27	1	21	667,011	116,600	707,710	17.0	1,107,010	8,017.07	2,006.00
25	397	65	1,130	1,617	2	1	3	107,895	26,908	134,803	49.2	274,137	10,239.31	2,435.17
1,891	37,562	2,352	83,026	124,831	3,378	162	3,540	8,724,094	2,620,847	11,344,947	51.8	21,887,614	13,254.30	2,638.66
3	911	68	2,279	3,261	0	2	2	195,368	79,435	274,803	57.2	480,116	15,559.89	2,592.87
9	456	43	1,062	1,570	1	2	3	112,901	33,612	146,512	51.5	284,261	11,377.29	2,653.57
12	2,406	88	3,585	6,091	3	1	4	444,130	131,748	575,878	53.3	1,081,075	13,950.08	2,184.82
0	597	23	1,396	2,016	0	0	0	151,925	65,117	217,043	52.7	411,800	17,956.65	3,884.68
555	7,536	500	17,620	26,220	393	20	421	2,315,339	757,457	3,072,790	55.0	5,522,408	14,903.27	2,957.65
82	1,927	157	4,351	6,517	42	6	48	521,748	163,965	685,713	53.2	1,288,895	10,417.42	2,318.37
8	917	23	1,219	2,167	16	0	16	169,362	68,511	237,873	49.5	480,744	14,407.35	2,517.54
1,091	12,861	866	26,257	41,075	1,071	67	1,138	2,355,893	688,388	3,044,279	51.6	5,902,742	10,032.31	2,154.40
1,066	7,366	333	17,075	25,840	967	45	1,012	2,208,121	621,070	2,829,192	51.6	5,045,715	17,052.56	3,435.72
67	1,122	62	2,899	4,150	38	0	38	387,738	176,405	564,143	60.2	937,851	16,828.18	3,326.11
943	11,865	516	20,325	33,649	802	10	821	2,303,864	650,201	2,063,065	50.5	5,064,591	13,105.20	2,582.90
903	6,936	366	16,499	24,704	239	19	258	2,615,723	734,559	3,350,280	52.9	6,338,375	20,635.89	3,009.39
759	7,501	244	16,405	24,909	1,321	104	1,425	2,191,957	1,023,821	3,215,778	54.2	5,936,452	22,401.79	4,527.10
4	761	18	1,092	1,875	4	0	4	142,160	39,315	181,476	54.5	332,772	11,727.65	2,955.16
108	10,577	347	21,426	32,458	133	8	141	2,017,220	715,760	2,732,980	49.4	5,536,768	12,868.27	2,753.93
16	1,368	93	2,837	4,314	56	0	56	321,222	101,486	422,708	54.6	773,761	15,033.25	2,470.83
62	712	47	1,801	2,622	25	2	27	193,504	52,240	245,743	51.6	475,911	11,809.80	2,695.16
46	1,122	71	2,702	3,941	8	4	12	303,984	117,677	421,660	51.8	813,264	12,753.88	2,897.80
154	2,185	144	5,214	7,697	61	11	72	467,166	122,858	590,025	55.4	1,065,419	8,932.68	2,119.72
61	1,231	46	2,802	4,140	31	6	37	239,510	68,183	307,693	50.3	611,980	13,968.32	3,128.32
13	1,231	115	3,048	4,407	7	4	11	258,659	76,206	334,866	56.8	589,599	9,797.91	1,781.07
0	445	32	1,039	1,516	0	0	0	70,052	36,486	106,538	47.0	226,881	13,418.57	3,121.26
364	3,999	251	10,187	14,801	39	21	60	990,721	280,574	1,271,296	53.1	2,391,952	11,906.42	1,704.57
85	966	132	2,763	3,946	14	1	15	260,717	84,860	345,576	56.8	608,776	8,865.62	1,128.86
279	3,033	119	7,424	10,855	25	20	45	730,004	195,715	925,720	51.9	1,783,177	13,485.52	2,063.92
279	3,033	119	7,424	10,855	25	20	45	730,004	195,715	925,720	51.9	1,783,177	13,485.52	2,063.92
1,433	14,210	263	32,577	48,483	1,096	24	1,120	3,406,230	1,115,229	4,521,461	51.8	8,726,772	12,662.75	2,966.71
312	2,431	103	7,448	10,294	0	3	3	667,460	209,566	877,026	58.6	1,496,842	9,318.80	2,163.98
1,121	11,779	160	25,129	38,189	1,096	21	1,117	2,738,770	905,663	3,644,435	50.4	7,229,931	13,678.98	3,213.51
38	673	4	1,662	2,377	0	0	0	177,313	56,948	234,260	51.0	459,641	15,664.95	4,171.01
95	334	15	1,010	1,454	52	4	56	130,113	42,363	172,476	54.8	314,986	17,637.37	4,011.79
120	1,160	34	3,006	4,320	0	1	1	264,590	81,442	346,033	46.0	752,234	12,290.21	3,063.07
42	803	15	1,885	2,745	0	1	1	188,689	76,622	265,312	49.8	533,184	13,881.74	3,329.78
706	7,566	74	14,725	23,071	1,044	15	1,059	1,689,020	568,369	2,257,390	50.0	4,510,586	13,873.90	3,150.01
120	1,243	18	2,841	4,222	0	0	0	289,045	79,918	368,964	56.0	659,299	11,645.52	2,949.77

Table continues

TABLE 8

U.S. CENSUS DIVISION 9, PACIFIC
CONTINUED

U.S. Community Hospitals
(Nonfederal, short-term general and other special hospitals)

2011 Utilization, Personnel and Finances

CLASSIFICATION	Hospitals	Beds	Admissions	Inpatient Days	Adjusted Patient Days	Average Daily Census	Adjusted Average Daily Census	Average Stay (days)	Surgical Operations	NEWBORNS Bassinets	NEWBORNS Births	OUTPATIENT VISITS Emergency	OUTPATIENT VISITS Total
Washington	85	11,670	576,214	2,613,217	5,171,999	7,292	14,400	4.5	428,877	935	77,238	2,321,612	12,457,930
Nonmetropolitan	32	1,360	41,964	246,734	744,819	676	2,039	5.9	59,145	153	7,986	297,162	1,802,421
Metropolitan	53	10,310	534,250	2,366,483	4,427,180	6,616	12,361	4.4	369,732	782	69,252	2,024,450	10,655,509
Bellingham	1	253	15,691	59,713	105,337	164	289	3.8	7,369	24	2,036	58,238	90,477
Bremerton-Silverdale	1	262	14,936	59,339	107,208	163	294	4.0	11,069	24	1,891	70,962	223,398
Kennewick-Richland-Pasco	4	419	22,138	84,887	172,853	232	473	3.8	14,973	37	4,828	101,188	355,810
Lewiston	1	35	1,364	5,727	19,859	16	54	4.2	2,474	0	0	13,678	71,130
Longview	1	202	9,729	41,162	74,367	113	204	4.2	3,810	27	834	61,712	300,194
Mount Vernon-Anacortes	3	205	12,831	44,507	114,106	122	312	3.5	16,349	27	1,665	61,919	658,951
Olympia	2	488	25,341	108,383	154,179	296	422	4.3	11,601	37	2,758	82,557	354,639
Portland-Vancouver-Beaverton	2	644	23,579	86,027	149,536	368	644	3.6	12,598	60	3,635	94,335	336,835
Seattle-Bellevue-Everett	19	4,368	238,409	1,123,083	2,175,080	3,077	5,960	4.7	171,931	323	31,406	794,222	5,857,618
Spokane	6	1,453	59,787	313,798	503,756	860	1,379	5.2	44,548	65	5,758	229,547	612,234
Tacoma	6	1,295	75,080	304,965	568,268	837	1,557	4.1	49,256	77	8,919	291,443	1,038,801
Wenatchee	3	162	10,262	39,817	88,889	108	243	3.9	5,997	25	1,462	14,322	106,038
Yakima	4	524	25,103	95,075	193,742	260	530	3.8	17,757	56	4,060	150,327	649,384

MSAs

TABLE 8

U.S. CENSUS DIVISION 9, PACIFIC CONTINUED

U.S. Community Hospitals
(Nonfederal, short-term general and other special hospitals)

2011 Utilization, Personnel and Finances

FULL-TIME EQUIVALENT PERSONNEL					FULL-TIME EQUIV. TRAINEES			EXPENSES						
								LABOR				TOTAL		
Physicians and Dentists	Registered Nurses	Licensed Practical Nurses	Other Salaried Personnel	Total Personnel	Medical and Dental Residents	Other Trainees	Total Trainees	Payroll (in thousands)	Employee Benefits (in thousands)	Total (in thousands)	Percent of Total	Amount (in thousands)	Adjusted per Admission	Adjusted per Inpatient Day
2,234	22,839	1,058	57,251	83,382	1,455	81	1,536	6,180,416	1,745,802	7,926,220	53.3	14,869,963	13,072.13	2,875.09
241	2,012	242	6,756	9,251	7	3	10	584,675	169,066	753,744	56.6	1,331,553	10,518.63	1,787.75
1,993	20,827	816	50,495	74,131	1,448	78	1,526	5,595,741	1,576,736	7,172,476	53.0	13,538,410	13,391.88	3,058.02
94	653	74	1,600	2,421	0	3	3	149,368	46,839	196,206	52.6	373,287	13,485.79	3,543.74
40	497	28	1,168	1,733	16	2	18	130,714	37,594	174,308	53.4	326,213	12,088.69	3,042.81
43	818	49	2,150	3,060	14	3	17	217,935	53,542	271,477	51.7	525,160	11,290.84	3,038.19
11	83	12	266	372	1	2	3	25,237	6,790	32,027	52.6	60,871	12,869.10	3,065.15
31	359	21	887	1,298	14	1	15	96,664	26,248	122,912	51.5	238,602	13,574.70	3,208.45
86	474	27	1,483	2,070	0	0	0	145,635	34,614	180,249	55.5	325,002	9,775.37	2,848.24
5	813	32	1,538	2,388	3	0	3	168,936	47,914	216,850	47.5	456,484	12,534.58	2,960.74
78	1,328	21	2,280	3,707	29	10	39	185,550	50,663	236,213	57.2	413,030	10,086.95	2,762.08
1,121	10,136	270	25,888	37,415	1,250	48	1,298	3,065,846	864,750	3,930,596	54.5	7,209,293	15,566.29	3,314.50
68	1,955	29	4,381	6,433	42	2	44	522,559	148,689	671,247	49.5	1,357,413	13,797.93	2,694.58
290	2,289	145	5,367	8,091	61	3	64	593,592	176,515	770,107	49.0	1,570,393	11,184.42	2,763.47
36	375	30	1,006	1,447	6	1	7	101,010	24,969	125,980	58.9	213,817	9,440.04	2,405.44
90	1,047	78	2,481	3,696	12	3	15	186,695	57,610	244,304	52.1	468,846	8,969.01	2,419.95

MSAs

Statistics for Multihospital Health Care Systems and their Hospitals

The following tables describing multihospital health care systems refers to information in section B of the 2012 *AHA Guide*.

Table 1 shows the number of multihospital health care systems by type of control. Table 2 provides a breakdown of the number of systems that own, lease, sponsor or contract manage hospitals within each control category. Table 3 gives the number of hospitals and beds in each control category as well as total hospitals and beds. Finally, Table 4 shows the percentage of hospitals and beds in each control category.

For more information on multihospital health care systems, please write to the Section for Health Care Systems, 155 N. Wacker Drive, Chicago, Illinois 60606 or call 312/422–3000.

Table 1. Multihospital Health Care Systems, by Type of Organizaton Control

Type of Control	Code	Number of Systems
Catholic (Roman) church–related	CC	37
Other church–related	CO	12
Subtotal, church–related		49
Other not–for–profit	NP	284
Subtotal, not–for–profit		333
Investor Owned	IO	80
Federal Government	FG	5
Total		418

Table 2. Multihospital Health Care Systems, by Type of Ownership and Control

Type of Ownership	Catholic Church–Related (CC)	Other Church–Related (CO)	Total Church–Related (CC + CO)	Other Not–for–Profit (NP)	Total Not–for–Profit (CC, CO, + NP)	Investor–Owned (IO)	Federal Government (FG)	All Systems
Systems that only own, lease or sponsor	31	8	39	255	294	74	5	373
Systems that only contract–manage	0	0	0	1	1	2	0	3
Systems that manage, own, lease, or sponsor	6	4	10	28	38	4	0	42
Total	37	12	49	284	333	80	5	418

Table 3. Hospitals and Beds in Multihospital Health Care Systems, by Type of Ownership and Control

Type of Ownership	Catholic Church–Related (CC) H	B	Other Church–Related (CO) H	B	Total Church–Related (CC + CO) H	B	Other Not–for–Profit (NP) H	B	Total Not–for–Profit (CC, CO, + NP) H	B	Investor–Owned (IO) H	B	Federal Government (FG) H	B	All Systems H	B
Owned, leased or sponsored	544	102,364	105	21,996	649	124,360	1,398	300,819	2,047	425,179	1,288	150,842	213	38,217	3,548	614,238
Contract–managed	39	1,470	6	546	45	2,016	84	5,687	129	7,703	129	8,681	0	0	258	16,384
Total	583	103,834	111	22,542	694	126,376	1,482	306,506	2,176	432,882	1,417	159,523	213	38,217	3,806	630,622

H = hospitals; B = beds.

Table 4. Hospitals and Beds in Multihospital Health Care Systems, by Type of Ownership and Control as a Percentage of All Systems

Type of Ownership	Catholic Church–Related (CC) H	B	Other Church–Related (CO) H	B	Total Church–Related (CC + CO) H	B	Other Not–for–Profit (NP) H	B	Total Not for–Profit (CC, CO, + NP) H	B	Investor–Owned (IO) H	B	Federal Government (FG) H	B	All Systems H	B
Owned, leased or sponsored	15.3	16.7	3.0	3.6	18.3	20.2	39.4	49.0	57.7	69.2	36.3	24.6	6.0	6.2	100.0	100.0
Contract–managed	15.1	9.0	2.3	3.3	17.4	12.3	32.6	34.7	50.0	47.0	50.0	53.0	0.0	0.0	100.0	100.0
Total	15.3	16.5	2.9	3.6	18.2	20.0	38.9	48.6	57.2	68.6	37.2	25.3	5.6	6.1	100.0	100.0

H = hospitals; B = beds.
*Please note that figures may not always equal the provided subtotal or total percentages due to rounding.

Glossary

This glossary explains specific terms as they are used in the tables and text of AHA Hospital Statistics

Ablation of Barrett's esophagus:
Premalignant condition that can lead to adenocarcinoma of the esophagus. The non surgical ablation of the premalignant tissue in Barrett's esophagus by the application of thermal energy or light through an endoscope passed from the mouth into the esophagus.

Acute long term care: Providers specialized acute hospital care to medically complex patients who are critically ill, have multisystem complications and/or failure, and require hospitalization averaging 25 days, in a facility offering specialized treatment programs and therapeutic intervention on a 24 hour/7day a week basis.

Adjusted average daily census: An estimate of the average number of patients (both inpatients and outpatients) receiving care each day during the reporting period, which is usually 12 months. The figure is derived by dividing the number of inpatient day equivalents (also called adjusted inpatient days) by the number of days in the reporting period.

Adjusted inpatient days: An aggregate figure reflecting the number of days of inpatient care, plus an estimate of the volume of outpatient services, expressed in units equivalent to an inpatient day in terms of level of effort. The figure is derived by first multiplying the number of outpatient visits by the ratio of outpatient revenue per outpatient visit to inpatient revenue per inpatient day. The product (which represents the number of patient days attributable to outpatient services) is then added to the number of *inpatient days*. Originally, the purpose of this calculation was to summarize overall productivity and calculate a unit cost that would include both inpatient and outpatient activities.

Formula 1:

$$\frac{\text{total expenses}}{\text{inpatient days} + \text{outpatient visits}\left(\dfrac{\dfrac{\text{outpatient revenue}}{\text{per outpatient visit}}}{\dfrac{\text{inpatient revenue}}{\text{per inpatient day}}}\right)}$$

However, the value of this calculation has changed over the years as the outpatient share of total revenue has grown and third-party payers have exerted a greater influence on pricing.

Admissions: The number of patients, excluding newborns, accepted for inpatient service during the reporting period; the number includes patients who visit the emergency room and are later admitted for inpatient service.

Adult Cardiac Surgery: Includes minimally invasive procedures that include surgery done with only a small incision or no incision at all, such as through a laparoscope or an endoscope and more invasive major surgical procedures that include open chest and open heart surgery.

Adult Cardiology Services: An organized clinical service offering diagnostic and interventional procedures to manage the full range of adult heart conditions.

Adult day care program: Program providing supervision, medical and psychological care, and social activities for older adults who live at home or in another family setting, but cannot be alone or prefer to be with others during the day. May include intake assessment, health monitoring, occupational therapy, personal care, noon meal, and transportation services.

Adult Diagnostic/invasive catheterization: (also called coronary angiography or coronary arteriography) is used to assist in diagnosing complex heart conditions. Cardiac angiography involves the insertion of a tiny catheter into the artery in the groin then carefully threading the catheter up into the aorta where the coronary arteries originate. Once the catheter is in place, a dye is injected which allows the cardiologist to see the size, shape, and distribution of the coronary arteries. These images are used to diagnose heart disease and to determine, among other things, whether or not surgery is indicated.

Adult Interventional cardiac catheterization: Non surgical procedure that utilizes the same basic principles as diagnostic catheterization and then uses advanced techniques to improve the heart's function. It can be a less-invasive alternative to heart surgery.

Airborne infection isolation room: A single-occupancy room for patient care where environmental factors are controlled in an effort to minimize the transmission of those infectious agents, usually spread person to person by droplet nuclei associated with coughing and inhalation. Such rooms typically have specific ventilation requirements for controlled ventilation, air pressure and filtration.

Alcoholism-drug abuse or dependency inpatient care: Provides diagnosis and therapeutic services to patients with alcoholism or other drug dependencies. Includes care for inpatient/residential treatment for patients whose course of treatment involves more intensive care than provided in an outpatient setting or where patient requires supervised withdrawal.

Alcoholism-drug abuse or dependency outpatient services: Organized hospital services that provide medical care and/or rehabilitative treatment services to outpatients for whom the primary diagnosis is alcoholism or other chemical dependency.

Alzheimer Center: Facility that offers care to persons with Alzheimer's disease and their families through an integrated program of clinical services, research, and education.

Ambulance services: Provision of ambulance services to the ill and injured who require medical attention on a scheduled or unscheduled basis.

Ambulatory Surgery Center: Facility that provides care to patients requiring surgery who are admitted and discharged on the same day. Ambulatory surgery centers are distinct from same day surgical units within the hospital outpatient departments for purposes of Medicare payments.

Arthritis treatment center: Specifically equipped and staffed center for the diagnosis and treatment of arthritis and other joint disorders.

Assisted living: A special combination of housing, supportive services, personalized assistance and health care designed to respond to the individual needs of those who need help in activities of daily living and instrumental activities of daily living. Supportive services are available, 24 hours a day, to meet scheduled and unscheduled needs, in a way that promotes maximum independence and dignity for each resident and encourages the involvement of a resident's family, neighbor and friends.

Assistive Technology Center: A program providing access to specialized hardware and software with adaptations allowing individuals greater independence with mobility, dexterity, or increased communication options.

Auxiliary: A volunteer community organization formed to assist the hospital in carrying out its purpose and to serve as a link between the institution and the community.

Average daily census: The average number of people served on an inpatient basis on a single day during the reporting period; the figure is calculated by dividing the number of inpatient days by the number of days in the reporting period.

Bariatric/weight control services: Bariatrics is the medical practice of weight reduction.

Beds: Number of beds regularly maintained (set up and staffed for use) for inpatients as of the close of the reporting period. Excludes newborn bassinets.

Bed-size category: Hospitals are categorized by the number of beds set up and staffed for use at the end of the reporting period. The eight categories in Hospital Statistics are: 6 to 24 beds; 25 to 49; 50 to 99; 100 to 199; 200 to 299; 300 to 399; 400 to 499; and 500 or more.

Birthing room-LDR room-LDRP room: A single-room type of maternity care with a more homelike setting for families than the traditional three-room unit (labor/delivery/recovery) with a separate postpartum area. A birthing room combines labor and delivery in one room. An LDR room accommodates three stages in the birthing process—labor, delivery, and recovery. An LDRP room accommodates all four stages of the birth process—labor, delivery, recovery, and postpartum.

Births: Total number of infants born in the hospital during the reporting period. Births do not include infants transferred from other institutions, and are excluded from admission and discharge figures.

Blood Donor Center: A facility that performs, or is responsible for the collection, processing, testing or distribution of blood and components.

Bone marrow transplant: See definition for Transplant service on page 213.

Breast cancer screening/mammograms: Mammography screening – The use of breast x-ray to detect unsuspected breast cancer in asymptomatic women. Diagnostic mammography – The x-ray imaging of breast tissue in symptomatic women who are considered to have a substantial likelihood of having breast cancer already.

Burn care: Provides care to severely burned patients. Severely burned patients are those with any of the following: (1) second-degree burns of more than 25% total body surface area for adults or 20% total body surface area for children: (2) third-degree burns of more than 10% total body surface area; (3) any severe burns of the hands, face, eyes, ears, or feet; or (4) all inhalation injuries, electrical burns, complicated burn injuries involving fractures and other major traumas, and all other poor risk factors.

Cardiac electrophysiology: Evaluation and management of patients with complex rhythm or conduction abnormalities, including diagnostic testing, treatment of arrhythmias by catheter ablation or drug therapy, and pacemaker/defibrillator implantation and follow-up.

Cardiac intensive care: Provides patient care of a more specialized nature than the usual medical and surgical care, on the basis of physicians' orders and approved nursing care plans. The unit is staffed with specially trained nursing personnel and contains monitoring and specialized support or treatment equipment for patients who, because of heart seizure, open-heart surgery, or other life-threatening conditions, require intensified, comprehensive observation and care. May include myocardial infarction, pulmonary care, and heart transplant units.

Cardiac Rehabilitation: A medically supervised program to help heart patients recover quickly and improve their overall physical and mental functioning. The goal is to reduce risk of another cardiac event or to keep an already present heart condition from getting worse. Cardiac rehabilitation programs include: counseling to patients, an exercise program, helping patients modify risk factors such as smoking and high blood pressure, providing vocational guidance to enable the patient to return to work, supplying information on physical limitations and lending emotional support.

Case management: A system of assessment, treatment planning, referral and follow-up that ensures the provision of comprehensive and continuous services and the coordination of payment and reimbursement for care.

Chaplaincy/pastoral care services: A service ministering religious activities and providing pastoral counseling to patients, their families, and staff of a health care organization.

Chemotherapy: An organized program for the treatment of cancer by the use of drugs or chemicals.

Children's wellness program: A program that encourages improved health status and a healthful lifestyle of children through health education, exercise, nutrition and health promotion.

Chiropractic services: An organized clinical service including spinal manipulation or adjustment and related diagnostic and therapeutic services.

Closed physician-hospital organization (Closed PHO): A joint venture between the hospital and physicians who have been selected on the basis of cost-effectiveness and/or high quality. The PHO can act as a unified agent in managed care contracting, own a managed care plan, own and operate ambulatory care centers or ancillary services projects, or provide administrative services to physician members.

Community health education: Education that provides health information to individuals and populations, as well as support for personal, family and community health decisions with the objective of improving health status.

Community hospitals: All nonfederal, short-term general, and special hospitals whose facilities and services are available to the public. (Special hospitals include obstetrics and gynecology; eye, ear, nose, and throat; rehabilitation; orthopedic; and other individually described specialty services.) Short-term general and special childrens hospitals are also considered to be community hospitals.

A hospital may include a nursing-home-type unit and still be classified as short-term, provided that the majority of its patients are admitted to units where the average length of stay is less than 30 days. Therefore, statistics for community hospitals often include some data about such nursing-home-type units. An example is furnished by Montana, where in 1995 63.6 percent of all hospitals classified as community hospitals include nursing-home-type units. Expense, revenue, utilization, and personnel data for these hospitals include data about their nursing-home-type units. Thus, total admissions to Montana community hospitals in 1995 were 96,154; total inpatient days, 997,759; total expenses, $791,806,393; and total payroll expenses, $352,583,331. If nursing-home-type unit data were excluded, these same items would be 94,034; 457,340; 752,567,865; and $328,911841, respectively.

Note that before 1972, hospital units of institutions such as prison and college infirmaries were included in the category of community hospitals. Including these units made this category equivalent to the short-term general and other special hospitals category. Although these hospital units are few in number and small in size, this change in definition should be taken into consideration when comparing data.

Community outreach: A program that systematically interacts with the community to identify those in need of services, alerting persons and their families to the availability of services, locating needed services, and enabling persons to enter the service delivery system.

Complementary and alternative medicine services: Organized hospital services or formal arrangements to providers that provide care or treatment not based solely on traditional western allopathic medical teachings as instructed in most U.S. medical schools. Includes any of the following: acupuncture, chiropractic, homeopathy, osteopathy, diet and lifestyle changes, herbal medicine, message therapy, etc.

Computer assisted orthopedic surgery (CAOS): Orthopedic surgery using computer technology, enabling three-dimensional graphic models to visualize a patient's anatomy.

Control: The type of organization responsible for establishing policy concerning the overall operation of hospitals. The three major categories are government (including federal, state, and local); nongovernment (nonprofit); and investor-owned (for-profit).

Crisis prevention: Services provided in order to promote physical and mental well being and the early identification of disease and ill health prior to the onset and recognition of symptoms so as to permit early treatment.

CT scanner: Computed tomographic scanner for head or whole body scans.

Deduction from revenue: The difference between revenue at full established rates (gross) and the payment actually received from payers (net).

Dental Services: An organized dental service or dentists on staff, not necessarily involving special facilities, providing dental or oral services to inpatients or outpatients.

Diagnostic radioisotope facility: The use of radioactive isotopes (Radiopharmaceuticals) as tracers or indicators to detect an abnormal condition or disease.

Electrodiagnostic Services: Diagnostic testing services for nerve and muscle function including services such as nerve conduction studies and needle electromyography.

Electron beam computed tomography (EBCT): A high tech computed tomography scan used to detect coronary artery disease by measuring coronary calcifications. This imaging procedure uses electron beams which are magnetically steered to produce a visual of the coronary artery and the images are produced faster than conventional CT scans.

Emergency department: Hospital facilities for the provision of unscheduled outpatient services to patients whose conditions require immediate care.

Emergency room visits: The number of visits to the emergency unit. When emergency outpatients are admitted to the inpatient areas of the hospital, they are counted as emergency room visits and subsequently, as inpatient admissions.

Emergency services: Health services that are provided after the onset of a medical condition that manifests itself by symptoms of sufficient severity, including severe pain, that the absence of immediate medical attention could reasonably be expected by a prudent layperson, who possesses an average knowledge of health and medicine, to result in placing the patient's health in serious jeopardy.

Enabling services: A program that is designed to help the patient access health care services by offering any of the following: transportation services and/or referrals to local social services agencies.

End of Life: Services offered to patients suffering from chronic, severe, and life-threatening diseases including comprehensive services that give patients and caregivers the resources and the confidence to manage symptoms, avoid emergency room admissions and frequent hospitalization, and remain in familiar and comfortable settings.

Endoscopic retrograde cholangiopancreatography (ERCP):
A procedure in which a catheter is introduced through an endoscope into the bile ducts and pancreatic ducts. Injection of contrast materials permits detailed x-ray of these structures. The procedure is used diagnostically as well as therapeutically to relieve obstruction or remove stones.

Endoscopic ultrasound: Specially designed endoscope that incorporates an ultrasound transductor used to obtain detailed images of organs in the chest and abdomen. The endoscope can be passed through the mouth or the anus. When combined with needle biopsy the procedure can assist in diagnosis and staging of cancer.

Enrollment (insurance) assistance services: A program that provides enrollment assistance for patients who are potentially eligible for public health insurance programs such as Medicaid, State Children's Health Insurance, or local/state indigent care programs. The specific services offered could include explanation of benefits, assist applicants in completing the application and locating all relevant documents, conduct eligibility interviews, and/or forward applications and documentation to state/local social service or health agency.

Equity model: An arrangement that allows established practitioners to become shareholders in a professional corporation in exchange for tangible and intangible assets of their existing practices.

Esophageal impedance study: A test in which a catheter is placed through the nose into the esophagus to measure whether gas or liquids are passing from the stomach into the esophagus and causing symptoms.

Expenses: Includes all expenses for the reporting period including payroll, non-payroll, and all nonoperating expenses. *Payroll expenses* include all salaries and wages. *Non-payroll expenses* are all professional fees and those salary expenditures excluded from payroll. *Labor related expenses* are defined as payroll expenses plus employee benefits.

Non-labor related expenses are all other non-payroll expenses. *Bad debt* has been reclassified from a "reduction in revenue" to an expense in accordance with the revised AICPA Audit Guide. However, for purposes of historical consistency, the expense total that appears throughout *AHA Hospital Statistics does not include "bad debt" as an expense item.* Note: Financial data may not add due to rounding.

Extracorporeal shock wave lithotripter (ESWL): A medical device used for treating stones in the kidney or urethra. The device disintegrates kidney stones noninvasively through the transmission of acoustic shock waves directed at the stones.

Fertility Clinic: A specialized program set in an infertility center that provides counseling and education as well as advanced reproductive techniques such as: injectable therapy, reproductive surgeries, treatment for endometriosis, male factor infertility, tubal reversals, in vitro fertilization (IVF), donor eggs, and other such services to help patients achieve successful pregnancies.

Fitness center: Provides exercise, testing, or evaluation programs and fitness activities to the community and hospital employees.

Foundation: A corporation, organized as a hospital affiliate or subsidiary, that purchases both tangible and intangible assets of one or more medical group practices. Physicians remain in a separate corporate entity but sign a professional services agreement with the foundation.

Freestanding outpatient care center: A facility owned and operated by the hospital, that is physically separate from the hospital and provides various medical treatments and diagnostic services on an outpatient basis only. Laboratory and radiology services are usually available.

Full-field digital mammography (FFDM): Combines the x-ray generators and tubes used in analog screen-film mammography (SFM) with a detector plate that converts the x-rays into a digital signal.

Full time equivalent employees (FTE): Full time personnel on payroll plus one half of the part time personnel on payroll. For purposes of *AHA Hospital Statistics*, full time and part time medical and dental residents/interns and other trainees are excluded from the calculation.

General medical-surgical care: Provides acute care to patients in medical and surgical units on the basis of physicians' orders and approved nursing care plans.

Genetic testing/counseling: A service equipped with adequate laboratory facilities and directed by a qualified physician to advise parents and prospective parents on potential problems in cases of genetic defects. A genetic test is the analysis of human DNA, RNA, chromosomes, proteins, and certain metabolites in order to detect heritable disease-related genotypes, mutations, phenotypes, or karyotypes for clinical purposes. Genetic tests can have diverse purposes, including the diagnosis of genetic diseases in newborns, children, and adults; the identification of future health risks; the prediction of drug responses; and the assessment of risks to future children.

Geriatric services: The branch of medicine dealing with the physiology of aging and the diagnosis and treatment of disease affecting the aged. Services could include: Adult day care; Alzheimer's diagnostic-assessment services; Comprehensive geriatric assessment; Emergency response system; Geriatric acute care unit; and/or Geriatric clinics.

Government, nonfederal, state, local: Controlled by an agency of state, county, or city government.

Gross inpatient revenue: Revenue from services rendered to inpatients at full established rates (also known as "charges").

Gross outpatient revenue: Revenue from services rendered to outpatients at full established rates.

Group practice without walls: In this organization, the hospital sponsors the formation of a physician group or provides capital to physicians to establish one. The group shares administrative expenses, although the physicians remain independent practitioners.

Group Purchasing Organization: An organization whose primary function is to negotiate contracts for the purpose of purchasing for members of the group or has a central supply site for its members.

Health fair: Community health education events that focus on the prevention of disease and promotion of health through such activities as audiovisual exhibits and free diagnostic services.

Health maintenance organization (HMO): A health care organization that acts as both insurer and provider of comprehensive but specified medical services in return for prospective per capita (capitation) payments.

Health Research: Organized hospital research program in any of the following areas: basic research, clinical research, community health research, and/or research on innovative health care delivery.

Health screening: A preliminary procedure such as a test or examination to detect the most characteristic sign or signs of a disorder that may require further investigation.

Heart transplant: See definition for Transplant services on page 213.

Hemodialysis: Provision of equipment and personnel for the treatment of renal insufficiency on an inpatient or outpatient basis.

HIV-AIDS services: (could include). *HIV-AIDS unit* – Special unit or team designated and equipped specifically for diagnosis, treatment, continuing care planning, and counseling services for HIV-AIDS patients and their families. *General inpatient care for HIV-AIDS* – Inpatient diagnosis and treatment for human immunodeficiency virus and acquired immunodeficiency syndrome patients, but dedicated unit is not available. *Specialized outpatient program for HIV-AIDS* – Special outpatient program providing diagnostic, treatment, continuing care planning, and counseling for HIV-AIDS patients and their families.

Home health services: Service providing nursing, therapy, and health-related homemaker or social services in the patient's home.

Hospice: A program providing palliative care, chiefly medical relief of pain and supportive services, addressing the emotional, social, financial, and legal needs of terminally ill patients and their families. Care can be provided in a variety of settings, both inpatient and at home.

Hospital unit: The hospital operation, excluding activity pertaining to nursing-home-type unit (as described below), for the following items: Admissions, Beds, FTEs (full-time, part-time, and total), Inpatient Days, Length of Stay, Net Revenue, and Total Expense.

Hospital unit of institutions: A hospital unit that is not open to the public and is contained within a nonhospital unit. An example is an infirmary that is contained within a college.

Hospitals in a network: Hospitals participating in a group that may include other hospitals, physicians, other providers, insurers, and/or community agencies that work together to coordinate and deliver a broad spectrum of services to the community.

Hospitals in a system: Hospitals belonging to a corporate body that owns and/or manages health provider facilities or health-related subsidiaries; the system may also own non-health-related facilities.

Image-guided radiation therapy (IGRT): Automated system for image-guided radiation therapy that enables clinicians to obtain high-resolution x-ray images to pinpoint tumor sites, adjust patient positioning when necessary, and complete a treatment, all within the standard treatment time slot, allowing for more effective cancer treatments.

Immunization program: Program that plans, coordinates and conducts immunization services in the community.

Indemnity fee for service: The traditional type of health insurance, in which the insured is reimbursed for covered expenses without regard to choice of provider. Payment up to a stated limit may be made either to the individual incurring and claiming the expense, or directly to providers.

Independent practice association (IPA): An IPA is a legal entity that holds managed care contracts and contracts with physicians, usually in solo practice, to provide care either on a fee-for-services or capitated basis. The purpose of an IPA is to assist solo physicians in obtaining managed care contracts.

Indigent care clinic: Health care services for uninsured and underinsured persons where care is free of charge or charged on a sliding scale. This would include "free clinics" staffed by volunteer practitioners, but could also be staffed by employees with sponsoring health care organizations subsidizing the cost of service.

Inpatient days: The number of adult and pediatric days of care, excluding newborn days of care, rendered during the entire reporting period.

Inpatient palliative care unit: An inpatient palliative care ward is a physically discreet, inpatient nursing unit where the focus is palliative care. The patient care focus is on symptom relief for complex patients who may be continuing to undergo primary treatment. Care is delivered by palliative medicine specialists.

Inpatient surgeries: Surgical services provided to patients who remain in the hospital overnight.

Insurance product: In tables 3 through 6, insurance product refers to a hospital-owned insurance product.

Integrated salary model: In this arrangement, physicians are salaried by the hospital or other entity of a health system to provide medical services for primary care and specialty care.

Intensity-Modulated Radiation Therapy (IMRT): A type of three-dimensional radiation therapy, which improves the targeting of treatment delivery in a way that is likely to decrease damage to normal tissues and allows varying intensities.

Intermediate nursing care: Provides health-related services (skilled nursing care and social services) to residents with a variety of physical conditions or functional disabilities. These residents do not require the care provided by a hospital or skilled nursing facility, but do need supervision and support services.

Intraoperative magnetic resonance imaging. An integrated surgery system which provides an MRI system in an operating room. The system allows for immediate evaluation of the degree to tumor resection while the patient is undergoing a surgical resection. Intraoperative MRI exists when a MRI (low-field or high-field) is placed in the operating theater and is used during surgical resection without moving the patient from the operating room to the diagnostic imaging suite.

Investor-owned, for-profit: Investor-owned, for-profit hospitals are those controlled on a for-profit basis by an individual, partnership, or profit-making corporation.

Kidney transplant: See definition for Transplant sevices on page 213.

Labor-related expenses: Payroll expenses plus employee benefits. *Non-labor-related expenses refers* to all other nonpayroll expenses, such as interest depreciation, supplies, purchased services, professional fees, and others.

Length of stay (LOS): LOS refers to the average number of days a patient stays at the facility. Short-term hospitals are those where the average LOS is less than 30 days. Long-term hospitals are those where the average LOS is 30 days or more. The figure is derived by dividing the number of inpatient days by the number of admissions.

Note that this publication carries two LOS variables: *total facility length of stay and hospital unit length of stay. Total facility* includes admissions and inpatient days from nursing-home-type units under control of the hospital. In *hospital unit length of stay*, nursing home utilization is subtracted.

Licensed practical nurse (LPN): A nurse who has graduated from an approved school of practical (vocational) nursing and works under the supervision of registered nurses and/or physicians.

Linguistic/Translation services: Services provided by the hospital designed to make health care more accessible to non-English speaking patients and their physicians.

Liver transplant: See definition for Transplant on page 213.

Long-term: Hospitals are classified either short-term or long-term according to the average length of stay (LOS). A long-term hospital is one in which the average LOS is 30 days or more.

Lung transplant: See definition for Transplant services on page 213.

Magnetic resonance imaging (MRI): The use of a uniform magnetic field and radio frequencies to study tissue and structure of the body. This procedure enables the visualization of biochemical activity of the cell in vivo without the use of ionizing radiation, radio-isotopic substances, or high-frequency sound.

Managed care: A term covering a broad spectrum of arrangements for health care delivery and financing, including managed indemnity plans (MIP), health maintenance organizations (HMO), preferred provider organizations (PPO), point-of-service plans (POS), and direct contracting arrangements between employers and providers.

Managed care contract: A contract between the hospital and a managed care organization.

Management services organization (MSO): A corporation owned by the hospital or a physician/hospital joint venture that provides management services to one or more medical group practices. As part of a full-service management agreement, the MSO purchases the tangible assets of the practices and leases them back, employs all non-physician staff, and provides all supplies/administrative systems for a fee.

Meals on wheels: A hospital sponsored program which delivers meals to people, usually the elderly, who are unable to prepare their own meals. Low cost, nutritional meals are delivered to individuals' homes on a regular basis.

Medical surgical intensive care: Provides patient care of a more intensive nature than the usual medical and surgical care, on the basis of physicians' orders and approved nursing care plans. These units are staffed with specially trained nursing personnel and contain monitoring and specialized support equipment for patients who, because of shock, trauma, or other life-threatening conditions, require intensified, comprehensive observation and care. Includes mixed intensive care units.

Mobile health services: Vans and other vehicles used to deliver primary care services.

Multi-slice spiral computed tomography (<64 slice CT): A specialized computed tomography procedure that provides three-dimensional processing and allows narrower and multiple slices with increased spatial resolution and faster scanning times as compared to a regular computed tomography scan.

Multi-slice spiral computed tomography (64+ slice CT): Involves the acquisition of volumetric tomographic x-ray absorption data expressed in Hounsfield units using multiple rows of detectors. 64+ systems reconstruct the equivalent of 64 or greater slices to cover the imaged volume.

Neonatal intensive care: A unit that must be separate from the newborn nursery providing intensive care to all sick infants including those with the very lowest birth weights (less than 1500 grams). NICU has potential for providing mechanical ventilation, neonatal surgery, and special care for the sickest infants born in the hospital or transferred from another institution. A full-time neonatologist serves as director of the NICU.

Neonatal intermediate care: A unit that must be separate from the normal newborn nursery and that provides intermediate and/or recovery care and some specialized services, including immediate resuscitation, intravenous therapy, and capacity for prolonged oxygen therapy and monitoring.

Net patient revenue: The estimated net realizable amounts from patients, third-party payers, and others for services rendered. The number includes estimated retroactive adjustments called for by agreements with third-party payers; retroactive adjustments are accrued on an estimated basis in the period the related services are rendered and then adjusted later as final settlements are determined.

Net total revenue: Net patient revenue plus all other revenue, including contributions, endowment revenue, governmental grants, and all other payments not made on behalf of individual patients.

Neurological services: Services provided by the hospital dealing with the operative and nonoperative management of disorders of the central, peripheral, and autonomic nervous system.

Nongovernment, nonprofit: Hospitals that are nongovernment, nonprofit are controlled by not-for-profit organizations, including religious organizations (Catholic hospitals, for example), fraternal societies, and others.

Nursing-home-type unit/facility: A unit/facility that primarily offers the following type of services to a majority of all admissions:

- *Skilled nursing*: The provision of medical and nursing care services, health-related services, and social services under the supervision of a registered nurse on a 24-hour basis.

- *Intermediate care*: The provision, on a regular basis, of health-related care and services to individuals who do not require the degree of care or treatment that a skilled nursing unit is designed to provide.

- *Personal care*: The provision of general supervision and direct personal care services for residents who require assistance in activities of daily living but who do not need nursing services or inpatient care. Medical and nursing services are available as needed.

- *Sheltered/residential care*: The provision of general supervision and protective services for residents who do not need nursing services or continuous personal care services in the conduct of daily life. Medical and nursing services are available as needed.

Nutrition programs: Those services within a health care facility which are designed to provide inexpensive, nutritionally sound meals to patients.

Obstetrics: Levels should be designated: (1) unit provides services for uncomplicated maternity and newborn cases; (2) unit provides services for uncomplicated cases, the majority of complicated problems, and special neonatal services; and (3) unit provides services for all serious illnesses and abnormalities and is supervised by a full-time maternal/fetal specialist.

Occupational health services: Includes services designed to protect the safety of employees from hazards in the work environment.

Oncology services: Inpatient and outpatient services for patients with cancer, including comprehensive care, support and guidance in addition to patient education and prevention, chemotherapy, counseling and other treatment methods.

Open physician hospital organization (Open PHO): A joint venture between the hospital and all members of the medical staff who wish to participate. The open PHO can act as a unified agent in managed care contracting, own a managed care plan, own and operate ambulatory care centers or ancillary services projects, or provide administrative services to physician members.

Optical colonoscopy: An examination of the interior of the colon using a long, flexible, lighted tube with a small built-in camera.

Orthopedic services: Services provided for the prevention or correction of injuries or disorders of the skeletal system and associated muscles, joints and ligaments.

Osteopathic hospitals: Osteopathic medicine is a medical practice based on a theory that diseases are due chiefly to a loss of structural integrity, which can be restored by manipulation of the neuro-muscular and skeletal systems, supplemented by therapeutic measures (such as medicine or surgery).

Other Intensive Care: A specially staffed, specialty equipped, separate section of a hospital dedicated to the observation, care, and treatment of patients with life threatening illnesses, injuries, or complications from which recovery is possible. It provides special expertise and facilities for the support of vital function and utilizes the skill of medical nursing and other staff experienced in the management of these problems.

Other long-term care: Provision of long-term care other than skilled nursing care or intermediate care for those who do not require daily medical or nursing services, but may require some assistance in the activities of daily living. This can include residential care, elderly care, or sheltered care facilities for developmentally disabled.

Other special care: Provides care to patients requiring care more intensive than that provided in the acute area, yet not sufficiently intensive to require admission to an intensive care unit. Patients admitted to this area are usually transferred here from an intensive care unit once their condition has improved. These units are sometimes referred to as definitive observation, step-down, or progressive care units.

Other transplant: See definition for Transplant services on page 213.

Outpatient care: Treatment provided to patients who do not remain in the hospital for overnight care. Hospitals may deliver outpatient care on site or through a facility owned and operated by the hospital, but physically separate from the hospital. In addition to treating minor illnesses or injuries, a free-standing center will stabilize seriously ill or injured patients before transporting them to a hospital. Laboratory and radiology services are usually available.

Outpatient care center (Freestanding): A facility owned and operated by the hospital, but physically separate from the hospital, that provides various medical treatments on an outpatient basis only. In addition to treating minor illnesses or injuries, the center will stabilize seriously ill or injured patients before transporting them to a hospital. Laboratory and radiology services are usually available.

Outpatient care center-services (Hospital-based): Organized hospital health care services offered by appointment on an ambulatory basis. Services may include outpatient surgery, examination, diagnosis, and treatment of a variety of medical conditions on a nonemergency basis, and laboratory and other diagnostic testing as ordered by staff or outside physician referral.

Outpatient surgery: Scheduled surgical services provided to patients who do not remain in the hospital overnight. The surgery may be performed in operating suites also used for inpatient surgery, specially designated surgical suites for outpatient surgery, or procedure rooms within an outpatient care facility.

Outpatient visit: A visit by a patient who is not lodged in the hospital while receiving medical, dental, or other services. Each visit an outpatient makes to a discrete unit constitutes one visit regardless of the number of diagnostic and/or therapeutic treatments that the patient receives. Total outpatient visits should include all clinic visits, referred visits, observation services, outpatient surgeries, and emergency room visits.

Pain Management Program: A recognized clinical service or program providing specialized medical care, drugs or therapies for the management of acute or chronic pain or other distressing symptom, administered by specially trained physicians and other clinicians, to patients suffering from acute illness of diverse causes.

Palliative Care Inpatient Unit: An inpatient palliative care ward is a physically discreet, inpatient nursing unit where the focus is palliative care. The patient care focus is on symptom relief for complex patients who may be continuing to undergo primary treatment. Care is delivered by palliative medicine specialists.

Palliative care program: An organized program providing specialized medical care, drugs or therapies for the management of acute or chronic pain and/or the control of symptoms administered by specially trained physicians and other clinicians; and supportive care services, such as counseling on advanced directives, spiritual care, and social services, to patients with advanced disease and their families.

Patient Controlled Analgesia (PCA). Patient-controlled Analgesia (PCA) is intravenously administered pain medicine under the patient's control. The patient has a button on the end of a cord than can be pushed at will, whenever more pain medicine is desired. This button will only deliver more pain medicine at pre-determined intervals, as programmed by the doctor's order.

Patient education center: Written goals and objectives for the patient and/or family related to therapeutic regimens, medical procedures, and self care.

Patient representative services: Organized hospital services providing personnel through whom patients and staff can seek solutions to institutional problems affecting the delivery of high-quality care and services.

Payroll expenses: Includes all salaries and wages. All professional fees and salary expenditures excluded from payroll, such as employee benefits, are defined as nonpayroll expenses and are included in total expenses.

Pediatric Cardiac Surgery: Includes minimally invasive procedures that include surgery done with only a small incision or no incision at all, such as through a laparoscope or an endoscope and more invasive major surgical procedures that include open chest and open heart surgery.

Pediatric Cardiology Services: An organized clinical service offering diagnostic and interventional procedures to manage the full range of pediatric heart conditions.

Pediatric Diagnostic/invasive catheterization: (also called coronary angiography or coronary arteriography) is used to assist in diagnosing complex heart conditions. Cardiac angiography involves the insertion of a tiny catheter into the artery in the groin then carefully threading the catheter up into the aorta where the coronary arteries originate. Once the catheter is in place, a dye is injected which allows the cardiologist to see the size, shape, and distribution of the coronary arteries. These images are used to diagnose heart disease and to determine, among other things, whether or not surgery is indicated.

Pediatric intensive care: Provides care to pediatric patients that is of a more intensive nature than that usually provided to pediatric patients. The unit is staffed with specially trained personnel and contains monitoring and specialized support equipment for treatment of patients who, because of shock, trauma, or other life-threatening conditions, require intensified, comprehensive observation and care.

Pediatric Interventional cardiac catheterization: Non surgical procedure that utilizes the same basic principles as diagnostic catheterization and then uses advanced techniques to improve the heart's function. It can be a less-invasive alternative to heart surgery.

Pediatric medical-surgical care: Provides acute care to pediatric patients on the basis of physicians' orders and approved nursing care plans.

Personnel: Number of persons on the hospital payroll at the end of the reporting period. Personnel are recorded in *Hospital Statistics* as full-time equivalents (FTEs), which are calculated by adding the number of full-time personnel to one-half the number of part-time personnel, excluding medical and dental residents, interns, and other trainees. *Per 100 adjusted census* indicates the ratio of personnel to adjusted average daily census, calculated on a per-100 basis.

Physical rehabilitation inpatient care: Provides care encompassing a comprehensive array of restoration services for the disabled and all support services necessary to help patients attain their maximum functional capacity.

Physical rehabilitation outpatient services: Outpatient program providing medical, health-related, therapy, social, and/or vocational services to help disabled persons attain or retain their maximum functional capacity.

Population: Population refers to the residential population of the United States. This includes both civilian and military personnel. Note that population is being used to calculate the values *for community health indicators per 1000 population.*

Positron emission tomography/CT (PET/CT): Provides metabolic functional information for the monitoring of chemotherapy, radiotherapy and surgical planning.

Positron emission tomography scanner (PET): A nuclear medicine imaging technology which uses radioactive (positron emitting) isotopes created in a cyclotron or generator and computers to produce composite pictures of the brain and heart at work. PET scanning produces sectional images depicting metabolic activity or blood flow rather than anatomy.

Preferred provider organization (PPO): A pre-set arrangement in which purchasers and providers agree to furnish specified health services to a group of employees/patients.

Primary care department: A unit or clinic within the hospital that provides primary care services (e.g. general pediatric care, general internal medicine, family practice, gynecology) through hospital-salaried medical and/or nursing staff, focusing on evaluating and diagnosing medical problems and providing medical treatment on an outpatient basis.

Prosthetic and Orthotic Services: Services providing comprehensive prosthetic and orthotic evaluation, fitting, and training.

Proton beam therapy: A form of radiation therapy which administers proton beams. While producing the same biologic effects as x-ray beams, the energy distribution of protons differs from conventional x-ray beams in that they can be more precisely focused in tissue volumes in a three-dimensional pattern resulting in less surrounding tissue damage than conventional radiation therapy permitting administration of higher doses.

Psychiatric child-adolescent services: Provides care to emotionally disturbed children and adolescents, including those admitted for diagnosis and those admitted for treatment.

Psychiatric consultation-liaison services: Provides organized psychiatric consultation/liaison services to nonpsychiatric hospital staff and/or departments on psychological aspects of medical care that may be generic or specific to individual patients.

Psychiatric education services: Provides psychiatric educational services to community agencies and workers such as schools, police, courts, public health nurses, welfare agencies, clergy, and so forth. The purpose is to expand the mental health knowledge and competence of personnel not working in the mental health field and to promote good mental health through improved understanding, attitudes, and behavioral patterns.

Psychiatric emergency services: Services of facilities available on a 24-hour basis to provide immediate unscheduled out-patient care, diagnosis, evaluation, crisis intervention, and assistance to persons suffering acute emotional or mental distress.

Psychiatric geriatric services: Provides care to emotionally disturbed elderly patients, including those admitted for diagnosis and those admitted for treatment.

Psychiatric inpatient care: Provides acute or long-term care to emotionally disturbed patients, including patients admitted for diagnosis and those admitted for treatment of psychiatric problems, on the basis of physicians' orders and approved nursing care plans. Long-term care may include intensive supervision to the chronically mentally ill, mentally disordered, or other mentally incompetent persons.

Psychiatric outpatient services: Provides medical care, including diagnosis and treatment, of psychiatric outpatients.

Psychiatric partial hospitalization program: Organized hospital services of intensive day/evening outpatient services of three hours of more duration, distinguished from other outpatient visits of one hour.

Radiology, diagnostic: The branch of radiology that deals with the utilization of all modalities of radiant energy in medical diagnoses and therapeutic procedures using radiologic guidance. This includes, but is not restricted to, imaging techniques and methodologies utilizing radiation emitted by x-ray tubes, radionnuclides, and ultrasonographic devices and the radiofrequency electromagnetic radiation emitted by atoms.

Radiology, therapeutic: The branch of medicine concerned with radioactive substances and using various techniques of visualization, with the diagnosis and treatment of disease using any of the various sources of radiant energy. Services could include: megavoltage radiation therapy; radioactive implants; stereotactic radiosurgery; therapeutic radioisotope facility; X-ray radiation therapy.

Registered nurse (RN): A nurse who has graduated from an approved school of nursing and who is currently registered by the state. RNs are responsible for the nature and quality of all nursing care that patients receive. In these tables, the number of RNs does not include those registered nurses more appropriately reported in other occupational categories, such as facility administrators, which are listed under *all other personnel* (Tables 1 and 2).

Rehabilitation services: A wide array of restoration services for disabled and recuperating patients, including all support services necessary to help them attain their maximum functional capacity.

Retirement housing: A facility which provides social activities to senior citizens, usually retired persons, who do not require health care but some short-term skilled nursing care may be provided. A retirement center may furnish housing and may also have acute hospital and long-term care facilities, or it may arrange for acute and long term care through affiliated institutions.

Robot-assisted walking therapy: A form of physical therapy that uses a robotic device to assist patients who are relearning how to walk.

Robotic surgery: The use of mechanical guidance devices to remotely manipulate surgical instrumentation.

Rural: A rural hospital is located outside a Metropolitan Statistical Area (MSA), as designated by the U.S. Office of Management and Budget (OMB) effective June 6, 2003. An urban area is a geographically defined, integrated social and economic unit with a large population nucleus. Micropolitan areas, which are new to the OMB June 6, 2003 definitions, continue to be classified as rural for purposes of this publication.

Rural Health Clinic: A clinic located in a rural, medically under-served area in the United States that has a separate reimbursement structure from the standard medical office under the Medicare and Medicaid programs.

Satellite Emergency Department: A facility owned and operated by the hospital but physically separate from the hospital for the provision of unscheduled outpatient services to patients whose conditions require immediate care. A freestanding ED is not physically connected to a hospital, but has all necessary emergency staffing and equipment on-site.

Shaped beam radiation system: A precise, non-invasive treatment that involves targeting beams of radiation that mirrors the exact size and shape of a tumor at a specific area of a tumor to shrink or destroy cancerous cells. This procedure delivers a therapeutic dose of radiation that conforms precisely to the shape of the tumor, thus minimizing the risk to nearby tissues.

Simulated rehabilitation environment: Rehabilitation focused on retraining functional skills in a contextually appropriate environment (simulated home and community settings) or in a traditional setting (gymnasium) using motor learning principles.

Single photon emission computerized tomography (SPECT): A nuclear medicine imaging technology that combines existing technology of gamma camera imaging with computed tomographic imaging technology to provide a more precise and clear image.

Skilled nursing care: Provides non-acute medical and skilled nursing care services, therapy, and social services under the supervision of a licensed registered nurse on a 24-hour basis.

Sleep Center: Specially equipped and staffed center for the diagnosis and treatment of sleep disorders.

Social work services (could include): Organized services that are properly directed and sufficiently staffed by qualified individuals who provide assistance and counseling to patients and their families in dealing with social, emotional, and environmental problems associated with illness or disability, often in the context of financial or discharge planning coordination.

Sports medicine: Provision of diagnostic screening and assessment and clinical and rehabilitation services for the prevention and treatment of sports-related injuries.

Stereotactic radiosurgery: Stereotactic radiosurgery (SRS) is a radiotherapy modality that delivers a high dosage of radiation to a discrete treatment area in as few as one treatment session. Includes gamma knife, cyberknife, etc.

Support groups: A hospital sponsored program that allows a group of individuals with the same or similar problems who meet periodically to share experiences, problems, and solutions in order to support each other.

Surgical operations: Those surgical operations, whether major or minor, performed in the operating room(s). A surgical operation involving more than one surgical procedure is still considered only one surgical operation.

Swing bed services: A hospital bed that can be used to provide either acute or long-term care depending on community or patient needs. To be eligible a hospital must have a Medicare provider agreement in place, have fewer than 100 beds, be located in a rural area, do not have a 24 hour nursing service waiver in effect, have not been terminated from the program in the prior two years, and meet various service conditions.

Teen outreach services: A program focusing on the teenager which encourages an improved health status and a healthful lifestyle including physical, emotional, mental, social, spiritual and economic health through education, exercise, nutrition and health promotion.

Tissue transplant: See definition for Transplant services on page 213.

Tobacco treatment/cessation program: Organized hospital services with the purpose of ending tobacco-use habits of patients addicted to tobacco/nicotine.

Transplant services. The branch of medicine that transfers an organ or tissue from one person to another or from one body part to another to replace a diseased structure or to restore function or to change appearance. Services could include: bone marrow transplant program; heart, lung, kidney, intestine, or tissue transplant. The other transplant services include transplant services other than bone marrow, heart, kidney, liver, lung, tissue and heart/lung or other multi-transplant surgeries.

Transportation to health facilities:
A long-term care support service designed to assist the mobility of the elderly. Some programs offer improved financial access by offering reduced rates and barrier-free buses or vans with ramps and lifts to assist the elderly or handicapped; others offer subsidies for public transport systems or operate mini-bus services exclusively for use by senior citizens.

Trauma center (certified): A facility to provide emergency and specialized intensive care to critically ill and injured patients. **Level 1:** A regional resource trauma center, which is capable of providing total care for every aspect of injury and plays a leadership role in trauma research and education. **Level 2:** A community trauma center, which is capable of providing trauma care to all but the most severely injured patients who require highly specialized care. **Level 3:** A rural trauma hospital, which is capable of providing care to a large number of injury victims and can resuscitate and stabilize more severely injured patients so that they can be transported to Level 1 or 2 facilities.

Ultrasound: The use of acoustic waves above the range of 20,000 cycles per second to visualize internal body structures.

Urban: An urban hospital is located inside a Metropolitan Statistical Area (MSA), designated by the U.S. Office of Management and Budget effective June 6, 2003. An urban areas is a geographically defined, integrated social and economic unit with a large population base. Micropolitan areas, which are new to the OMB June 6, 2003 definitions, are not considered to be urban for purposes of this publication.

Urgent care center: A facility that provides care and treatment for problems that are not life-threatening but require attention over the short term.

Virtual colonoscopy: Noninvasive screening procedure used to visualize, analyze and detect cancerous or potentially cancerous polyps in the colon.

Volunteer services department:
An organized hospital department responsible for coordinating the services of volunteers working within the institution.

Women's health center/services:
An area set aside for coordinated education and treatment services specifically for and promoted to women as provided by this special unit. Services may or may not include obstetrics but include a range of services other than OB.

Wound Management Services:
Services for patients with chronic wounds and nonhealing wounds often resulting from diabetes, poor circulation, improper seating and immunocompromising conditions. The goals are to progress chronic wounds through stages of healing, reduce and eliminate infections, increase physical function to minimize complications from current wounds and prevent future chronic wounds. Wound management services are provided on an inpatient or outpatient basis, depending on the intensity of service needed.

2011 AHA Annual Survey
Health Forum, L.L.C.

Please return to:
AHA Annual Survey

A. REPORTING PERIOD (please refer to the instructions and definitions at the end of this questionnaire)

Report data for a full 12-month period, preferably your last completed fiscal year (365 days). (Be consistent in using the same reporting period for responses throughout various sections of this survey.)

1. Reporting Period used (beginning and ending date) ...... __ __ / __ __ / __ __ __ __ to __ __ / __ __ / __ __ __ __
   Month   Day   Year   Month   Day   Year

2. a. Were you in operation 12 full months
      at the end of your reporting period .... YES ☐ NO ☐

   b. Number of days open
      during reporting period .... _____

3. Indicate the beginning of your current fiscal year .... __ __ / __ __ / __ __ __ __
   Month   Day   Year

B. ORGANIZATIONAL STRUCTURE

1. CONTROL

Indicate the type of organization that is responsible for establishing policy for overall operation of your hospital. CHECK ONLY ONE:

Government, nonfederal
- ☐ 12 State
- ☐ 13 County
- ☐ 14 City
- ☐ 15 City-County
- ☐ 16 Hospital district or authority

Nongovernment, not-for profit (NFP)
- ☐ 21 Church-operated
- ☐ 23 Other not-for-profit (including NFP Corporation)

Investor-owned, for-profit
- ☐ 31 Individual
- ☐ 32 Partnership
- ☐ 33 Corporation

Government, federal
- ☐ 41 Air Force
- ☐ 42 Army
- ☐ 43 Navy
- ☐ 44 Public Health Service

- ☐ 45 Veterans' Affairs
- ☐ 46 Federal other than 41-45 or 47-48
- ☐ 47 PHS Indian Service
- ☐ 48 Department of Justice

2. SERVICE

Indicate the ONE category that BEST describes your hospital or the type of service it provides to the MAJORITY of patients:

- ☐ 10 General medical and surgical
- ☐ 11 Hospital unit of an institution (prison hospital, college infirmary)
- ☐ 12 Hospital unit within an institution for the mentally retarded
- ☐ 13 Surgical
- ☐ 22 Psychiatric
- ☐ 33 Tuberculosis and other respiratory diseases
- ☐ 41 Cancer
- ☐ 42 Heart
- ☐ 44 Obstetrics and gynecology
- ☐ 45 Eye, ear, nose, and throat

- ☐ 46 Rehabilitation
- ☐ 47 Orthopedic
- ☐ 48 Chronic disease
- ☐ 62 Institution for the mentally retarded
- ☐ 80 Acute long-term care hospital
- ☐ 82 Alcoholism and other chemical dependency
- ☐ 49 Other-specify treatment area: _____

3. OTHER

a. Does your hospital restrict admissions primarily to children? .... YES ☐ NO ☐

B. ORGANIZATIONAL STRUCTURE (continued)

b. Does the hospital itself operate subsidiary corporations? .... YES ☐ NO ☐

c. Is the hospital contract managed? If yes, please provide the name, city, and state of the organization .. YES ☐ NO ☐

    Name: _____ City: _____ State: _____

d. Is the hospital a participant in a network? ....YES ☐ NO ☐
    If yes, please provide the name, city and state and telephone number of the network. If the hospital participates in more than one network, please provide the name, city, and state and telephone number of the network on page 15, under supplemental information.

    Name: _____ City: _____ State: _____ Telephone_____

e. Is your hospital owned in whole or in part by physicians or a physician group?... YES ☐ NO ☐

f. If you checked 80 Acute long-term care hospital (LTCH) in the Section B2 (Service), please indicate if you are a freestanding LTCH or a LTCH arranged within a general acute care hospital.
    ☐ Free standing LTCH   ☐ LTCH arranged in a general acute care hospital

    If you are arranged in a general acute care hospital, what is your host hospital's name?
    Name_____ City_____ State_____

4. NATIONAL PROVIDER IDENTIFIER (NPI)

a. Does your hospital have its new National Provider Identifier (NPI) from the National Plan and Provider Enumeration System?
    Yes☐   No☐

If yes, please report the ten digit NPI __ __ __ __ __ __ __ __ __ __

b. Does your hospital also have a Subpart NPI? Yes_____ No___

If yes, please report the Subpart NPI and provide the relevant taxonomy code to indicate the type of service provided. If you have multiple Subpart NPIs please report them all (in the supplemental section on page 15, at the end of this questionnaire or on a separate sheet).

Subpart NPI 1 __ __ __ __ __ __ __ __ __ __   Taxonomy Code __ __

Subpart NPI 2 __ __ __ __ __ __ __ __ __ __   Taxonomy Code __ __

Subpart NPI 3 __ __ __ __ __ __ __ __ __ __   Taxonomy Code __ __

```
Taxonomy Codes

Ambulatory Health Care Facility    01
Medicare Defined Swing Bed Unit   02
Psychiatric Unit         03
Rehabilitation Unit    04
Rehabilitation, Substance Use Disorder Unit  05
Laboratory   06
Nursing and Custodial Care Facility   07
Residential Treatment Facility   08
Respite Care Facility   09
Other 10
```

C. FACILITIES AND SERVICES

For each service or facility listed below, please check all the categories that describe how each item is provided **as of the last day of the reporting period**. Check all categories that apply for an item. Leave all categories blank for a facility or service that is not provided. Column 3 refers to the networks that were identified in section B, question 3d. If you check column (1) C1-19, please include the number of staffed beds.
The sum of the beds reported in 1-19 should equal Section D(1b), beds set up and staffed on page 9.

	(1) Owned or provided by my hospital or its subsidiary	(2) Provided by my Health System (in my local community)	(3) Provided by my network (in my local community)	(4) Provided through a formal contractual arrangement or joint venture with another provider that is not in my system or network (in my local community)
1. General medical-surgical care.........................(# Beds: _____)	☐	☐	☐	☐
2. Pediatric medical-surgical care ....(# Beds: _____)	☐	☐	☐	☐
3. Obstetrics [Level of unit (1-3): (___)].................(# Beds: _____)	☐	☐	☐	☐
4. Medical-surgical intensive care....................... (# Beds: _____)	☐	☐	☐	☐
5. Cardiac intensive care ....(# Beds: _____)	☐	☐	☐	☐
6. Neonatal intensive care............................. (# Beds: _____)	☐	☐	☐	☐
7. Neonatal intermediate care...........................(# Beds: _____)	☐	☐	☐	☐
8. Pediatric intensive care................................ (# Beds:_____)	☐	☐	☐	☐
9. Burn care................................ (# Beds: _____)	☐	☐	☐	☐
10. Other special care _____..... (# Beds: _____)	☐	☐	☐	☐
11. Other intensive care_____......(# Beds: _____)	☐	☐	☐	☐
12. Physical rehabilitation...................................(# Beds: _____)	☐	☐	☐	☐
13. Alcoholism-drug abuse or dependency care.......(# Beds: _____)	☐	☐	☐	☐
14. Psychiatric care.. (# Beds: _____)	☐	☐	☐	☐
15. Skilled nursing care...................................... (# Beds: _____)	☐	☐	☐	☐
16. Intermediate nursing care............................(# Beds: _____)	☐	☐	☐	☐
17. Acute long-term care.................................... (# Beds: _____)	☐	☐	☐	☐
18. Other long-term care................................ (# Beds: _____)	☐	☐	☐	☐
19. Other care (specify): _____...... (# Beds: _____)	☐	☐	☐	☐
20. Adult day care program..	☐	☐	☐	☐
21. Airborne infection isolation room (# rooms _____).....................	☐	☐	☐	☐
22. Alcoholism-drug abuse or dependency outpatient services..........	☐	☐	☐	☐
23. Alzheimer Center..	☐	☐	☐	☐
24. Ambulance services..	☐	☐	☐	☐
25. Ambulatory surgery center..	☐	☐	☐	☐
26. Arthritis treatment center..	☐	☐	☐	☐
27. Assisted living..	☐	☐	☐	☐
28. Auxiliary...	☐	☐	☐	☐
29. Bariatric/weight control services......................................	☐	☐	☐	☐
30. Birthing room/LDR room/LDRP room..................................	☐	☐	☐	☐
31. Blood Donor Center...	☐	☐	☐	☐
32. Breast cancer screening/mammograms...............................	☐	☐	☐	☐

C. FACILITIES AND SERVICES (continued)

	(1) Owned or provided by my hospital or its subsidiary	(2) Provided by my Health System (in my local community)	(3) Provided by my network (in my local community)	(4) Provided through a formal contractual arrangement or joint venture with another provider that is not in my system or network (in my local community)
33. Cardiology and cardiac surgery services				
a. Adult cardiology services	☐	☐	☐	☐
b. Pediatric cardiology services	☐	☐	☐	☐
c. Adult diagnostic catheterization	☐	☐	☐	☐
d. Pediatric diagnostic catheterization	☐	☐	☐	☐
e. Adult interventional cardiac catheterization	☐	☐	☐	☐
f. Pediatric interventional cardiac catheterization	☐	☐	☐	☐
g. Adult cardiac surgery	☐	☐	☐	☐
h. Pediatric cardiac surgery	☐	☐	☐	☐
i. Adult cardiac electrophysiology	☐	☐	☐	☐
j. Pediatric cardiac electrophysiology	☐	☐	☐	☐
k. Cardiac rehabilitation	☐	☐	☐	☐
34. Case management	☐	☐	☐	☐
35. Chaplaincy/pastoral care services	☐	☐	☐	☐
36. Chemotherapy	☐	☐	☐	☐
37. Children's wellness program	☐	☐	☐	☐
38. Chiropractic services	☐	☐	☐	☐
39. Community outreach	☐	☐	☐	☐
40. Complementary and alternative medicine services	☐	☐	☐	☐
41. Computer assisted orthopedic surgery (CAOS)	☐	☐	☐	☐
42. Crisis prevention	☐	☐	☐	☐
43. Dental services	☐	☐	☐	☐
44. Emergency services				
a. Emergency department	☐	☐	☐	☐
b. Pediatric emergency department	☐	☐	☐	☐
c. Satellite emergency department	☐	☐	☐	☐
d. If you checked column 1 (44c), is the department open 24 hours a day, 7 days a week? Yes ☐ No ☐				
e. Trauma center (certified) [Level of unit (1-3) _____]	☐	☐	☐	☐
45. Enabling services	☐	☐	☐	☐
46. Endoscopic services				
a. Optical colonoscopy	☐	☐	☐	☐
b. Endoscopic ultrasound	☐	☐	☐	☐
c. Ablation of Barrett's esophagus	☐	☐	☐	☐
d. Esophageal impedance study	☐	☐	☐	☐
e. Endoscopic retrograde cholangiopancreatography (ERCP)	☐	☐	☐	☐
47. Enrollment (insurance) assistance services	☐	☐	☐	☐
48. Extracorporeal shock wave lithotripter (ESWL)	☐	☐	☐	☐
49. Fertility clinic	☐	☐	☐	☐
50. Fitness center	☐	☐	☐	☐
51. Freestanding outpatient care center	☐	☐	☐	☐
52. Geriatric services	☐	☐	☐	☐
53. Health fair	☐	☐	☐	☐

C. FACILITIES AND SERVICES (continued)

	(1) Owned or provided by my hospital or its subsidiary	(2) Provided by my Health System (in my local community)	(3) Provided by my network (in my local community)	(4) Provided through a formal contractual arrangement or joint venture with another provider that is not in my system or network (in my local community)
54. Community health education	☐	☐	☐	☐
55. Genetic testing/counseling	☐	☐	☐	☐
56. Health screenings	☐	☐	☐	☐
57. Health research	☐	☐	☐	☐
58. Hemodialysis	☐	☐	☐	☐
59. HIV/AIDS services	☐	☐	☐	☐
60. Home health services	☐	☐	☐	☐
61. Hospice program	☐	☐	☐	☐
62. Hospital-based outpatient care center services	☐	☐	☐	☐
63. Immunization program	☐	☐	☐	☐
64. Indigent care clinic	☐	☐	☐	☐
65. Linguistic/translation services	☐	☐	☐	☐
66. Meal on wheels	☐	☐	☐	☐
67. Mobile health services	☐	☐	☐	☐
68. Neurological services	☐	☐	☐	☐
69. Nutrition program	☐	☐	☐	☐
70. Occupational health services	☐	☐	☐	☐
71. Oncology services	☐	☐	☐	☐
72. Orthopedic services	☐	☐	☐	☐
73. Outpatient surgery	☐	☐	☐	☐
74. Pain management program	☐	☐	☐	☐
75. Palliative care program	☐	☐	☐	☐
76. Palliative care inpatient unit	☐	☐	☐	☐
77. Patient controlled analgesia (PCA)	☐	☐	☐	☐
78. Patient education center	☐	☐	☐	☐
79. Patient representative services	☐	☐	☐	☐
80. Physical rehabilitation services				
a. Assistive technology center	☐	☐	☐	☐
b. Electrodiagnostic services	☐	☐	☐	☐
c. Physical rehabilitation outpatient services	☐	☐	☐	☐
d. Prosthetic and orthotic services	☐	☐	☐	☐
e. Robot-assisted walking therapy	☐	☐	☐	☐
f. Simulated rehabilitation environment	☐	☐	☐	☐
81. Primary care department	☐	☐	☐	☐
82. Psychiatric services				
a. Psychiatric child-adolescent services	☐	☐	☐	☐
b. Psychiatric consultation-liaison services	☐	☐	☐	☐
c. Psychiatric education services	☐	☐	☐	☐
d. Psychiatric emergency services	☐	☐	☐	☐
e. Psychiatric geriatric services	☐	☐	☐	☐
f. Psychiatric outpatient services	☐	☐	☐	☐
g. Psychiatric partial hospitalization services	☐	☐	☐	☐
h. Psychiatric residential treatment	☐	☐	☐	☐

C. FACILITIES AND SERVICES (continued)

	(1) Owned or provided by my hospital or its subsidiary	(2) Provided by my Health System (in my local community)	(3) Provided by my network (in my local community)	(4) Provided through a formal contractual arrangement or joint venture with another provider that is not in my system or network (in my local community)
83. Radiology, diagnostic				
a. CT Scanner	☐	☐	☐	☐
b. Diagnostic radioisotope facility	☐	☐	☐	☐
c. Electron beam computed tomography (EBCT)	☐	☐	☐	☐
d. Full-field digital mammography (FFDM)	☐	☐	☐	☐
e. Magnetic resonance imaging (MRI)	☐	☐	☐	☐
f. Intraoperative magnetic resonance imaging	☐	☐	☐	☐
g. Multi-slice spiral computed tomography (<64+ slice CT)	☐	☐	☐	☐
h. Multi-slice spiral computed tomography (64+ slice CT)	☐	☐	☐	☐
i. Positron emission tomography (PET)	☐	☐	☐	☐
j. Positron emission tomography/CT (PET/CT)	☐	☐	☐	☐
k. Single photon emission computerized tomography (SPECT)	☐	☐	☐	☐
l. Ultrasound	☐	☐	☐	☐
84. Radiology, therapeutic				
a. Image-guided radiation therapy (IGRT)	☐	☐	☐	☐
b. Intensity-modulated radiation therapy (IMRT)	☐	☐	☐	☐
c. Proton beam therapy	☐	☐	☐	☐
d. Shaped beam radiation system	☐	☐	☐	☐
e. Stereotactic radiosurgery	☐	☐	☐	☐
85. Retirement housing	☐	☐	☐	☐
86. Robotic surgery	☐	☐	☐	☐
87. Rural health clinic	☐	☐	☐	☐
88. Sleep center	☐	☐	☐	☐
89. Social work services	☐	☐	☐	☐
90. Sports medicine	☐	☐	☐	☐
91. Support groups	☐	☐	☐	☐
92. Swing bed services	☐	☐	☐	☐
93. Teen outreach services	☐	☐	☐	☐
94. Tobacco treatment/cessation program	☐	☐	☐	☐
95. Transplant services				
a. Bone marrow	☐	☐	☐	☐
b. Heart	☐	☐	☐	☐
c. Kidney	☐	☐	☐	☐
d. Liver	☐	☐	☐	☐
e. Lung	☐	☐	☐	☐
f. Tissue	☐	☐	☐	☐
g. Other	☐	☐	☐	☐
96. Transportation to health services	☐	☐	☐	☐
97. Urgent care center	☐	☐	☐	☐
98. Virtual colonoscopy	☐	☐	☐	☐
99. Volunteer services department	☐	☐	☐	☐
100. Women's health center/services	☐	☐	☐	☐
101. Wound management services	☐	☐	☐	☐

C. FACILITIES AND SERVICES (continued)

102a. In which of the following physician arrangements does your hospital or system/network participate? Column 3 refers to the networks that were identified in section B, question 3d. For hospital level physician arrangements that are reported in column 1, please report the number of physicians involved.

		(1) My Hospital		(2) My Health System	(3) My Health Network
a.	Independent Practice Association (IPA).............................	☐	(# of physicians _____)	☐	☐
b.	Group practice without walls	☐	(# of physicians _____)	☐	☐
c.	Open Physician-Hospital Organization (PHO)	☐	(# of physicians _____)	☐	☐
d.	Closed Physician-Hospital Organization (PHO)	☐	(# of physicians _____)	☐	☐
e.	Management Service Organization (MSO)	☐	(# of physicians _____)	☐	☐
f.	Integrated Salary Model	☐	(# of physicians _____)	☐	☐
g.	Equity Model	☐	(# of physicians _____)	☐	☐
h.	Foundation...	☐	(# of physicians _____)	☐	☐
i.	Other, please specify _____	☐	(# of physicians _____)	☐	☐

102b. Looking across all the relationships identified in question 102a, what is the total number of physicians (count each physician only once) that are engaged in an arrangement with your hospital that allows for joint contracting with payers or shared responsibility for financial risk or clinical performance between the hospital and physician (arrangement may be at the hospital, system or network level)?   # of physicians _____

103a. Does your hospital participate in any joint venture arrangements with physicians or physician groups?   YES ☐   NO ☐

103b. If your hospital participates in any joint ventures with physicians or physician groups, please indicate which types of services are involved in those joint ventures (Check all that apply)

- a. ☐ Limited service hospital
- b. ☐ Ambulatory surgical centers
- c. ☐ Imaging centers
- d. ☐ Other _____

103c. If you selected 'a. Limited Service Hospital', please tell us what type(s) of services are provided. (Check all that apply.)

- a. ☐ Cardiac
- b. ☐ Orthopedic
- c. ☐ Surgical
- d. ☐ Other _____

103d. Does your hospital participate in joint venture arrangements with organizations other than physician groups?   YES ☐   NO ☐

104a. Has your hospital or health care system established an accountable care organization (ACO)?   YES ☐   NO ☐

104b. If yes, please indicate the patient population that participates in the ACO. (Check all that apply):

- a. ☐ Medicaid
- b. ☐ Medicare
- c. ☐ Privately Insured
- d. ☐ Other, please specify _____

105. Does your hospital have an established medical home program?   YES ☐   NO ☐

106. Does your hospital participate in a bundled payment program involving inpatient, physician, and/or post acute care services where the hospital receives a single payment from a payer for a package of services and then distributes payments to participating providers of care (such as a single fee for hospital and physician services for a specific procedure, e.g. hip replacement, CABG)?   YES ☐   NO ☐

107. Please indicate below what percentage of your hospital's net patient revenue is paid based on the following payment mechanisms:

Type of Payment Arrangement

Percent of Net Patient Revenue
(must sum to 100%)

a. Fee for Service – DRG   _____

b. Fee for Service – Per Diem   _____

c. Fee for Service plus Shared Savings   _____

d. Bundled payments (inpatient plus physician and/or post acute care)   _____

e. Partial and global capitation payments   _____

f. Other, please specify_____   _____

108. Does your hospital, health system or health network have an equity interest in any of the following insurance products? (Check all that apply) Contractual relationships with HMOs and PPOs should not be reported here but in Question 109. Column 3 refers to the networks that were identified in section B, question 3d.

	(1) My Hospital	(2) My Health System	(3) My Health Network	(4) Joint Venture with Insurer
a. Health Maintenance Organization..	☐	☐	☐	☐
b. Preferred Provider Organization...	☐	☐	☐	☐
c. Indemnity Fee for Service Plan..	☐	☐	☐	☐

109. Does your hospital have a formal written contract that specifies the obligations of each party with:

a. Health maintenance organization (HMO) .... YES ☐   NO ☐   b. If YES, how many contracts?   _____

c. Preferred provider organization (PPO) ....YES ☐   NO ☐   d. If YES, how many contracts?   _____

110. What percentage of the hospital's net patient revenue is paid on a capitated basis? If the hospital does not participate in capitated arrangements, please enter "0")   _____ %

111. What percentage of the hospital's net patient revenue is paid on a shared risk basis?   _____ %

112. Does your hospital contract directly with employers or a coalition of employers to provide care on a capitated, predetermined, or shared risk basis? ....YES ☐   NO ☐

113. If your hospital has arrangements to care for a specific group of enrollees in exchange for a capitated payment, how many lives are covered?

D. TOTAL FACILITY BEDS, UTILIZATION, FINANCES, AND STAFFING

Please report beds, utilization, financial, and staffing data for the 12-month period that is consistent with the period reported on page 1. Report financial data for reporting period only. Include within your operations all activities that are wholly owned by the hospital, including subsidiary corporations regardless of where the activity is physically located. Please do not include within your operations distinct and separate divisions that may be owned by your hospital's parent corporation. If final figures are not available, please estimate. Round to the nearest dollar. Report all personnel who were on the payroll and whose payroll expenses are reported in D3f. (Please refer to specific definitions on pages 23-26.)

	(1) Total Facility	(2) Nursing Home Unit/Facility
Fill out column (2) if hospital owns and operates a nursing home type unit/facility. Column (1) should be the combined total of hospital plus nursing home unit/facility.		

1. BEDS AND UTILIZATION

a. Total licensed beds..

b. Beds set up and staffed for use at the end of the reporting period ....

c. Bassinets set up and staffed for use at the end of the reporting period ....

d. Births (exclude fetal deaths) ....

e. Admissions (exclude newborns, include neonatal & swing admissions) ....

f. Inpatient days (exclude newborns, include neonatal & swing days) ....

g. Emergency department visits..

h. Total outpatient visits (include emergency department visits & outpatient surgeries)....

i. Inpatient surgical operations ....

j. Number of operating rooms ....

k. Outpatient surgical operations..

2. MEDICARE/MEDICAID UTILIZATION (exclude newborns, include neonatal & swing days and deaths)

a1. Total Medicare (Title XVIII) inpatient discharges (including Medicare Managed Care) ....

a2. How many Medicare inpatient discharges were Medicare Managed Care ....

b1. Total Medicare (Title XVIII) inpatient days (including Medicare Managed Care) ....

b2. How many Medicare inpatient days were Medicare Managed Care ....

c1. Total Medicaid (Title XIX) inpatient discharges (including Medicaid Managed Care) ....

c2. How many Medicaid inpatient discharges were Medicaid Managed Care ....

d1. Total Medicaid (Title XIX) inpatient days (including Medicaid Managed Care) ....

d2. How many Medicaid inpatient days were Medicaid Managed Care ....

3. FINANCIAL

*a. Net patient revenue .... .00 .00

*b. Tax appropriations .... .00

*c. Other operating revenue .... .00

*d. Nonoperating revenue .... .00

*e. **TOTAL REVENUE (add 3a thru 3d)** .... .00 .00

f. Payroll expenses (only) .... .00 .00

g. Employee benefits .... .00 .00

h. Depreciation expense (for reporting period only) .... .00

i. Interest expense .... .00

j. Supply expense... .00

k. **TOTAL EXPENSES (Payroll plus all non-payroll expenses, including bad debt)** .00 .00

l. Due to differing accounting standards in use, please indicate whether or not bad debt is included in:

Total Expenses YES ☐ NO ☐

Deductions from net Patient Revenue YES ☐ NO ☐

4. REVENUE BY TYPE

a. Total gross inpatient revenue .... _____.00

b. Total gross outpatient revenue .... _____.00

c. Total gross patient revenue .... _____.00

*5. UNCOMPENSATED CARE & PROVIDER TAXES

a. Bad debt expense .... _____.00

b. Financial Assistance (includes Charity Care) (Revenue forgone at full-established rates. Include in gross revenue.) .... _____.00

c. Is your bad debt reported here (5a) reported on the basis of full charges?   YES ☐   NO ☐

d. Does your state have a provider Medicaid tax/assessment program .... YES ☐   NO ☐

e. If yes, please report the total gross amount paid into the program .... _____.00

f. Due to differing accounting standards please indicate whether the provider tax/assessment amount is included in:

    1. Total expense   YES ☐   NO ☐

    2. Deductions from net Patient Revenue   YES ☐   NO ☐

*6. REVENUE BY PAYOR (report total facility gross and net figures)

	(1) Gross	(2) Net
*a. GOVERNMENT (1) Medicare:		
a) Fee for service patient revenue	_____.00	_____.00
b) Managed care revenue	_____.00	_____.00
c) Total (a + b)	**_____.00**	**_____.00**
(2) Medicaid:		
a) Fee for service patient revenue	_____.00	_____.00
b) Managed care revenue	_____.00	_____.00
c) Medicaid Disproportionate Share Hospital Payments (DSH)		_____.00
d) Medicaid supplemental payments: not including Medicaid Disproportionate Share Hospital Payments (DSH)		_____.00
e) Total (a + b + c + d)	**_____.00**	**_____.00**
(3) Other government:	_____.00	_____.00
*b. NONGOVERNMENT (1) Self-pay	_____.00	_____.00
(2) Third-party payors:		
a) Managed care (includes HMO and PPO)	_____.00	_____.00
b) Other third-party payors	_____.00	_____.00
c) Total third-party payors (a + b)	**_____.00**	**_____.00**
(3) All Other nongovernment:	_____.00	_____.00
*c. TOTAL	**_____.00**	**_____.00**

(Total gross should equal 4c on page 9. Total net should equal 3a on page 9.)

Are the financial data on pages 9 and 10 from your audited financial statement? .... YES ☐   NO ☐

---

7. FIXED ASSETS

a. Property, plant and equipment at <u>cost</u> .... _____.00

b. Accumulated <u>depreciation</u> .... _____.00

c. Net property, plant and equipment (a-b) .... _____.00

d. Total gross square feet of your physical plant used for or in support of your healthcare activities .... _____

8. TOTAL CAPITAL EXPENSES

Include all expenses used to acquire assets, including buildings, remodeling projects, equipment, or property. _____.00

9. ENERGY CONSUMPTION

a. Have obtained an Energy Star rating from the EPA?   **YES**☐   **NO**☐

b. If you have obtained an Energy Star rating from the EPA, what is your rating?   _____

10. INFORMATION TECHNOLOGY

*a. IT operating expense..._____.00

*b. IT capital expense... ...._____.00

*c. Number of employed IT staff (in FTEs) ...._____

*d. Number of outsourced IT staff (in FTEs)..._____

e. Does your hospital have an electronic health record (see definition)?

☐ Yes, fully implemented   ☐ Yes, partially implemented   ☐ No

f. **Do you plan to attest as a Meaningful User of certified EHR technology and if so, in what federal fiscal year (FFY) will you achieve meaningful use for the first time?**

☐ Yes, attested in FFY 2011 (by Sep 30, 2011)

☐ Yes, in FFY 2012 (by Sep 30, 2012)

☐ Yes, in FFY 2013 (by Sep 30, 2013)

☐ Yes, by FFY 2015 (by Sep 30, 2015)

☐ Not planning to attest

☐ Not eligible for either Medicare or Medicaid EHR incentives

☐ Do Not Know

Note: To qualify as a meaningful user for Medicare and Medicaid, a hospital must (1) possess EHR technology certified against all 24 objectives of meaningful use; (2) meet each of 14 "core" objectives of meaningful use, at least 1 public health objective, and at least 4 additional "menu set" objectives; and (3) report on each of 15 clinical quality measures generated directly from the certified EHR.

> For additional questions regarding use of an electronic health record, please respond to the 2011 AHA Annual Survey Information Technology Supplement sent under separate cover.

*These data will be treated as confidential and not released without written permission. AHA will however, share these data with your respective state hospital association and, if requested, with your appropriate metropolitan/regional association.

For members of the Catholic Health Association of the United States (CHA), AHA will also share these data with CHA unless there are objections expressed by checking this box ☐. The state/metropolitan/regional association and CHA may not release these data without written permission from the hospital.

11. STAFFING

Report full-time (35 hours or more) and part-time (less than 35 hours) personnel who were on the hospital/facility **payroll at the end of your reporting period**. Include members of religious orders for whom dollar equivalents were reported. Exclude private-duty nurses, volunteers, and all personnel whose salary is financed entirely by outside research grants. Exclude physicians and dentists who are paid on a fee basis. FTE is the total number of hours worked by all employees over the full (12 month) reporting period divided by the normal number of hours worked by a full-time employee for that same time period. For example, if your hospital considers a normal workweek for a full-time employee to be 40 hours, a total of 2,080 would be worked over a full year (52 weeks). If the total number of hours worked by all employees on the payroll is 208,000, then the number of Full-Time Equivalents (FTE) is 100 (employees). The FTE calculation for a specific occupational category such as Registered nurses is exactly the same. The calculation for each occupational category should be based on the number of hours worked by staff employed in that specific category.

For each occupational category, please report the number of staff vacancies as of the last day of your reporting period. A vacancy is defined as a budgeted staff position which is unfilled as of the last day of the reporting period and for which the hospital is actively seeking either a full-time or part-time permanent replacement. Personnel who work in more than one area should be included only in the category of their primary responsibility and should be counted only once.

	(1) Full-Time (35 hr/wk or more) On Payroll	(2) Part-Time (Less than 35hr/wk) On Payroll	(3) FTE	(4) Vacancies
a. Physicians				
b. Dentists				
c. Medical and dental residents/interns				
d. Other trainees				
e. Registered nurses				
f. Licensed practical (vocational) nurses				
g. Nursing assistive personnel				
h. Radiology technicians				
i. Laboratory technicians				
j. Pharmacists, licensed				
k. Pharmacy technicians				
l. Respiratory therapists				
m. All other personnel				
n. Total facility personnel (add 11a through 11m)				

(Total facility personnel should include hospital plus nursing home type unit/facility personnel reported in 11o and 11p.)

o. Nursing home type unit/facility registered nurses				
p. Total nursing home type unit/facility personnel				

12. PRIVILEGED PHYSICIANS

Report the total number of physicians with privileges at your hospital by type of relationship with the hospital. The sum of the physicians reported in 12a-12f should equal the total number of privileged physicians (12g) in the hospital.

	(1) Total Employed	(2) Total Individual Contract	(3) Total Group Contract	(4) Not Employed or Under Contract	(5) Total Privileged
a. Primary care (general practitioner, general internal medicine, family practice, general pediatrics, obstetrics/gynecology, geriatrics)					
b. Emergency medicine					
c. Hospitalist					
d. Intensivist					
e. Radiologist/pathologist/anesthesiologist					
f. Other specialist					
g. Total (add 12a-12f)					

13. HOSPITALISTS

a. Do hospitalists provide care for patients in your hospital? .... YES ☐   NO ☐ **(if yes, please report in D.12c.)**

b. If yes, please report the total number of full-time equivalents (FTE) hospitalists..................... FTE _____

14. INTENSIVISTS

a.   Do intensivists provide care for patients in your hospital? (If no, please skip to 15.) YES ☐   NO ☐ **(if yes, please report in D.12d.)**

b.   If yes, please report the total number of FTE intensivists and assign them to the following areas. Please indicate whether the intensive care area is closed to intensivists. (Meaning that only intensivists are authorized to care for ICU patients.)

		FTE	Closed to Intensivists
1.	Medical-surgical intensive care	_____	☐
2.	Cardiac intensive care	_____	☐
3.	Neonatal intensive care	_____	☐
4.	Pediatric intensive care	_____	☐
5.	Other intensive care	_____	☐
6.	**Total** (Should equal total in 12d)	_____	

15. ADVANCED PRACTICE REGISTERED NURSES

a. Do advanced practice nurses provide care for patients in your hospital? .... YES ☐   NO ☐   (if no, please skip to 16.)

b. If yes, please report the number of full time, part time and FTE advanced practice nurses employed or contracted to provide care for patients in your hospital.

_____ Full-time   _____ Part-time   _____ FTE

c. If yes, please indicate the type of service the nurses provide (Please check all that apply).

☐ Primary care   ☐ Anesthesia services (Certified registered nurse **anesthetist**)   ☐ Emergency department care

☐ Other specialty care   ☐ Patient education   ☐ Case management   ☐ Other

16. FOREIGN EDUCATED NURSES

a.   Did your facility hire more foreign-educated nurses (including contract or agency nurses) to help fill RN vacancies in 2011 vs. 2010?

More ☐   Less ☐   Same ☐   Did not hire foreign nurses ☐

b.   From which countries/continents are you recruiting foreign-educated nurses?

Africa ☐   South Korea ☐   Canada ☐   Philippines ☐   China ☐   India ☐   Other ☐

E. SUPPLEMENTAL INFORMATION

1. CARE COORDINATION

Please indicate activities that your organization is engaged in to coordinate care across setting and extent to which they are used.

	Not used at all	Used minimally	Used moderately	Used Widely	Used hospital-wide
a. Chronic care management processes or programs to manage patients with high-volume, high-cost diseases.	☐	☐	☐	☐	☐
b. Use of predictive analytic tools to identify individual patients at high risk for poor outcomes or extraordinary resource use.	☐	☐	☐	☐	☐
c. Prospective management of patients at high-risk for poor outcomes or extraordinary resource use by experienced case managers	☐	☐	☐	☐	☐
d. Assignment of case managers to patients at risk for hospital admission or readmission for outpatient follow-up.	☐	☐	☐	☐	☐
e. Medication reconciliation as part of an established plan of care.	☐	☐	☐	☐	☐
f. Provision of visit summaries to patients as part of all outpatient encounters and scheduling of follow-up visits and/or specialty referrals at the time of the initial encounter.	☐	☐	☐	☐	☐
g. Post-hospital discharge continuity of care program with scaled intensiveness based upon a severity or risk profile for adult medical-surgical patients in defined diagnostic categories or severity profiles	☐	☐	☐	☐	☐
h. Arrangement of home visits by physicians, advanced practice nursed or other professionals for homebound and complex patients for whom office visits constitute a physical hardship.	☐	☐	☐	☐	☐

Describe your hospital's processes for facilitating safe transitions. Check the appropriate box for each process administered.

	How is the process administered? (Check all that apply.)				Is the process:	
	Verbally	Paper (mail or fax)	Electronic	Other	Standard?	Ad hoc?
a. Identifying patients who transition between setting of care.	☐	☐	☐	☐	☐	☐
b. Sharing clinical information between setting of care.	☐	☐	☐	☐	☐	☐
c. Providing patient discharge summaries to primary care providers.	☐	☐	☐	☐	☐	☐
d. Providing patient discharge summaries to other providers (e.g. rehabilitation hospitals).	☐	☐	☐	☐	☐	☐
e. Tracking the status of transitions including the timing of information exchange.	☐	☐	☐	☐	☐	☐

2. DIVERSITY, LANGUAGE AND LEADERSHIP

		YES	NO
a.	Does your hospital gather information on a patient's race/ethnicity at any point during their stay?	☐	☐
b.	Does your hospital gather information on a patient's primary language at any point during their stay?	☐	☐
c.	Does your hospital or health system currently have or plan to develop, execute, or evaluate a diversity strategy or plan?	☐	☐
d.	Does your hospital educate all clinical staff during orientation about how to address the unique cultural and linguistic factors affecting the care of diverse patients and communities?	☐	☐
e.	Does your hospital require all employees to attend diversity training?	☐	☐
f.	Does the hospital's strategic plan include goals for improving quality of care of culturally and linguistically-diverse patient population?	☐	☐

3. OTHER

a. Does your hospital provide services through one or more satellite facilities?   YES ☐   NO ☐

b. Does the hospital participate in a group purchasing arrangement?   YES ☐   NO ☐

If yes, please provide the name, city, and state of the group purchasing organization. If the hospital participates in more than one group purchasing organization, please provide the name, city, state and telephone number of the group purchasing organization(s) on page 15 (3i), under supplemental information

Name: _____   City: _____   State: _____

Does the hospital purchase medical/surgical supplies directly through a distributor?   YES ☐   NO ☐
    If yes, please provide the name of the distributor.

Name: _____

d. Which of the following best describes the type of triage system your emergency department uses on a daily basis to determine which patients can wait to be seen and which need to be seen immediately.

  1. Three (3) level system (emergent, urgent, non urgent, red, yellow, green)   ☐
  2. Four (4) level system (emergent, unstable urgent, stable urgent, non-urgent)   ☐
  3. Five (5) level Emergency Severity Index (ESI)   ☐
  4. Five (5) level system (Australasian, Manchester or Acuity Scale)   ☐
  5. Other (please specify) _____   ☐
  6. Don't know   ☐

e. Does your hospital outsource the HIM coding function under any of the following conditions?

	YES	NO
1. To handle backlog due to staff vacations or shortages.	☐	☐
2. Partially outsource during normal operations.	☐	☐
3. Completely outsourced during normal operations	☐	☐

f. Does your hospital use social media applications to conduct patient outreach or engage patients?

    ☐ Yes   . ☐ No   . ☐ Do not know

g. If yes, which social media applications does your hospital use for patient outreach or engagement (check all that apply)?

    1. ☐ Social networking service (e.g. Facebook, Google+, LinkedIn, etc.)

    2. ☐ Microblogging service (e.g. Twitter, Tumblr, etc.)

    3. ☐ Online video sharing

    4. ☐ Hospital's own website

    5. ☐ Hospital patient portal or personal health record

    6. ☐ Smart phone applications

    7. ☐ Other: Please describe _____

    8. ☐ Don't know

h. If your hospital hired RNs during the reporting period, how many were new graduates from nursing schools? _____

i. Use this space to describe your community benefit activities as well as any partners you are currently working with on such activities. Also use this space or additional sheets if more space is required for comments or to elaborate on any information supplied on this survey. Refer to the response by page, section and item name.

As declared previously, hospital specific revenue data are treated as confidential. AHA's policy is not to release these data without written permission from your institution. The AHA will however, share these data with your respective state hospital association and if requested with your appropriate metropolitan/regional association.

On occasion, the AHA is asked to provide these data to external organizations, both public and private, for their use in analyzing crucial health care policy or research issues. The AHA is requesting your permission to allow us to release your confidential data to those requests that we consider legitimate and worthwhile. In every instance of disclosure, the receiving organization will be prohibited from releasing hospital specific information.

Please indicate below whether or not you agree to these types of disclosure:

[ ] I hereby grant AHA permission to release my hospital's revenue data to external users that the AHA determines have a legitimate and worthwhile need to gain access to these data subject to the user's agreement with the AHA not to release hospital specific information.

_____
Chief Executive Officer   Date

[ ] I do not grant AHA permission to release my confidential data.

_____
Chief Executive Officer   Date

Does your hospital or health system have an Internet or Homepage address?   Yes ☐ No ☐

If yes, please provide the address: http:// _____

Thank you for your cooperation in completing this survey. If there are any questions about your responses to this survey, who should be contacted?

_____   (____)_____
Name (please print)   Title   (Area Code) Telephone Number

_____/_____/_____   _____   (____)_____
Date of Completion   Chief Executive Officer   Hospital's Main Fax Number

Contact Email address: _____

NOTE: PLEASE PHOTOCOPY THE INFORMATION FOR YOUR HOSPITAL FILE BEFORE RETURNING THE ORIGINAL FORM TO THE AMERICAN HOSPITAL ASSOCIATION. ALSO, PLEASE FORWARD A PHOTOCOPY OF THE COMPLETED QUESTIONNAIRE TO YOUR STATE HOSPITAL ASSOCIATION.

THANK YOU

SECTION A
REPORTING PERIOD
Instructions

INSTRUCTIONS AND DEFINITIONS FOR THE 2011 ANNUAL SURVEY OF HOSPITALS.
For purposes of this survey, a hospital is defined as the organization or corporate entity licensed or registered as a hospital by a state to provide diagnostic and therapeutic patient services for a variety of medical conditions, both surgical and nonsurgical.

1. Reporting period used (beginning and ending date): Record the beginning and ending dates of the reporting period in an eight-digit number: for example, January 1, 2009 should be shown as 01/01/2009. Number of days should equal the time span between the two dates that the hospital was open. If you are reporting for less than 365 days, utilization and finances should be presented for days reported only.
2. Were you in operation 12 full months at the end of your reporting period? If you are reporting for less than 365 days, utilization and finances should be presented for days reported only.
3. Number of days open during reporting period: Number of days should equal the time span between the two dates that the hospital was open.

SECTION B
ORGANIZATIONAL STRUCTURE
Instructions and Definitions

1. **CONTROL**
   Check the box to the left of the type of organization that is responsible for establishing policy for overall operation of the hospital.
   Government, nonfederal.
   State. Controlled by an agency of state government.
   County. Controlled by an agency of county government.
   City. Controlled by an agency of municipal government.
   City-County. Controlled jointly by agencies of municipal and county governments.
   Hospital district or authority. Controlled by a political subdivision of a state, county, or city created solely for the purpose of establishing and maintaining medical care or health-related care institutions.
   Nongovernment, not for profit. Controlled by not-for-profit organizations, including religious organizations (Catholic hospitals, for example), community hospitals, cooperative hospitals, hospitals operated by fraternal societies, and so forth.
   Investor owned, for profit. Controlled on a for profit basis by an individual, partnership, or a profit making corporation.
   Government, federal. Controlled by an agency or department of the federal government.

2. **SERVICE**
   Indicate the ONE category that best describes the type of service that your hospital provides to the majority of patients.
   General medical and surgical. Provides diagnostic and therapeutic services to patients for a variety of medical conditions, both surgical and nonsurgical.
   Hospital unit of an institution. Provides diagnostic and therapeutic services to patients in an institution.
   Hospital unit within an institution for the mentally retarded. Provides diagnostic and therapeutic services to patients in an institution for the mentally retarded.
   Surgical. An acute care specialty hospital where 2/3 or more of its inpatient claims are for surgical/diagnosis related groups.
   Psychiatric. Provides diagnostic and therapeutic services to patients with mental or emotional disorders.
   Tuberculosis and other respiratory diseases. Provides medical care and rehabilitative services to patients for whom the primary diagnosis is tuberculosis or other respiratory diseases.
   Cancer. Provides medical care to patients for whom the primary diagnosis is cancer.
   Heart. Provides diagnosis and treatment of heart disease.
   Obstetrics and gynecology. Provides medical and surgical treatment to pregnant women and to mothers following delivery. Also provides diagnostic and therapeutic services to women with diseases or disorders of the reproductive organs.
   Eye, ear, nose, and throat. Provides diagnosis and treatment of diseases and injuries of the eyes, ears, nose, and throat.
   Rehabilitation. Provides a comprehensive array of restoration services for the disabled and all support services necessary to help them attain their maximum functional capacity.
   Orthopedic. Provides corrective treatment of deformities, diseases, and ailments of the locomotive apparatus, especially affecting the limbs, bones, muscles, and joints.
   Chronic disease. Provides medical and skilled nursing services to patients with long-term illnesses who are not in an acute phase, but who require an intensity of services not available in nursing homes.
   Institution for the mentally retarded. Provides health-related care on a regular basis to patients with psychiatric or developmental impairment who cannot be treated in a skilled nursing unit.
   Acute long term care hospital. Provides high acuity interdisciplinary services to medically complex patients that require more intensive recuperation and care than can be provided in a typical nursing facility.
   Alcoholism and other chemical dependency. Provides diagnostic and therapeutic services to patients with alcoholism or other drug dependencies.

3. **OTHER**
   a. **Children admissions.** A hospital whose primary focus is the health and treatment of children and adolescents.
   b. **Subsidiary.** A company that is wholly controlled by another or one that is more than 50% owned by another organization.
   c. **Contract managed.** General day-to-day management of an entire organization by another organization under a formal contract. Managing organization reports directly to the board of trustees or owners of the managed organization; managed organization retains total legal responsibility and ownership of the facility's assets and liabilities.
   d. **Network.** A group of hospitals, physicians, other providers, insurers and/or community agencies that voluntarily work together to coordinate and deliver health services

4. **National Provider Identifier (NPI)** is a unique identification number for covered health care providers. Covered health care providers and all health plans and health care clearinghouses must use the NPIs in the administrative and financial transactions adopted under HIPAA. The NPI is a 10-position, intelligence-free numeric identifier (10-digit number).

SECTION C
FACILITIES AND SERVICES
Definitions

Owned/provided by the hospital or its subsidiary. All patient revenues, expenses and utilization related to the provision of the service are reflected in the hospital's statistics reported elsewhere in this survey.

Provided by my Health System (in my local community). Another health care provider in the same system as your hospital provides the service and patient revenue, expenses, and utilization related to the provision of the service are recorded at the point where the service was provided and would not be reflected in your hospital's statistics reported elsewhere in this survey. (A system is a corporate body that owns, leases, religiously sponsors and/or manages health provider)

Provided by my network (in my local community). Another health care provider in the same network as your hospital provides the service and patient revenue, expenses and utilization related to the provision of the service are recorded at the point where the service was provided and would not be reflected in your hospital's statistics reported elsewhere in this survey. (A network is a group of hospitals, physicians, other providers, insurers and/or community agencies that voluntarily work together to coordinate and deliver health services. When reporting a service for a network, please indicate the name of the network in Section B, question d.)

Provided through a formal contractual arrangement or joint venture with another provider that is not in my system or network. All patient revenues and utilization related to the provision of the service are recorded at the site where the service was provided and would not be reflected in your hospital statistics reported elsewhere in this survey. (A joint venture is a contractual arrangement between two or more parties forming an unincorporated business. The participants in the arrangement remain independent and separate outside of the venture's purpose.)

1. **General medical-surgical care.** Provides acute care to patients in medical and surgical units on the basis of physicians' orders and approved nursing care plans.
2. **Pediatric medical-surgical care.** Provides acute care to pediatric patients on the basis of physicians' orders and approved nursing care plans.
3. **Obstetrics.** Level should be designated: (1) unit provides services for uncomplicated maternity and newborn cases; (2) unit provides services for uncomplicated cases, the majority of complicated problems, and special neonatal services; and (3) unit provides services for all serious illnesses and abnormalities and is supervised by a full-time maternal/fetal specialist.
4. **Medical surgical intensive care.** Provides patient care of a more intensive nature than the usual medical and surgical care, on the basis of physicians' orders and approved nursing care plans. These units are staffed with specially trained nursing personnel and contain monitoring and specialized support equipment for patients who because of shock, trauma or other life-threatening conditions require intensified comprehensive observation and care. Includes mixed intensive care units.
5. **Cardiac intensive care.** Provides patient care of a more specialized nature than the usual medical and surgical care, on the basis of physicians' orders and approved nursing care plans. The unit is staffed with specially trained nursing personnel and contains monitoring and specialized support or treatment equipment for patients who, because of heart seizure, open-heart surgery, or other life-threatening conditions, require intensified, comprehensive observation and care. May include myocardial infarction, pulmonary care, and heart transplant units.
6. **Neonatal intensive care.** A unit that must be separate from the newborn nursery providing intensive care to all sick infants including those with the very lowest birth weights (less than 1500 grams). NICU has potential for providing mechanical ventilation, neonatal surgery, and special care for the sickest infants born in the hospital or transferred from another institution. A full-time neonatologist serves as director of the NICU.
7. **Neonatal intermediate care.** A unit that must be separate from the normal newborn nursery and that provides intermediate and/or recovery care and some specialized services, including immediate resuscitation, intravenous therapy, and capacity for prolonged oxygen therapy and monitoring.
8. **Pediatric intensive care.** Provides care to pediatric patients that is of a more intensive nature than that usually provided to pediatric patients. The unit is staffed with specially trained personnel and contains monitoring and specialized support equipment for treatment of patients who, because of shock, trauma, or other life-threatening conditions, require intensified, comprehensive observation and care.
9. **Burn care.** Provides care to severely burned patients. Severely burned patients are those with any of the following: (1) second-degree burns of more than 25% total body surface area for adults or 20% total body surface area for children: (2) third-degree burns of more than 10% total body surface area; (3) any severe burns of the hands, face, eyes, ears, or feet; or (4) all inhalation injuries, electrical burns, complicated burn injuries involving fractures and other major traumas, and all other poor risk factors.
10. **Other special care.** Provides care to patients requiring care more intensive than that provided in the acute area, yet not sufficiently intensive to require admission to an intensive care unit. Patients admitted to this area are usually transferred here from an intensive care unit once their condition has improved. These units are sometimes referred to as definitive observation, step-down or progressive care units.
11. **Other intensive care.** A specially staffed, specialty equipped, separate section of a hospital dedicated to the observation, care, and treatment of patients with life threatening illnesses, injuries, or complications from which recovery is possible. It provides special expertise and facilities for the support of vital function and utilizes the skill of medical nursing and other staff experienced in the management of these problems.
12. **Physical rehabilitation.** Provides care encompassing a comprehensive array of restoration services for the disabled and all support services necessary to help patients attain their maximum functional capacity.
13. **Alcoholism-drug abuse or dependency care.** Provides diagnosis and therapeutic services to patients with alcoholism or other drug dependencies. Includes care for inpatient/residential treatment for patients whose course of treatment involves more intensive care than provided in an outpatient setting or where patient requires supervised withdrawal.
14. **Psychiatric care.** Provides acute or long-term care to emotionally disturbed patients, including patients admitted for diagnosis and those admitted for treatment of psychiatric problems, on the basis of physicians' orders and approved nursing care plans. Long-term care may include intensive supervision to the chronically mentally ill, mentally disordered, or other mentally incompetent persons.
15. **Skilled nursing care.** Provides non-acute medical and skilled nursing care services, therapy, and social services under the supervision of a licensed registered nurse on a 24-hour basis.
16. **Intermediate nursing care.** Provides health-related services (skilled nursing care and social services) to residents with a variety of physical conditions or functional disabilities. These residents do not require the care provided by a hospital or skilled nursing facility, but do need supervision and support services.
17. **Acute long-term care.** Provides specialized acute hospital care to medically complex patients who are critically ill, have multisystem complications and/or failure, and require hospitalization averaging 25 days, in a facility offering specialized treatment programs and therapeutic intervention on a 24-hour/7 day a week basis.
18. **Other long-term care.** Provision of long-term care other than skilled nursing care or intermediate care for those who do not require daily medical or nursing services, but may requires some assistance in the activities of daily living. This can include residential care, elderly care, or sheltered care facilities for developmentally disabled.
19. **Other care.** (specify) Any type of care other than those listed above.
    The sum of the beds reported in Section C 1-19 should equal what you have reported in Section D(1b) for beds set up and staffed.
20. **Adult day care program.** Program providing supervision, medical and psychological care, and social activities for older adults who live at home or in another family setting, but cannot be alone or prefer to be with others during the day. May include intake assessment, health monitoring, occupational therapy, personal care, noon meal, and transportation services.

21. **Airborne infection isolation room.** A single-occupancy room for patient care where environmental factors are controlled in an effort to minimize the transmission of those infectious agents, usually spread person to person by droplet nuclei associated with coughing and inhalation. Such rooms typically have specific ventilation requirements for controlled ventilation, air pressure and filtration.

22. **Alcoholism-drug abuse or dependency outpatient services.** Organized hospital services that provide medical care and/or rehabilitative treatment services to outpatients for whom the primary diagnosis is alcoholism or other chemical dependency.

23. **Alzheimer center.** Facility that offers care to persons with Alzheimer's disease and their families through an integrated program of clinical services, research, and education.

24. **Ambulance services.** Provision of ambulance service to the ill and injured who require medical attention on a scheduled and unscheduled basis.

25. **Ambulatory surgery center.** Facility that provides care to patients requiring surgery that are admitted and discharged on the same day. Ambulatory surgery centers are distinct from same day surgical units within the hospital outpatient departments for purposes of Medicare payment.

26. **Arthritis treatment center.** Specifically equipped and staffed center for the diagnosis and treatment of arthritis and other joint disorders.

27. **Assisted living.** A special combination of housing, supportive services, personalized assistance and health care designed to respond to the individual needs of those who need help in activities of daily living and instrumental activities of daily living. Supportive services are available, 24 hours a day, to meet scheduled and unscheduled needs, in a way that promotes maximum independence and dignity for each resident and encourages the involvement of a resident's family, neighbor and friends.

28. **Auxiliary.** A volunteer community organization formed to assist the hospital in carrying out its purpose and to serve as a link between the institution and the community.

29. **Bariatric/weight control services.** Bariatrics is the medical practice of weight reduction.

30. **Birthing room/LDR room/LDRP room.** A single-room type of maternity care with a more homelike setting for families than the traditional three-room unit (labor/delivery/recovery) with a separate postpartum area. A birthing room combines labor and delivery in one room. An LDR room accommodates three stages in the birthing process--labor, delivery, and recovery. An LDRP room accommodates all four stages of the birth process--labor, delivery, recovery, and postpartum.

31. **Blood donor center.** A facility that performs, or is responsible for the collection, processing, testing or distribution of blood and components.

32. **Breast cancer screening/mammograms.** Mammography screening - The use of breast x-ray to detect unsuspected breast cancer in asymptomatic women. Diagnostic mammography - The x-ray imaging of breast tissue in symptomatic women who are considered to have a substantial likelihood of having breast cancer already.

33. **Cardiology and cardiac surgery services.** Services which include the diagnosis and treatment of diseases and disorders involving the heart and circulatory system.

    a-b Cardiology services. . An organized clinical service offering diagnostic and interventional procedures to manage the full range of heart conditions.

    c-d. Diagnostic catheterization. (also called coronary angiography or coronary arteriography) is used to assist in diagnosing complex heart conditions. Cardiac angiography involves the insertion of a tiny catheter into the artery in the groin then carefully threading the catheter up into the aorta where the coronary arteries originate. Once the catheter is in place, a dye is injected which allows the cardiologist to see the size, shape, and distribution of the coronary arteries. These images are used to diagnose heart disease and to determine, among other things, whether or not surgery is indicated.

    e-f. Interventional cardiac catheterization. Nonsurgical procedure that utilizes the same basic principles as diagnostic catheterization and then uses advanced techniques to improve the heart's function. It can be a less-invasive alternative to heart surgery.

    g-h. Cardiac surgery. Includes minimally invasive procedures that include surgery done with only a small incision or no incision at all, such as through a laparoscope or an endoscope and more invasive major surgical procedures that include open chest and open heart surgery.

    i-j. Cardiac electrophysiology. Evaluation and management of patients with complex rhythm or conduction abnormalities, including diagnostic testing, treatment of arrhythmias by catheter ablation or drug therapy, and pacemaker/defibrillator implantation and follow-up.

    k. Cardiac rehabilitation. A medically supervised program to help heart patients recover quickly and improve their overall physical and mental functioning. The goal is to reduce risk of another cardiac event or to keep an already present heart condition from getting worse. Cardiac rehabilitation programs include: counseling to patients, an exercise program, helping patients modify risk factors such as smoking and high blood pressure, providing vocational guidance to enable the patient to return to work, supplying information on physical limitations and lending emotional support.

34. **Case management.** A system of assessment, treatment planning, referral and follow-up that ensures the provision of comprehensive and continuous services and the coordination of payment and reimbursement for care.

35. **Chaplaincy/pastoral care services.** A service ministering religious activities and providing pastoral counseling to patients, their families, and staff of a health care organization.

36. **Chemotherapy.** An organized program for the treatment of cancer by the use of drugs or chemicals.

37. **Children's wellness program.** A program that encourages improved health status and a healthful lifestyle of children through health education, exercise, nutrition and health promotion.

38. **Chiropractic services.** An organized clinical service including spinal manipulation or adjustment and related diagnostic and therapeutic services.

39. **Community outreach.** A program that systematically interacts with the community to identify those in need of services, alerting persons and their families to the availability of services, locating needed services, and enabling persons to enter the service delivery system.

40. **Complementary and alternative medicine services.** Organized hospital services or formal arrangements to providers that provide care or treatment not based solely on traditional western allopathic medical teachings as instructed in most U.S. medical schools. Includes any of the following: acupuncture, chiropractic, homeopathy, osteopathy, diet and lifestyle changes, herbal medicine, massage therapy, etc.

41. **Computer assisted orthopedic surgery (CAOS).** Orthopedic surgery using computer technology, enabling three-dimensional graphic models to visualize a patient's anatomy.

42. **Crisis prevention.** Services provided in order to promote physical and mental well being and the early identification of disease and ill health prior to the onset and recognition of symptoms so as to permit early treatment.

43. **Dental Services.** An organized dental service or dentists on staff, not necessarily involving special facilities, providing dental or oral services to inpatients or outpatients.

44. **Emergency services.** Health services that are provided after the onset of a medical condition that manifests itself by symptoms of sufficient severity, including severe pain, that the absence of immediate medical attention could reasonably be expected by a prudent layperson, who possesses an average knowledge of health and medicine, to result in placing the patient's health in serious jeopardy.

    a-b. Emergency department. Hospital facilities for the provision of unscheduled outpatient services to patients whose conditions require immediate care.

    c. Satellite Emergency Department. A facility owned and operated by the hospital but physically separate from the hospital for the provision of unscheduled outpatient services to patients whose conditions require immediate care. A freestanding ED is not physically connected to a hospital, but has all necessary emergency staffing and equipment on-site.

    e. Trauma center (certified). A facility to provide emergency and specialized intensive care to critically ill and injured patients. Level 1: A regional resource trauma center, which is capable of providing total care for every aspect of injury and plays a leadership role in trauma research and education. Level 2: A community trauma center, which is capable of providing trauma care to all but the most severely injured patients who require highly specialized care. Level 3: A rural trauma hospital, which is capable of providing care to a large number of injury victims and can resuscitate and stabilize more severely injured patients so that they can be transported to level 1 or 2 facilities. Please provide explanation on page 15 if necessary.

45. **Enabling services.** A program that is designed to help the patient access health care services by offering any of the following: transportation services and/or referrals to local social services agencies.

46. **Endoscopic services.**
    a. **Optical colonoscopy.** An examination of the interior of the colon using a long, flexible, lighted tube with a small built-in camera.
    b. **Endoscopic ultrasound.** Specially designed endoscope that incorporates an ultrasound transducer used to obtain detailed images of organs in the chest and abdomen. The endoscope can be passed through the mouth or the anus. When combined with needle biopsy the procedure can assist in diagnosis of disease and staging of cancer.
    c. **Ablation of Barrett's esophagus.** Premalignant condition that can lead to adenocarcinoma of the esophagus. The nonsurgical ablation of premalignant tissue in Barrett's esophagus by the application of thermal energy or light through an endoscope passed from the mouth into the esophagus.
    d. **Esophageal impedance study.** A test in which a catheter is placed through the nose into the esophagus to measure whether gas or liquids are passing from the stomach into the esophagus and causing symptoms.
    e. **Endoscopic retrograde cholangiopancreatography (ERCP).** A procedure in which a catheter is introduced through an endoscope into the bile ducts and pancreatic ducts. Injection of contrast material permits detailed x-ray of these structures. The procedure is used diagnostically as well as therapeutically to relieve obstruction or remove stones.

47. **Enrollment (insurance) assistance services.** A program that provides enrollment assistance for patients who are potentially eligible for public health insurance programs such as Medicaid, State Children's Health Insurance, or local/state indigent care programs. The specific services offered This could include explanation of benefits, assist applicants in completing the application and locating all relevant documents, conduct eligibility interviews, and/or forward applications and documentation to state/local social service or health agency.

48. **Extracorporeal shock wave lithotripter (ESWL).** A medical device used for treating stones in the kidney or urethra. The device disintegrates kidney stones noninvasively through the transmission of acoustic shock waves directed at the stones.

49. **Fertility clinic.** A specialized program set in an infertility center that provides counseling and education as well as advanced reproductive techniques such as: injectable therapy, reproductive surgeries, treatment for endometriosis, male factor infertility, tubal reversals, in vitro fertilization (IVF), donor eggs, and other such services to help patients achieve successful pregnancies.

50. **Fitness center.** Provides exercise, testing, or evaluation programs and fitness activities to the community and hospital employees.

51. **Freestanding outpatient care center.** A facility owned and operated by the hospital, that is physically separate from the hospital and provides various medical treatments and diagnostic services on an outpatient basis only. Laboratory and radiology services are usually available.

52. **Geriatric services.** The branch of medicine dealing with the physiology of aging and the diagnosis and treatment of disease affecting the aged. Services could include: Adult day care; Alzheimer's diagnostic-assessment services; Comprehensive geriatric assessment; Emergency response system; Geriatric acute care unit; and/or Geriatric clinics.

53. **Health fair.** Community health education events that focus on the prevention of disease and promotion of health through such activities as audiovisual exhibits and free diagnostic services.

54. **Community health education.** Education that provides health information to individuals and populations as well as support for personal, family and community health decisions with the objective of improving health status.

55. **Genetic testing/counseling.** A service equipped with adequate laboratory facilities and directed by a qualified physician to advise parents and prospective parents on potential problems in cases of genetic defects. A genetic test is the analysis of human DNA, RNA, chromosomes, proteins, and certain metabolites in order to detect heritable disease-related genotypes, mutations, phenotypes, or karyotypes for clinical purposes. Genetic tests can have diverse purposes, including the diagnosis of genetic diseases in newborns, children, and adults; the identification of future health risks; the prediction of drug responses; and the assessment of risks to future children.

56. **Health screening.** A preliminary procedure such as a test or examination to detect the most characteristic sign or signs of a disorder that may require further investigation.

57. **Health research.** Organized hospital research program in any of the following areas: basic research, clinical research, community health research, and/or research on innovative health care delivery.

58. **Hemodialysis.** Provision of equipment and personnel for the treatment of renal insufficiency on an inpatient or outpatient basis.

59. **HIV-AIDS services.** Could include: HIV-AIDS unit-Special unit or team designated and equipped specifically for diagnosis, treatment, continuing care planning, and counseling services for HIV-AIDS patients and their families. General inpatient care for HIV-AIDS-Inpatient diagnosis and treatment for human immunodeficiency virus and acquired immunodeficiency syndrome patients, but dedicated unit is not available. Specialized outpatient program for HIV-AIDS-Special outpatient program providing diagnostic, treatment, continuing care planning, and counseling for HIV-AIDS patients and their families.

60. **Home health services.** Service providing nursing, therapy, and health-related homemaker or social services in the patient's home.

61. **Hospice.** A program providing palliative care, chiefly medical relief of pain and supportive services, addressing the emotional, social, financial, and legal needs of terminally ill patients and their families. Care can be provided in a variety of settings, both inpatient and at home.

62. **Hospital-based outpatient care center-services.** Organized hospital health care services offered by appointment on an ambulatory basis. Services may include outpatient surgery, examination, diagnosis, and treatment of a variety of medical conditions on a nonemergency basis, and laboratory and other diagnostic testing as ordered by staff or outside physician referral.

63. **Immunization program.** Program that plans, coordinates and conducts immunization services in the community.

64. **Indigent care clinic.** Health care services for uninsured and underinsured persons where care is free of charge or charged on a sliding scale. This would include "free clinics" staffed by volunteer practitioners, but could also be staffed by employees with the sponsoring health care organization subsidizing the cost of service.

65. **Linguistic/translation services.** Services provided by the hospital designed to make health care more accessible to non-English speaking patients and their physicians.

66. **Meals on wheels.** A hospital sponsored program which delivers meals to people, usually the elderly, who are unable to prepare their own meals. Low cost, nutritional meals are delivered to individuals' homes on a regular basis.

67. **Mobile health services.** Vans and other vehicles used for delivery to primary care services.

68. **Neurological services.** Services provided by the hospital dealing with the operative and nonoperative management of disorders of the central, peripheral, and autonomic nervous systems.

69. **Nutrition programs.** Services within a health care facility which are designed to provide inexpensive, nutritionally sound meals to patients.

70. **Occupational health services.** Includes services designed to protect the safety of employees from hazards in the work environment.

71. **Oncology services.** Inpatient and outpatient services for patients with cancer, including comprehensive care, support and guidance in addition to patient education and prevention, chemotherapy, counseling and other treatment methods.

72. **Orthopedic services.** Services provided for the prevention or correction of injuries or disorders of the skeletal system and associated muscles, joints and ligaments.

73. **Outpatient surgery.** Scheduled surgical services provided to patients who do not remain in the hospital overnight. The surgery may be performed in operating suites also used for inpatient surgery, specially designated surgical suites for outpatient surgery, or procedure rooms within an outpatient care facility.

74. **Pain management program.** A recognized clinical service or program providing specialized medical care, drugs or therapies for the management of acute or chronic pain and other distressing symptoms, administered by specially trained physicians and other clinicians, to patients suffering from an acute illness of diverse causes.

75. **Palliative care program.** An organized program providing specialized medical care, drugs or therapies for the management of acute or chronic pain and/or the control of symptoms administered by specially trained physicians and other clinicians; and supportive care services, such as counseling on advanced directives, spiritual care, and social services, to patients with advanced disease and their families.

76. **Palliative care inpatient unit.** An inpatient palliative care ward is a physically discreet, inpatient nursing unit where the focus is palliative care. The patient care focus is on symptom relief for complex patients who may be continuing to undergo primary treatment. Care is delivered by palliative medicine specialists.

77. **Patient controlled analgesia (PCA).** Patient-controlled analgesia (PCA) is intravenously administered pain medicine under the patient's control. The patient has a button on the end of a cord than can be pushed at will, whenever more pain medicine is desired. This button will only deliver more pain medicine at pre-determined intervals, as programmed by the doctor's order.

78. **Patient education center.** Written goals and objectives for the patient and/or family related to therapeutic regimens, medical procedures, and self care.

79. **Patient representative services.** Organized hospital services providing personnel through whom patients and staff can seek solutions to institutional problems affecting the delivery of high quality care and services.

80. **Physical rehabilitation services.** Program providing medical, health-related, therapy, social, and/or vocational services to help disabled persons attain or retain their maximum functional capacity.
    a. **Assistive technology center.** A program providing access to specialized hardware and software with adaptations allowing individuals greater independence with mobility, dexterity, or increased communication options.
    b. **Electrodiagnostic services.** Diagnostic testing services for nerve and muscle function including services such as nerve conduction studies and needle electromyography.
    c. **Physical rehabilitation outpatient services.** Outpatient program providing medical, health-related, therapy, social, and/or vocational services to help disabled persons attain or retain their maximum functional capacity.
    d. **Prosthetic and orthotic services.** Services providing comprehensive prosthetic and orthotic evaluation, fitting, and training.
    e. **Robot-assisted walking therapy.** A form of physical therapy that uses a robotic device to assist patients who are relearning how to walk.
    f. **Simulated rehabilitation environment.** Rehabilitation focused on retraining functional skills in a contextually appropriate environment (simulated home and community settings) or in a traditional setting (gymnasium) using motor learning principles.

81. **Primary care department.** A unit or clinic within the hospital that provides primary care services (e.g. general pediatric care, general internal medicine, family practice, gynecology) through hospital-salaried medical and/or nursing staff, focusing on evaluating and diagnosing medical problems and providing medical treatment on an outpatient basis.

82. **Psychiatric services.** Services provided by the hospital that offer immediate initial evaluation and treatment to patients with mental or emotional disorders.
    a. **Psychiatric child-adolescent services.** Provides care to emotionally disturbed children and adolescents, including those admitted for diagnosis and those admitted for treatment.
    b. **Psychiatric consultation-liaison services.** Provides organized psychiatric consultation/liaison services to nonpsychiatric hospital staff and/or departments on psychological aspects of medical care that may be generic or specific to individual patients.
    c. **Psychiatric education services.** Provides psychiatric educational services to community agencies and workers such as schools, police, courts, public health nurses, welfare agencies, clergy, and so forth. The purpose is to expand the mental health knowledge and competence of personnel not working in the mental health field and to promote good mental health through improved understanding, attitudes, and behavioral patterns.
    d. **Psychiatric emergency services.** Services of facilities available on a 24-hour basis to provide immediate unscheduled out-patient care, diagnosis, evaluation, crisis intervention, and assistance to persons suffering acute emotional or mental distress.
    e. **Psychiatric geriatric services.** Provides care to emotionally disturbed elderly patients, including those admitted for diagnosis and those admitted for treatment.
    f. **Psychiatric outpatient services.** Provides medical care, including diagnosis and treatment, of psychiatric outpatients.
    g. **Psychiatric partial hospitalization program.** Organized hospital services of intensive day/evening outpatient services of three hours or more duration, distinguished from other outpatient visits of one hour.
    h. **Psychiatric Residential Treatment.**

83. **Radiology, diagnostic.** The branch of radiology that deals with the utilization of all modalities of radiant energy in medical diagnoses and therapeutic procedures using radiologic guidance. This includes, but is not restricted to, imaging techniques and methodologies utilizing radiation emitted by x-ray tubes, radionuclides, and ultrasonographic devices and the radiofrequency electromagnetic radiation emitted by atoms.
    a. **CT Scanner.** Computed tomographic scanner for head or whole body scans.
    b. **Diagnostic radioisotope facility.** The use of radioactive isotopes (Radiopharmaceuticals) as tracers or indicators to detect an abnormal condition or disease.
    c. **Electron beam computed tomography (EBCT).** A high tech computed tomography scan used to detect coronary artery disease by measuring coronary calcifications. This imaging procedure uses electron beams which are magnetically steered to produce a visual of the coronary artery and the images are produced faster than conventional CT scans.
    d. **Full-field digital mammography (FFDM).** Combines the x-ray generators and tubes used in analog screen-film mammography (SFM) with a detector plate that converts the x-rays into a digital signal.
    e. **Magnetic resonance imaging (MRI).** The use of a uniform magnetic field and radio frequencies to study tissue and structure of the body. This procedure enables the visualization of biochemical activity of the cell in vivo without the use of ionizing radiation, radioisotopic substances or high-frequency sound.
    f. **Intraoperative magnetic resonance imaging.** An integrated surgery system which provides an MRI system in an operating room. The system allows for immediate evaluation of the degree to tumor resection while the patient is undergoing a surgical resection. Intraoperative MRI exists when a MRI (low-field or high-field) is placed in the operating theater and is used during surgical resection without moving the patient from the operating room to the diagnostic imaging suite.
    g. **Multi-slice spiral computed tomography (<64+slice CT).** A specialized computed tomography procedure that provides three-dimensional processing and allows narrower and multiple slices with increased spatial resolution and faster scanning times as compared to a regular computed tomography scan.
    h. **Multi-slice spiral computed tomography (64+ slice CT).** Involves the acquisition of volumetric tomographic x-ray absorption data expressed in Hounsfield units using multiple rows of detectors. 64+ systems reconstruct the equivalent of 64 or greater slices to cover the imaged volume.

i. **Positron emission tomography (PET).** A nuclear medicine imaging technology which uses radioactive (positron emitting) isotopes created in a cyclotron or generator and computers to produce composite pictures of the brain and heart at work. PET scanning produces sectional images depicting metabolic activity or blood flow rather than anatomy.

j. **Positron emission tomography/CT (PET/CT).** Provides metabolic functional information for the monitoring of chemotherapy, radiotherapy and surgical planning.

k. **Single photon emission computerized tomography (SPECT).** Single photon emission computerized tomography is a nuclear medicine imaging technology that combines existing technology of gamma camera imaging with computed tomographic imaging technology to provide a more precise and clear image.

l. **Ultrasound.** The use of acoustic waves above the range of 20,000 cycles per second to visualize internal body structures.

84. **Radiology, therapeutic.** The branch of medicine concerned with radioactive substances and using various techniques of visualization, with the diagnosis and treatment of disease using any of the various sources of radiant energy. Services could include: megavoltage radiation therapy; radioactive implants; stereotactic radiosurgery; therapeutic radioisotope facility; X-ray radiation therapy.

   a. **Image-guided radiation therapy (IGRT).** Automated system for image-guided radiation therapy that enables clinicians to obtain high-resolution x- ray images to pinpoint tumor sites, adjust patient positioning when necessary, and complete a treatment, all within the standard treatment time slot, allowing for more effective cancer treatments.

   b. **Intensity-Modulated Radiation Therapy (IMRT).** A type of three-dimensional radiation therapy, which improves the targeting of treatment delivery in a way that is likely to decrease damage to normal tissues and allows varying intensities.

   c. **Proton beam therapy.** A form of radiation therapy which administers proton beams. While producing the same biologic effects as x-ray beams, the energy distribution of protons differs from conventional x-ray beams in that they can be more precisely focused in tissue volumes in a three-dimensional pattern resulting in less surrounding tissue damage than conventional radiation therapy permitting administration of higher doses.

   d. **Shaped beam radiation system.** A precise, non-invasive treatment that involves targeting beams of radiation that mirrors the exact size and shape of a tumor at a specific area of a tumor to shrink or destroy cancerous cells. This procedure delivers a therapeutic dose of radiation that conforms precisely to the shape of the tumor, thus minimizing the risk to nearby tissues.

   e. **Stereotactic radiosurgery.** Stereotactic radiosurgery (SRS) is a radiotherapy modality that delivers a high dosage of radiation to a discrete treatment area in as few as one treatment session. Includes gamma knife, cyberknife, etc.

85. **Retirement housing.** A facility that provides social activities to senior citizens, usually retired persons, who do not require health care but some short-term skilled nursing care may be provided. A retirement center may furnish housing and may also have acute hospital and long-term care facilities, or it may arrange for acute and long-term care through affiliated institutions.

86. **Robotic surgery.** The use of mechanical guidance devices to remotely manipulate surgical instrumentation.

87. **Rural health clinic.** A clinic located in a rural, medically under-served area in the United States that has a separate reimbursement structure from the standard medical office under the Medicare and Medicaid programs.

88. **Sleep center.** Specially equipped and staffed center for the diagnosis and treatment of sleep disorders.

89. **Social work services.** Could include: organized services that are properly directed and sufficiently staffed by qualified individuals who provide assistance and counseling to patients and their families in dealing with social, emotional, and environmental problems associated with illness or disability, often in the context of financial or discharge planning coordination.

90. **Sports medicine.** Provision of diagnostic screening and assessment and clinical and rehabilitation services for the prevention and treatment of sports-related injuries.

91. **Support groups.** A hospital sponsored program that allows a group of individuals with the same or similar problems who meet periodically to share experiences, problems, and solutions in order to support each other.

92. **Swing bed services.** A hospital bed that can be used to provide either acute or long-term care depending on community or patient needs. To be eligible a hospital must have a Medicare provider agreement in place, have fewer than 100 beds, be located in a rural area, do not have a 24 hour nursing service waiver in effect, have not been terminated from the program in the prior two years, and meet various service conditions.

93. **Teen outreach services.** A program focusing on the teenager which encourages an improved health status and a healthful lifestyle including physical, emotional, mental, social, spiritual and economic health through education, exercise, nutrition and health promotion.

94. **Tobacco treatment/cessation program.** Organized hospital services with the purpose of ending tobacco-use habits of patients addicted to tobacco/nicotine.

95. **Transplant services.** The branch of medicine that transfers an organ or tissue from one person to another or from one body part to another to replace a diseased structure or to restore function or to change appearance. Services could include: Bone marrow transplant program; heart, lung, kidney, intestine, or tissue transplant. Please include heart/lung or other multi-transplant surgeries in 'other'.

96. **Transportation to health facilities.** A long-term care support service designed to assist the mobility of the elderly. Some programs offer improved financial access by offering reduced rates and barrier-free buses or vans with ramps and lifts to assist the elderly or handicapped; others offer subsidies for public transport systems or operate mini-bus services exclusively for use by senior citizens.

97. **Urgent care center.** A facility that provides care and treatment for problems that are not life threatening but require attention over the short term.

98. **Virtual colonoscopy.** Noninvasive screening procedure used to visualize, analyze and detect cancerous or potentially cancerous polyps in the colon.

99. **Volunteer services department.** An organized hospital department responsible for coordinating the services of volunteers working within the institution.

100. **Women's health center/services.** An area set aside for coordinated education and treatment services specifically for and promoted to women as provided by this special unit. Services may or may not include obstetrics but include a range of services other than OB.

101. **Wound management services.** Services for patients with chronic wounds and nonhealing wounds often resulting from diabetes, poor circulation, improper seating and immunocompromising conditions. The goals are to progress chronic wounds through stages of healing, reduce and eliminate infections, increase physical function to minimize complications from current wounds and prevent future chronic wounds. Wound management services are provided on an inpatient or outpatient basis, depending on the intensity of service needed.

102a. **Physician arrangements.** An integrated healthcare delivery program implementing physician compensation and incentive systems for managed care services.

   a. **Independent practice association (IPA).** AN IPA is a legal entity that holds managed care contracts. The IPA then contracts with physicians, usually in solo practice, to provide care either on a fee-for-services or capitated basis. The purpose of an IPA is to assist solo physicians in obtaining managed care contracts.

   b. **Group practice without walls.** Hospital sponsors the formation of, or provides capital to physicians to establish, a "quasi" group to share administrative expenses while remaining independent practitioners.

   c. **Open physician-hospital organization (PHO).** A joint venture between the hospital and all members of the medical staff who wish to participate. The PHO can act as a unified agent in managed care contracting, own a managed care plan, own and operate ambulatory care centers or ancillary services projects, or provide administrative services to physician members.

   d. **Closed physician-hospital organization (PHO).** A PHO that restricts physician membership to those practitioners who meet criteria for cost effectiveness and/or high quality.

   e. **Management services organization (MSO).** A corporation, owned by the hospital or a physician/hospital joint venture, that provides management services to one or more medical group practices. The MSO purchases the tangible assets of the practices and leases them back as part of a full-service management agreement, under which the MSO employs all non-physician staff and provides all supplies/administrative systems for a fee.

   f. **Integrated salary model.** Physicians are salaried by the hospital or another entity of a health system to provide medical services for primary care and specialty care.

   g. **Equity model.** Allows established practitioners to become shareholders in a professional corporation in exchange for tangible and intangible assets of their existing practices.

   h. **Foundation.** A corporation, organized either as a hospital affiliate or subsidiary, which purchases both the tangible and intangible assets of one or more medical group practices. Physicians remain in a separate corporate entity but sign a professional services agreement with the foundation.

102b. Of all physician arrangements listed in question 102a (a-i), indicate the total number of physicians (count each physician only once) that are engaged in an arrangement with your hospital that allows for joint contracting with payers or shared responsibility for financial risk or clinical performance between the hospital and physician (arrangement may be at the hospital, system or network level). *Joint contracting* does not include contracting between physicians participating in an independent practice.

103a. Joint venture. A contractual arrangement between two or more parties forming an unincorporated business. The participants in the arrangement remain independent and separate outside of the ventures purpose.

104a. Accountable Care Organization (ACO) Contract. An ACO contract as having two essential elements: (1) accountability for the total costs of care for the population of patients attributed to the primary care physicians in the organization; (2) financial incentives that link the magnitude of bonus payments to performance on quality measures (which could include technical quality, patient experience and/or health outcome measures). This will generally involve a contract where the payer establishes a target budget for one or more years for the total costs of care for the agreed-upon patient population, the payer tracks actual spending and performance on quality; and the provider receives bonus payments that could include a share of savings that are (or are not) contingent on meeting quality targets, with (or without) additional bonuses related to performance on those quality measures.

105. Patient-Centered Medical Home. The medical home concept refers to the provision of comprehensive primary care services that facilitates communication and shared decision-making between the patient, his/her primary care providers, other providers, and the patient's family.

106. Bundling. Bundling is a payment mechanism whereby a provider entity receives a single payment for services provided across one or parts of the care continuum. For example, an entity might receive a single payment for the hospital and physician services provided as part of an inpatient stay or might receive a single payment for the post acute care services involved in a single episode of care. The entity then has responsibility for compensating each of the individual providers involved in the episode of care.

110. Capitation. An at-risk payment arrangement in which an organization receives a fixed prearranged payment and in turn guarantees to deliver or arrange all medically necessary care required by enrollees in the capitated plan. The fixed amount is specified within contractual agreements between the payor and the involved organization. The fixed payment amount is based on an actuarial assessment of the services required by enrollees and the costs of providing these services, recognizing enrollees' adjustment factors such as age, sex, and family size.

111.. Shared risk payments. A payment arrangement in which a hospital and a managed care organization share the risk of adverse claims experience. Methods for sharing risk could include: capitation with partial refunds or supplements if billed hospital charges or costs differ from capitated payments, and service or discharge-based payments with withholds and bonus payouts that depend on expenditure targets.

SECTION D
TOTAL FACILITY BEDS, UTILIZATION, FINANCES, AND STAFFING

Instructions and Definitions

For the purposes of this survey, nursing home type unit/facility provides **long-term care for the elderly or other patients requiring chronic care** in a non-acute setting in any of the following categories: *Skilled nursing care *Intermediate care *Other Long-term Care (*see page 18 definitions)The nursing home type units/facilities are to be owned and operated by the hospital. Only one legal entity may be vested with title to the physical property or operate under the authority of a duly executed lease of the physical property.

1 a. **Total licensed beds** is the total number of beds authorized by the state licensing (certifying agency).

   b. Report the number of **beds** regularly available (those **set up and staffed for use**) at the end of the reporting period. Report only operating beds, not constructed bed capacity. Include all bed facilities that are set up and staffed for use by inpatients that have no other bed facilities, such as pediatric bassinets, isolation units, quiet rooms, and reception and observation units assigned to or reserved for them. Exclude newborn bassinets and bed facilities for patients receiving special procedures for a portion of their stay and who have other bed facilities assigned to or reserved for them. Exclude, for example, labor room, post anesthesia, or postoperative recovery room beds, psychiatric holding beds, and beds that are used only as holding facilities for patients prior to their transfer to another hospital.

   c. Report the number of normal newborn **bassinets**. Do not include neonatal intensive care or intermediate care bassinets. These should be reported on page 3, C6 and C7.

   d. Total **births** should exclude fetal deaths.

   e. Include the number of adult and pediatric **admissions** only (exclude births). This figure should include all patients admitted during the reporting period, including neonatal and swing admissions.

   f. Report the number of adult and pediatric **days of care** rendered during the entire reporting period. Do not include days of care rendered for normal infants born in the hospital, but do include those for their mothers. Include days of care for infants born in the hospital and transferred into a neonatal care unit. Also include swing bed inpatient days. **Inpatient day** of care (also commonly referred to as a **patient day** or a **census day**, or by some federal hospitals as an **occupied bed day**) is a period of service between the census-taking hours on two successive calendar days, the day of discharge being counted only when the patient was admitted the same day.

   g. **Emergency department visits** should reflect the number of visits to the emergency unit. Emergency outpatients can be admitted to the inpatient areas of the hospital, but they are still counted as emergency visits and subsequently as inpatient admissions.

   h. An **Outpatient visit** is a visit by a patient who is not lodged in the hospital while receiving medical, dental, or other services. Each appearance of an outpatient in each unit constitutes one visit regardless of the number of diagnostic and/or therapeutic treatments that the patient receives. Total outpatient visits should include all clinic visits, referred visits, observation services, outpatient surgeries (also reported on line D1j), home health service visits, and emergency department visits (also reported on line D1g).
   Clinic visits should reflect total number of visits to each specialized medical unit that is responsible for the diagnosis and treatment of patients on an outpatient, nonemergency basis (i.e., alcoholism, dental, gynecology, etc.). Visits to the satellite clinics and primary group practices should be included if revenue is received by the hospital.

Referred visits should reflect total number of outpatient ancillary visits to each specialty unit of the hospital established for providing technical aid used in the diagnosis and treatment of patients. Examples of such units are diagnostic radiology, EKG, pharmacy, etc.

Observation services are those services furnished on a hospital's premises, including use of a bed and periodic monitoring by a hospital's nursing or other staff, which are reasonable and necessary to evaluate an outpatient's condition or determine the need for a possible admission to the hospital as an inpatient. Observation services usually do not exceed 24 hours. However, there is no hourly limit on the extent to which they may be used.

Home health service visits are visits by home health personnel to a patient's residence.

i. **Inpatient surgical operation.** Count each patient undergoing surgery as one surgical operation regardless of the number of surgical procedures that were performed while the patient was in the operating or procedure room.

j. **Operating room.** A unit/room of a hospital or other health care facility in which surgical procedures requiring anesthesia are performed.

k. **Outpatient surgical operation.** For outpatient surgical operations, please record operations performed on patients who do not remain in the hospital overnight. Include all operations whether performed in the inpatient operating rooms or in procedure rooms located in an outpatient facility. Include an endoscopy only when used as an operative tool and not when used for diagnosis alone. Count each patient undergoing surgery as one surgical operation regardless of the number of surgical procedures that were performed while the patient was in the operating or procedure room.

2a2. Managed Care Medicare Discharges. A discharge day where a Medicare Managed Care Plan is the source of payment.

2b2. Managed Care Medicare Inpatient Days. An inpatient day where a Medicare Managed Care Plan is the source of payment.

2c2. Managed Care Medicaid Discharges. A discharge day where a Medicaid Managed Care Plan is the source of payment.

2d2. Managed Care Medicaid Inpatient Days. An inpatient day where a Medicaid Managed Care Plan is the source of payment.

3a. Net patient revenue. Reported at the estimated net realizable amounts from patients, third-party payors, and others for services rendered, including estimated retroactive adjustments under reimbursement agreements with third-party payors. Retroactive adjustments are accrued on an estimated basis in the period the related services are rendered and adjusted in future periods, as final settlements are determined.

3b. Tax appropriations. A predetermined amount set aside by the government from its taxing authority to support the operation of the hospital.

3c. Other operating revenue. Revenue from services other than health care provided to patients, as well as sales and services to nonpatients. Revenue that arises from the normal day-to-day operations from services other than health care provided to patients. Includes sales and services to nonpatients, and revenue from miscellaneous sources (rental of hospital space, sale of cafeteria meals, gift shop sales). Also include operating gains in this category.

3d. Nonoperating revenue. Includes investment income, extraordinary gains and other nonoperating gains.

3e. Total revenue. Add net patient revenue, tax appropriations, other operating revenue and nonoperating revenue.

3f. Payroll expenses. Include payroll for all personnel including medical and dental residents/interns and trainees.

3g. Employee benefits. Includes social security, group insurance, retirement benefits, workman's compensation, unemployment insurance, etc.

3h. Depreciation expense (for reporting period only) report only the depreciation expense applicable to the reporting period. The amount also Should be included in accumulated depreciation (D7b).

3i. Interest expense. Report interest expense for the reporting period only.

3j. Supply expense. The net cost of all tangible items that are expensed including freight, standard distribution cost, and sales and use tax minus rebates. This would exclude labor, labor-related expenses and services as well as some tangible items that are frequently provided as part of labor costs.

3k. Total expenses. Includes all payroll and non-payroll expenses (including bad debt) as well as any nonoperating losses (including extraordinary losses).

4a. Total gross inpatient revenue. The hospitals full-established rates(charges) for all services rendered to inpatients.

4b. Total gross outpatient revenue. The hospitals full-established rates(charges) for all services rendered to outpatients.

4c. Total gross patient revenue. Total gross patient revenue (add total gross inpatient revenue and total gross outpatient revenue).

5. Uncompensated care. Care for which no payment is expected or no charge is made. It is the sum of bad debt and charity care absorbed by a hospital or other health care organization in providing medical care for patients who are uninsured or are unable to pay.

5a. Bad debt expense. The provision for actual or expected uncollectibles resulting from the extension of credit. Because bad debts are reported as an expense and not a deduction from revenue, the gross charges that result in bad debts will remain in net revenue (D3a).

5b. Financial Assistance (Includes **Charity care).** Financial assistance and charity care refer to health services provided free of charge or at reduced rates to individuals who meet certain financial criteria . For purposes of this survey, charity care is measured on the basis of revenue forgone, at full established rates.

5d. Medicaid Provider Tax, Fee or Assessment. Dollars paid as a result of a state law that authorizes collecting revenue from specified categories of providers. Federal matching funds may be received for the revenue collected from providers and some or all of the revenues may be returned directly or indirectly back to providers in the form of a Medicaid payment.

6. REVENUE BY PAYOR

6a1 Medicare. Should agree with the Medicare utilization reported in questions D21-Db2.

6a1a Fee for service patient revenue. Include traditional Medicare fee-for-service.

6a1c. Total. Medicare revenue (add Medicare fee for service patient revenue and Medicare managed care revenue).

6a2. Medicaid. Should agree with Medicaid utilization reported in questions D2c1-D2d2.

6a2a. Fee for service patient revenue. Do not include Medicaid disproportionate payments(DSH) or Medicaid supplemental payments that are non-Medicaid disproportionate payments (DSH).

6a2c. Medicaid disproportionate share payments. DSH minus associated provider taxes or assessments. Report in 'Net' column only.

6a2d. Medicaid supplemental payments. Not including Medicaid DSH payments (these are supplemental payments the Medicaid program pays the hospital that are NOT Medicaid DSH) and minus associated provider taxes or assessments. Report in 'Net' column only.

7. Fixed Assets. Represent land and physical properties that are consumed or used in the creation of economic activity by the health care entity. The historical or acquisition costs are used in recording fixed assets. Net plant, property, and equipment represent the original costs of these items less accumulated depreciation and amortization.

7d. Gross Square Footage. Include all inpatient, outpatient, office, and support space used for or in support of your health care activities. Exclude exterior, roof, and garage space in the figure.

8. Capital Expenses. Expenses used to acquire assets, including buildings, remodeling projects, equipment, or property.

9. Energy Consumption.

a. **Energy Star rating is a** national energy performance rating system, which utilizes a 1-100 scale to give meaning to the energy usage. To qualify, each building must meet specific guidelines in four areas: energy performance; thermal comfort; indoor air quality; illumination levels.

10. Information Technology.

a. **IT Operating expense.** Exclude department depreciation and operating dollars paid against capital leases.

b. **IT Capital expense.** Include IT capital expense for the current year only. Any capital expense that is carried forward from the previous year should be excluded from this figure. Include IT related capital included in the budget of other departments. (i.e. lab, radiology, etc., if known or can be reasonably estimated.) Include the total value of capital leases to be signed in the current year.

c. **Number of Employed IT staff (in FTEs).** Number of full-time equivalent (FTE) staff employed in the IT department/organization and on the hospital payroll.

d. **Total number of outsourced IT staff.** (i.e. contracted staff).

e. **Electronic Health Record.** An electronic health record (EHR) integrates electronically originated and maintained patient-level clinical health information, derived from multiple sources, into one point of access. An EHR replaces the paper medical record as the primary source of patient information.

STAFFING

11. **Full-Time Equivalent (FTE)** is the total number of hours worked by all employees over the full (12 month) reporting period divided by the normal number of hours worked by a full-time employee for that same time period. For example, if your hospital considers a normal workweek for a full-time employee to be 40 hours, a total of 2,080 would be worked over a full year (52 weeks). If the total number of hours worked by all employees on the payroll is 208,000, then the number of Full-Time Equivalents (FTE) is 100 (employees). The FTE calculation for a specific occupational category such as registered nurses is exactly the same. The calculation for each occupational category should be based on the number of hours worked by staff employed in that specific category.

a-b. **Physicians and dentists.** Include only those physicians and dentists engaged in clinical practice and on the payroll. Those who hold administrative positions should be reported in "All other personnel."

d. **Other trainees.** A trainee is a person who has not completed the necessary requirements for certification or met the qualifications required for

full salary under a related occupational category. Exclude medical and dental residents/interns who should be reported on line 7b.

e. **Registered nurses.** Nurses who have graduated from approved schools of nursing and who are currently registered by the state. They are responsible for the nature and quality of all nursing care that patients receive. Do not include any registered nurses more appropriately reported in other occupational categories, such as facility administrators, and therefore listed under "All other personnel."

f. **Licensed practical (vocational) nurses.** Nurses who have graduated from an approved school of practical (vocational) nursing who work under the supervision of registered nurses and/or physicians.

g. **Nursing assistive personnel.** Certified nursing assistant or equivalent unlicensed staff assigned to patient care units and reporting to nursing.

h. **Radiology Technicians.** Technical positions in imaging fields, including, but not limited to, radiology, sonography, nuclear medicine, radiation therapy, CT, MRI.

i. **Laboratory professional/technical.** Professional and technical positions in all areas of the laboratory, including, but not limited to, histology, phlebotomy, microbiology, pathology, chemistry, etc.

j. **Pharmacists, licensed.** Persons licensed within the state who are concerned with the preparation and distribution of medicinal products.

k. **Pharmacy technicians.** Persons who assist the pharmacist with selected activities, including medication profile reviews for drug incompatibilities, typing labels and prescription packaging, handling of purchase records and inventory control.

l. **Respiratory Therapists.**

m. **All other personnel.** This should include all other personnel not already accounted for in other categories.

n. **Total facility personnel.** This line is to include the total facility personnel - hospital plus nursing home type unit/facility personnel (for those hospitals that own and operate a nursing home type unit/facility).

o-p. **Nursing home type unit/facility personnel.** These lines should be filled out only by hospitals that own and operate a nursing home type unit/facility, where only one legal entity is vested with title to the physical property or operates under the authority of a duly executed lease of the physical property. If nursing home type unit/facility personnel are reported on the total facility personnel line, but cannot be broken out, please write "cannot break out" on this line.

12. **Privileged Physicians.** Report the total number of physicians (by type) on the medical staff with privileges except those with courtesy, honorary and provisional privileges. Do not include residents or interns.

Employed by your hospital. Physicians that are either direct hospital employees or employees of a hospital subsidiary corporation. Physicians that are employed for non-clinical services (administrative services, medical director services, etc.) should be excluded.

Individual contract. An independent physician under a formal contract to provide services at your hospital including at outpatient facilities, clinics and offices. Physicians that are contracted only for non-clinical services (administrative services, medical director services, etc.) should be excluded.

Group contract. A physician that is part of a group (group practice, faculty practice plan or medical foundation) under a formal contract to provide services at your hospital including at inpatient and outpatient facilities, clinics and offices. Physicians that are contracted only for non-clinical services (administrative services, medical director services, etc.) should be excluded.

Not employed or under contract. Other physicians with privileges that have no employment or contractual relationship with the hospital to provide services.

The sum of the physicians reported in 12a-12f should equal the total number of privileged physicians in the hospital.

a. **Primary care.** A physician that provides primary care services including general practice, general internal medicine, family practice, general pediatrics, obstetrics/gynecology and geriatrics.

b. **Emergency medicine.** Physicians who provide care in the emergency department.

c. **Hospitalist.** Physician whose primary professional focus is the care of hospitalized medical patients (through clinical, education, administrative and research activity).

d. **Intensivist.** A physician with special training to work with critically ill patients. Intensivists generally provided medical-surgical, cardiac, neonatal, pediatric and other types of intensive care.

e. **Radiologist/pathologist/anesthesiologist**
Radiologist. A physician who has specialized training in imaging, including but not limited to radiology, sonography, nuclear medicine, radiation therapy, CT, MRI.
Pathologist. A physician who examines samples of body tissues for diagnostic purposes.
Anesthesiologist. A physician who specializes in administering medications or other agents that prevent or relieve pain, especially during surgery.

f. **Other specialist.** Other physicians (not included above) that specialize in a specific type of medical care.

15. **Advanced Practice Registered Nurses.** Registered nurses with advanced didactic and clinical education, knowledge, skills, and scope of practice. Includes: **Physician assistant.** A healthcare professional licensed to practice medicine with supervision of a licensed physician. **Nurse practitioner.** A registered nurse with at least a master's degree in nursing and advanced education in primary care, capable of independent practice in a variety of settings. **Clinical nurse specialist (CNS).** A registered nurse who, through a formal graduate degree (masters or doctorate) CNS education program, is prepared as CNS with expertise in a specialty area of nursing practice. CNSs are clinical experts in the diagnosis and treatment of illness, and the delivery of evidence-based nursing interventions. **Certified Registered Nurse Anesthetist (CRNA). Midwives.**

15c. **Primary care.** Medical services including general practice, general internal medicine, family practice, general pediatrics, obstetrics/gynecology.

Emergency department care. The provision of unscheduled outpatient services to patients whose conditions require immediate care in the emergency department setting.

NOTES

NOTES

NOTES

NOTES